...m Lincoln
...th president of the
...States

...s Attucks
...an colonist killed
...Boston Massacre

...e Washington
...esident of
...ted States

Creating America

A History of the United States

**Beginnings
through
World War I**

Jesus Garcia

Donna M. Ogle

C. Frederick Risinger

Joyce Stevos

McDougal Littell
A DIVISION OF HOUGHTON MIFFLIN COMPANY

Jesus Garcia is Professor of Social Studies at the University of Nevada at Las Vegas. A former social studies teacher, Dr. Garcia has co-authored many books and articles on subjects that range from teaching social studies in elementary school to seeking diversity in education. Dr. Garcia will serve as President of the National Council for the Social Studies in 2004–2005.

Donna M. Ogle is Professor of Reading and Language Arts at National-Louis University in Evanston, Illinois, and is a specialist in reading in the content areas with an interest in social studies. She is past president of the International Reading Association. A former social studies teacher, Dr. Ogle is also Director of a Goals 2000 grant for Reading and Thinking in the Content Areas for four Chicago high schools. She developed the K-W-L reading strategy that is so widely used in schools.

C. Frederick Risinger is Director of Professional Development and Coordinator for Social Studies Education at Indiana University. He is past president of the National Council for the Social Studies. Mr. Risinger also served on the coordinating committee for the National History Standards Project. He writes a monthly column on technology in the social studies classroom for *Social Education.*

Joyce Stevos recently retired from 36 years of service to the Providence, Rhode Island, Public Schools. For 15 of those years, she was the social studies area supervisor and developed programs on Holocaust studies, the Armenian genocide, character education, voter education, and government and law. Currently, she is a Ph.D. candidate in education focusing on how youth develop a citizen identity.

Acknowledgments begin on page R95.

ISBN 0-618-37708-5

Printed in the United States of America
4 5 6 7 8 9 – DWO – 07 06 05

nsultants and Reviewers

ntent Consultants

content consultants reviewed the manuscript for historical
h and accuracy and for clarity of presentation.

r Beck
rtment of History
rn Illinois University
eston, Illinois

Joseph Kett
Department of History
University of Virginia
Charlottesville, Virginia

Christopher Waldrep
Department of History
Eastern Illinois University
Charleston, Illinois

l Farber
rtment of History
rsity of New Mexico
querque, New Mexico

Jack N. Rakove
Department of History
Stanford University
Stanford, California

Nancy Woloch
Department of History
Barnard College
New York, New York

yl Johnson-Odim
rtment of History
a University
go, Illinois

Virginia Stewart
Department of History
University of North Carolina,
    Wilmington
Wilmington, North Carolina

lticultural Advisory Board

nulticultural advisors reviewed the manuscript for appropriate historical content.

Dean
l Studies Consultant
and, Texas

Pat Payne
Office of Multicultural Education
Indianapolis Public Schools
Indianapolis, Indiana

Jon Reyhner
Department of Education
Northern Arizona University
Flagstaff, Arizona

ne C. Howard
ge of Education
Ohio State University
nbus, Ohio

Betto Ramirez
Former Teacher, La Joya, Texas
Social Studies Consultant
Mission, Texas

Ronald Young
Department of History
Georgia Southern University
Statesboro, Georgia

C. Moya
rtment of History
rsity of California
Los Angeles
ngeles, California

Consultants and Reviewers

Teacher Consultants

The following educators contributed activity options for the Pupil's Edition and teaching ideas and activities for the Teacher's Edition.

Paul C. Beavers
J. T. Moore Middle School
Nashville, Tennessee

Holly West Brewer
Buena Vista Paideia Magnet School
Nashville, Tennessee

Ron Campana
Social Studies Consultant
New York, New York

Patricia B. Carlson
Swanson Middle School
Arlington, Virginia

Ann Cotton
Ft. Worth Independent School
   District
Ft. Worth, Texas

Kelly Ellis
Hamilton Junior High School
Cypress, Texas

James Grimes
Middlesex County Vocational–
Technical High School
Woodbridge, New Jersey

Brent Heath
De Anza Middle School
Ontario, California

Suzanne Hidalgo
Serrano Middle School
Highland, California

Barbara Kennedy
Sylvan Middle School
Citrus Heights, California

Pamela Kniffin
Navasota Junior High School
Navasota, Texas

Tammy Leiber
Navasota Junior High School
Navasota, Texas

Lori Lesslie
Cedar Bluff Middle School
Knoxville, Tennessee

Brian McKenzie
Dr. Charles R. Drew Science
   Magnet School
Buffalo, New York

W. W. Bear Mills
Goddard Junior High School
Midland, Texas

Lindy Poling
Millbrook High School
Raleigh, North Carolina

Jean Price
T. H. Rogers Middle School
Houston, Texas

Meg Robbins
Wilbraham Middle School
Wilbraham, Massachusetts

Philip Rodriguez
McNair Middle School
San Antonio, Texas

Leslie Schubert
Parkland School
McHenry, Illinois

Robert Sisko
Carteret Middle School
Carteret, New Jersey

Marci Smith
Hurst-Euless-Bedford Indeper
   School District
Bedford, Texas

James Sorenson
Chippewa Middle School
Des Plaines, Illinois

Nicholas G. Sysock
Carteret Middle School
Carteret, New Jersey

Lisa Williams
Lamberton Middle School
Carlisle, Pennsylvania

Michael Yell
Hudson Middle School
Hudson, Wisconsin

Pontiac

JOIN, or DIE.

George Washington

California gold miner

Frances Ellen
Watkins Harper

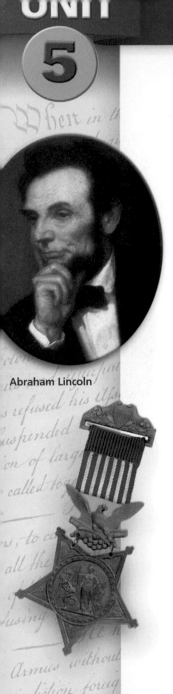

Abraham Lincoln

THE JUNGLE

UPTON SINCLAIR

Queen Liliuokalani

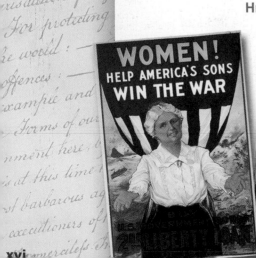

xvi

Buzz Aldrin

Features

Features

HISTORY through ART

Now and then

Connections TO

STRANGE but True

oices from the Past

A VOICE FROM THE PAST

The land is the finest for cultivation that I ever in my life set foot upon, and it also abounds in trees of every description.

Henry Hudson, quoted in *Discoverers of America*

A VOICE FROM THE PAST

These, with the pictures, busts [sculptures of the head and shoulders], and prints (of which copies upon copies are spread everywhere), have made your father's face as well known as that of the moon.

Benjamin Franklin, letter to his daughter Sally

Voices from the Past

A VOICE FROM THE PAST

I do not recollect of [remember] ever seeing my mother by the light of day. She was with me in the night. She would lie down with me, and get me to sleep, but long before I waked she was gone.

Frederick Douglass, *Narrative of the Life of Frederick Douglass*

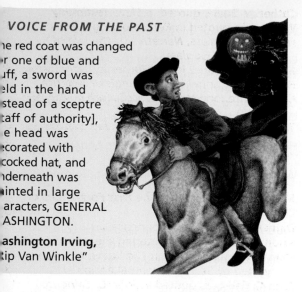
A VOICE FROM THE PAST

From the time of the Chicago fire I became more and more engrossed [interested] in the labor struggle and I decided to take an active part in the efforts of the working people to better the conditions under which they worked and lived.

Mary Harris Jones,
Autobiography of Mother Jones

Voices from the Past

A VOICE FROM THE PAST

[I was determined] to adopt an entirely contrary plan of proceedings from that of all others who had . . . visited Japan on the same errand.

Commodore Matthew Perry, *Personal Journal*

A VOICE FROM THE PAST

I have a dream that my four little children will one day live in a nation where they will not be judged by the color of their skin but by the content of their character. I have a dream today.

Dr. Martin Luther King, Jr., "I Have a Dream," August 28, 1963

Visual Primary Sources for Assessment

Historical Maps

Charts and Graphs

Causes of the War of 1812

Impressment of U.S. Citizens

Interference with American shipping

British support of Native-American resistance

WAR

Charts

Graphs

CONNECTIONS TO MATH

Military Deaths in the American Revolution

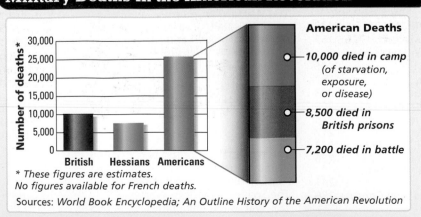

American Deaths

10,000 died in camp (of starvation, exposure, or disease)

8,500 died in British prisons

7,200 died in battle

* These figures are estimates.
No figures available for French deaths.

Sources: *World Book Encyclopedia; An Outline History of the American Revolution*

Time Lines and Infographics

Time Lines

Infographics

The Rise and Decline of Feudalism

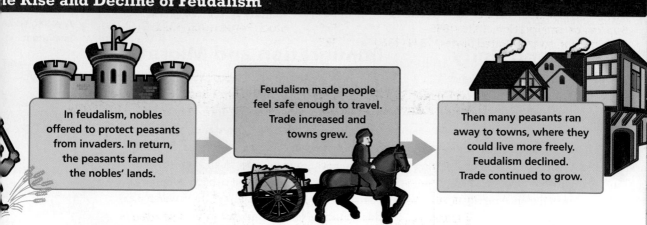

In feudalism, nobles offered to protect peasants from invaders. In return, the peasants farmed the nobles' lands.

Feudalism made people feel safe enough to travel. Trade increased and towns grew.

Then many peasants ran away to towns, where they could live more freely. Feudalism declined. Trade continued to grow.

Imagine life in Jamestown, America's first permanent English settlement. The nation we inhabit now is a much different place than it was then, more than three centuries ago. Yet there are repeating themes—ideas and issues—in American history that tie the past and present together. This book focuses on nine significant themes in U.S. history. Understanding these themes will help you to make sense of American history.

Democratic Ideals

From the day they declared themselves citizens of a new nation, Americans have built their society around the principles of democracy. In a democracy, power lies with the people, and every individual enjoys basic rights that cannot be taken away. Throughout the nation's history, however, some Americans—mainly women and minorities—have had to struggle to gain their full rights. Still, the ideals of democracy remain the guiding principles of this land.

What right or freedom do you consider the most important? Why?

Citizenship

The citizens of the United States enjoy rights and freedoms found in very few other places in the world. Yet Americans know that with such freedoms come responsibilities and duties. Whether they stand in line to vote or spend a weekend to clean up a local river, Americans recognize that citizen participation is what keeps a democracy strong.

How do citizens that you know contribute to your community?

Dr. Martin Luther King, Jr.

Impact of the Individual

The history of the United States is the story not only of governments and laws but of individuals. Indeed, individuals have made the United States what it is today through their extraordinary achievements. American history provides a variety of examples of the impact of the individual on society in both the United States and the world.

Name several individuals who have an impact on American society today. What impact do they have?

Diversity and Unity

The United States has been a land of many peoples, cultures, and faiths. Throughout the nation's history, this blend of ethnic, racial, and religious groups has helped to create a rich and uniquely American culture. The nation's many different peoples are united in their belief in American values and ideals.

What things do you enjoy that came to the United States from other cultures?

Immigration and Migration

The movement of people has played a vital role in American history. This country was settled by and has remained a magnet for immigrants. Even within the United States, large numbers of people have migrated to different regions of the country. However, movements to and within the United States have not always been voluntary. Africans were brought against their will to this country. Native Americans were forced from their homelands in order to make room for European settlers.

Why do you think people continue to immigrate to the United States?

A young Asian immigrant

xpansion

nen the United States declared its inde-
dence from Great Britain, it was only a
ection of states along the Atlantic Ocean.
the new country would not remain that
for long. Many Americans shared a
se of curiosity, adventure, and a strong
ef that their destiny was to expand all the
to the Pacific Ocean. Driven by this
ef, they pushed westward. Americans'
rts to increase the size of their nation is
curring theme in early U.S. history.

*ere do you predict that the exploration
pace—the final frontier—will lead?*

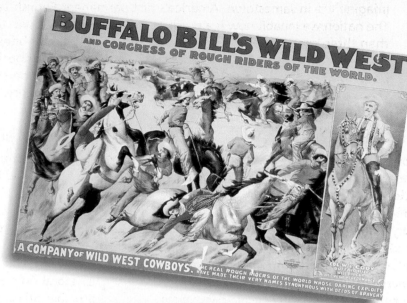

Poster for Buffalo Bill's Wild West show

merica and the World

the power and prestige of the United States have
vn, the nation has played a much more active
in world affairs. Indeed, throughout the 20th
ury, the United States focused much of its
gy on events beyond its borders. The nation
ght in two world wars and tried to promote
ocracy, peace, and economic growth around the
e. As one of the world's political and economic
ers, the United States will continue to be a key
er in world affairs throughout the new century.

*t do you think the role of the United States in
world should be today?*

Science and Technology

Americans have always been quick to embrace
inventions and new ways of doing things.
After all, this country was settled by
people who turned away from old ways
and tried new ones. In the past two
centuries, new inventions, new
technologies, and scientific break-
throughs have transformed the
United States—and will continue
to do so in the new century.

*What recent inventions or
innovations affect your life?*

onomics in History

nomics has had a powerful impact on the course of U.S. history. For example,
desire for wealth led thousands to join the California Gold Rush in 1849.
nation as a whole has grown wealthy, thanks to its abundant resources and
hard work of its citizens. An important economic issue, however, has been
to make sure that all people have opportunities to share fully in the nation's
th. This issue will continue to be important in the 21st century.

*t do you think are the most exciting economic opportunities
Americans today?*

Thomas Edison's first light bulb

This section of the textbook helps you develop and practice the skills you need to study history and to take standardized tests. Part 1, **Strategies for Studying History,** takes you through the features of the textbook and offers suggestions on how to use these features to improve your reading and study skills.

Part 2, **Test-Taking Strategies and Practice,** offers specific strategies for tackling many of the items you'll find on a standardized test. It gives tips for answering multiple-choice, constructed-response, extended-response, and document-based questions. In addition, it offers guidelines for analyzing primary and secondary sources, maps, political cartoons, charts, graphs, and time lines. Each strategy is followed by a set of questions you can use for practice.

CONTENTS

Part 1: Strategies for Studying History

Reading is the central skill in the effective study of history or any other subject. You can improve your reading skills by using helpful techniques and through practice. The better your reading skills, the more you'll remember what you read. Below you'll find several strategies that involve built-in features of this textbook. Careful use of these strategies will help you learn and understand history more effectively.

Preview Chapters Before You Read

Each chapter begins with a two-page chapter opener and a one-page **Reading Strategy** feature. Study the materials to help you get ready to read.

1 Read the chapter and section titles and study the chapter-opening visual. Look for clues that indicate what will be covered in the chapter.

2 Preview the time line. Note the years that the chapter covers. What important events took place during this time period?

3 Study the **Interact with History** feature. Experience what it was like to live in the past by answering **What Do You Think?** questions.

4 Read the **Reading Strategy** feature (see page S3). **What Do You Want to Know?** and the note taking chart will help focus your reading.

CHAPTER 6

The Road to Revolution 1763-1776

Section 1
Tighter British Control

Section 2
Colonial Resistance Grows

Section 3
The Road to Lexington and Concord

Section 4
Declaring Independence

The bayonets, or blades, on the soldiers' gun were very dangerous in close combat.

Angry confrontations between colonial protestors and British Red Coats became common as the colonies moved towards independence.

The fife and drum corps played music to keep soldiers at a steady march. During battle, the drummers beat out orders and the fifers carried messages and stratadies.

Interact with Histo

The year is 1765. Your neighbors are or by Britain's demand that British troops housed in American cities at American expense. Britain has never done this b There are protests in many cities. You to decide what you would do.

Would you join the protest?

What Do You Think?
- What is the best way to show opposit policies you consider unjust?
- Is there anything to be gained by prot Anything to be lost?
- Does government have the right to ma demands without consent of the peop Why or why not?

RESEARCH LINKS
CLASSZONE.COM
Visit the Chapter 6 links for more inform about the American Revolution.

1763
Proclamation of 1763 becomes law.

1765
Stamp Act is passed.

1767
Townshend Acts are passed.

1769
Spanish begin to establish military posts and missions in California.

1770
Boston Massacre

1773
Boston Tea Party

Intolerable Acts are passed. First Continental Congress meets.

1775
Battles of Lexington and Concord

1776
Declaration of Independence is signed

USA World 1763

1763
Treaty of Paris ends Seven Years' War in Europe.

1765
Chinese forces invade Burma.

1769
Scotland's James Watt patents a steam engine capable of running other machines.

1772
Captain Cook explores the South Pacific.

1774
Reign of Louis XVI begins in Russia.

The Road to Rev

 chapter consists of three, four, or five sections. These
ns focus on shorter periods of time or on particular historical
es. Use the section openers to help you prepare to read.

 tudy the sentences under the headings **Main Idea** and **Why It
Matters Now.** These tell you what's important in the material that
 ou're about to read.

 review the **Terms & Names** list. This will give you an idea of the
 sues and personalities you will read about in the section.

 ead **One American's Story** and **A Voice from the Past.** These
 rovide one individual's view of an important issue of the time.

 otice how the section is divided into smaller chunks, each with a
 d headline. These headlines give you a quick outline of the section.

TERMS & NAMES	
King George III	Stamp Act
Quartering Act	Patrick Henry
revenue	boycott
Sugar Act	Sons of Liberty

4

Reading Strategy: Sequencing Events

What Do You Know?
What do you already know about the time before the Revolution? What were
the issues that caused the colonists to choose independence?

Think About
- what you have learned about this period from
  movies, television, or historical fiction
- reasons people in history have chosen to fight for
  freedom from oppression
- your responses to the Interact with History about
  joining the protest (see page 157)

What Do You Want to Know?
 What questions do you have about the issues and events that pushed the
American colonists toward rebellion? Record them in your notebook before you
read the chapter.

Sequencing Events
Sequencing means putting events in the order in which they happen in time. In learning
about how the American colonies moved toward independence, it would be helpful to list
the important events. Place them in the order in which they occurred. You might record the
event and its date in a graphic organizer such as the one below. Copy this organizer in your
notebook. Fill it in as you read the chapter.

S See Skillbuilder Handbook, page R4.

Taking Notes

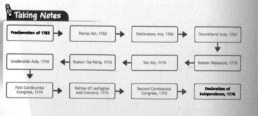

1

Tighter British Control

5

MAIN IDEA	WHY IT MATTERS NOW	**6** TERMS & NAMES	
Americans saw British efforts to tax them and to increase control over the colonies as violations of their rights.	Colonial protests were the first steps on the road to American independence.	King George III Quartering Act revenue Sugar Act	Stamp Act Patrick Henry boycott Sons of Liberty

7
ONE AMERICAN'S STORY
James Otis, Jr., a young Massachusetts lawyer, stormed through the
streets of Boston one day in 1760. He was furious. His father had just
been denied the post of chief justice of the Massachusetts colony by the
royal governor. To Otis, this was one more example of Britain's lack of
respect for colonial rights. Another example was its use of search warrants
that allowed customs officers to enter any home or business to look for
smuggled goods. Otis believed these searches were illegal.

In court in February 1761, Otis spoke with great emotion for five
hours about the search warrant and its use.

A VOICE FROM THE PAST
It appears to me the worst instrument of arbitrary power, the most
destructive of English liberty and the fundamental principles of law,
that was ever found in an English law-book.
James Otis, Jr., quoted in *James Otis: The Pre-Revolutionist* by J. C. Ridpath

In making the first public speech demanding English liberties for
the colonists, James Otis planted a seed of freedom. In this section,
you will read more about the early protests against Britain's policies
in America.

James Otis, Jr.,
argues in court
against illegal search
warrants in 1761.

8
The Colonies and Britain Grow Apart
During the French and Indian War, Britain and the colonies fought side
by side. Americans took great pride in being partners in the victory over
the French. However, when the war ended, problems arose. Britain
wanted to govern its 13 original colonies and the territories gained in the
war in a uniform way. So the British Parliament in London imposed new
laws and restrictions. Previously, the colonies had been allowed to develop
largely on their own. Now they felt that their freedom was being limited.

Taking Notes
Use your chart to
take notes about
the tightening of
British control.

The Road to Revolution 159

What Do You Want to Know?

 What questions do you have about the issues and events that pushed
the American colonists toward rebellion? Record them in your notebook before you read the chapter.

Use Active Reading Strategies As You Read

Now you're ready to read the chapter. Read one section at a time, from beginning to end.

1 Ask and answer questions as you read. Look for the **Reading History** questions in the margin. Answering these will show whether you understand what you've just read.

2 Try to visualize the people, places, and events you read about. Studying the pictures and any illustrated features will help you do this.

3 Read to build your vocabulary. Use the marginal **Vocabulary** notes to find the meaning of unfamiliar terms.

4 Look for the story behind the events. Read **Background** notes in the margin for additional information on people, places, events, and ideas.

> ### *Reading* History
> **A. Summarizing**
> Who was upset by the Proclamation of 1763?

The first of Parliament's laws was the Proclamation of 1763. (See Chapter 5.) It said that colonists could not settle west of the Appalachian Mountains. Britain wanted this land to remain in the hands of its Native American allies to prevent another revolt like Pontiac's Rebellion.

The proclamation angered colonists who had hoped to move to the fertile Ohio Valley. Many of these colonists had no land of their own. It also upset colonists who had bought land as an investment. As a result, many ignored the law.

> **1**
> *Reading* History
> A. Summarizing
> Who was upset by the Proclamation of 1763?

British Troops and Taxes

King George III, the British monarch, wanted to enforce the proclamation and also keep peace with Britain's Native American allies. To do this, he decided to keep 10,000 soldiers in the colonies. In 1765, Parliament passed the **Quartering Act**. This was a cost-saving measure that required the colonies to quarter, or house, British soldiers and provide them with supplies. General Thomas Gage, commander of these forces, put most of the troops in New York.

Britain owed a large debt from the French and Indian War. Keeping troops in the colonies would raise that debt even higher. Britain needed more **revenue**, or income, to meet its expenses. So it attempted to have the colonies pay part of the war debt. It also wanted them to contribute toward the costs of frontier defense and colonial government.

In the past, the king had asked the colonial assemblies to pass taxes to support military actions that took place in the colonies. This time, however, Parliament voted to tax the Americans directly.

In 1764, Parliament passed the **Sugar Act**. This law placed a tax on sugar, molasses, and other products shipped to the colonies. It also called for strict enforcement of the act and harsh punishment of smugglers. Colonial merchants, who often traded in smuggled goods, reacted with anger.

Colonial leaders such as James Otis claimed that Parliament had no right to tax the colonies, since the colonists were not represented in Parliament. As Otis exclaimed, "Taxation without representation is tyranny!" British finance minister George Grenville disagreed. The colonists were subjects of Britain, he said, and enjoyed the protection of its laws. For that reason, they were subject to taxation.

The colonial view of the hated stamp tax is shown by the skull and crossbones on this emblem (above); a royal stamp is pictured at right.

> **2**

> **3**
> Vocabulary
> tyranny:
> absolute power in the hands of a single ruler

Britain Passes the Stamp Act

The Sugar Act was just the first in a series of acts that increased tension between the mother country and the colonies. In 1765, Parliament passed the **Stamp Act**. This law required all legal and commercial documents to carry an official stamp showing that a tax had been paid. All diplomas, contracts, and wills had to carry a stamp.

160

Even published materials such as newspapers had to be written on special stamped paper.

The Stamp Act was a new kind of tax for the colonies. The Sugar Act had been a tax on imported goods. It mainly affected merchants. In contrast, the Stamp Act was a tax applied within the colonies. It fell directly on all colonists. Even more, the colonists had to pay for stamps in silver coin—a scarce item in the colonies.

Colonial leaders vigorously protested. For them, the issue was clear. They were being taxed without their consent by a Parliament in which they had no voice. If Britain could pass the Stamp Act, what other taxes might it pass in the future? Samuel Adams, a leader in the Massachusetts legislature, asked, "Why not our lands? Why not the produce of our lands and, in short, everything we possess and make use of?" **Patrick Henry**, a member of Virginia's House of Burgesses, called for resistance to the tax. When another member shouted that resistance was treason, Henry replied, "If this be treason, make the most of it!"

The Colonies Protest the Stamp Act

Colonial assemblies and newspapers took up the cry—"No taxation without representation!" In October 1765, nine colonies sent delegates to the Stamp Act Congress in New York City. This was the first time the colonies met to consider acting together in protest. Delegates drew up a petition to the king protesting the Stamp Act. The petition declared that the right to tax the colonies belonged to the colonial assemblies, not to Parliament. Later, colonial merchants organized a **boycott** of British goods. A boycott is a refusal to buy.

Meanwhile, some colonists formed secret societies to oppose British policies. The most famous of these groups was the **Sons of Liberty**. Many Sons of Liberty were lawyers, merchants, and craftspeople—the colonists most affected by the Stamp Act. These groups staged protests against the act.

Not all of their protests were peaceful. The Sons of Liberty burned the stamped paper whenever they could find it. They also attacked customs officials, whom they covered with hot tar and feathers and paraded in public. Fearing for their safety, many customs officials quit their jobs.

The protests in the colonies had an effect in Britain. Merchants thought that their trade with America would be hurt. Some British political leaders, including

> *Reading* History
> **B. Making Inferences** Why did the colonists boycott goods?

> **4**
> Background
> To voice their protests, the Sons of Liberty in Boston met under a huge, 120-year-old elm tree that they called the Liberty Tree.

> ## Vocabulary
> **tyranny:**
> absolute power in the hands of a single ruler

> ## Background
> To voice their protests, the Sons of Liberty in Boston met under a huge, 120-year-old elm tree that they called the Liberty Tree.

ew and Summarize What You Have Read

 you finish reading a section, review and summarize what you've
If necessary, go back and reread information that was not clear the
ime through.

eread the red headlines for a quick summary of the major points
overed in the section.

tudy any charts, graphs, and maps in the section. These visual
materials usually provide a condensed version of information in
he section.

eview the pictures and note how they relate to the section content.

omplete all the questions in the **Section Assessment**. This will help
ou think critically about what you have just read.

---

mediately offered Massachusetts their support. They sent food and
ney to Boston. The committees of correspondence also called for a
eting of colonial delegates to discuss what to do next.

he First Continental Congress Meets

September 1774, delegates from all the colonies except Georgia met
Philadelphia. At this meeting, called the **First Continental
ongress**, delegates voted to ban all trade with Britain until the
olerable Acts were repealed. They also called on each colony to begin
ning troops. Georgia agreed to be a part of the actions of the
ngress even though it had voted not to send delegates.

The First Continental Congress marked a key step in American his-
y. Although most delegates were not ready to call for independence,
y were determined to uphold colonial rights. This meeting planted
seeds of a future independent government. John Adams called it "a
ery of American statesmen." The delegates agreed to meet in seven
nths, if necessary. By that time, however, fighting with Britain
 begun.

etween War and Peace

 colonists hoped that the trade boycott would force a repeal of the
olerable Acts. After all, past boycotts had led to the repeal of the Stamp
 and the Townshend Acts. This time, however, Parliament stood firm.
ven increased restrictions on colonial trade and sent more troops.
 by the end of 1774, some colonists were preparing to fight. In
ssachusetts, John Hancock headed the Committee of Safety, which had
 power to call out the militia. The colonial troops continued to train.

CAUSE AND EFFECT: Growing Conflict Between Britain and America

ATE	BRITISH ACTION	COLONIAL REACTION
63	Proclamation of 1763 issued	Proclamation leads to anger
65	Stamp Act passed	Boycott of British goods; Stamp Act Resolves passed
66	Stamp Act repealed; Declaration Act passed	Boycott ended
67	Townshend Acts passed	New boycotts; Boston Massacre (March 1770)
70	Townshend Acts repealed (April)	Tension between colonies and Britain reduced
73	Tea Act passed	Boston Tea Party
74	Intolerable Acts passed	First Continental Congress bans trade; militia organized
75	Troops ordered to Lexington and Concord, Massachusetts	Militia fights British troops; Second Continental Congress; Continental Army established

ILLBUILDER Interpreting Charts
What British action caused the first violence in the growing conflict between Britain and America?
How might the Intolerable Acts be seen as a reaction as well as an action?

171

When the British moved, so did Revere and Dawes.
They galloped over the countryside on their "midnight
ride," spreading the news. In Lexington, they were
joined by Dr. Samuel Prescott. When Revere and
Dawes were stopped by a British patrol, Prescott broke
away and carried the message to Concord.

Lexington and Concord

At dawn on April 19, some 700 British troops reached
Lexington. They found Captain John Parker and about 70
militiamen waiting. The British commander ordered the
Americans to drop their muskets. They refused. No one
knows who fired first, but within a few minutes eight militiamen lay dead. The British then marched to Concord,
where they destroyed military supplies. A battle broke out
at a bridge north of town, forcing the British to retreat.

Nearly 4,000 Minutemen and militiamen arrived in
the area. They lined the road from Concord to
Lexington and peppered the retreating redcoats with
musket fire. "It seemed as if men came down from the
clouds," one soldier said. Only the arrival of 1,000
more troops saved the British from destruction as they
scrambled back to Boston.

Background
British losses
totaled 273 sol-
diers compared to
95 militiamen.

Reading History
C. Drawing
Conclusions
Why did Emerson
call it the "shot
heard 'round
the world"?

Lexington and Concord were the first battles of the
Revolutionary War. As Ralph Waldo Emerson later wrote,
colonial troops had fired the "shot heard 'round the world." Americans
would now have to choose sides and back up their political opinions by
force of arms. Those who supported the British were called **Loyalists**.
Those who sided with the rebels were **Patriots**. The conflict between the
two sides divided communities, families, and friends. The war was on!

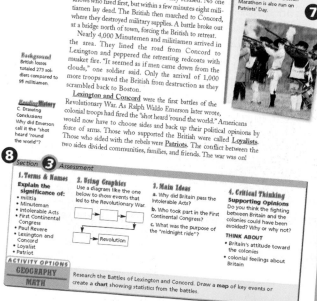

Now and then

PATRIOTS' DAY
The "shot heard 'round the
world" is celebrated every year
in Massachusetts and Maine.
Patriots' Day, as it is called, is
the third Monday of April. In
Concord and nearby towns,
modern-day Minutemen like
those below reenact the battle
that began the Revolution on
April 19, 1775. The Boston
Marathon is also run on
Patriots' Day.

7

8

Section 3 Assessment

1. Terms & Names
Explain the
significance of:
• militia
• Minuteman
• Intolerable Acts
• First Continental Congress
• Paul Revere
• Lexington and Concord
• Loyalist
• Patriot

2. Using Graphics
Use a diagram like the one
below to show events that
led to the Revolutionary War.

[ ] → [ ] → [ ]
        ↓
[ ] → Revolution

3. Main Ideas
a. Why did Britain pass the
Intolerable Acts?

b. Who took part in the First
Continental Congress?

c. What was the purpose of
the "midnight ride"?

4. Critical Thinking
Supporting Opinions
Do you think the fighting
between Britain and the
colonies could have been
avoided? Why or why not?

THINK ABOUT
• Britain's attitude toward
the colonies
• colonial feelings about
Britain

ACTIVITY OPTIONS
GEOGRAPHY
MATH

Research the Battles of Lexington and Concord. Draw a **map** of key events or
create a **chart** showing statistics from the battles.

Part 2: Test-Taking Strategies and Practi[ce]

Improve your test-taking skills by practicing the strategies discussed in this section. Read the tips on the left-hand page. Then apply them to the practice items on the right-hand page.

Multiple Choice

A multiple-choice question consists of a stem and a set of choices. The stem is usually in the form of a question or an incomplete sentence. One of the choices correctly answers the question or completes the sentence.

1 Read the stem carefully and try to answer the question or complete the sentence without looking at the choices.

2 Pay close attention to key words in the stem. They may direct you toward the correct answer.

3 Read each choice with the stem. Don't jump to conclusions about the correct answer until you've read all of the choices.

4 Think carefully about questions that include *All of the above* among the choices.

5 After reading all of the choices, eliminate any that you know are incorrect.

6 Use modifiers to help narrow your choice.

7 Look for the best answer among the remaining choices.

stem

1 1. At the beginning of the Revolution, (most) Americans were **2**

3 choices

   A. united in support of the war.

   B. Patriots who wanted independence from Great Britain.

   C. against a war with Great Britain.

   D. Loyalists who supported the British point of view.

Most is a key[word] Replacing it w[ith] or *some* cha[nges the] sentence and [may lead to a] different answ[er]

2. Which of the following weapons were first used effectiv[ely] during World War I?

   A. airplanes

   B. machine guns

   C. tanks

   D. all of the above **4** If you select this answer, be sure that all of the choices are correct.

3. At the outset of the Civil War, both the Union and the Confederacy wanted the support of the border states—

   A. Delaware, Maryland, Kentucky, and Oklahoma.

   B. Delaware, Maryland, Kentucky, and Missouri.

   C. Delaware, Maryland, West Virginia, Kentucky, and Missouri.

   D. (all) the states bordering the Missouri Compromise line.

5 You can elim[inate A if you] remember th[at Oklahoma] was not a st[ate at the] time of the C[ivil War.]

6 Absolute words, such as *all, never, always, every,* and *only,* often signal an incorrect choice.

7 In **C**, West Virginia did [not exist as a] border between the Un[ion and the] Confederacy. However, [it broke] away from Virginia earl[y in the war] and became a state in [1863.] Therefore, **B** is the corre[ct answer.]

Directions: Read the following questions and choose the *best* answer from the four choices.

1. New inventions that helped open the Great Plains to farming included

   A. the steel windmill.

   B. barbed wire.

   C. the spring-tooth harrow.

   D. all of the above

2. Which of the following statements *best* explains why, by the year 1500, there were hundreds of Native American groups with diverse religious beliefs, economies, and languages?

   A. The local environment influenced each group in different ways.

   B. Spiritual beliefs dictated many groups' distinct cultural growth.

   C. Contagious disease caused the people to form smaller groups.

   D. Trading practices led to the establishment of specialized cultures.

3. During the presidency of Thomas Jefferson, the United States was able to foster westward expansion when it acquired territory in what is known as

   A. Seward's Folly.

   B. the Missouri Compromise.

   C. the Kansas-Nebraska Act.

   D. the Louisiana Purchase.

4. Who commanded the Texan forces at the Alamo?

   A. James Fannin

   B. David Crockett

   C. William Travis

   D. Sam Houston

Primary Sources

Primary sources are materials written or made by people who took part in or witnessed historical events. Letters, diaries, speeches, newspaper articles, and autobiographies are all primary sources. So, too, are legal documents, such as wills, deeds, and financial records.

1 Look at the source line and identify the author. Consider what qualifies the author to write about the events discussed in the passage.

2 Skim the document to form an idea of what it is about.

3 Note special punctuation. Ellipses indicate that words or sentences have been removed from the original passage. Brackets indicate words that were not in the original. Bracketed words often are replacements for difficult or unfamiliar terms.

4 Carefully read the passage and distinguish between facts and the author's opinions. (That the groups of soldiers were wandering in all directions is a fact. The reasons for their wandering offered by Madison are her opinions.)

5 Consider for whom the author was writing. The intended audience may influence what and how an author writes.

6 Before rereading the passage, skim the questions to identify the information you need to find.

answers: 1 (D), 2 (B)

The Flight from the White House

Wednesday Morning, twelve o'clock. Since sunrise I have been turning my spy-glass in every direction, . . but alas! I can see only groups of military, wandering in all directions, as if there a lack of arms, or of spirit to fight for their own fireside.

Three o'clock. Will you believe it, my sister? we have had a battle, or skirmish, near Bladensburg, and here I am still, within sound of the cannon!. . . Two messengers covered with dust come to bid me fly. . . . At this late hour a wagon has bee [found], and I have had it filled with plate and the most valua portable articles belonging to the house. Whether it will reach destination . . . or fall into the hands of British soldiery, event must determine. Our kind friend, Mr. Carroll, has come to ha my departure, and is in a very bad humor with me, because I on waiting until the large picture of General Washington is secured. . . . It is done! and the precious portrait placed in the hands of two gentlemen of New York, for safe keeping. And dear sister, I must leave this house. . . . When I shall again wr to you, or where I shall be tomorrow, I cannot tell!

The author is Dolley Madison, the wife of President James Madison. She personally oversaw the evacuation of the White House in 1814.

—Dolley Madison, in a letter to her describing her flight from the Whi House in August 1814

This is a letter. If it were report to Congress, the content would be much

1. Dolley Madison's letter describes her preparations to flee the White House in advance of a British attack. In whic war did this attack take place?

A. War of Jenkins' Ear
B. French and Indian War
C. Revolutionary War
D. War of 1812

2. Why might Dolley Madison be considered a good sourc information on the British attack on Washington, D.C.:

A. She was the wife of President James Madison.
B. She was an eyewitness to the attack.
C. She helped her husband develop military policy.
D. She had intercepted British war plans.

Directions: Use this passage, from a letter on conservation written by President Theodore Roosevelt, and your knowledge of U.S. history to answer questions 1 through 3.

> In the east, the States are now painfully, and at great expense, endeavoring to undo the effects of their former shortsighted policy in throwing away their forest lands. Congress has before it bills to establish by purchase great forest reserves in the White Mountains and the Southern Appalachians, and the only argument against the bills is that of their great expense. New York and Pennsylvania are now, late in the day, endeavoring themselves to protect the forests which guard the headwaters of their streams. Michigan and Wisconsin have already had their good timber stript from their forests by the great lumber companies. But the western States, far more fortunate than their eastern sisters in this regard, can now reserve their forests for the good of all their citizens, without expense, if they choose to show the requisite foresight.
>
> —President Theodore Roosevelt, in a private letter in 1907

1. According to President Roosevelt, forests not yet damaged by timber companies could be set aside at no expense in the

   A. Midwest.

   B. East.

   C. South.

   D. West.

2. You can tell from this letter that President Roosevelt

   A. favored changing forests to farmland.

   B. was a good president.

   C. supported environmental protection.

   D. was an owner of a large lumber company.

3. Which one of the following statements from the letter is most strictly a fact?

   A. "Congress has before it bills to establish by purchase great forest reserves in the White Mountains."

   B. "New York and Pennsylvania are now, late in the day, endeavoring themselves to protect the forests."

   C. ". . . States are now painfully, and at great expense, endeavoring to undo the effects of . . . throwing away their forest lands."

   D. "But the western States, far more fortunate than their eastern sisters . . . can now reserve their forests."

Secondary Sources

Secondary sources are descriptions or interpretations of historical events made by people who were not at those events. The most common types of written secondary sources are history books, encyclopedias, and biographies. A secondary source often combines information from several primary sources.

❶ Read titles to preview what the passage is about.

❷ Look for topic sentences. These, too, will help you preview the content of the passage.

❸ As you read, use context clues to help you understand difficult or unfamiliar words. (You can tell from the description of the battle in the previous sentences that the word *fiasco* must mean something like "disaster," "failure," or "blunder.")

❹ As you read, ask and answer questions that come to mind. You might ask: Why would the Washington raid embarrass and anger Americans? Why did the Washington raid achieve little?

❺ Before rereading the passage, skim the questions to identify the information you need to find.

❶ **The British Offensive**

❷ Ironically, Britain's most spectacular success began as a diversi [its main] offensive [in the North]. A British army that had from Bermuda entered Chesapeake Bay and on August 24, 1 a larger American force . . . at Bladensburg, Maryland. The E Bladensburg deteriorated into the "Bladensburg Races" as the American troops fled, virtually without firing a shot. The Bri then descended on Washington, D.C. Madison, who had wit ❸ the Bladensburg fiasco, fled into the Virginia hills. His wife, loaded her silver, a bed, and a portrait of George Washington her carriage before joining him. British troops ate the supper prepared for the Madisons and then burned the presidential ❹ and other public buildings in the capital. Beyond embarrassin angering Americans, the Washington raid accomplished little after a failed attack on Baltimore, the British broke off the o

—Paul S. Boyer, et al., *The Enduring*

❺ 1. Why do you think the authors refer to the Battle of Bla as a "fiasco"?

A. because the American forces fled almost without a fight

B. because President Madison had to flee the White House

C. because it allowed the British to attack Washington, D.C

D. because it was a famous victory for the British forces

2. What, according to the authors, did the British raid on Washington, D.C., accomplish?

A. It paved the way for the British capture of Baltimore.

B. It burned down all the public buildings in the city.

C. It helped the British offensive in the North.

D. It embarrassed and angered many Americans.

Remember t of choices th absolutes, su *every*, or on

answers: 1 (A), 2 (D)

Directions: Use this passage and your knowledge of U.S. history to answer questions 1 through 3.

African-American Sailors

African Americans contributed greatly to the growth of maritime commerce in the United States. Beginning in colonial times, slaves, with their masters' permission, hired themselves out as sailors. Some served as translators on slave ships. Merchant ships also offered a means of escape for runaway slaves. A few escapees even took to the sea as pirates.

Seafaring was one of the few occupations open to free African Americans. They served on clippers, naval vessels, and whaling ships from the 1700s into the late 1800s. Federal crew lists from Atlantic seaports show that during this time African Americans made up 10 percent or more of sailors on American ships. Seafaring was an especially dangerous line of work for free blacks. They risked capture in southern ports, where they were often thrown in jail or sold into slavery.

1. What records show that African Americans made up 10 percent or more of sailors on American ships?

   A. shipyard records

   B. family Bibles

   C. federal crew lists

   D. ships' logs

2. The passage implies that free and enslaved African Americans went to sea for all of the following reasons *except* to

   A. escape slavery.

   B. live as pirates.

   C. earn wages as sailors.

   D. discover new lands.

3. The author states that life was especially dangerous for free African-American sailors because

   A. American prosperity depended on their work alone.

   B. the worst jobs on board ship were always assigned to them.

   C. they ran the risk of capture and enslavement in southern ports.

   D. they were more likely than white sailors to contract scurvy.

Political Cartoons

Political cartoons are drawings that express views on political issues of the day. Cartoonists use symbols and such artistic styles as caricature—exaggerating a person's physical features—to get their message across.

1 Identify the subject of the cartoon. Titles and captions often indicate the subject matter.

2 Identify the main characters in the cartoon. Here, the main character is Horace Greeley, a candidate in the 1872 presidential election.

3 Note the symbols—ideas or images that stand for something else—used in the cartoon.

4 Study labels and other written information in the cartoon.

5 Analyze the point of view. How cartoonists use caricature often indicates how they feel. The exaggeration of Greeley's physical appearance—short and overweight—makes him appear comical.

6 Interpret the cartoonist's message.

The cartoonist shows Tammany Hall, New York's Democratic political machine, as a tiger. Uncle Sam, a symbol for the United States, is shown looking on.

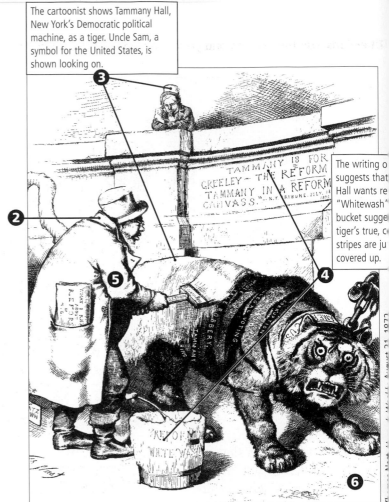

The writing o
suggests that
Hall wants re
"Whitewash"
bucket sugge
tiger's true, c
stripes are ju
covered up.

1 "What are you going to do about it, if 'Old Honesty' lets him loose again?"

1. Based on the cartoon, what do you think was Horace G
major issue in the 1872 presidential campaign?

    A. political reform

    B. states' rights

    C. abolition

    D. temperance

2. Which one of the following statements do you think *be*
represents the cartoonist's point of view?

    A. Horace Greeley is an honest man.

    B. Tammany Hall supports political reform.

    C. Tammany Hall, regardless of Greeley's view, is still corru

    D. Horace Greeley, like most Tammany politicians, is corrup

answers: 1 (A), 2 (C)

Directions: Use the cartoon and your knowledge of U.S. history to answer questions 1 through 3.

BATTLE OF PICARDY

U.S.A.

Rollin Kirby, *New York World*, 1917

"That's my fight, too!"

1. The cartoon character is a symbol of

A. Americans opposed to war.

B. the president of the United States.

C. old soldiers retired from the United States Army.

D. the United States as a whole.

2. The "fight" in the cartoon caption refers to

A. the War of 1812.

B. World War II in Europe.

C. World War II in the Pacific.

D. World War I in Europe.

3. The cartoonist's point of view is *best* described by which of the following statements?

A. The United States believes it has an obligation to join in this foreign war.

B. Uncle Sam is too old and too late for every battle.

C. The United States should stay out of other countries' wars.

D. A country should equip its soldiers with the best weapons and other supplies.

Charts

Charts present information in a visual form. History textbooks use several types of charts, including tables, flow charts, Venn diagrams, and infographics. The type of chart most commonly found in standardized tests is the table. It organizes information in columns and rows for easy viewing.

❶ Read the title and identify the broad subject of the chart.

❷ Read the column and row headings and any other labels. This will provide more details about the subject of the chart.

❸ Compare and contrast the information from column to column and row to row.

❹ Try to draw conclusions from the information in the chart. Ask yourself: What trends does the chart show?

❺ Read the questions and then study the chart again.

Review difficult or unfamiliar words. Here, the term *nativity* means "place of birth."

❶ **United States Population by Region and Nativity, 1890–192**

❷

	1890	1900	1910	192
Northeast				
Total Population	17,407,000	21,047,000	25,869,000	29,
% Native Born	78	77	74	77
% Foreign Born	22	23	26	23
North Central				
Total Population	22,410,000	26,333,000	29,889,000	34,
% Native Born	82	84	84	86
% Foreign Born	18	16	16	14
South				
Total Population	20,028,000	24,524,000	29,389,000	33,
% Native Born	97	98	97	97
% Foreign Born	3	2	3	3
West				
Total Population	3,134,000	4,309,000	7,082,000	9,2
% Native Born	76	79	79	82
% Foreign Born	24	21	21	18

Source: *Historical Statistics of the U*

Compare changes in population over time and contrast statistics among regions.

❸

❺ 1. The two regions with the highest percentage of foreign-b inhabitants are the

   A. Northeast and the West.

   B. West and the South.

   C. South and the North Central.

   D. North Central and the Northeast.

2. When did immigration to the Northeast peak?

   A. between 1910 and 1920

   B. before 1900

   C. between 1900 and 1910

   D. after 1920

answers: 1 (A), 2 (C)

Directions: Use the charts and your knowledge of U.S. history to answer questions 1 through 4.

Percentage of Population Free and Enslaved, by States and Territories, 1790

North		
State/Territory	Free	Enslaved
Connecticut	98.9	1.1
Delaware	85.0	15.0
Maine	100.0	0.0
Massachusetts	100.0	0.0
New Hampshire	99.9	0.1
New Jersey	93.8	6.2
New York	93.8	6.2
Pennsylvania	99.1	0.9
Rhode Island	98.6	1.4
Vermont	100.0	0.0

South		
State/Territory	Free	Enslaved
Georgia	64.5	35.5
Kentucky	83.1	16.9
Maryland	67.8	32.2
North Carolina	74.5	25.5
South Carolina	57.0	43.0
Virginia	60.9	39.1

Source: Inter-University Consortium for Political and Social Research

1. The state with the highest percentage of enslaved people was

A. New Hampshire.

B. North Carolina.

C. Rhode Island.

D. South Carolina.

2. Which of the following *best* describes most states in the North?

A. The population was more than 98 percent free.

B. More than 10 percent of the population was enslaved.

C. Less than 60 percent of the population was free.

D. The population was more than 20 percent enslaved.

3. Which statement about the percentage of enslaved people is true?

A. It was much lower in the South.

B. It was much higher in the South.

C. There was no difference between the regions.

D. There was a slight difference between the regions.

4. What economic factor *best* explains the population differences between the regions?

A. The North focused on manufacturing.

B. The North was wealthy enough to free enslaved people.

C. The South focused on plantation agriculture.

D. The South needed enslaved people for factory work.

Line and Bar Graphs

Graphs show statistics in a visual form. Line graphs are particularly useful for showing changes over time. Bar graphs make it easy to compare numbers or sets of numbers.

① Read the title and identify the broad subject of the graph.

② Study the labels on the vertical and horizontal axes to see the kinds of information presented in the graph. Note the intervals between amounts and between dates. This will help you read the graph more efficiently.

③ Look at the source line and evaluate the reliability of the information in the graph. Government statistics on education tend to be reliable.

④ Study the information in the graph and note any trends.

⑤ Draw conclusions and make generalizations based on these trends.

⑥ Read the questions carefully, and then study the graph again.

① High School Graduates, 1880–1920

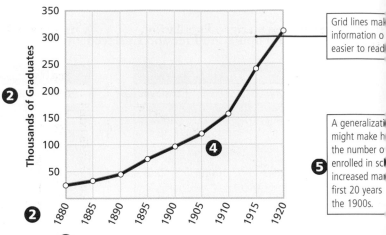

Grid lines ma[ke] information o[n] easier to read

A generalizat[ion] might make h[...] the number o[f] enrolled in sc[hool] increased ma[...] first 20 years [of] the 1900s.

③ Source: *Historical Statistics of the United States*

⑥ 1. How many students graduated from high school in 190[5]?

    A. exactly 100,000

    B. about 125,000

    C. about 150,000

    D. exactly 175,000

① Public Secondary School Enrollment, 1880–1920

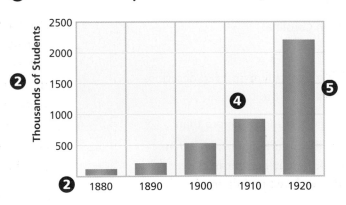

③ Source: *Historical Statistics of the United States*

⑥ 2. Which one of the following sentences do you think *best* describes the trend shown in the bar graph?

    A. The number of students enrolled steadily increased.

    B. The number of students enrolled showed little change.

    C. The number of students enrolled rose and fell.

    D. The number of students enrolled steadily decreased.

answers: 1 (B), 2 (A)

ctions: Use the graphs and your knowledge of U.S. history to answer questions 1 through 4.

th of the African-American Population, -1860

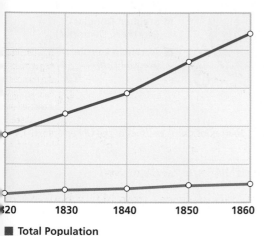

■ Total Population
■ Free Population

Churches by Denomination, 1750

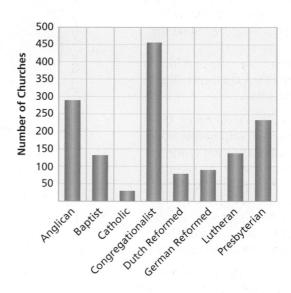

. In which year did the total African-American population first exceed 3.5 million?

A. 1830

B. 1840

C. 1850

D. 1860

. About how many times larger than the free African-American population was the enslaved population in 1860?

A. four

B. five

C. six

D. eight

3. Which one of the following statements accurately reflects information in the graph?

A. There were more Congregationalist churches than all other denominations combined.

B. There were more Presbyterian churches than Anglican churches.

C. The Baptists had the fewest churches.

D. The Congregationalists had the most churches.

4. Which statement about religion in the colonies of the mid-18th century does the graph support?

A. All of the colonists were Anglicans.

B. By 1750, there were many religions in the colonies.

C. The colonists of 1750 were not religious.

D. Only immigrants from England established churches.

Pie Graphs

A pie, or circle, graph shows relationships among the parts of a whole. These parts look like slices of a pie. The size of each slice is proportional to the percentage of the whole that it represents.

❶ Read the title and identify the broad subject of the pie graph.

❷ Look at the legend to see what each slice of the pie represents.

❸ Read the source line and note the origin of the data shown in the pie graph.

❹ Compare the slices of the pie and try to make generalizations and draw conclusions from your comparisons.

❺ Read the questions carefully and review difficult or unfamiliar terms.

❻ Eliminate choices that you know are wrong.

❶ The Popular Vote in the 1860 Presidential Election

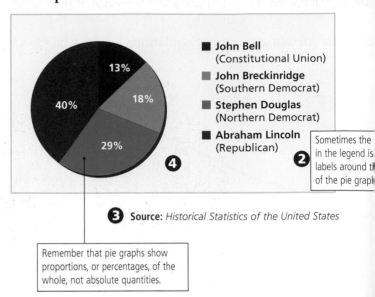

- John Bell (Constitutional Union)
- John Breckinridge (Southern Democrat)
- Stephen Douglas (Northern Democrat)
- Abraham Lincoln (Republican)

Sometimes the in the legend is labels around th of the pie graph **❷**

❸ Source: *Historical Statistics of the United States*

Remember that pie graphs show proportions, or percentages, of the whole, not absolute quantities.

1. In the 1860 presidential election, Abraham Lincoln won

   A. by a landslide.
   B. a majority of the votes cast.
   C. a plurality of the votes cast.
   D. by a narrow margin.

   In electoral ter word *landslid* to an overwhe victory, *major* "more than 50 and *plurality* "the most but 50 percent." **❺**

2. What political situation in 1860 does the pie graph show

   A. The Democratic Party was split into northern and southe before the 1860 election.
   B. The Republican Party was not yet an important force in national politics.

   You can elimin you notice tha Republican Pa more votes tha other. **❻**

   C. Douglas won fewer popular votes than Lincoln but won more electoral votes.
   D. Because no candidate won a majority of the popular vot House of Representatives decided the election.

answers: 1 (C), 2 (A)

Directions: Use the pie graphs and your knowledge of U.S. history to answer questions 1 through 4.

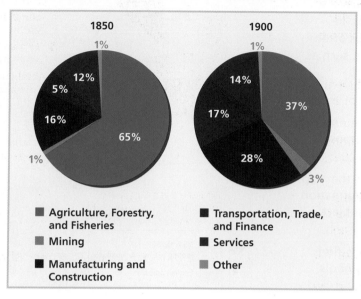

Distribution of Workers in the United States, 1850 and 1900

1850

1%
12%
5%
16%
65%
1%

1900

1%
14%
37%
17%
28%
3%

- ■ Agriculture, Forestry, and Fisheries
- ■ Mining
- ■ Manufacturing and Construction
- ■ Transportation, Trade, and Finance
- ■ Services
- ■ Other

Source: *Historical Statistics of the United States*

1. In 1850, most people worked in

   A. agriculture, forestry, and fisheries.

   B. mining.

   C. services.

   D. transportation, trade, and finance.

2. In 1900, more people worked in manufacturing and construction than in

   A. agriculture, forestry, and fisheries.

   B. mining and agriculture, forestry, and fisheries combined.

   C. services and transportation, trade, and finance combined.

   D. transportation, trade, and finance.

3. Which occupation category showed an increase between 1850 and 1900?

   A. manufacturing and construction

   B. services

   C. transportation, trade, and finance

   D. all of the above

4. What helped to bring about the changes reflected in the two pie graphs?

   A. the passage of new immigration laws

   B. the growth of industry

   C. the decline of world agricultural markets

   D. all of the above

Political Maps

Political maps show countries and the political divisions within countries—states, for example. They also show the location of major cities. In addition, political maps often show physical features, such as rivers, seas, oceans, and mountain ranges.

1 Read the title to determine the subject and purpose of the map.

2 Read the labels on the map. This will reveal information about the map's subject and purpose.

3 Study the legend to find the meaning of symbols used on the map.

4 Look at the lines of latitude and longitude. This grid makes locating places much easier.

5 Use the compass rose to determine directions on the map.

6 Use the scale to estimate the distances between places shown on the map.

7 Read the questions, and then carefully study the map to determine the answers.

Instead of a c[o]
rose, some ma[p]
North arrow.

1 Middle Colonies to 1700

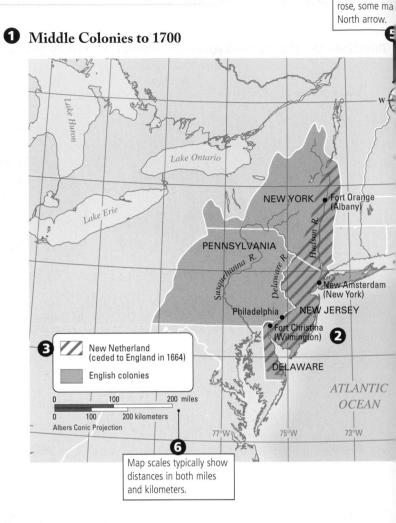

3 New Netherland (ceded to England in 1664)

English colonies

0   100   200 miles
0   100   200 kilometers
Albers Conic Projection

6 Map scales typically show distances in both miles and kilometers.

7 1. Which of the following bodies of water formed part of t[he] border between New Netherland and the English middl[e] colonies?

  A. Lake Erie

  B. Lake Huron

  C. Delaware River

  D. Hudson River

2. Which entire English colony was once part of New Net[herland?]

  A. New York

  B. New Jersey

  C. Pennsylvania

  D. all of the above

answers: 1 (C), 2 (B)

Directions: Use the map and your knowledge of U.S. history to answer questions 1 through 4.

New States, 1816–1848

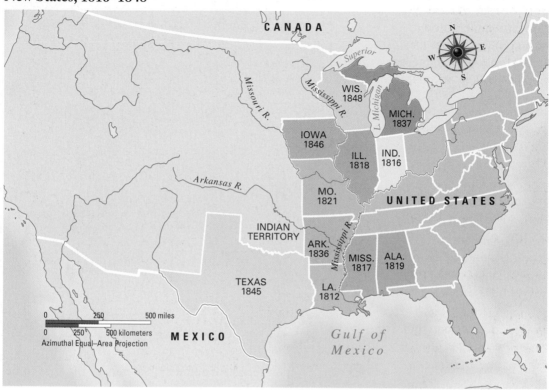

1. Which state joined the Union in 1845?

   A. Iowa

   B. Illinois

   C. Wisconsin

   D. Texas

2. The Mississippi River forms the western border of which of the following states?

   A. Missouri, Arkansas, and Louisiana

   B. Illinois and Mississippi

   C. Iowa and Missouri

   D. Iowa, Missouri, and Arkansas

3. A barge filled with logs from Wisconsin is going to the Gulf of Mexico. It is most likely traveling

   A. south on the Mississippi River.

   B. west across the Great Plains.

   C. north on the Arkansas River.

   D. southwest through Indian Territory.

4. The states admitted to the Union in the 1840s were

   A. Missouri, Wisconsin, and Illinois.

   B. Kansas, Texas, and Iowa.

   C. Texas, Wisconsin, and Iowa.

   D. Illinois, Texas, and Wisconsin.

Thematic Maps

A thematic map, or special-purpose map, focuses on a particular topic. The location of baseball parks, a country's natural resources, election results, and major battles in a war are all topics you might see illustrated on a thematic map.

1 Read the title to determine the subject and purpose of the map.

2 Examine the labels on the map to find more information about the map's subject and purpose.

3 Study the legend to find the meaning of the symbols and colors used on the map.

4 Look at the colors and symbols on the map and try to identify patterns.

5 Read the questions and then carefully study the map to determine the answers.

1 **Southern Military Districts, 1867**

3 While a thematic map focuses one topic, it often offers sever kinds of information on that to Therefore, the legend for a the map is usually very detailed.

5 **1.** Which former Confederate state was the first to be readmitted to the Union?

A. Tennessee

B. South Carolina

C. Florida

D. Alabama

2. The military district in which Texas was located was commanded by

A. General Edward Ord.

B. General John Pope.

C. General Philip Sheridan.

D. General Daniel Sickles.

answers: 1 (A), 2 (C)

Directions: Use the map and your knowledge of U.S. history to answer questions 1 through 4.

The Battle of San Jacinto, 1836

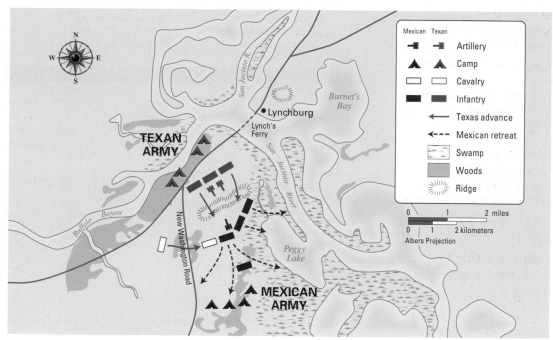

1. The Texas camp was located in what type of area?

   A. swamp

   B. ridge

   C. woods

   D. open plains

2. In which direction did the Texan forces move to attack the Mexican army?

   A. directly south

   B. northeast

   C. directly east

   D. southeast

3. An attack was launched on the Mexican forces from the west by

   A. Texan artillery.

   B. Texan cavalry.

   C. Texan infantry.

   D. all of the above

4. What was the importance of the Battle of San Jacinto?

   A. Texas won its independence from Mexico.

   B. It avenged the defeats at Goliad and the Alamo.

   C. Texas gained U.S. support in the struggle for freedom.

   D. It proved that the Texans were better fighters than the Mexicans.

Time Lines

A time line is a type of chart that lists events in the order in which they occurred. In other words, time lines are a visual method of showing what happened when.

1 Read the title to discover the subject of the time line.

2 Identify the time period covered by the time line by noting the earliest and latest dates shown. On vertical time lines, the earliest date is shown at the top. On horizontal time lines, it is on the far left.

3 Read the events and their dates in sequence. Notice the intervals between events.

4 Use your knowledge of history to develop a fuller picture of the events listed in the time line. For example, you might try to identify some of the leading individuals involved in the events.

5 Note how events are related to one another. Look particularly for cause-effect relationships.

6 Use the information you have gathered from the above strategies to answer the questions.

1 **The Road to Revolution, 1765–1775**

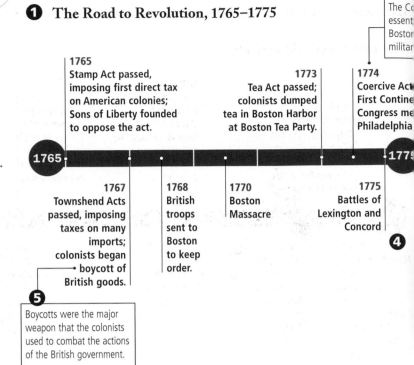

The C
essent
Bostor
militar

1765
Stamp Act passed, imposing first direct tax on American colonies; Sons of Liberty founded to oppose the act.

1773
Tea Act passed; colonists dumped tea in Boston Harbor at Boston Tea Party.

1774
Coercive Act
First Contine
Congress me
Philadelphia

1765 — 1775

1767
Townshend Acts passed, imposing taxes on many imports; colonists began boycott of British goods.

1768
British troops sent to Boston to keep order.

1770
Boston Massacre

1775
Battles of Lexington and Concord

4

5
Boycotts were the major weapon that the colonists used to combat the actions of the British government.

6 1. How did the colonists respond to the passage of the Townshend Acts?

A. They founded the Sons of Liberty.

B. They dumped British tea in Boston Harbor.

C. They began a boycott of British goods.

D. They called the First Continental Congress.

2. About how much time passed between the Coercive Act the first battles of the Revolutionary War?

A. one year

B. three years

C. seven years

D. nine years

Directions: Use the time line and your knowledge of U.S. history to answer questions 1 through 3.

The Erie Canal, 1816–1840s

1816
Former New York City Mayor DeWitt Clinton proposes building a canal to connect the Great Lakes to Albany.

1825
Erie Canal completed; shipping time from New York City to Buffalo reduced from 3 weeks to 8 days.

1836
Toll receipts exceed entire cost of construction; work begins to enlarge canal.

1840
New York City is now the busiest port in the U. S.

1815 ─────────────────────────────────── 1845

1817
New York state authorizes $7 million to build the 363-mile-long Erie Canal; construction begins.

1819
Mid-section of canal completed; first boat travels from Rome to Utica.

1829
3,640 bushels of wheat shipped down the canal.

1837
500,000 bushels of wheat transported down the canal.

1841
One million bushels of wheat shipped down the canal.

---

1. The Erie Canal was completed and ready for water traffic between Buffalo and Albany in

A. 1817.

B. 1819.

C. 1825.

D. 1840.

2. About how many years after the canal was finished did work begin to enlarge it?

A. 4 years

B. 6 years

C. 11 years

D. 21 years

3. Which of the following statements about the Erie Canal is *not* true?

A. The canal greatly reduced the time it took to ship goods between the Great Lakes and New York.

B. From 1837 to 1841, the volume of wheat shipped through the canal doubled.

C. The cost of building the canal was greater than the amount of tolls collected.

D. The mid-section of the canal was completed in 1819.

Constructed Response

Constructed-response questions focus on various kinds of documents. Each document usually is accompanied by a series of questions. These questions call for short answers that, for the most part, can be found directly in the document. Some answers, however, require knowledge of the subject or time period addressed in the document.

1 Read the title of the document to discover the subject addressed in the questions.

2 Study and analyze the document. Take notes on what you see.

3 Read the questions and then study the document again to locate the answers.

4 Carefully write your answers. Unless the directions say otherwise, your answers need not be complete sentences.

1 Joseph Glidden's Patent

2 Constructed-response que use a wide range of docu including short passages, charts, graphs, maps, time posters, and other visual r This is a copy of a legal d called a patent.

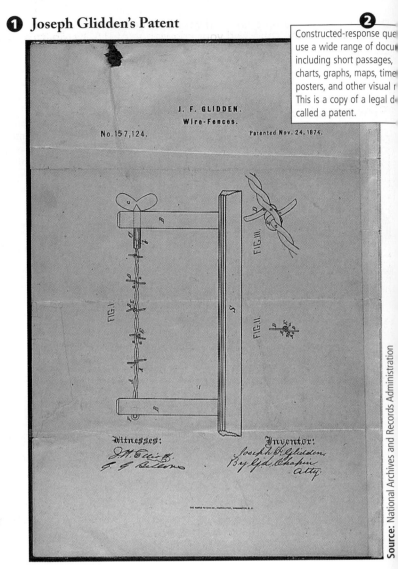

J. F. GLIDDEN.
Wire-Fences.

No. 157,124.

Patented Nov. 24, 1874.

Witnesses:

Inventor:

Source: National Archives and Records Administration

3 **4** 1. What invention is illustrated on this patent?

barbed wire fence

2. What suggests that this is a legal document?

It is signed by witnesses and an attorney.

3. What other developments had a major impact on farmin the plains in the 1800s?

steel plows, reapers, threshers, dry farming

Directions: Use the chart and your knowledge of U.S. history to answer questions 1 through 3.

First Amendment Rights: the Five Basic Freedoms

Freedom of Religion	People have the right to practice the religion of their choice.
Freedom of Speech	People have the right to state their ideas.
Freedom of the Press	People have the right to publish their ideas.
Freedom of Assembly	People have the right to meet peacefully in groups.
Freedom to Petition	People have the right to petition the government.

1. Does the First Amendment guarantee you the right to belong to any religion you like?

2. You write a letter to the mayor asking for a stop sign to be placed at an intersection near your school. Which of the five basic freedoms are you exercising?

3. What specific activities are covered by freedom of speech, and what activities are covered by freedom of the press? How are the two freedoms related?

Extended Response

Extended-response questions, like constructed-response questions, usually focus on one kind of document. However, they are more complex and require more time to complete than typical short-answer constructed-response questions. Some extended-response questions ask you to complete a chart, graph, or diagram. Still others ask you to write an essay, a report, or some other lengthier piece based on the document.

1 Read the title of the document to get an idea of the subject.

2 Study and analyze the document. Take notes on your ideas.

3 Carefully read the extended-response questions. (Question 1 asks you to present the information in the chart in a time line. Question 2 asks you to write an essay by applying your knowledge of history to information in the chart.)

4 If the question calls for some type of diagram, make a rough sketch on scrap paper first. Then, make a final copy of your diagram on the answer sheet.

5 If the question requires an extended piece of writing, jot down ideas in outline form. Use this outline to write your answer.

1 Ratifying the Constitution

State	Date Ratified
Connecticut	January 9, 1788
Delaware	December 7, 1787
Georgia	January 2, 1788
Maryland	April 28, 1788
Massachusetts	February 6, 1788
New Hampshire	June 21, 1788
New Jersey	December 18, 1787
New York	July 26, 1788
North Carolina	November 21, 1789
Pennsylvania	December 12, 1787
Rhode Island	May 29, 1790
South Carolina	May 23, 1788
Virginia	June 25, 1788

4 For time other d rememb include all appr labels.

3 1. Use the information in the chart and your knowledge of U.S. history to create a time line for the ratification of the Constitution.

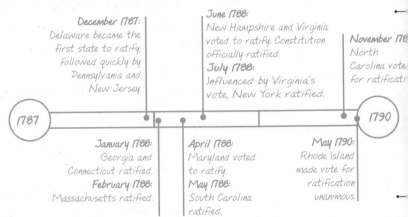

The Ratification of the Constitution

December 1787:
Delaware became the first state to ratify, followed quickly by Pennsylvania and New Jersey.

June 1788:
New Hampshire and Virginia voted to ratify, Constitution officially ratified.

July 1788:
Influenced by Virginia's vote, New York ratified.

November 178
North Carolina vote for ratificati

1787

1790

January 1788:
Georgia and Connecticut ratified.
February 1788:
Massachusetts ratified.

April 1788:
Maryland voted to ratify.
May 1788:
South Carolina ratified.

May 1790:
Rhode Island made vote for ratification unanimous.

3 2. Write a brief essay explaining the significance of the Bill Rights to the ratification of the Constitution.

5 Sample Response The best essays will point out that the promise of a Bill of Rights was key to getting enough support to ensure ratification of the Constitution. The vot for ratification by Virginia—the largest of the states—was contingent upon the passage of a Bill of Rights.

Directions: Use the passage, chart, and your knowledge of U.S. history to answer question 1.

A Country Dividing

As the United States grew during the 1800s, Congress and the people argued about what form of government each new territory and state would have. The differences of opinion centered on one issue more than any other: slavery. Eventually, those sectional arguments led to the Civil War.

The chart below lists three acts of Congress that addressed the issue of slavery in the West. On the right are the provisions of each of these acts.

Act	Provisions
Missouri Compromise, 1820	**1.** Slavery was to be prohibited in the Louisiana territory north of the 36° 30' parallel. **2.** Missouri would enter the Union as a slave state. **3.** Maine would enter the Union as a free state.
Compromise of 1850	**1.** The territories of New Mexico and Utah were created without restrictions on slavery. **2.** California would enter the Union as a free state. **3.** The slave trade would be prohibited in Washington, D.C. **4.** Congress would pass a strong fugitive slave law for mandatory return of escaped slaves.
Kansas-Nebraska Act, 1854	**1.** Two new territories, Kansas and Nebraska, were created. **2.** The people residing in the Kansas and Nebraska territories would have the right to decide whether their territory would enter the Union as a free or slave state (popular sovereignty). **3.** The Kansas-Nebraska Act repealed the Missouri Compromise of 1820, which prohibited slavery in territories north of 36° 30'.

. Write an essay explaining how the Missouri Compromise, the Compromise of 1850, and the Kansas-Nebraska Act promoted sectionalism.

Document-Based Questions

A document-based question focuses on several documents—both visual and written. These documents often are accompanied by short-answer questions. You then use the answers to these questions and information from the documents to write an essay on a specified subject.

1 Carefully read the "Historical Context" to get an indication of the issue addressed in the question.

2 Note the action words used in the "Task" section. These words tell you exactly what the essay question requires.

3 Study and analyze each document. Think about how the documents are connected to the essay question. Take notes on your ideas.

4 Read and answer each of the document-specific questions.

Introduction

1 **Historical Context:** During President George Washington's first te parties started to develop around the beliefs of two members of cabinet, Secretary of the Treasury Alexander Hamilton and Secre Thomas Jefferson. Despite Washington's opposition to political p had a great influence in American domestic and foreign policy.

2 **Task:** Discuss the role of the Federalist and Democratic-Republica the early Republic, and explain why George Washington believe political parties were divisive.

Part 1: Short Answer

Study each document carefully and answer the questions that fc

Document 1: Washington's Farewell Address

3 Let me . . . warn you in the most solemn manner against the [harmful] effects of the spirit of party generally. This spirit, u is inseparable from our nature, having its root in the stronges the human mind. . . .

It serves always to distract the public councils and enfeebl the public administration. It agitates the community with illf jealousies and false alarms; kindles the animosity [hatred] of against another; foments occasionally riot and insurrection. I door to foreign influence and corruption, which find a facilit [easy entry] to the government itself through the channels of passions.

—Georg

4 **Why did Washington believe that political parties wou nation?**

He believed that political parties would have a bac the nation by playing upon the jealousies of differen and stirring up considerable trouble for the nation. governments might also find it easy to use political influence our national affairs.

Document 2: Positions of the First United States Political Parties

Federalist Party	Democratic-Republican Party
Strong central government	Weak central government
Loose interpretation of the Constitution	Strict interpretation of the Constitution
Government should pay states' Revolutionary War debts	Each state should pay its own debts
Favored a national bank	Opposed a national bank
Favored business interests	Favored agricultural interests
Pro-British foreign policy	Pro-French foreign policy

How were the policies favored by the Federalists different from those favored by the Democratic-Republicans?

The parties held opposite views on major policy issues.

Document 3: Policy Dispute in Congress Hall, Philadelphia

The cartoon shows the two parties fighting over foreign policy. What does it imply about their ability to settle disagreements?

Their disputes, if not settled by debate, threatened to destroy the federal government.

Part 2: Essay

Using information from the documents, your answers to the questions in Part 1, and your knowledge of U.S. history, write an essay in which discuss the different views the first political parties held on major issues between 1789 and 1801 and explain why Washington believed political parties were divisive. ❻

❺ Carefully read the essay question. Then write an outline for your essay.

❻ Write your essay. Be sure that it has an introductory paragraph that introduces your argument, main body paragraphs that explain it, and a concluding paragraph that restates your position. In your essay, include extracts or details from specific documents to support your ideas. Add other supporting facts or details that you know from your study of American history.

Sample Response The best essays will point out the differences between the Federalists and Democratic-Republicans (Document 2), and will show how political disagreements, such as those portrayed in the cartoon (Document 3), supported Washington's warning in his Farewell Address (Document 1). Essays should draw upon information not specifically included in the documents that illustrates an understanding of the political debate during the Washington and Adams administrations. Students may also refer to the Alien and Sedition Acts passed by the Federalist Congress during Adams's presidency, and the opposing viewpoint expressed in the Kentucky and Virginia Resolutions authored by Jefferson and Madison, respectively.

Introduction

Historical Context: In 1775, Great Britain had an army of 48,647 men located throughout the world, about 8,000 of them in the Americas. A rebellion by the small group of 13 colonies in America did not scare the keepers of such a large colonial empire.

Task: Discuss how the colonists' beliefs and military actions contributed to their victory in the Revolution. Include the significance of the American alliances with European nations.

Part 1: Short Answer

Study each document carefully and answer the questions that follow.

Document 1: First Georgia Regiment of Infantry Continental Line, 1777

The hunting shirt, or rifle dress, shown here was recommended by George Washington in his general order of July 24, 1776. Declaring it a practical item to be given to the troops, he also claimed that "... it is a dress justly supposed to carry no small terror to the enemy, who think every such person a complete marksman."

Source: New-York Historical Society

What unusual military tactics did patriots like the man in the picture use to surprise and outsmart the British during the Revolution?

Document 2: Philadelphia, September 12, 1777

I close this paper with a short address to General Howe. . . . We know the cause which we are engaged in, and though a passionate fondness for it may make us grieve at every injury. . . . We are not moved by the gloomy smile of a worthless king, but by the ardent glow of generous patriotism. We fight not to enslave, but to set a country free, and to make room upon the earth for honest men to live in. In such a case we are sure that we are right; and we leave to you the despairing reflection of being the tool of a miserable tyrant.

—Thomas Paine, *The American Crisis No. IV*

Although this excerpt is addressed to the British General Howe, how might it also have encouraged the colonists to continue their fight against the British?

Document 3: The Battle of Yorktown, 1781: Winning the American Revolution

Estimated American, French, and British Forces and Casualties		
Generals and Their Divisions	Forces	Casualties
General Washington (American colonies)	11,100	90
General Rochambeau (France)	7,800	250
General Cornwallis (Britain)	8,900	550

Estimated French and British Naval Strength*		
French and British Fleets	Ships	Guns on Board Ship
Admiral Graves (Britain)	25	1,450
Lieutenant General DeGrasse (France)	35	2,610

*Does not include small craft or transport ships

Source: U.S. Army Center of Military History

What support was provided by the French in the Battle of Yorktown?

Part 2: Essay

Using information from the documents, your answers to the questions in Part 1, and your knowledge of U.S. history, write an essay that discusses how the colonists' beliefs and military actions contributed to their victory in the Revolution. Include in your essay the significance of American alliances with European nations.

The Landscape of America

The best place to begin your study of American history is with the geography of America. Geography is more than the study of the land and people. It also involves the relationship between people and their environment.

The United States is part of the North American continent. The United States ranks third in both total area and population in the world. It is filled with an incredible variety of physical features, natural resources, climatic conditions, and people. This handbook will help you to learn about these factors and to understand how they affected the development of the United States.

A timber company collects logs in the North

NORTHWEST

WEST

SOUTHWEST

0   500 Miles
0   1,000 Kilometers

0   100 Miles
0   200 Kilometers

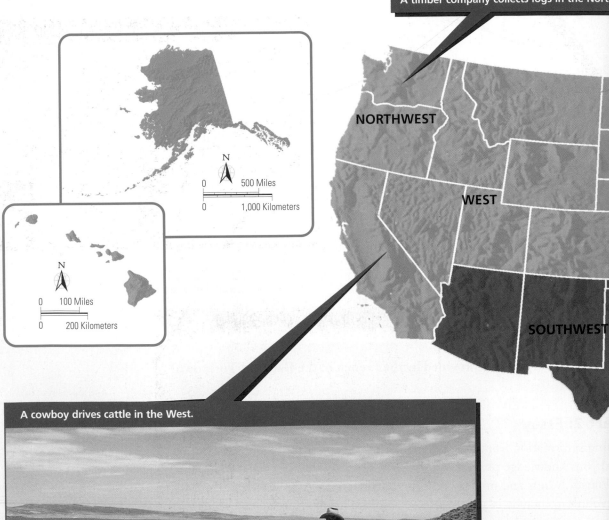

A cowboy drives cattle in the West.

...bine harvests wheat in the Midwest.

NORTHEAST

EST

SOUTHEAST

Fishers haul their catch toward shore in the Northeast.

N

500 Miles

1,000 Kilometers

Oranges are big business in the Southeast.

Themes of Geography

One useful way to think about geography is in terms of major themes or ideas. These pages examine the five major themes of geography and show how they apply to Boston, Massachusetts. Recognizing and understanding these themes will help you to understand all the different aspects of geography.

Location

"Where am I?" Your answer to this question is your *location*. One way to answer it is to use *absolute* location. That means you'll use the coordinates of longitude and latitude to give your answer (see page 8). For example, if you're in Boston, its absolute location is approximately 42° north latitude and 71° west longitude.

Like most people, however, you'll probably use *relative* location to answer the question. Relative location describes where a certain area is in relation to another area. For example, Boston lies in the northeast corner of the United States, next to the Atlantic Ocean.

THINKING ABOUT GEOGRAPHY What is the relative location of your school?

Boston is located on the shores of the Atlantic Ocean.

Place

"What is Boston like?" *Place* can help you answer this question. Place refers to the physical and human factors that make one area different from another. Physical characteristics are natural features, such as physical setting, plants, animals, and weather. For example, Boston sits on a hilly peninsula.

Human characteristics include cultural diversity and the things people have made—including language, the arts, and architecture. For instance, Boston includes African Americans, as well as people of Irish, Italian, Chinese, and Hispanic ancestry.

THINKING ABOUT GEOGRAPHY What physical and human characteristics make where you live unique?

Boston has gr[...] and changed [...] this 1722 map[...]

Region

Geographers can't easily study the whole world at one time. So they break the world into regions. A *region* can be as large as a continent or as small as a neighborhood. A region has certain shared characteristics that set it apart. These characteristics might include political division, climate, language, or religion. Boston is part of the northeast region. It shares a climate—continental temperate—with the cities of New York and Philadelphia.

THINKING ABOUT GEOGRAPHY What characteristics does your city or town share with nearby cities or towns?

Airplanes from Boston's Logan International Airport move people and ideas around the globe.

People shop, eat, and interact at Boston's famous Quincy Market.

Movement

Movement refers to the shifting of people, goods, and ideas from one place to another. People constantly move in search of better places to live, and they trade goods with one another over great distances. Movement also causes ideas to travel from place to place. In recent years, technology has quickened the movement of ideas and goods.

Boston became known as the *Cradle of Liberty* because of the movement of ideas. The concepts of freedom and self-government that developed in Boston spread to the other colonies and helped to start the American Revolution.

THINKING ABOUT GEOGRAPHY What are some of the different ways you spread information and ideas?

Human-Environment Interaction

Human-environment interaction refers to ways people interact with their environment, such as building a dam, cutting down a tree, or even sitting in the sun.

In Boston, human-environment interaction occurred when officials filled in swampy areas to make the city larger. In other ways, the environment has forced people to act. For example, people have had to invent ways to protect themselves from extreme weather and natural disasters.

THINKING ABOUT GEOGRAPHY What are ways that people in your city or town have changed their environment?

---

mes of Geography Assessment

Main Ideas

What is the relative location of your home?

What are three characteristics of the region in ch you live?

What are at least three ways in which you have ntly interacted with the environment?

2. Critical Thinking

Forming and Supporting Opinions Which aspect of geography described in these themes do you think has most affected your life? Explain.

THINK ABOUT

• ways that you interact with your environment

• how you travel from place to place

Map Basics

Geographers use many different types of maps, and these maps all have a variety of features. The map on the next page gives you information on a historical event—the War of 1812. But you can use it to learn about different parts of a map, too.

Types of Maps

Physical maps Physical maps show mountains, hills, plains, rivers, lakes, oceans, and other physical features of an area.

Political maps Political maps show political units, such as countries, states, provinces, counties, districts, and towns. Each unit is normally shaded a different color, represented by a symbol, or shown with a different typeface.

Historical maps Historical maps illustrate such things as economic activity, migrations, battles, and changing national boundaries.

Tools of Geography

The ancient Greeks developed some of the first ways to study geography. Today, geographers and map makers use advanced technology to study geography.

GPS

A Global Positioning System (GPS) is a navigational system that uses at least three satellites to identify a person's absolute location. It is also used to study other aspects of geography.

Surveyors

An American surveys the land in the 19th century.

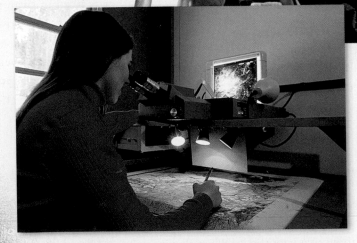

Computers

Computers can create electronic maps in which geographers can quickly add or remove features that keep the map current. Computers can also be used to monitor environmental problems such as deforestation and global warming.

ading a Map

Lines Lines indicate political boundaries, roads and highways, human movement, and rivers and other waterways.

Symbols Symbols represent such items as capital cities, battle sites, or economic activities.

Labels Labels are words or phrases that explain various items or activities on a map.

Compass Rose A compass rose shows which way the directions north (N), south (S), east (E), and west (W) point on the map.

Scale A scale shows the ratio between a unit of length on the map and a unit of distance on the earth. A typical one-inch scale indicates the number of miles and kilometers that length represents on the map.

F **Colors** Colors show a variety of information on a map, such as population density or the physical growth of a country.

G **Legend or Key** A legend or key lists and explains the symbols, lines, and colors on a map.

H **Lines of Longitude** These are imaginary, north-south lines that run around the globe.
Lines of Latitude These are imaginary, east-west lines that run around the globe. Together, latitude and longitude lines form a grid on a map or globe to indicate an area's absolute location.

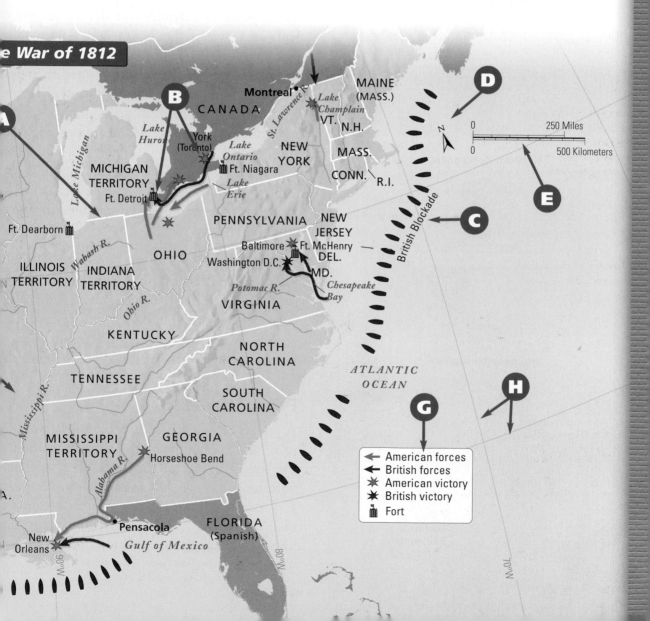

e War of 1812

American forces
British forces
American victory
British victory
Fort

Longitude Lines (Meridians)

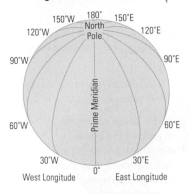

Latitude Lines (Parallels)

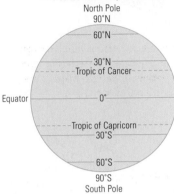

Northern Hemisphere

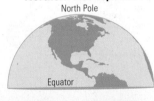

Southern Hemisphere

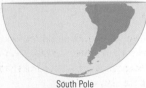

Longitude lines

- are imaginary lines that run north to south arou[nd] the globe and are known as meridians
- show the distance in degrees east or west of th[e] prime meridian

The prime meridian is a longitude line that runs fr[om] the North Pole to the South Pole. It passes thro[ugh] Greenwich, England, and measures 0° longitude.

Latitude lines

- are imaginary lines that run east to west arou[nd] the globe and are known as parallels
- show distance in degrees north or south [of] the equator

The equator is a latitude line that circles the e[arth] halfway between the North and South poles [and] measures 0° latitude.

The tropics of Cancer and Capricorn are pa[ral]lels that form the boundaries of the Tropic[s, a] region that stays warm all year.

Latitude and longitude lines appear togethe[r on] a map and allow you to pinpoint the abso[lute] location of cities and other geographic featu[res.] You express this location through coordinate[s, or] intersecting lines. These are measured in degre[es.]

Hemisphere

Hemisphere is a term for half the globe. The g[lobe] can be divided into Northern and Southern he[mi]spheres (separated by the equator) or into Eas[tern] and Western hemispheres. The United State[s is] located in the Northern and Western hemisph[eres.]

Projections

A projection is a way of showing the curved su[rface] of the earth on a flat map. Flat maps cannot s[how] the size, shape, and direction of a globe all at [once] with total accuracy. As a result, all projections [dis]tort some aspect of the earth's surface. Some m[aps] distort distances, while other maps distort a[rea.] On the next page are four projections.

Mercator Projection

90°W   0°   90°E

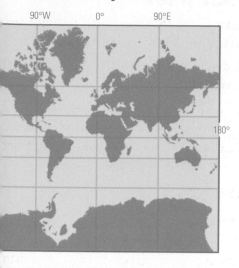

180°

Mercator projection shows most of the continents as
ook on a globe. However, the projection stretches
e lands near the North and South poles. The
tor is used for all kinds of navigation.

Azimuthal Projection

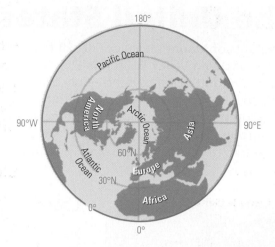

An azimuthal projection shows the earth so that a straight
line from the central point to any other point on the map
gives the shortest distance between the two points. Size
and shape of the continents are also distorted.

Homolosine Projection

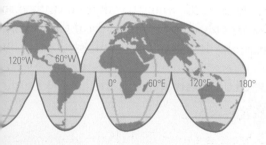

rojection shows the accurate shapes and sizes of the
asses, but distances on the map are not correct.

Robinson Projection

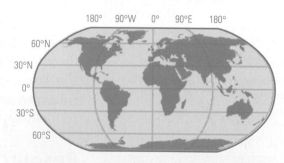

Textbook maps commonly use the Robinson projection.
It shows the entire earth with nearly the true sizes and
shapes of the continents and oceans. However, the shapes
of the landforms near the poles appear flat.

p Basics Assessment

Main Ideas

What is the longitude and latitude of your city
own?

What information is provided by the legend on the
o on page 7?

Vhat is a projection? Compare and contrast Antarctica
he Mercator and the Robinson projections.

2. Critical Thinking

Making Inferences Why do you think latitude
and longitude are so important to sailors?

THINK ABOUT
• the landmarks you use to find your way around
• the landmarks available to sailors on the ocean

Physical Geography of the United States

From the heights of Mount McKinley (20,320 feet above sea level) in Alaska to the depths of Death Valley, California (282 feet below sea level), the geography of the United States is incredibly diverse. In between these extremes lie such varied features and conditions as scorching Arizona deserts, lush Oregon forests, freezing Vermont winters, and sunny Florida beaches. Physical geography involves all the natural features on the earth. This includes the land, resources, climate, and vegetation.

Flowers and brush cover the Coral Pink Sand Dunes in southern Utah.

Land

Separated from much of the world by two oceans, the United States covers 3,717,796 square miles and spans the entire width of North America. To the west, Hawaii stretches the United States into the Pacific Ocean. To the north, Alaska extends the United States to the Arctic Circle. On the U.S. mainland, a central plain separates large mountains in the West and low mountains in the East. Plains make up almost half of the country, while mountains and plateaus make up a quarter each.

An abundance of lakes—Alaska alone has three million—rivers also dot the landscape. Twenty percent of the United States is farmed, providing the country with a steady food supply. Urban areas cover only about two percent of the nation. Refer to the map on the next page for a complete look at the U.S. landscape.

THINKING ABOUT GEOGRAPHY What is the land like around your city or state?

Resources

The United States has a variety of natural resources. Vast amounts of coal, oil, and natural gas lie underneath America's soil. Valuable deposits of lead, zinc, uranium, gold, and silver exist. These resources have helped the United States become the world's leading industrial nation—producing nearly 21 percent of the world's goods and services.

These resources have also helped the United States become both the world's largest producer of energy (natural gas, oil, nuclear power, and electricity) and the world's largest consumer of it. Other natural resources include the Great Lakes, which is shared with Canada. They contain about 20 percent of the world's total supply of fresh surface water. Refer to the map on the next page to examine the nation's natural resources.

THINKING ABOUT GEOGRAPHY What are the different natural resources that you and your family use in your daily lives?

Oil drilled from Alaska helps power the nation's planes, trains, cars, and factories.

and and Resources

250 Miles
500 Kilometers

Miners extract such minerals as gold, silver, and copper from the Rocky Mountains.

40°N

ATLANTIC
OCEAN

30°N

The Appalachians are among the earth's oldest mountains.

70°N

60°N

20°N

num

er

re

🪵 Lumber
🔥 Natural gas
🛢 Oil
📜 Silver
⚛ Uranium
🪙 Zinc

Elevation Key

Feet	Meters
13,120	4,000
9,840	3,000
6,560	2,000
3,280	1,000
1,640	500
656	200
0	0
Below sea level	

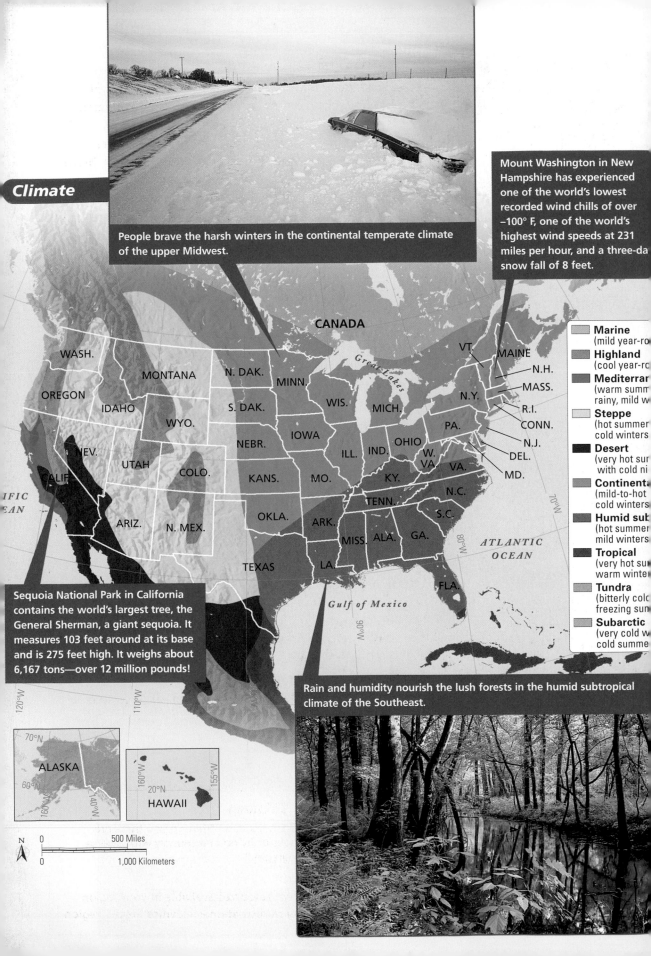

Climate

People brave the harsh winters in the continental temperate climate of the upper Midwest.

Mount Washington in New Hampshire has experienced one of the world's lowest recorded wind chills of over –100° F, one of the world's highest wind speeds at 231 miles per hour, and a three-day snow fall of 8 feet.

Sequoia National Park in California contains the world's largest tree, the General Sherman, a giant sequoia. It measures 103 feet around at its base and is 275 feet high. It weighs about 6,167 tons—over 12 million pounds!

Rain and humidity nourish the lush forests in the humid subtropical climate of the Southeast.

CANADA

Great Lakes

WASH.
OREGON
MONTANA
IDAHO
WYO.
NEV.
CALIF.
UTAH
COLO.
ARIZ.
N. MEX.
N. DAK.
S. DAK.
NEBR.
KANS.
OKLA.
TEXAS
MINN.
IOWA
MO.
ARK.
LA.
WIS.
ILL.
IND.
KY.
TENN.
MISS.
ALA.
GA.
MICH.
OHIO
W. VA.
VA.
N.C.
S.C.
FLA.
PA.
N.Y.
VT.
MAINE
N.H.
MASS.
R.I.
CONN.
N.J.
DEL.
MD.

PACIFIC OCEAN

ATLANTIC OCEAN

Gulf of Mexico

70°W
80°W
90°W
100°W
110°W
120°W

Marine
(mild year-ro
Highland
(cool year-ro
Mediterran
(warm summe
rainy, mild w
Steppe
(hot summer
cold winters
Desert
(very hot sur
with cold ni
Continent
(mild-to-hot
cold winters
Humid sub
(hot summer
mild winters
Tropical
(very hot su
warm winte
Tundra
(bitterly cold
freezing sur
Subarctic
(very cold w
cold summe

70°N
ALASKA
60°N
160°W
140°W

160°W
155°W
20°N
HAWAII

N

| 0 | 500 Miles |
| 0 | 1,000 Kilometers |

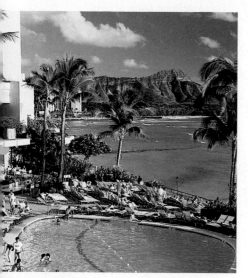

sts and residents bask in the sunshine of
ki Beach in Hawaii.

Climate

The United States contains a variety of climates. For example, the mean temperature in January in Miami, Florida, is 67° F, while it is 11° F in Minneapolis, Minnesota. Most of the United States experiences a continental climate, or distinct change of seasons. Some regional climatic differences include hot and humid summers in the Southeast versus hot and dry summers in the Southwest. Harsh winters and heavy snow can blanket parts of the Midwest, the Northeast, and the higher elevations of the West and Northwest. Refer to the map on the previous page to see the nation's climatic regions.

Human activities have affected the climate, too. For example, pollution from cars and factories can affect local weather conditions and may be contributing to a dangerous rise in the earth's temperature.

THINKING ABOUT GEOGRAPHY How would you describe the climate where you live?

ountainside burns with the autumn
e of New Hampshire.

Vegetation

Between 20,000 and 25,000 species and subspecies of plants and vegetation grow in the United States—including over 1,000 different kinds of trees. Climate often dictates the type of vegetation found in a region. For instance, cold autumns in the Northeast contribute to the brilliantly colored autumn leaves. Rain nourishes the forests in the Northwest and Southeast. The central plains, where rainfall is less heavy, are covered by grass. Cactus plants thrive in the dry southwestern deserts.

Along with natural vegetation, climate dictates the nation's variety of planted crops. For example, temperate weather in the Midwest helps wheat to grow, while warm weather nourishes citrus fruit in Florida and California.

THINKING ABOUT GEOGRAPHY What kinds of trees or plants grow in your region?

sical Geography Assessment

Main Ideas

What are the different aspects of physical graphy?

Which state contains the largest variety of ates?

What two states contain most of the country's esources?

2. Critical Thinking

Drawing Conclusions What do you think are the advantages of living in a country with diverse physical geography?

THINK ABOUT

• the different resources available in your region
• the variety of recreational activities in your region

Geographic Dictionary

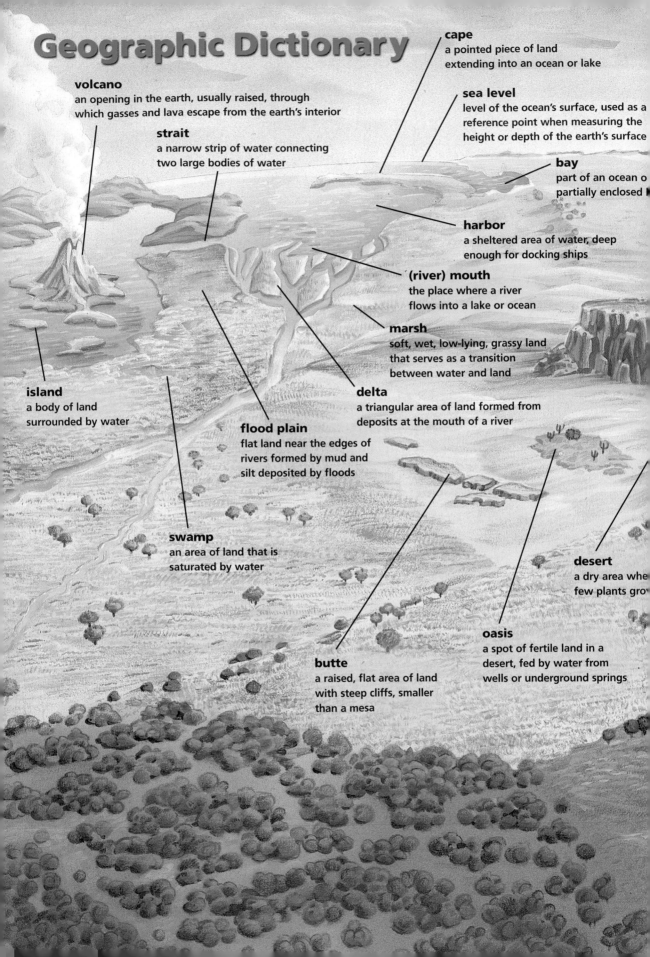

volcano
an opening in the earth, usually raised, through which gasses and lava escape from the earth's interior

cape
a pointed piece of land extending into an ocean or lake

sea level
level of the ocean's surface, used as a reference point when measuring the height or depth of the earth's surface

strait
a narrow strip of water connecting two large bodies of water

bay
part of an ocean o partially enclosed

harbor
a sheltered area of water, deep enough for docking ships

(river) mouth
the place where a river flows into a lake or ocean

marsh
soft, wet, low-lying, grassy land that serves as a transition between water and land

island
a body of land surrounded by water

delta
a triangular area of land formed from deposits at the mouth of a river

flood plain
flat land near the edges of rivers formed by mud and silt deposited by floods

desert
a dry area whe few plants gro

swamp
an area of land that is saturated by water

oasis
a spot of fertile land in a desert, fed by water from wells or underground springs

butte
a raised, flat area of land with steep cliffs, smaller than a mesa

irie
ge, level area
rassland with
or no trees

steppe
a wide, treeless plain

mountain
natural elevation of the earth's
surface with steep sides and
greater height than a hill

valley
low land between hills or
mountains

glacier
a large ice mass that
moves slowly down a
mountain or over land

a
le, flat-topped mountain with
sides, larger than a butte

cataract
a large, powerful
waterfall

canyon
a narrow, deep valley
with steep sides

cliff
the steep, almost vertical edge
of a hill, mountain, or plain

eau
ad, flat area of
higher than the
unding land

Human Geography of the United Stat

Human geography focuses on people's relationships with each other and the surrounding environment. It includes two main themes of geography: human-environment interaction and movement. The following pages will help you to better understand the link between people and geography.

Humans Adapt to Their Surroundings

Humans have always adapted to their environment. For example, in North America, many Native American tribes burned forest patches to create grazing area to attract animals and to clear area for farmland. In addition, Americans have adapted to their environment by building numerous dams, bridges, and tunnels. More recently, scientists and engineers have been developing building materials that will better withstand the earthquakes that occasionally strike California.

THINKING ABOUT GEOGRAPHY What are some of the ways in which you interact with your environment on a daily basis?

Early Americans of the Southwest protect themselves from the weather by building dwellings.

The Hoover Dam, located on the Colorado River between Arizona and Nevada, provides electri for Arizona, Nevada, and Southern California.

An oil spill from the ship *Exxon Valdez* harmed wildlife, such as this bird, in Prince William Sound, Alaska, in 1989.

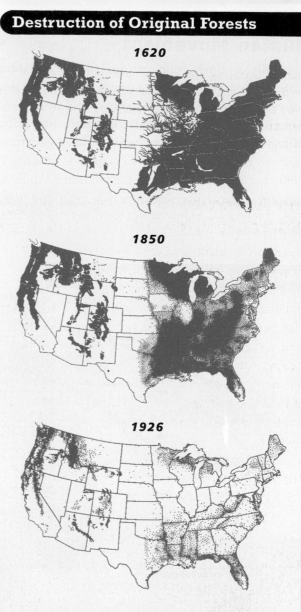

Destruction of Original Forests

1620

1850

1926

These maps show that, over the years, human beings have nearly cut down all the original forests in the United States. Each dot represents 25,000 acres.

mans Affect
e Environment

n humans interact with the environment, times nature suffers. In the United States, xample, major oil leaks or spills occur each —fouling shorelines and harming wildlife. ling suburbs and strip malls has also oyed forests, farmland, and valuable wetlands.

KING ABOUT GEOGRAPHY What are e of the environmental problems in city or town?

n plant trees along ago expressway.

Preserving and Restoring

Americans—as well as people all over the world—have been working hard to balance economic progress with conservation. For example, car companies in the United States and around the world are working to develop pollution-free vehicles. In 1994, the average American family of four recycled around 1,100 pounds of waste. And, in the 1990s, Americans have planted more than two million acres of new trees each year.

THINKING ABOUT GEOGRAPHY What are some of the ways in which you help the environment?

Human Movement

In prehistoric times, people roamed the earth in search of food. Today in the United States, people move from place to place for many different reasons. Among them are cost of living, job availability, and climate. Since the 1970s, many Americans—as well as many new immigrants—moved to the Sunbelt. This region runs through the southern United States from Virginia to California. Between 1950 and 1990, that region's population soared from 52 million to 118 million.

THINKING ABOUT GEOGRAPHY Has your family ever moved? If so, what were some of the reasons?

This map shows human moveme the 1970s. The information belov explains some of the results of th movement in the 1990s.

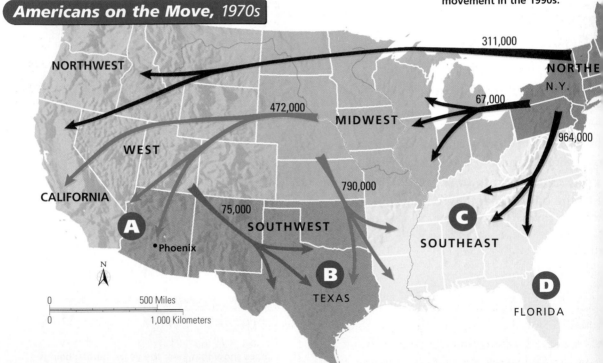

Americans on the Move, *1970s*

NORTHWEST

NORTHE
N.Y.

311,000

67,000

472,000

MIDWEST

WEST

790,000

964,000

CALIFORNIA

75,000

A

SOUTHWEST

•Phoenix

C

SOUTHEAST

N

B

D

500 Miles

TEXAS

FLORIDA

0
0   1,000 Kilometers

A By 1996, the Phoenix-Mesa metropolitan area reached a population of 2.75 million, more than the number of pe living in the entire state in 1980.

B Between 1990 and 1994, Texas overtook New York as th nation's second most populous state, behind California.

C One of the nation's fastest growing areas was the South where population growth ranged from six to nine perce between 1990 and 1994. Jobs grew in the area by 14 pe

D Florida's population is growing so much that it could be as populous as New York state by around 2020.

New home developments cover
the desert in Las Vegas, Nevada.

late 19th century, millions of immigrants
d on the shores of the United States.

The Sears Tower
overlooks Chinatown
in Chicago.

mans Spread Ideas and Information

oughout U.S. history, people from all over the world have come to the
ed States. They have brought with them food, music, language, tech-
gy, and other aspects of their culture. As a result, the United States is
of the most culturally rich and diverse nations in the world. Look
nd your town or city. You'll probably notice different people, lan-
es, and foods.

oday, the spreading of ideas and customs does not rely solely on human
ement. Technology—from the Internet to television to satellites—
ds ideas and information throughout the world faster than ever. This
created an ever-growing, interconnected world. As the 21st century
s, human geography will continue to play a key role in shaping the
ed States and the world.

KING ABOUT GEOGRAPHY How have computers and the
rnet affected your life?

---

man Geography Assessment

Main Ideas

What are some of the ways that people have helped
restore the environment?

What are some of the ways that residents of your
gion have successfully modified their landscape?

What are some of the reasons that people move from
ce to place?

2. Critical Thinking

Recognizing Effects In what ways has technology
helped bring people in the world together?

THINK ABOUT

- the different ways in which people communicate
  today
- the speed in which people today can communicate
  over long distances

TERMS

Briefly explain the significance of each of the following.

1. physical map
2. political map
3. longitude
4. latitude
5. hemisphere
6. projection
7. flood plain
8. sea level
9. human geography
10. human movement

REVIEW QUESTIONS

Themes of Geography (pages 4–5)

1. What is the difference between *absolute* location and *relative* location?
2. What is meant by the theme of place?
3. What are the themes of movement and human-environment interaction?

Map Basics (pages 6–9)

4. What do you think are some of the benefits of using technology to study geography?
5. What are the three major kinds of maps?
6. What are latitude and longitude lines?

Physical Geography (pages 10–13)

7. How have the natural resources in the United States helped its economic development?
8. What are the different climates within the United States?

Human Geography (pages 16–19)

9. How is human geography different from physic geography?
10. What aspects of human geography might cause people to move?

CRITICAL THINKING

1. **Forming and Supporting Opinions** Which of the five themes of geography do you think has the most impact on history? Why?
2. **Analyzing Causes** How do the climate and natural resources of an area affect its economy
3. **Drawing Conclusions** How have computers helped geographers make more accurate maps
4. **Making Inferences** Why do you think the Mercator projection is used for all types of navigation?
5. **Recognizing Effects** How does a diverse land-scape help or hurt the economy of an area?

GEOGRAPHY SKILLS

1. INTERPRETING MAPS: Movement

Basic Map Elements

a. What region of the United States is shown?
b. Compare the number of teams on the 1987 map and the 2000 map. How many more teams are on the 2000 map?

Interpreting the Map

c. What geographic theme(s) is most responsible fo the increase in sports teams in this region?
d. According to the map, which sport enjoyed the biggest surge in popularity in this region?

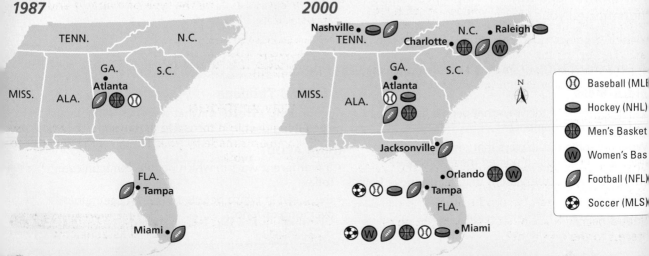

Major League Sports in Southeast Cities

TERPRETING MAPS: Region

y the map and then answer the questions.

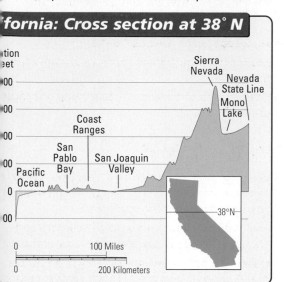

fornia: Cross section at 38° N

Map Elements

hat are the different landforms on the map?

preting the Map

hat is the level of the San Joaquin Valley? How
any miles does it take to get from there to the
ghest point in California at the 38th parallel?

TERPRETING PRIMARY SOURCES

03, President Thomas Jefferson appointed
wether Lewis to explore the lands of the Louisiana
ase. Jefferson gave him these instructions:

object of your mission is to explore the Missouri
. . . by its course & communication with the waters
e Pacific Ocean, may offer the most direct &
ticable water communication across this continent,
he purposes of commerce. . . .
her objects worthy of notice will be the soil & face
e country, its growth & vegetable productions . . .
mineral productions of every kind. . . . climate as
acterized by the thermometer . . . the dates at
h particular plants put forth or lose their flowers,
af, times of appearance of particular birds, reptiles,
sects.

mas Jefferson, quoted in *The Journals of Lewis
Clark*

What was Jefferson expecting to find in the West?

Why might the president want to know about the
and's soil and vegetable production?

What aspect of human geography might be of
terest to the president?

ALTERNATIVE ASSESSMENT

1. INTERDISCIPLINARY ACTIVITY: Math

Plotting Latitude and Longitude On a piece of
graph paper, sketch a map of the United States. Be
sure to draw in state boundaries, too. Then, using an
atlas as a reference, draw and mark the latitude and
longitude lines that cross the nation at five degree
intervals. Plot the estimated longitude and latitude
location of your city or town. Determine at which
degrees the lines intersect where you live. Repeat this
exercise for at least five different places you have visited or would like to visit within the United States.

2. COOPERATIVE LEARNING ACTIVITY

Making a Map How well do you know the neighborhood around your school? Form groups of three to
four students. Then work together to draw a map of
the neighborhood around your school. Include:

- streets
- residences
- stores
- geographic features
- important landmarks

The map should be accurate but not too cluttered
with unnecessary details. Compare your group's map
with those of the other groups in the class.

3. TECHNOLOGY ACTIVITY

Writing Directions Several Internet sites provide
detailed maps of the United States. They also provide
driving directions to most places in the country.

- Locate one of these map sites on the Internet.
- Think of a place in the United States that you would
  like to visit.
- Work with the computer to find the best route for
  reaching it.

Write out clear directions as well as the total mileage
of your trip. Also, note the type of map it is and the
features it highlights.

For more important geography sites . . .

INTERNET ACTIVITY
CLASSZONE.COM

4. HISTORY PORTFOLIO

Review your alternative assessment activities. Use
comments made by your teacher or classmates to
improve your work.

Additional Test Practice,
pp. S1–S33

TEST PRACTICE
CLASSZONE.COM

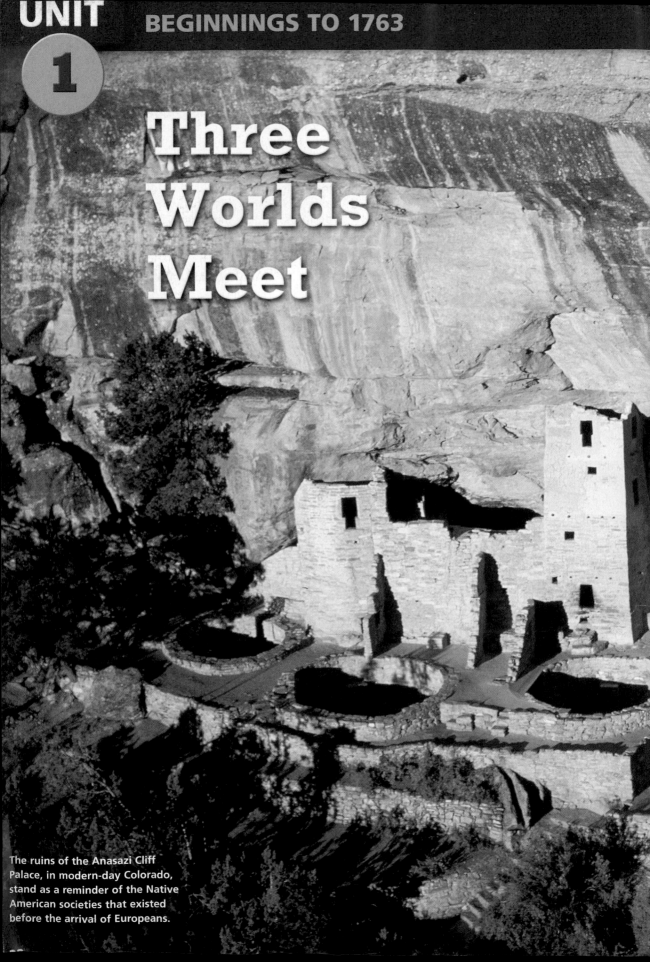

Three Worlds Meet

The ruins of the Anasazi Cliff Palace, in modern-day Colorado, stand as a reminder of the Native American societies that existed before the arrival of Europeans.

"The story of my people and the story of this place are one single story."

—Taos Pueblo man

These Native Americans may well be seeing ships this size for the first time.

400 B.C.–200 B.C.
Hopewell culture, which created this mica birdclaw, flourishes in the Midwest.

200s
The Maya are using hieroglyphic writing.

Americas
World

200 B.C.

About 6 B.C.
Jesus of Nazareth is born. His teachings become the basis for Christianity.

476
Western Roman Empire ends. Over time, Europe splits into small kingdoms.

You are a Native American living on the northeastern coast of North America. One day you see a giant boat topped by strange white cloths. Men climb into smaller boats and row toward you. You have never seen men like this. They have pale skin and wear heavy, colorful clothing. You wonder what will happen when they land.

This European ship spent weeks at sea to reach the coast of North America.

What happens when different societies meet?

What Do You Think?

- What can different societies learn from each other?
- What might they gain from each other?
- What positive and negative things might happen when they meet?

RESEARCH LINKS
CLASSZONE.COM

Visit the Chapter 1 links for more information about the first Americans or European voyagers.

800s
grown
now the
States.

1000
Viking Leif Erikson reaches what is now Newfoundland.

1100s
The city of Cahokia flourishes in what is now Illinois.

1200s
The Aztecs conquer much of central Mexico.

1492
The European explorer Columbus lands in the Americas.

A.D. 1500

1096
Europeans begin the Crusades to capture the Holy Land from followers of Islam.

1324
Mansa Musa, emperor of Mali, travels to Islam's holy city. Word of his gold spreads to Europe.

Reading Strategy: Categorizing Information

What Do You Know?

What do you know about the history of the Americas, West Africa, and Europe? How advanced must a society be to build large structures like the ones at the right?

Think About

- what you know about other societies, such as Egypt, that built large structures
- what you've read in books
- your responses to the Interact with History about when different societies meet (see page 25)

AFRICA This Muslim mosque in Timbuktu, Mali, was built in the 1300s and 1400s.

EUROPE St Basilica (a C church) in V Italy, was b 1500s and

What Do You Want to Know?

 What questions do you have about the past societies of the Americas, West Africa, and Europe? What do you want to know about how they met? Record those questions in your notebook before you read the chapter.

Categorizing Information

One way to make better sense of what you read is to categorize. To categorize is to sort information into groups. The chart below will help you record information about the societies of the Americas, West Africa, and Europe. As you read, look for information relating to the categories of trade, technology, religion, and art. Record that informatio on your chart.

S See Skillbuilder Handbook, page R6.

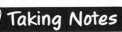 Taking Notes

	Trade	Technology	Religion	Art
AMERICAS				
WEST AFRICA				
EUROPE				

Crossing to the Americas

MAIN IDEA	WHY IT MATTERS NOW	TERMS & NAMES

peoples came from Asia to
…ericas and over time
…ed complex civilizations.

Archaeologists and other scientists
continue to make new discoveries
about these ancient people.

archaeologist
artifact
migrate
culture

domestication
civilization
irrigation
Mound Builders

ONE AMERICAN'S STORY

For many years, Solveig Turpin has searched Texas for paintings that
ancient people drew on rock walls. Turpin is an **archaeologist**.
That is a scientist who studies the human past by examining
the things people left behind. Turpin believes that one of the
paintings she found shows a religious leader who turned
himself into a panther.

A VOICE FROM THE PAST

This is the Shaman [religious leader] who transforms into the
largest and most powerful animal here. . . . I like to call [the
shamans] supramen because they were over everything.

Solveig Turpin, quoted in *In Search of Ancient North America*

Archaeologist Solveig
Turpin wears a shirt
displaying the rock
paintings of ancient
peoples as she
discusses her work.

Archaeologists make theories about the past based on what they learn
from bones and artifacts. **Artifacts** are tools and other objects that humans
made. Section 1 discusses some theories about early Americans.

The First People in America

As many societies do, many Native Americans have stories explaining
the origin of their people. Some believe the gods created their ancestors.
Others believe their ancestors were born of Mother Earth. In contrast,
scientists think that the first Americans **migrated**, or moved, here from
Asia. But scientists disagree about how and when this move took place.

Some ancient people may have crossed a land bridge that joined Asia
and North America during the last Ice Age. The Ice Age was a time of
extreme cold that lasted for thousands of years. Glaciers trapped so much
water that ocean levels dropped. A bridge of land, now called Beringia,
appeared where the Bering Strait is now. (See map, page 28.) When the
earth grew warm again, the glaciers melted and flooded Beringia. Some
scientists who hold this theory believe the earliest Americans arrived

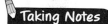

Taking Notes

Use your chart to
take notes about
the Americas.

	Trade
AMERICAS	
WEST AFRICA	
EUROPE	

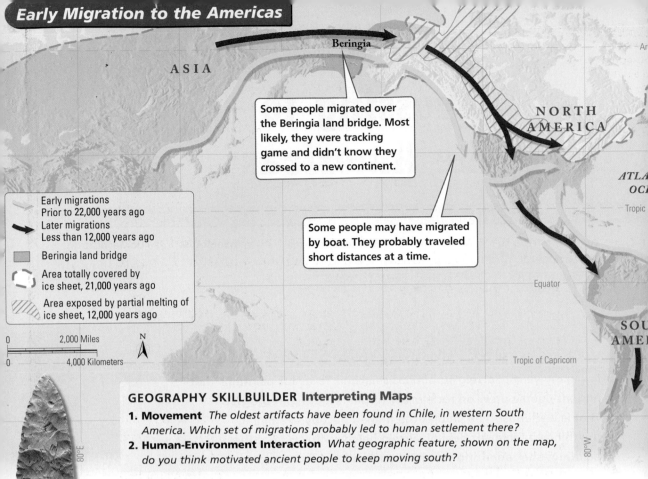

ASIA

Beringia

NORTH
AMERICA

Some people migrated over
the Beringia land bridge. Most
likely, they were tracking
game and didn't know they
crossed to a new continent.

ATLA
OC

Tropic

Some people may have migrated
by boat. They probably traveled
short distances at a time.

Equator

SOU
AME

Tropic of Capricorn

Legend

Early migrations
Prior to 22,000 years ago

Later migrations
Less than 12,000 years ago

Beringia land bridge

Area totally covered by
ice sheet, 21,000 years ago

Area exposed by partial melting of
ice sheet, 12,000 years ago

0   2,000 Miles
0   4,000 Kilometers

N

GEOGRAPHY SKILLBUILDER Interpreting Maps
1. **Movement** *The oldest artifacts have been found in Chile, in western South America. Which set of migrations probably led to human settlement there?*
2. **Human-Environment Interaction** *What geographic feature, shown on the map, do you think motivated ancient people to keep moving south?*

12,000 years ago. Other scientists believe humans came to the Americas much earlier. They have found artifacts in South America that tests show to be 30,000 years old. These scientists believe that people came to the Americas by many routes, over thousands of years. Some came by boat, sailing short distances from island to island. This theory may also change as scientists find more evidence of ancient Americans.

Ancient hunters used spear points such as this one, which is about 10,000 years old.

Agriculture Leads to Civilization

A <u>culture</u> is a way of life shared by people with similar arts, beliefs, and customs. The first Americans lived in hunting and gathering cultures. They hunted small animals, such as rabbits, and large animals, such as the woolly mammoth. They gathered wild seeds, nuts, and berries.

In time, people started to plant the seeds they found. This was the beginning of agriculture. About 5,000 years ago, humans began domestication. <u>**Domestication**</u> is the practice of breeding plants or taming animals to meet human needs. By trial and error, people in central Mexico learned which seeds grew the best crops. By selecting the right seeds, they improved the quality of maize, or corn, until its ears were large. Dried and stored for future use, corn became a main food source.

Knowledge of agriculture spread throughout the Americas. Having a stable food supply changed the way people lived. Once they no longer had to travel to find food, they built permanent villages. Farmers were able to produce large harvests, so that fewer people needed to farm.

Vocabular
woolly ma
moth: a ha
ancestor o
elephant, r
extinct

*ding*History

awing
usions Why
d a culture
to learn
ulture before
ld develop a
ation?

Some people began to practice other crafts, such as weaving or making pots. A few people became religious leaders.

Slowly, some cultures grew complex and became civilizations. A **civilization** has five features: (1) cities that are centers of trade, (2) specialized jobs for different people, (3) organized forms of government and religion, (4) a system of record keeping, and (5) advanced tools.

Early Mesoamerican Civilizations

About 1200 B.C., an advanced civilization arose in Mesoamerica, a region that stretches from central Mexico to present-day Nicaragua. For 800 years, a people called the Olmec thrived along the Gulf of Mexico. The Olmec set up a network of trade routes and constructed earthen mounds shaped like pyramids. They built large, busy cities like La Venta.

> ### A VOICE FROM THE PAST
>
> La Venta was not just an empty ceremonial spot visited by Olmec priests and nobles but a prosperous community of fishers, farmers, traders, and specialists, such as the artisans and the sculptors.
>
> **Rebecca González,** quoted in "New Light on the Olmec," *National Geographic*

Around 400 B.C., the Olmec abandoned La Venta and other cities. Scientists don't know why. By then, Olmec culture had spread along trade routes and influenced others. Later people in Mesoamerica adapted Olmec religious practices and carved designs inspired by Olmec art.

By A.D. 250, about 650 years after the Olmec vanished, the Maya had developed a great civilization. Their cities were in southern Mexico and Guatemala, where they built pyramid mounds topped by temples. From artifacts, archaeologists know that the Maya had an accurate yearly calendar. They were the first people in the Americas to create a number system using zero. Their written language used picture symbols.

By 900, the Maya had abandoned many of their cities. Scientists think that revolts, disease, or crop failures may have caused their society to fail.

The Hohokam and the Anasazi

During the Mayan period, an agricultural people inhabited the American Southwest. The Hohokam lived in what is now Arizona from about 300 B.C. to A.D. 1400. That desert region has little rain, so farming is difficult. But the Hohokam altered their dry environment. They dug hundreds of miles of canals to carry river water to their crops. The practice of bringing water to crops is called **irrigation**.

The Hohokam raised corn, beans, and squash. They also gathered wild plants and hunted animals. They traded widely—with people in Mexico, the Southwest, and California. Hohokam pottery and religious practices show the influence of Mesoamerican cultures, which they learned about through trade.

ground
maticians
a also
ped the
f using a
l for zero.
s later car-
e idea
Asia to
e.

Ancient peoples of the American Southwest used images like this to communicate with each other. Such images are called petroglyphs.

The Mound Builders

During the 1700s, Europeans discovered several mysterious earthen mounds in what is now the American Southeast and Midwest. They believed a lost civilization had built the mounds. Historians now know that different Native American groups, known as the Mound Builders, built these structures. The builders may have used the mounds for burial tombs, as a tribute to their gods, or for some other religious purpose. One famous mound is the Great Serpent Mound in present-day Ohio. The Adena, Fort Ancient, or Hopewell cultures possibly built it. An aerial photograph of the Great Serpent Mound is shown below.

The ancient builders carefully outlined the shape of the serpent using rocks and clay mixed with ashes. This allowed them to design the image accurately and to give it a strong foundation.

Workers dug with stones and should bones from deer a They used about baskets of soil to mound. Construct likely took betwe ten years and req hundreds of labo

The mound is a quarter mile long, averages 20 feet wide, and is about 5 feet high.

0   1/4 mile

CONNECT TO HISTORY

1. **Drawing Conclusions** R the five characteristics of a civilization on page 29. W of these characteristics wo a culture need to be able build something like the Great Serpent Mound?

S See Skillbuilder Handbook, page R13.

CONNECT TO TODAY

2. **Researching** How do mo monuments to the dead d from those constructed by Mound Builders?

For more about Mound Builders

Beginning about A.D. 100, the Anasazi lived in the area where Utah, Arizona, Colorado, and New Mexico now meet. Scientists don't know their origin. Like the Hohokam, the Anasazi were mainly farmers who also traded widely.

The Anasazi built houses with hundreds of rooms and many stories. For protection, they placed some buildings against overhanging canyon walls. The 800-room Pueblo Bonito in Chaco Canyon, New Mexico, housed perhaps 1,000 people. In the 1500s, when Spanish explorers first saw these houses, they called them *pueblos,* meaning villages. Around 1300, drought or warfare caused the Anasazi to leave their homes.

The Mound Builders

In the eastern part of what is now the United States lived several groups of people called Mound Builders. The **Mound Builders** were early Native Americans who built large earthen structures.

The two oldest Mound Builder societies were the Adena and the Hopewell. Archaeologists know little about the Adena. The Hopewell, located in what is now the Midwest, lived from 400 B.C. to A.D. 400. Like the Hohokam, they grew corn. Artifacts show that they had a large trade network. It stretched from the Atlantic to the Rocky Mountains, and from the Great Lakes to Florida. Hopewell mounds served as burial sites. Their tombs contained jewelry and other gifts for the dead.

The last group of Mound Builders, the Mississippians, lived from A.D. 800 to 1700. They built some of the first cities in North America. For example, Cahokia in Illinois has more than 100 mounds. One of them, Monks Mound, rises 100 feet and covers 16 acres. In some cities, the Mississippians built flat-topped, pyramid-shaped temple mounds.

By the 1700s, most of the Mississippians had died from diseases they caught from Europeans. But many Native American groups continued to thrive throughout the United States, as you will read in Section 2.

ng History
paring
ther
American
built
d-shaped
s?

---

ion ❶ Assessment

erms & Names

lain the
gnificance of:

haeologist
ifact
grate
ture
mestication
ilization
gation
ound Builders

2. Using Graphics

Use a chart like the one below to list ancient cultures of Mesoamerica and North America and their locations.

Ancient Culture	Location

Which of these cultures was closest to where you live?

3. Main Ideas

a. By what land bridge did some ancient people migrate to North America, and how was it created?

b. How did the development of farming lead to the growth of civilization?

c. How did trade help to spread culture?

4. Critical Thinking

Comparing How did the Hohokam and the Anasazi adapt to living in their environment?

THINK ABOUT
• Hohokam agriculture
• Anasazi dwellings

VITY OPTIONS

SCIENCE
GUAGE ARTS

Research the growing of corn. Draw a **diagram** of a corn plant with its parts labeled or write a **description** of how corn grows.

2

Societies of North America

MAIN IDEA	WHY IT MATTERS NOW	TERMS & NAMES
By 1500, a variety of Native American groups—each with a distinct culture—lived in North America.	Many Americans today claim one or more of these cultures as part of their heritage.	technology slash-and-~~agricultu~~ tundra kayak Deganawi~~ matrilineal Iroquois Le~~

ONE AMERICAN'S STORY

Many Native Americans today work to save their culture. Haida artist Bill Reid took part in this effort. When he was a teenager in the 1930s, few Haida artists were making totem poles or other Haida crafts. Reid began to learn about Haida arts from his grandfather.

Reid studied Northwest Coast native arts and jewelry making. Soon he created gold jewelry with Haida designs and carved sculptures. When Reid died, his work was praised.

> *A VOICE FROM THE PAST*
>
> Canada has lost one of its greatest artists. A descendant of a lineage of great Haida artists . . . , Bill Reid revived an artistic tradition that had survived only in museum collections.
>
> **Dr. George MacDonald,** at Bill Reid's memorial service, March 24, 1998

Creating s
of traditio
was one v
Reid kept
culture ali

Written records and people like Reid have preserved knowledge of the cultures that flourished in the Americas when Europeans arrived. This section explains the diversity of Native American groups in 1500.

Taking Notes

Use your chart to take notes about the societies of North America.

	Trade
MERICAS	
EST FRICA	
UROPE	

Native American Diversity

By 1500, Native Americans had divided into hundreds of cultural groups, speaking perhaps 2,000 languages. One reason Native Americans were so diverse was that each group adapted to its own environment—whether subzero ice fields, scorching deserts, or dense forests.

Environment shaped each group's economy, technology, and religion. **Technology** is the use of tools and knowledge to meet human needs. In some regions, Native Americans based their economy on farming. In others, they relied on hunting or fishing. Different environments caused technology to vary. In coastal areas, farmers made tools from shells. In

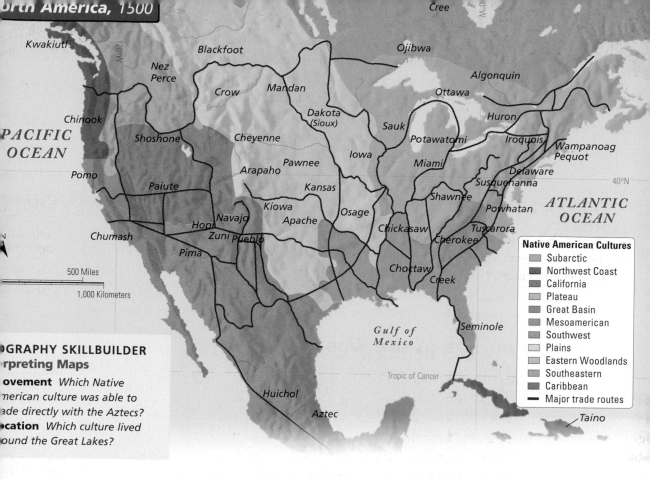

Cree

Kwakiutl
Blackfoot
Ojibwa

Nez Perce
Crow
Mandan
Algonquin
Ottawa

Chinook
PACIFIC OCEAN
Shoshone
Cheyenne
Dakota (Sioux)
Sauk
Huron
Iroquois

Pomo
Paiute
Cheyenne
Pawnee
Arapaho
Iowa
Potawatomi
Miami
Wampanoag
Pequot
Delaware
Susquehanna
40°N

Chumash
Hopi
Navajo
Zuni Pueblo
Apache
Kiowa
Osage
Shawnee
Powhatan
Tuscarora
ATLANTIC OCEAN

Pima
Chickasaw
Cherokee

500 Miles
1,000 Kilometers
Choctaw
Creek

Gulf of Mexico

Seminole

Tropic of Cancer

Native American Cultures
- Subarctic
- Northwest Coast
- California
- Plateau
- Great Basin
- Mesoamerican
- Southwest
- Plains
- Eastern Woodlands
- Southeastern
- Caribbean
- — Major trade routes

Huichol
Aztec
Taino

GRAPHY SKILLBUILDER
rpreting Maps
ovement Which Native
merican culture was able to
ade directly with the Aztecs?
cation Which culture lived
ound the Great Lakes?

deserts, they used irrigation. Environment affected religion, too. Native Americans strongly believed that certain places were sacred—and that animals, plants, and natural forces had spiritual importance.

Although Native American groups had many differences, they all felt closely connected to nature, as shown in the following chant.

A VOICE FROM THE PAST

Earth's body has become my body
  by means of these I shall live on.
Earth's mind has become my mind
  by means of these I shall live on.

Navajo Blessing Way, quoted in *America in 1492*

In addition, trade linked Native Americans. Trading centers developed across North America, especially at points where two cultures met.

Peoples of the North and Northwest Coast

round
it are
led the

The Aleut (uh•LOOT) and the Inuit (IHN•yoo•iht) were peoples of the far North. The Aleut lived on islands off Alaska, and the Inuit lived near the coast on tundra. **Tundra** is a treeless plain that remains frozen under its top layer of soil. Ice and snow cover the ground most of the year.

Because their climate was too cold for farming, the Inuit and Aleut were hunters. They paddled **kayaks**, small boats made of animal skins, into icy seas to spear whales, seals, and walruses. They hunted these mammals for food, and they made seal and walrus skins into clothes. Some Inuit religious ceremonies honored the spirits of the whales and seals they caught. The Inuit also hunted such land animals as caribou. They made arrowheads and spear points from bones and antlers.

Farther south, Northwest Coast people also hunted sea mammals. But they mostly fished for salmon. Living by forests, Northwest Coast people used wood for houses, boats, and carved objects. They traded such coastal products as shells for items from the inland, such as furs.

Northwest Coast groups such as the Kwakiutl (KWAH•kee•OOT•uhl) and Haida had a special ceremony—the potlatch. Individuals would give away most or all of their goods as a way to claim status and benefit their community. They held potlatches to mark life events, such as naming a child or mourning the dead.

> *The term [potlatch] comes from Chinook . . . and means 'to give.'*
>
> Gloria Cranmer Webster, U'mista Cultural Centre

Reading His
A. Making Inferences W would inlan people trade seashells?

Peoples of the West

Unlike the Native Americans of the Northwest Coast, those of the West did not rely mainly on the sea. The peoples of the West included tribes in California, the Columbia Plateau, and the Great Basin. Much of the West is desert or is not suitable for farming. The people who lived there existed mainly by hunting and gathering.

The men hunted deer, elk, antelope, rabbits, and birds. They also fished, especially for salmon that swam up the western rivers. Women gathered such wild foods as nuts, seeds, and berries. Many western groups moved with the seasons to collect food.

Reading His
B. Reading a On the map page 33, loc the cultures California, t Plateau, and Great Basin Notice why three toget are called t peoples of West.

The women of some western tribes became expert weavers. Pomo women wove beautiful baskets that they used to gather and store food. They wove some baskets tightly enough to be watertight.

The peoples of the West had strong spiritual beliefs, often linked to nature. Some held ceremonies to ensure a large food supply. Others held dances to ask for rain, for plant growth, and for good hunting. Still others believed that their religious leaders could contact the spirit world.

Peoples of Mexico

Far to the south, the Aztecs ruled a great civilization in what is now central Mexico. The origin of the Aztecs is unclear. They may have been hunters and gatherers like the Native Americans of the West. Sometime during the 1100s, they migrated into the Valley of Mexico.

In 1325, they began to build their capital city, Tenochtitlán (teh•NAWCH•tee•TLAHN), on islands in Lake Texcoco. Two things helped the Aztecs become a strong empire. First, they drained swamps and built an

The Aztec Calendar

This stone is the Aztec calender wheel. In the center is the sun god. Around it are symbols for the 20 days of the Aztec month. Three are enlarged below.

Rabbit   Deer   Death

irrigation system. This enabled them to grow plenty of food. Second, they were a warlike people who conquered most of their neighbors. The defeated people then had to send the Aztecs food and resources.

The Aztecs had a complex society. Rulers were the highest class. Priests and government workers ranked next. Slaves and servants were at the bottom. The Aztecs had elaborate religious ceremonies linked to their calendar and their study of the sun, moon, and stars. Many of their beliefs came from earlier Mesoamerican cultures.

The Aztecs' most important ritual involved feeding their sun god human blood. To do this, the Aztecs sacrificed prisoners of war by cutting out the person's heart while he was still alive. One reason the Aztecs fought so many wars was to capture prisoners to sacrifice.

Peoples of the Southwest

North of the Aztec, in what is now the American Southwest, lived the Pueblo people. Their ancestors were the ancient Hohokam and Anasazi. Like their ancestors, the Pueblo used irrigation to alter their desert region for farming. They lived in many-storied houses of adobe—dried mud bricks. These large buildings sometimes held an entire village.

Pueblo Indian farmers raised corn, beans, and squash. For meat, they hunted game and raised turkeys. Men did most of the farming, hunting, weaving, and building. Women ground the corn and cooked the food, repaired the adobe houses, and crafted pottery.

The Navajo and the Apache were nomadic, or wandering, hunter-gatherers who came to the region later than the Pueblo. For food, they relied mainly on game and on cactus, roots, and piñon nuts. Often, they traded these wild products for crops that the Pueblo had grown. Over time, the Navajo adopted farming and other Pueblo practices.

Peoples of the Great Plains

Farther north, the Great Plains is a flat grassland region stretching from the Mississippi River west to the Rocky Mountains. Today, most people think of Plains Indians on horseback, but originally they had no horses. The Spanish first brought horses to the Americas in the 1500s.

Some Plains groups were nomads. Others lived in villages by rivers, where land was easier to farm. In summer, entire villages set out to track bison. Hunting bison on foot was difficult, but Plains tribes used their environment to help them. Working together, the villagers stampeded the herd over a cliff, so the fall would kill or disable the animals. Plains Indians not only ate the bison's meat. They also made its hide into clothes and its bones into tools.

daily *life*

KACHINA DANCES
Every year in summer the Hopi, Zuni, and other Pueblo Indians held a religious celebration. The ceremony called on the kachinas, or spirits of the ancestors. The Pueblo believed the kachinas had the power to bring a plentiful harvest. At the festival, masked dancers played the role of different kachinas. They danced and sang songs to bring rain in the year ahead. Today, the Pueblo also carve kachina dolls, shown below, as well as hold dances.

In winter such northern Plains groups as the Mandans and Pawnee lived in large circular lodges. Wooden beams held up the earthen walls. A hole at the top provided air, light, and an outlet for smoke from the fire. Buried partly underground, the earth lodge protected the people from the extreme cold and wind of the Plains climate.

The spiritual beliefs of Plains tribes varied. Some felt a close tie to regional animals such as the bison or plants such as corn. Some honored sacred places, such as the Black Hills of South Dakota and Wyoming. Many Plains tribes held a ceremony called the Sun Dance, which involved making a vow and asking the Creator for aid.

Peoples of the Southeast

The Southeast, which stretches from east Texas to the Atlantic Ocean, has mild winters and warm summers with plentiful rainfall. The long growing season led the Choctaw (CHAHK•taw), Chickasaw (CHIHK•uh•SAW), and other southeastern groups to become farmers. As many other Native Americans did, they grew corn, beans, squash, and pumpkins.

Women did most of the farming, while men hunted, fished, and cleared land. The men spent months in the forest tracking deer. In the Southeast, people traced their family ties through the women. Societies in which ancestry is traced through the mother are called **matrilineal**.

In southeastern villages, people gathered at a central square for public meetings and such religious ceremonies as the Green Corn Festival. Held once a year, this festival offered thanks for the corn harvest and also served as a kind of New Year's celebration. People cleaned their houses, threw away old pots, and settled quarrels as a sign of a fresh start for the year.

Reading **Hi**
D. Analyzin
Causes Wh
would a lor
growing sea
lead peopl
become far

Peoples of the Eastern Woodlands

Like the Southeast, the Northeast had plenty of fish, game, and rain. But the climate was colder with snowy winters. Forests covered much of the region, so it is called the Eastern Woodlands. Most of the people living there spoke either an Iroquoian or Algonquian language.

Many Native Americans in the Southeast and Eastern Woodlands played lacrosse using sticks like these. Modern Americans have adopted the game.

Like all Native Americans, the Iroquois learned to live in their environment. They hunted wild game. They adapted the forest for farming by using slash-and-burn agriculture. In **slash-and-burn agriculture**, farmers chopped down and then burned trees on a plot of land. The ashes from the fire enriched the soil. When a field's soil became worn out, the farmer abandoned it and cleared a new field. The Iroquois lived in longhouses, bark-covered shelters as long as 300 feet. One longhouse held eight to ten families.

The Algonquin lived in wigwams, domelike houses covered with deerskin and slabs of bark. For protection, both the Iroquois and Algonquin surrounded their villages with high fences made of poles. Iroquois villagers often needed protection not only from the enemies of the Iroquois, but from each other. The Iroquois often raided neighboring villages for food and captives.

In the late 1500s, five northern Iroquois nations took the advice of a peace-seeking man named **Deganawida**. They stopped warring with each other and formed an alliance. This alliance of the Cayuga, Mohawk, Oneida, Onondaga, and Seneca was the **Iroquois League**. The League brought a long period of peace to the Iroquois. A council of leaders from each nation governed the League. They followed rules called the Great Law of Peace. The Iroquois were also a matrilineal society. If a leader did something wrong, the women of his clan could vote him out of office.

Across the Atlantic, the peoples of West Africa also adapted to their environment and engaged in trade. West Africa was the region from which most Africans were brought to the Americas. You will read about it in the next section.

ground
ugh it is a
way to
fields, slash-
urn agricul-
loes cause
onmental
ge by
oying
s.

AMERICA'S HISTORY MAKERS

DEGANAWIDA (THE PEACEMAKER)

Iroquois tradition honors Deganawida as the Peacemaker. Seeing how destructive warfare was for the Iroquois, Deganawida went from tribe to tribe and described his dream of peace. A poor speaker, he persuaded few warriors. Finally, an Iroquois chief named Hiawatha spoke for him. After long negotiations, the leaders of the warring nations made peace. However, Deganawida's own tribe, the Huron, did not join the League.

How did both Deganawida and Hiawatha lead the Iroquois toward peace?

---

ion ② Assessment

erms & Names
lain the
gnificance of:
chnology
ndra
yak
atrilineal
sh-and-burn
griculture
eganawida
quois League

2. Using Graphics

Use a cluster diagram to record how Native Americans from each region adapted to their environment.

People of the North

Adapted to Environment

3. Main Ideas

a. What were some of the religious ceremonies of Native Americans?

b. How were the Pueblo like their ancestors, the Hohokam?

c. How did the formation of the Iroquois League benefit its member nations?

4. Critical Thinking

Drawing Conclusions
How did trade benefit both groups that took part in it?

THINK ABOUT

• who the Northwest Coast people traded with and what they exchanged

• what the Pueblo exchanged with nomadic groups

VITY OPTIONS

ART

GUAGE ARTS

Reread the Navajo chant on page 33. Draw an **illustration** to go with the chant or write additional **verses**.

The Iroquois Great Law of Peac

Setting the Stage The five nations of the Iroquois League created a constitution, called the Great Law of Peace, that had 117 laws and custom These laws governed all aspects of life and war. In this excerpt, Deganawi introduces the Great Law by describing a tree that symbolizes the perman and stability of the league. **See Primary Source Explorer** ◎

1 I am Deganawida and with the Five Nations' Confederate **Lords**[1] I the Tree of Great Peace. I plant it in your territory, **Adodarhoh**,[2] an Onondaga Nation, in the territory of you who are Firekeepers.

I name the tree the Tree of the Great Long Leaves. Under the shade o Tree of the Great Peace we spread the soft white feathery down of the thistle as seats for you, Adodarhoh, and your cousin Lords.

We place you upon those seats, spread soft with the feathery down c globe thistle, there beneath the shade of the spreading branches of the of Peace. There shall you sit and watch the Council Fire of the **Confed of the Five Nations**,[3] and all the affairs of the Five Nations shall be t acted at this place before you, Adodarhoh, and your cousin Lords, b Confederate Lords of the Five Nations.

2 Roots have spread out from the Tree of the Great Peace, one to the r one to the east, one to the south, and one to the west. The name of roots is The Great White Roots and their nature is Peace and Strength

If any man or any nation outside the Five Nations shall obey the la the Great Peace and make known their disposition to the Lords c Confederacy, they may trace the Roots to the Tree and if their mine clean and they are obedient and promise to obey the wishes o Confederate Council, they shall be welcomed to take shelter beneat Tree of the Long Leaves.

A CLOSER LOOK

THE COUNCIL FIRE

The council fire of the Iroquois League was kept burning for about 200 years.

1. What do you think it would mean if the council fire were allowed to die?

A CLOSER LOOK

THE GREAT WHITE ROOTS

The roots of a tree help to anchor it in the ground, and they draw water and food from the soil.

2. Why might Deganawida say the nature of the roots is "Peace and Strength"?

1. **Lords:** chiefs.

2. **Adodarhoh:** the name of the office of the Onondaga chief.

3. **Confederacy of the Five Nations:** the Iroquois League

Interactive Primary Source Assessment

1. Main Ideas

a. In what territory was the Tree of the Great Peace planted?

b. Where will the affairs of the Five Nations be conducted?

c. Where have the Tree's roots spread?

2. Critical Thinking

Making Inferences Were outsiders welcome to join Iroquois League? Explain.

THINK ABOUT

• the phrase *they may trace the Roots to the Tree*

• the phrase *take shelter beneath the Tree*

3

Societies of West Africa

MAIN IDEA	WHY IT MATTERS NOW	TERMS & NAMES	
...ples of West Africa developed ...cated kingdoms, trade ...s, and artistic achievements.	It was from this region that many Africans were brought to the Americas.	Ghana Muslims Islam Mali	Songhai Hausa Yoruba Benin

ONE AFRICAN'S STORY

King Tenkaminen (TEHN•kah•MEE•nehn) of the West African empire of **Ghana** was a powerful ruler. He grew rich by taxing gold traders who traveled through his land. In 1067, a geographer wrote a description of the royal court.

A VOICE FROM THE PAST

The king adorns himself . . . wearing necklaces round his neck and bracelets on his forearms. . . . Behind the king stand ten pages holding shields and swords decorated with gold.

al-Bakri, quoted in *The Horizon History of Africa*

Kumasi, a modern West African chief, wears gold to show his status.

West Africa was the homeland of many of the enslaved Africans who were brought to the Americas after 1500. You will read about West Africa in this section.

African Geography and World Trade

Africa is the world's second largest continent after Asia. (See the map on page 40.) Although Africa has a variety of land forms and climates, almost three quarters of it lies within the tropics. The equator runs east-west across the center of Africa. Dense rain forests stretch along the equator in central and western Africa. North and south of the rain forests are broad savannas, which are grassy plains with thorny bushes and scattered trees. Beyond the savanna in the North lies the Sahara, the world's largest desert. Beyond the savanna in the South lies the smaller Kalahari Desert.

By A.D. 1500, coastal ports had linked Africa with the rest of the world for many centuries. Ships from ports on the Mediterranean and the Red Sea carried goods to Arabia and Persia. On Africa's east coast, city-states carried on a brisk trade with ports across the Indian Ocean.

Taking Notes

Use your chart to take notes about West Africa.

	Trade	
AMERICAS		
WEST AFRICA		
EUROPE		

Like other parts of Africa, West Africa has rain forest along the equator and savanna to the north. The Niger River arcs across those grasslands and forests and then empties into the Atlantic Ocean. Along its northern edge, West Africa borders the Sahara.

Ghana Grows Wealthy

On a map, the Sahara appears to be a barrier between West Africa and the ports on the Mediterranean coast. But by A.D. 500, camel caravans led by eager merchants made regular journeys across the great desert. This connected West Africa to the wider world.

Ghana became the first West African kingdom to grow rich through trade. From the 700s to the mid-1000s, Ghana prospered by controlling the busy trade in gold and salt. Located on the southern edge of the Sahara, Ghana became a marketplace for traders going north and south in search of salt and gold. (Ancient Ghana was northwest of modern Ghana.) Salt was important because it helps the human body retain water in hot weather. Traders carried salt from the Saharan salt mines in the north. In Ghana's markets, they met other traders offering gold from the forests of West Africa.

Ghana's king benefited from this trade. He imposed taxes on all gold and salt passing through his kingdom. The taxes had to be paid in gold. The king also claimed all gold nuggets found in his kingdom. Ghana's king used the resulting wealth to pay for an army and build an empire.

Backgroun
The camel i
in the deser
because it c
travel up to
days withou
water.

Reading H
A. Analyzin
Causes Wh
the king w
taxes to be
in gold and
gold nugge
be given t

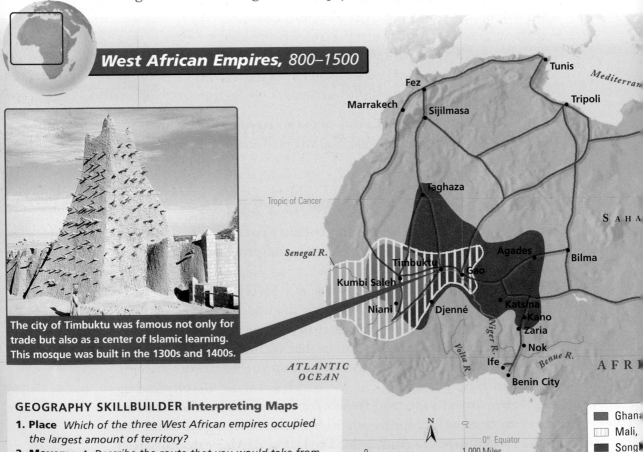

West African Empires, 800–1500

The city of Timbuktu was famous not only for trade but also as a center of Islamic learning. This mosque was built in the 1300s and 1400s.

GEOGRAPHY SKILLBUILDER Interpreting Maps

1. **Place** Which of the three West African empires occupied the largest amount of territory?
2. **Movement** Describe the route that you would take from the port city of Tunis to the trade city of Timbuktu.

Islam Enters Ghana

Many of the traders who came to Ghana from North Africa were Muslims. **Muslims** are followers of the religion of Islam. Founded by the prophet Muhammad in the 600s, **Islam** teaches that there is one God, named Allah. Muslims must perform such duties as praying five times a day and making a pilgrimage to the holy city of Mecca in Arabia. Muslim traders crossing the Sahara brought Islam from North Africa to West Africa. Ghana's rulers allowed those Muslims to build mosques, or houses of worship, in Ghana's capital, Kumbi Saleh. In time, Ghana's rulers employed Muslims as advisers.

bulary
mage: a trip
oly place

The Muslim empires of North Africa wanted to convert Ghana's people to Islam and to control Ghana's gold trade. In 1076, a Muslim army conquered Kumbi Saleh. This lessened Ghana's power. A number of local leaders took advantage of Ghana's weakness. They built up their own small states on the edges of the once mighty empire. Ghana never regained its former strength.

Over the next several centuries, more and more West Africans converted to Islam. In fact, many of the enslaved Africans who were brought to the Americas were Muslims.

Mali Replaces Ghana

By the 1200s, another West African kingdom had taken over most of Ghana's territory. This kingdom, called **Mali,** became West Africa's most powerful state. Its wealth also came from control of the gold-salt trade. But because it was located farther south than Ghana, Mali was better able to control the trade on the upper Niger River. (Ancient Mali stretched farther west than modern Mali and not as far north.)

Mali's first great ruler, Sundiata (sun•JAHT•ah), reigned from about 1230 to 1255. He came to power by crushing a cruel, unpopular leader. Sundiata's armies conquered many important trading cities. This made Mali's hold on trade stronger and made Mali more prosperous. Sundiata was a Muslim, but he did not force his people to accept Islam. Most of the people of Mali retained their traditional African beliefs.

ulary
: very
is

Mali's other great leader was Mansa Musa (MAHN•sah moo•SAH), who was a devout Muslim. Mansa Musa came to the throne in 1312. Under his leadership, the empire became one of the largest in the world.

ngHistory
ing
ces How
think the
ns reacted
sa Musa's
1?

Mansa Musa is best remembered for making the Muslim pilgrimage to Mecca in 1324 and 1325. On his way to Mecca, he stopped in Cairo, Egypt. According to some stories, Mansa Musa entered the city leading a huge caravan that included 500 servants who waved staffs decorated with gold. Each of the 80 camels in his caravan struggled under the weight of a 300-pound sack of gold. The legend of Mali's wealth spread

A European mapmaker placed this picture of Mansa Musa on a map in 1375. It was drawn from his imagination.

all the way to Europe. This was one reason that Europeans began to trade with Africa about 150 years later.

On his return to Mali, Mansa Musa brought back many Muslim scholars, artists, and architects. They helped spread Islamic culture and learning throughout the empire. The city of Timbuktu (TIHM•buhk•TOO) in eastern Mali became a leading center of trade and Islamic learning. After Mansa Musa's death in 1337, Mali slowly grew weaker.

The Empire of Songhai

As Mali's power decreased, the **Songhai** (SAWNG•HY) people living at the Great Bend in the Niger River broke away from its control. In 1464, under the leader Sunni Ali, they began their own empire. Sunni Ali was a Muslim, but he also practiced the traditional Songhai religion.

Under Sunni Ali, the Songhai captured the great city of Timbuktu. Then they put the important trading city of Djenné (jeh•NAY) under siege and captured it after seven years. In addition to conquering territory, Sunni Ali set up an organized system of government.

After Sunni Ali died in 1492, conflicts arose. Some Muslims began a rebellion because they wanted Islam to be the only religion of Songhai. The leader of the revolt was Askia Muhammad, a devoted Muslim.

Askia Muhammad won his fight and became Songhai's second great ruler. For 35 years, he ably governed the empire. He chose capable officials who made the government run smoothly. He also expanded trade and set up an efficient tax system. Askia Muhammad used his wealth to build mosques and support Muslim scholars.

After Askia Muhammad's reign, several weak rulers succeeded him. Even when a strong ruler took the throne again, the empire faced problems. In spite of Songhai's wealth and learning, it lacked modern weapons. In 1591, a Moroccan fighting force from North Africa invaded Songhai with gunpowder and cannon. They easily defeated Songhai's soldiers, who were defending their empire with swords and spears.

Vocabulary
siege: surrounding a castle with an army until it surrenders

Reading **Hi**
C. Recogniz
Effects Hov
would Askia
Muhammac
actions pror
Islam in Sor

Other West African Kingdoms

As empires rose and fell in some parts of West Africa, small city-states arose in other parts of the region. The **Hausa** (HOW•suh) states emerged after A.D. 1000 in what is now northern Nigeria. Hausa city-states, such as Katsina and Kano, thrived on trade. Although the Hausa people shared a language, their city-states were independent of each other.

The **Yoruba** (YAWR•uh•buh) lived in the forests southwest of the Niger River. Ife and Oyo, the largest Yoruba states, had kings

Now and then

AFRICAN HERITAGE

One way many African Americans show pride in their heritage is by wearing kente cloth. Kente cloth, shown below, is a colorful fabric woven by the Akan and Ewe people of Ghana.

Some African Americans celebrate the holiday of Kwanzaa in December. Based on traditional African harvest festivals, Kwanzaa lasts a week. Each day honors a value held by Africans: unity, self-determination, collective responsibility, cooperative economics, purpose, creativity, and faith.

who were considered to be partly divine. The Yoruba were mostly farmers, but they also had gifted artists, who carved wood and ivory and cast metal sculptures. Yoruba statues are still considered great art.

Another kingdom famous for its art was Benin. **Benin,** located in the delta of the Niger River, lay on main trade routes and prospered because of that. The capital, Benin City, was large and surrounded by thick, earthen walls. About 1600, a Dutch visitor compared Benin City to his home city of Amsterdam in Europe.

ling History

alyzing
s of View
u think
er's view of
City is posi-
r negative?
n.

A VOICE FROM THE PAST

The houses in this town stand in good order, each one close and evenly placed with its neighbor, just as the houses in Holland stand. . . . The king's court is very great. It is built around many square-shaped yards.

Olfert Dapper, quoted in *Centuries of Greatness*

Benin artists produced sophisticated bronze statues such as this figure of a horn-blower.

In the late 1400s, Europeans reached Benin. Portuguese ships arrived, and the Portuguese set up a trade center near Benin City. Benin traders sold the Portuguese pepper, ivory, and leopard skins in exchange for copper and guns. In time, the Portuguese and other Europeans also began to trade for enslaved Africans. The Europeans who came to West Africa were not seeking information about its rich history or culture. They wanted a supply of laborers to work on large farms, called plantations. Chapter 2 explains more about plantations and slavery.

Trade was just one reason Europeans were sailing far beyond their lands. Social changes were also spurring them to explore the world. Those changes are discussed in Section 4.

tion ❸ Assessment

Terms & Names

plain the
gnificance of:

hana
Muslims
lam
Mali
onghai
ausa
oruba
enin

2. Using Graphics

Compare the Ghana Empire and the Mali Empire using a Venn diagram like the one shown.

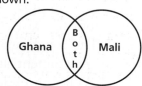

How was the influence of Islam different in each?

3. Main Ideas

a. How did Ghana's ruler benefit from controlling the gold-salt trade?

b. How did Islam spread within West Africa?

c. For what artistic achievements are the Yoruba and the people of Benin known?

4. Critical Thinking

Identifying Facts and Opinions Is the description of Benin City above mainly a statement of fact or opinion?

THINK ABOUT

• whether Dapper's statement can be proven by measurement or observation

• whether his statement expresses his own bias

IVITY OPTIONS

SPEECH

EOGRAPHY

Retell Mansa Musa's famous journey as an **oral history** or create a **map** that shows the route you think he took from Mali to Mecca.

4

Societies of Europe

MAIN IDEA	WHY IT MATTERS NOW	TERMS & NAMES
By 1500, Europe was going through a period of social change that sparked interest in learning and exploration.	The changes taking place in Europe led to the exploration of the Americas.	European Middle Ages Renaissan● feudalism printing p● manor system Reformati● Crusades profit

ONE EUROPEAN'S STORY

Ermentrude gathered up a chicken and five eggs and went to see the steward. He was the man who managed the land where she lived for its owners. Ermentrude and her husband, Bodo, were farmers who worked on a small piece of a large estate owned by someone else.

Ermentrude gave the chicken and eggs to the steward as part of her rent. Then she hurried home to weave cloth and cook supper.

Ermentrude lived in the early 800s, but her life was typical of the way many Europeans lived for centuries. This section explains that way of life and how it had changed by 1500.

The peasant●
11th-centur●
are probabl●
land owned ●
someone el●
European p●
Ermentrude ●
ever left the ●
where they ●

Taking Notes

●se your chart to ●ake notes about ●urope.

	Trade
●ICAS	
●A	
●PE	

Feudalism in Europe

Ermentrude lived in the **European Middle Ages,** which lasted from the late 400s, when the Western Roman Empire ended, to about the 1300s. (In some parts of Europe, the Middle Ages lasted to the 1400s.) The Romans used written laws and a mighty army to keep order. But over time, the empire grew weak. Germanic tribes from the east and north invaded the empire and contributed to its fall. The rough, uneducated Germanic tribes destroyed the strong Roman government and trade networks, and the tribes set up small kingdoms. With no trade, people stopped using money. They paid in goods, such as chickens and eggs.

Other groups also disrupted Europe. During the 800s to 1000s, Vikings swept down from the north. From their warships, they carried out lightning raids, looting villages and then racing back out to sea. To survive such difficult times, Europeans turned to feudalism. **Feudalism** is a political system in which a king allows nobles, or lords, to use lands

*ding*History

ntifying
ems What
ems were
eans trying
ve with feu-
n and the
r system?

that belong to him. In return, the lords owe the king military service and protection for the people living on the land.

Along with feudalism, Europeans developed the **manor system.** In this system, lords divided their lands into manors, or large estates, that were farmed mostly by serfs. Serfs were landless peasants who weren't allowed to leave the manor. In return for the serfs' work, the lord promised to protect them. The lords built heavily walled castles where people could go in times of danger.

The Roman Catholic Church also gained power during these uncertain times. Taking on the roles once filled by government officials, the Church collected taxes, aided the sick, and punished criminals. It became a powerful, unifying force throughout Europe.

Revival of Trade and Towns

By the 1000s, feudalism had brought more stability to society. As strong lords gained more control over their lands, long periods of peace and security followed. Merchants once again felt safe to travel. New farming methods, such as better ways to plant and plow fields, led to a food surplus. With more to eat, the population increased. More people meant more demand for goods, which spurred trade. Old towns near busy trade routes revived, and new towns grew up near manor houses and churches. Money came back into use.

As the economy grew, many serfs ran away to towns. Some became craftspeople who practiced such trades as shoemaking. Others became merchants who sold the goods that craftspeople made. Merchants and craftspeople formed a new social class, the middle class. They had fewer riches, rights, and privileges than lords, but far more freedom than they had known as serfs.

Trade with the East

Trade increased, not only within Europe, but also with places outside Europe. Located on the Mediterranean, Italy had an advantage in this trade. Italian cities such as Venice traded with other port cities, such as Constantinople, located in what is now Turkey.

*ng*History

gnizing
 What
did the
es have
an trade?

War also spurred trade. Many European Christians were angry that Muslims held the Holy Land, where Jesus had lived. In 1096, European Christians launched the **Crusades,** a series of wars to capture the Holy Land. They ultimately failed to keep the Holy Land, but the Crusades changed European life. Italians supplied the ships that carried Crusaders to the Middle East. On the return trip, the ships brought Asian goods to Europe. These goods had traveled across the Indian Ocean and then overland to the Mediterranean.

STRANGE *but* True

PEPPER MILLIONAIRES

Europeans were desperate to get spices, such as pepper and cloves. Before refrigeration, meat often spoiled. Spices helped disguise the taste of rotten meat.

In the 1500s, just one shipload of spices could make a merchant wealthy for life. The average working person would have to work at least 1,000 years to earn as much as a merchant could earn from one load of pepper!

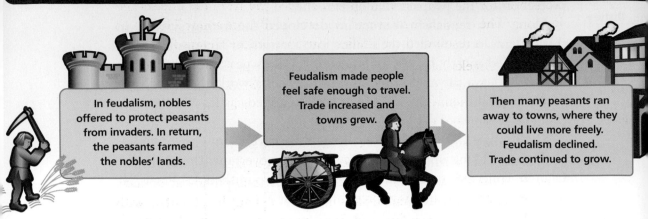

In feudalism, nobles offered to protect peasants from invaders. In return, the peasants farmed the nobles' lands.

Feudalism made people feel safe enough to travel. Trade increased and towns grew.

Then many peasants ran away to towns, where they could live more freely. Feudalism declined. Trade continued to grow.

After the Crusades, Italians continued to trade with Muslims in other Mediterranean cities.

An Italian merchant named Marco Polo also stirred European curiosity about distant lands. Polo had spent 24 years traveling in China and central Asia. A book written about Polo's travels described China's riches and wonders. It increased European interest in Asia.

The Decline of Feudalism

The growth of trade and towns weakened feudalism because so many serfs left the manors for town life. The power of the lords shrank because they had fewer people under their control. Beginning in 1347, a deadly disease also weakened feudalism. The bubonic plague swept across Europe, killing about one-fourth of the population and reducing the number of workers. Lords competed for the laborers who survived, so they began to pay wages to peasants, such as John of Cayworth.

A VOICE FROM THE PAST

John of Cayworth . . . ought to carry in autumn beans or oats for 2 days with a cart and 3 animals of his own, the value of the work being 12 denarii [about a penny]. And he shall receive from the lord each day 3 meals.

Contract of John of Cayworth, from *Readings in European History*

As feudal lords lost power, kings grew stronger. They won the support of townspeople because they could raise large armies to enforce order. In return, townspeople agreed to support their kings by paying taxes. The armies enforced order and imposed the king's authority over lesser lords. As countries became safer, trade flourished even more.

The Renaissance and Reformation

Italy, which was thriving because of trade, became the birthplace of the **Renaissance**—a time of increased interest in art and learning. *Renaissance* is a French term meaning "rebirth." Lasting from the 1300s to 1600, the Renaissance spread from Italy throughout Europe.

Several forces led to this rebirth of learning. As feudalism weakened and the plague brought great suffering, Europeans began to question

Reading **H**
C. Analyzin
Causes Wh
three cause
to the decli
feudalism?

what life meant. In their search for new answers, some people turned to old sources. They read the writings and studied the art of the Greeks and Romans. The classical Greeks and Romans lived from about 750 B.C. to A.D. 476. As a result of these studies, European ideas changed.

bulary
sophy: the
of the
ing of life

1. The Greeks had praised human achievement. European scholars began humanism, the study of human worth, ideas, and potential.
2. Classical education stressed such subjects as history, philosophy, and literature. Europeans spent more time studying those subjects.
3. From classical art, European artists learned to make art more realistic. They created some of the world's finest paintings and statues.
4. Muslim scholars had saved classical manuscripts about science. Also, Muslim mathematicians had invented algebra. Contact with Muslim societies influenced European science and mathematics.

ground
nting press
novable
–blocks of
or wood
ave raised
cters. The
se invented
ble type in
1045.
berg re-
ted it.

A new invention helped spread Renaissance ideas. In about 1455, a German named Johannes Gutenberg invented the **printing press,** a machine that mechanically prints pages. People no longer had to copy books by hand. Printers could make hundreds of copies of a book cheaply and accurately. More people read, and ideas spread quickly.

By the early 1500s, Renaissance ideas and other forces weakened the Catholic Church. Many church leaders were corrupt. Some claimed to grant God's forgiveness for money. Martin Luther, a German monk, publicly posted 95 statements that criticized such practices. This began the **Reformation,** a movement to correct problems in the Church.

The Reformation split the Church into two groups—Catholics and Protestants. In time, Protestants divided into many different churches.

ISTORY through ART

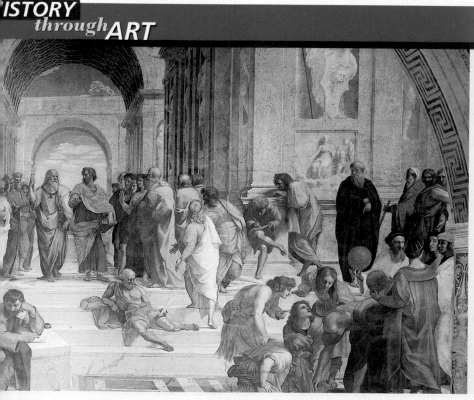

This painting, _School of Athens_ by Raphael, shows many aspects of Renaissance art and culture.

- Like much Renaissance art, it looks more realistic than the art of the Middle Ages. (See page 44 for comparison.)
- It honors the Greek thinkers Aristotle and Plato, who are the two men in the center arch.
- It also honors Renaissance artists. Raphael himself is in the group to the right.

Why might Raphael have wanted to include himself in a painting with famous Greeks?

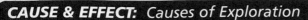

CAUSE & EFFECT: *Causes of Exploration*

After the Crusades, Europeans want Asian goods.

CAUSE

EFFECT
Italy dominates trade because it developed a network during the Crusades.

CAUSE

EFFECT
Other European nations want a share of Italy's profits.

CAUSE

EFFECT
Other nations seek water route to Asia.

SKILLBUILDER Interpreting Charts
What economic activity was the primary cause of exploration?

When European colonists came to America, they carried their religious disagreements and hopes for religious freedom with them.

Changes in Trade

The Renaissance period saw not only changes in learning and religion, but also in trade. As trade grew, Italian merchants needed to improve the way they did business. They began to use more exact ways of keeping track of a business's income and its costs. By subtracting the costs from the income, the merchants determined the **profit**.

Italian merchants made huge profits by trading in Asian goods. Because Italians had done business with Muslims for centuries, they had a special relationship. In addition to that, the Italians used military strength to control the trade on the Mediterranean—and didn't allow other Europeans to take part in it.

Merchants in other European countries envied the profits made by Italian merchants. As a result, other Europeans began to want a share of the rich trade in Asian goods. They had to find different routes to Asia from the ones controlled by the Italians and Muslims. Other European countries began to search for a non-Mediterranean water route to Asia, as you will read in Section 5.

Reading **His**
D. Making Generalizati
If a country
to complete
dominate tr
in a certain
how will oth
countries
respond?

Section **4** Assessment

1. Terms & Names

Explain the significance of:
• European Middle Ages
• feudalism
• manor system
• Crusades
• Renaissance
• printing press
• Reformation
• profit

2. Using Graphics

On a chart like this one, list how the Renaissance changed art and learning.

Changes to Art and Learning
•
•
•
•

3. Main Ideas

a. What caused feudalism to develop?

b. What led to the revival of trade and towns?

c. How did Italy come to control European trade with Asia?

4. Critical Thinking

Contrasting How did the Renaissance differ from the European Middle Ages?

THINK ABOUT
• the economy
• how power was distributed
• the authority of the church

ACTIVITY OPTIONS

TECHNOLOGY
MUSIC

Design a **Web site** or compose a **song** advertising the great new Renaissance invention—the printing press.

5

Early European Explorers

MAIN IDEA	WHY IT MATTERS NOW	TERMS & NAMES
•peans searched for sea to Asia, Christopher •us reached the Americas.	Columbus's journey permanently linked the Americas to the rest of the world.	navigator Christopher Columbus caravel

ONE EUROPEAN'S STORY

Sailors seeking a route to Asia depended on the skill of their navigator. A **navigator** plans the course of a ship by using instruments to find its position. In the 1400s, Portugal had a famous prince called Henry the Navigator. Yet, Henry wasn't a navigator. He lived at Sagres, on the southwestern coast of Portugal. In this town, he began a school of navigation.

Henry decided to organize and pay for sailing expeditions to explore the Atlantic and the west coast of Africa. He was hoping to find African gold, to learn more about geography, and to spread Christianity. His ships traveled farther down the African coast than Europeans had ever gone. Because Henry sponsored the voyages, the English named him "the navigator." As you will read in this section, those voyages began Europe's age of discovery.

Henry the Navigator sponsored voyage that helped Portuga find a water route to Asia.

A Water Route to Asia

Under Prince Henry, the Portuguese developed an improved ship called the **caravel**. The caravel had triangular sails as well as square sails. Square sails carried the ship forward when the wind was at its back. Triangular sails allowed the caravel to sail into the wind. The caravel was better than other European ships of the time at sailing into the wind.

In January 1488, the Portuguese explorer Bartolomeu Dias (DEE•uhs) reached the southern tip of Africa. After sailing around it, he returned to Portugal at the urging of his crew. Portugal's king named the tip the Cape of Good Hope because he hoped they had found a route to Asia.

Ten years later, another Portuguese explorer, Vasco da Gama, followed Dias's route around the cape. He continued north along the eastern coast of Africa. Then he sailed east across the Indian Ocean to India. At last, someone had found an all-water route to Asia.

Taking Notes

Use your chart to take notes about European explorers.

	Trade		
AMERICAS			
WEST AFRICA			
EUROPE			

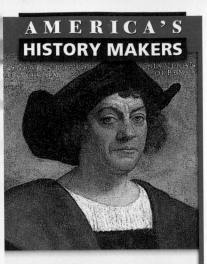

CHRISTOPHER COLUMBUS
1451–1506

Christopher Columbus's son Ferdinand wrote that his father "took to the sea at the age of 14 and followed it ever after."

Columbus's early voyages nearly cost him his life. When he was 25, pirates off the coast of Portugal sank his ship. Columbus survived by grabbing a floating oar and swimming to shore.

But he also learned a lot from sailing on Portuguese ships. The sailors taught Columbus about Atlantic wind patterns. This knowledge later helped him on his history-making voyage.

What character traits, shown in Columbus's early life, might have made him a good leader?

That route meant that the Portuguese could now trade with Asia without dealing with the Muslims or Italians. Portugal took control of the valuable spice trade. The merchants of Lisbon, Portugal's capital, grew rich. Spain and other European rivals wanted to take part in this profitable trade. They began to look for their own water routes to Asia.

Columbus's Plan

By the time of da Gama's voyage, an Italian sailor named **Christopher Columbus** thought he knew a faster way to reach Asia. Europeans had known for centuries that the earth is round. Columbus decided that instead of sailing around Africa and then east, he would sail west across the Atlantic. He calculated that it would be a short journey.

But Columbus made several mistakes. First, he relied on the writings of two people—Marco Polo and a geographer named Paolo Toscanelli—who were wrong about the size of Asia. They claimed that Asia stretched farther from west to east than it really did.

Second, Columbus underestimated the distance around the globe. He thought the earth was only two thirds as large as it actually is! Because of Polo and Toscanelli, Columbus thought that Asia took up most of that distance. Therefore, he believed that the Atlantic Ocean must be small. And a voyage west to Asia would be short.

In 1483, Columbus asked the king of Portugal to finance a voyage across the Atlantic. The king's advisers opposed the plan. They argued that Columbus had miscalculated the distance to Asia. They also reminded the king of the progress that Portuguese explorers had made sailing down the coast of Africa looking for a route to Asia. The advisers persuaded the king not to finance the voyage. So in 1486, Columbus turned to Portugal's rival, Spain.

Help from Spain's Rulers

Spain's rulers, King Ferdinand and Queen Isabella, liked Columbus's plan because they wanted a share of the rich Asian trade. As a strong Catholic, the Queen also welcomed a chance to spread Christianity. But there were also reasons not to support Columbus. First, a royal council had doubts about Columbus's calculations and advised Ferdinand and Isabella not to finance him. Second, the Spanish monarchs were in the middle of a costly war to drive the Muslims out of Spain. Third, Columbus was asking a high payment for his services.

The years of waiting had made Columbus determined to profit from his explorations. As a reward for his efforts, he demanded the high title

Reading His

A. Comparin
Compare wh
happened af
Portugal beg
to control th
spice trade t
what happen
when Italy c
trolled it.

Backgrour
As you read
Section 4, M
Polo's book
about his tr
had increas
European in
est in Asia.

Vocabular
monarch: a
or queen

Admiral of the Ocean Sea and a percentage of any wealth he brought from Asia. He also expected to be made the ruler of the lands he found.

Finally in January of 1492, the Spanish conquered the last Muslim stronghold in Spain. The Spanish monarchs could now afford to finance Columbus but still had doubts about doing so. Columbus left the palace to return home. But after listening to a trusted adviser, the king and queen changed their minds and sent a rider on horseback to bring Columbus back. He and the rulers finally reached an agreement.

ding **History**
awing
usions Did
greement
Columbus
he was ask-
or? Explain.

A VOICE FROM THE PAST

Your Highnesses . . . accorded me great rewards and ennobled me so that from that time henceforth I might . . . be high admiral of the Ocean Sea and perpetual Governor of the islands and continent which I should discover.

Christopher Columbus, letter to King Ferdinand and Queen Isabella

Preparing to sail, Columbus assembled his ships—the *Niña*, the *Pinta*, and the *Santa María*—at the port of Palos de la Frontera in southern Spain.

Setting Sail

At first, Columbus had trouble finding a crew. Then a respected local shipowner agreed to sign on as captain of the *Pinta*. Other crew members soon followed. About 90 men loaded the ships with enough food for one year, casks of fresh water, firewood, and other necessities.

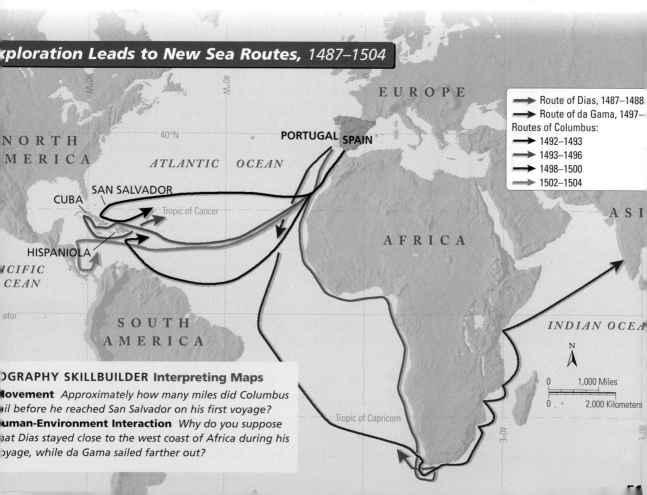

xploration Leads to New Sea Routes, *1487–1504*

Route of Dias, 1487–1488
Route of da Gama, 1497–
Routes of Columbus:
1492–1493
1493–1496
1498–1500
1502–1504

EUROPE

PORTUGAL SPAIN

ATLANTIC OCEAN

NORTH
MERICA

40°N

SAN SALVADOR

CUBA

Tropic of Cancer

HISPANIOLA

ICIFIC
CEAN

ator

SOUTH
AMERICA

AFRICA

ASI

INDIAN OCEA

N

0   1,000 Miles
0   2,000 Kilometers

Tropic of Capricorn

GRAPHY SKILLBUILDER Interpreting Maps
Movement *Approximately how many miles did Columbus
il before he reached San Salvador on his first voyage?*
uman-Environment Interaction *Why do you suppose
at Dias stayed close to the west coast of Africa during his
oyage, while da Gama sailed farther out?*

The tiny fleet of wooden ships glided out of the harbor on August 3, 1492. First they sailed southwest toward the Canary Islands off the northwest coast of Africa. From there, Columbus was relying on trade winds that blew toward the west to speed his ships across the ocean.

Once aboard ship, Columbus kept a log, or daily record of each day's sailing. In fact, he kept two logs. One he showed to his men and one he kept secret. Columbus's secret log recorded the truth about the journey.

Reading **His**
C. Analyzing Causes What caused Colun to decide to two logs?

> ### A VOICE FROM THE PAST
>
> [We] made 15 leagues [this] day and . . . [I] decided to report less than those actually traveled so in case the voyage were long the men would not be frightened and lose courage.
>
> **Christopher Columbus,** quoted in *Columbus and the Age of Discovery*

By October 10, the men had lost both courage and confidence in their leader. They had been at sea for almost ten weeks and had not seen land for over a month. Afraid that they would starve if the trip went on longer, they talked of returning home. To avoid mutiny, Columbus and the crew struck a bargain. The men agreed to sail on for three more days, and Columbus promised to turn back if they had not sighted land by then. Two days later in the early morning hours of October 12, a sailor on the *Pinta* called out "Tierra, tierra" [Land, land].

Reaching the Americas

By noon, the ships had landed on an island in the Caribbean Sea. Columbus believed that he had reached the Indies, islands in Southeast Asia where spices grew. The islanders who greeted Columbus and his men were Taino (TY•noh) people, but Columbus mistakenly called them Indians.

Columbus named the island San Salvador. After unfurling the royal banner and flags, he ordered his crew to "bear witness that I was taking possession of this island for the King and Queen." Eager to reach the rich country of Japan, which he believed was nearby, he left San Salvador. He took six or seven Taino with him as guides. For the next three months, he visited several of the Caribbean islands.

Finally, he reached an island that he named Española, which we call Hispaniola today. (See map on page 51.) On that island, Columbus and his men found some gold and precious objects such as pearls. This convinced Columbus that he had reached Asia. He decided to return home, leaving 39 of his men on Hispaniola. Even before Columbus left, his men had angered the Taino people by stealing from them and committing violence. By the time Columbus returned ten months later, the Taino had killed the men.

Backgroun
Today, the In are called th East Indies. T islands of the Caribbean ar called the W Indies.

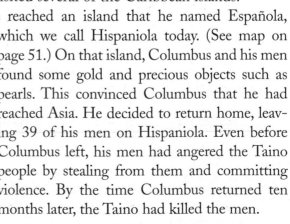

Now *and* **then**

NATIVE AMERICAN VIEW OF COLUMBUS

In 1992, many Native Americans protested the 500th anniversary of Columbus's voyage. Suzan Shown Harjo, who is Cheyenne and Creek, explained why.

As Native American peoples in this red quarter of Mother Earth, we have no reason to celebrate an invasion that caused the demise [death] of so many of our people and is still causing destruction today.

The Spanish enslaved the Taino, who nearly all died from disease and bad treatment. This statue is one of the few Taino artifacts left from the 1500s.

In January 1493, he sailed back to Spain. Firmly believing that he had found a new water route to Asia, he wrote to Ferdinand and Isabella. The Spanish rulers called him to the royal court to report on his voyage. Neither Columbus nor the king and queen suspected that he had landed near continents entirely unknown to Europeans.

A French map-maker uses an instrument to learn his exact position on the globe.

An Expanding Horizon

Columbus made three more voyages to the Americas, but never brought back the treasures he had promised Spain's rulers. He also failed to meet Queen Isabella's other goal. She wanted Christianity brought to new people. When she learned that Columbus had mistreated and enslaved the people of Hispaniola, she became angry.

After the fourth voyage, Spain's rulers refused to give Columbus any more help. He died in 1506, still believing he had reached Asia and bitter that he had not received the fame or fortune that he deserved.

In time, the geographic knowledge Columbus brought back changed European views of the world. People soon realized that Columbus had reached continents that had been unknown to them previously. And Europeans were eager to see if these continents could make them rich.

For centuries, Europeans had seen the ocean as a barrier. With one voyage, Columbus changed that. Instead of a barrier, the Atlantic Ocean became a bridge that connected Europe, Africa, and the Americas. As you will learn in Chapter 2, Columbus's explorations began an era of great wealth and power for Spain. As Spain grew rich, England, France, and other European countries also began to send ships to the Americas.

*ing*History

king

nces How e Atlantic he a bridge cting e, Africa, he Americas?

---

tion **5** *Assessment*

Terms & Names

plain the ignificance of:

avigator

aravel

hristopher Columbus

2. Using Graphics

On a diagram like the one shown, list the effects of Columbus's voyages.

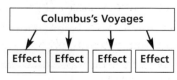

Columbus's Voyages			
Effect	Effect	Effect	Effect

Which effects were negative and which were positive?

3. Main Ideas

a. Why was Prince Henry eager to find an all-water route to Asia?

b. Why did Spain's king and queen decide to support Columbus's first voyage?

c. Why was Columbus disappointed by the outcome of his four voyages to the Americas?

4. Critical Thinking

Analyzing Points of View
Explain how each of the following people might have viewed Columbus's first voyage. Give reasons for their points of view.

THINK ABOUT
• Columbus
• Queen Isabella
• a Taino chief

IVITY OPTIONS

EOGRAPHY

MATH

Use the map on page 51. Create an enlarged **map** of Columbus's first voyage, or measure the distance of each voyage to list on a **table**.

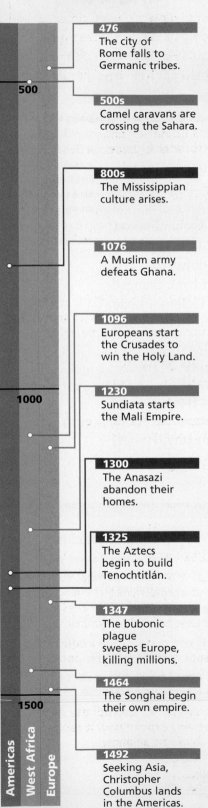

VISUAL SUMMARY

The World in 1500

476
The city of Rome falls to Germanic tribes.

500

500s
Camel caravans are crossing the Sahara.

800s
The Mississippian culture arises.

1076
A Muslim army defeats Ghana.

1096
Europeans start the Crusades to win the Holy Land.

1000

1230
Sundiata starts the Mali Empire.

1300
The Anasazi abandon their homes.

1325
The Aztecs begin to build Tenochtitlán.

1347
The bubonic plague sweeps Europe, killing millions.

1464
The Songhai begin their own empire.

1500

1492
Seeking Asia, Christopher Columbus lands in the Americas.

Americas
West Africa
Europe

TERMS & NAMES

Briefly explain the significance of each of the following.

1. migrate
2. civilization
3. technology
4. Iroquois League
5. Islam
6. feudalism
7. Crusades
8. Renaissance
9. navigator
10. Christopher Columbus

REVIEW QUESTIONS

Crossing to the Americas (pages 27–31)

1. What are two theories about migration to the Americas?
2. For what purposes did the Mound Builders construct earthen mounds?

Societies of North America (pages 32–38)

3. What enabled the Aztecs to become a strong empire?
4. How did the Iroquois League come about?

Societies of West Africa (pages 39–43)

5. What enabled Ghana, Mali, and Songhai all to grow rich?
6. Did Islam become more or less influential in West Africa from the 700s to the 1400s? Explain.

Societies of Europe (pages 44–48)

7. How did the manor system work during the Middle Ages?
8. How did the Crusades increase European interest in trade?

Early European Explorers (pages 49–53)

9. Why did non-Italian Europeans seek new trade routes to Asia?
10. How did Columbus miscalculate the distance to Asia?

CRITICAL THINKING

1. USING YOUR NOTES: CATEGORIZING INFORMATION

Using your completed chart, answer the questions below.

	Trade	Technology	Religion
AMERICAS (Sections 1 and 2)			
WEST AFRICA (Section 3)			
EUROPE (Sections 4 and 5)			

a. What was one instance in wh trade spread knowledge?

b. Which of the technologies th you listed are still used today

c. What religions were practice each of the three regions?

2. ANALYZING LEADERSHIP

Do you think Columbus was a g leader or a bad one? Use detai from the chapter to explain yo answer.

3. THEME: DIVERSITY AND UNITY

How have Native Americans, Africans, and Europeans all influ enced American culture? Give e ples from your own experience.

4. MAKING GENERALIZATION

What types of goods are peop most likely to seek through tra Think about the trade goods m tioned in the chapter and why ple wanted them.

5. APPLYING CITIZENSHIP SK

Compare the Iroquois League t what you know of the U.S. gov ment. How are they similar?

Interact with Histor

Think about the various encou between societies mentioned i chapter. What do you think ha pened when more Europeans to the Americas and met Nativ Americans?

Use the map and your knowledge of U.S. history to answer questions 1 and 2.

Additional Test Practice, pp. S1–S33.

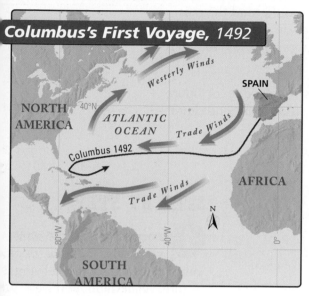

Columbus's First Voyage, 1492

How did the winds affect Columbus's journey?

A. The westerly winds across the Atlantic made the voyage faster.

B. The trade winds across the Atlantic slowed down the voyage.

C. The trade winds across the Atlantic made the voyage faster.

D. The winds had little effect on Columbus's voyage.

2. If Columbus's route had been farther north, which of the following would have happened?

A. The voyage would have taken less time.

B. The voyage would have taken more time.

C. The voyage would not have been different.

D. The voyage would not have been possible.

This quotation from Olfert Dapper is about Benin City in Africa. Use this quotation and your knowledge of West Africa to answer question 3.

PRIMARY SOURCE

The houses in this town stand in good order, each one close and evenly placed with its neighbor, just as the houses in Holland stand . . . The king's court is very great. It is built around many square-shaped yards.

Olfert Dapper, *Centuries of Greatness*

3. The passage best supports which point of view?

A. Benin City, and other African cities, should be unique, not modeled after European cities.

B. The king's court of Benin City was great in contrast to the rest of the city.

C. The design of Benin City made it an extremely valuable trade center.

D. The design of Benin City was appealing in its resemblance to European cities.

TEST PRACTICE
CLASSZONE.COM

ALTERNATIVE ASSESSMENT

WRITING ABOUT HISTORY

Imagine you have been hired to write the **brochure** for a Native American exhibit at a museum.

Choose a Native American group discussed in the chapter. Use library resources to learn more about the group.

Highlight their economy, religion and spiritual beliefs, or arts and crafts in your exhibit. Write a description of the exhibit for your brochure that would encourage people to come.

COOPERATIVE LEARNING

Work with a group to create a radio program of Columbus's first voyage. Group members can find his in the library, select parts to record, or create sound effects to play in the background.

INTEGRATED TECHNOLOGY

DOING INTERNET RESEARCH

Countries and alliances often use a symbol to represent who they are. The Iroquois League chose a tree as their symbol. Use the Internet and library resources to research the Iroquois League and its symbol.

• Research the beliefs and goals of the Iroquois League. Make a list of their beliefs and goals.

• Also search Native American museum sites and/or reservation sites in New York state.

• Describe why the tree was an appropriate symbol for the Iroquois League and explain how it represented the beliefs and goals of the alliance.

For more about the Iroquois League . . .

INTERNET ACTIVITY
CLASSZONE.COM

Create and Decode a Pictograph

Native Americans of the Southwest created thousands of images to communicate with each other. These images, known as pictographs, helped people recall certain events, ideas, or information. Even if the people who created them were no longer present, others could read the messages. Most images were painted or carved on the surfaces of rock. There are three types of pictographs: petroglyphs, petrograms, and geoglyphs. (See HELP DESK on the next page.)

ACTIVITY Create a pictograph that other students will decode, or figure out. Then, acting as an anthropologist, interview students in one other group about their pictograph.

TOOLBOX

Each group will need:

drawing paper or poster board

markers

regular and colored pencils

watercolor paints and brushes (optional)

an envelope

The Fremont culture carved this petroglyph. It is currently located in Dinosaur National Monument—most of which sits in northwestern Colorado.

STEP BY STEP

1 **Form a group of 4 or 5 students.** Together, think message to tell someone living in future. What might you want fut generations to know about your ture, or way of life? If you're hav trouble coming up with a messag copy the chart below into your n book. Write information for each category that you think would be interesting to future generations Then choose one of these catego for your message.

Sports	
Politics	
Fashion	
Music	
Entertainment	
Weather	
Daily Life	

2 **Examine reference mate** In the library or on the Inte research Native American pictogra Use the information you find to he start your project. (See HELP DESK the next page.)

3 Create your pictograph.
Communicate your message with symbols like the ones that you have researched. Sketch your pictograph on the drawing paper or poster board with a pencil first. Make the pictograph simple so that the decoders will understand your message. Remember to use symbols—not letters.

4 Decorate your pictograph.
Use markers or watercolor paints to finish your pictograph. Also, record the translation of your pictograph in your notebook.

5 Exchange your pictograph with another group of students.
Try to decode the message in the pictograph that the other group of students has given you. Write your translation and place it in your envelope. Give the envelope to the group whose pictograph you decoded.

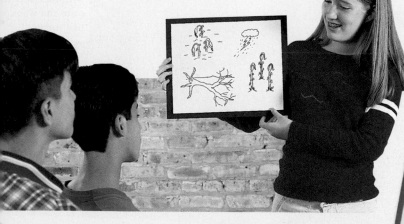

Compare the other students' translation with your actual message. Did the other students understand your ~ge? Let them know how accurate they were.

TE AND SPEAK
the information in the pictograph that you decoded,
a description of the people who created the message.
e symbols as well as the message itself to help you in
description. Explain to the class how you came to your
usions.

HELP DESK
For related information see Chapter 1, p. 29.

Researching Your Project
• *On the Trail of Spider Woman: Petroglyphs, Pictographs, and Myths of the Southwest* by Carol Patterson-Rudolph. Shows variety of actual pictographs.

• *21 Kinds of American Folk Art and How to Make Each One* by Jean and Cle Kinney. Explains process of making pictographs.

For more about pictographs . . .

RESEARCH LINKS
CLASSZONE.COM

Did You Know?
Petroglyphs are images carved into a rock using stone tools. **Petrograms** are images painted on a rock. **Geoglyphs** are images formed on the ground by scraping away soil or by arranging stones to form an image.

REFLECT & ASSESS
• Which symbols in your pictograph were clear to the decoders? Which were not clear?

• What methods did you use to decode the messages of others?

• What did you learn about language and communication from doing this pictograph decoding activity?

Ships in a harbor in Lisbon, Portugal, are preparing for a voyage of exploration.

Smaller b[...] ferry the [...] the sailin[...]

A crane loads su[...] onto the ships, [...] like today.

1497
Cabot searches for Northwest Passage.

1521
Cortés conquers the Aztec Empire.

1535
Cartier leads expedition up St. Lawrence River.

1539–1542
Coronado, de Soto, and Cabrillo explore different parts of North America.

1565
Spanish found St. Augustine.

**N. America
World** (**1492**)

1494
Spain and Portugal agree to Treaty of Tordesillas.

1534
English Parliament declares Henry VIII head of the English Church.

1542
King of Spain issues the New Laws for better treatment of Native Americans.

The year is 1510. You live in a European port town and have heard exciting tales about mysterious lands across the sea. You decide to join a voyage of exploration in search of fortune.

Would you join a voyage of exploration?

What Do You Think?

- What do you think led Europeans to explore distant lands?
- What reasons would make you want to join a voyage of exploration?
- What reasons would keep you from joining such a voyage?

RESEARCH LINKS
CLASSZONE.COM
Visit the Chapter 2 links for more information about exploration of the Americas.

1626
Dutch buy Manhattan Island.

1680
Popé leads Pueblo Revolt and forces Spanish from New Mexico.

1700

1644
Manchus establish Qing Dynasty in China.

1651
English Parliament passes Navigation Act.

es for
age.

Reading Strategy: Finding Main Ideas

What Do You Know?

What comes to mind when someone uses the word *explorer*?
Why do you think people explored different territories?

Think About

- what you've learned about explorers from movies, school, or your parents
- reasons that people travel throughout the world today
- your responses to the Interact with History about joining a voyage of exploration (see page 59)

What Do You Want to Know?

What questions do you have about exploration or the early colonization of the Americas? Write those questions in your notebook before you read the chapter.

Vasco Núñez de Balboa cl
the Pacific Ocean for Spai

Finding Main Ideas

To help you remember what you read, take notes about the events and ideas discussed i
the chapter. Taking notes means writing down important information. The chart below l
the major events and ideas covered in the chapter. Use the chart to take notes about the
important events and ideas.

S See Skillbuilder Handbook, page R3.

 Taking Notes

Event/Idea	Notes
Exploration	
Establishing Colonies	
European Competition	
Columbian Exchange	
Origins of Slavery	

Spain Claims an Empire

MAIN IDEA	WHY IT MATTERS NOW	TERMS & NAMES
laimed a large empire in ericas.	The influence of Spanish culture remains strong in modern America.	Treaty of Tordesillas missionary mercantilism Amerigo Vespucci *conquistador* Hernando Cortés Montezuma Francisco Pizarro

ONE EUROPEAN'S STORY

In 1493, the rulers of Spain and Portugal wanted Pope Alexander VI to decide who would control the lands that sailors from their countries were exploring.

In May 1493, Alexander VI issued his ruling. He drew an imaginary line around the world. It was called the Line of Demarcation. Portugal could claim all non-Christian lands to the east of the line. Spain could claim the non-Christian lands to the west. In this section, you will learn how Spain and Portugal led Europe in the race to gain colonies in the Americas.

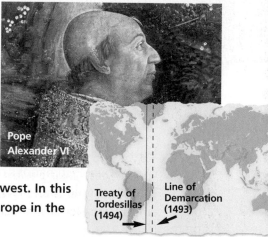

Pope Alexander VI

Treaty of Tordesillas (1494)

Line of Demarcation (1493)

Spain and Portugal Compete

King John II was unhappy with the pope's placement of the line. He believed that it favored Spain. So he demanded that the Spanish rulers meet with him to change the pope's decision. In June 1494, the two countries agreed to the **Treaty of Tordesillas** (TAWR•day•SEEL•yahs). This treaty moved the Line of Demarcation more than 800 miles farther west.

The change eventually allowed Portugal to claim much of eastern South America, which later became the Portuguese colony of Brazil. After making this agreement, Spain and Portugal increased their voyages of exploration in search of wealth, power, and glory.

European countries had three main goals during this age of exploration. First, they wanted to spread Christianity beyond Europe. Each expedition included **missionaries,** or people sent to convert the native peoples to Christianity. Second, they wanted to expand their empires. Third, they wanted to become rich.

By increasing their wealth, European countries could gain power and security. An economic system called **mercantilism** describes how

✏️ **Taking Notes**

Use your chart to take notes about exploring and establishing colonies.

Event/Idea	Notes
Exploration	
Establishing Colonies	
European Competition	
Columbian Exchange	
Origins of Slavery	

Economics *in* History

Mercantilism

The main goal of mercantilism was to increase the money in a country's treasury by creating a favorable balance of trade. A country had a favorable balance of trade if it had more exports than imports. Colonies helped a country have the goods to maintain a favorable balance of trade.

For example, say Spain sold $500 in sugar to France, and France sold $300 in cloth to Spain. France would also have to pay Spain $200 worth of precious metals to pay for all the sugar. Spain would then have a favorable balance of trade because the value of its exports (sugar) was greater than the value of its imports (cloth). Spain would become richer because of the precious metals it received from France.

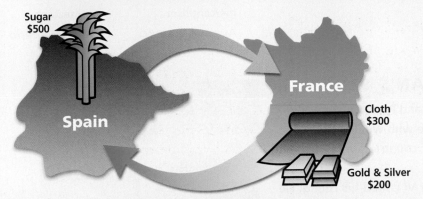

Sugar
$500

Spain

France

Cloth
$300

Gold & Silver
$200

CONNECT TO HISTORY
1. **Finding Main Ideas** Unde
   mercantilism, what did a
   country need to do to beco
   rich? Discuss the way coloni
   enriched a country accordir
   mercantilism.

    See Skillbuilder
   Handbook, page R5.

CONNECT TO TODAY
2. **Making Inferences** Think
   about your own family bud
   What do you think would
   happen if your family colle
   less money than it paid for
   goods for several years? Do
   think this situation would b
   the same for a nation as it
   would for a family?

For more about mercantilism . . .

 **RESEARCH LINKS**
CLASSZONE.COM

Europeans enriched their treasuries. (See *Economics in History,* above.) Colonies helped nations do this in several ways. They provided mines that produced gold and silver. They also produced goods such as crops that could be traded for gold and silver. Finally, they served as a market for the home country. The search for riches spurred European exploration.

Vocabulary
colony: a re
or people th
politically a
economicall
trolled by
another cou

Europeans Explore Foreign Lands

After Columbus's first voyage, many explorers went to sea. **Amerigo Vespucci** (vehs•POO•chee) was one of the first. He was an Italian sailor who set out in 1501 to find a sea route to Asia. Vespucci realized that the land he saw on this voyage was not Asia. A German mapmaker was impressed by Vespucci's account of the lands, so he named the continent "America" after him.

Another famous explorer was the Spaniard Vasco Núñez de Balboa. Balboa heard Native American reports of another ocean. In 1513, he led an expedition through the jungles of Panama and reached the Pacific Ocean. Raising his sword, Balboa stepped into the surf and claimed the ocean and all the lands around it for Spain. (See page 59.)

Perhaps no explorer was more capable than the Portuguese sailor Ferdinand Magellan. He proposed to reach Asia by sailing west around South America. The Spanish king agreed to fund Magellan's voyage.

In 1519, Magellan set out from Spain with five ships and about 240 men. After a stormy passage around South America, Magellan entered the Pacific Ocean. For several months his crew crossed the Pacific, suffering great hardship. A member of the crew described what they ate.

A VOICE FROM THE PAST

We were three months and twenty days without . . . fresh food. We ate biscuit, which was no longer biscuit, but powder of biscuits swarming with worms. . . . We drank . . . water that had been putrid for many days.

Antonio Pigafetta, quoted in *The Discoverers*

*ing***History**
ding **Main**
What
the main
butions of
cci, Balboa,
agellan
lorers?

Eventually, Magellan reached the Philippines, where he became involved in a local war and was killed. But his crew traveled on. In 1522, the one remaining ship arrived back in Spain. The sailors in Magellan's crew became the first people to sail around the world.

The Invasion of Mexico

While Magellan's crew was sailing around the world, the Spanish began their conquest of the Americas. Soldiers called **_conquistadors_** (kahn•KWIHS•tuh•DAWRZ), or conquerors, explored the Americas and claimed them for Spain. **Hernando Cortés** was one of these *conquistadors*. He landed on the Central American coast with 508 men in 1519.

The Spanish arrival shook the Aztec Empire, which dominated most of Mexico. The Aztec emperor **Montezuma** feared that Cortés had been

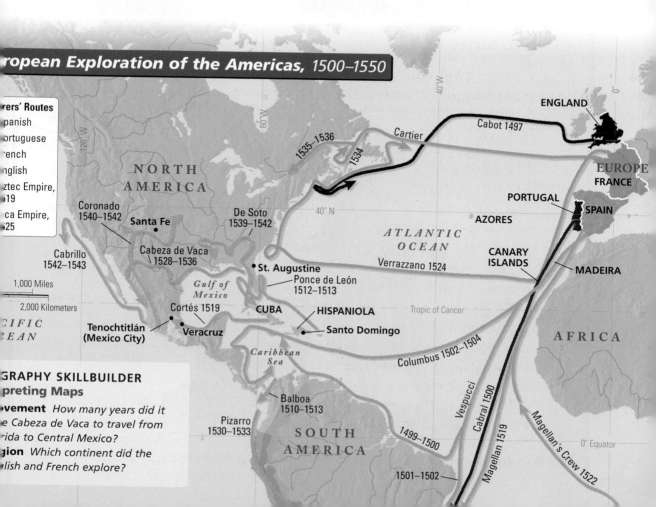

ropean Exploration of the Americas, *1500–1550*

rers' Routes
panish
ortuguese
rench
nglish
ztec Empire,
19
ca Empire,
25

1,000 Miles
2,000 Kilometers

NORTH AMERICA

Coronado 1540–1542
Santa Fe
Cabrillo 1542–1543
Cabeza de Vaca 1528–1536
De Soto 1539–1542
1535–1536
1534
Cartier
Cabot 1497
ENGLAND
EUROPE
FRANCE
PORTUGAL
SPAIN
AZORES
CANARY ISLANDS
MADEIRA

40° N
ATLANTIC OCEAN
Verrazzano 1524

St. Augustine
Ponce de León 1512–1513
Gulf of Mexico
Tropic of Cancer
CUBA
HISPANIOLA
Santo Domingo

IFIC EAN
Cortés 1519
Tenochtitlán (Mexico City)
Veracruz
Caribbean Sea
AFRICA
Columbus 1502–1504

Balboa 1510–1513
Pizarro 1530–1533
SOUTH AMERICA
Vespucci
1499–1500
Cabral 1500
Magellan 1519
Magellan's Crew 1522
0° Equator
1501–1502

GRAPHY SKILLBUILDER
preting Maps
vement *How many years did it*
e Cabeza de Vaca to travel from
rida to Central Mexico?
gion *Which continent did the*
lish and French explore?

sent by an Aztec god to rule Mexico. Montezuma sent Cortés gifts—including two disks of solid gold and silver—to get him to leave. But the gifts only excited Spanish dreams of riches.

The Spaniards marched inland and formed alliances (agreements with friendly peoples) with the native peoples who hated Aztec rule. After a few months, Cortés reached the Aztec capital, Tenochtitlán (teh•NAWCH•tee•TLAHN). Montezuma received Cortés with great ceremony and housed the *conquistadors* in a magnificent palace. But Cortés took Montezuma captive and tried to rule the Aztec Empire by giving commands through Montezuma. The Aztecs rebelled.

The Aztecs surrounded the Spaniards and their allies in their headquarters in Tenochtitlán. On the night of June 30, 1520, the Spaniards tried to sneak out of the city, but the Aztecs discovered them and vicious fighting broke out. About 800 Spaniards and more than 1,000 of their allies were killed that night. The Spaniards later called the event *La Noche Triste* (lah NAW•cheh TREES•teh)—the Sad Night.

Despite this defeat, the Spaniards and their allies regrouped. In May 1521, Cortés led his forces back to Tenochtitlán. At this point, the Spaniards got help from an invisible ally. Many Aztecs fell victim to an outbreak of smallpox, which severely weakened their ranks. The germs

Background
One of the
people who
Cortés broug
into his grou
was Malintz
She was the
daughter of
local chief a
served as
an interpret
for Cortés.

AMERICA'S HISTORY MAKERS

HERNANDO CORTÉS
1485–1547

Hernando Cortés was born in Spain to a noble but poor family. In 1504, at the age of 19, he sailed to the Americas to seek his fortune. Although he became a wealthy landowner in Cuba, he was not satisfied. "I have come to win gold," he said, "not to plow the fields like a peasant." His great chance came when he was picked to lead the expedition to Mexico. Strongwilled, shrewd, and cruel, Cortés succeeded against great odds.

MONTEZUMA
1466–1520

Montezuma, ruler of the Aztec Empire, rose to the throne in 1502. His words carried weight with his subjects.

According to Juan de Tovar, a Jesuit, "When he spoke, he drew the sympathy of others by his subtle phrases and . . . by his profound reasoning." Montezuma lived in great luxury, receiving officials and commoners alike at his lavish palace. His subjects treated him almost as a god and were not allowed to look at him. Though brutal at times, he was said to be a just and effective ruler.

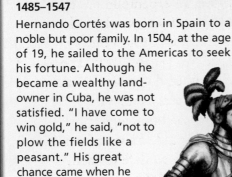

Which man would you prefer to have as leader of your country? Why?

that caused this disease had been brought to America by the Europeans.

Cortés placed Tenochtitlán under siege for three months. When Tenochtitlán finally fell, the Aztec Empire lay in ruins. An Aztec poet described the scene.

A VOICE FROM THE PAST

Broken spears lie in the roads; we have torn our hair in our grief. The houses are roofless now, and their walls are red with blood. . . . We have pounded our hands in despair against the adobe walls, for our inheritance, our city, is lost and dead.

Aztec poet, quoted in *Seeds of Change*

On the rubble of the Aztec capital, the Spanish built Mexico City. Over time, the populations and cultures of Spain and Mexico merged and produced a new society, that of the present-day nation of Mexico.

The Conquest of the Incan Empire

Despite the fall of the Aztecs, a people called the Inca still had a powerful empire centered in the Cuzco Valley in what is now Peru. By 1525, the Inca ruled a 2,000-mile-long territory in the Andes Mountains along the western coast of South America. The Inca also possessed much gold and silver.

Native American stories of Incan wealth reached the Spanish. In 1531, a *conquistador* named **Francisco Pizarro** led an expedition of 180 men into Peru. Like the Aztecs, the Incas feared that the Spanish might be gods. The Incan emperor Atahualpa (AH•tuh•WAHL•puh) ordered his troops not to fight. Then he went to meet the *conquistadors*. The Spanish attacked quickly. They killed thousands of Incas and took Atahualpa captive. In an attempt to free himself, the Incan emperor gave the Spanish a treasure of gold. The Spaniards strangled him anyway.

With Atahualpa dead, the Incan Empire collapsed. Having been ordered by Atahualpa not to fight, the Incas refused to defend themselves even after his death. Then Pizarro took control of this area for Spain. The Spanish called the area Peru.

Reasons for Spanish Victories

People have long been amazed that the great Aztec and Incan empires fell to such small groups of Spanish *conquistadors*. But Spanish success can be explained by four major reasons.

1. The spread of European diseases killed millions of Native Americans and weakened their resistance to conquest.
2. The Spanish were excellent soldiers and sailors. They also had superior weapons, such as guns, that helped them defeat much larger Native American armies.

This Aztec mask represents Quetzalcoatl, the god that Montezuma feared had sent Cortés.

bulary
surround-
a city

ing**History**
ding a Map
e map on
3 to find
an Empire.

ng**History**
ving
sions Why
Incan
fall to
anish?

3. Spain made alliances with Native Americans who were enemies of the Aztecs and Incas.

4. The Spanish *conquistadors* acted brutally toward the Native Americans under their control.

Having conquered the major Native American empires in Central and South America, the Spaniards began to explore other parts of North and South America.

Reading His
D. Drawing Conclusions
What was th
most import.
reason for th
Spanish succ
in conquerin
territory in t
Americas?

Other Spanish Explorers

The Spaniards hoped to collect treasures from North America as they had from Mexico and Peru. Rumors of golden cities kept Spanish hopes high. For example, a few men, including the Spaniard Álvar Núñez Cabeza de Vaca and Estevanico, a slave of North African descent, survived a shipwreck off the North American mainland. As the men wandered across the continent, they heard Native American stories about cities of gold. When they reached Mexico, Cabeza de Vaca and Estevanico thrilled the Spaniards with these rumors.

Estevanico was a slave who helped the Spanish explore parts of North America. He was killed during Coronado's search for golden cities.

Between 1539 and 1542, three expeditions set out to find these cities. Francisco Vázquez de Coronado traveled through present-day Arizona and New Mexico. Hernando de Soto set out from Florida to explore the southeast. Juan Rodríguez Cabrillo sailed up the California coast. But all three failed to find the fabled cities of gold.

For a while, it seemed that the Spaniards would explore the Americas all by themselves. As you will read in the next section, however, the Spanish would soon face competition from other Europeans.

Section 1 Assessment

1. Terms & Names

Explain the significance of:

- Treaty of Tordesillas
- missionary
- mercantilism
- Amerigo Vespucci
- *conquistador*
- Hernando Cortés
- Montezuma
- Francisco Pizarro

2. Using Graphics

Review the section and find four events to place on a time line that shows how Spain built its empire.

Spain Builds an Empire

1492 ├──┼──┼──┼──┤ 1542

Which event do you think is the most important? Why?

3. Main Ideas

a. Why did Europeans explore different territories?

b. Why did Spain succeed in conquering so much of the Americas?

c. What was significant about the Magellan expedition?

4. Critical Thinking

Comparing What was similar about the conques of Mexico and Peru?

THINK ABOUT

- the *conquistadors*
- the Incan and Aztec lea

ACTIVITY OPTIONS

ART

LANGUAGE ARTS

Use the library or the Internet to find a photograph of an Aztec or Incan artifact. Create a **replica** or write a **description** of the object.

2

European Competition in North America

MAIN IDEA	WHY IT MATTERS NOW	TERMS & NAMES

uropean countries competed
ain for control over territory
mericas.

European culture has strongly
influenced American culture.

Henry Hudson

John Cabot

Giovanni da
Verrazzano

Jacques Cartier

Spanish Armada

Samuel de Champlain

New France

ONE EUROPEAN'S STORY

In 1609, the Englishman **Henry Hudson** sailed under the Dutch flag from Europe. He hoped to find a route to China. Arriving at the coast of present-day New York, he sailed up the river that now bears his name. Hudson described what he saw.

A VOICE FROM THE PAST

The land is the finest for cultivation that I ever in my life set foot upon, and it also abounds in trees of every description. The natives are a very good people; for, when they saw that I would not remain, they . . . broke [their arrows] in pieces and threw them into the fire.

Henry Hudson, quoted in *Discoverers of America*

Hudson did not find a passage to Asia, but he led another expedition in 1610, this time for the English. In Canada, he disovered a large bay, today called Hudson Bay. After enduring a harsh winter, his crew rebelled. They put Hudson, his young son, and several loyal sailors in a small boat and set them adrift. Hudson's party was never heard from again.

The Search for the Northwest Passage

Hudson's voyages showed that some European countries hoped to find a westward route to Asia as late as the 1600s. While Spain was taking control of the Americas, other Europeans were sending out expeditions to find the Northwest Passage, a water route through North America to Asia.

One of the first explorers to chart a northern route across the Atlantic in search of Asia was the Italian sailor **John Cabot**. In 1497, Cabot crossed the Atlantic Ocean to explore for the English. He landed in the area of Newfoundland, Canada. He was certain that he had reached Asia and claimed the land for England. The next year he set sail once more,

Taking Notes

Use your chart to take notes about European competition for colonies.

Event/Idea	Notes
Exploration	
Establishing Colonies	
European Competition	
Columbian Exchange	
Origins of Slavery	

hoping to reach Japan. He was never seen again. Even so, his voyages were the basis for future English colonies along North America's Atlantic shore.

In 1524, another Italian, **Giovanni da Verrazzano,** set out under the French flag to find the Northwest Passage. He explored the Atlantic coastline of North America, but there was no passage to be found.

France tried again between 1534 and 1536 with the voyages of **Jacques Cartier** (ZHAHK kahr•TYAY). Cartier traveled up the St. Lawrence River to the site of present-day Montreal. At that point, rapids blocked the way and ended his search for the Northwest Passage. It would be almost 75 years before the French would return to colonize the region.

Spain Responds to Competition

French and English claims to North America angered Spain, which had claimed the land under the Treaty of Tordesillas. The tensions between Spain, England, and France stemmed from religious conflicts in Europe, such as the Reformation, which you read about in Chapter 1. These conflicts also led to fighting in the Americas.

Florida was one of the battlegrounds between the Spanish and the French. In 1564, a group of French Protestants, called Huguenots (HYOO•guh•NAHTS), founded a colony called Fort Caroline. Before long, Spanish troops under the command of Pedro Menéndez de Avilés arrived in that area. "This is the armada of the King of Spain," he announced, "who has sent me [here] to burn and hang the Lutheran [Protestant] French." Menéndez built a fort, St. Augustine, a short distance away. Then he brutally massacred the French.

Spain and England Clash

Religious differences and the quest for national power also led to conflict between Spain and England. In 1558, Queen Elizabeth I, a Protestant, came to the English throne. Spain, which was Catholic, plotted to remove the Protestant queen. But Elizabeth fought to defend England and challenge Spain's power at sea.

Although England's navy was not as powerful as Spain's, the English fleet had many speedy ships with skillful sailors. Daring sailors, known as sea dogs, used these ships to attack the bulky Spanish sailing ships—called galleons—that brought gold and silver from the Americas.

Sir Francis Drake became the most famous of the sea dogs because of his bold adventures and attacks against the Spanish. In 1577, Drake began a three-year voyage that took him around the world. During this voyage,

Reading **Hi**

A. Reading
Use the map
pages 63 an
to see the a
Cabot, Huds
Verrazzano,
Cartier visite

Vocabular
armada: a
of warships

America's HERITAGE

ST. AUGUSTINE
The thick stone walls of the fort at St. Augustine (shown below) still stand guard over the Florida coast today. Founded in 1565, St. Augustine is the oldest permanent European settlement in the United States. For more than two centuries, St. Augustine was an important outpost of Spain's empire in the Americas. Many Spanish colonial buildings remain at the site. The fort is now a national monument.

he raided Spanish ports and ships in South America. He stole great amounts of treasure from them. When he arrived home in 1580, he was a national hero. Not only had Drake and his men hounded the Spanish, but they were also the first Englishmen to sail around the world.

The English navy used its smaller, quicker ships to defeat the larger, slower galleons of the Spanish Armada.

The Defeat of the Spanish Armada

The attacks of Drake and other sea dogs enraged Philip II, the Spanish king. Determined to teach the English a lesson, Philip sent the **Spanish Armada** to conquer England and restore Catholicism to that nation. This fleet, made up of 130 ships, set out for England in the summer of 1588.

The English and Spanish navies met in the English Channel, which separates England from the European continent. In their smaller but faster craft, the English darted among the Spanish warships, firing deadly rounds with their cannons. Confused and crippled, the armada was retreating when it was hit by a severe storm. With half of its ships destroyed, the armada barely made it home.

Spain was still quite strong after the defeat of the armada. It quickly rebuilt its navy and maintained its large colonial possessions. But Spain would never again be as powerful as it was in 1588.

The English victory over Spain had two important effects. First, England remained independent and Protestant. Although England was less powerful than Spain, it had shown that it could defend itself. Second, Spain's image suffered. The world saw that Spain could be beaten. Other nations joined England in challenging Spain.

ngHistory
ving
ions
s the
of the
Armada
nt?

English adventurers like Drake continued to attack Spanish interests abroad. In addition, England challenged Spanish claims to lands in North America, such as California and Newfoundland. Even so, England took a cautious approach to overseas expansion. The English government refused to provide money to start colonies. Instead, private citizens had to provide the money for colonization. As a result, England did not establish a successful colony in America until after 1600.

The French and Dutch Seek Trade

France and the Netherlands were also looking for ways to gain wealth through exploration and colonization. At first, their goal in the Americas was to find the Northwest Passage to Asia. When that search failed, they began to focus on North America itself.

The Frenchman **Samuel de Champlain** (sham•PLAYN) explored the St. Lawrence River. In 1608, he founded a fur-trading post at Quebec. This post became the first permanent French settlement in North America. Champlain's activities opened a rich fur trade with local Native Americans. After a couple of decades, **New France,** as the colony was called, began to thrive.

At the same time, the Dutch were building a colony called New Netherland. It was located along the Hudson River in present-day New York. After Hudson's voyage up the river in 1609, the Dutch built Fort Nassau in 1614, near the site of the modern city of Albany.

In 1626, the Dutch bought Manhattan Island from Native Americans. The Dutch then founded the town of New Amsterdam on that site, where New York City is currently located. New Netherland was soon thriving from the fur trade with Native Americans.

These early French and Dutch colonies, however, were small compared to the large empire Spain was building in the Americas. You will read about the growth of Spain's American empire in the next section.

Reading **H**
C. Making
Inferences
do you thir
took France
the Nether
so long to s
colonies in
Americas?

Section **2** Assessment

1. Terms & Names

Explain the significance of:
- Henry Hudson
- John Cabot
- Giovanni da Verrazzano
- Jacques Cartier
- Spanish Armada
- Samuel de Champlain
- New France

2. Using Graphics

Use a chart like the one below to show how European nations competed for power.

England	
France	
Netherlands	
Spain	

3. Main Ideas

a. What were the English, French, and Dutch searching for in their early voyages of exploration?

b. How did England defeat the Spanish Armada?

c. Where did the French and Dutch set up their first American colonies?

4. Critical Thinking

Making Inferences Wh do you think England founded colonies later th Spain did?

THINK ABOUT
- conditions in Spain and England
- the lands each country discovered

ACTIVITY OPTIONS

MUSIC

TECHNOLOGY

Research the life of one of the explorers discussed in this section. Compose a **song** or design a **Web page** about that person.

The Spanish and Native Americans

ONE AMERICAN'S STORY

Huamán Poma, a Peruvian Native American, wrote to King Philip III of Spain to complain about the abuse the Spanish heaped upon Native Americans.

A VOICE FROM THE PAST

It is their [the Spanish] practice to collect Indians into groups and send them to forced labor without wages, while they themselves receive the payment.

Huamán Poma, *Letter to a King*

A Spanish priest forces a Native American woman to work at a loom.

In his letter, Poma asked the king to help the Native Americans and uphold the rule of law in Peru. If the king actually read the letter, it made no difference. Spanish colonists continued to mistreat Native Americans as the Spanish Empire expanded in the Americas.

Spanish Colonies in the Americas

The Spanish Empire grew rapidly, despite efforts by other European countries to compete with Spain. By 1700, it controlled much of the Americas. Spain took several steps to establish an effective colonial government. First, it divided its American empire into two provinces called New Spain and Peru. Each province was called a **viceroyalty**. The top official of each viceroyalty was called the viceroy. He ruled in the king's name.

The Spanish also built new roads to transport people and goods across the empire. These roads stretched outward from the capitals at Mexico City and Lima. The roads helped Spain to control the colonies by allowing soldiers to move quickly from place to place. Roads also improved the Spanish economy because materials, such as gold and silver, could be transported efficiently to the coast and then to Spain.

Taking Notes

Use your chart to take notes about establishing colonies and the Columbian Exchange.

Event/Idea	Notes
Exploration	
Establishing Colonies	
European Competition	
Columbian Exchange	
Origins of Slavery	

Life in Spanish America

Spanish colonists received *encomiendas* to help them make the colonies productive. An **_encomienda_** was a grant of Native American labor. Hernando Cortés received a grant of more than 100,000 Native Americans to work his estate.

The Spanish rulers also created large estates, called **_haciendas_**, to provide food for the colony. *Haciendas* usually became large farms where Native Americans worked to grow cash crops, such as coffee and cotton. The *encomienda* and *hacienda* systems put much of the power and land in the hands of a few people.

The Spaniards made sure that people with Spanish backgrounds held power in the colonies. Spanish-born colonists such as Cortés made up the top layer of colonial society. Just below the Spanish were the Creoles—people of Spanish descent who were born in the colonies. The next step down the social order were the *mestizos*. *Mestizos* are people of mixed Spanish and Native American ancestry. The people with the least power and fewest rights were Native Americans and enslaved Africans.

Background•
The problem•
unequal we
especially in
continues to
trouble Lati
American
societies too

The Role of the Church

The Catholic Church played an important role in Spanish colonial society. In places like New Mexico and California, the church built **missions,** settlements that included a church, a town, and farmlands. The goal of the missions was to convert Native Americans to Christianity. The missions also increased Spanish control over the land.

Missionaries helped the Native Americans to create a better supply of food. They also offered Native Americans protection against enemies. Many Native Americans learned how to read and write in the missions. Others developed skills such as carpentry and metalworking.

Over time, however, many Native Americans grew increasingly unhappy. The missionaries often worked them as if they were slaves. The missionaries also tried to replace Native American religions and traditions. As a result, some Native Americans ran away, while others rebelled. Some destroyed churches and killed missionaries.

In 1680, a man named **Popé** led the Pueblo Indians in a rebellion against the Spanish. His forces surrounded the Spanish settlement at

*Reading*B
A. Summar
How did th
Spanish mi
change the
lives of Na
Americans

Santa Fe, in present-day New Mexico, and forced the colonists to flee. Popé ordered the churches and other Spanish buildings to be destroyed. He then tried to revive native customs that had been lost under Spanish rule. But before long, attacks from neighboring tribes weakened Pueblo control. In 1692, the Spanish regained control of Santa Fe.

Sugar Plantations Develop

The Spanish also forced Native Americans to work on **plantations,** large farms that raised cash crops. These crops were usually exported to Europe. The most important crop was sugar.

Although sugar was in great demand in Europe, there was not much land there to grow it. The resulting demand led to the development of sugar plantations in the Americas. On his second voyage to the Americas, in 1493, Columbus brought sugar cane to Hispaniola, one of the Caribbean islands he had landed on in 1492. He found ideal conditions for sugar production there. Spanish planters soon expanded operations to the nearby islands that Spain colonized.

Sugar plantations required many workers, so the Spanish planters turned to native peoples, such as the Taino. Through *encomiendas*, the Spaniards forced thousands of Taino to work in the fields. The plantations thrived, but many of the Taino suffered and died.

The Abuse of Native Americans

Most Spaniards treated the Native Americans as little more than beasts of burden. According to Fray Toribio de Benavente, a Catholic missionary, the Spanish "do nothing but command. They are the drones who suck the honey which is made by the poor bees, the Indians."

Not all Spaniards approved of this treatment. One man in particular fought for better treatment of Native

ground
plantation
included
co, cotton,
heal (a dye),
acao.

HISTORY through ART

Theodore de Bry created this picture, *Sugar: the greatest gift of the Old World to the New,* in the 1600s. It shows workers processing sugar in the Americas. Europeans brought sugar production to the Americas from the Mediterranean.

How does the picture help explain why the Europeans used slaves to make sugar?

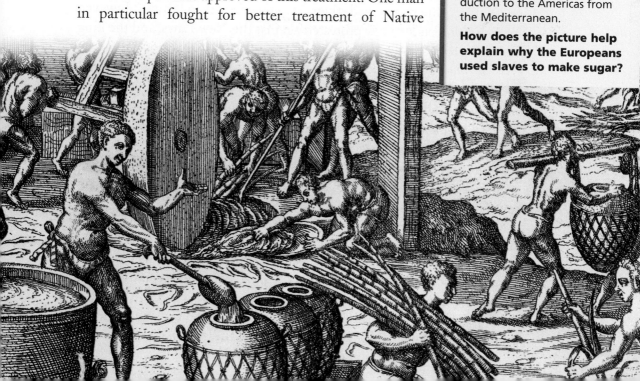

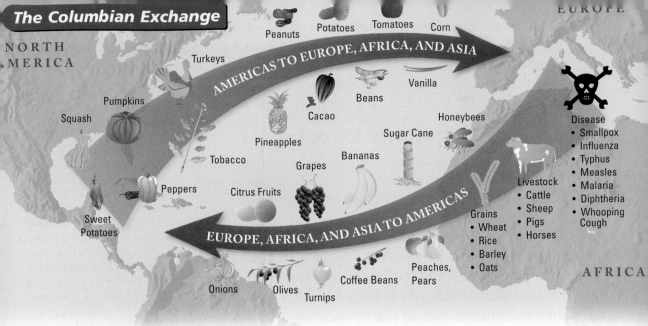

The Columbian Exchange

AMERICAS TO EUROPE, AFRICA, AND ASIA

NORTH AMERICA

Peanuts · Potatoes · Tomatoes · Corn

Turkeys

Pumpkins

Squash

Beans

Vanilla

Cacao

Honeybees

Pineapples

Sugar Cane

Tobacco

Bananas

Grapes

Peppers

Citrus Fruits

Sweet Potatoes

Disease
• Smallpox
• Influenza
• Typhus
• Measles
• Malaria
• Diphtheria
• Whooping Cough

Livestock
• Cattle
• Sheep
• Pigs
• Horses

Grains
• Wheat
• Rice
• Barley
• Oats

EUROPE

AFRICA

EUROPE, AFRICA, AND ASIA TO AMERICAS

Onions · Olives · Turnips · Coffee Beans · Peaches, Pears

Americans. His name was **Bartolomé de Las Casas.** Las Casas had come to Hispaniola in 1502 and taken part in the conquest of Cuba a decade later. For his part in the conquest, he received an *encomienda.* Las Casas was also a Catholic priest, however, and he soon faced a moral dilemma: How can a person serve God and enslave Native Americans at the same time?

In 1514, Las Casas gave up his claim to the Native Americans who worked for him. For the next 50 years, he fought against the abuse of Native Americans, earning the title "Protector of the Indians."

Because of his efforts, the Spanish king issued the New Laws in 1542. These laws ordered the gradual freeing of all enslaved Native Americans. Holders of *encomiendas* who were found guilty of mistreating Native Americans had their *encomiendas* taken away. However, Spanish colonists strongly protested against the New Laws, and the king eventually reversed many of them.

The Columbian Exchange

The arrival of the Spanish in the Americas brought more than a clash of peoples and cultures. It also brought a movement of plants, animals, and diseases between the Eastern and Western hemispheres. This movement of living things between hemispheres is called the **Columbian Exchange.**

One result of the Columbian Exchange was the transfer of germs from Europe to the Americas. When Europeans came to America, they brought with them germs that caused diseases such as smallpox, measles, and influenza. Native Americans had no immunity to them.

Although exact numbers are unknown, historians estimate that diseases brought by Europeans killed more than 20 million Native Americans in Mexico in the first century after conquest. Many scholars agree that the population of Native Americans in Central America decreased by 90 to 95 percent between the years 1519 and 1619. The

Reading **Hi**
B. Making Inferences might have pened if Na Americans h been immu to Europea diseases?

result was similar in Peru and other parts of the Americas. A Spanish missionary in Mexico described the effects of smallpox on the Aztecs.

A VOICE FROM THE PAST

There was a great havoc. Very many died of it. They could not walk. . . . They could not move; they could not stir; they could not change position, nor lie on one side; nor face down, nor on their backs. And if they stirred, much did they cry out. Great was its destruction.

Bernardino de Sahagún, quoted in *Seeds of Change*

Other effects of the Columbian Exchange were more positive. The Spanish brought many plants and animals to the Americas. European livestock—cattle, pigs, and horses—all thrived in the Americas. Crops from the Eastern Hemisphere, such as grapes, onions, and wheat, also thrived in the Western Hemisphere.

The Columbian Exchange benefited Europe, too. Many American crops became part of the European diet. Two that had a huge impact were potatoes and corn, which are highly nutritious. They helped feed European populations that might otherwise have gone hungry. Potatoes, for example, became an important food in Ireland, Russia, and other parts of northern Europe. Without potatoes, Europe's population might not have grown as rapidly as it did.

By mixing the products of two hemispheres, the Columbian Exchange brought the world closer together. Of course, people were also moving from one hemisphere to the other, blending their cultures in the process. The next section focuses on one important aspect of the movement of peoples: the forced migration of enslaved Africans to the Americas.

Now and then

KILLER BEES

Even today, plant and animal species continue to move from one hemisphere to the other. A recent example of this is the killer bee (shown below).

Killer bees were first brought to Brazil from Africa to help make honey in the 1950s. Killer bees are aggressive, however, and can kill large animals when they swarm. After some of these bees escaped from a Brazilian laboratory in 1957, they began to migrate. In recent years, they have been responsible for the deaths of a number of pets in the American Southwest.

ground
and, the
ation
sed from
llion in
:o more
million
5, largely
se of the
evel of
nts in
oes.

tion 3 Assessment

Terms & Names

plain the gnificance of:

- ceroyalty
- ncomienda
- acienda
- ission
- opé
- antation
- artolomé de as Casas
- olumbian Exchange

2. Using Graphics

Use a cluster diagram like the one below to show how Spain organized its colonies.

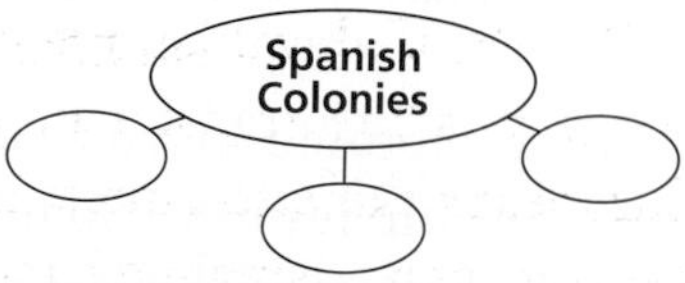

How did these actions help the Spanish control the Americas?

3. Main Ideas

a. What were the four levels of Spanish colonial society?

b. What was the main crop grown on colonial plantations?

c. How were Native Americans abused in the colonies?

4. Critical Thinking

Recognizing Effects
What were the positive and negative effects of the Columbian Exchange?

THINK ABOUT
- disease
- food
- livestock

IVITY OPTIONS

ART
NGUAGE ARTS

Make a **collage** that shows the plants and animals involved in the Columbian Exchange, or write a **story** that tells how Native Americans reacted to the animals.

Beginnings of Slavery in the Americas

4

MAIN IDEA	WHY IT MATTERS NOW	TERMS & NAMES
Slavery in the Americas began in order to provide cheap labor for the colonies.	The effects of slavery, including racism, helped shape attitudes and social conditions in the United States.	slavery slave codes African Diaspora racism middle passage

ONE AMERICAN'S STORY

In 1546, Diego de Campo was the leader of 7,000 maroons, or runaway slaves on the island of Hispaniola. There were only about 1,000 European men on the island.

The Spanish planters greatly feared de Campo. When the Spanish attacked the maroons, de Campo and his followers defeated the Spanish.

Eventually the Spaniards captured de Campo. He offered to lead the fight against the maroons. The Spanish accepted the offer. With de Campo's help, the Spanish defeated the maroons, and slavery in Hispaniola grew. In this section, you will read how slave labor expanded in the Americas.

Colonial tro
searched fo
communitie
of maroons
destroy the

Taking Notes

se your chart
o take notes
bout the origins
f slavery.

nt/Idea	Notes
oration	
blishing nies	
pean petition	
mbian ange	
ins of ery	

The Origins of American Slavery

By the 1600s, <u>slavery</u>, the practice of holding a person in bondage for labor, was firmly established in the Americas. But slavery was not new. Its roots went back to the world's ancient civilizations.

Slavery took many different forms throughout history. In some societies, slaves were mainly domestic servants in wealthy households. Some slaves also labored in mines and fields.

People were often enslaved when they were captured in battle or sold to pay off debts. Some slaves were treated with respect. Some were allowed to marry and own property. The children of many slaves were allowed to go free.

Slavery began to change, however, with the rise of sugar plantations. Europeans had used slaves to grow sugar in the eastern Mediterranean since the 1100s. Then, in the 1400s and 1500s, Portugal and Spain set up sugar plantations on islands in the eastern Atlantic. To work these plantations, they used African slaves bought from traders in Africa.

When the Spanish and Portuguese founded their colonies in the Americas, they brought the plantation system with them. At first they tried to enslave Native Americans to work in the fields and mines. But the Native Americans quickly died from overwork and disease. In some cases, they rebelled with the help of local allies.

The Spaniards then looked to other sources of slave labor, including Spanish slaves, black Christian slaves, and Asian slaves. But there was not enough of any of these groups to meet demand.

Finally, the Spanish and Portuguese enslaved Africans to provide labor. They enslaved Africans for four basic reasons. First, Africans were immune to most European diseases. Second, Africans had no friends or family in the Americas to help them resist or escape enslavement. Third, enslaved Africans provided a permanent source of cheap labor. Even their children could be held in bondage. Fourth, many Africans had worked on farms in their native lands.

ing History

wing
usions Why
lonists
that
n slaves
more useful
Native
can slaves?

The Slave Trade

The slave trade grew slowly at first. In 1509, the Spanish governor of Hispaniola, Diego Colón—Columbus's son—wrote to King Ferdinand to complain about a labor shortage on the island. In response, the king sent 50 African slaves to Hispaniola. The slave trade increased with the demand for slaves to work in the colonies. Eventually the colonies came to depend on slave labor. As one Spanish official in Peru wrote, "The black slave is the basis of the *hacienda* and the source of all wealth which this realm produces."

European slave traders carried out the shipment of Africans to the Americas. The rulers of West African kingdoms participated in the trade, too. On the coast of Africa, local kings gathered captives from inland. The local kings then traded these captives for European goods, such as textiles, ironware, wine, and guns.

This trade made the coastal kingdoms rich while weakening inland African societies. In 1526, King Afonso, a West African ruler, protested against the slave trade in a letter to Portugal's king. Afonso wrote, "Everyday these [slave] merchants take our people. . . . So great is this corruption and evil that our country is becoming completely depopulated."

ulary
lated: to
pulation

CONNECTIONS TO MATH

Slaves Imported to the Americas, *1493–1810*

Number of slaves (in millions)

7
6
5
4
3
2
1
0

1493–1600   1601–1700   1701–1810

Dates

Source: Philip D. Curtin, *The Atlantic Slave Trade*

SKILLBUILDER Interpreting Graphs

1. *About how many slaves were imported to the Americas between 1493 and 1810?*
2. *Why do you think the numbers increased?*

The diagram above shows how slave traders packed enslaved Africans onto slave ships for the middle passage. A British naval officer painted the picture on the right, which also shows the crowded conditions on slave ships.

The Middle Passage

Afonso's protest did not stop the forced removal of people from Africa. This removal has become known as the **African Diaspora**. Before the slave trade ended in the late 1800s, approximately 12 million Africans had been enslaved and shipped to the Western Hemisphere. Of these, perhaps two million died during the voyage.

The voyage from Africa to the Americas was called the **middle passage.** The voyage was given this name because it was the middle leg of the triangular trade. The triangular trade refers to the movement of trade ships between Europe, Africa, and the Americas. You will learn more about the triangular trade in Chapter 4.

Olaudah Equiano (oh•LOW•duh EHK•wee•AHN•oh) was one of these kidnapped Africans. He made this journey in the 1700s. He was about 11 years old when he was taken from his home and sold into slavery. Later, after he bought his freedom, he wrote his life story and told what the middle passage was like.

A VOICE FROM THE PAST

The first object which saluted my eyes when I arrived on the coast, was the sea, and a slave ship . . . waiting for its cargo. These filled me with astonishment, which was soon converted into terror, when I was carried on board.

Olaudah Equiano, quoted in *Great Slave Narratives*

Equiano saw a row of men shackled together in chains. He also saw a large boiling kettle. He feared that he was going to be cooked and eaten "by those white men with horrible looks, red faces, and long hair."

The scene on the slave deck below was even worse. Several hundred slaves were crammed into a space so small that there was not even enough room to stand up. Foul smells and disease, along with the shrieks and groans of the dying, made the middle passage a terrifying experience. The captives who did not die faced new horrors in the Americas.

Vocabulary
diaspora: th
scattering o
people outs
their homel

Reading
B. Making
Inferences
would slav
traders pac
many capt
onto slave

Slavery in the Americas

Once the enslaved Africans arrived in the colonies, they were sold at auction. Some were taken to large homes where they worked as servants. Most were forced to do hard labor in *haciendas* or mines. They were also fed and housed poorly.

Many slaves resisted slavery by running away. Across Peru and New Spain, maroons formed communities, often with Native Americans. Sometimes enslaved Africans rebelled. To prevent rebellion, the Spanish government passed **slave codes,** laws to regulate the treatment of slaves. Some of these laws tried to soften the harsh conditions of slavery, but most were designed to punish slaves and keep them in bondage.

Over time, Europeans came to associate slavery with black Africans. To many Europeans, dark skin color became a sign of inferiority. Slavery, which developed to provide a labor force, led to racism. **Racism** is the belief that some people are inferior because of their race.

The slave trade lasted for nearly 400 years, from the early 1500s to the mid-1800s. This contact between Africa and the Americas also formed part of the Columbian Exchange that you read about in Section 3. Africans brought to the Americas a vast knowledge about farming and animals. At the same time, American crops such as sweet potatoes, peanuts, and chilies made their way to Africa.

Enslaved Africans also brought with them a strong artistic heritage of dance, music, and storytelling. The slave trade brought together people from different parts of Africa with different cultural traditions. The experience of slavery helped create a common African-based culture in the Americas. By the 1700s, all the American colonies of European countries had African slaves. As you will read in the next chapter, African culture would be one of the forces that shaped life in the American colonies.

ling **History**

alyzing
es What
have
d slave
rs to treat
humans
such
y?

---

tion 4 Assessment

1. Terms & Names

plain the ignificance of:
avery
frican Diaspora
iiddle passage
ave codes
acism

2. Using Graphics

Use a diagram like the one below to compare the experience of Native Americans and Africans under slavery.

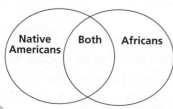

Native Americans | Both | Africans

3. Main Ideas

a. When did slavery begin?

b. Why did Europeans bring Africans to the Americas?

c. What are three examples of bad conditions faced by enslaved Africans?

4. Critical Thinking

Recognizing Effects What were the long-term effects of slavery in the Americas?

THINK ABOUT
• the economy in the Americas
• the African Diaspora
• cultural diversity in the Americas

IVITY OPTIONS

| ART |
| MATH |

Research some aspect of the slave trade, such as the middle passage or the number of people enslaved. Paint a **picture** or draw a **graph** to show what you learned.

TERMS & NAMES

Briefly explain the significance of each of the following.

1. mercantilism
2. Hernando Cortés
3. Montezuma
4. Spanish Armada
5. New France
6. *encomienda*
7. Columbian Exchange
8. slavery
9. African Diaspora
10. middle passage

REVIEW QUESTIONS

Spain Claims an Empire (pages 61–66)

1. What were three reasons for the European voyages of exploration in the 1400s and 1500s?
2. Who conquered the Aztecs and Incas?
3. What three reasons explain Spain's success in building an empire in the Americas?

European Competition in North America (pages 67–70)

4. What was the Northwest Passage?
5. Why did the Spanish Armada attack England?
6. What did the French and Dutch colonists trade?

The Spanish and Native Americans (pages 71–75)

7. How did Spanish rule affect Native Americans?
8. How did the Columbian Exchange affect Europe?

Beginnings of Slavery in the Americas (pages 76–79)

9. Why did the Spanish and Portuguese use slave labor in their colonies?
10. How did the slave trade work?

CRITICAL THINKING

1. USING YOUR NOTES: FINDING MAIN IDEAS

Event/Idea	Notes
Exploration	
Establishing Colonies	
European Competition	
Columbian Exchange	
Origins of Slavery	

Using your completed chart, answer the questions be

a. What causes did European competition and exploration have in common?

b. How did the establishment of colonies in the Americas lead to slavery?

c. Which concept in the chart contributed most to Columbian Exchange?

2. ANALYZING LEADERSHIP

Think about the explorers and *conquistadors* discu in this chapter. What qualities did they possess tha made them successful in their efforts?

3. THEME: IMMIGRATION AND MIGRATION

What were the causes and effects of the migratior Europeans and Africans to the Americas?

4. APPLYING CITIZENSHIP SKILLS

What kind of values did Bartolomé de Las Casas demonstrate in his actions? How effective was he improving his society?

Interact *with* History

Have your answers about whether or not you wou join a voyage of exploration changed after readin the chapter? Explain.

VISUAL SUMMARY

European Exploration of the Americas

Causes

National Competition

Desire for Wealth

Spread Christianity

European Exploration of the Americas

Effects

Destruction of Aztec and Incan Empires

The Columb Exchange

European Colonies in Americas

Slavery

e the chart and your knowledge of U.S. history to
swer questions 1 and 2.

dditional Test Practice, pp. S1–S33.

	1601–1810	
laves Imported to the Americas (in thousands)		
EGION/COUNTRY	**1601–1700**	**1701–1810**
ritish N. America	*	348
ritish Caribbean	263.7	1,401.3
rench Caribbean	155.8	1,348.4
panish America	292.5	578.6
utch Caribbean	40	460
anish Caribbean	4	24
razil (Portugal)	560	1,891.4

*=less than 1,000

Source: Philip D. Curtin, *The Atlantic Slave Trade*

Which region or country imported the most slaves
to the Americas?

A. British Caribbean

B. French Caribbean

C. Brazil (Portugal)

D. Spanish Caribbean

2. Which region imported less than 1,000 slaves
before 1700?

A. Brazil (Portugal)

B. British North America

C. Danish Caribbean

D. Dutch Caribbean

**This quotation is from Olaudah Equiano, an African
slave. Use the quotation and your knowledge of
U.S. history to answer question 3.**

PRIMARY SOURCE

The first object which saluted my eyes when I arrived
on the coast, was the sea, and a slave ship . . . waiting for its cargo. These filled me with astonishment,
which was soon converted into terror, when I was
carried on board.

Olaudah Equiano, *Great Slave Narratives*

3. The passage supports which of the following conclusions?

A. Equiano and the others on board felt safe.

B. The conditions on the ship were horrifying.

C. Because he protested, Equiano was allowed to
return home.

D. Equiano's circumstances improved after he
arrived in the colonies.

TEST PRACTICE
CLASSZONE.COM

ERNATIVE ASSESSMENT

✎ WRITING ABOUT HISTORY

e a **newspaper article** about one of these events:
oche Triste in Mexico or the murder of the Incan
eror Atahualpa.

e library resources to research Mexican or Incan
tory.

ur article should explain what happened and who
s involved. Add details that explain when, where,
hy, and how the event occurred.

ve your article an interesting headline.

OPERATIVE LEARNING

a group, create a diorama to depict one of the
nunities of Spanish America in the 1600s. Your
ma should include features such as a mission, a
nda, roads, mines or sugar mills. Use drawings,
and written descriptions that depict daily life

INTEGRATED TECHNOLOGY

DOING INTERNET RESEARCH

The Columbian Exchange is the movement of plants
and animals around the world as a result of exploration. Use the Internet and other library resources to
research the movement of a plant or animal around
the world.

- Choose a specific plant or animal. You might choose
  corn, potatoes, chocolate, tea, coffee, sugar, or
  horses, cattle, or pigs.

- Use your plant or animal as a keyword. Search
  the Internet to find where the plant or animal
  first existed and where it moved.

For more about the Columbian Exchange . . .

INTERNET ACTIVITY
CLASSZONE.COM

The settlers at Jamestown, Virginia, built a fort with three walls rather than four to make it easier to defend.

These soldiers are training to defend the Jamestown fort and settlers.

1585
First English colony established at Roanoke.

1607
John Smith and other English settlers establish Jamestown.

1620
Pilgrims land at Plymouth.

1630
Puritans found Massachusetts Bay Colony.

N. America
World 1585

1587
Foreign missionaries are banished from Japan.

1588
England defeats Spanish Armada.

1605
Akbar, Mughal emperor of India, dies.

Cha
En
be

The settlers' houses were built inside the fort walls for protection.

The year is 1607. You have just sailed across the ocean and arrived in a strange land. Your family has traveled to the eastern coast of North America in search of freedom and prosperity. Your first task in the new land is to decide what you need to do to survive.

What dangers would you face as a settler?

What Do You Think?

- What do you need to survive in the wilderness?
- This settlement is actually a fort, with an armed force and high fences. What reasons might there be for building a fort?
- What kind of settlement would you build?

RESEARCH LINKS
CLASSZONE.COM

Visit the Chapter 3 links for more information about the English colonies.

kes
1675
King
Philip's
War
erupts.

1681
William Penn receives charter for Pennsylvania.

1692
Salem witchcraft trials are held.

1732
Colony of Georgia is founded by James Oglethorpe.

1732

rchy
en
rns

1688
William and Mary take power in Britain's Glorious Revolution.

Reading Strategy: Sequencing Events

What Do You Know?

What do you already know about the American colonies? What sort of person might choose to leave his or her native country and cross the ocean to settle in a new land?

Think About

- what you've learned about American settlers from movies, television, historical fiction, or science fiction about space travel
- opportunities and challenges offered in a new land
- your responses to the Interact with History about facing dangers as a settler (see page 83)

What Do You Want to Know?

 What questions do you have about the Europeans who settled in North America? about those who were already here? Record your questions in your notebook before read this chapter.

Sequencing Events

Sequencing means putting events in order. In learning about the early colonies, for exam it will be useful to you to list the 13 original colonies and an important early date mentioned for each in the chapter. You might record the name and a date for each colony in graphic organizer such as the one below. Copy this organizer in your notebook. Fill it in you read the chapter.

S See Skillbuilder Handbook, page R4.

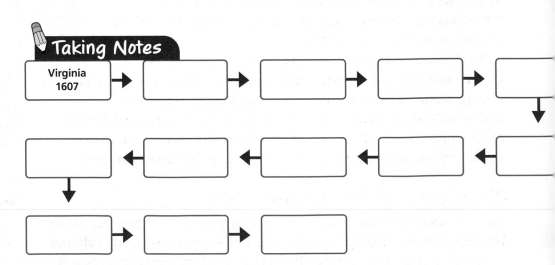

✏️ **Taking Notes**

| Virginia 1607 |

Early Colonies Have Mixed Success

MAIN IDEA	WHY IT MATTERS NOW	TERMS & NAMES
...rly English colonies failed, but ...own survived—partly through ...al effort and hard work.	Jamestown's survival led to more English colonies and a lasting English influence in the United States.	joint-stock company indentured servant charter House of Burgesses Jamestown Bacon's Rebellion John Smith

ONE AMERICAN'S STORY

In 1585, John White traveled with the first English expedition to Roanoke, an island off North Carolina. White sailed back to England in 1586 and then returned to Roanoke as governor the next year, bringing with him more than 100 settlers. Soon White's daughter Elinor gave birth to a baby girl. John White described the event.

A VOICE FROM THE PAST

On August 18 a daughter was born to Elinor, . . . wife of Ananias Dare. . . . The child was christened on the following Sunday and was named Virginia because she was the first Christian born in Virginia.

John White, *The New World*

In 1587, White was forced to sail back to England a second time to get needed supplies. He left the colonists, including his granddaughter, Virginia, in Roanoke. White was delayed and did not return to Roanoke until 1590.

To his shock and grief, he found no trace of the colonists or his granddaughter, all of whom had disappeared. The only clues to their whereabouts were the letters *CRO* carved in a tree and the word *Croatoan* carved in a doorpost. White never discovered the fate of his family and the other colonists. In this section, you will learn why English settlers such as White came to America despite such hardships.

Drawing by John White of an old man of the Pomeiock tribe.

The English Plan Colonies

As you read in Chapter 2, religious and political rivalries increased between England and Spain in the late 1500s. Spain had many colonies in the Americas, but England had none. England began directing its resources toward establishing colonies after its defeat of the Spanish Armada in 1588.

Taking Notes

Use your chart to take notes about the early colonies.

Virginia 1607 →

Richard Hakluyt (HAK•LOOT), an English geographer, urged England to start a colony. Hakluyt thought that colonies would provide a market for English exports. They also would serve as a source of raw materials. By having colonies, England hoped to increase its trade and build up its gold supply. This is the economic theory of mercantilism (see page 62). In mercantilism, the state controls trade and attempts to transfer wealth from colonies to the parent country. Hakluyt also thought that English colonies would help to plant the Protestant faith in the Americas.

The earliest English colonists had many reasons for going to America. The lack of economic opportunity in England forced many to seek their fortunes abroad. Stories of gold mines lured some to leave England. Others left to escape religious persecution.

Reading His
A. Summariz
Why did Eng
colonists sett
America?

Two Early Colonies Fail

Sir Walter Raleigh was a soldier, statesman, and adventurer who served under Queen Elizabeth I of England. She gave him permission to sponsor the colony at Roanoke. He named England's first colony Virginia after the unmarried, or virgin, queen. Financed by Raleigh, the colony began in 1585 on Roanoke Island. The colonists relied on the Native Americans for food. But when the Native Americans realized that the settlers wanted their land, they cut off the colonists' food supply. Those who survived returned to England in 1586.

Vocabulary
financed: pa
raised funds

In 1587, artist John White convinced Raleigh to try again to establish the Roanoke colony, with the disastrous results described in One American's Story (page 85). To this day, no one knows for sure what happened. Some historians think that the colonists mingled with the neighboring Native Americans. Others believe that they moved to Chesapeake Bay and were killed by Native Americans defending their land.

In 1607, the Plymouth Company sponsored the Sagadahoc colony at the mouth of the Kennebec River in Maine. Some of the settlers were English convicts. One colonist wrote of George Popham, the governor, "He stocked or planted [the colony] out of all the jails of England." Within the first year, arguments among colonists, a harsh winter, fights with Native Americans, and food shortages forced most of the colonists to return to England.

Financing a Colony

Raleigh had financed the colony at Roanoke. When the colony failed, he lost his investment. The English learned from Raleigh's financial loss at Roanoke that one person could not finance a colony. To raise money, they turned to the **joint-stock company**. Joint-stock companies were backed by investors, people who put money into a project to earn profits. Each investor received pieces of ownership of the company called

Now and then

THE LUMBEE AND THE LOST COLONISTS

The Lumbee tribe lives mainly in North Carolina. Some of the Lumbee believe they are descendants of the lost colonists of Roanoke. Among the evidence cited is the fact that 41 of the 95 last names of the Lumbee were last names of the colonists.

Other Lumbee don't believe that they are descended from English ancestors. The Lumbee are trying to win federal recognition as a Native American tribe. English ancestry might weaken their claim for federal financial support.

shares of stock. In this way, the investors split any profits and divided any losses.

Merchants organized the Virginia Company of London and the Virginia Company of Plymouth. King James I of England granted charters to both companies in 1606. A **charter** was a written contract, issued by a government, giving the holder the right to establish a colony.

Jamestown Is Founded in 1607

In 1607, the Virginia Company of London financed an expedition to Chesapeake Bay that included more than 100 colonists. They sailed up the James River until they found a spot to settle. They named the first permanent English settlement **Jamestown** in honor of King James.

From the start, the Jamestown colonists endured terrible hardships. The site of the colony was swampy and full of malaria-carrying mosquitoes. This disease made the colonists sick with fever. Many also became ill from drinking the river water. To make matters worse, the London Company had incorrectly told the settlers that the colony would be rich in gold. They spent their days searching for gold rather than building houses and growing food.

The climate was also a hardship. The colonists soon learned that the summers were hot and humid and the winters bitter cold. As one colonist recalled, "There were never Englishmen left in a foreign country in such misery as we were in this newly discovered Virginia."

Jamestown Grows

By January 1608, only 38 colonists remained alive. Later that year, **John Smith,** a soldier and adventurer, took control. To make sure the colonists worked, Smith announced, "He that will not work shall not eat." Smith's methods worked. He ordered an existing wall extended around Jamestown. He also persuaded the Powhatan tribe to trade their corn to the colonists. In 1609, Smith was injured in a gunpowder explosion and returned to England. That same year, 800 more English settlers arrived in Jamestown.

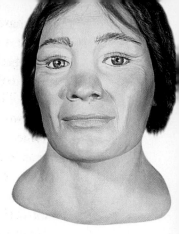

This is a computer reconstruction of the face of Mistress Forrest, believed to be the first English woman to come to Jamestown.

Early English Settlements, 1585–1607

Sagadahoc R. (Kennebec)

Sagadahoc, 1

Massachusetts Bay

Hudson R.

0 100 Miles
0 200 Kilometers

ATLANTIC OCEAN

Potomac R.

Chesapeake Bay

James R.

Jamestown, 1607

Roanoke R.

Roanoke I., 1585, 1587

GEOGRAPHY SKILLBUILDER Interpreting Maps
1. **Location** Which colony was located northeast of Jamestown? How many miles northeast was it?
2. **Human-Environment Interaction** Why did the colonists settle near the coast?

ground
rians used
lieve that
olony's origi-
te had been
ed by the
s River.
t archaeo-
l digs, how-
have
ered the
n higher
d.

ing **History**
ving
ms If you
een John
how
you have
the
sts to work?

Because of growing tensions between the settlers and Native Americans, the Powhatan stopped trading food and attacked the settlers. The settlers did not dare leave the fort. During the "starving time," the colonists ate rats, mice, and snakes. Only 60 of the colonists were still alive when two ships arrived in 1610. Lord De La Warr, the new governor, imposed discipline, and the "starving time" ended.

In 1612, John Rolfe developed a high-grade tobacco that the colonists learned to grow. It quickly became very popular in England. The success of tobacco growing changed Jamestown in many ways. The Virginia Company thought of the colonists as employees. The colonists, however, wanted a share of the profits.

The company responded by letting settlers own land. Settlers worked harder when the land was their own. The company offered a 50-acre land grant for each man, woman, or child who could pay his or her way to the colony. In 1619, the first African Americans arrived in Jamestown. The population of Virginia jumped from about 600 in 1619 to more than 2,000 in 1621.

Even more laborers were needed. Those who could not afford passage to America were encouraged to become **indentured servants.** These men and women sold their labor to the person who paid their passage to the colony. After working for a number of years, they were free to farm or take up a trade of their own.

The colonists soon became annoyed at the strict rule of the governor, who represented the Virginia Company's interests back in London. To provide for more local control, the company decided that burgesses, or elected representatives, of the colonists would meet once a year in an assembly. The **House of Burgesses,** created in 1619, became the first representative assembly in the American colonies.

Conflicts with the Powhatan

Cultural differences put the Powhatan and the English on a collision course. At first, the Powhatan traded food with the colonists. Then, as more colonists arrived and wanted land, relations grew worse. In an effort to improve relations between the English colonists and the Powhatan, John Rolfe married Chief Powhatan's daughter, Pocahontas, in 1614.

For a time, there was an uneasy peace. The colonists learned from the Powhatan how to grow corn, catch fish, and capture wild fowl. However, the expanding tobacco plantations took over more and more Powhatan land. In 1622, in response to land grabs by the colonists, the Powhatan killed hundreds of Jamestown's residents.

Reading His
C. Analyzing
Causes Wha
the main rea
for the vario
arrangemen
Virginia Com
came up wit
bring people
America?

Reading Hi
D. Finding N
Ideas What
the central
pute betwee
Powhatan a
the settlers?

AMERICA'S HISTORY MAKERS

POCAHONTAS
1595?–1617

Pocahontas met John Smith when she was about 12 years old. Smith taught her English and admired her spirit. She admired Smith's bravery and saved his life twice. After Smith returned to England, she married the colonist John Rolfe in 1614. Shown below is a portrait of Pocahontas, done in 1616.

Two years later, the Rolfes went to England to raise money for the Jamestown colony. While getting ready to sail home, Pocahontas died of smallpox.

How did Pocahontas show that Native Americans and white settlers might live in peace?

Bacon's Rebellion in 1676

As you have seen, many of the English colonists who came to Virginia during the 1600s fought with the Native Americans. They also battled one another. By the 1670s, one-fourth of the free white men were former indentured servants. These colonists, who did not own land, resented the wealthy eastern landowners. The poor settlers lived mostly on Virginia's western frontier, where they battled the Native Americans for land.

Nathaniel Bacon and a group of landless frontier settlers opposed Governor William Berkeley. They complained about high taxes and Governor Berkeley's favoritism toward large plantation owners. Bacon demanded that Berkeley approve a war against the Native Americans to seize their land for tobacco plantations. Governor Berkeley's refusal of Nathaniel Bacon's demand sparked **Bacon's Rebellion** in 1676.

Bacon marched into Jamestown, took control of the House of Burgesses, and burned Jamestown to the ground. Bacon's sudden illness and death ended the rebellion. Berkeley hanged Bacon's followers. Angered by Berkeley's actions, King Charles II recalled the governor to England. After that incident, the House of Burgesses passed laws to prevent a royal governor from assuming such power again. The burgesses had taken an important step against tyranny. In the next section, you will read about the New England colonies and their steps toward independence.

Nathaniel Bacon (right) confronts Virginia governor William Berkeley at Jamestown in 1676.

ulary
y: a govern-
n which a
ruler has
te power

---

tion **1** Assessment

Terms & Names

plain the
gnificance of:
oint-stock company
harter
amestown
ohn Smith
ndentured servant
ouse of Burgesses
acon's Rebellion

2. Using Graphics

Use a series-of-events chain to review events that led to the founding of Jamestown.

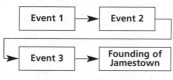

What were reasons England wanted colonies in America?

3. Main Ideas

a. Why did the first English settlement at Roanoke fail?

b. How did the English finance their colonies after 1606?

c. What was the outcome of Bacon's Rebellion?

4. Critical Thinking

Drawing Conclusions
What were the main reasons that Jamestown survived and prospered?

THINK ABOUT

- how, after the "starving time," Lord De La Warr took control
- John Rolfe's development of a high-grade tobacco plant

IVITY OPTIONS

ART
NGUAGE ARTS

You need indentured servants to work on your plantation. Draw a **poster** or write an **advertisement** that will attract people to your plantation.

Report from the New World

You are a settler who has landed on the wild eastern shore of North America. You and your 93 fellow colonists survived a frightening nine-week Atlantic voyage. Now you are struggling to build a new home in the wilderness. There are no roads, inns, or towns in this land. The game, berries, and fish here taste strange, sometimes unpleasant. Your only neighbors are small groups of Native Americans.

COOPERATIVE LEARNING On these pages are challenges you face as you put down roots in America. Working with a small group, decide how to deal with each challenge. Choose an option, assign a task to each group member, and do the activity. You will find useful information in the Data File. Be prepared to present your solutions to the class as part of a report to your sponsors back in England.

CIVICS CHALLENGE

"They had little or no care of any other thing, but to pamper their bellies."

As your colony takes root, most members work hard to farm, cook, wash, mend, trade, and defend the colony. But a few colonists think only of their own comfort. You call a meeting to set some rules about work. Present your solution to this problem using one of these options:

- Make a poster for the meeting hall that states the new work rules and punishments.

- Write a report describing the problem and how the colony solved it.

CONOMICS CHALLENGE

ight tin dish
t pleased him."

e spring arrives, your stores of English
running low. You and your friends decide
ling with the neighboring Native
. They could provide a steady supply of
, and vegetables until your harvest comes
p a plan for opening trade. Present your
one of these options:

up, role-play the meeting in which you
our trading plan.

structions for the team of colonists who
trade with the Native Americans.

ACTIVITY WRAP-UP

the class As a group, review your solution to each
Consider the following:

each solution meets its particular challenge
lution shows the most creativity

ave made your decision, present your solutions to the
group member should take part in the presentation.

The Journey

Distance: more than 5,000 nautical miles from Europe to the east coast of North America

Length: 6–14 weeks

Dangers: storms, scurvy, dysentery, malnutrition, seasickness, overcrowding

Food and Livestock Taken

barrels of salted beef, oatmeal, dried grains, cheese, oil, vinegar, and salt; seeds for peas, barley, herbs, and other crops; cows, horses, goats, pigs, sheep, and chickens

Equipment Taken

axes, hoes, nails, hooks for doors, hammers, chisels, hatchets, spades, pickaxes, iron pots, copper kettles, skillets, platters, dishes, wooden spoons, rugs

Weapons Taken

swords, muskets, daggers, gunpowder, light armor, cannon

Clothes Taken

shirts, several pairs of shoes, leather for mending, waistcoats, caps, skirts, jackets, trousers

Dangers in America

Biggest killers: typhoid, dysentery, famine

Other dangers: pneumonia, malaria, and other diseases; exposure to harsh weather; fire; wild animals; attacks by Native Americans

Benefits in America

religious and political freedom; opportunity to own land; abundant timber for shelters, forts, heat, ships, and trade; rich food resources

For more about the American colonies . . .

RESEARCH LINKS
CLASSZONE.COM

2

New England Colonies

MAIN IDEA	WHY IT MATTERS NOW	TERMS & NAMES
Religion influenced the settlement and government of the New England colonies.	The Puritan work ethic and religious beliefs influence American culture today.	Pilgrims Fundamen~ of Conne~ Mayflower Compact Roger Will~ Puritans Anne Hut~ Great Migration King Phili~

ONE AMERICAN'S STORY

In 1605, Englishmen captured and enslaved a Native American named Squanto and took him to England. Squanto returned to America in 1619. There he discovered that his Pawtuxet tribe had been killed by disease. In 1621, Squanto set about helping the English plant crops on tribal lands. Colonist William Bradford made the following comment.

A VOICE FROM THE PAST

Squanto . . . was a special instrument sent of God for their [the colonists'] good beyond their expectation. . . . He directed them how to set their corn, where to take fish, and to procure other commodities, and was also their pilot to bring them to unknown places.

William Bradford, quoted in *The Pilgrim Reader*

In this section, you will learn about the Pilgrims and Puritans, their relations with the Native Americans, and their settlement of the New England colonies.

Squanto t~
Pilgrims h~
grow corn

Taking Notes

Use your chart to take notes about the New England colonies.

Virginia 1607 → [ ]

The Voyage of the *Mayflower*

In the early 1500s, King Henry VIII of England broke that country's ties with the Catholic Church and established the Church of England, an official state church under his control. In the early 1600s, a religious group called the Separatists called for a total break with the Church of England. They thought it was too much like the Catholic Church.

The **Pilgrims** were a Separatist group. King James attacked them for rejecting England's official church. To escape this harsh treatment, the Pilgrims fled to Holland, a country known for its acceptance of different opinions. Eventually, the Pilgrims became dissatisfied with life in Holland. They approached the Virginia Company and asked if they could settle in America "as a distinct body by themselves." The Virginia

The *Mayflower* brings the Pilgrims to Plymouth in 1620.

Company arranged for them to settle on land within its boundaries on the eastern coast of North America.

On a cold, raw November day in 1620, a ship called the *Mayflower* arrived off Cape Cod on the Massachusetts coast. Blown north of its course, the *Mayflower* landed in an area that John Smith had mapped and called New England. They landed at a site that had been named Plymouth.

Because the Pilgrims landed outside the limits of the Virginia Company, their charter did not apply. For the sake of order, the men aboard the *Mayflower* signed an agreement called the **Mayflower Compact**. In it, they vowed to obey laws agreed upon for the good of the colony. The Mayflower Compact helped establish the idea of self-government and majority rule. (See Interactive Primary Sources, page 98.)

The Pilgrims Found Plymouth

Like the early settlers at Jamestown, the Pilgrims at Plymouth endured a starving time. That first winter, disease and death struck with such fury that "the living were scarce able to bury the dead." Half the group had died by spring.

However, energy, hope, and help returned. One day a Native American walked up to a group of colonists. To their astonishment, he called out, "Welcome, Englishmen." This was Samoset, a Pemaquid who had learned to speak English from European fishermen. Samoset introduced the settlers to another Native American named Squanto, a Pawtuxet, who also spoke English.

"Welcome, Englishmen."
Samoset

The Pilgrims had angered the Native Americans by taking their corn. Squanto acted as an interpreter between the Pilgrims and Chief Massasoit. He helped them to negotiate a peace treaty and showed them how to plant, hunt, and fish. While their crops grew, the colonists began trading with the Native Americans for furs and preparing lumber to ship back to England in order to make a profit.

Sometime in the fall—no one knows exactly when—the Plymouth settlement celebrated the blessings of a good harvest by holding a three-day feast. It was the first Thanksgiving. This Thanksgiving came to represent the peace that existed at that time between the Native Americans and Pilgrims.

*ng***History**
ing
ces
> you
quanto
helpful
Pilgrims?

Thanks to the help of Squanto and other Native Americans, the Pilgrims learned to survive in their new environment. Soon more people would sail to New England seeking religious freedom.

The Puritans Come to Massachusetts Bay

Between about 1630 and 1640, a religious group called the **Puritans** left England to escape bad treatment by King James I. Unlike the Separatists, who wanted to break away from the Church of England, the Puritans wanted to reform, or "purify," its practices. By the thousands, Puritan families left for the Americas. Their leaving is known as the **Great Migration.** Many thousands of Puritans left their homeland to found new settlements around the world. Of these settlers, about 20,000 crossed the Atlantic Ocean to New England.

Many Puritan merchants had invested in the Massachusetts Bay Company. In 1629, the company received a royal charter to settle land in New England. In 1630, 11 well-supplied ships carried about 1,000 passengers to the Massachusetts Bay Colony. Unlike earlier colonists, the Puritans were well prepared and did not suffer through a starving time. John Winthrop was the colony's Puritan governor. He stated that the new colony would be a commonwealth, a community in which people work together for the good of the whole.

Background
During the Great Migration, the Puritans also went to Ireland, the Netherlands, the Rhineland, and the West Indies.

Reading **Hi**
B. Making Inferences Winthrop, politicians sometimes spoke of America as "a city upon a hill." What does this phrase suggest about America's role in the world?

> *A VOICE FROM THE PAST*
>
> So shall we keep the unity of the spirit, in the bond of peace. . . . Ten of us will be able to resist a thousand of our enemies. . . . For we must consider that we shall be as a City upon a Hill, the eyes of all people are on us.
>
> **John Winthrop,** *"Model of Christian Charity"*

The New England Way

The basic unit of the commonwealth was the congregation—a group of people who belong to the same church. Each Puritan congregation set up its own town. The meetinghouse was the most important building in each town. There people gathered for town meetings, a form of self-government in which people made laws and other decisions for the community. In the Massachusetts Bay Colony, only male church members could vote or hold office. They elected representatives to a lawmaking body called the General Court, which in turn chose the governor.

By law, everyone in town had to attend church services held in the meetinghouse. The sermon, the most important part of the church service, provided instruction in the "New England Way." This was a term used by the Puritans to describe both their beliefs and their society, which emphasized duty, godliness, hard work, and honesty. The Puritans thought that amusements such as dancing and playing games would lead to laziness. They believed that God required them to work long and hard at their vocation.

The Puritan work ethic helped contribute to the rapid growth and success of the New England colonies. The New England Way also depended on education. Because the Puritans wanted everyone to be able to read the Bible, laws required that all children learn to read.

*ing*History
marizing
were some
tant ele-
of the New
d Way?

Some Puritan congregations set up new colonies. In 1636, Thomas Hooker moved his congregation to the Connecticut Valley. There they wrote and adopted the **Fundamental Orders of Connecticut** in 1639 (see page 98). In effect, these laws were a constitution. The Fundamental Orders extended voting rights to non-church members and limited the power of the governor. They expanded the idea of representative government.

The first European settlement in New Hampshire was a village near Portsmouth in 1623. In 1638, John Wheelwright established the town of Exeter. The town's founders drew up the Exeter Compact, which was based on the Mayflower Compact.

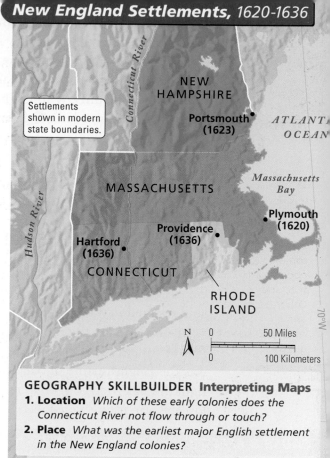

New England Settlements, 1620-1636

Settlements shown in modern state boundaries.

NEW HAMPSHIRE

Portsmouth (1623)

ATLANTIC OCEAN

Connecticut River

Hudson River

MASSACHUSETTS

Massachusetts Bay

Plymouth (1620)

Providence (1636)

Hartford (1636)

CONNECTICUT

RHODE ISLAND

N

0   50 Miles

0   100 Kilometers

70°W

GEOGRAPHY SKILLBUILDER Interpreting Maps
1. **Location** *Which of these early colonies does the Connecticut River not flow through or touch?*
2. **Place** *What was the earliest major English settlement in the New England colonies?*

Challenges to Puritan Leaders

Not everyone agreed with the New England Way. **Roger Williams** was a minister in Salem, Massachusetts, who founded the first Baptist church in America. He opposed forced attendance at church. He also opposed the English colonists' taking of Native American lands by force. Because of his beliefs, the General Court forced Williams to leave the colony. In 1636, he fled southward and founded the colony of Rhode Island, which guaranteed religious freedom and the separation of church and state.

Anne Hutchinson believed that a person could worship God without the help of a church, minister, or Bible. She conducted discussions in her home that challenged church authority. Hutchinson was brought to trial and forced to leave Massachusetts. In 1638, she fled to Rhode Island.

Anne Hutchinson preaches in her home in Boston.

Another religious group was the Quakers. Their name came from an early leader's statement that they should "tremble [quake] at the word of the Lord." Opponents coined the name as an insult. Quakers challenged the Massachusetts commonwealth. They believed that each person could know God directly through "an inner light." Neither ministers nor the Bible was needed. Quakers also believed in treating Native Americans fairly, which set them apart from other colonists. For such beliefs, Quakers were whipped, imprisoned, and hanged. Many left for Rhode Island.

*Reading*Hi
D. Forming
Opinions W
it odd that t
Puritans per
cuted certai
individuals a
groups for t
religious be

King Philip's War

The growing population of colonists began to force the Native Americans from their land. Europeans and Native Americans defined land ownership differently. To Europeans, land could be owned by individuals. To Native Americans, land belonged to everyone. Conflict over land resulted in warfare.

In 1675–1676, the Puritan colonies fought a brutal war with the Native Americans. This was known as **King Philip's War**. "King Philip" was the English name of Metacom, leader of the Wampanoag. To help fight the war, Metacom organized an alliance of tribes. The Wampanoag lost the war. Many were killed, while others were sold into slavery in the West Indies. Those who remained lost their land and were forced to become laborers. English settlers expanded even farther into Native American land.

Backgroun
Metacom w
the son of
Massasoit, f
of the Pilgr

CAUSE & EFFECT: King Philip's War, 1675–1676

Reasons for Conflict
- **Land ownership**
- **Religion**
- **Increased population of Europeans**

KING PHILIP'S WAR

Native American Losses
- **Approximately 3,000 killed**
- **King Philip (Metacom) killed**
- **About 500 Native Americans enslaved**

European Losses
- **About 600 settlers killed**
- **More than 45 villages attacked**
- **About 12 villages destroyed**

Sources: *Encyclopedia Britannica, World Book Encyclopedia*

SKILLBUILDER Interpreting Charts
1. *Was there a greater loss of life among the settlers or the Native Americans?*
2. *How might the growing population of Europeans have created more conflict with the Native Americans?*

The Salem Witchcraft Trials

Puritan New England was originally a society centered on the church. By the late 1600s, however, this had begun to change. Societal changes in Puritan New England had led to an atmosphere of fear and suspicion. Then, several Salem village girls were told frightening stories about witches by Tituba, a slave from the West Indies. Pretending to be bewitched, the girls falsely accused others of witchcraft. The witch-hunts began in 1692. The clergy viewed the Salem witch-hunts and trials as a sign from God for the village to return to a strict Puritan lifestyle.

This mid-nineteenth-century oil painting, *The Trial of George Jacobs, August 5, 1692,* was painted by T. H. Matteson in 1855. It captures the horrors of the Salem witch trials. As the young women cry out, the accused tries to defend himself against charges that he bewitched them.

Jacobs's own granddaughter testified against him. He was tried and convicted on August 5, 1692, and executed two weeks later along with four neighbors.

How accurately do you think the painting shows the strong emotions in the courtroom?

Hysteria spread through Salem. Those accused were forced to name others as witches. More than 100 people were arrested and tried. Of those, 20 were found guilty and put to death. Nineteen persons were hanged, and another was pressed to death by heavy stones when he refused to enter a plea in response to the charge of witchcraft. The panic was short-lived, and Salem came to its senses. The experience showed, however, how a society can create scapegoats for its problems.

In the next section, you will read about the Middle and Southern colonies, how they were founded, and how they provided the new settlers with economic opportunities.

ulary
oat: one
made to
e blame
ers

:ion ② Assessment

Terms & Names

plain the significance of:
- lgrims
- ayflower Compact
- uritans
- reat Migration
- ndamental Orders
  Connecticut
- oger Williams
- ne Hutchinson
- ng Philip's War

2. Using Graphics

Use a cluster diagram to review details about the New England Way.

New England Way

Which parts would you find easy to accept? Which difficult?

3. Main Ideas

a. What is the Mayflower Compact?

b. What is the meaning of the term the "Great Migration"?

c. What were some of the causes of King Philip's War?

4. Critical Thinking

Recognizing Effects What impact did the arrival of the English in New England have on the Native Americans?

THINK ABOUT
- Squanto
- Chief Massasoit
- King Philip's War

IVITY OPTIONS

NGUAGE ARTS

SPEECH

Choose one of the Puritan dissenters from this section and retell his or her story. Either write a **newspaper article** about the person or give an **oral history**.

The Mayflower Compact

Setting the Stage In 1620, 41 of the colonists aboard the *Mayflower* dr[e]
up the Mayflower Compact. This document refers to the area where they
landed as "Virginia" because the land grants of the Virginia Company
extended into New England. The colonists provided for self-government
under majority rule of the male voters. **See Primary Source Explorer**

A CLOSER LOOK

REASONS FOR VOYAGE

The three reasons the colonists
give for their voyage to the
eastern seaboard of North
America are the glory of God,
the advancement of Christianity,
and the honor of the king.

**1. Why might sailing to new
lands advance Christianity?**

A CLOSER LOOK

GUIDING PURPOSE

The general good of the colony
is the guiding purpose of the
colonists in signing the compact.

**2. What does this suggest about
the relationship between the
individual and the community?**

We, whose names are underwritten, . . . having undertaken for the glo[ry]
God, and advancement of the Christian faith, and the honor of our Kin[g]
country, a voyage to plant the first colony in the northern parts of Virg[inia]
do by these presents, solemnly and mutually in the presence of God an[d]
another **covenant**[1] and combine ourselves together into a civil **body po[litic]**
for our better ordering and preservation; and furtherance of the ends a[fore]
said . . . do enact, constitute, and frame such just and equal laws, ordina[nces]
acts, constitutions, and offices from time to time as shall be thought
[proper] and convenient for the general good of the colony unto whic[h]
promise all due submission and obedience. In witness whereof we have
unto subscribed our names at Cape Cod the eleventh of November, i[n]
year of our **sovereign**[3] lord King James of England . . . Anno Domini [1620.]

From B. P. Poore, ed., *The Federal and State Constitutions*, Part I, p. 931.

1. **covenant:** promise in a
   binding agreement.

2. **body politic:** the
   people of a politically
   organized group.

3. **sovereign:** suprem[e]

The Fundamental Orders of Connecticut

Setting the Stage In January 1639, male citizens of three townships
in Connecticut (Hartford, Windsor, and Wethersfield) assembled and dr[ew]
up the Fundamental Orders of Connecticut. This document is often call[ed]
the first written constitution in America. It contains a preamble,
or introduction, and a set of laws. **See Primary Source Explorer**

Preamble

Forasmuch as it has pleased the Almighty God by the wise disposition [of]
Divine Providence so to order and dispose of things that we, the inhab[itants]
and residents of Windsor, Hartford, and Wethersfield are now coha[bitating]

dwelling in and upon the river of Conectecotte [Connecticut] and the
 thereunto adjoining; and well knowing where a people are gathered
ther the Word of God requires that, to maintain the peace and union of
 a people, there should be an orderly and decent government established
ding to God, to order and dispose of the affairs of the people at all sea-
 as occasion shall require; do therefore associate and **conjoin**[1] ourselves
 as one public state or commonwealth. . . . As also in our civil affairs to
ded and governed according to such laws, rules, orders, and decrees as
 be made, ordered and decreed, as follows:

s, Rules, and Orders

s ordered, sentenced, and decreed that there shall be yearly two general
blies or courts. . . . The first shall be called the Court of Election,
in shall be yearly chosen . . . so many magistrates and other public offi-
s shall be found **requisite**.[2] . . .

s ordered . . . that no person be chosen governor above once in two years,
hat the governor be always a member of some approved congregation. . . .

s ordered . . . that to the aforesaid Court of Election the several towns
send their deputies. . . . Also, the other General Court in September
be for making of laws, and any other public occasion which concerns
od of the Commonwealth. . . .

s ordered . . . that after there are warrants given out for any of the said
al Courts, the constable or constables of each town shall forthwith give
 distinctly to the inhabitants of the same . . . that at a place and time
ey meet and assemble themselves together to elect and choose certain
es to be at the General Court then following to [manage] the affairs of
ommonwealth. . . .

oin: unite.
isite: required.

A CLOSER LOOK

GOOD GOVERNMENT

Good government is pleasing to
God in the eyes of the colonists.
An orderly and decent government helps to maintain peace
and order within a community
and between people.

**3. How would you define good
government today?**

A CLOSER LOOK

THE GOVERNOR'S ROLE

The person serving as governor
can serve only once every two
years and must be a member of
an approved congregation.

**4. Why might the colonists have
wished to limit the power of
the chief executive?**

A CLOSER LOOK

THE COURTS

The Court of Election chooses
officials to serve; the General
Court makes laws.

**5. Why might it be a good idea
to separate these two functions?**

ractive Primary Sources Assessment

ain Ideas

hose rights did the Mayflower Compact protect?

hy are written documents useful in setting up
vernment?

ow were the Fundamental Orders based on
ion?

2. Critical Thinking

Supporting Opinions
How do you think these documents reflect the English
contribution to American democracy?

THINK ABOUT
• self-government
• majority rule

3

Founding the Middle and Southern Colonies

MAIN·IDEA

The founding of the Middle and Southern colonies provided settlers with many economic opportunities.

WHY IT MATTERS NOW

America is still a place where immigrants seek freedom and economic opportunity.

TERMS & NAMES

Peter Stuyvesant
patroon
Duke of York
proprietary colony

William
Quaker
royal co
James (

ONE AMERICAN'S STORY

In 1624, the Dutch founded the colony of New Netherland (later New York) on the eastern coast of North America. **Peter Stuyvesant**, the new governor, arrived in the city of New Amsterdam in May 1647. Because of his rough manner, he lost the support of the Dutch colonists. In 1664, a British fleet ordered the city of New Amsterdam to surrender itself to British control. Unable to gain the support of the Dutch colonists, Stuyvesant surrendered. He then defended his decision to his superiors back in the Netherlands.

A VOICE FROM THE PAST

Powder and provisions failing, and no relief or reinforcements being expected, we were necessitated [forced] to come to terms with the enemy, not through neglect of duty or cowardice . . . but in consequence of an absolute impossibility to defend the fort.

Peter Stuyvesant, quoted in *Peter Stuyvesant and His New York*

In this section, you will read about the founding of the Middle Colonies (such as New York) and the Southern Colonies.

Peter Stuy
governor
Dutch colc
Netherlan
leg in 164
military ac
against th
St. Martin
Caribbean

Taking Notes

Use your chart to take notes about the middle and southern colonies.

Virginia
1607 →

The Middle Colonies

The Middle Colonies were New York, New Jersey, Pennsylvania, and Delaware. They were located between New England to the north and the Chesapeake region to the south. (See the map on page 102.) Swedes, Dutch, English, Germans, and Africans were among the groups who came to these colonies.

Religious freedom attracted many groups, including Protestants, Catholics, Quakers, and Jews. The Hudson and Delaware rivers supported shipping and commerce. The river valleys had rich soil and mild winters. These conditions were favorable for farming and raising livestock.

New Netherland Becomes New York

In 1624, Dutch settlers financed by the Dutch West India Company founded the colony of New Netherland. New Netherland included the Hudson River valley, Long Island, and the land along the Delaware River.

To attract more settlers, the Dutch West India Company employed the patroon system. A **patroon** was a person who brought 50 settlers to New Netherland. As a reward, a patroon received a large land grant. He also received special privileges in hunting, fishing, and fur trading on his land.

In the early years, many different kinds of people settled in New Netherland. Twenty-three Jewish settlers arrived in 1654, and others soon followed. Later, Africans were brought to the colony as slaves and indentured servants. Many Puritans also came.

Peter Stuyvesant, the colony's governor, wanted to add land to New Netherland. He attacked the nearby charter colony of New Sweden in 1655. This colony was located along the Delaware River. The main settlement was Fort Christina (later named Wilmington, Delaware). It had been settled by Swedes in 1638. After an attack by the Dutch, the Swedes surrendered Fort Christina.

England's King Charles II decided that his brother, the **Duke of York,** should drive the Dutch out of New Netherland. The Dutch colony was a threat to England because of its trade. It was also a threat because of its expanding settlements and its location. There were English colonies in New England to the north and Virginia to the south. As you have seen, when the duke's ships appeared off New Amsterdam in August 1664, the colony surrendered. New Netherland became the **proprietary colony** of New York. The Duke of York was now the proprietor, or owner, of the colony.

New Jersey, Pennsylvania, and Delaware

The Duke of York had become the largest single landowner in America. He gave part of his claim, the province of New Jersey, to his friends Sir George Carteret and Lord John Berkeley in 1664. They encouraged settlers to come by promising freedom of religion. They also promised large grants of land and a representative assembly.

William Penn became another large landowner in America. Born into a wealthy English family, Penn joined the **Quakers,** to his father's disapproval. The young Penn was attacked for his Quaker beliefs. King Charles II owed the Penn family money. In repayment, in 1681 he gave Penn a large piece of land in America that came to be called Pennsylvania. The name means "Penn's woods."

round
ke of York
e King
in 1685.

History
ing
s Why
he prom-
ligious
encour-
verse
ion in a

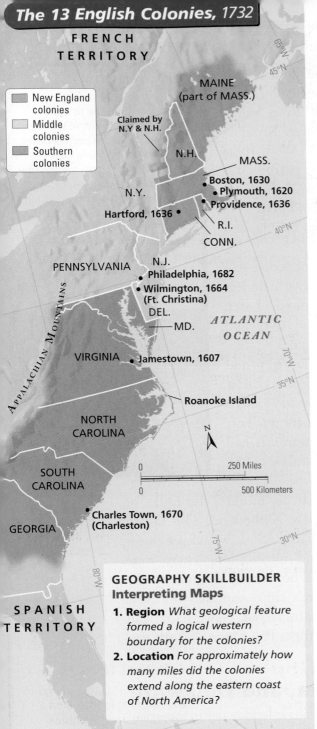

The 13 English Colonies, 1732

FRENCH TERRITORY

New England colonies
Middle colonies
Southern colonies

MAINE (part of MASS.)

Claimed by N.Y & N.H.

N.H.

MASS.
Boston, 1630
Plymouth, 1620
Providence, 1636

N.Y.
Hartford, 1636

R.I.
CONN.

PENNSYLVANIA
N.J.
Philadelphia, 1682
Wilmington, 1664 (Ft. Christina)
DEL.
MD.

ATLANTIC OCEAN

VIRGINIA
Jamestown, 1607

Roanoke Island

NORTH CAROLINA

SOUTH CAROLINA

GEORGIA

Charles Town, 1670 (Charleston)

APPALACHIAN MOUNTAINS

N

0   250 Miles

0   500 Kilometers

SPANISH TERRITORY

GEOGRAPHY SKILLBUILDER
Interpreting Maps

1. **Region** What geological feature formed a logical western boundary for the colonies?
2. **Location** For approximately how many miles did the colonies extend along the eastern coast of North America?

Penn used this land to create a colony where Quakers could live according to their beliefs. Among other things, the Quakers believed that all people should live in peace and harmony. They welcomed different religions and ethnic groups. In Pennsylvania, Penn extended religious freedom and equality to all. He especially wanted the Native Americans to be treated fairly. In a letter to them in 1681, Penn said, "May [we] always live together as neighbors and friends."

Penn's policies helped make Pennsylvania one of the wealthiest of the American colonies. Many settlers came to Pennsylvania seeking religious freedom and a better life. In 1704, Penn granted the three lower counties of Delaware their own assembly. The counties later broke away to form the colony of Delaware.

*Reading*Hi
B. Comparin
Contrasting
did Penn's p
toward Nati
Americans c
pare with th
of other col
you have re
about?

The Southern Colonies

The new Southern Colonies were Maryland, the Carolinas, and Georgia. The Appalachian Mountains bordered parts of these colonies in the west. In the east, the colonies bordered the Atlantic Ocean. The soil and climate of this region were suitable for warm-weather crops such as tobacco, rice, and indigo.

Maryland and the Carolinas

Lord Baltimore established Maryland in 1632 for Roman Catholics fleeing persecution in England. To attract other settlers besides Catholics, Lord Baltimore promised religious freedom. In 1649, Maryland passed the Toleration Act.

Maryland based its economy on tobacco, which required backbreaking work. Every three or four years, the tobacco crop used up the soil, and workers had to clear new land. Most laborers came as either servants or slaves. Maryland attracted few women as settlers.

In 1663, Carolina was founded as a colony. English settlers from Barbados built Charles Town, later called Charleston, in 1670. They

bulary
na: The
of the
y is based
atin form
harles," in
of King
es II.

busied themselves cutting timber, raising cattle, and trading with the Native Americans. After 1685, Charleston became a refuge for Huguenots, French Protestants seeking religious freedom.

Carolina's colonists needed laborers to grow rice and indigo. The English settlers encouraged the use of enslaved Africans. They also sold local Native Americans into slavery. As a result, wars broke out between the settlers and the Tuscarora and Yamasee tribes. The settlers' taking of tribal lands also fueled the wars.

Carolina's proprietors, or owners, refused to send help to stop a threatened Spanish attack on Charleston. Because of this, the colonists overthrew the colony's proprietary rule in 1719. In 1729, Carolina became a **royal colony**. Then it was ruled by governors appointed by the king. The colony was divided into North Carolina and South Carolina.

Georgia

In 1732, **James Oglethorpe** founded Georgia as a refuge for debtors. The English government wanted to use the colony as a military outpost against Spanish Florida to the south and French Louisiana to the west. In 1739, during a war between England and Spain, the Spanish tried to force the English colonists out of Georgia but were unsuccessful. English, German, Swiss, and Scottish colonists settled in Georgia. All religions were welcome. As the colony's leader, Oglethorpe set strict rules that upset the colonists. The king, in response to unrest, made Georgia a royal colony in 1752.

By the early 1700s, there were 13 English colonies along the eastern coast of North America. In the next chapter, you will read about how these colonies developed.

James Oglethorpe was the founder of Georgia.

ing **History**
ding a Map
e map on
02 to check
ation of
a in relation
Spanish ter-
of Florida.

---

erms & Names

plain the
gnificance of:

eter Stuyvesant

atroon

uke of York

oprietary colony

illiam Penn

uaker

yal colony

mes Oglethorpe

2. Using Graphics

Identify an effect for each cause listed in the chart below.

Cause	Effect
New Netherland threat to English	
English attacked Quakers	
Laborers needed in Carolinas	
Oglethorpe too strict in Georgia	

3. Main Ideas

a. What were the goals of the patroon system?

b. What three Middle Colonies offered religious freedom?

c. What were three crops grown in the Southern Colonies?

4. Critical Thinking

Analyzing Causes Why did colonists in Maryland and the Carolinas enslave Native Americans and use African slaves?

THINK ABOUT
• the crops being grown
• the nature of farm work

VITY OPTIONS

IGUAGE ARTS

SCIENCE

What are the health effects of tobacco? Write a **news article** or give a **television report** for a science show about the effects of tobacco on the body.

TERMS & NAMES

Briefly explain the significance of each of the following.

1. joint-stock company
2. Jamestown
3. John Smith
4. House of Burgesses
5. Pilgrims
6. Mayflower Compact
7. Great Migration
8. Fundamental Orders of Connecticut
9. proprietary colony
10. William Penn

REVIEW QUESTIONS

Early Colonies Have Mixed Success (pages 85–91)

1. What were the reasons given by Richard Hakluyt that England should start a colony?
2. Why were Jamestown and Plymouth financed by joint-stock companies?
3. How did John Rolfe change the Virginia colony?

New England Colonies (pages 92–99)

4. What was John Winthrop's vision for Massachusetts Bay?
5. What was the system of government in the Massachusetts Bay Colony?
6. What were some of the effects of King Philip's War?

Founding the Middle and Southern Colonies (pages 100–103)

7. Why did Charles II want New Netherland?
8. What were relations like between Native Americans and settlers in Pennsylvania?
9. What was the Toleration Act of 1649?
10. What ethnic and racial groups settled in the Middle Colonies and why did they do so?

CRITICAL THINKING

1. USING YOUR NOTES: SEQUENCING EVENTS

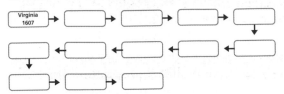

Using your completed chart, answer these question

a. Which was the earliest successful settlement in Virginia?
b. Which colony was founded last?

2. ANALYZING LEADERSHIP

Why do you think William Penn was a more succes leader than Peter Stuyvesant?

3. APPLYING CITIZENSHIP SKILLS

What were some of the common ideals that link t Mayflower Compact, the establishment of the Hou of Burgesses, and town meetings?

4. THEME: IMPACT OF THE INDIVIDUAL

How did individual effort help ensure the success of England's colonies in America?

5. ANALYZING CAUSES

What were the political, economic, and social caus for the founding of the different British colonies North America?

Interact *with* History

How do the dangers you discussed before you read this chapter compare with the dangers peop actually faced?

VISUAL SUMMARY

The 13 Colonies

		Important Early Dates	Founder(s)
England Colonies	Massachusetts	Plymouth, 1620; Mass. Bay, 1630	Pilgrims; Puritans
	New Hampshire	Portsmouth, 1623	Proprietors
	Rhode Island	Providence, 1636	Roger Williams
	Connecticut	Hartford, 1636	Thomas Hooker
Middle Colonies	New York (New Netherland)	Dutch settlers arrive, 1624	Dutch West India Company
	Delaware	Fort Christina, 1638	Swedes
	New Jersey	Duke of York establishes, 1664	George Carteret, John Berkel
	Pennsylvania	Charles II bestows land, 1681	William Penn
Southern Colonies	Virginia	Jamestown, 1607	Virginia Company of London
	Maryland	Founded as religious haven, 1632	Lord Baltimore
	North Carolina	Founded, 1663	Proprietors
	South Carolina	Founded, 1663	Proprietors
	Georgia	Founded as debtors' refuge, 1732	James Oglethorpe

e the graph and your knowledge of U.S. history
answer questions 1 and 2.

ditional Test Practice, pp. S1–S33.

Population of the Colonies

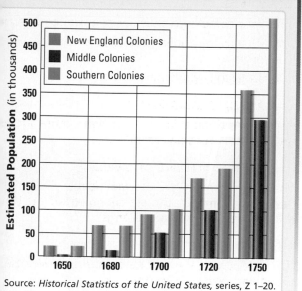

Source: *Historical Statistics of the United States*, series, Z 1–20.

About how much did the population of the
Southern colonies increase between 1720 and
1750?

A. 100,000

B. 200,000

C. 300,000

D. 500,000

2. Between what time periods was the increase in the
population of the New England colonies greatest?

A. between 1650 and 1680

B. between 1680 and 1700

C. between 1700 and 1720

D. between 1720 and 1750

**This quotation is from Peter Stuyvesant, Dutch
governor of New Amsterdam, about his encounter
with British forces. Use the quotation and your
knowledge of U.S. history to answer question 3.**

PRIMARY SOURCE

Powder and provisions failing, and no relief or reinforcements being expected, we were necessitated
[forced] to come to terms with the enemy, not
through neglect of duty or cowardice . . . but in consequence of an absolute impossibility to defend the fort.

Peter Stuyvesant, *Peter Stuyvesant and His New York*

3. The passage best supports which conclusion?

A. Stuyvesant surrendered to the British.

B. The citizens of New Amsterdam did not want to
use their supplies.

C. Stuyvesant feared the British forces.

D. The people of New Amsterdam refused to
surrender to the British.

TEST PRACTICE
CLASSZONE.COM

ERNATIVE ASSESSMENT

WRITING ABOUT HISTORY

vould an attorney have defended an accused
n during the Salem witchcraft trials? Write a
nent to the court defending the woman.

can do research for your statement in books
ut the Salem witchcraft trials.

er sources of information include historical soci-
s, archives, and museums.

r statement should persuade a jury of the time.

PERATIVE LEARNING

few of your classmates, write and perform a
oout the "lost colonists" of Roanoke. Depict
ts dealing with food shortages, illness, and rela-
with Native Americans.

INTEGRATED TECHNOLOGY

DOING INTERNET RESEARCH

The Mayflower Compact was devised in response to
the need for some sort of government. Use it as a
model for planning a government for your class.

- Use the Internet or other library resources to learn
  more about the Mayflower Compact.

- Adapt ideas from the Mayflower Compact that
  might work for your class.

- Make decisions about what rules are needed, who
  will hold office, how they will be selected and how
  long they will serve, and whether or not there
  should be limits on majority rule.

For more about the Mayflower Compact . . .

INTERNET ACTIVITY
CLASSZONE.COM

In 1702, a vast countryside surrounded Philadelphia. Most colonists earned their living in the country. Fewer than one in ten lived in cities.

Some Native Americans lived close to the American cities.

c. 1700
Colonial population reaches 257,000.

1712
Slave uprising occurs in New York City.

1718
French fou Orleans at Mississippi

Spanish pri in Texas.

USA World 1700

1701
War of the Spanish Succession begins in Europe.

1707
Act of Union unites England with Scotland and creates Great Britain.

Philadelphia was a major center of commerce.

It is the early 1700s when you arrive in one of America's larger port cities. After nearly a month of ocean travel, you are thrilled to see land. As you leave the ship, you wonder where you will live and how you will earn a living.

Would you settle on a farm or in a town?

What Do You Think?

- Will you choose to live where other people from your homeland live? Or will you try somewhere new?

- How did you make a living in your old country? Will this influence your choice?

RESEARCH LINKS
CLASSZONE.COM

Visit the Chapter 4 links for more information about the development of the colonies.

1733
ranklin
s *Poor*
manac.

1739
Enslaved Africans revolt in Stono Rebellion.

1742
First European settlement west of Allegheny Mountains is established.

c. 1750 Population of the English colonies passes the one million mark.

1753

becomes eat Britain.

1739
Nadir Shah of Persia conquers Delhi, India.

1752
China suppresses Tibetan rebellion and forces Dalai Lama to accept its authority.

Reading Strategy: Analyzing Causes and Eff●

What Do You Know?

What ideas and pictures come to mind when you hear people talk about "the South" or "the North"? Why do you think these distinct regions developed?

Think About
- what you have learned about these regions from books or movies
- the way geography affects people's choices
- your responses to the Interact with History about settling on a farm or in a town (see page 107)

What Do You Want to Know?

What questions do you have about how the four colonial regions developed? Record these questions in your notebook before you read the chapter.

NEW ENGLAND COLONIES

MIDDLE COLONIES

Backcountry

SOUTHERN COLONIES

Analyzing Causes and Effects

As you read about history, it is important to understand not only what happened in the past, but also the reasons why it happened. Clue words that indicate cause—such as *because* and *since*—can help you look for causes of historical events. Use the chart belo● to list causes that contributed to the different economic developments in each of the colonial regions.

S See Skillbuilder Handbook, page R11.

Taking Notes

		NEW ENGLAND COLONIES	MIDDLE COLONIES	SOUTHERN COLONIES	BACKCOUNTRY
CAUSES	Climate				
	Resources				
	People				
EFFECT	Economic Development				

1

New England: Commerce and Religion

MAIN IDEA	WHY IT MATTERS NOW	TERMS & NAMES
and trade contributed to the and prosperity of the New Colonies.	Coastal cities in New England continue to engage in trade.	Backcountry subsistence farming	triangular trade Navigation Acts smuggling

ONE AMERICAN'S STORY

Peleg Folger, a New England sailor, kept a journal that describes what whaling was like in the 1750s. In one entry, he explained what happened after whales were sighted and small boats were launched to pursue them.

A VOICE FROM THE PAST

So we row'd about a mile and a Half from the [ship], and then a whale come up under us, & [smashed in] our boat . . . and threw us every man overboard [except] one. And we all came up and Got Hold of the Boat & Held to her until the other boat (which was a mile and half off) came up and took us in, all Safe, and not one man Hurt.

Peleg Folger, quoted in *The Sea-Hunters*

Whales hunted by New Englanders, such as Peleg Folger, might weigh as much as 50 tons and be over 60 feet in length.

When Folger and his mates killed a whale, they cut a hole in its head, and removed large amounts of oil from the animal. When the ship returned to port, this oil was sold to colonists, who used it as fuel in their lamps.

Many settlers in the New England Colonies—Massachusetts, New Hampshire, Connecticut, and Rhode Island—made a living from the sea. The majority of New Englanders, however, were farmers.

Distinct Colonial Regions Develop

Between 1700 and 1750, the population of England's colonies in North America doubled and then doubled again. At the start of the century, the colonial population stood at about 257,000. By 1750, more than 1,170,000 settlers called the English colonies home.

By the 1700s, the colonies formed three distinct regions: the New England Colonies, the Middle Colonies, and the Southern Colonies. Another area was the **Backcountry**. It ran along the Appalachian Mountains through the far western part of the other regions.

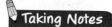

Taking Notes

Use your chart to take notes about the New England colonies.

		NEW ENGLAND COLONIES	MIDD
CAUSES	Climate		
	Resources		
	People		
EFFECT	Economic Development		

Several factors made each colonial region distinct. Some of the most important were each region's climate, resources, and people.

1. New England had long winters and rocky soil. English settlers made up the largest group in the region's population.
2. The Middle Colonies had shorter winters and fertile soil. The region attracted immigrants from all over Europe.
3. The Southern Colonies had a warm climate and good soil. There, some settlers used enslaved Africans to work their plantations.
4. The Backcountry's climate and resources varied, depending on the latitude. Many Scots-Irish immigrants settled there.

During the colonial era, the majority of people made their living by farming. However, the type of agriculture they practiced depended on the climate and resources in the region where they settled.

Vocabulary
latitude: the tance north south of the equator, me ured in degr

The Farms and Towns of New England

Life in New England was not easy. The growing season was short, and the soil was rocky. Most farmers practiced **subsistence farming**. That is, they produced just enough food for themselves and sometimes a little extra to trade in town.

Most New England farmers lived near a town. This was because colonial officials usually did not sell scattered plots of land to individual

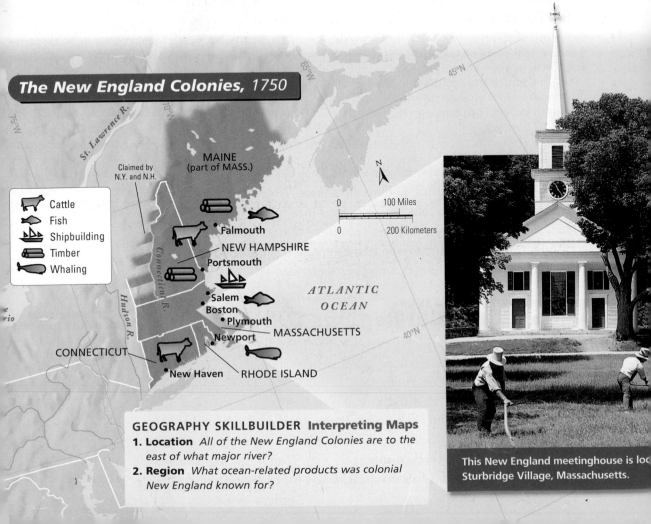

The New England Colonies, 1750

MAINE (part of MASS.)

Claimed by N.Y. and N.H.

Cattle
Fish
Shipbuilding
Timber
Whaling

Falmouth
NEW HAMPSHIRE
Portsmouth
Salem
Boston
Plymouth
Newport
MASSACHUSETTS
CONNECTICUT
New Haven
RHODE ISLAND

St. Lawrence R.
Connecticut R.
Hudson R.

ATLANTIC OCEAN

0   100 Miles
0   200 Kilometers

GEOGRAPHY SKILLBUILDER Interpreting Maps
1. **Location** All of the New England Colonies are to the east of what major river?
2. **Region** What ocean-related products was colonial New England known for?

This New England meetinghouse is loc
Sturbridge Village, Massachusetts.

farmers. Instead, they sold larger plots of land to groups of people—often to the congregation of a Puritan church. A congregation then settled the town and divided the land among the members of its church.

This pattern of settlement led New England towns to develop in a unique way. Usually, a cluster of farmhouses surrounded a green—a central square where a meetinghouse was located and where public activities took place. Because people lived together in small towns, shopkeepers had enough customers to make a living. Also, if the townspeople needed a blacksmith or a carpenter, they could pool their money and hire one.

Harvesting the Sea

New England's rocky soil made farming difficult. In contrast, the Atlantic Ocean offered many economic opportunities. In one story, a group of settlers was standing on a hill overlooking the Atlantic. One of them pointed out to sea and exclaimed, "There is a great pasture where our children's grandchildren will go for bread!"

The settler's prediction came true. Not far off New England's coast were some of the world's best fishing grounds. The Atlantic was filled with mackerel, halibut, cod, and many other types of fish.

New England's forests provided everything needed to harvest these great "pastures" of fish. The wood cut from iron-hard oak trees made excellent ship hulls. Hundred-foot-tall white pines were ideal for masts. Shipbuilders used about 2,500 trees to produce just one ship!

New England's fish and timber were among its most valuable articles of trade. Coastal cities like Boston, Salem, New Haven, and Newport grew rich as a result of shipbuilding, fishing, and trade.

Atlantic Trade

New England settlers engaged in three types of trade. First was the trade with other colonies. Second was the direct exchange of goods with Europe. The third type was the triangular trade.

Triangular trade was the name given to a trading route with three stops. For example, a ship might leave New England with a cargo of rum

ding**History**

cognizing
ts How did
ay land was
n New
nd affect
ay people

ground
2, over
people
Boston.

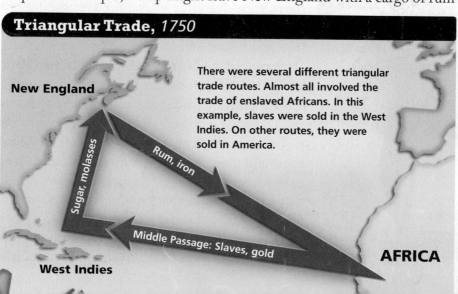

Triangular Trade, 1750

New England

There were several different triangular trade routes. Almost all involved the trade of enslaved Africans. In this example, slaves were sold in the West Indies. On other routes, they were sold in America.

Sugar, molasses

Rum, iron

Middle Passage: Slaves, gold

AFRICA

West Indies

and iron. In Africa, the captain would trade his cargo for slaves. Slaves then endured the horrible Middle Passage to the West Indies, where they were exchanged for sugar and molasses. Traders then took the sugar and molasses back to New England. There, colonists used the molasses to make rum, and the pattern started over.

Background
See Olaudah Equiano's de tions of the Middle Passa on page 78.

New England won enormous profits from trade. England wanted to make sure that it received part of those profits. So the English government began to pass the **Navigation Acts** in 1651. The Navigation Acts had four major provisions designed to ensure that England made money from its colonies' trade.

1. All shipping had to be done in English ships or ships made in the English colonies.
2. Products such as tobacco, wood, and sugar could be sold only to England or its colonies.
3. European imports to the colonies had to pass through English ports.
4. English officials were to tax any colonial goods not shipped to England.

But even after the passage of the Navigation Acts, England had trouble controlling colonial shipping. Merchants ignored the acts whenever possible. **Smuggling**—importing or exporting goods illegally—was common. England also had great difficulty preventing pirates—like the legendary Blackbeard—from interfering with colonial shipping.

STRANGE *but* True

BLACKBEARD THE PIRATE

Of all the pirates who attacked colonial ships, Blackbeard (shown below) was the most famous. He was a fearsome man known to stick matches in his hair to light up his face during battle.

Blackbeard's pirate career finally came to an end in 1718, when Virginia's governor sent an expedition against him. Nearly half the expedition's men died in the key battle. Blackbeard himself did not fall until he had suffered nearly 25 wounds. Before sailing back to port, sailors cut off his head and put it on the front of their ship.

African Americans in New England

There were few slaves in New England. Slavery simply was not economical in this region of small farms. Also, because the growing season was short, there was little work for slaves during the long winter months. Farmers could not afford to feed and house slaves who were not working.

Reading H
B. Analyzin Causes Why there relati few enslave workers in England?

Even so, some New Englanders in larger towns and cities did own slaves. They worked as house servants, cooks, gardeners, and stable-hands. In the 1700s, slave owners seldom had enough room to house more than one or two slaves. Instead, more and more slave owners hired out their slaves to work on the docks or in shops or warehouses. Slave owners sometimes allowed their slaves to keep a portion of their wages.

Occasionally, some enslaved persons were able to save enough to buy their freedom. In fact, New

England was home to more free blacks than any other region. A free black man might become a merchant, sailor, printer, carpenter, or landowner. Still, white colonists did not treat free blacks as equals.

Changes in Puritan Society

The early 1700s saw many changes in New England society. One of the most important was the gradual decline of the Puritan religion. There were a number of reasons for this decline.

*ding*History

aking
ences Why
t an interest
aterial things
pete with the
an religion?

One reason was that the drive for economic success competed with Puritan ideas. Many colonists, especially those who lived along the coast, seemed to care as much about business and material things as they did about religion. One observer had this complaint.

"[Boston] is so conveniently Situated for Trade."

An observer in 1713

A VOICE FROM THE PAST

[Boston] is so conveniently Situated for Trade and the Genius of the people are so inclined to merchandise, that they seek no other Education for their children than writing and Arithmetick.

An observer in 1713, quoted in *A History of American Life*

Another reason for the decline of the Puritan religion was the increasing competition from other religious groups. Baptists and Anglicans established churches in Massachusetts and Connecticut, where Puritans had once been the most powerful group.

Political changes also weakened the Puritan community. In 1691, a new royal charter for Massachusetts guaranteed religious freedom for all Protestants, not just Puritans. The new charter also granted the vote based on property ownership instead of church membership. This change put an end to the Puritan churches' ability to control elections.

To the south of New England were the Middle Colonies, which developed in quite different ways—as the next section shows.

---

tion **1** Assessment

Terms & Names

plain the
ignificance of:
ackcountry
ubsistence farming
riangular trade
lavigation Acts
muggling

2. Using Graphics

Use a chart like the one shown to record how New Englanders prospered from the Atlantic Ocean.

Economic Activity	Benefits to Colonists

How did some profit illegally from the ocean?

3. Main Ideas

a. How did most people in New England earn a living?

b. Why did England pass the Navigation Acts?

c. What factors led to the decline of the Puritan religion in New England?

4. Critical Thinking

Making Inferences What advantages might there be in living near other people in small towns, such as those in New England?

THINK ABOUT

- the transportation options available to colonists
- why shopkeepers chose to open businesses in towns

IVITY OPTIONS

ART

ECHNOLOGY

Read more about whaling. Make a **mobile** that shows different kinds of whales or plan a **multimedia presentation** on whaling today.

The Middle Colonies: Farms and Cities

MAIN IDEA	WHY IT MATTERS NOW	TERMS & NAMES
The people who settled in the Middle Colonies made a society of great diversity.	States in this region still boast some of the most diverse communities in the world.	cash crop artisan gristmill Conestoga diversity

ONE AMERICAN'S STORY

Elizabeth Ashbridge was only 19 years old when she arrived in America from England in the 1730s. Although she was an indentured servant, she hoped to earn her freedom and find a way to express her strong religious feelings.

After several years, Elizabeth did gain freedom. In Pennsylvania, she joined a religious group called the Society of Friends, or Quakers. The new Quaker longed to share her beliefs openly.

> ### A VOICE FROM THE PAST
>
> I was permitted to see that all I had gone through was to prepare me for this day; and that the time was near, when it would be required of me, to go and declare to others what the God of mercy had done for my soul.
>
> **Elizabeth Ashbridge,** *Some Account . . . of the Life of Elizabeth Ashbridge*

The Quakers believed that people of different beliefs could live together in harmony. They helped to create a climate of tolerance and acceptance in the Middle Colonies of New York, New Jersey, Pennsylvania, and Delaware, as you will read in this section.

A woman sp[...]
at a Quaker [...]
The Society [...]
allowed wo[...]
more active [...]
other religio[...]

A Wealth of Resources

The Middle Colonies had much to offer in addition to a climate of tolerance. A Frenchman named Michel Guillaume Jean de Crèvecoeur (krehv•KUR) praised the region's "fair cities, substantial villages, extensive fields . . . decent houses, good roads, orchards, meadows, and bridges, where an hundred years ago all was wild, woody, and uncultivated."

The prosperity that Crèvecoeur described was typical of the Middle Colonies. Immigrants from all over Europe came to take advantage of this region's productive land. Their settlements soon crowded out Native Americans, who had lived in the region for thousands of years.

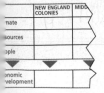

aking Notes

se your chart to
ke notes about
e middle colonies.

	NEW ENGLAND COLONIES	MIDD...
...nate		
...sources		
...ople		
...onomic ...velopment		

Among the immigrants who came to the Middle Colonies were Dutch and German farmers. They brought the advanced agricultural methods of their countries with them. Their skills, knowledge, and hard work would soon result in an abundance of foods.

The Middle Colonies boasted a longer growing season than New England and a soil rich enough to grow **cash crops**. These were crops raised to be sold for money. Common cash crops included fruits, vegetables, and, above all, grain. The Middle Colonies produced so much grain that people began calling them the "breadbasket" colonies.

The Importance of Mills

After harvesting their crops of corn, wheat, rye, or other grains, farmers took them to a **gristmill**. There, millers crushed the grain between heavy stones to produce flour or meal. Human or animal power fueled some of these mills. But water wheels built along the region's plentiful rivers powered most of the mills.

The bread that colonists baked with these products was crucial to their diet. Colonists ate about a pound of grain in some form each day—nearly three times more than Americans eat today. Even though colonists ate a great deal of grain, they had plenty left over to send to the region's coastal markets for sale.

bulary
another
for grain,
e-seeded
of cereal
s like
t and rye

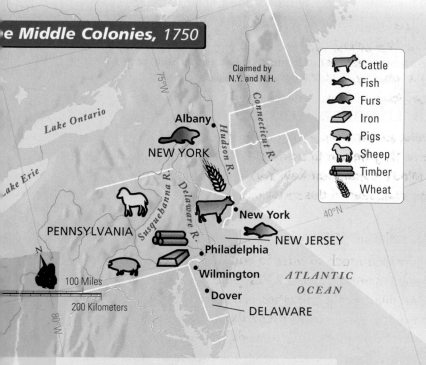

e Middle Colonies, 1750

Claimed by N.Y. and N.H.

Cattle
Fish
Furs
Iron
Pigs
Sheep
Timber
Wheat

Lake Ontario

Albany

NEW YORK

Hudson R.

Connecticut R.

Lake Erie

PENNSYLVANIA

Susquehanna R.

Delaware R.

New York

NEW JERSEY

Philadelphia

100 Miles
200 Kilometers

Wilmington

Dover

DELAWARE

ATLANTIC OCEAN

40°N

75°W

80°W

35°N

Philipsburg Manor, in Sleepy Hollow, New York, has a working 18th-century farm and a water-powered gristmill.

G.APHY SKILLBUILDER Interpreting Maps
ace/ *What are the three major rivers in the Middle Colonies?*
ovement *Why might the Middle Colonies' rivers that empty the ocean be important for farmers?*

The Cities Prosper

The excellent harbors along the coasts of the Middle Colonies were ideal sites for cities. New York City grew up at the mouth of the Hudson River, and Philadelphia was founded on the Delaware River. The merchants who lived in these growing port cities exported cash crops, especially grain, and imported manufactured goods.

Because of its enormous trade, Philadelphia was the fastest growing city in the colonies. The city owed its expansion to a thriving trade in wheat and other cash crops. By 1720, it was home to a dozen large shipyards—places where ships are built or repaired.

The city's wealth also brought many public improvements. Large and graceful buildings, such as Philadelphia's statehouse—which was later renamed Independence Hall—graced the city's streets. Streetlights showed the way along paved roads. In 1748, a Swedish visitor named Peter Kalm exclaimed that Philadelphia had grown up overnight.

Reading Hi

A. Reading a
Map Locate
York and
Philadelphia
the map on
115. Note th
rivers next to
which they v
built.

daily *life*

NAMES AND OCCUPATIONS

Many English colonists had names like Miller and Smith—names that reflected how their families had made a living in England. For example, a colonist named Miller probably had an ancestor who had operated a mill. Similarly, Smith probably had an ancestor who had been a blacksmith.

Sometimes colonists continued in the same occupations as their ancestors. But as time went on, colonists turned to other occupations, and their names no longer reflected how they earned a living. Yet names like Smith and Miller remain common in the United States, reflecting the country's past as English colonies.

A VOICE FROM THE PAST

And yet its natural advantages, trade, riches and power, are by no means inferior to any, even of the most ancient towns in Europe.

Peter Kalm, quoted in *America at 1750*

New York could also thank trade for its rapid growth. This bustling port handled flour, bread, furs, and whale oil. At midcentury, an English naval officer admired the city's elegant brick houses, paved streets, and roomy warehouses. "Such is this city," he said, "that very few in England can rival it in its show."

A Diverse Region

Many different immigrant groups arrived in the port cities of the Middle Colonies. Soon, the region's population showed a remarkable

Backgroun
In 1742, Nev
York City's p
lation was a
11,000, and
nearly 13,00
people lived
Philadelphia

A. Cooper

A. Sawyer

A. Smith

A. Potter

diversity, or variety, in its people. One of the largest immigrant groups in the region, after the English, was the Germans.

Many of the Germans arrived between 1710 and 1740. Most came as indentured servants fleeing religious intolerance. Known for their skillful farming, these immigrants soon made a mark on the Middle Colonies. "German communities," wrote one historian, "could be identified by the huge barns, the sleek cattle, and the stout workhorses."

Germans also brought a strong tradition of craftsmanship to the Middle Colonies. For example, German gunsmiths first developed the long rifle. Other German **artisans**, or craftspeople, became ironworkers and makers of glass, furniture, and kitchenware.

Germans built **Conestoga wagons** to carry their produce to town. These wagons used wide wheels suitable for dirt roads, and the wagons' curved beds prevented spilling when climbing up and down hills. The wagons' canvas covers offered protection from rain. Conestoga wagons would later be important in settling the West.

The Middle Colonies became home to many people besides the Germans. There were also the English, Dutch, Scots-Irish, African, Irish, Scottish, Welsh, Swedish, and French. Because of the diversity in the Middle Colonies, different groups had to learn to accept, or at least tolerate, one another.

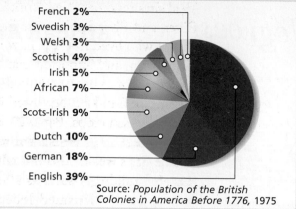

ground
e second
of the 1700s,
than one in
colonists in
sylvania
ed German
try.

ling History
mmarizing
would you
be the pop-
n of the
e Colonies?

The Middle Colonies, 1750
Population Diversity

French 2%
Swedish 3%
Welsh 3%
Scottish 4%
Irish 5%
African 7%
Scots-Irish 9%
Dutch 10%
German 18%
English 39%

Source: *Population of the British Colonies in America Before 1776*, 1975

SKILLBUILDER Interpreting Graphs
1. *What group made up nearly one-fifth of the population in the Middle Colonies?*
2. *What were the two main languages spoken in the Middle Colonies?*

A Climate of Tolerance

While the English Puritans shaped life in the New England Colonies, many different groups contributed to the culture of the Middle Colonies. Because of the greater number of different groups, it was difficult for any single group to dominate the others. Thus, the region's diversity helped to create a climate of tolerance. Some of the region's religious groups also helped to promote tolerance.

The Middle Colonies' earliest settlers, the Dutch in New York and the Quakers in Pennsylvania, both practiced religious tolerance. That is, they honored the right of religious groups to follow their own beliefs without interference. Quakers also insisted on the equality of men and women. As a result, Quaker women served as preachers, and female missionaries traveled the world spreading the Quaker message.

SERVATIONS

…aving, importing and purchasing of

Negroes;

…e Advice thereon, extracted from the
…of the Yearly-Meeting of the People called
…s, held at *London* in the Year 1748.

Anthony Benezet

…spread forth your Hands, I will hide mine …om you, yea when ye make many Prayers I …t hear; your Hands are full of Blood. Wash …e you clean, put away the Evil of your Doings …efore mine Eyes Isai. 1, 15.

…his the Fast that I have chosen, to loose the …of Wickedness, to undo the heavy Burden, to …e Oppressed go free, and that ye break every … Chap. 58, 7.

Second Edition.

GERMANTOWN:
…ted by CHRISTOPHER SOWER. 1760.

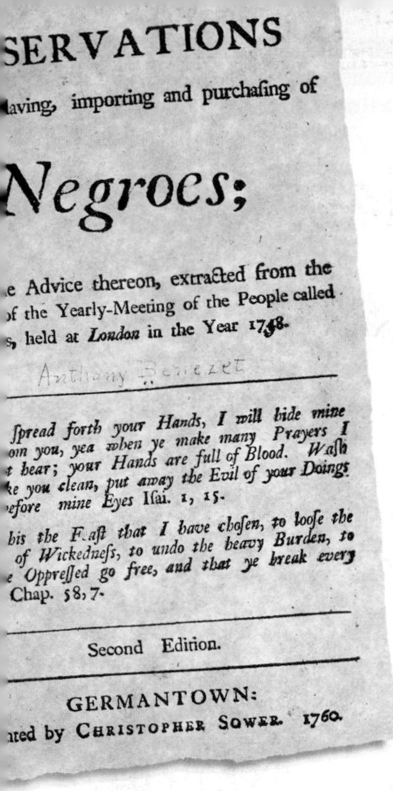

Most Quakers were opposed to slavery. Shown here is a Quaker antislavery pamphlet printed in the Middle Colonies.

Quakers were also the first to raise their voices against slavery. Quaker ideals influenced immigrants in the Middle Colonies—and eventually the whole nation.

African Americans in the Middle Colonies

The tolerant attitude of many settlers in the Middle Colonies did not prevent slavery in the region. In 1750, about 7 percent of the Middle Colonies' population was enslaved. As in New England, many people of African descent lived and worked in cities.

New York City had a larger number of people of African descent than any other city in the Northern colonies. In New York City, enslaved persons worked as manual laborers, servants, drivers, and as assistants to artisans and craftspeople. Free African-American men and women also made their way to the city, where they worked as laborers, servants, or sailors.

*Reading*His…
C. Forming Opinions W… you think th… force was ne… to keep Afric… enslaved?

Tensions existed between the races in New York City, sometimes leading to violence. In 1712, for example, about 24 rebellious slaves set fire to a building. They then killed nine whites and wounded several others who came to put out the fire. Armed colonists caught the suspects, who were punished horribly. Such punishments showed that whites would resort to force and violence to control slaves. Even so, the use of violence did little to prevent the outbreak of other slave rebellions.

Force would also be used in the South, which had far more enslaved Africans than the North. In the next section, you will learn how the South's plantation economy came to depend on the labor of enslaved Africans.

Section 2 Assessment

1. Terms & Names

Explain the significance of:

- cash crop
- gristmill
- diversity
- artisan
- Conestoga wagon

2. Using Graphics

Use a cluster diagram like the one shown to indicate where different immigrants in the Middle Colonies came from.

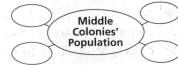

What was the third largest group in the region?

3. Main Ideas

a. What attracted settlers to the Middle Colonies?

b. What service was performed at gristmills?

c. Why might enslaved Africans be able to join in rebellion more easily in the city than the country?

4. Critical Thinking

Analyzing Causes Wha… factors allowed large coas… cities to develop in the Middle Colonies?

THINK ABOUT

- geography
- people
- trade

ACTIVITY OPTIONS

MATH
GEOGRAPHY

Read more about Philadelphia. Create a **database** of the city's population growth in the 1700s or draw a **map** that shows its physical growth.

3

The Southern Colonies: Plantations and Slavery

MAIN IDEA	WHY IT MATTERS NOW	TERMS & NAMES
•nomy of the Southern ⋅s relied heavily on ⋅bor.	The existence of slavery deeply affected the South and the nation.	indigo overseer Eliza Lucas Stono Rebellion William Byrd II

ONE AMERICAN'S STORY

George Mason was born to a wealthy Virginia family in 1725. Mason—who later described the slave trade as "disgraceful to mankind"—wrote about the contributions of enslaved persons on his family's plantation.

A VOICE FROM THE PAST

My father had among his slaves carpenters, coopers [barrel makers], sawyers, blacksmiths, tanners, curriers, shoemakers, spinners, weavers and knitters, and even a distiller.

George Mason, quoted in *Common Landscape of America*

Because the Masons and other wealthy landowners produced all that they needed on their own plantations, they appeared to be independent. But their independence usually depended on the labor of enslaved Africans. Although planters were only a small part of the Southern population, the plantation economy and slavery shaped life in the Southern Colonies: Maryland, Virginia, the Carolinas, and Georgia.

George Mason was active in local affairs in Virginia. He would later play a role in the drafting of the United States Constitution.

The Plantation Economy

The South's soil and almost year-round growing season were ideal for plantation crops like rice and tobacco. These valuable plants required much labor to produce, but with enough workers they could be grown as cash crops. Planters had no trouble transporting their crops because the region's many waterways made it easy for oceangoing ships to tie up at plantation docks.

Like George Mason's boyhood home, most plantations were largely self-sufficient. That is, nearly everything that planters, their families, and their workers needed was produced on the plantation. Because plantations were so self-sufficient, large cities like those in the North were rare

Taking Notes

Use your chart to take notes about the Southern colonies.

		NEW ENGLAND COLONIES	MIDD
CAUSES	Climate		
	Resources		
	People		
EFFECT	Economic Development		

The Southern Colonies, 1750

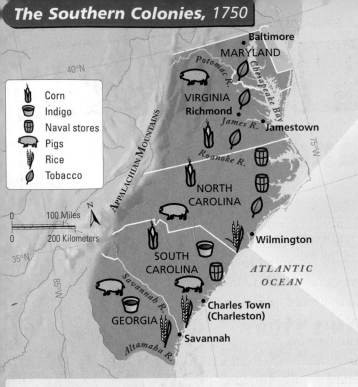

Legend:
- Corn
- Indigo
- Naval stores
- Pigs
- Rice
- Tobacco

0 — 100 Miles
0 — 200 Kilometers

40°N, 35°N, 75°W, 85°W

Baltimore, MARYLAND, Potomac R., Chesapeake Bay, VIRGINIA, Richmond, James R., Jamestown, Roanoke R., NORTH CAROLINA, Wilmington, SOUTH CAROLINA, ATLANTIC OCEAN, Savannah R., Charles Town (Charleston), GEORGIA, Savannah, Altamaha R., APPALACHIAN MOUNTAINS

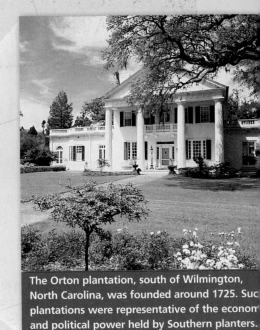

The Orton plantation, south of Wilmington, North Carolina, was founded around 1725. Such plantations were representative of the econom and political power held by Southern planters.

GEOGRAPHY SKILLBUILDER Interpreting Maps
1. **Location** *The Southern Colonies were south of what latitude?*
2. **Place** *Which Southern Colonies grew crops of both rice and indigo?*

in the Southern Colonies. The port city of Charles Town (later called Charleston) in South Carolina was an early exception.

As the plantation economy continued to grow, planters began to have difficulty finding enough laborers to work their plantations. Toward the end of the 1600s, the planters began to turn to enslaved Africans for labor.

The Turn to Slavery

For the first half of the 1600s, there were few Africans in Virginia, whether enslaved or free. In 1665, fewer than 500 Africans had been brought into the colony. At that time, African and European indentured servants worked in the fields together.

Starting in the 1660s, the labor system began to change as indentured white servants started to leave the plantations. One reason they left was the large amount of land available in the Americas. It was fairly easy for white men to save enough money to buy land and start their own farms. White servants could not be kept on the plantations permanently. As Bacon's Rebellion showed, it was also politically dangerous for planters to try to keep them there (see page 89). As a result, the landowners had to find another source of labor.

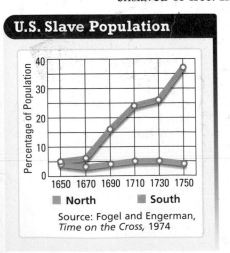

U.S. Slave Population

Percentage of Population

40, 30, 20, 10, 0

1650 1670 1690 1710 1730 1750

■ North   ■ South

Source: Fogel and Engerman, *Time on the Cross,* 1974

Backgrour
In 1742, Cha
Town's popu
tion was 6,8

Reading H
A. Reading
Graph Ask
and answe
question ab
the geopgr
pattern of
changes in
slave popu

Planters tried to force Native Americans to work for them. But European diseases caused many Native Americans to die. Those who survived usually knew the country well enough to run away.

To meet their labor needs, the planters turned to enslaved Africans. As a result, the population of people of African descent began to grow rapidly. By 1750, there were over 235,000 enslaved Africans in America. About 85 percent lived in the Southern Colonies. Enslaved Africans made up about 40 percent of the South's population.

Plantations Expand

The growth of slavery allowed plantation farming to expand in South Carolina and Georgia. Without slave labor, there probably would have been no rice plantations in the region's swampy lowlands.

Enslaved workers drained swamps, raked fields, burned stubble, and broke ground before planting. They also had to flood, drain, dry, hoe, and weed the same fields several times before the harvest.

The cultivation of rice required not only back-breaking labor but also considerable skill. Because West Africans had these skills, planters sought out slaves who came from Africa's rice-growing regions.

On higher ground, planters grew **indigo,** a plant that yields a deep blue dye. A young woman named **Eliza Lucas** had introduced indigo as a successful plantation crop after her father sent her to supervise his South Carolina plantations when she was 17.

The Planter Class

Slave labor allowed planters, such as the Byrd family of Virginia, to become even wealthier. These families formed an elite planter class. They had money or credit to buy the most slaves. And because they had more slaves, they could grow more tobacco, rice, or indigo to sell.

Small landowners with just one or two slaves simply could not compete. Many gave up their land and moved westward. As a result, the powerful planter class gained control of the rich land along the coast. The planter class was relatively small compared to the rest of the population. However, this upper class soon took control of political and economic power in the South. A foreign traveler in the South commented that the planters "think and act precisely as do the nobility in other countries."

Some planters, following the traditions of nobility, did feel responsible for the welfare of their enslaved

ding **History**
alyzing
es What fac-
ed to the
rtation of
ved Africans
he South?

ng **History**
gnizing
How did
wth of
affect
l power in
th?

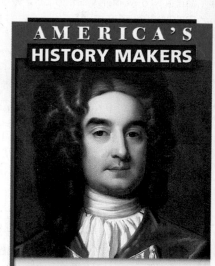

AMERICA'S HISTORY MAKERS

WILLIAM BYRD II
1674–1744

William Byrd II was one of the best known of the Southern planters. His family owned a large estate in Virginia. After his father died, Byrd took on his father's responsibilities, including membership in the House of Burgesses.

But Byrd is best remembered for his writing. His most famous work is *History of the Dividing Line betwixt Virginia and North Carolina.* In it, Byrd celebrates the land and climate of the South. At times, however, he is critical of its people. Even today, the book creates a vivid picture of life in the Southern Colonies.

How did William Byrd II demonstrate his leadership abilities?

workers. Power, they believed, brought with it the responsibility to do good. Many planters, though, were tyrants. They held complete authority over everyone in their households. Planters frequently used violence against slaves to enforce their will.

Vocabulary
tyrant: harsh ruler

Life Under Slavery

On large Southern plantations, slaves toiled in groups of about 20 to 25 under the supervision of **overseers.** Overseers were men hired by planters to watch over and direct the work of slaves. Enslaved persons performed strenuous and exhausting work, often for 15 hours a day at the peak of the harvest season. If slaves did not appear to be doing their full share of work, they were often whipped by the overseer.

Enslaved people usually lived in small, one-room cabins that were furnished only with sleeping cots. For a week's food, a slave might receive only around a quarter bushel of corn and a pound of pork. Some planters allowed their slaves to add to this meager ration by letting them raise their own potatoes, greens, fruit, or chicken.

In spite of the brutal living conditions, Africans preserved many customs and beliefs from their homelands. These included music, dances, stories, and, for a time, African religions—including Islam. African kinship customs became the basis of African-American family culture. A network of kin was a source of strength even when families were separated.

Reading **H**
D. Finding Ideas Wha toms and b from their lands provi strength fo enslaved Africans?

Resistance to Slavery

At the same time that enslaved Africans struggled to maintain their own culture, they fought against their enslavement. They sometimes worked slowly, damaged goods, or purposely carried out orders the wrong way. A British traveler in 1746 noted that many slaves pretended not to understand tasks they often had performed as farmers in West Africa.

A VOICE FROM THE PAST

You would really be surpriz'd at their Perseverance; let an hundred Men shew him how to hoe, or drive a wheelbarrow, he'll still take the one by the Bottom, and the other by the Wheel; and they often die before they can be conquer'd.

Edward Kimber, quoted in *White over Black*

At times, slaves became so angry and frustrated by their loss of freedom that they rose up in rebellion. One of the most famous incidents was the **Stono Rebellion.** In September 1739, about 20 slaves gathered at the Stono River just south of Charles Town. Wielding guns and other weapons, they killed several planter families and marched south, beating drums and loudly inviting other slaves to join them in their plan to seek freedom in Spanish-held Florida. By late that afternoon, however, a white militia had surrounded the group of escaping slaves. The two sides clashed, and many slaves died in the fighting. Those captured were executed.

Stono and similar revolts led planters to make slave codes even stricter. Slaves were now forbidden from leaving plantations without permission. The laws also made it illegal for slaves to meet with free blacks. Such laws made the conditions of slavery even more inhumane.

The Southern Colonies' plantation economy and widespread use of slaves set the region on a very different path from that of the New England and Middle Colonies. In the next section, you will learn how settlers used the unique resources of the Backcountry to create settlements there.

ground
codes were
designed to
ol slaves and
them in
ge.

---

tion **3** **Assessment**

Terms & Names

plain the
gnificance of:
ndigo
liza Lucas
William Byrd II
verseer
tono Rebellion

2. Using Graphics

Use a diagram like the one shown to review the factors that led to the use of slaves in the South.

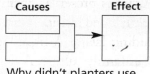

Why didn't planters use Native American workers?

3. Main Ideas

a. What percentage of the South's population was enslaved in 1750?

b. What crops did plantations in Georgia and South Carolina grow?

c. How did enslaved persons resist their slavery?

4. Critical Thinking

Contrasting How did geographic differences between the Southern Colonies and the New England Colonies affect their labor systems?

THINK ABOUT

• the climate of the regions
• the nature of the soil

IVITY OPTIONS

ART

SCIENCE

Do more research on rice plantations. Draw a **diagram** of a typical plantation or write a **report** on how rice is cultivated today.

Differences Among the Colonies

Many factors shape a region's economy and the way its settlers make a living. One of the most important is its physical geography—the climate, soil, and natural resources of the region. The geography of the American colonies varied from one colony to another. For example, in some areas, farmers could dig into rich, fertile soil. In others, they could not stick their shovels in the ground without hitting rocks.

Major Regional Exports (by export value*)

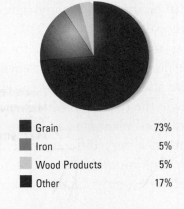

NEW ENGLAND COLONIES

New England had a short growing season and rocky soil. Colonists took advantage of other opportunities in the region, especially fishing and whaling.

Dried Fish and Whale Oil	44%
Livestock	17%
Wood Products	13%
Other	26%

MIDDLE COLONIES

The longer growing season of the Middle Colonies—the "breadbasket colonies"—allowed farmers to grow cash crops of grain.

Grain	73%
Iron	5%
Wood Products	5%
Other	17%

SOUTHERN COLONIES

The South had a nearly year-round growing season. The use of enslaved Africans allowed Southern planters produce cash crops of tobacco and

Tobacco	48%
Rice	20%
Bread, Flour, Grain (not rice)	13%
Indigo	7%
Other	12%

*Export Value in Pounds Sterling (Five-Year Average, 1768–1772)

Source: James F. Shepherd and Gary M. Walton, *Shipping, Maritime Trade, and the Economic Development of Colonial North America* (Cambridge: Cambridge University Press, 1972.)

ARTIFACT FILE

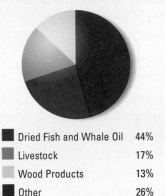

Farmer's Plow Middle colonists relied on the heavy blades of plows to cut seed rows into the region's fertile soil.

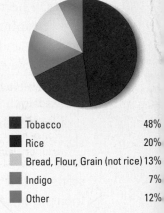

Indigo On some plantations in the South, planters grew crops of indigo plants—like the one pictured here—to produce the rich blue dyes used to color this yarn.

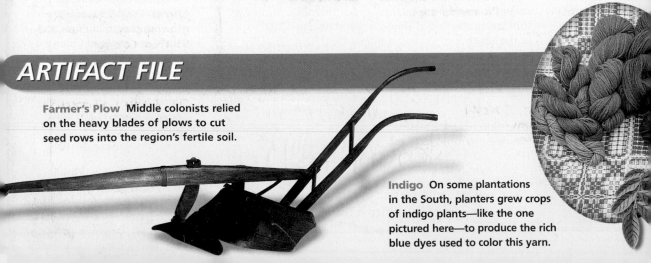

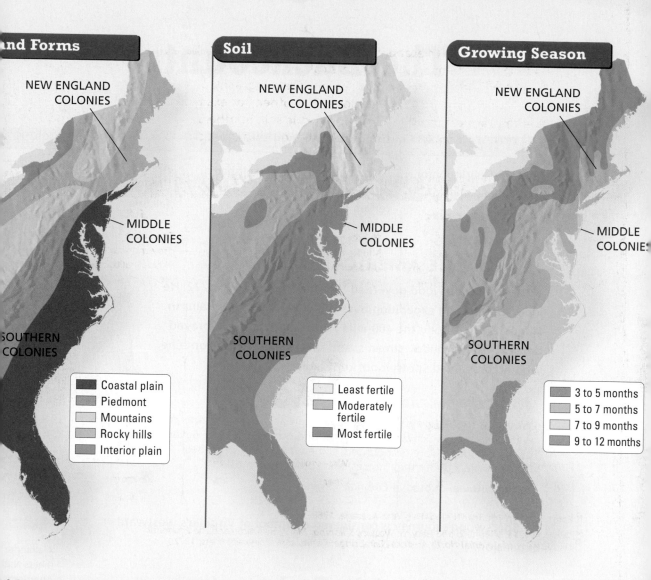

and Forms

NEW ENGLAND COLONIES

MIDDLE COLONIES

SOUTHERN COLONIES

- Coastal plain
- Piedmont
- Mountains
- Rocky hills
- Interior plain

Soil

NEW ENGLAND COLONIES

MIDDLE COLONIES

SOUTHERN COLONIES

- Least fertile
- Moderately fertile
- Most fertile

Growing Season

NEW ENGLAND COLONIES

MIDDLE COLONIES

SOUTHERN COLONIES

- 3 to 5 months
- 5 to 7 months
- 7 to 9 months
- 9 to 12 months

al Geography The maps above show the different types of land forms, d growing seasons that were found in the different colonial regions. These helped to shape the economies of each of the regions, which were quite t, as the pie graphs show on the previous page.

Line Field Trip

ew Bedford Whaling Museum
achusetts has many objects
to whaling, including bone
objects called scrimshaws.
carved this whale's tooth
ackknife or sail needle and
the design with ink.

about whaling . . .

RESEARCH LINKS
CLASSZONE.COM

CONNECT TO GEOGRAPHY

1. **Region** How long was the growing season in most of the Southern Colonies?
2. **Human-Environment Interaction** How might the soil quality in the Middle Colonies have influenced the region's population?

   [G] See Geography Handbook, pages 10–13.

CONNECT TO HISTORY

3. **Analyzing Causes** Why did the land forms and soil of New England cause many to turn to the Atlantic Ocean for a living?

The Backcountry

MAIN IDEA	WHY IT MATTERS NOW	TERMS & NAMES
Settlers moved to the Backcountry because land was cheap and plentiful.	Backcountry settlers established a rural way of life that still exists in certain parts of the country.	Appalachian Mountains · piedmont fall line · clan

ONE AMERICAN'S STORY

Alexander Spotswood governed Virginia from 1710 to 1722. He led a month-long expedition over the Blue Ridge Mountains in August 1716. During the 400-mile journey, adventurers braved dense thickets, muddy streams, and rattlesnakes. John Fontaine, who accompanied Spotswood, kept a diary of the trip.

A VOICE FROM THE PAST

We had a rugged way; we passed over a great many small runs of water, some of which were very deep, and others very miry. Several of our company were dismounted, some were down with their horses, others under their horses, and some thrown off.

John Fontaine, quoted in *Colonial Virginia*

Spotswood's journey is considered a symbol of Virginia's westward expansion.

Alexander
meets Nati
Americans
Ridge Mou
segment o
Appalachia
Mountains

Taking Notes

Use your chart to take notes about the backcountry.

	NEW ENGLAND COLONIES	MIDD
Climate		
Resources		
People		
Economic Development		

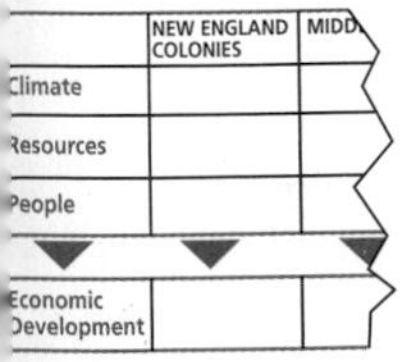

Geography of the Backcountry

Just as Spotswood predicted, settlers soon began to move into the Backcountry. This was a region of dense forests and rushing streams in or near the **Appalachian Mountains**. The Appalachians stretch from eastern Canada south to Alabama.

In the South, the Backcountry began at the **fall line**. The fall line is where waterfalls prevent large boats from moving farther upriver. Beyond the fall line is the **piedmont**. Piedmont means "foot of the mountains." It is the broad plateau that leads to the Blue Ridge Mountains of the Appalachian range.

The Backcountry's resources made it relatively easy for a family to start a small farm. The region's many springs and streams provided water, and forests furnished wood that settlers could use for log cabins and fences.

Backcountry Settlers

The first Europeans in the Backcountry made a living by trading with the Native Americans. Backcountry settlers paid for goods with deerskins. A unit of value was one buckskin or, for short, a "buck."

Farmers soon followed the traders into the region, but they had to be cautious. As the number of settlements grew, the farmers often clashed with the Native Americans whose land they were taking.

Farmers sheltered their families in log cabins. They filled holes between the logs with mud, moss, and clay. Then they sawed out doors and windows. Lacking glass, settlers used paper smeared with animal fat to cover their windows.

William Byrd—on his expedition to establish the southern border of Virginia—described a long night that he spent in one such cabin. He complained that he and at least ten other people were "forc't to pig together in a Room . . . troubled with the Squalling of peevish, dirty children into the Bargain."

Backcountry life may have been harsh, but by the late 1600s many families had chosen to move there. Some of them went to escape the plantation system, which had crowded out many small farmers closer to the seacoast. Then, in the 1700s, a new group of emigrants—the Scots-Irish—began to move into the Backcountry.

The Scots-Irish

The Scots-Irish came from the borderland between Scotland and England. Most of them had lived for a time in northern Ireland. In 1707, England and Scotland merged and formed Great Britain. The merger caused many hardships for the Scots-Irish. Poverty and crop failures made this bad situation even worse.

As a result, Scots-Irish headed to America by the thousands. After they arrived, they quickly moved into the Backcountry. The Scots-Irish brought their clan system with them to the Backcountry. **Clans** are large groups of families—sometimes in the thousands—that claim a common ancestor. Clan members were suspicious of outsiders and banded together when danger threatened. These clans helped families to deal with the dangers and problems of the Backcountry.

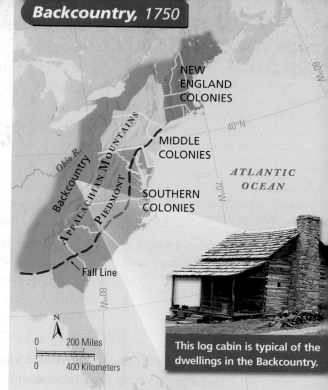

Backcountry, 1750

NEW ENGLAND COLONIES

MIDDLE COLONIES

SOUTHERN COLONIES

APPALACHIAN MOUNTAINS

PIEDMONT

Ohio R.

Backcountry

Fall Line

ATLANTIC OCEAN

40°N

70°W

80°W

60°W

N

0   200 Miles
0   400 Kilometers

This log cabin is typical of the dwellings in the Backcountry.

GEOGRAPHY SKILLBUILDER Interpreting Maps
Region *What geographical feature did the northern and southern areas of the Backcountry have in common?*

Backcountry Life

Life in the Backcountry was very different from life along the seaboard. Settlers along the coast carried on a lively trade with England. But in the Backcountry, rough roads and rivers made it almost impossible to move goods.

As a result, Backcountry farmers learned quickly to depend on themselves. They built log cabins and furnished them with cornhusk mattresses and homemade benches and tables. They fed their families with the hogs and cattle they raised and with the fish and game they killed. They grew yellow corn to feed their livestock and white corn to eat. Popcorn was probably their only snack food. To protect their precious corn from pests, daytime patrols of women, children, and the elderly served as human scarecrows.

Women in the Backcountry worked in the cabin and fields, but they also learned to use guns and axes. An explorer who traveled in the region described one of these hardy Backcountry women.

A VOICE FROM THE PAST

She is a very civil woman and shows nothing of ruggedness or Immodesty in her carriage, yett she will carry a gunn in the woods and kill deer, turkeys, etc., shoot doun wild cattle, catch and tye hoggs, knock down [cattle] with an ax and perform the most manfull Exercises.

A visitor to the Backcountry, quoted in *A History of American Life*

Settlers in the Backcountry often acted as if there were no other people in the region, but this was not so. In the woods and meadows that surrounded their cabins, settlers often encountered Native Americans and other groups that had made America their home.

Other Peoples in North America

The Backcountry settlers started a westward movement that would play a critical role in American history. Most settlers' motivation to move west was simple—the desire for land.

Yet the push to the west brought settlers into contact with other peoples of North America. Native Americans had made their homes there for thousands of years. In addition, France and Spain claimed considerable territory in North America.

Sometimes this contact led to changes in people's cultures. For instance, North America had no horses until the Spanish colonists brought them into Mexico in the 1500s. Horses migrated north, and Native Americans caught them and made them an important part of their culture.

Reading **Hi**
B. Making
Inferences H
would you
describe the
people in th
Backcountry
lived?

Reading **H**
C. Summari
As England
colonies
expanded
ward, wha
groups did
encounter?

Contact also led to conflict. As English settlers pushed into the Backcountry, they put pressure on Native American tribes. Some tribes reacted by raiding isolated homesteads and small settlements. White settlers struck back, leading to more bloodshed.

This painting shows Native Americans catching wild horses. Many would later use the horses to hunt buffalo on the Great Plains.

The English colonists also came into conflict with the French. The French had colonized eastern Canada and had moved into the territories, rich with fur, along the Mississippi River. French fur traders wanted to prevent English settlers from moving west and taking away part of the trade. One Native American told an Englishman, "You and the French are like two edges of a pair of shears, and we are the cloth that is cut to pieces between them."

Spain also controlled large areas of North America—including territories that today form part or all of the states of Arizona, California, Colorado, Florida, Nevada, New Mexico, Texas, Utah, and Wyoming. Spanish settlers were farmers, ranchers, and priests. Priests, who established missions to convert Native Americans, built forts near the missions for protection. In 1718, Spaniards built Fort San Antonio de Bexar to guard the mission of San Antonio de Valero, later renamed the Alamo.

These different groups continued to compete—and sometimes fight—with one another. Frequently, England's colonies had to unite against these other groups. As a result, a common American identity began to take shape, as you will read in Chapter 5.

ulary
: scissors

---

ion **4** Assessment

erms & Names

lain the gnificance of:
- •palachian ountains
- l line
- •dmont
- n

2. Using Graphics

Use a chart like the one shown to list some of the geographic characteristics of the Backcountry.

Backcountry Geography
1.
2.
3.
4.

3. Main Ideas

a. Which settlers migrated to the Backcountry?

b. How did clans help the Scots-Irish survive?

c. What economic activities did women carry out in the region?

4. Critical Thinking

Identifying Problems As England's colonies expanded farther west, what problems would they face?

THINK ABOUT
- • other inhabitants of the Americas
- • the resources desired by the colonists

VITY OPTIONS

GUAGE ARTS

ART

Read an account of the Backcountry written in the 1700s. Write a **newspaper article** or draw a series of **cartoons** that describe what you have read.

VISUAL SUMMARY

The Colonies Develop

New England: Commerce and Religion

New England was distinguished by its small farming towns and profitable fishing and trade.

The Middle Colonies: Farms and Cities

The Middle Colonies' farms produced large cash crops that fueled trade in its coastal cities.

The Southern Colonies: Plantations and Slavery

The South's plantation economy and large number of enslaved Africans made it different from the other regions.

The Backcountry

The Backcountry was distant from the denser coastal populations, so settlers there developed an independent and rugged way of life.

TERMS & NAMES

Briefly explain the significance of the following.

1. Backcountry
2. subsistence farming
3. triangular trade
4. Navigation Acts
5. cash crop
6. gristmill
7. Conestoga wagon
8. overseer
9. Stono Rebellion
10. Appalachian Mountains

REVIEW QUESTIONS

New England: Commerce and Religion (pages 109–113)

1. How would you describe the life of a New England farmer?
2. In what ways did settlers in the region take advantage of the Atlantic Ocean?
3. How were New England towns settled?

The Middle Colonies: Farms and Cities (pages 114–118)

4. How were farms in the Middle Colonies different from those in New England?
5. What characterized the population of the Middle Colonies?

The Southern Colonies: Plantations and Slavery (pages 119–125)

6. Why did Southern planters infrequently travel to towns to sell their crops or to buy food and supplies?
7. Why did planters turn to enslaved Africans for labor?
8. In what ways did slaves resist?

The Backcountry (pages 126–129)

9. Where was the Backcountry located in the 1700s?
10. How was life in the Backcountry different from that along the coast?

CRITICAL THINKING

1. USING YOUR NOTES: ANALYZING CAUSES AND EFFECTS

Using your completed chart, answer the questions below.

a. How was the Middle Coloni climate different from the Backcountry's?
b. How did the South's labor sy differ from the North's?
c. How did the resources of Ne England affect its economy?

2. ANALYZING LEADERSHIP

How did the South's plantation economy influence who becam leaders in the region?

3. THEME: ECONOMICS IN HISTORY

What factors influenced the e nomic development of each o four colonial regions?

4. APPLYING CITIZENSHIP SH

How did the Quaker influence the Middle Colonies contribut the behavior of citizens of the region?

5. SEQUENCING EVENTS

What changes took place in t population and treatment of African Americans between 1 and 1750?

Interact with Histo

How would the choice that y made at the beginning of the ter have varied according to region in which you lived? W you still make the same choic

e the map and your knowledge of U.S. history to
swer questions 1 and 2.

ditional Test Practice, pp. S1–S33.

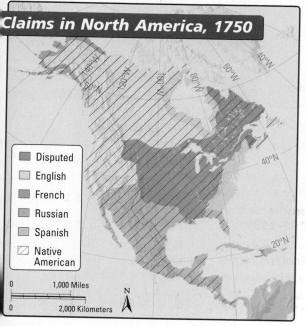

Claims in North America, 1750

Legend:
- Disputed
- English
- French
- Russian
- Spanish
- Native American

0 — 1,000 Miles
0 — 2,000 Kilometers

N

Vhich of the groups shown inhabited the largest
rea of North America?

A. English

. Native American

. Russian

. Spanish

2. Which European group claimed the northernmost
territory?

A. English

B. French

C. Russian

D. Spanish

**This quotation from Edward Kimber is about slaves
in the United States. Use the quotation and your
knowledge of U.S. history to answer question 3.**

PRIMARY SOURCE

You would really be surpriz'd at their Perseverance;
let an hundred Men shew him how to hoe, or drive a
wheelbarrow, he'll still take the one by the Bottom,
and the other by the Wheel; and they often die
before they can be conquer'd.

Edward Kimber, quoted in *White over Black*

3. The speaker uses the word *Perseverance* to emphasize which of the following?

A. the slave's belief in working hard at his or
her tasks

B. the slave's determination to resist enslavement

C. the slave's confusion about what is expected of
him or her

D. the slave's submission to the condition of
slavery

TEST PRACTICE
CLASSZONE.COM

RNATIVE ASSESSMENT

WRITING ABOUT HISTORY

e that you are a Quaker living in colonial
a. Write a **diary** entry about your typical day.

can learn more about Quaker life in colonial
s by reading primary sources found in the library.
re you begin to write, make a list of the ways in
h you might spend a typical day as a Quaker. Use
notes to write your diary entry.

PERATIVE LEARNING

ith a few of your classmates to design and con-
model of a log cabin. Group members can
e responsibilities for researching the history of
ns, recording details about the location of your
n, and designing and building the cabin.

INTEGRATED TECHNOLOGY

DOING INTERNET RESEARCH

You can learn about different aspects of colonial farm
life from primary sources. Use the Internet or library
resources to begin your research.

- Use the Internet to find primary sources such as
diaries, journal entries, or letters.

- Another source of information might be historical
or living history museums.

- Use your research to create a chart listing the differences between your family's lifestyle and a colonial
family's.

For more about colonial farming . . .

INTERNET ACTIVITY
CLASSZONE.COM

Patrick Henry argues against the king in 1763.

For colonists like these, conflicts with the British government have helped shape a separate identity.

1689
Massachusetts colonists overthrow royal governor Andros.

1704
Boston Newsletter is founded.

USA
World 1680

1689
William and Mary replace James II as rulers of England.

1707
England and Scotland join to form Great Britain.

1709
About 13,500
the German s
emigrate to E

You are outraged by the attacks on British traders and settlers. You wonder whether it is wise to join with other colonies, though. Will it mean that Virginians or New Englanders will be able to make laws for Pennsylvania?

What do you have in common with other British colonists?

What Do You Think?

- What are some good reasons to join with the other British colonies?

- How great are the differences between the British colonies?

- What separates British and French colonists?

RESEARCH LINKS
CLASSZONE.COM

Visit the Chapter 5 links for more information about early-American identity.

1735
Decision in
trial supports
of the press.

1738
Minister George Whitefield arrives in Georgia.

1754
French and Indian War begins.

1759
Quebec falls to the British.

1763
French and Indian War ends.

1763

comes
at Britain.

1756
Seven Years' War between France and Britain is declared.

Colonial Social Ranks

HIGH

- large landowners
- church officials
- government officials
- wealthy merchants

UPPER MIDDLE

- small farmers
- tradespeople

LOWER MIDDLE

- renters
- unskilled workers

LOW

- indentured servants
- slaves

Land ownership also helped determine colonists' social position. Unlike England, America had no class of nobles whose titles passed from parent to child. But people were still divided into high, middle, and low ranks, as they were in England. Large landholders were high in rank. Small farmers who owned their land were in the middle rank. Most colonists fit this category. People who did not own land, such as servants, slaves, or hired workers, were low in rank. Colonial women held the same rank as their husbands or fathers.

Colonists showed respect to their "betters" by curtsying or tipping a hat, for example. Seats in church were assigned by rank, with wealthy families in the front pews and poor people in the back. Despite such divisions, the wealthy were expected to aid the poor.

Women and the Economy

Although women were not landholders, their work was essential to the colonial economy. As you learned in Chapter 4, enslaved African women helped raise cash crops such as tobacco and indigo. Most white women were farm wives who performed tasks and made products their families needed. They cooked, churned butter, made soap and candles, spun fibers, wove cloth, sewed and knitted clothes, and did many other chores. They usually tended a garden and looked after farm animals. At harvest time, they often worked in the fields alongside men and older children.

Because cash was scarce, farm wives bartered, or traded, with their neighbors for goods and services. For example, a woman who nursed a sick neighbor or helped deliver a baby might be paid in sugar or cloth.

Women in towns and cities usually did the same types of housework that rural women did. In addition, some urban women ran inns or other businesses. Madam Knight, whose journey was described in One American's Story on page 135, sold writing paper, taught handwriting, and rented rooms to guests. A few women, usually the wives or widows of tradesmen, practiced trades themselves.

Although women contributed to the colonial economy, they did not have many rights. Women could not vote. In most churches, they could not preach or hold office. (Quaker meetings were an exception.) A married woman could not own property without her husband's permission. By law, even the money a woman earned belonged to her husband.

Young People at Work

Children's work also supported the colonial economy. Families were large. New England families, for example, had an average of six to eight children. More children meant more workers. Children as young as three or four were expected to be useful. They might help look after farm animals, gather berries, and watch younger children.

Reading **Hi**
A. Finding M
Ideas What
colonists ga
owning land

Reading **I**
B. Finding
Ideas In w
ways was
women's v
essential t
economy?

Around age six, boys were "breeched." This meant that they no longer wore the skirts or smocks of all young children but were given a pair of pants. They then began to help their fathers at work. Sons of farmers worked all day clearing land and learning to farm. Sons of craftsmen tended their fathers' shops and learned their fathers' trades.

Around age 11, many boys left their fathers to become apprentices. An **apprentice** learned a trade from an experienced craftsman. The apprentice received food, clothing, lodging, and a general education, as well as training in the specific craft or business. He worked for free, usually for four to seven years, until his contract was fulfilled. Then he could work for wages or start his own business.

Girls rarely were apprenticed. They learned sewing and other household skills from their mothers. In New England, girls of 13 or 14 often were sent away to other households to learn specialized skills such as weaving or cheese making. Orphaned girls and boys worked as servants for families who housed and fed them until adulthood.

ing **History**

trasting
did the
1g of boys
irls differ?

Colonial Schooling

If land, wealth, and hard work were valued across the colonies, so was education. Most children were taught to read so that they could understand the Bible. Only children from wealthy families went beyond reading to learn writing and arithmetic. These children learned either from private tutors or in private schools. Poorer children sometimes learned to read from their mothers.

HISTORY through ART

This drawing shows the inside of an 18th-century one-room schoolhouse.

What does the picture suggest to you about colonial schooling?

Or they attended "dame schools," where women taught the alphabet and used the Bible to teach reading. Most children finished their formal education at age seven.

Children's textbooks emphasized religion. The widely used *New England Primer* paired the letter *A* with the verse "In *Adam's* fall / We Sinned all." Beside the letter *B* was a picture of the Bible. The primer contained the Lord's Prayer and *The Shorter Catechism,* more than 100 questions and answers about religion.

Colonial America had a high literacy rate, as measured by the number of people who could sign their names. In New England, 85 percent of white men were literate, compared with 60 percent of men in England. In the Middle Colonies, 65 percent of white men were literate, and in the South, about 50 percent were. In each region of the colonies, roughly half as many white women as men were literate. Most colonists thought schooling was more important for males. Educated African Americans were rare. If they were enslaved, teaching them to read was illegal. If they were free, they were often kept out of schools.

Newspapers and Books

Colonial readers supported a publishing industry that also drew the colonies together. In the early 1700s, the colonies had only one local newspaper, the *Boston News-letter.* But over the next 70 years, almost 80 different newspapers appeared in America. Many were published for decades.

Most books in the colonies were imported from England, but colonists slowly began to publish their own books. Almanacs were very popular. A typical almanac included a calendar, weather predictions, star charts, farming advice, home remedies, recipes, jokes, and proverbs. In 1732, Benjamin Franklin began to publish *Poor Richard's Almanack.* It contained sayings that are still repeated today, such as "Haste makes waste."

Colonists also published poetry, regional histories, and autobiographies. Most personal stories told of struggles to maintain religious faith during hard times. A form of literature unique to the Americas was the captivity narrative. In it, a colonist captured by Native Americans described living among them.

Mary Rowlandson's 1682 captivity narrative, *The Sovereignty and Goodness of God,* was one of the first colonial bestsellers. Native Americans attacked Rowlandson's Massachusetts village in 1676, during King Philip's War. They held her hostage for 11 weeks. During that time, she was a servant to a Narragansett chieftain, knitting stockings and making shirts for his family and others. "I told them it was Sabbath day," she recalled, "and desired them to let me rest, and told them I

Reading Hi
D. Contrasti
How was co
education di
from educat
today?

Reading H
E. Categori
What were
types of co
literature?

would do as much more tomorrow. To which they answered me, they would break my face." After townspeople raised money to ransom Rowlandson, she was released. Although she mourned a young daughter who had died in captivity, she praised God for returning her safely.

The Great Awakening

Mary Rowlandson's religious faith was central to her life. But in the early 1700s, many colonists feared they had lost the religious passion that had driven their ancestors to found the colonies. Religion seemed dry, dull, and distant, even to regular churchgoers.

In the 1730s and 1740s, a religious movement called the **Great Awakening** swept through the colonies. The traveling ministers of this movement preached that inner religious emotion was more important than outward religious behavior. Their sermons appealed to the heart and drew large crowds. **Jonathan Edwards,** one of the best-known preachers, terrified listeners with images of God's anger but promised they could be saved.

ground
ous
ngs with
intensely
onal crowds
n part of
ican reli-
tradition.

A VOICE FROM THE PAST

And now you have an extraordinary opportunity, a day wherein Christ has thrown the door of mercy wide open, and stands in calling and crying with a loud voice to poor sinners. . . . How awful it is to be left behind at such a day!

Jonathan Edwards, "Sinners in the Hands of an Angry God"

The Great Awakening lasted for years and changed colonial culture. Congregations argued over religious practices and often split apart. People left their old churches and joined other Protestant groups such as Baptists. Some of these groups welcomed women, African Americans, and Native Americans. Overall, churches gained 20,000 to 50,000 new members. To train ministers, religious groups founded colleges such as Princeton and Brown.

The Great Awakening inspired colonists to help others. **George Whitefield** (HWIT·feeld) drew thousands of people with his sermons and raised funds to start a home for orphans. Other ministers taught Christianity and reading to Native Americans and African Americans. The

George Whitefield preaching to a crowd

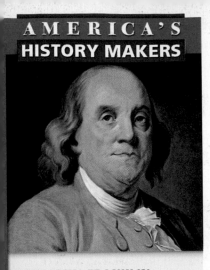

BENJAMIN FRANKLIN

1706–1790

As an Enlightenment thinker, Benjamin Franklin used reason to improve society. At 42, he retired from business to devote his life to science and public service. He proved that lightning was a form of electricity. Then he invented the lightning rod to protect buildings. The Franklin stove and bifocal eyeglasses were also his inventions. He organized a fire department, a lending library, and a society to discuss philosophy. Later he helped draft the Declaration of Independence.

How did Franklin help improve colonial society?

Great Awakening encouraged ideas of equality and the right to challenge authority. In this way, the movement contributed to the revolutionary fervor of the colonists when they declared independence from England years later.

The Enlightenment

Unlike the Great Awakening, which stressed religious emotion, the **Enlightenment** emphasized reason and science as the paths to knowledge. **Benjamin Franklin** was a famous American Enlightenment figure. This intellectual movement appealed mostly to wealthy, educated men. But it, too, had far-reaching effects on the colonies.

The Enlightenment began in Europe, as scientists discovered natural laws governing the universe. Isaac Newton, for example, explained the law of gravity.

Other Enlightenment thinkers applied the idea of natural law to human societies. The English philosopher **John Locke** argued that people have natural rights. These are rights to life, liberty, and property. People create governments to protect their natural rights, he claimed. If a government fails in this duty, people have the right to change it. Locke challenged the belief that kings had a God-given right to rule.

Enlightenment ideas of natural rights and government by agreement influenced leaders across Europe and the colonies. As you will see in Section 2, colonists began to wonder whether the British government protected their rights and freedoms. Eventually, they would rebel and form a new government.

Reading His

F. Recognizin Effects Wha were five eff of the Great Awakening?

Backgroun Locke argued against the i that the king a God-given to rule. But believed tha natural right individuals c from God.

---

1. Terms & Names

Explain the significance of:

- apprentice
- Great Awakening
- Jonathan Edwards
- George Whitefield
- Enlightenment
- Benjamin Franklin
- John Locke

2. Using Graphics

Describe the parts of colonial culture in a chart.

Economy	
Education	
Publishing	
Religion	

Why was each important in colonial culture?

3. Main Ideas

a. Why was land ownership so important to the colonists?

b. How did women and young people contribute to the colonial economy?

c. How did the Great Awakening affect the colonies?

4. Critical Thinking

Contrasting How were t Great Awakening and the Enlightenment different?

THINK ABOUT

- the ideas each moveme promoted
- the people to whom ea movement appealed

ACTIVITY OPTIONS

LANGUAGE ARTS

ART

Make up a **saying** that reflects some part of colonial culture, or draw an **illustration** of a saying from colonial times.

Roots of Representative Government

ONE AMERICAN'S STORY

In 1688, the Puritan minister Increase Mather sailed to England to get relief for Massachusetts. The English government had canceled the charter of Massachusetts and sent a royal governor to rule.

The colonists thought the governor trampled their rights as English subjects. After four years in England, Mather came home with a new charter that he hoped would satisfy the colonists.

A VOICE FROM THE PAST

For all English liberties are restored to them: No Persons shall have a Penny of their Estates taken from them; nor any Laws imposed on them, without their own Consent by Representatives chosen by themselves.

Increase Mather, quoted in *The Last American Puritan*

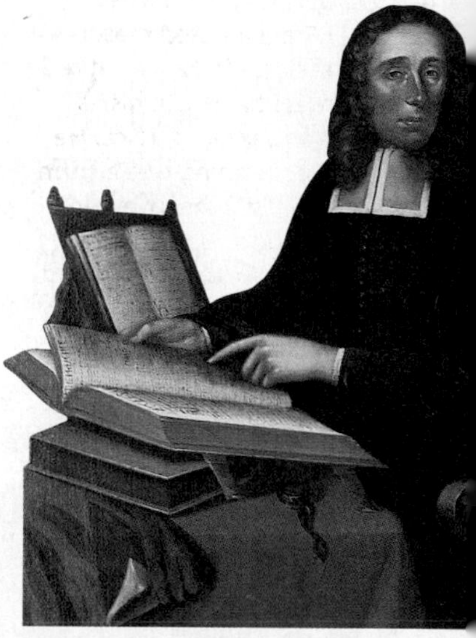

This is a detail of *Increase Mather* by Jan van der Spriett.

Mather called the new charter "a Magna Carta for New England." In this section, you will learn about the rights of English people set forth in the Magna Carta and later documents. These rights are the basis for the rights Americans enjoy today.

The Rights of Englishmen

English colonists expected certain rights that came from living under an English government. These "rights of Englishmen" had developed over centuries.

The first step toward guaranteeing these rights came in 1215. That year, a group of English noblemen forced King John to accept the **Magna Carta** (Great Charter). The king needed the nobles' money to finance a war. This document guaranteed important rights to noblemen and freemen—those not bound to a master. They could not have their property seized by the king or his officials. They could not be taxed, in most

Taking Notes

Use your chart to take notes about the roots of representative government in the American colonies.

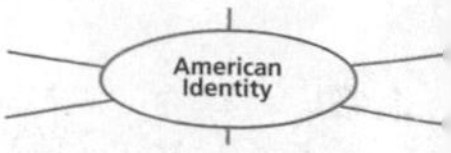

American Identity

cases, unless a council of prominent men agreed. They could not be put to trial based only on an official's word, without witnesses. They could be punished only by a jury of their peers, people of the same social rank.

A VOICE FROM THE PAST

No freeman shall be seized, imprisoned, dispossessed, outlawed, or exiled, . . . nor will we proceed against or prosecute him except by the lawful judgment of his peers, or by the law of the land.

Magna Carta, translated in *A Documentary History of England*

Reading **His**
A. Comparin
What rights
the Magna C
remain right
America tod

The Magna Carta limited the powers of the king. Over time, the rights it listed were granted to all English people, not just noblemen and freemen.

Parliament and Colonial Government

One of the most important English rights was the right to elect representatives to government. **Parliament,** England's chief lawmaking body, was the colonists' model for representative government. Parliament was made up of two houses. Members of the House of Commons were elected by the people. Members of the House of Lords were nonelected nobles, judges, and church officials.

The king and Parliament were too far away to manage every detail of the colonies. Also, like the citizens of England, English colonists in America wanted to have a say in the laws governing them. So they formed

CITIZENSHIP TODAY

The Importance of Juries

The right to a trial by jury, established in the Magna Carta, is an important legal right. When you become an adult, you will likely be asked to serve on a jury.

Many young people in Knox County, Illinois, have already served as jurors on a teen court (shown below, with an advisor). They decide the best punishment for other teenagers who have admitted breaking a law. For example, shoplifters might be sentenced to write an apology to the store. Knox County is one of more than 500 U.S. communities that have teen courts.

How Can You Serve on a Teen Court?

1. Search the library or Interr learn more about teen cou

2. Ask the police department whether your town has a t court. If it does, volunteer.

3. If you want to start a teen court, seek advice from a community that has one.

4. Invite a lawyer to your cla talk about a juror's role.

5. Find a group to sponsor yc court, and get support fro youth officers and judges.

See the Citizenship Handb page 280.

For more about courts and juries .

RESEARCH LINKS
CLASSZONE.COM

Knox County Teen Court volunteers

their own elected assemblies, similar to the House of Commons. Virginia's House of Burgesses was the first of these. In Pennsylvania, William Penn allowed colonists to have their own General Assembly. These Virginia and Pennsylvania assemblies imposed taxes and managed the colonies.

Although the colonists governed themselves in some ways, England still had authority over them. The king appointed royal governors to rule some colonies on his behalf. Parliament had no representatives from the colonies. Even so, it passed laws that affected the colonies. The colonists disliked these laws, and they began to clash with royal governors over how much power England should have in America. These conflicts became more intense in the late 1600s.

*ding*History
aking
ences Why
he colonists
e laws
ed by
ament?

A Royal Governor's Rule

The reign of James II threatened the colonies' tradition of self-government. James became king in 1685. He wanted to rule England and its colonies with total authority. One of his first orders changed the way the Northern colonies were governed. These colonies, especially Massachusetts, had been smuggling goods and ignoring the Navigation Acts (see Chapter 4). When challenged, the people of Massachusetts had claimed that England had no right to make laws for them. The previous king, Charles II, had then canceled their charter.

"You have no more privileges left you."
a Boston court officia[l]

*ding*History
cognizing
ts How did
s II weaken
overnment
e colonies?

King James combined Massachusetts and the other Northern colonies into one Dominion of New England, ruled by royal governor **Edmund Andros.** Andros angered the colonists by ending their representative assemblies and allowing town meetings to be held only once a year.

With their assemblies outlawed, some colonists refused to pay taxes. They said that being taxed without having a voice in government violated their rights. Andros jailed the loudest complainers. At their trial, they were told, "You have no more privileges left you than not to be Sould [sold] for Slaves."

The colonists hated Governor Andros.

The colonists sent Increase Mather to England to plead with King James (see One American's Story on page 141). However, a revolution in England swept King James and Governor Andros from power.

England's Glorious Revolution

The English Parliament had decided to overthrow King James for not respecting its rights. Events came to a head in 1688. King James, a Catholic, had been trying to pack his next Parliament with officials who would overturn anti-Catholic laws. He had dismissed the last Parliament in 1685. The Protestant leaders of Parliament were outraged. They offered

ground
nd had
ne
stant in the
entury.
lics were
out of high

the throne to James's Protestant daughter, Mary, and her husband, William of Orange. William was the ruler of the Netherlands. Having little support from the people, James fled the country at the end of 1688. Parliament named William and Mary the new monarchs of England. This change in leadership was called England's **Glorious Revolution**.

After accepting the throne, William and Mary agreed in 1689 to uphold the **English Bill of Rights**. This was an agreement to respect the rights of English citizens and of Parliament. Under it, the king or queen could not cancel laws or impose taxes unless Parliament agreed. Free elections and frequent meetings of Parliament must be held. Excessive fines and cruel punishments were forbidden. People had the right to complain to the king or queen in Parliament without being arrested.

Background
The English B
Rights was th
model for the
of Rights in t
U.S. Constitu

The English Bill of Rights established an important principle: the government was to be based on laws made by Parliament, not on the desires of a ruler. The rights of English people were strengthened.

The American colonists were quick to claim these rights. When the people of Boston heard of King James's fall, they jailed Governor Andros and asked Parliament to restore their old government.

Shared Power in the Colonies

After the Glorious Revolution, the Massachusetts colonists regained some self-government. They could again elect representatives to an assembly. However, they still had a governor appointed by the crown.

Backgroun
Massachuset
colonists also
gained more
ious freedom
They no long
had to be ch
members to

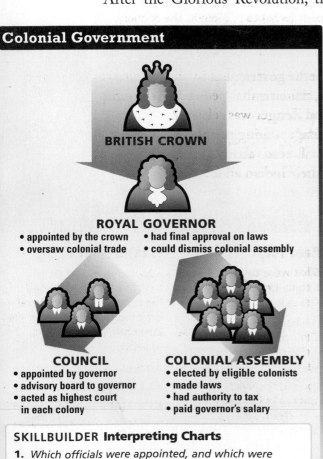

Colonial Government

BRITISH CROWN

ROYAL GOVERNOR
- appointed by the crown
- oversaw colonial trade
- had final approval on laws
- could dismiss colonial assembly

COUNCIL
- appointed by governor
- advisory board to governor
- acted as highest court in each colony

COLONIAL ASSEMBLY
- elected by eligible colonists
- made laws
- had authority to tax
- paid governor's salary

SKILLBUILDER Interpreting Charts
1. *Which officials were appointed, and which were elected?*
2. *How were lawmaking powers shared?*

The diagram on this page shows how most colonial governments were organized by 1700. Note how the royal governor, his council, and the colonial assembly shared power. The governor could strike down laws passed by the assembly, but the assembly was responsible for the governor's salary. If he blocked the assembly, the assembly might refuse to pay him.

During the first half of the 1700s, England interfered very little in colonial affairs. This hands-off policy was called **salutary neglect**. Parliament passed many laws regulating trade, the use of money, and even apprenticeships in the colonies. But governors rarely enforced these laws. The colonists got used to acting on their own.

Vocabulary
salutary: he
ful or benef

The Zenger Trial

Colonists moved toward gaining a new right, freedom of the press, in 1735. That year, **John Peter Zenger,** publisher of the *New-York Weekly Journal,* stood trial for printing criticism of New York's governor. The governor had removed a judge and tried to fix an election.

Government officials burn the *New-York Weekly Journal.*

A VOICE FROM THE PAST

A Governor turns rogue [criminal], does a thousand things for which a small rogue would have deserved a halter [hanging], and because it is difficult . . . to obtain relief against him, . . . it is prudent [wise] to . . . join in the roguery.

New-York Weekly Journal, quoted in *Colonial America, 1607–1763*

*ding*History

awing
usions Why
he Zenger
a step
rd freedom
e press?

At that time, it was illegal to criticize the government in print. Andrew Hamilton defended Zenger at his trial, claiming that people had the right to speak the truth. The jury agreed, and Zenger was released.

English rights were part of the heritage uniting people in the British colonies. In the next section, you will read about another unifying force—a war against the French and their Indian allies.

:tion ② Assessment

Terms & Names

xplain the significance of:
Magna Carta
Parliament
Edmund Andros
Glorious Revolution
English Bill of Rights
alutary neglect
ohn Peter Zenger

2. Using Graphics

In the boxes, show how the rights of English people developed in the three years mentioned.

English Rights

| 1215 | 1689 | 1735 |

Which right is most important to you?

3. Main Ideas

a. What were three of the traditional rights expected by English colonists?

b. In what ways did the English government anger the colonists in the late 1600s?

c. How did England's policies toward the colonies change after the Glorious Revolution?

4. Critical Thinking

Supporting Opinions
In your opinion, who had the most power—the royal governor, the council, or the assemblies? Defend your opinion.

THINK ABOUT
• their roles in making laws
• their roles in raising money
• who had final approval in matters

TIVITY OPTIONS

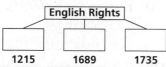

SPEECH

ART

Deliver **closing arguments** or create a **leaflet** defending John Peter Zenger and freedom of the press.

The French and Indian War

MAIN IDEA	WHY IT MATTERS NOW	TERMS & NAMES
Britain's victory in the French and Indian War forced France to give up its North American colonies.	British influence spread over North America, though French populations and place names still exist here.	French and Indian War · Albany Plan of Union · Battle of Qu[e] · Treaty of Pa[ris] · Pontiac's Re[bellion] · Proclamatio[n]

ONE AMERICAN'S STORY

The Frenchman, Charles de Langlade, and his family controlled the fur trade around what is now Green Bay, Wisconsin.

In 1752, Charles commanded 250 Ottawa and Chippewa warriors in an attack on a village in present-day Ohio. His reason: the Miami people there had stopped trading with the French and were now trading with the British. Charles and his men destroyed the village's British trading post. This attack helped lead to the French and Indian War.

This section describes the war, in which French forces fought British forces in North America. Each side had Native American allies.

This 1903 pa[inting] Edward Den[ny] shows Char[les] de Langlade attacking Br[itish] forces in 17[52].

[Ta]king Notes

[Us]e your chart to [ta]ke notes about [th]e French and [In]dian War.

American Identity

France Claims Western Lands

As you learned in Chapters 2 and 4, the French were exploring the North American interior while English colonists were settling the eastern coast. By the late 1600s, French explorers had claimed the Ohio River valley, the Mississippi River valley, and the entire Great Lakes region. The French territory of Louisiana, claimed by the explorer La Salle in 1682, stretched from the Appalachian Mountains to the Rocky Mountains.

The French built their main settlements, Quebec and Montreal, along the St. Lawrence River in Canada. (See the map on page 148.) They also built forts along the Great Lakes and along rivers draining into the Mississippi. By 1760, the French colony, New France, had a European population of about 80,000. By contrast, the British colonies had more than a million settlers.

Some Europeans in New France were Jesuit priests. They wanted to convert Native Americans to Christianity. Other Europeans in New France worked as fur traders. Native Americans brought furs to French forts and exchanged them for goods such as iron pots and steel knives. Many French traders carried goods by canoe into remote parts of New France.

Native American Alliances

kground
n French
rs lived
ng and
ied Native
ricans.

The English competed with the French for furs. Also, different Native American groups competed to supply furs to the Europeans. The fur trade created economic and military alliances between the Europeans and their Native American trading partners. The Huron and Algonquin peoples of the Great Lakes region were allied with the French. The Iroquois of upper New York often were allied with the Dutch and, later, the English.

kground
roquois
a union of
ations.

Alliances between Europeans and Native Americans led to their involvement in each other's wars. For example, by the mid-1600s, the Iroquois had trapped all the beavers in their own lands. To get more furs, they made war on their Huron and Algonquin neighbors, driving them west. Eventually the Iroquois controlled an area ranging from Maine west to the Ohio Valley and north to Lake Michigan. Iroquois expansion threatened the French fur trade. In response, the French armed the Huron and Algonquin peoples to fight the Iroquois. The Iroquois were armed by the English.

ding History
cognizing
ts How did
ur trade lead
ars?

When France and England declared war on each other in Europe in 1689, French and English colonists in America also began to fight. With their Native American allies, they attacked each other's settlements and forts. During the 1700s, two more wars between France and England fueled wars in their colonies. Neither side won a clear victory in these wars. A final war, the **French and Indian War** (1754–1763), decided which nation would control the northern and eastern parts of North America.

A French trader visits a Native American family.

Conflict in the Ohio River Valley

The seeds for the French and Indian War were planted when British fur traders began moving into the Ohio River valley in the 1750s. British land companies were also planning to settle colonists there. The French and their Native American allies became alarmed. To keep the British out of the valley, Charles de Langlade destroyed the village of Pickawillany and its British trading post (see One American's Story on page 146).

ding History
king
nces Why
he Ohio
Valley
tant to the
h and British
nments?

The British traders left, and the French built forts to protect the region linking their Canadian and Louisiana settlements. This upset the Virginia colony, which claimed title to the land. In 1753, the lieutenant governor of Virginia sent a small group of soldiers to tell the French to leave. Their leader was a 21-year-old major named George Washington. Washington reported the French commander's reply.

A VOICE FROM THE PAST

He told me the Country belong'd to them, that no English Man had a right to trade upon them Waters; & that he had Orders to make every Person Prisoner that attempted it on the Ohio or the Waters of it.

George Washington, *"Journey to the French Commandant"*

Virginia's lieutenant governor sent about 40 men to build a fort at the head of the Ohio River, where Pittsburgh stands today. French and Native American troops seized the partially built fort in April 1754 and completed it themselves. The French named it Fort Duquesne (du•KAYN).

War Begins and Spreads

George Washington was on his way to defend Fort Duquesne when he learned of its surrender. He and his men pushed on and built another small fort, Fort Necessity. Following Washington's surprise attack on a French force, the French and their allies attacked Fort Necessity on July 3, 1754. After Washington surrendered, the French let him march back to Virginia. The French and Indian War had begun. This war became part of the Seven Years' War (1756–1763), a worldwide struggle for empire between France and Great Britain.

Background
The Seven Years' War was fought not only in North America but in the Caribbean, throughout Europe, and India and Africa.

French and Indian War, 1754–1763

GEOGRAPHY SKILLBUILDER
Interpreting Maps
1. **Place** Which nation controlled territory along the St. Lawrence and Ohio rivers?
2. **Place** Which forts were the sites of British victories?

British territory
French territory
Disputed territory
★ British victory
✶ French victory

While Washington was surrendering Fort Necessity, representatives from the British colonies and the Iroquois nations were meeting at Albany, New York. The colonists wanted the Iroquois to fight with them against the French. The Iroquois would not commit to this alliance.

Benjamin Franklin, who admired the union of the six Iroquois nations, suggested that the colonies band together for defense. His **Albany Plan of Union** was the first formal proposal to unite the colonies. The plan called for each colony to send representatives to a Grand Council. This council would be able to collect taxes, raise armies, make treaties, and start new settlements. The leaders in Albany supported Franklin's plan, but the colonial legislatures later defeated it because they did not want to give up control of their own affairs.

Braddock's Defeat

Britain realized that to win the war, it could not rely solely on the colonists for funding or for troops. Therefore, the British sent General Edward Braddock and two regiments to Virginia. In 1755, Braddock marched toward the French at Fort Duquesne. George Washington was at his side. Their red-coated army of 2,100 moved slowly over the mountains, weighed down by a huge cannon.

On July 9, on a narrow trail eight miles from Fort Duquesne, fewer than 900 French and Indian troops surprised Braddock's forces. Washington suggested that his men break formation and fight from behind the trees, but Braddock would not listen. The general held his position and had four horses shot out from under him. Washington lost two horses. Four bullets went through Washington's coat, but, miraculously, none hit him. In the end, nearly 1,000 men were killed or wounded. General Braddock died from his wounds. American colonists were stunned by Braddock's defeat and by many other British losses over the next two years.

The British Take Quebec

In 1757, Britain had a new secretary of state, William Pitt, who was determined to win the war in the colonies. He sent the nation's best generals to America and borrowed money to pay colonial troops for fighting. The British controlled six French forts by August 1759, including Fort Duquesne (rebuilt as Fort Pitt). In late summer, the British began to attack New France at its capital, Quebec.

ding **History**
awing
usions Why
Braddock
ted by a
er enemy
?

ground
se the
seemed
to win the
ome
ois had
them as

America's
HERITAGE

ACADIANS TO CAJUNS

Braddock's defeat and other early losses in the war increased British concern about the loyalty of the French people in Acadia (now Nova Scotia). The British had won Acadia from France in 1713.

In 1755, British officers forced out 6,000 Acadians who would not take a loyalty oath. The British burned Acadian villages and spread the people to various British colonies, as shown. Eventually, some Acadians made their way to the French territory of Louisiana. There they became known as Cajuns.

Quebec sat on cliffs 300 feet above the St. Lawrence River. Cannon and thousands of soldiers guarded its thick walls. British general James Wolfe sailed around the fort for two months, unable to capture it. Then, in September, a scout found a steep, unguarded path up the cliffs to the plains just west of Quebec. At night, Wolfe and 4,000 of his men floated to the path and secretly climbed the cliffs.

When the French awoke, the British were lined up on the plains, ready to attack. In the short, fierce battle that followed, Wolfe was killed. The French commander, Montcalm, died of his wounds the next day. Quebec surrendered to the British. The **Battle of Quebec** was the turning point of the war. When Montreal fell the next year, all of Canada was in British hands.

Reading**His**
D. Finding M
Ideas How w
the British at
capture Queb

The Treaty of Paris

Britain and France battled in other parts of the world for almost three more years. Spain made a pact in 1761 to aid France, but its help came too late. When the Seven Years' War ended in 1763, Britain had won.

By the **Treaty of Paris,** Britain claimed all of North America east of the Mississippi River. To reward Spain for its help, France gave it New Orleans and Louisiana, the French territory west of the Mississippi. Britain, which had seized Cuba and the Philippines from Spain, gave them back in exchange for Florida. The treaty ended French power in North America.

Background
France kept
a few islands
Newfoundla
and in the W
Indies.

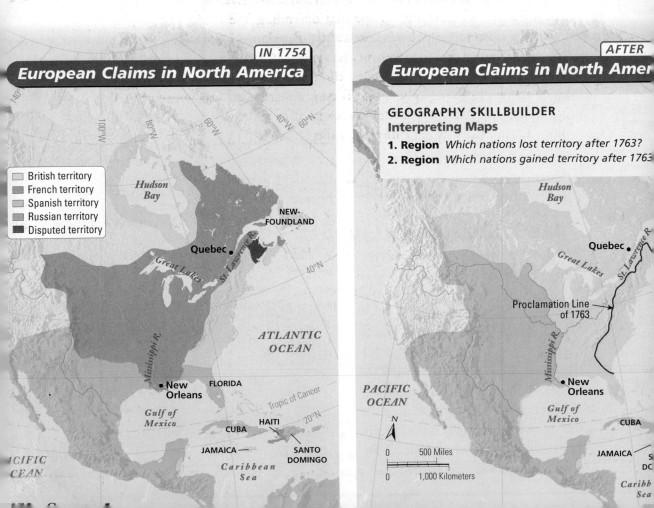

IN 1754
European Claims in North America

- British territory
- French territory
- Spanish territory
- Russian territory
- Disputed territory

Hudson Bay

NEW-FOUNDLAND

Quebec

Great Lakes

St. Lawrence R.

ATLANTIC OCEAN

Mississippi R.

New Orleans

FLORIDA

Tropic of Cancer

Gulf of Mexico

CUBA

HAITI

JAMAICA

SANTO DOMINGO

Caribbean Sea

ACIFIC CEAN

AFTER
European Claims in North Amer

GEOGRAPHY SKILLBUILDER
Interpreting Maps
1. **Region** Which nations lost territory after 1763?
2. **Region** Which nations gained territory after 1763

Hudson Bay

Quebec

Great Lakes

St. Lawrence R.

Proclamation Line of 1763

PACIFIC OCEAN

Mississippi R.

New Orleans

Gulf of Mexico

CUBA

JAMAICA

Caribb Sea

N

0   500 Miles
0   1,000 Kilometers

Pontiac's Rebellion

After French forces withdrew, the British took over their forts. They refused to give supplies to the Native Americans, as the French had. British settlers also moved across the mountains onto Native American land. In the spring and summer of 1763, Native American groups responded by attacking settlers and destroying almost every British fort west of the Appalachians. They surrounded the three remaining forts. This revolt was called **Pontiac's Rebellion,** although the Ottawa war leader Pontiac was only one of many organizers.

British settlers reacted with equal viciousness, killing even Indians who had not attacked them. British officers came up with a brutal plan to end the Delaware siege at Fort Pitt.

Pontiac

A VOICE FROM THE PAST

Could it not be contrived to send the Small Pox among those disaffected [angry] tribes of Indians? We must on this occasion use every stratagem in our power to reduce them.

Major General Jeffrey Amherst, quoted in *The Conspiracy of Pontiac*

The officers invited Delaware war leaders in to talk and then gave them smallpox-infected blankets as gifts. This started a deadly outbreak.

By the fall, the Native Americans had retreated. Even so, the uprising made the British government see that defending Western lands would be costly. Therefore, the British issued the **Proclamation of 1763,** which forbade colonists to settle west of the Appalachians.

The colonists were angry. They thought they had won the right to settle the Ohio River Valley. The British government was angry at the colonists, who did not want to pay for their own defense. This hostility helped cause the war for American independence, as you will read.

Section 3 Assessment

Terms & Names

Explain the significance of:

French and Indian War
Albany Plan of Union
Battle of Quebec
Treaty of Paris
Pontiac's Rebellion
Proclamation of 1763

2. Using Graphics

Write the month and year each battle occurred. Classify each as a French or British victory.

Date	Incident	Victor
	Seizure of Fort Duquesne	
	Surrender of Fort Necessity	
	Braddock's defeat	
	Battle of Quebec	

Which was most important?

3. Main Ideas

a. How did the fur trade contribute to the French and Indian War?

b. Why did the British begin to win the war after 1758?

c. What were some causes and effects of Pontiac's Rebellion?

4. Critical Thinking

Analyzing Points of View
Why did the French, British, and Native Americans fight over the Ohio River Valley?

THINK ABOUT
• how the British viewed the valley
• how the French viewed it
• how the Native Americans viewed it

ACTIVITY OPTIONS

GEOGRAPHY

MUSIC

Learn more about the Battle of Quebec and its setting. Make a three-dimensional **model** of the battle or write a **song** about it.

Beginnings of an American Identity

Separate Colonies

Early American Culture

English colonists shared certain values, such as land ownership and hard work. The Great Awakening and the Enlightenment also drew colonists together.

Roots of Representative Government

English colonists expected the right to elect representatives to government and other political rights that had developed in England over centuries.

The French and Indian War

English colonists were also drawn together as they fought against common enemies—the French and their Native American allies.

Common Identity

TERMS & NAMES

Briefly explain the significance of each of the following.

1. Great Awakening
2. Enlightenment
3. John Peter Zenger
4. Magna Carta
5. Parliament
6. Glorious Revolution
7. Edmund Andros
8. French and Indian War
9. Treaty of Paris
10. Proclamation of 1763

REVIEW QUESTIONS

Early American Culture (pages 135–140)

1. Why did colonists want to own land?
2. What was women's role in the colonial economy?
3. What were the effects of the Great Awakening on colonial culture and politics?

Roots of Representative Government (pages 141–145)

4. Why did colonies have representative assemblies?
5. What was one important right granted in the Magna Carta?
6. How did the Zenger trial help lead to freedom of the press?
7. How was the English Bill of Rights related to the Glorious Revolution?

The French and Indian War (pages 146–151)

8. What was George Washington's role in the French and Indian War?
9. What did England gain as a result of the French and Indian War?
10. What was one reason for Pontiac's Rebellion?

CRITICAL THINKING

1. USING YOUR NOTES: FINDING MAIN IDEAS

Using your completed chart, answer the questions below.

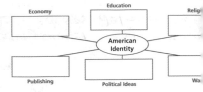

a. What were some political ide shared by people in the American colonies?
b. How was religion important American identity?
c. How did publishing help buil an American identity?

2. THEME: DEMOCRATIC IDEA

What democratic ideals did Americans inherit from Englanc

3. APPLYING CITIZENSHIP SKI

Why is jury duty an example of responsible citizenship?

4. CONTRASTING

How did colonial government d fer from present-day governme in the United States?

5. ANALYZING CAUSES

What do you think was the mo: important cause of the French a Indian War?

6. ANALYZING LEADERSHIP

Give an example of bad militar political leadership from the ch ter. What mistake was made?

Interact *with* Histor

Now that you have read the cha what would you say British colo in America had in common?

se the map and your knowledge of U.S. history to
nswer questions 1 and 2.

dditional Test Practice, pp. S1–S33.

French Explorers on the Mississippi

Where did La Salle's journey begin?

A. Lake Erie

B. Lake Huron

C. Lake Michigan

D. Lake Ontario

2. Along which river did both teams of explorers travel?

A. Illinois River

B. Mississippi River

C. Ohio River

D. Wisconsin River

This is a quotation from Increase Mather about colonial government. Use the quotation and your knowledge of U.S. history to answer question 3.

PRIMARY SOURCE

For all English liberties are restored to them: No Persons shall have a Penny of their Estates taken from them; nor any Laws imposed on them, without their own Consent by Representatives chosen by themselves.

Increase Mather, quoted in *The Last American Puritan*

3. The passage best represents which point of view?

A. The colonists were entitled to the basic rights of English subjects.

B. The colonists' land belonged to the government.

C. Colonists did not have to pay taxes to the English government.

D. Colonists were not entitled to liberties granted to English subjects.

TEST PRACTICE
CLASSZONE.COM

ERNATIVE ASSESSMENT

WRITING ABOUT HISTORY

ng colonial times, children often had to learn
skills. Imagine that you were a young person
g this time. Write a **letter** to your family describ-
our life and the work you do.

e library resources to learn more about the roles
children during colonial times.

plain what you have learned about your work,
d describe what you like or don't like about it.

OOPERATIVE LEARNING

ing in a group, hold a diplomatic council trying
event the French and Indian War. Group members
ssume different roles: English and French officials,
sh settlers, French fur traders, English-allied
ois, French-allied Huron or Algonquin.

INTEGRATED TECHNOLOGY

DOING INTERNET RESEARCH

Colonial American culture was not like modern American culture. Use the Internet to do research about life in 18th century colonial America. Then prepare a dramatic presentation featuring one of the important figures from the time, such as Benjamin Franklin, Madam Sarah Knight, or Pontiac.

- On the Internet, find images, stories, poems, or novels, and articles about daily life, interests, or entertainment in the early and middle 1700s.

- Historical societies or living history museums in the original 13 states may also provide information about this period of time in American history.

For more about colonial American culture . . .

INTERNET ACTIVITY
CLASSZONE.COM

Creating a New Nation

"By the rude bridge . . . the embattled farmers stood and fired the shot heard round the world."

—Ralph Waldo Emerson, "Concord Hymn"

Americans battled British troops at Old North Bridge, Concord, Massachusetts, in April 1775.

The Road to Revolution 1763–1776

Angry confrontations between colonial protestors and British Red Coats became common as the colonies moved towards independence.

1763
Proclamation of 1763 becomes law.

1765
Stamp Act is passed.

1767
Townshend Acts are passed.

Sp
es
pos

**USA
World** 1763

1763
Treaty of Paris ends Seven Years' War in Europe.

1765
Chinese forces invade Burma.

Scotland's James
steam eng
running o

nets, or blades, on rs' gun were very s in close combat.

The fife and drum corps played music to keep soldiers at a steady march. During battle, the drummers beat out orders and the fifers carried messages and stretchers.

The year is 1765. Your neighbors are enraged by Britain's demand that British troops be housed in American cities at American expense. Britain has never done this before. There are protests in many cities. You have to decide what you would do.

Would you join the protest?

What Do You Think?

- What is the best way to show opposition to policies you consider unjust?

- Is there anything to be gained by protesting? Anything to be lost?

- Does government have the right to make demands without consent of the people? Why or why not?

RESEARCH LINKS
CLASSZONE.COM

Visit the Chapter 6 links for more information about the American Revolution.

1772
Captain Cook explores the South Pacific.

cre

1773
Boston Tea Party

1774
Intolerable Acts are passed; First Continental Congress meets.

1774
Reign of Louis XVI begins in France.

1775
Battles of Lexington and Concord

1776
Declaration of Independence is signed.

1776

Reading Strategy: Sequencing Events

What Do You Know?

What do you already know about the time before the Revolution? What were the issues that caused the colonists to choose independence?

Think About
- what you have learned about this period from movies, television, or historical fiction
- reasons people in history have chosen to fight for freedom from oppression
- your responses to the Interact with History about joining the protest (see page 157)

What Do You Want to Know?

What questions do you have about the issues and events that pushed the American colonists toward rebellion? Record them in your notebook before you read the chapter.

Sequencing Events

Sequencing means putting events in the order in which they happen in time. In learning about how the American colonies moved toward independence, it would be helpful to li the important events. Place them in the order in which they occurred. You might record event and its date in a graphic organizer such as the one below. Copy this organizer in y notebook. Fill it in as you read the chapter.

 See Skillbuilder Handbook, page R4.

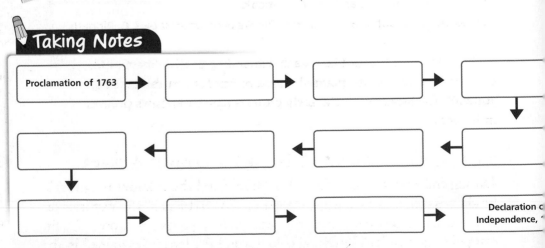

Taking Notes

Proclamation of 1763 →

Declaration of Independence,

1

Tighter British Control

MAIN IDEA	WHY IT MATTERS NOW	TERMS & NAMES
...ans saw British efforts to tax ...d to increase control over the ... as violations of their rights.	Colonial protests were the first steps on the road to American independence.	King George III Stamp Act Quartering Act Patrick Henry revenue boycott Sugar Act Sons of Liberty

ONE AMERICAN'S STORY

James Otis, Jr., a young Massachusetts lawyer, stormed through the streets of Boston one day in 1760. He was furious. His father had just been denied the post of chief justice of the Massachusetts colony by the royal governor. To Otis, this was one more example of Britain's lack of respect for colonial rights. Another example was its use of search warrants that allowed customs officers to enter any home or business to look for smuggled goods. Otis believed these searches were illegal.

In court in February 1761, Otis spoke with great emotion for five hours about the search warrant and its use.

A VOICE FROM THE PAST

It appears to me the worst instrument of arbitrary power, the most destructive of English liberty and the fundamental principles of law, that was ever found in an English law-book.

James Otis, Jr., quoted in *James Otis: The Pre-Revolutionist* by J. C. Ridpath

In making the first public speech demanding English liberties for the colonists, James Otis planted a seed of freedom. In this section, you will read more about the early protests against Britain's policies in America.

James Otis, Jr., argues in court against illegal search warrants in 1761.

The Colonies and Britain Grow Apart

During the French and Indian War, Britain and the colonies fought side by side. Americans took great pride in being partners in the victory over the French. However, when the war ended, problems arose. Britain wanted to govern its 13 original colonies and the territories gained in the war in a uniform way. So the British Parliament in London imposed new laws and restrictions. Previously, the colonies had been allowed to develop largely on their own. Now they felt that their freedom was being limited.

Taking Notes

Use your chart to take notes about the tightening of British control.

Proclamation of 1763 →

The first of Parliament's laws was the Proclamation of 1763. (See Chapter 5.) It said that colonists could not settle west of the Appalachian Mountains. Britain wanted this land to remain in the hands of its Native American allies to prevent another revolt like Pontiac's Rebellion.

The proclamation angered colonists who had hoped to move to the fertile Ohio Valley. Many of these colonists had no land of their own. It also upset colonists who had bought land as an investment. As a result, many ignored the law.

*Reading*His
A. Summariz
Who was up:
by the Procla
tion of 1763

British Troops and Taxes

<u>King George III,</u> the British monarch, wanted to enforce the proclamation and also keep peace with Britain's Native American allies. To do this, he decided to keep 10,000 soldiers in the colonies. In 1765, Parliament passed the **Quartering Act.** This was a cost-saving measure that required the colonies to quarter, or house, British soldiers and provide them with supplies. General Thomas Gage, commander of these forces, put most of the troops in New York.

Britain owed a large debt from the French and Indian War. Keeping troops in the colonies would raise that debt even higher. Britain needed more <u>revenue,</u> or income, to meet its expenses. So it attempted to have the colonies pay part of the war debt. It also wanted them to contribute toward the costs of frontier defense and colonial government.

In the past, the king had asked the colonial assemblies to pass taxes to support military actions that took place in the colonies. This time, however, Parliament voted to tax the Americans directly.

In 1764, Parliament passed the <u>Sugar Act.</u> This law placed a tax on sugar, molasses, and other products shipped to the colonies. It also called for strict enforcement of the act and harsh punishment of smugglers. Colonial merchants, who often traded in smuggled goods, reacted with anger.

Colonial leaders such as James Otis claimed that Parliament had no right to tax the colonies, since the colonists were not represented in Parliament. As Otis exclaimed, "Taxation without representation is tyranny!" British finance minister George Grenville disagreed. The colonists were subjects of Britain, he said, and enjoyed the protection of its laws. For that reason, they were subject to taxation.

Vocabular
tyranny:
absolute po
in the hand
a single rul

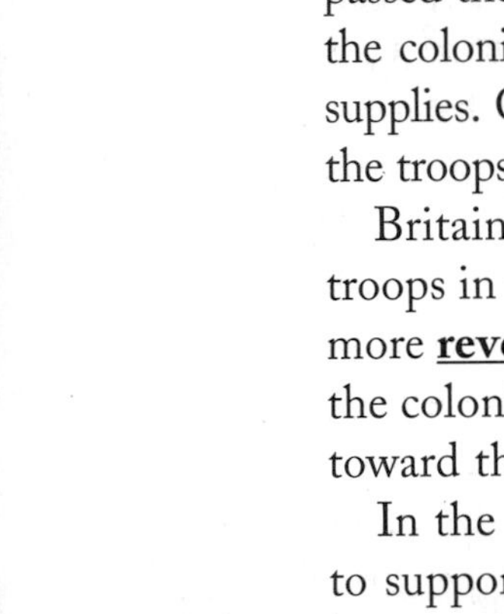

Britain Passes the Stamp Act

The Sugar Act was just the first in a series of acts that increased tension between the mother country and the colonies. In 1765, Parliament passed the <u>Stamp Act.</u> This law required all legal and commercial documents to carry an official stamp showing that a tax had been paid. All diplomas, contracts, and wills had to carry a stamp.

The colonial view of the hated stamp tax is shown by the skull and crossbones on this emblem (above); a royal stamp is pictured at right.

Even published materials such as newspapers had to be written on special stamped paper.

The Stamp Act was a new kind of tax for the colonies. The Sugar Act had been a tax on imported goods. It mainly affected merchants. In contrast, the Stamp Act was a tax applied within the colonies. It fell directly on all colonists. Even more, the colonists had to pay for stamps in silver coin—a scarce item in the colonies.

Colonial leaders vigorously protested. For them, the issue was clear. They were being taxed without their consent by a Parliament in which they had no voice. If Britain could pass the Stamp Act, what other taxes might it pass in the future? Samuel Adams, a leader in the Massachusetts legislature, asked, "Why not our lands? Why not the produce of our lands and, in short, everything we possess and make use of?" **Patrick Henry**, a member of Virginia's House of Burgesses, called for resistance to the tax. When another member shouted that resistance was treason, Henry reportedly replied, "If this be treason, make the most of it!"

The Colonies Protest the Stamp Act

Colonial assemblies and newspapers took up the cry—"No taxation without representation!" In October 1765, nine colonies sent delegates to the Stamp Act Congress in New York City. This was the first time the colonies met to consider acting together in protest. Delegates drew up a petition to the king protesting the Stamp Act. The petition declared that the right to tax the colonies belonged to the colonial assemblies, not to Parliament. Later, colonial merchants organized a **boycott** of British goods. A boycott is a refusal to buy.

Meanwhile, some colonists formed secret societies to oppose British policies. The most famous of these groups was the **Sons of Liberty**. Many Sons of Liberty were lawyers, merchants, and craftspeople—the colonists most affected by the Stamp Act. These groups staged protests against the act.

Not all of their protests were peaceful. The Sons of Liberty burned the stamped paper whenever they could find it. They also attacked customs officials, whom they covered with hot tar and feathers and paraded in public. Fearing for their safety, many customs officials quit their jobs.

The protests in the colonies had an effect in Britain. Merchants thought that their trade with America would be hurt. Some British political leaders, including

ing **History**
king
nces Why
e colonists
t goods?

ground
e their
ts, the
f Liberty in
met
a huge,
ar-old elm
at they
the Liberty

Colonists protest the Stamp Act.

THE FOLLY OF ENGLAND AND THE RUIN OF AMERICA

Bostonians Paying the Taxman

In this British political cartoon, Americans are depicted as barbarians who would tar and feather a customs official, or tax collector, and pour hot tea down his throat.

A Liberty Tree as a gallows

B Stamp Act posted upside down

C Protesters in Boston

D Customs official tarred and feathered

the popular parliamentary leader William Pitt, agreed with American thinking about taxing the colonies. Pitt spoke out against the Stamp Act.

A VOICE FROM THE PAST

The Americans have not acted in all things with prudence and [good] temper. They have been driven to madness by injustice. Will you punish them for the madness you have [caused]? . . . My opinion . . . is that the Stamp Act be repealed absolutely, totally and immediately.

William Pitt, quoted in *Patriots* by A. J. Langguth

Parliament finally saw that the Stamp Act was a mistake and repealed it in 1766. But at the same time, Parliament passed another law—the Declaratory Act. This law said that Parliament had supreme authority to govern the colonies. The Americans celebrated the repeal of the Stamp Act and tried to ignore the Declaratory Act. A great tug of war between Parliament and the colonies had begun. The central issue was control of the colonies, as you will learn in the next section.

Reading **Hi**
C. Drawing
Conclusions
was it impo
for Parliame
to pass the
Declaratory

Section 1 Assessment

1. Terms & Names

Explain the significance of:

- King George III
- Quartering Act
- revenue
- Sugar Act
- Stamp Act
- Patrick Henry
- boycott
- Sons of Liberty

2. Using Graphics

Use a cluster diagram like the one below to review points of conflict between Britain and the colonies.

Points of Conflict

Which do you think was the most serious? Explain.

3. Main Ideas

a. Why did the Proclamation of 1763 anger colonists?

b. How did colonists react to the Stamp Act?

c. What was the goal of secret societies such as the Sons of Liberty?

4. Critical Thinking

Analyzing Points of Vi
What were the two sides
the debate over British ta
tion of the colonies?

THINK ABOUT

- how Parliament viewe
  the colonies
- what concerned the
  colonists about taxes

ACTIVITY OPTIONS

ART

MUSIC

Imagine that you are a colonial leader who wants to get your fellow colonists to protest British policy. Design a **poster** or write a **song of protest**.

2

Colonial Resistance Grows

MAIN IDEA

Americans began to organize
ose British policies.

WHY IT MATTERS NOW

Americans continue to protest what
they view as wrongs and injustices.

TERMS & NAMES

Crispus Attucks

Townshend Acts

writs of assistance

Samuel Adams

Boston Massacre

John Adams

committee of
   correspondence

Boston Tea Party

ONE AMERICAN'S STORY

<u>Crispus Attucks</u> knew about the struggle for freedom. The son of an
African-American father and a Native American mother, Attucks was
born into slavery in Framingham, Massachusetts, around 1723. As a
young man, Attucks escaped by running away to sea.

In March 1770, Attucks found himself in Boston, where feelings
against British rule were hot. One night Attucks took part in a
disturbance between colonists and British troops. He was about to
play a key role in U.S. history—losing his life to a British bullet in a
protest that came to be called the Boston Massacre. In Section 2, you
will read how tension between Britain and its colonies led to violence.

Crispus Attucks, a
sailor of African-
American and Native
American ancestry,
was an early hero of
America's struggle
for freedom.

The Townshend Acts Are Passed

After the uproar over the Stamp Act, Britain hoped to avoid further
conflict. Even so, it still needed to raise money to pay for troops and
other expenses in America. The Quartering Act was not working.
Most of the British army was in New York, and New York saw that as
an unfair burden. Its assembly refused to pay to house the troops.

The king's finance minister, Charles Townshend, told Parliament that he
had a way to raise revenue in the colonies. So in 1767, Parliament passed
his plan, known as the **Townshend Acts**.

The first of the Townshend Acts suspended New York's assembly until
New Yorkers agreed to provide housing for the troops. The other acts
placed duties, or import taxes, on various goods brought into the
colonies, such as glass, paper, paint, lead, and tea. Townshend thought
that duties, which were collected before the goods entered the colonies,
would anger the colonists less than the direct taxes of the Stamp Act.
The money raised would be used to pay the salaries of British governors
and other officials in the colonies. To enforce the acts, British officers

✏ Taking Notes

Use your chart to
take notes about
colonial resistance.

Proclamation
of 1763 ➔ [ ]

would use **writs of assistance,** or search warrants, to enter homes or businesses to search for smuggled goods.

The Reasons for Protest

Protests immediately broke out at news of the Townshend Acts. New Yorkers were angry that their elected assembly had been suspended. People throughout the colonies were upset that Britain was placing new taxes on them. "The issue," said John Dickinson, an important Pennsylvania lawyer, was "whether Parliament can legally take money out of our pockets without our consent." He explained his opposition to the Townshend Acts in essays called *Letters from a Farmer in Pennsylvania,* published in 1767.

WOMEN AND PROTEST

Women were not allowed to participate in political life in the colonies. So their role in protesting British actions was not as prominent as that of men. However, women made their beliefs known by taking part in demonstrations.

Also, some women formed the Daughters of Liberty. This was a patriotic organization that joined in the boycott of British tea and other goods. The refusal of these colonial women to use British imports caused them personal hardship. They were forced to make many of the boycotted items, such as clothing, themselves.

A VOICE FROM THE PAST

Let these truths be . . . impressed on our minds—that we cannot be happy without being free—that we cannot be free without being secure in our property—that we cannot be secure in our property if without our consent others may . . . take it away—that taxes imposed on us by Parliament do thus take it away—that duties laid for the sole purpose of raising money are taxes—that attempts to lay such duties should be instantly and firmly opposed.

John Dickinson, quoted in *A New Age Now Begins* by Page Smith

Reading **His**

A. Making Inferences does Dickins believe that interfere wi happiness?

The colonists were also angry about the writs of assistance. Many believed, as James Otis had argued (see page 159), that the writs went against their natural rights. These rights had been described by English philosopher John Locke during the Enlightenment. The law of nature, said Locke, teaches that "no one ought to harm another in his life, health, liberty, or possessions." The colonists felt that the Townshend Acts were a serious threat to their rights and freedoms.

Tools of Protest

To protest the Townshend Acts, colonists in Boston announced another boycott of British goods in October 1767. The driving force behind this protest was **Samuel Adams,** a leader of the Boston Sons of Liberty. Adams urged colonists to continue to resist British controls.

The boycott spread throughout the colonies. The Sons of Liberty pressured shopkeepers not to sell imported goods. The Daughters of Liberty called on colonists to weave their own cloth and use American products. As a result, trade with Britain fell sharply.

Colonial leaders asked for peaceful protests. Articles in the *Boston Gazette* asked the people to remain calm—

This engraving, *The Bloody Massacre Perpetrated in King Street* by Boston silversmith Paul Revere, appeared in the *Boston Gazette*.

"no mobs. . . . Constitutional methods are best." However, tempers were running high. When customs officers in Boston tried to seize the American merchant ship *Liberty*, which was carrying smuggled wine, a riot broke out. The rioters forced the customs officers to flee.

Fearing a loss of control, officials called for more British troops. A defiant Samuel Adams replied, "We will destroy every soldier that dares put his foot on shore. . . . I look upon them as foreign enemies."

The Boston Massacre

In the fall of 1768, 1,000 British soldiers (known as redcoats for their bright red jackets) arrived in Boston under the command of General Thomas Gage. With their arrival, tension filled the streets of Boston.

Since the soldiers were poorly paid, they hired themselves out as workers, usually at rates lower than those of American workers. Resentment against the redcoats grew. Soldiers and street youths often yelled insults at each other. "Lobsters for sale!" the youths would yell, referring to the soldiers' red coats. "Yankees!" the soldiers jeered. *Yankee* was supposed to be an insult, but the colonists soon took pride in the name.

On March 5, 1770, tensions finally exploded into violence. A group of youths and dockworkers—among them Crispus Attucks—started trading insults in front of the Custom House. A fight broke out, and the soldiers began firing. Attucks and four laborers were killed.

The Sons of Liberty called the shooting the **Boston Massacre**. They said that Attucks and the four others had given their lives for freedom. The incident became a tool for anti-British propaganda in newspaper articles, pamphlets, and posters. The people of Boston were outraged.

Meanwhile, the redcoats who had fired the shots were arrested for murder. **John Adams,** a lawyer and cousin of Samuel Adams, defended them in court. Adams was criticized for taking the case. He replied that the law should be "deaf . . . to the clamors of the populace." He supported

activity
the Boston
re . . .

MULATION
NE.COM

gHistory
gnizing
anda How
use of the
assacre
anti-
iew?

SAMUEL ADAMS
1722–1803

Samuel Adams was a Harvard graduate. But unlike his cousin John, also a Harvard graduate, he showed little skill for the law. Later, when he took control of the family business, he lost his father's fortune. Yet he succeeded in one important undertaking—moving America toward independence.

Adams's true talent lay in rousing people to action in support of a cause. A fiery orator and a master of propaganda, he used words as a weapon. One British official said that "every dip of his pen stings."

JOHN ADAMS
1735–1826

John Adams, unlike Samuel, was considered a moderate in the struggle against Britain. He was an important voice of reason and at first opposed resisting by force.

Adams believed in the rule of law. He called his defense of the soldiers in the Boston Massacre "one of the best pieces of service I ever rendered my country."

Eventually, Adams became convinced that only outright resistance would gain liberty for America. He said, "Britain has at last driven America, to the last Step, a compleat Seperation from her."

How did the cousins John and Samuel Adams differ in the way they protested British actions?

the colonial cause but wanted to show that the colonists followed the rule of law. Adams argued that the soldiers had acted in self-defense. The jury agreed. To many colonists, however, the Boston Massacre would stand as a symbol of British tyranny.

The Tea Act

The colonists were unaware that on the day of the Boston Massacre, Parliament proposed the repeal of the Townshend Acts. One month later, all the acts except the tax on tea were repealed. The colonial boycott had been effective—British trade had been hurt. But Parliament kept the tea tax to show that it still had the right to tax the colonists. For most Americans, the crisis was over.

Samuel Adams, however, wanted to make sure people did not forget the cause of liberty. He started a drive to form **committees of correspondence** in various towns in Massachusetts. These groups exchanged letters on colonial affairs. Before long, committees throughout Massachusetts were corresponding with one another and with committees in other colonies.

Then, in 1773, Parliament opened up old wounds when it passed the Tea Act. Tea was very popular in the colonies, but much of it was smuggled in from Holland. The Tea Act gave the British East India Company control over the American tea trade. The tea would arrive in the colonies only in the trading company's ships and be sold there by its merchants. Colonists who had not been paying any tax on smuggled tea would now have to pay a tax on this regulated tea. This enraged colonial shippers and merchants. The colonists wondered what Parliament would do next.

Reading **H**
C. Drawing
Conclusion
Why did Sa
Adams thir
the colonis
might forg
cause of lib

The Boston Tea Party

Protests against the Tea Act took place all over the colonies. In Charleston, South Carolina, colonists unloaded tea and let it rot on the docks. In New York City and Philadelphia, colonists blocked tea ships from landing. In Boston, the Sons of Liberty organized what came to be known as the **Boston Tea Party**.

Colonists dumped hundreds of chests of tea into Boston Harbor in 1773 to protest the Tea Act.

On the evening of December 16, 1773, a group of men disguised as Native Americans boarded three tea ships docked in Boston Harbor. One of the men, George Hewes, a Boston shoemaker, later recalled the events.

ding **History**

ading a
Find Boston
r on the
on page 172.

A VOICE FROM THE PAST

We then were ordered by our commander to open the hatches and take out all the chests of tea and throw them overboard. . . . In about three hours from the time we went on board, we had thus broken and thrown overboard every tea chest to be found on the ship, while those in the other ships were disposing of the tea in the same way, at the same time.

George Hewes, quoted in *A Retrospect of the Boston Tea-Party*

That night, Hewes and the others destroyed 342 chests of tea. Many colonists rejoiced at the news. They believed that Britain would now see how strongly colonists opposed taxation without representation.

Others doubted that destroying property was the best way to settle the tax debate. Some colonial leaders offered to pay for the tea if Parliament would repeal the Tea Act. Britain rejected the offer. It not only wanted repayment, but it also wanted the men who destroyed the tea to be brought to trial. The British reaction to the Boston Tea Party would fan the flames of rebellion in the 13 colonies, as you will read in the next section.

ing **History**

ognizing
How did
react to
Party?

tion ❷ Assessment

Terms & Names	2. Using Graphics	3. Main Ideas	4. Critical Thinking
plain the gnificance of:	Create a time line like the one below to show the significant people and events described in this section.	**a.** Why did colonists oppose the Townshend Acts?	**Drawing Conclusions** Do you think colonial outrage over the Boston Massacre was justified? Explain.
rispus Attucks		**b.** Why were British troops sent to Boston?	
ownshend Acts			
rits of assistance	1767 1773	**c.** What prompted the Boston Tea Party?	**THINK ABOUT**
muel Adams			• how the British troops were taunted
oston Massacre			
hn Adams	Which event do you think was the most important? Explain.		• whether troops have the right to fire on citizens
mmittee of rrespondence			
oston Tea Party			

VITY OPTIONS

SPEECH

ECHNOLOGY

Read more about the Boston Massacre or the Boston Tea Party. Present an **oral report** or plan a **multimedia presentation** about the event.

Fight for Representative Government

You are a colonist living in Boston on the eve of the American Revolution. Nearly a decade of protest against British policies has failed to secure American rights. Redcoats continue to be quartered in the city. The Tea Act still stands. Now the dumping of tea in Boston Harbor by some Patriots has charged the atmosphere with tension. Trouble lies ahead, but you are determined to fight for a government that will protect your rights.

COOPERATIVE LEARNING On this page are two challenges that you face as the conflict with Britain unfolds. Working with a small group, decide how to deal with each challenge. Choose an option, assign a task to each group member, and do the activity. You will find useful information in the Data File. Present your solutions to the class.

ART CHALLENGE

"Do not . . . sip the accursed, dutied STUFF"

People all over Boston are worried about the Tea Act. It taxes tea, but it also lets the British East India Company sell tea through its own agents. In time, the plan could drive American tea sellers out of business. How can you protest these threats to American commerce and liberty? Present your viewpoint using one of these options:

- Design an anti–Tea Act poster.
- Draw a political cartoon showing the dangers of the Tea Act.

"Wear none but your own country linen"

ears of struggle have taken their toll on Boston. People
e tired of soldiers and of boycotting British goods, such as
othing. But the Tea Act presents a huge threat. The Boston
a Party took care of only one shipment. How can you help
ncourage the boycott of other British goods, such as cloth-
g? Look at the Data File for help. Present your appeal using
e of these options:

Make a graph showing the effect of colonial boycotts on
mports of British goods to America.

Write an editorial using statistics to show how American
oycotts have hurt the British.

sent to the Class Meet as a group to review your responses to
ish attacks on American liberty. Pick the most creative solution
each challenge and present these solutions to the class.

DATA FILE

Population in 1774–1775

Britain: 7,860,000
  London: 700,000

The 13 colonies: 2,350,000
  Philadelphia: 33,000
  New York: 22,000
  Boston: 16,000

North American Imports from Britain

(in millions of pounds sterling)

Year		Year	
1763	1.6	1770	1.9
1764	2.3	1771	4.2
1765	1.9	1772	3.0
1766	1.8	1773	2.1
1767	1.9	1774	2.6
1768	2.2	1775	0.2
1769	1.3	1776	0.1

North American Exports to Britain

(in millions of pounds sterling)

Year		Year	
1763	1.1	1770	1.0
1764	1.1	1771	1.3
1765	1.2	1772	1.3
1766	1.0	1773	1.4
1767	1.1	1774	1.4
1768	1.3	1775	1.9
1769	1.1	1776	0.1

Key Boycott Dates

1764 Boycott after passage of Sugar Act
1765 Boycott after passage of Stamp Act
1766 Boycott relaxed after Stamp Act repealed
1767 Boycott after passage of Townshend Acts
1770 Townshend Acts repealed
1774 Boycott after passage of Intolerable Acts

Sales and Consumption of Tea at the Time of the Boston Tea Party

British sales: fourth most important product shipped to America
American consumption: 1.2 million pounds per year

For more on Revolutionary America . . .

RESEARCH LINKS
CLASSZONE.COM

The Road to Lexington and Concord

MAIN IDEA	WHY IT MATTERS NOW	TERMS & NAMES
The tensions between Britain and the colonies led to armed conflict in Massachusetts.	Americans at times still find themselves called upon to fight for their principles.	militia — Paul Rever... Minuteman — Lexington Concord Intolerable Acts — Loyalist First Continental Congress — Patriot

ONE AMERICAN'S STORY

On April 19, 1775, some 70 militiamen led by Captin John Parker gathered in Lexington, Massachusetts, a town near Boston. A **militia** is a force of armed civilians pledged to defend their community. About one-third of the Lexington militia were **Minutemen**, trained to "act at a minute's warning." They had heard that the British were coming.

Parker's troops had never faced soldiers. Soon they would meet the British on Lexington Green in the first battle of the Revolutionary War. According to tradition, Parker told his men, "Stand your ground; don't fire unless fired upon, but if they mean to have war, let it begin here."

In this section, you will read how colonial protests led to revolution.

This statue
Captain Jo...
stands in L...
Massachus...

Taking Notes

Use your chart to take notes about the beginning of the American Revolution.

oclamation
of 1763 →

The Intolerable Acts

The Boston Tea Party had aroused fury in Britain. One British official said that the people of Boston "ought to be knocked about their ears." King George III declared, "We must master them or totally leave them to themselves and treat them as aliens." Britain chose to "master" the colonies.

In 1774, Parliament passed a series of laws to punish the Massachusetts colony and to serve as a warning to other colonies. The British called these laws the Coercive Acts, but they were so harsh that the colonists called them the **Intolerable Acts**.

One of the acts would close the port of Boston until colonists paid for the destroyed tea. Others banned committees of correspondence, allowed Britain to house troops wherever necessary, and let British officials accused of crimes in the colonies stand trial in Britain. To enforce the acts, Parliament appointed General Thomas Gage governor of Massachusetts.

In 1773, Sam Adams had written, "I wish we could arouse the continent." The Intolerable Acts answered his wish. Other colonies immediately offered Massachusetts their support. They sent food and money to Boston. The committees of correspondence also called for a meeting of colonial delegates to discuss what to do next.

The First Continental Congress Meets

In September 1774, delegates from all the colonies except Georgia met in Philadelphia. At this meeting, called the **First Continental Congress,** delegates voted to ban all trade with Britain until the Intolerable Acts were repealed. They also called on each colony to begin training troops. Georgia agreed to be a part of the actions of the Congress even though it had voted not to send delegates.

The First Continental Congress marked a key step in American history. Although most delegates were not ready to call for independence, they were determined to uphold colonial rights. This meeting planted the seeds of a future independent government. John Adams called it "a nursery of American statesmen." The delegates agreed to meet in seven months, if necessary. By that time, however, fighting with Britain had begun.

Between War and Peace

The colonists hoped that the trade boycott would force a repeal of the Intolerable Acts. After all, past boycotts had led to the repeal of the Stamp Act and the Townshend Acts. This time, however, Parliament stood firm. It even increased restrictions on colonial trade and sent more troops.

By the end of 1774, some colonists were preparing to fight. In Massachusetts, John Hancock headed the Committee of Safety, which had the power to call out the militia. The colonial troops continued to train.

ing **History**

aluating
do you
the First
nental
ress was
tant?

CAUSE AND EFFECT: *Growing Conflict Between Britain and America*

DATE	BRITISH ACTION		COLONIAL REACTION
1763	Proclamation of 1763 issued	▶	Proclamation leads to anger
1765	Stamp Act passed	▶	Boycott of British goods; Stamp Act Resolves passed
1766	Stamp Act repealed; Declaration Act passed	▶	Boycott ended
1767	Townshend Acts passed	▶	New boycotts; Boston Massacre (March 1770)
1770	Townshend Acts repealed (April)	▶	Tension between colonies and Britain reduced
1773	Tea Act passed	▶	Boston Tea Party
1774	Intolerable Acts passed	▶	First Continental Congress bans trade; militias organized
1775	Troops ordered to Lexington and Concord, Massachusetts	▶	Militia fights British troops; Second Continental Congress; Continental Army established

SKILLBUILDER Interpreting Charts
1. *What British action caused the first violence in the growing conflict between Britain and America?*
2. *How might the Intolerable Acts be seen as a reaction as well as an action?*

Most colonial leaders believed that any fight with Britain would be short. They thought that a show of force would make Britain change its policies. Few expected a war. One who did was Patrick Henry.

> **A VOICE FROM THE PAST**
>
> Gentlemen may cry peace, peace—but there is no peace. The war is actually begun! The next gale that sweeps from the north will bring to our ears the clash of resounding arms! Our brethren are already in the field! Why should we idle here? . . . I know not what course others may take. But as for me, give me liberty or give me death.
>
> **Patrick Henry,** quoted in *Patriots* by A. J. Langguth

Henry delivered what became his most famous speech in the Virginia House of Burgesses in March 1775.

The Midnight Ride

Meanwhile, spies were busy on both sides. Sam Adams had built a spy network to keep watch over British activities. The British had their spies too. They were Americans who were loyal to Britain. From them, General Gage learned that the Massachusetts militia was storing arms and ammunition in Concord, about 20 miles northwest of Boston. He also heard that Sam Adams and John Hancock were in Lexington. On the night of April 18, 1775, Gage ordered his troops to arrest Adams and Hancock in Lexington and to destroy the supplies in Concord.

The Sons of Liberty had prepared for this moment. **Paul Revere,** a Boston silversmith, and a second messenger, William Dawes, were charged with spreading the news about British troop movements. Revere had arranged a system of signals to alert colonists in Charlestown, on the shore opposite Boston. If one lantern burned in the Old North Church steeple, the British troops were coming by land; if two, they were coming by water. Revere would go across the water from Boston to Charlestown and ride to Lexington and Concord from there. Dawes would take the land route.

Reading **Hi**
B. Recogniz
Effects Wha
effect migh
ing have ha
the people
of Boston?

Backgrou
The signals
a backup sy
in case Reve
was captur

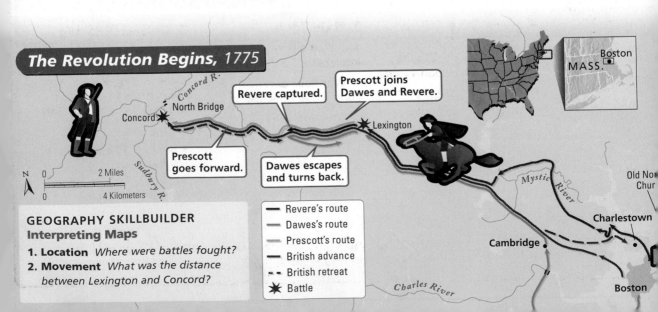

The Revolution Begins, *1775*

Revere captured.

Prescott joins
Dawes and Revere.

Concord — North Bridge

Prescott
goes forward.

Dawes escapes
and turns back.

Lexington

Old No
Chur

Charlestown

Cambridge

Concord R.

Sudbury R.

Mystic River

Charles River

Boston

N
0   2 Miles
0   4 Kilometers

GEOGRAPHY SKILLBUILDER
Interpreting Maps
1. **Location** *Where were battles fought?*
2. **Movement** *What was the distance between Lexington and Concord?*

— Revere's route
— Dawes's route
— Prescott's route
— British advance
-- British retreat
✶ Battle

MASS.
Boston

When the British moved, so did Revere and Dawes. They galloped over the countryside on their "midnight ride," spreading the news. In Lexington, they were joined by Dr. Samuel Prescott. When Revere and Dawes were stopped by a British patrol, Prescott broke away and carried the message to Concord.

Lexington and Concord

At dawn on April 19, some 700 British troops reached Lexington. They found Captain John Parker and about 70 militiamen waiting. The British commander ordered the Americans to drop their muskets. They refused. No one knows who fired first, but within a few minutes eight militiamen lay dead. The British then marched to Concord, where they destroyed military supplies. A battle broke out at a bridge north of town, forcing the British to retreat.

Nearly 4,000 Minutemen and militiamen arrived in the area. They lined the road from Concord to Lexington and peppered the retreating redcoats with musket fire. "It seemed as if men came down from the clouds," one soldier said. Only the arrival of 1,000 more troops saved the British from destruction as they scrambled back to Boston.

Lexington and Concord were the first battles of the Revolutionary War. As Ralph Waldo Emerson later wrote, colonial troops had fired the "shot heard 'round the world." Americans would now have to choose sides and back up their political opinions by force of arms. Those who supported the British were called **Loyalists**. Those who sided with the rebels were **Patriots**. The conflict between the two sides divided communities, families, and friends. The war was on!

ground
losses
d 273 sol-
:ompared to
itiamen.

'ing History
wing
usions
lid Emerson
the "shot
'round
orld"?

Now and then

PATRIOTS' DAY

The "shot heard 'round the world" is celebrated every year in Massachusetts and Maine. Patriots' Day, as it is called, is the third Monday of April. In Concord and nearby towns, modern-day Minutemen like those below reenact the battle that began the Revolution on April 19, 1775. The Boston Marathon is also run on Patriots' Day.

---

tion ③ Assessment

Terms & Names

plain the gnificance of:
- ilitia
- linuteman
- ntolerable Acts
- rst Continental ongress
- aul Revere
- exington and oncord
- oyalist
- atriot

2. Using Graphics

Use a diagram like the one below to show events that led to the Revolutionary War.

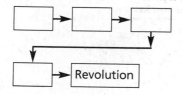

3. Main Ideas

a. Why did Britain pass the Intolerable Acts?

b. Who took part in the First Continental Congress?

c. What was the purpose of the "midnight ride"?

4. Critical Thinking

Supporting Opinions

Do you think the fighting between Britain and the colonies could have been avoided? Why or why not?

THINK ABOUT
- Britain's attitude toward the colonies
- colonial feelings about Britain

IVITY OPTIONS

EOGRAPHY

MATH

Research the Battles of Lexington and Concord. Draw a **map** of key events or create a **chart** showing statistics from the battles.

From

JOHNNY
TREMAIN

by Esther Forbes

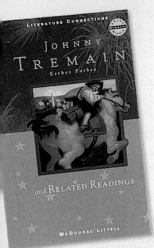

In 1775, 16-year-old Johnny Tremain lives in Boston and works as a delivery boy for a newspaper. Because he travels so much around the city, he is able to help the Patriots gather information about what the British are doing.

On the night of April 18, Johnny learns that British troops will be leaving on an expedition to seize the gunpowder at Lexington and Concord. He rushes to tell this news to Dr. Joseph Warren, who is a Patriot. Then Johnny goes to bed, wondering if the war has started and worried about his friend Rab, who has gone to join the Minutemen at Lexington.

So Johnny slept. It was daylight when he woke with Warren's hand upon his shoulder. Outside on Tremont Street he could hear the clumping of army boots. A sergeant was swearing at his men. The soldiers were paraded so close to the house, which stood **flush**[1] with the sidewalk-less street, that Johnny at first thought they must be in the room.

Doctor Warren dared speak no louder than a whisper.

"I'm going now."

"Something's happened?"

"Yes." He motioned Johnny to follow him into the kitchen. This room was on the back of the house. They could talk without danger of being overheard by the troops in the street.

Doctor Warren had on the same clothes as the day before. He had not been to bed. But now his hat was on his head. His black bag of instruments and medicines was packed and on the table. Silently he put milk, bread, herrings be[...] it, and gestured to Johnny to join him.

"Where did it begin?" asked Johnny.

"Lexington."

"Who won?"

"They did. Seven hundred against seven[...] wasn't a battle. It was . . . just target practic[...] for them. Some of our men were killed an[...] British **huzzaed**[2] and took the road to Conc[...]

"And did they get our supplies there?"

"I don't know. Paul Revere sent for m[...] after the firing on Lexington Green."

The young man's usually fresh-colored[...] was **haggard**[3]. He knew the seriousness o[...] day for himself and for his country.

"But everywhere the alarm is sprea[...] Men are grabbing their guns—marching[...] Concord. Paul Revere did get through in[...] last night. Billy Dawes a little later. Hundre[...] maybe thousands—of Minute Men are o[...] march. Before the day's over, there'll be[...] fighting—not target practice. But Gage d[...] know that it's begun. You see, long b[...] Colonel Smith got to Lexington—just as[...] as he heard that Revere had warned the [...] try—he sent back for reinforcements. For[...] Percy. You and I, Johnny, are just about the[...] people in Boston who know that bloo[...] already been shed."

"Were many killed—at Lexington?"

"No, not many. They stood up—just a [...] ful. The British fired on them. It was dawr[...]

Johnny licked his lips. "Did they tell y[...] names of those killed?"

---

1. **flush:** in a line with.

2. **huzzaed:** cheered.

3. **haggard:** tired.

"No. Did Rab get out in time?"

"Yes. Last Sunday."

The Doctor's clear blue eyes darkened. He
[k]new what was in Johnny's mind. He picked up
[his b]ag. "I've got to get to them. They'll need sur-
[geon]s. Then, too, I'd rather die fighting than on
[gal]lows. Gage won't be so **lenient**[4] now—soon
[as h]e learns war has begun."

"Wait until I get my shoes on."

"No, Johnny, you are to stay here today. Pick
[up f]or me any information. For instance, out of
[my b]edroom window I can see soldiers standing
[the] length of the street 'way over to the
[Com]mon. You find out what regiments are being
[sent]—and all that. And today go about and lis-
[ten t]o what folk are saying. And the names of any
[the] British arrest. We know Gage expects to
[have] his men back here tonight. If so, there'll be
[lots] of confusion getting them into town. You
[watc]h your chance and slip out to me."

"Where'll I find you?"

". . . Ask about."

"I will do so."

"They've begun it. We'll end it, but this war
[it] may last quite a long time."

[len]ient: not strict.

[sur]gery: operating room.

[Britis]h troops fire on the Lexington militia
[on Ap]ril 19, 1775. The war begins here!

They shook hands silently. Johnny knew that
Warren was always conscious of the fact that he
had a crippled hand. Everybody else had
accepted and forgotten it. The back door closed
softly. Warren was gone.

Johnny went to the **surgery**,[5] put on his
boots and jacket. The wall clock said eight
o'clock. It was time to be about. There was no
leaving by the front door. The soldiers were
leaning against it. Through the curtains of the
windows he could see the muskets. He noticed
the facings on their uniforms. The Twenty-
Third Regiment. The narrow course of Tremont
Street was filled to the brim and overflowing
with the waiting scarlet-coated men. Like a river
of blood. He left by the kitchen.

CONNECT TO HISTORY

1. **Recognizing Effects** What
was Johnny's reaction to the
news about Lexington? Discuss
what roles Johnny and Dr.
Warren were to play in the early
days of the Revolutionary War.

 See Skillbuilder Handbook,
page R11.

CONNECT TO TODAY

2. **Researching** Where are there
revolutions in the world today?

For more about revolutions . . .

RESEARCH LINKS
CLASSZONE.COM

Declaring Independence

MAIN IDEA	WHY IT MATTERS NOW	TERMS & NAMES	
Fighting between American and British troops led the colonies to declare their independence.	The United States of America was founded at this time.	Ethan Allen artillery Second Continental Congress Continental Army	Benedict Declarati Indepe Thomas .

ONE AMERICAN'S STORY

Abigail Adams and her husband, John Adams, would spend most of the Revolutionary War apart. He was often away in Philadelphia meeting with other Patriot leaders. In his absence, she ran the household and farm in Braintree, Massachusetts, and raised their four children. During their separation, they exchanged many letters. Abigail was a very sharp observer of the political scene. In one letter, she shared her concerns about the future of the American government.

A VOICE FROM THE PAST

If we separate from Britain, what Code of Laws will be established? How shall we be governed so as to retain our Liberties? Can any government be free which is not administered by general stated Laws? Who shall frame these Laws? Who will give them force and energy?

Abigail Adams, quoted in *Abigail Adams: Witness to a Revolution* by Natalie S. Bober

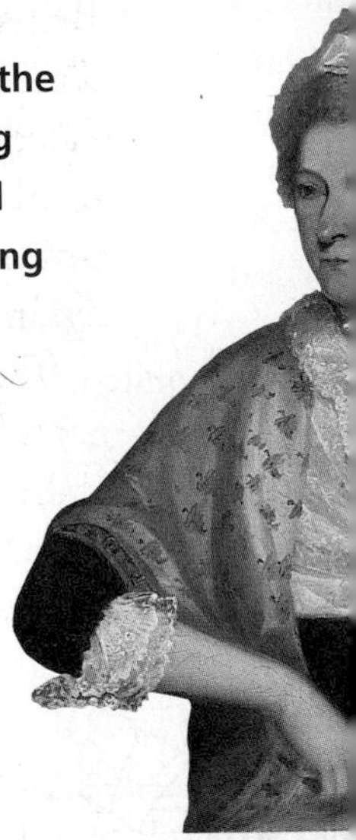

Abigail Ad an early ac women's r one of the letter writ in history.

These questions would be answered later. First, a war had to be fought and won.

aking Notes

se your chart to ke notes about e start of the evolution and the eclaration of dependence.

clamation of 1763 → [ ]

The Continental Army Is Formed

After the fighting at Lexington and Concord, militiamen from Massachusetts and other colonies began gathering around Boston. Their numbers eventually reached some 20,000. General Gage decided to move his soldiers from the peninsula opposite Boston to the city itself. Boston was nearly surrounded by water. This fact, he thought, made a colonial attack by land almost impossible.

Not long after, on May 10, 1775, Americans attacked Britain's Fort Ticonderoga on the New York side of Lake Champlain. **Ethan Allen** led this band of backwoodsmen known as the Green Mountain Boys. They captured the fort and its large supply of **artillery**—cannon and large guns. These guns would be used later to drive the British from Boston.

Also on May 10, the **Second Continental Congress** began meeting in Philadelphia. Delegates included John and Samuel Adams, John Hancock, Benjamin Franklin, George Washington, and Patrick Henry. They agreed to form the **Continental Army**. Washington, who was from Virginia, was chosen as its commanding general. He had served as a colonial officer with the British during the French and Indian War. Congress also authorized the printing of paper money to pay the troops. It was beginning to act as a government.

The Battle of Bunker Hill

xground
pattle was
d Bunker Hill
use the origi-
lan was to
the battle

Meanwhile, tensions were building in Boston in June 1775. Militiamen seized Bunker Hill and Breed's Hill behind Charlestown. They built fortifications on Breed's Hill. Alarmed, the British decided to attack.

General William Howe crossed the bay with 2,200 British soldiers. Forming in ranks, they marched up Breed's Hill. On the hilltop, the militia waited. According to the legend, Colonel William Prescott ordered, "Don't fire until you see the whites of their eyes!" When the British got close, the militia unleashed murderous fire. The British fell back and then charged again. Finally, they forced the militia off the hill.

"Don't fire until you see the whites of their eyes!"
Colonel William Prescott

The redcoats had won the Battle of Bunker Hill, but at tremendous cost. More than 1,000 were killed or wounded, compared with some 400 militia casualties. "The loss we have sustained is greater than we can bear," wrote General Gage. The inexperienced colonial militia had held its own against the world's most powerful army.

The bloody fighting between militiamen and British troops is shown in *The Death of General Warren at Bunker Hill* by John Trumbull (1786).

A Last Attempt at Peace

Despite this deepening conflict, most colonists still hoped for peace. Even some Patriot leaders considered themselves loyal subjects of the king. They blamed Parliament for the terrible events taking place.

In July 1775, moderates in Congress drafted the Olive Branch Petition and sent it to London. This document asked the king to restore harmony between Britain and the colonies. Some members opposed the petition but signed it anyway as a last hope.

The king rejected the petition, however, and announced new measures to punish the colonies. He would use the British navy to block American ships from leaving their ports. He also would send thousands of hired German soldiers, called Hessians, to fight in America. "When once these rebels have felt a smart blow, they will submit," he declared.

The colonial forces were not going to back down, though. They thought they were equal to the British troops. George Washington knew otherwise. The British soldiers were professionals, while the colonial troops had little training and were poorly equipped. The Massachusetts militia barely had enough gunpowder to fight one battle.

During the summer of 1775, Washington arrived at the militia camp near Boston. He immediately began to gather supplies and train the army. In the fall, Washington approved a bold plan. Continental Army troops would invade Quebec, in eastern Canada. They hoped to defeat British forces there and draw Canadians into the Patriot camp. One of the leaders of this expedition was **Benedict Arnold**. He was an officer who had played a role in the victory at Fort Ticonderoga.

After a grueling march across Maine, Arnold arrived at Quebec in November 1775. By that time, however, winter had set in. Under harsh conditions, the Americans launched their attack but failed. After several months, they limped home in defeat.

The British Retreat from Boston

In Massachusetts, the Continental Army had surrounded British forces in Boston. Neither side was able or willing to break the standoff. However, help for Washington was on the way. Cannons were being hauled from Fort Ticonderoga. This was a rough job, since there were no roads across the snow-covered mountains. It took soldiers two months to drag the 59 heavy weapons to Boston, where they arrived in January 1776.

Background
The olive bra
is considered
symbol of pea

Reading His
A. Analyzing
Points of Vie
Why did King
George rejec
petition?

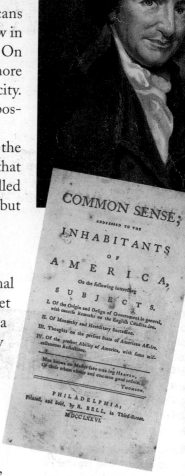

Armed with these cannons, Washington moved his troops to Dorchester Heights, overlooking Boston. The Americans threatened to bombard the city. General Howe, who was now in charge of the British forces, decided to withdraw his troops. On March 17, about 9,000 British soldiers departed Boston in more than 100 ships. Boston Patriots joyfully reclaimed their city. Although the British had damaged homes and destroyed possessions, Boston was still standing.

*ling*History

ming

ons Did the

sts deserve

ment?

n.

More than 1,000 Loyalist supporters left along with the British troops. Anti-British feeling in Boston was so strong that the Loyalists feared for their safety. Some Patriots even called for Loyalists to be hanged as traitors. This did not happen, but Loyalists' homes and property were seized.

Common Sense Is Published

In early 1776, most Americans still wanted to avoid a final break with Britain. However, the publication of a pamphlet titled *Common Sense* helped convince many Americans that a complete break with Britain was necessary. Written by Thomas Paine, a recent immigrant from England, this pamphlet made a strong case for American independence.

Paine ridiculed the idea that kings ruled by the will of God. Calling George III "the Royal Brute," Paine argued that all monarchies were corrupt. He also disagreed with the economic arguments for remaining with Britain. "Our corn," he said, "will fetch its price in any market in Europe." He believed that America should follow its own destiny.

This is the front page of *Common Sense* by Thomas Paine (above). It was one of the most influential political documents in history.

A VOICE FROM THE PAST

Everything that is right or natural pleads for separation. The blood of the slain, the weeping voice of nature cries, "'Tis time to part." Even the distance at which the Almighty has placed England and America is a strong and natural proof that the authority of the one over the other was never the design of heaven.

Thomas Paine, *Common Sense*

Common Sense was an instant success. Published in January, it sold more than 100,000 copies in three months. The call for independence had become a roar.

A Time of Decision

The Continental Congress remained undecided. A majority of the delegates still did not support independence. Even so, in May 1776, Congress adopted a resolution authorizing each of the 13 colonies to establish its own government.

On June 7, Richard Henry Lee of Virginia introduced a key resolution. It called the colonies "free and independent states" and declared

The Declaration of Independence

Setting the Stage On July 4, 1776, the Second Continental Congress ado
what became one of America's most cherished documents. Written by Tho
Jefferson, the Declaration of Independence voiced the reasons for separat
from Britain and provided the principles of government upon which
the United States would be built. **See Primary Source Explorer**

[Preamble]

When in the Course of human events, it becomes necessary for one pe
to dissolve the political bands which have connected them with another,
to assume among the powers of the earth, the separate and equal statio
which the Laws of Nature and of Nature's God entitle them, a decent res
to the opinions of mankind requires that they should declare the ca
which impel them to the separation.

[The Right of the People to Control Their Governmer

We hold these truths to be self-evident, that all men are created equal, that
are **endowed**[1] by their Creator with certain **unalienable**[2] Rights, that ar
these are Life, Liberty and the pursuit of Happiness; that, to secure these ri
Governments are instituted among Men, deriving their just powers from
consent of the governed; that whenever any Form of Government bec
destructive of these ends, it is the Right of the People to alter or to aboli
and to institute new Government, laying its foundation on such principle:
organizing its powers in such form, as to them shall seem most likely to
their Safety and Happiness. Prudence, indeed, will dictate that Governn
long established should not be changed for light and transient causes;
accordingly all experience hath shewn that mankind are more disposed to
fer, while evils are sufferable, than to right themselves by abolishing the f
to which they are accustomed. But when a long train of abuses
usurpations,[3] pursuing invariably the same Object, evinces a design to re
them under absolute **Despotism,**[4] it is their right, it is their duty, to thro
such Government, and to provide new Guards for their future security.

Such has been the patient sufferance of these Colonies; and such is no
necessity which constrains them to alter their former System
Government. The history of the present King of Great Britain is a histc
repeated injuries and usurpations, all having in direct object the estab
ment of an absolute Tyranny over these States. To prove this, let fac
submitted to a **candid**[5] world.

A CLOSER LOOK

RIGHTS OF THE PEOPLE

The ideas in this passage reflect
the views of John Locke. Locke was
an English philosopher who
believed that the natural rights of
individuals came from God, but
that a government's power comes
from the consent of the governed.
This belief is the foundation of
modern democracy.

**1. In what way can American
voters bring about changes in
their government?**

---

1. **endowed:** provided.
2. **unalienable:** unable to be taken away.
3. **usurpations:** unjust seizures of power.
4. **Despotism:** rule by tyrant with absolute power.
5. **candid:** fair, impart

rannical Acts of the British King]

has refused his Assent to Laws, the most wholesome and necessary for
public good.

e has forbidden his Governors to pass Laws of immediate and pressing
ortance, unless suspended in their operation till his assent should be
ined; and, when so suspended, he has utterly neglected to attend to them.
e has refused to pass other Laws for the accommodation of large districts
eople, unless those people would **relinquish**[6] the right of Representation
e Legislature, a right inestimable to them, and formidable to tyrants only.
e has called together legislative bodies at places unusual, uncomfortable,
distant from the depository of their public Records, for the sole purpose
tiguing them into compliance with his measures.

has dissolved Representative Houses repeatedly, for opposing with
ly firmness his invasions on the rights of the people.

has refused for a long time, after such dissolutions, to cause others to be
ed; whereby the Legislative powers, incapable of Annihilation, have
ned to the people at large for their exercise; the State remaining in the
n time exposed to all the dangers of invasions from without, and
ulsions[7] within.

has endeavoured to prevent the population of these States; for that pur-
obstructing the Laws for **Naturalization**[8] of Foreigners; refusing to pass
rs to encourage their migration hither, and raising the conditions of new
ropriations of Lands.

has obstructed the Administration of Justice, by refusing his Assent to
s for establishing Judiciary powers.

has made Judges dependent on his Will alone, for the **tenure**[9] of their
es, and the amount and payment of their salaries.

has erected a multitude of New Offices, and sent hither swarms of
ers to harass our people and **eat out their substance**.[10]

has kept among us, in times of peace, Standing Armies, without the
ent of our legislatures.

has affected to render the Military independent of and superior to the
power. He has combined with others to subject us to a jurisdiction for-
to our constitution and unacknowledged by our laws; giving his Assent
eir Acts of pretended Legislation:

quartering[11] large bodies of armed troops among us;

protecting them, by a mock Trial, from punishment for any Murders
n they should commit on the Inhabitants of these States;

cutting off our Trade with all parts of the world;

---

nquish: give up.
vulsions: violent
rbances.

8. **Naturalization:** process of becoming a citizen.

9. **tenure:** term.

10. **eat out their substance:** drain their resources.

11. **quartering:** housing or giving lodging to.

A CLOSER LOOK

GRIEVANCES AGAINST BRITAIN

The list contains 27 offenses by the British king and others against the colonies. It helps explain why it became necessary to seek independence.

2. Which offense do you think was the worst? Why?

A CLOSER LOOK

LOSS OF REPRESENTATIVE GOVERNMENT

One of the Intolerable Acts of 1774 stripped the Massachusetts Legislature of many powers and gave them to the colony's British governor.

3. Why was this action so "intolerable"?

A CLOSER LOOK

QUARTERING TROOPS WITHOUT CONSENT

The Quartering Act of 1765 required colonists to provide housing and supplies for British troops in America.

4. Why did colonists object to this act?

For imposing Taxes on us without our Consent;

For depriving us, in many cases, of the benefits of Trial by Jury;

For transporting us beyond Seas to be tried for pretended offenses;

For abolishing the free System of English Laws in a neighboring Provi[nce] establishing therein an **Arbitrary**[12] government, and enlarging its Bounda[ries] so as to render it at once an example and fit instrument for introducing [the] same absolute rule into these Colonies;

For taking away our Charters, abolishing our most valuable laws, and a[lter]ing fundamentally the Forms of our Governments;

For suspending our own Legislatures, and declaring themselves inve[sted] with power to legislate for us in all cases whatsoever.

He has **abdicated**[13] Government here, by declaring us out of his Protec[tion] and waging War against us.

He has plundered our seas, ravaged our Coasts, burnt our towns, [and] destroyed the lives of our people.

He is at this time transporting large Armies of **foreign Mercenaries** [to] compleat the works of death, desolation, and tyranny, already begun with [cir]cumstances of Cruelty & **perfidy**[15] scarcely paralleled in the most barba[rous] ages, and totally unworthy the Head of a civilized nation.

He has constrained our fellow Citizens, taken Captive on the high Se[as to] bear Arms against their Country, to become the executioners of their fr[iends] and Brethren, or to fall themselves by their Hands.

He has excited **domestic insurrections**[16] amongst us, and has endeavo[red] to bring on the inhabitants of our frontiers the merciless Indian Sav[ages,] whose known rule of warfare is an undistinguished destruction of all [ages,] sexes and conditions.

[Efforts of the Colonies to Avoid Separation]

In every stage of these Oppressions We have **Petitioned for Redress**[17] i[n the] most humble terms; Our repeated Petitions have been answered on[ly by] repeated injury. A Prince, whose character is thus marked by every act w[hich] may define a Tyrant, is unfit to be the ruler of a free people.

Nor have We been wanting in attentions to our British brethren. We [have] warned them from time to time of attempts by their legislature to exte[nd an] unwarrantable jurisdiction over us. We have reminded them of the cir[cum]stances of our emigration and settlement here. We have appealed to [their] native justice and **magnanimity,**[18] and we have conjured them by the t[ies of] our common kindred, to disavow these usurpations, which would inev[itably] interrupt our connections and correspondence. They too have been de[af]

12. **Arbitrary:** not limited by law.

13. **abdicated:** given up.

14. **foreign Mercenaries:** professional soldiers hired to serve in a foreign army.

15. **perfidy:** dishonesty, disloyalty.

16. **domestic insurrections:** rebellions at home.

17. **Petitioned for Re[dress:]** asked for the corre[ction] of wrongs.

18. **magnanimity:** generosity, forgive[ness.]

voice of justice and of **consanguinity**.[19] We must, therefore, **acquiesce**[20]
he necessity, which denounces our Separation, and hold them, as we hold
rest of mankind, Enemies in War, in Peace Friends.

e Colonies Are Declared Free and Independent]

therefore, the Representatives of the United States of America, in General
gress, Assembled, appealing to the Supreme Judge of the world for the
tude[21] of our intentions, do, in the name, and by the Authority of the good
le of these Colonies solemnly publish and declare, That these United
nies are, and of Right ought to be, Free and Independent States; that they
bsolved from all Allegiance to the British Crown, and that all political
ction between them and the State of Great Britain is, and ought to be,
y dissolved; and that as Free and Independent States, they have full Power
vy War, conclude Peace, contract Alliances, establish Commerce, and do
her Acts and Things which Independent States may of right do.
d for the support of this Declaration, with a firm reliance on the protec-
of divine Providence, we mutually pledge to each other our Lives, our
ines, and our sacred Honor. [Signed by]

Hancock *President, from Massachusetts*
gia] Button Gwinnett; Lyman Hall;
e Walton
e Island] Stephen Hopkins;
m Ellery
ecticut] Roger Sherman;
l Huntington; William Williams;
Wolcott
Carolina] William Hooper;
Hewes; John Penn
Carolina] Edward Rutledge;
as Heyward, Jr.; Thomas Lynch, Jr.;
Middleton
and] Samuel Chase; William Paca;
as Stone; Charles Carroll
ia] George Wythe;
d Henry Lee; Thomas Jefferson;

Benjamin Harrison; Thomas Nelson, Jr.;
Francis Lightfoot Lee; Carter Braxton

[Pennsylvania] Robert Morris;
Benjamin Rush; Benjamin Franklin;
John Morton; George Clymer; James Smith;
George Taylor; James Wilson; George Ross

[Delaware] Caesar Rodney; George Read;
Thomas McKean

[New York] William Floyd; Philip Livingston;
Francis Lewis; Lewis Morris

[New Jersey] Richard Stockton; John
Witherspoon; Francis Hopkinson; John
Hart; Abraham Clark

[New Hampshire] Josiah Bartlett; William
Whipple; Matthew Thornton

[Massachusetts] Samuel Adams; John
Adams; Robert Treat Paine; Elbridge Gerry

A CLOSER LOOK

POWERS OF AN INDEPENDENT GOVERNMENT

The colonists identified the ability to wage war and agree to peace; to make alliances with other nations; and to set up an economic system as powers of a free and independent government.

7. What other powers are held by an independent government?

A CLOSER LOOK

DECLARATION SIGNERS

The Declaration was signed by 56 representatives from the 13 original states.

8. Which signers do you recognize? Write one line about each of those signers.

sanguinity:
tionship by a
mon ancestor;
e connection.

20. **acquiesce:** accept
without protest.

21. **rectitude:** moral
uprightness.

ractive Primary Source Assessment

ain Ideas

/hat is the purpose of the Declaration of
pendence as stated in the Preamble?

/hat are the five main parts of the Declaration?

hat are three rights that all people have?

2. Critical Thinking

Drawing Conclusions Why did the colonies feel that
they had to declare their independence?

THINK ABOUT
- colonial grievances against Britain
- Britain's response to these grievances

VISUAL SUMMARY

The Road to Revolution

1763 — Proclamation of 1763

1764 Sugar Act

1765 Quartering Act; Stamp Act; Sons of Liberty; Stamp Act Congress

1766 Repeal of Stamp Act; Declaratory Act

1767 Townshend Acts; Suspension of New York Assembly

1768 Occupation of Boston by British troops

1769 Daughters of Liberty

1770 Boston Massacre; Repeal of all Townshend Acts except tea tax

1772 Committees of Correspondence

1773 Tea Act; Boston Tea Party

1774 Intolerable Acts; First Continental Congress; Boycott of British goods

1775 Battles of Lexington and Concord; Second Continental Congress; Appointment of Washington as commander of Continental Army; Battle of Bunker Hill; Olive Branch Petition

1776 *Common Sense*; Declaration of Independence

TERMS & NAMES

Briefly explain the significance of each of the following.

1. Stamp Act
2. Sons of Liberty
3. writs of assistance
4. Samuel Adams
5. Boston Tea Party
6. militia
7. Lexington and Concord
8. Loyalist
9. Declaration of Independence
10. Thomas Jefferson

REVIEW QUESTIONS

Tighter British Control (pages 159–162)

1. How did relations between Britain and the colonies change after the Seven Years' War?
2. Why did Britain try to tax the colonies?
3. Why did the colonists cry, "No taxation without representation"?

Colonial Resistance Grows (pages 163–169)

4. How did the colonists protest the Townshend Acts?
5. How was the Boston Massacre used for propaganda purposes?
6. How did the committees of correspondence help keep people informed?

The Road to Lexington and Concord (pages 170–175)

7. Why was the First Continental Congress held?
8. What was the Midnight Ride?

Declaring Independence (pages 176–185)

9. What was the Battle of Bunker Hill?
10. What was the core idea of the Declaration of Independence?

CRITICAL THINKING

1. USING YOUR NOTES: SEQUENCING EVENTS

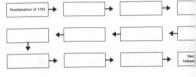

Using your completed chart, answer the questions below.

a. What city was the site of ea[r] protest activity?
b. What event happened after Tea Act?

2. ANALYZING LEADERSHIP

How did colonial leaders differ their methods of defending an securing basic rights for the colonies?

3. APPLYING CITIZENSHIP SK[ILLS]

Did colonial leaders have a res[pon]sibility to include women, Afri[can] Americans, and other groups i[n] the Declaration of Independen[ce] Explain.

4. THEME: IMPACT OF THE INDIVIDUAL

How did John Adams's role as lawyer for the British soldiers involved in the Boston Massac[re] help set a tone for the Revolutionary cause?

5. DRAWING CONCLUSIONS

What factors and events led th[e] colonies to seek independence

6. SUPPORTING OPINIONS

Do you think the American Revolution would have occurr[ed] Britain had not taxed the colo[nies] Why or why not?

Interact *with* Histo[ry]

Now that you have read abou[t] road to revolution, do you co[n] sider your decision made at th[e] beginning of the chapter to j[oin] not join the protest a wise ch[oice] or a poor choice? Explain.

STANDARDS-BASED ASSESSMENT

Use the map and your knowledge of U.S. history to answer questions 1 and 2.

Additional Test Practice, pp. S1–S33.

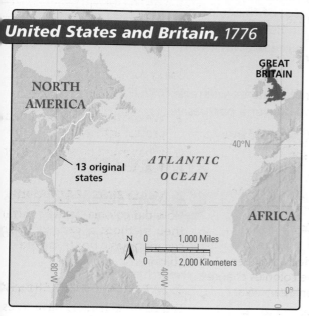

United States and Britain, 1776

What does the yellow shaded area on the map represent?

A. the original colonies

B. Great Britain

C. North America

D. the United States

2. What is the approximate distance between the northernmost colony and Great Britain?

A. 1,000 miles

B. 2,000 kilometers

C. 3,000 miles

D. 5,000 kilometers

This quotation from James Otis is about the use of search warrants by the British. Use the quotation and your knowledge of U.S. history to answer question 3.

PRIMARY SOURCE

It appears to me the worst instrument of arbitrary power, the most destructive of English liberty and the fundamental principles of law, that was ever found in an English law-book.

James Otis, Jr., quoted in *James Otis: The Pre-Revolutionist* by J. C. Ridpath

3. What conclusion can you draw about Otis's point of view?

A. Otis believed that the searches would benefit the colonists.

B. Otis realized that British searches were more important than colonial liberties.

C. Otis believed that colonists were entitled to certain liberties.

D. Otis thought the searches were right.

TEST PRACTICE
CLASSZONE.COM

ALTERNATIVE ASSESSMENT

WRITING ABOUT HISTORY

Colonists had divided opinions about the Boston Tea Party. Suppose you are a pollster, attempting to gather data about public opinion. Write **quotations** from five colonists who support the Tea Party and another five quotations from people who condemn the act.

You can write your quotations based on information found in books or on the Internet.

Using a word processor, you can use different type sizes and fonts to emphasize the question you pose and the two opposing responses.

COOPERATIVE LEARNING

Participate in a class debate modeled after the discussion held by members of the Continental Congress concerning independence and the slave trade.

INTEGRATED TECHNOLOGY ACTIVITY

PARTICIPATING IN A NET SIMULATION

Go to *NetSimulations: Boston Massacre* at **classzone.com** to participate in the jury trial of Captain Thomas Preston. He and the soldiers of the 29th British Regiment have been arrested for the murder of five citizens.

• Use the information in this chapter and the simulation to review the events surrounding the Boston Massacre. Use the Juror's Journal to take notes.

• Read Captain Preston's statement, then begin questioning the prosecution and defense witnesses. Answer the questions in the Juror's Journal to record the evidence you hear.

• Listen to each attorney's closing arguments, then enter your verdict.

NET SIMULATION
CLASSZONE.COM

Raise the Liberty Pole

In 1765, the Sons of Liberty gathered around a huge elm tree in Boston that they named the Liberty Tree. It became a meeting place where people voiced their protests against British policies. Replicas of the Liberty Tree—giant poles sometimes decorated with the flags of the colonies—were raised throughout the colonies. These liberty poles represented the unity of the American colonies as they struggled to break away from British rule.

ACTIVITY Like the American Patriots, each group of students will raise its own liberty pole. Each group also will write and deliver a persuasive speech supporting the cause of the American colonies.

TOOLBOX

Each group will need:

scissors

poster board

pencil

markers

masking tape

3 cardboard tubes from wrapping paper

construction paper

twine

stapler

STEP BY STEP

1 **Form groups.** Each group should consist of four or fiv students. The members of your gro will do the following jobs:

- research each colony
- design and create flags
- construct a pole
- write and deliver a speech

2 **Do research on the 13 colonies.** For each colony, your group should find a person, p or object that represents that colo For example, a Pilgrim's hat might resent Massachusetts. The 13 color are listed below.

New England Colonies	Middle Colonies	Souther Colonies
Massachusetts (including Maine)	New York	North Ca
New Hampshire	Delaware	Virginia
Connecticut	New Jersey	Marylan
Rhode Island	Pennsylvania	South Ca
		Georgia

Members of the Sons of Liberty raise a liberty pole in July 1776 to celebrate America's independence.

3 Design and create 13 flags for the colonies.

Decide what person, place, or object you will use on your flag for each colony. Cut each flag out of the poster board. Sketch your design on the flag with a pencil. Then use markers to decorate it. On the back of each flag, explain how your design portrays the characteristics of that colony.

Construct the pole.

Using masking tape, fasten the cardboard tubes together to one long tube. Then reinforce ube by taping construction r around it.

String the flags on the pole.

Feed a piece of twine gh the open ends of the long Tie the ends of the twine her to form a tight loop. Now all 13 flags to the twine.

6 Raise your liberty pole.

Lean your liberty pole next to a small table or desk. Take turns with members of your group and visit other liberty poles. As students visit your station, explain the significance of your flag designs.

TE AND SPEAK

a persuasive speech to recruit others to join the cause of . In your speech, explain what is wrong with British poli- ive reasons why the colonies should become independent. ead your speech to the other groups as part of the ment process.

HELP DESK

For related information on the Liberty Tree, see pages 161–162 in Chapter 6.

Researching Your Project

- *The Revolutionary War* by Bart McDowell
- *The American Revolutionaries* edited by Milton Meltzer

For more about the American Revolution . . .

RESEARCH LINKS
CLASSZONE.COM

Did You Know?

The numbers 45 and 92 played an important part in the history of these liberty poles. The 45th issue of a British newspaper openly criti- cized the king in 1763 and was reprinted in the colonies. In 1768, 92 members of the Massachusetts General Assembly voted against canceling a letter to the other 12 colonies that called for action against Britain. To represent the numbers, 92 members of the Sons of Liberty would often raise liberty poles to a height of about 45 feet.

REFLECT & ASSESS

- How well do your flags represent the colonies?
- How clearly does your speech explain grievances against the British?
- Why do you think the practice of raising liberty poles spread to many of the colonies?

This painting shows General Washington and his troops in their winter camp at Valley Forge.

1776
British capture New York, but Americans win a battle in New Jersey.

1777
Battles of Saratoga convince Europeans that America might win the war.

1778
France enters the war on the American side.

1
A
fr
ta
fo
n

USA World 1776

1776
Scotsman Adam Smith publishes a book saying that government shouldn't control the economy.

1778
Voltaire, who wrote about the rights of people, dies in Paris.

It is 1777. Your brother is an American soldier. In his last letter to you, he wrote that the army has no shoes or bullets and little food. But he plans to keep fighting.

Now, a British army is coming toward your farm. You hear that the soldiers are stealing crops to feed themselves and their horses.

What would you sacrifice to win freedom?

What Do You Think?

- What sacrifices do civilians make during wartime?
- What sacrifices do soldiers make?
- Is it worth such sacrifices to win independence for your country? Why or why not?

RESEARCH LINKS
CLASSZONE.COM

Visit the Chapter 7 links for more information about the American Revolution.

1781
In the war's last big battle, the Americans and French defeat the British at Yorktown.

1783
Treaty of Paris ends the war.

1783

1781
oseph II of Austria
dom, which forced
s to farm someone
else's land for life.

1783
Simón Bolívar, who will become a revolutionary leader in South America, is born in what is now Venezuela.

CHAPTER 7

Reading Strategy: Sequencing Events

What Do You Know?

What stories do you know about the people or events of the Revolution? How do people display courage and self-sacrifice during wartime?

Think About

- what you've learned about American settlers from movies, television, historical fiction, or science fiction about space travel
- opportunities and challenges offered in a new land
- your responses to the Interact with History about sacrificing to win freedom (see page 191)

Colonists burn the harvest to keep it the British.

What Do You Want to Know?

 What would you like to learn about the steps that people took to win the American Revolution? In your notebook, record what you hope to learn from this chapter.

Sequencing Events

To sequence is to put events in the order in which they happened. You learned this skill i Chapter 6 by sequencing the events that led to the American Revolution. Now as you rea Chapter 7, practice sequencing again. Put the major battles and events of the war in ord by recording them on a time line. Copy the time line below in your notebook. You may want to make it bigger.

S See Skillbuilder Handbook, page R4.

 Taking Notes

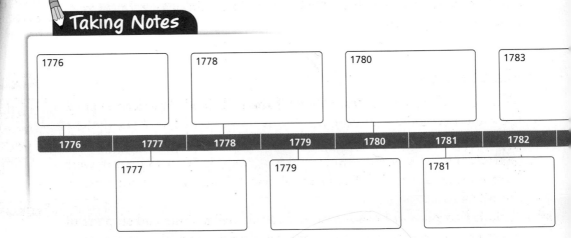

The Early Years of the War

ONE AMERICAN'S STORY

In search of liberty, Haym Salomon moved from Europe to New York sometime between 1764 and 1775. He was a Jew from Poland. Salomon soon became a successful merchant and banker. During the war, Salomon supported the Patriot cause.

When the British captured New York in 1776, many Patriots fled but Salomon stayed. The British arrested him. Salomon spoke many languages. The British thought he could help them deal with foreign merchants, so they let him out of prison. Salomon used this opportunity to help other prisoners escape.

In 1778, the British wanted to arrest him again, so he fled to Philadelphia and continued to aid the Patriots. He loaned the new government more than $600,000, which was never repaid.

Like Salomon, many people made hard choices about which side to support during the Revolutionary War. This section discusses those choices and the obstacles Americans faced in the war's early years.

Haym Salomon sacrificed his health and his fortune to help his new country.

Americans Divided

The issue of separating from Great Britain divided American society. Opinion polls did not exist in the 1700s, so we don't know exactly how many people were on each side. But historians estimate that roughly 20 to 30 percent of Americans were Loyalists, roughly 40 to 45 percent were Patriots, and the rest remained neutral. Most Americans did not support the Revolution.

Both Patriots and Loyalists came from all walks of life and all parts of America. In general, New England and Virginia had high numbers of Patriots. Loyalists were numerous in cities, in New York State, and in the

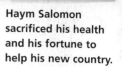

Taking Notes

Use your chart to take notes about the early years of the American Revolution.

1776	1777	1778

South. Many Loyalists worked for the British government or were clergy in the Church of England. Some Quakers were Loyalists, although many wanted peace. (Their faith taught that war was wrong.)

The war divided Native Americans, too. For instance, some Iroquois nations fought with the British and others with the Americans. Those Native Americans who joined the British feared that if the Americans won, they would take Native American land. Some Native Americans who lived near colonists and interacted with them sided with the Americans.

Background
The Iroquois
League had
erally kept p
among the
Iroquois nati
for about 20
years—until
American
Revolution.

African Americans also fought on both sides. At first, slave owners feared that African Americans who had guns might lead slave revolts. Therefore, few states allowed African Americans to enlist, or sign up with the army. Then a British governor offered freedom to any enslaved person who joined the British army. Many slaves ran away to fight for the British. In response, most states began to accept African-American soldiers. In all, about 5,000 African Americans served in the Continental Army. Many African Americans who did so hoped that American independence would bring greater equality.

Differences over the war split families, too. For example, Benjamin Franklin's son William took Britain's side. The father and son stopped speaking.

Creating an Army

Reading H
A. Analyzin
Causes Wh
would the
agreement
the war ma
hard to rais
army?

Because not everyone supported the war, raising an army was difficult. The army also faced other problems. In June 1775, **George Washington** became the commander of the Continental Army. At first, this new national army was formed from state militias, made up of untrained and undisciplined volunteers.

After Congress created the Continental Army, men began to enlist, but most of them didn't stay long. At the start of the war, Congress asked men to enlist only for one year. Later Congress did lengthen the term of service. When the soldiers' time was up, they went home. As a result, Washington's army never numbered more than 17,000 men.

Congress's inability to supply the army also frustrated Washington. The soldiers needed everything—blankets, shoes, food, and even guns and ammunition. Angrily, Washington wrote, "Could I have foreseen what I have, and am likely to experience, no consideration upon earth should have induced [persuaded] me to accept this command."

Many women tried to help the army. Martha Washington and other wives followed their husbands to army camps. The women cooked, did laundry, and

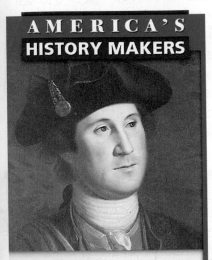

AMERICA'S HISTORY MAKERS

GEORGE WASHINGTON

1732–1799

At the age of 16, George Washington worked as a surveyor, setting land boundaries in the wilderness. He learned to handle hardship by hunting for food and sleeping outdoors.

In the French and Indian War, Washington had many brushes with death. Yet he wrote, "I heard the bullets whistle, and, believe me, there is something charming in the sound."

That war made him the most famous American officer. People loved him for his courage. As commander of the Continental Army, Washington's popularity helped unite Americans.

How did Washington's early life prepare him to lead the army?

dingHistory

lving

ems How
Washington
solve the
em of lead-
small, inex-
nced force
st a large
ssional

nursed sick or wounded soldiers. A few women even helped fight. Mary Hays earned the nickname "Molly Pitcher" by carrying water to tired soldiers during a battle. Deborah Sampson dressed as a man, enlisted, and fought in several engagements.

Building an army was crucial to Washington's plan. To the British, the Americans were disorganized, inexperienced rebels. The British thought that if they won a decisive battle, the Americans would give up. By contrast, Washington's main goal was to survive. To do so, he needed to keep an army in the field, win some battles—no matter how small—and avoid a crushing defeat. He knew he could not hope to win a major battle until he had a large, well-equipped army.

These Hessian boots weighed about 12 pounds a pair.

Struggle for the Middle States

As Chapter 6 explains, Washington had forced the British to retreat from Boston in March 1776. He then hurried his army to New York City, where he expected the British to go next. One British goal was to occupy coastal cities so that their navy could land troops and supplies in those cities. From there, they could launch their military campaigns.

Washington's hunch was correct. In July 1776, Britain's General William Howe arrived in New York with a large army. Then in August, more soldiers arrived, including about 9,000 Hessian mercenaries. A **mercenary** is a professional soldier hired to fight for a foreign country. British soldiers usually signed up for life—which discouraged enlistment. So Britain needed mercenaries, whom it hired from the German states.

ground

itish-hired
naries came
part of
ny called
which is
gin of the
lessian.

For several months, the British and American armies fought for New York State. Finally, the British forced Washington to retreat through New Jersey. By December, when the American army crossed the Delaware River into Pennsylvania, it was in terrible condition. Charles Willson Peale, a Philadelphia painter who watched the crossing, saw one muddy soldier who "had lost all his clothes. He was in an old, dirty blanket jacket, his beard long, and his face so full of sores he could not clean it." To Peale's shock, the soldier called his name. He was Peale's brother!

Political writer Thomas Paine also witnessed the hard conditions and the soldiers' low spirits on the retreat. To

War in the Middle States, 1776–1777

- ← American forces
- ← British forces
- ✳ American victory
- ✳ British victory

MAINE (part of Mass.)

N.H.

MASS.   Boston

CONN.

N.Y.

Morristown
PENNSYLVANIA
Germantown
Brandywine
MARYLAND   N.J.
Washington
DEL.

R.I.

New York
Princeton
Trenton
Philadelphia

ATLANTIC OCEAN

Chesapeake Bay

VIRGINIA

Lake Champlain

Washington

Howe

GEOGRAPHY SKILLBUILDER Interpreting Maps
1. **Place** In what state did the American victories take place?
2. **Movement** How did the British general Howe travel from New York to Brandywine?

Thomas Sully's *Passage of the Delaware* shows Washington at the Delaware River, leading to the American attack on the British at Trenton, New Jersey.

urge them to keep fighting, Paine published the first in a series of pamphlets called *The American Crisis*.

Reading **H**
C. Recogniz
Propaganda
does this pa
promote th
American c

A VOICE FROM THE PAST

These are the times that try men's souls. The summer soldier and the sunshine patriot will, in this crisis, shrink from the service of their country; but he that stands it *now*, deserves the love and thanks of man and woman.

Thomas Paine, *The American Crisis*

Washington hoped a victory would encourage his weary men. He also knew that he must attack the British quickly because most of his soldiers would leave once their enlistments ended on December 31.

Late on December 25, 1776, Washington's troops rowed across the icy Delaware River to New Jersey. From there, they marched in bitter, early-morning cold to Trenton to surprise the Hessians, some of whom were sleeping after their Christmas celebration. The Americans captured or killed more than 900 Hessians and gained needed supplies. Washington's army won another victory at Princeton eight days later. These victories proved that the American general was better than the British had thought. The American army began to attract new recruits.

Britain's Strategy

Meanwhile, the British were pursuing a **strategy**—an overall plan of action—to seize the Hudson River Valley. If successful, they would cut off New England from the other states. The strategy called for three armies to meet at Albany, New York. General John Burgoyne would lead a force south from Canada. Lieutenant Colonel Barry St. Leger would lead his army from Lake Ontario down the Mohawk Valley. Burgoyne expected General Howe to follow the Hudson north from New York City.

Burgoyne left Canada in June 1777 with an army that included British, Hessians, and Iroquois. In July, they captured Fort Ticonderoga.

Called "Gentleman Johnny" by his soldiers, Burgoyne enjoyed traveling slowly and throwing parties to celebrate victories. After Ticonderoga, his delays gave the Americans time to cut down trees to block his route. They also burned crops and drove off cattle, leaving the countryside bare of supplies for the British troops.

Things grew rougher during the last 25 miles of Burgoyne's march to Albany. On a map, the route looked easy, but it really crossed a swampy wilderness. The army had to build bridges and roads. Burgoyne took four weeks to reach the Hudson. Still confident, he looked forward to the **rendezvous**, or meeting, with St. Leger and Howe in Albany.

On August 4, Burgoyne received a message from Howe. He would not be coming north, Howe wrote, because he had decided to invade Pennsylvania to try to capture General Washington and Philadelphia—where the Continental Congress met. "Success be ever with you," wrote Howe. Yet Burgoyne needed Howe's soldiers, not his good wishes.

Howe did invade Pennsylvania. In September 1777, he defeated but did not capture Washington at the Battle of Brandywine. Howe then occupied Philadelphia. In October, Washington attacked Howe at Germantown. Washington lost the battle, however, and retreated.

Battles Along the Mohawk

As Burgoyne received Howe's message, St. Leger faced his own obstacle in reaching Albany. In the summer of 1777, he was trying to defeat a small American force at Fort Stanwix in the Mohawk River valley of New York. St. Leger's forces included Iroquois led by Mohawk chief Joseph Brant, also called Thayendanegea (THĪ•ehn•DAHG•ee).

Brant and his sister, Molly, had strong ties to the British. Molly was a British official's wife, and Joseph was a convert to the Church of England. Both Joseph and Molly tried to convince the Iroquois to fight for the British, who upheld Iroquois rights to their land.

During August 1777, American general Benedict Arnold led a small army up the Mohawk River. He wanted to chase the British away from

War in the North, 1777

0   100 Miles
0   200 Kilometers

- → American forces
- ← British forces
- ✳ American victory
- ✳ British victory

Quebec
St. Lawrence R.
MAINE (part of Mass.)
Montreal
Lake Champlain
St. Leger
Mohawk R.
Ft. Ticonderoga
Saratoga
N.H.
Ft. Ontario
Bennington
Ft. Stanwix
Oriskany
Arnold
Gates MASS.
NEW YORK
Albany Boston
Hudson R.
ATLANTIC OCEA
Delaware R.
PENNSYLVANIA
CONN.
R.I.

GEOGRAPHY SKILLBUILDER Interpreting Maps
1. **Place** From which two cities did the British invade the United States?
2. **Movement** What did St. Leger want to capture by taking the longer route by way of Lake Ontario?

The Iroquois chief Joseph Brant was a British ally.

ing**History**
luating
Howe's
als for
asion of
lvania. Was
essful?

lary
: a person
anges
s

Fort Stanwix. Arnold sent a captured Loyalist and some Iroquois who were American allies to spread the rumor that he had a large army.

The trick worked. St. Leger's troops were afraid they were about to be outnumbered. The army retreated so fast that it left behind tents, cannon, and supplies. Because of St. Leger's flight and Howe's refusal to follow the strategy, no one was left to rendezvous with Burgoyne.

Saratoga: A Turning Point

By this time, Burgoyne's army was running out of supplies, and it needed horses. The general sent a raiding party into Vermont to see what it could find. The raiding party encountered New England troops, who badly defeated it at the Battle of Bennington on August 16, 1777.

Despite this setback, Burgoyne's army headed slowly toward Albany. On the way, it met a powerful Continental Army force led by General Horatio Gates. Gates's soldiers were waiting on a ridge called Bemis Heights, near Saratoga, New York. There the Americans had created fortifications, or built-up earthen walls, behind which to fight. The Polish engineer Tadeusz Kosciuszko (TAH•deh•oosh KAWSH•choosh•kaw) had helped the Americans do this.

Burgoyne would have to break through the fortifications to proceed to Albany. On September 19, he attacked. While Gates commanded the Americans on the ridge, Benedict Arnold led an attack on nearby

Reading **Hi**
E. Reading a
Find Saratog
the map on
197. Notice
close it is to
Burgoyne's
of Albany.

Freeman's Farm. His men repeatedly charged the British and inflicted heavy casualties. Still, the British held their position.

On October 7, another battle broke out. Again Arnold led daring charges against the British. Although hundreds of muskets were firing at him, he galloped through the battlefield "like a madman," a sergeant later said. Frightened, Burgoyne's Hessian mercenaries began to fall back. Eventually, a bullet tore into Arnold's leg and stopped him. Even so, the Americans forced Burgoyne to retreat.

Burgoyne's army moved slowly through heavy rain to a former army camp at Saratoga. By the time they arrived, the men were exhausted. Some fell in the mud and slept in their wet uniforms. The Continental Army then surrounded Burgoyne's army and fired on it day and night without stopping. Burgoyne decided to surrender. The series of conflicts that led to this surrender is known as the **Battles of Saratoga.**

The Battles of Saratoga had two very different consequences. As Benedict Arnold was recovering from his wound, he married a woman who was a Loyalist. Over time, Arnold came to feel that Congress had not rewarded him enough for his heroic actions at Saratoga and other battles. Influenced by his bitterness and his wife, he betrayed his army. In 1780, he agreed to turn over an American fort to the British. Although his plot was discovered before he could carry it out, he escaped. Even today, the name *Benedict Arnold* is used to mean traitor.

On the positive side, the victory at Saratoga was a turning point in the Revolution. It caused European nations to think that the Americans might win their war for independence. As you will read in Section 2, several European nations decided to help America in its struggle.

ing **History**
ning and
rting
ns Which
two conse-
s of the
of
ga was
ignificant?

---

ion **1** *Assessment*

erms & Names

lain the
gnificance of:
eorge Washington
ercenary
ategy
ndezvous
ttles of Saratoga

2. Using Graphics

Use a cluster diagram like the one shown to list the difficulties Americans faced in the early years of the war.

American Difficulties

Which difficulty do you think was hardest to overcome?

3. Main Ideas

a. How were Americans divided over the issue of separating from Great Britain?

b. Why was it difficult for George Washington to form and keep a large army?

c. How did the Battles of Saratoga mark a turning point in the war?

4. Critical Thinking

Contrasting How did the British and American strategies differ during the early years of the war?

THINK ABOUT
• what the British expected from the Americans
• Washington's main goals for the American army
• why Burgoyne invaded from Canada

VITY OPTIONS

GUAGE ARTS

ART

Learn more about a Revolutionary War leader. Write a brief **biography** or create a **trading card** with a picture on one side and important facts on the other.

2

The War Expands

MAIN IDEA	WHY IT MATTERS NOW	TERMS & NAMES

MAIN IDEA	WHY IT MATTERS NOW	TERMS & NAMES	
Some Europeans decided to help America. As the war continued, it spread to the sea and the frontier.	This was the beginning of the United States' formal relationships with other nations.	ally Marquis de Lafayette bayonet	desert privateer James Fort John Paul

ONE AMERICAN'S STORY

To defeat the British Empire, the United States needed a foreign ally. An **ally** is a country that agrees to help another country achieve a common goal. The ideal ally would share America's goal of defeating Britain. So the United States turned to France—Britain's long-time enemy.

In 1776, Congress sent Benjamin Franklin to France to persuade it to be the ally of the United States. Famous for his experiments with electricity, Franklin became a celebrity in Paris. He wrote to his daughter, saying that medallions with his likeness were popular there.

> **A VOICE FROM THE PAST**
>
> These, with the pictures, busts [sculptures of the head and shoulders], and prints (of which copies upon copies are spread everywhere), have made your father's face as well known as that of the moon.
>
> **Benjamin Franklin,** letter to his daughter Sally

After America's victory at Saratoga, the French agreed to an alliance. This section explains how the war expanded with foreign aid.

Franklin's
Quaker co
hat amuse
French. Th
fit the ima
had of hin
noble mar
wild coun

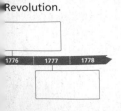

Taking Notes

Use your chart to take notes about the expansion of the American Revolution.

Help from Abroad

France was still bitter over its defeat by Britain in the French and Indian War, in which France lost its North American colonies. The French hoped to take revenge on the British by helping Britain's American colonies break free. In 1776, France began to give secret aid to the Americans. However, the French didn't want to lose to Britain a second time. That is why they didn't publicly ally themselves with the United States until after the Americans had proved they could win battles.

After hearing of the American victory at Saratoga, King Louis XVI of France recognized U.S. independence. In 1778, France signed two treaties of alliance with the United States. By doing so, France went to war with Britain. As part of its new alliance, France sent badly needed funds, supplies, and troops to America.

In 1779, France persuaded its ally Spain to help the Americans. Spain was also Britain's rival. The Spanish governor of Louisiana, General Bernardo de Gálvez, acted quickly. He captured the British strongholds of Natchez and Baton Rouge in the lower Mississippi Valley.

From there, his small army went on to take Mobile, and in 1781 Pensacola in West Florida. These victories prevented the British from attacking the United States from the southwest. In addition, Britain had to keep thousands of troops fighting Gálvez—instead of fighting the Americans. However, like France, Spain's motives were not simply to help the United States. Gálvez's victories helped extend Spain's empire in North America.

By entering the war on America's side, France and Spain forced the British to fight a number of enemies on land and sea. The British had to spread their military resources over many fronts. For example, they were afraid they might have to fight the French in the West Indies, so they sent troops there. This prevented the British from concentrating their strength to defeat the inexperienced Americans.

Europeans Help Washington

The Americans gained some of the military experience they needed from Europe. Several European military officers came to Washington's aid, including men from France, Poland, and the German states.

The **Marquis de Lafayette** (LAF•ee•EHT) was a 19-year-old French nobleman who volunteered to serve in Washington's army. He wanted a military career, and he believed in the American cause. He quickly gained Washington's confidence and was given the command of an army division. Lafayette won respect and love from his men by sharing their hardships. Called "the soldier's friend," he used his own money to buy warm clothing for his ragged troops. Washington regarded him almost as a son.

Lafayette fought in many battles and also persuaded the French king to send a 6,000-man army to America. He became a hero in both France and the United States. Later he took part in France's own revolution.

Along with Lafayette came the Baron de Kalb, a German officer who had served in the French army. He became one of Washington's generals and earned a reputation for bravery. In 1780, he received 11 wounds in the Battle of Camden and died.

Another German, Baron von Steuben, helped turn the inexperienced Americans

ground
•ston, Texas,
•ned for
•z.

ing History
•ognizing
•s How did
•ca's allies
•nt Britain
•ocusing all
•ght on the
•cans?

ground
•of these
•ean officers
•rofessional
•s looking
•army that
•hire them.
•like
•tte, also
•d in the
•an cause.

Lafayette stands with the slave James Armistead, whose owner allowed him to spy for Lafayette. After the war, the state of Virginia set Armistead free. Armistead then took Lafayette's last name as his own.

into a skilled fighting force. Washington asked him to train the army. In 1778, Steuben began by forming a model company of 100 men. Then he taught them how to move in lines and columns and how to handle weapons properly. Under Steuben's direction, the soldiers practiced making charges with **bayonets**—long steel knives attached to the ends of guns. Within a month, the troops were executing drills with speed and precision. Once the model company succeeded, the rest of the army adopted Steuben's methods.

Winter at Valley Forge

Help from Europeans came at a time when the Americans desperately needed it. In late 1777, Britain's General Howe forced Washington to retreat from Philadelphia. Beginning in the winter of 1777–1778, Washington and his army camped at Valley Forge in southeast Pennsylvania.

On the march to Valley Forge, Washington's army was so short on supplies that many soldiers had only blankets to cover themselves. They also lacked shoes. The barefoot men left tracks of blood on the frozen ground as they marched. The soldiers' condition did not improve at camp. The Marquis de Lafayette described what he saw.

A VOICE FROM THE PAST

The unfortunate soldiers were in want of everything; they had neither coats, nor hats, nor shirts, nor shoes; their feet and their legs froze till they grew black and it was often necessary to amputate them. . . . The Army frequently passed whole days without food.

Marquis de Lafayette, quoted in *Valley Forge: Pinnacle of Courage*

Reading **Hi**
B. Identifyin
Facts and
Opinions Is
Lafayette m
recounting
or expressin
opinions? E

Because of this, the name *Valley Forge* came to stand for the great hardships that Americans endured in the Revolutionary War. Over the winter, the soldiers at Valley Forge grew weak from not having enough food or warm clothing. Roughly a quarter of them died from malnutrition, exposure to the cold, or diseases such as smallpox and typhoid fever.

daily *life*

CAMP LIFE IN WINTER

At Valley Forge, soldiers slept in small huts, 12 men to a hut. They slept in shifts so they could take turns using the scarce blankets. The men also shared clothing. If one went on guard duty, the others lent him their clothes and stayed by the fire in the hut until he came back. Guards had to stand in old hats to keep their shoeless feet warm.

The soldiers cooked on hot stones, in iron kettles, or on portable iron braziers. Often the only food they had was fire cakes—a bread made of flour and water paste.

These iron kettles were so heavy that soldiers often threw them away on a march.

This surgeon's kit includes a saw, used perform amputation

Soldiers would place burning coals in braziers like this. Braziers were used to cook food and heat huts.

Washington appealed to Congress to send the soldiers supplies, but it was slow in responding. Luckily, private citizens sometimes came to the soldiers' aid. According to one story, on New Year's Day 1778, a group of Philadelphia women drove ten teams of oxen into camp. The oxen were pulling wagons loaded with supplies and 2,000 shirts. The women had the oxen killed to provide food for the men.

Despite the hardships, Washington and his soldiers showed amazing endurance. Under such circumstances, soldiers often **desert,** or leave military duty without intending to return. Some soldiers did desert, but Lieutenant Colonel John Brooks wrote that the army stayed together because of "Love of our Country." The men also stayed because of Washington. Private Samuel Downing declared that the soldiers "loved him. They'd sell their lives for him."

ding **History**

alyzing
s of View
are two dif-
t explana-
for why
ican soldiers
ot desert?

War on the Frontier

Elsewhere, other Americans also took on difficult challenges. In 1777, a 24-year-old frontiersman named George Rogers Clark walked into the office of Virginia's governor, Patrick Henry. Clark said he had come to take part in defending the Western frontier. He lived in Kentucky, which was claimed by Virginia. Clark wanted Virginia to defend that region against British soldiers and their Native American allies in what is now Indiana and Illinois. "If a country is not worth protecting," he said, "it is not worth claiming."

"If a country is not worth protecting, it is not worth claiming."
George Rogers Clark

ground

late 1700s,
estern fron-
as the
between
palachian
tains and
ississippi

Clark was difficult to ignore. He stood six feet tall, had red hair, and displayed a dramatic personality. He persuaded Governor Henry that he was right. The governor told Clark to raise an army to capture British posts on the Western frontier.

In May of 1778, Clark and a group of frontiersmen began to travel down the Ohio River. He recruited others on the way, until he had a force of 175 to 200. They went by boat and later on foot to Kaskaskia, a British post on the Mississippi River. They captured Kaskaskia without a fight.

Then they moved east to take Fort Sackville at Vincennes, in present-day Indiana. Earlier, a small force sent by Clark had taken Vincennes, but British forces under Henry Hamilton had recaptured it. Settlers called Hamilton the "Hair Buyer" because he supposedly paid rewards for American scalps.

War on the Frontier, 1778

In 1778, George Rogers Clark captures British outposts on the American frontier without firing a shot. Though the British retake Vincennes, Clark regains it after a short battle in 1779.

L. Huron
PROVINCE OF QUEBEC
L. Erie
Ft. Detroit
Hamilton
Wabash R.
40°N
Vincennes (Ft. Sackville)
Cahokia
Kaskaskia
Ohio R.
Clark
Ft. Pi
Mississippi R.

American forces
British forces
American victory
American fort
British fort

N
0   100 Miles
0   200 Kilometers

GEOGRAPHY SKILLBUILDER Interpreting Maps
1. **Movement** *From what fort did British general Hamilton travel to Vincennes?*
2. **Region** *What rivers form the boundaries of the region captured by Clark and his men?*

Determined to retake Fort Sackville, Clark and his men set out for Vincennes from Kaskaskia in February 1779. Hamilton wasn't expecting an attack because the rivers were overflowing their banks and the woods were flooded. Clark's men slogged through miles of icy swamps and waded through chest-deep water. They caught the British at Vincennes by surprise.

When Hamilton and his troops tried to remain in the fort, Clark pretended to have a larger force than he really had. He also found a way to frighten the British into leaving. Clark and his men had captured several Native Americans, who were allies of the British and had American scalps on their belts. Clark executed some of them in plain view of the fort. He promised to do the same to Hamilton and his men if they didn't surrender immediately. The British gave up.

Clark's victory gave the Americans a hold on the vast region between the Great Lakes and the Ohio River. This area was more than half the total size of the original 13 states. However, Fort Detroit on Lake Erie remained in the hands of the British.

Reading His
D. Making
Decisions W
factors do yc
think influer
Clark's decisi
to execute h
prisoners?

STRANGE but True

THE FIRST COMBAT SUBMARINE

During the Revolution, the Americans built the first combat submarine—the *Turtle*, shown below. It held only a pilot, who steered with one hand and cranked a propeller with the other. To submerge, the pilot used a foot pump to let in water.

In 1776, the *Turtle* failed on its mission to attach a bomb to a British warship in New York harbor. It reached the ship but couldn't drill through its copper-clad hull. The *Turtle* failed at later missions, too.

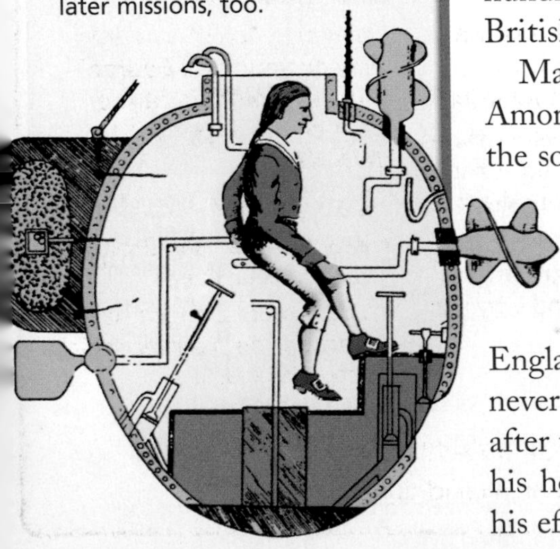

War at Sea

The war expanded not only to the frontier but also to the sea. By 1777, Britain had about 100 warships off the American coast. This allowed Britain to control the Atlantic trade routes. There was no way the Americans could defeat the powerful British navy.

But American privateers attacked British merchant ships. A **privateer** is a privately owned ship that a wartime government gives permission to attack an enemy's merchant ships. After capturing a British merchant ship, the crew of a privateer sold its cargo and shared the money. As a result, a desire for profit as well as patriotism motivated privateers. The states and Congress commissioned more than 1,000 privateers to prey on the British. During the war, they captured hundreds of British ships. This disrupted trade, causing British merchants to call for the war to end.

Many men answered the privateers' call for volunteers. Among them was 14-year-old **James Forten**, who was the son of a free African-American sail maker. In 1780, Forten signed up to sail on the *Royal Louis* to earn money for his family after his father died. When a British ship captured the *Royal Louis* in 1781, the British offered Forten a free trip to England. Reportedly, Forten refused, saying he would never betray his country. Released from a British prison after the war, Forten walked barefoot from New York to his home in Philadelphia. He later became famous for his efforts to end slavery.

Vocabulary
merchant sh
a ship used
trade

A Naval Hero

Though outnumbered, the Continental Navy scored several victories against the British. An officer named **John Paul Jones** won the most famous sea battle.

In 1779, Jones became the commander of a ship named *Bonhomme Richard*. With four other ships, he patrolled the English coast. In September, Jones's vessels approached a convoy in which two British warships were guarding a number of supply ships.

Jones closed in on the *Serapis,* the larger of the two warships. At one point, the *Bonhomme Richard* rammed the better-armed British vessel. As the two ships locked together, the confident British captain demanded that Jones surrender. In words that have become a famous U.S. Navy slogan, Jones replied, "I have not yet begun to fight!"

The two warships were so close together that the muzzles of their guns almost touched. They blasted away, each seriously damaging the other. On the shore, crowds of Britons gathered under a full moon to watch the fighting. After a fierce three-and-a-half-hour battle, the main mast of the *Serapis* cracked and fell. The ship's captain then surrendered. The *Bonhomme Richard* was so full of holes that it eventually sank, so Jones and his crew had to sail away in the *Serapis!*

Jones's success against the best navy in the world angered the British and inspired the Americans. Even so, the Americans knew that the war had to be won on land. The next section discusses the major land battles in the closing years of the war.

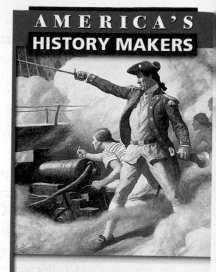

AMERICA'S HISTORY MAKERS

JOHN PAUL JONES
1747–1792

The most famous naval officer of the Revolution is known by a fake name. He was born John Paul in Scotland and first went to sea as a 12-year-old. By age 21, he had command of a merchant ship.

In 1773, Paul killed the leader of a mutiny on his ship. To avoid a murder trial, he fled to America and added Jones to his name.

Bold and daring, Jones scored many victories against the British. But his battle with the *Serapis* is what earned his place in history.

What are the two words that you think best describe Jones's character? Explain.

---

tion ➋ Assessment

Terms & Names

plain the gnificance of:
• ly
• Marquis de Lafayette
• ayonet
• esert
• rivateer
• mes Forten
• hn Paul Jones

2. Using Graphics

Use this diagram to list the effects of the entry of France and Spain into the war.

```
Cause: France and Spain
enter the war.
   │        │        │
   ▼        ▼        ▼
┌──────┐ ┌──────┐ ┌──────┐
│Effect│ │Effect│ │Effect│
└──────┘ └──────┘ └──────┘
```

3. Main Ideas

a. What role did Benjamin Franklin play in helping America win the Revolution?

b. How did European officers such as Lafayette aid America in the Revolutionary War?

c. What was John Paul Jones's major contribution during the war, and why was it important?

4. Critical Thinking

Analyzing Points of View Why do you think George Rogers Clark thought the frontier was important to defend?

THINK ABOUT

• why General Hamilton was called "Hair Buyer"

• why America might have wanted the frontier region after the war

IVITY OPTIONS

ART

SPEECH

Imagine yourself at Valley Forge in the winter of 1777–1778. Create a **comic strip** or give a **talk** describing your response to the harsh conditions.

bulary
by: a group
ps traveling
her for
y

The Path to Victory

MAIN IDEA	WHY IT MATTERS NOW	TERMS & NAMES
Seeking Loyalist support, the British invaded the South—but ultimately lost the war there.	For more than two centuries, the American Revolution has inspired other people to fight tyranny.	Lord Cornwallis pacifist guerrillas Battle of Y[...]

ONE AMERICAN'S STORY

Patriot Nancy Hart glared at the five armed Loyalists who burst into her Georgia cabin. Tradition says that the men had shot her last turkey and ordered her to cook it for them. Raids like this were common in the South, where feuding neighbors used the war as an excuse to fight each other. Both Patriots and Loyalists took part in the raids.

As Hart prepared the food, she planned her attack. When dinner was ready, the men sat down to eat. Seizing one of their muskets, Hart shot and killed one man and wounded another. She aimed the gun at the others as her daughter ran for help. A group of Patriots arrived and hanged the Loyalists.

As Nancy Hart's story demonstrates, the fighting between Patriots and Loyalists in the South was vicious. In this section, you will learn why the British war effort shifted to the South and why it failed.

The state o[...]
named a co[...]
Nancy Hart [...]
shown here[...]
Loyalists pr[...]

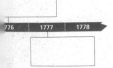

Taking Notes

Use your chart to [m]ake notes about [t]he events that [l]ed to an American [v]ictory.

776   1777   1778

Savannah and Charles Town

The British believed that most Southerners were Loyalists. Because of this, in 1778 the British decided to move the war to the South. After three years of fighting in the North, the British were no closer to victory. Although they had captured Northern cities, they couldn't control the countryside because they did not have enough troops to occupy it. The British believed that if they gained territory in the South, Southern Loyalists would hold it for them.

The British also expected large numbers of Southern slaves to join them because they had promised to grant the slaves freedom. Although thousands of African Americans did run away to join the British, not all of them were set free. Instead, some British officers sold African Americans into slavery in the West Indies.

ding History
awing
lusions Why
t an advan-
to be able
ove troops
een the
Indies and
outh?

Britain's West Indian colonies were a third reason the British invaded the South. Southern seaports were closer to the West Indies, where British troops were stationed. If the British captured Southern ports, they could move troops back and forth between the two regions.

In December 1778, the British captured the port of Savannah, Georgia. Using Savannah as a base, they then conquered most of Georgia. In 1780, a British army led by General Henry Clinton landed in South Carolina. They trapped American forces in Charles Town (now Charleston), which was the largest Southern city. When the city's 5,000 defenders surrendered, the Americans lost almost their entire Southern army. It was the worst American defeat of the war.

The Swamp Fox and Guerrilla Fighting

After that loss, Congress assigned General Horatio Gates—the victor at Saratoga—to form a new Southern army. Continental soldiers led by Baron de Kalb formed the army's core. Gates added about 2,000 new and untrained militia. He then headed for Camden, South Carolina, to challenge the army led by the British general **Lord Cornwallis.**

On the way, a band of Patriots from South Carolina approached Gates. "Their number did not exceed 20 men and boys, some white, some black, and all mounted, but most of them miserably equipped," wrote an officer. Their leader was Francis Marion, called the "Swamp Fox." He provided Gates with helpful knowledge of South Carolina's coastal swamplands. Gates sent Marion to destroy boats on the Santee River behind Camden. (See the map on page 209.) This would cut off British communications with Charles Town.

In August 1780, Gates's army ran into British troops outside Camden. The Americans were in no condition to fight. They were out of supplies and half-starved. Even worse, Gates put the inexperienced militia along part of the frontline instead of behind the veterans. When the British attacked, the militia panicked and ran. Gates also fled, but Kalb remained with his soldiers and received fatal wounds. This second defeat in the South ended Gates's term as head of an army and caused American spirits to fall to a new low.

ing History
luating
do you
was most
sible for
nerican loss
nden?

After Camden, a small British force set out for Charles Town with a column of American prisoners. Marion's band overwhelmed the British and freed the prisoners. Fighting from a base in the swamps, Marion's men cut the British supply line that led inland and north from Charles Town. Marion used the methods of a guerrilla. **Guerrillas** are small bands of fighters who weaken the enemy with surprise raids and hit-and-run attacks. Both Patriots and Loyalists formed guerrilla bands in the South. They carried out vicious raids.

Now and then

BATTLE TACTICS

A difference in battle tactics affected future warfare. British soldiers marched shoulder to shoulder in three rows. When they neared the enemy, the first row knelt, the second crouched, and the third remained standing. They all fired without aiming.

The Americans were better shots. They often marched in rows, but sometimes they hid in woods or behind walls to take aim. Guerrillas attacked swiftly, then fled into the countryside. Those tactics succeeded and are still used today. This photograph shows modern U.S. soldiers learning guerrilla tactics.

Artillery of the Revolution

Artillery—large guns and cannon—played a key role in the American Revolution. The ability of these guns to kill and destroy from a distance made them essential in war. One witness of a battle described the destruction: "Many men were badly injured and mortally wounded by the fragments of bombs, . . . their arms and legs severed or themselves struck dead." Most cannon used in the Revolution were made of cast bronze. During the 1700s, artillery design did not change significantly. However, artillery became more mobile (more easily moved).

After each shot, a soldier sponged the inside of the barrel. This put out sparks and cleaned away any dirt left from the last shot.

A soldier loaded the cannon with gunpowder and a cannonball. He did so by ramming them down the barrel.

Soldiers aimed the gun by turning the entire carriage. An instrument called a quadrant told them how high to raise the barrel to reach their target.

Cannon were classified by weight of the iron ball they American artillery ranged f 3-pounders to 32-pounders

Soldiers lit the cannon by applying a red-hot wire or a tube of burning powder to a touchhole drilled through the back of the barrel, where the gunpowder lay. The gunpowder exploded, forcing the projectile out of the open end of the barrel.

In the 1700s, most cannon were accurate at ranges of up to 1,000 yards. That is the length of ten football fields laid end to end.

CONNECT TO HISTORY

1. **Recognizing Effects** Wh would it be an advantage army to have mobile artille

S See Skillbuilder Handbook, page R11.

CONNECT TO TODAY

2. **Researching** Find inform about modern artillery in encyclopedia or on the Int How did artillery change i 20th century?

For more about artillery . . .

RESEARCH LINKS
CLASSZONE.COM

The Tide Turns

Even battles in the South sometimes turned vicious. One example was the Battle of Kings Mountain, fought on the border of North and South Carolina in October 1780. After surrounding a force of about 1,000 Loyalist militia and British soldiers, the Americans slaughtered most of them. James P. Collins, a 16-year-old American, described the scene.

> ***A VOICE FROM THE PAST***
>
> The dead lay in heaps on all sides, while the groans of the wounded were heard in every direction. I could not help turning away from the scene before me with horror and, though exulting in victory, could not refrain from shedding tears.
>
> **James P. Collins,** quoted in *The Spirit of Seventy-Six*

Many of the dead had been shot or hanged after they surrendered. The Americans killed them in revenge for Loyalist raids and an earlier incident in which the British had butchered Americans. Kings Mountain was one of Britain's first losses in the South. It soon suffered more.

After Gates's defeat at Camden, Washington put a new general, Nathanael Greene, in charge of the Southern army. Greene was one of Washington's most able officers. He had been a Quaker, but his church had cast him out because of his belief in the armed struggle against the British. Most Quakers are **pacifist,** or opposed to war.

Under Greene's command, the American army avoided full-scale battles, in which the British had the edge because of superior firepower. So the American forces let the British chase them around the countryside and wear themselves out. When the Americans did fight, they did their best to make sure the British suffered heavy losses.

As the fighting dragged on into its sixth year, opposition to the war grew in Britain. As a result, some British leaders began to think that American independence would not be so bad.

*ing***History**
trasting
lid Greene's
gy as a gen-
iffer from
f Gates at
en?

The End of the War

In 1781, most of the fighting took place in Virginia. In July of that year, the British general Cornwallis set up his base at Yorktown, located on a peninsula in Chesapeake Bay. From there, his army could receive supplies by ship from New York.

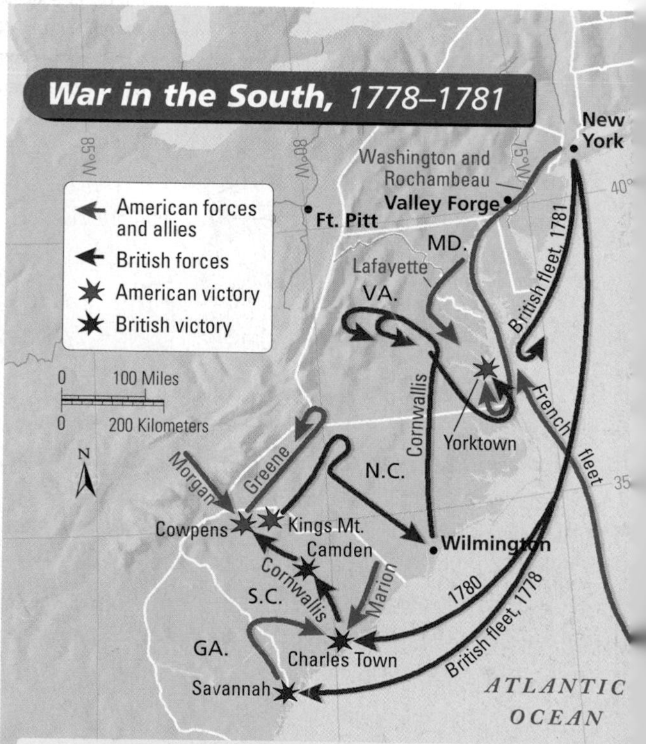

War in the South, 1778–1781
American forces and allies
British forces
American victory
British victory
0 100 Miles
0 200 Kilometers
N
85°W
80°W
75°W
40°
35°
New York
Washington and Rochambeau
Valley Forge
Ft. Pitt
MD.
Lafayette
VA.
British fleet, 1781
Yorktown
French fleet
Cornwallis
N.C.
Wilmington
1780
British fleet, 1778
Morgan
Greene
Cowpens
Kings Mt.
Camden
Cornwallis
Marion
S.C.
GA.
Charles Town
Savannah
ATLANTIC OCEAN

GEOGRAPHY SKILLBUILDER Interpreting Maps

1. **Place** *What ports did the British use to invade the South?*
2. **Movement** *Who traveled from Wilmington to Yorktown, and who traveled from New York?*

The victorious American forces accept the British surrender at Yorktown. George Washington is to the left of the American flag.

Washington saw Cornwallis's decision as a golden opportunity. In August 1781, a large French fleet arrived from the West Indies and blocked Chesapeake Bay. These ships prevented the British from receiving supplies—and from escaping. They also allowed Washington to come from the North and trap Cornwallis on the peninsula. Washington had enough men to do this because a large French force led by General Jean Rochambeau had joined his army.

Washington and Rochambeau moved south. When British ships tried to reach Cornwallis, French ships drove them back. In the **Battle of Yorktown,** the American and French troops bombarded Yorktown with cannon fire, turning its buildings to rubble. Cornwallis had no way out. On October 19, 1781, he surrendered his force of about 8,000.

Vocabulary
bombard: to attack with artillery

Although some fighting continued, Yorktown was the last major battle of the war. When the British prime minister, Lord North, heard the news, he gasped, "It is all over!" Indeed, he and other British leaders were soon forced to resign. Britain's new leaders began to negotiate a peace treaty, which is discussed in the next section.

Section 3 Assessment

1. Terms & Names

Explain the significance of:
- Lord Cornwallis
- guerrillas
- pacifist
- Battle of Yorktown

2. Using Graphics

Use a chart like the one below to list the geographic factors that made the British move their war effort to the South.

Physical factors, such as location	Human factors, such as who lived there

Were the human factors as helpful as the British hoped?

3. Main Ideas

a. Why did the fighting between Patriots and Loyalists in the South turn vicious?

b. What type of warfare did Francis Marion and his men employ?

c. How did Gates's errors in leadership contribute to the American loss at Camden?

4. Critical Thinking

Analyzing Causes How di each of the following help bring about the British defeat at Yorktown?

THINK ABOUT
- the location chosen by Cornwallis
- the French fleet
- the French troops unde Rochambeau
- Washington's planning

ACTIVITY OPTIONS

TECHNOLOGY / **MUSIC**

Imagine that Congress has asked you to commemorate the Battle of Yorktown. Design a **Web page** or write a **song** celebrating the U.S. victory.

The Legacy of the War

MAIN IDEA	WHY IT MATTERS NOW	TERMS & NAMES
he war, the new nation faced such as a high national debt ds for equality.	To promote liberty, some states passed laws outlawing slavery and protecting religious freedom.	Treaty of Paris of 1783 Elizabeth Freeman republicanism Richard Allen

ONE AMERICAN'S STORY

In 1776, 15-year-old Joseph Plumb Martin of Connecticut signed up to fight for the Americans. He stayed with the army until the war ended. Many years later, Martin wrote about leaving the army.

A VOICE FROM THE PAST

There was as much sorrow as joy. . . . We had lived together as a family of brothers for several years, . . . had shared with each other the hardships, dangers, and sufferings incident to a soldier's life; had sympathized with each other in trouble and sickness; . . . And now we were to be . . . parted forever.

Joseph Plumb Martin, quoted in *The Revolutionaries*

At war's end, Martin and his country faced an uncertain future. How would the United States recover from the war? What issues would confront the new nation? Section 4 discusses those questions.

Although this painting is not of Jos Plumb Martin himself, he may have dressed like this American soldier.

Why the Americans Won

In November 1783, the last British ships and troops left New York City, and American troops marched in. As Washington said good-bye to his officers in a New York tavern, he hugged each one. Tears ran down his face. He became so upset that he had to leave the room.

Earlier in the fall, Washington had written a farewell letter to his armies. In it, he praised them by saying that their endurance "through almost every possible suffering and discouragement for the space of eight long years, was little short of a standing miracle."

By their persistence, the Americans won independence even though they faced many obstacles. As you have read, they lacked training and experience. They were often short of supplies and weapons. By contrast, the British forces ranked among the best trained in the world. They were

Taking Notes

Use your chart to take notes about the results of the American Revolution.

1776	1777	1778

experienced and well-supplied professional soldiers. Yet the Americans had certain advantages that enabled them to win.

Reading **His**
A. Evaluating
What do you think was Washington's best character as a leader?

1. **Better leadership.** British generals were overconfident and made poor decisions. By contrast, Washington learned from his mistakes. After early defeats, he developed the strategy of dragging out the war to wear down the British. Despite difficulties, he never gave up.
2. **Foreign aid.** Britain's rivals, especially France, helped America. Foreign loans and military aid were essential to America's victory.
3. **Knowledge of the land.** The Americans knew the land where the war took place and used that knowledge well. The British could control coastal cities but could not extend their control to the interior.
4. **Motivation.** The Americans had more reason to fight. At stake were not only their lives but also their property and their dream of liberty.

The Treaty of Paris

As the winners, the Americans won favorable terms in the **Treaty of Paris of 1783,** which ended the Revolutionary War. The treaty included the following six conditions:

1. The United States was independent.
2. Its boundaries would be the Mississippi River on the west, Canada on the north, and Spanish Florida on the south.
3. The United States would receive the right to fish off Canada's Atlantic Coast, near Newfoundland and Nova Scotia.
4. Each side would repay debts it owed the other.
5. The British would return any enslaved persons they had captured.
6. Congress would recommend that the states return any property they had seized from Loyalists.

Neither Britain nor the United States fully lived up to the treaty's terms. Americans did not repay the prewar debts they owed British merchants or return Loyalist property. For their part, the British did not return

HISTORY *through* ART

The American painter Benjamin West began a portrait of the men who negotiated the Treaty of Paris. But the British officials refused to pose, so West never finished the painting. From left to right are the American officials John Jay, John Adams, Benjamin Franklin, and two others.

What does this painting reveal about the British response to losing the war?

runaway slaves. They also refused to give up military outposts in the Great Lakes area, such as Fort Detroit.

Costs of the War

No one knows exactly how many people died in the war, but eight years of fighting took a terrible toll. An estimated 25,700 Americans died in the war, and 1,400 remained missing. About 8,200 Americans were wounded. Some were left with permanent disabilities, such as amputated limbs. The British suffered about 10,000 military deaths.

Many soldiers who survived the war left the army with no money. They had received little or no pay for their service. Instead of back pay, the government gave some soldiers certificates for land in the West. Many men sold that land to get money for food and other basic needs.

Both the Congress and the states had borrowed money to finance the conflict. The war left the nation with a debt of about $27 million—a debt that would prove difficult to pay off.

The losers of the war also suffered. Thousands of Loyalists lost their property. Between 60,000 and 100,000 Loyalists left the United States during and after the war. Among them were several thousand African Americans and Native Americans, including Joseph Brant. Most of the Loyalists went to Canada. There they settled new towns and provinces. They also brought English traditions to areas that the French had settled. Even today, Canada has both French and English as official languages.

ground
after
ge Rogers
's Western
ies, the
n stayed at
Detroit.

ing History
alyzing
s Why do
nink the
sts left the
d States?

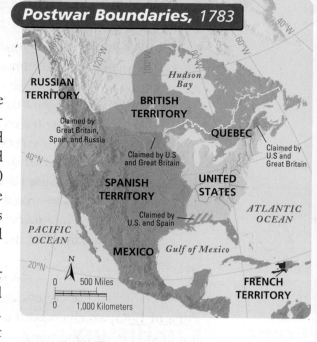

Postwar Boundaries, 1783

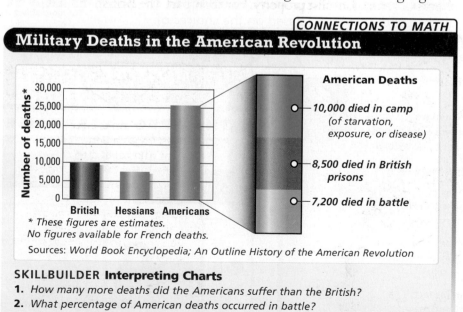

CONNECTIONS TO MATH

Military Deaths in the American Revolution

Number of deaths*

British   Hessians   Americans

* These figures are estimates.
No figures available for French deaths.

American Deaths

10,000 died in camp (of starvation, exposure, or disease)

8,500 died in British prisons

7,200 died in battle

Sources: *World Book Encyclopedia; An Outline History of the American Revolution*

SKILLBUILDER Interpreting Charts
1. How many more deaths did the Americans suffer than the British?
2. What percentage of American deaths occurred in battle?

Issues After the War

The American Revolution was not just a war, but a change in ideas about government. Before the war, Americans had demanded their rights as English citizens. But after declaring their independence, they replaced that goal with the idea of **republicanism**. This idea stated that instead of a king, the people would rule. The government would obtain its authority from the citizens and be responsible to them.

For this system to work, individuals would have to place the good of the country above their own interests. At first, only men were allowed to take part in governing by voting or holding public office—and not even all men. However, women could help the nation by teaching their children the virtues that benefited public life. Such virtues included honesty, duty, and the willingness to make sacrifices.

Economics *in* History

Free Enterprise

One cause of the Revolution was the colonists' resentment of British mercantilism. Parliament passed laws to discourage the colonists from developing their own manufacturing and to force them to buy British goods. During the war, British economic control weakened. British exports of woolens to the colonies dropped from £645,900 in 1774 to only £2,540 in 1776. As a result, the colonists were able to make more economic choices—for example, they could choose to manufacture wool clothing.

The end of Britain's mercantilist control allowed free enterprise to begin to develop in the United States. In a free-enterprise system, business can be conducted freely based on the choices of individuals. The government does not control the system, but only protects and regulates it.

CONNECT TO HISTORY

1. **Analyzing Causes** Why d you think the colonists wer able to manufacture their wool clothing during the w

   See Skillbuilder
   Handbook, page R11.

CONNECT TO TODAY

2. **Comparing** Think about a where you shop. Name examples of businesses tha compete with each other. Compare the methods they use to attract customers.

For more about free enterprise . . .

RESEARCH LINKS
CLASSZONE.COM

A Competition encourages businesses to improve goods and services and to keep prices down.

B Property is owned by individuals and businesses.

C The desire to make a profit motivates businesspeople.

D Individuals, not the government, decide what to buy and what to manufacture and sell.

E The government protects private property and makes sure businesses operate fairly.

THE FREE ENTERPRISE MALL

THE BARGAIN STORE

PAY LESS GET MORE STOR

As part of their liberty, Americans called for more religious freedom. Before the war, some laws discriminated against certain religions. Some states had not allowed Jews or Catholics to hold public office. After the war, states began to abolish those laws. They also ended the practice of using tax money to support churches.

Many people began to see a conflict between slavery and the ideal of liberty. Vermont outlawed slavery, and Pennsylvania passed a law to free slaves gradually. Individual African Americans also tried to end slavery. For example, **Elizabeth Freeman** sued for her freedom in a Massachusetts court and won. Her victory in 1781 and other similar cases ended slavery in that state. Freeman later described her desire for freedom.

A VOICE FROM THE PAST

Anytime while I was a slave, if one minute's freedom had been offered to me, and I had been told I must die at the end of that minute, I would have taken it—just to stand one minute on God's earth a free woman.

Elizabeth Freeman, quoted in *Notable Black American Women*

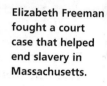

Elizabeth Freeman fought a court case that helped end slavery in Massachusetts.

…ing**History**
…ving
…ems How
…ee African
…icans take
…e responsi-
…of trying to
…ve their

With freedom, African Americans began to form their own institutions. For example, the preacher **Richard Allen** helped start the Free African Society. That society encouraged African Americans to help each other. Allen also founded the African Methodist Episcopal Church, the first African-American church in the United States.

Perhaps the main issue facing Americans after the war was how to shape their national government. American anger over British taxes, violation of rights, and control of trade had caused the war. Now the United States needed a government that would protect citizens' rights and economic freedom. In Chapter 8, you will read how U.S. leaders worked to create such a government.

…tion **4** Assessment

Terms & Names

…plain the
…gnificance of:

…eaty of Paris
… 1783
…publicanism
…izabeth Freeman
…chard Allen

2. Using Graphics

Use a chart like the one below to classify the terms of the Treaty of Paris according to which side they favored. (Do not list terms that don't favor either side.)

Terms of the Treaty of Paris	
Favorable to America	Favorable to Britain

3. Main Ideas

a. What advantages helped the Americans win the Revolutionary War?

b. How did the end of the war affect Loyalists?

c. What were the economic costs of the war to individuals and to the government?

4. Critical Thinking

Recognizing Effects How did republicanism shape the United States after the war?

THINK ABOUT

• American ideas about government
• the roles men and women could play in public life
• religious freedom
• the antislavery movement

…VITY OPTIONS

SPEECH

MATH

Look up the U.S. population in 1780. Calculate what percentage of American people died in the war. Report your findings in a **speech** or a **pie graph**.

TERMS & NAMES

Briefly explain the significance of each of the following.

1. George Washington
2. mercenary
3. Battles of Saratoga
4. ally
5. Marquis de Lafayette
6. John Paul Jones
7. Lord Cornwallis
8. Battle of Yorktown
9. Treaty of Paris of 1783
10. republicanism

REVIEW QUESTIONS

The Early Years of the War (pages 193–199)

1. What motives led African Americans to fight for the British? The Americans?
2. How did women help the American war effort?
3. What events led to the British defeat at Saratoga?

The War Expands (pages 200–205)

4. What foreign countries helped America? How?
5. What were conditions like at Valley Forge?

The Path to Victory (pages 206–210)

6. What two Southern ports did the British capture?
7. How did America's ally France contribute to the victory at Yorktown?

The Legacy of the War (pages 211–215)

8. For what did Washington praise his army in his farewell letter?
9. What land did the United States acquire from Britain as a result of the Treaty of Paris?
10. What three states outlawed slavery after the war?

CRITICAL THINKING

1. USING YOUR NOTES: SEQUENCING EVENTS

Using your completed time line, answer the questio below.

| 1776 | 1777 | 1778 | 1779 | 1780 | 1781 | 1782 | 1783 |

a. What were the main events of 1776 and 1777?
b. While George Rogers Clark was capturing Kaska what was happening in the South?

2. ANALYZING LEADERSHIP

George Washington was the most beloved Americ leader of his time. What qualities do you think ma him such a respected leader?

3. THEME: CITIZENSHIP

What Revolutionary leaders displayed civic virtue b putting the good of the nation ahead of their own interests? Explain your answer.

4. RECOGNIZING EFFECTS

How did Britain's loss in the war allow free enterp to develop in the United States?

5. APPLYING CITIZENSHIP SKILLS

How was the writing of *The American Crisis* an ex ple of good U.S. citizenship?

Interact *with* History

How did the sacrifices you discussed before you re the chapter compare with what Patriots really did

VISUAL SUMMARY

The American Revolution

People and Events of the Revolution

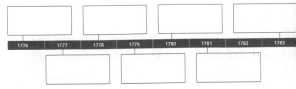

Military		Civilian	
George Washington	commanded the Continental Army.	Haym Salomon	helped finance the war for America.
Marquis de Lafayette	fought for the Americans.	Molly Pitcher	aided soldiers by bringing them water in battle.
John Burgoyne	surrendered to the Americans at Saratoga.	Thomas Paine	wrote *The American Crisis* to inspire Americans.
John Paul Jones	won a major naval victory for America.	Benjamin Franklin	was a diplomat to France and Britain.
George Rogers Clark	helped hold the Western frontier for America.	James Forten	was captured by the British but would not betray America.
Lord Cornwallis	surrendered at Yorktown, ending the war.	Nancy Hart	defended her Georgia home against Loyalist raiders.

se the map and your knowledge of U.S. history to nswer questions 1 and 2.

dditional Test Practice, pp. S1–S33.

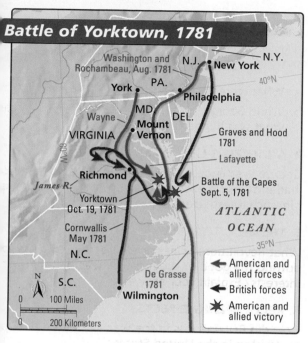

Battle of Yorktown, 1781

In what state was the Battle of Yorktown fought?

A. North Carolina

B. Pennsylvania

C. South Carolina

D. Virginia

2. Which of the following describes the route of the forces led by Cornwallis?

A. south from York, PA to Yorktown, VA

B. south from New York to Yorktown, VA

C. north from Wilmington, NC to Richmond, VA

D. north from Richmond, VA to Wilmington, NC

This quotation is from Thomas Paine discussing the Revolutionary War. Use the quotation and your knowledge of U.S. history to answer question 3.

PRIMARY SOURCE

These are the times that try men's souls. The summer soldier and the sunshine patriot will, in this crisis, shrink from the service of their country; but he that stands it now, deserves the love and thanks of man and woman.

Thomas Paine, *The American Crisis*

3. Who is Paine referring to as "the summer soldier and the sunshine patriot"?

A. Americans who support the war only when it is going well

B. Loyalists who never support the war efforts

C. Americans who show continuous support for the war

D. soldiers who perform best in good weather

TEST PRACTICE
CLASSZONE.COM

ERNATIVE ASSESSMENT

WRITING ABOUT HISTORY

se you are a soldier at Valley Forge during the r of 1777–1778. Write daily **journal** entries for veek, describing the harsh conditions of the camp our physical and emotional state.

earch Valley Forge in books or encyclopedias.

to locate primary sources such as letters, diaries, journals of soldiers at Valley Forge.

OPERATIVE LEARNING

ng in groups, prepare a talk show in which discuss which side to take in the Revolutionary One group member should be the host. Other ers should be guests. Consider some of the fol- g guests: the wife of an American soldier, an ed African American, an Iroquois chief, a Quaker er, and an employee of the British government.

INTEGRATED TECHNOLOGY

CREATING A MULTIMEDIA PRESENTATION

Choose a major battle of the Revolution. Then use the Internet and other library resources to research that battle. Gather information that represents the American and British points of view.

- Locate details about the battle, as well as primary sources, such as quotations from participants on both sides. Make copies of any images you find, being careful to credit your sources.

- Find music of the time period and sound effects.

- Once you have collected these audio and visual materials, combine them to create a multimedia presentation.

For more about the battles . . .

INTERNET ACTIVITY
CLASSZONE.COM

Confederation to Constitution 1776–1791

Delegates kept the windows closed during meetings so that the proceedings would be secret.

Some of the most respected men in the nation served as delegates, including Alexander Hamilton and Benjamin Franklin.

1777
Patriots win Battles of Saratoga.
Continental Congress passes the
Articles of Confederation.

1781
Articles of Confederation
go into effect.
British surrender at
Yorktown.

the

USA
World 1776

1779
Spain
declares war
on Britain.

1781
Joseph II allo
religious fre
Christians in

The delegates of the Constitutional Convention chose George Washington, hero of the Revolutionary War, to be president of the convention.

The year is 1787, and your young country needs to reform its government. Now everyone is wondering what the new government will be like. You have been called to a convention to decide how the new government should be organized.

How do you form a government?

What Do You Think?

- What will be your main goal in creating a new government?
- How will you get the people at the convention to agree on important issues?

 **RESEARCH LINKS**
CLASSZONE.COM

Visit the Chapter 8 links for more information about America after the revolution.

1786–1787
I Shays leads a rebellion of Massachusetts farmers.

1787
Constitutional Convention is held in Philadelphia.

1788
U.S. Constitution is ratified.

1789
George Washington becomes the first president of the United States.

1791
Bill of Rights is ratified.

1791

1785
Jean-Paul Blanchard and John Jefferies cross the English Channel in a balloon.

1787
Freetown, Sierra Leone, is made a home for freed slaves.

1789
French Revolution begins.

Reading Strategy: Solving Problems

What Do You Know?

What do you think of when people talk about the U.S. government? Why do nations have governments? What does the U.S. government do?

Think About
- what you've learned about the U.S. government from the news or your teachers
- what the purpose of a government is
- how the government affects your everyday life
- your responses to the Interact with History about forming a government (see page 219)

The Constitutional Convention in what is now known as Independence Hall (shown abc

What Do You Want to Know?

 What questions do you have about how the four colonial regions developed? Recor these questions in your notebook before you read the chapter.

Solving Problems

When you read history, look for how people solved problems they faced in the past. Cop the chart below in your notebook. Use it to identify the methods that Americans used to solve the problems faced by the nation after declaring its independence.

S See Skillbuilder Handbook, page R18.

 Taking Notes

Problems	Solutions
Western lands	
Postwar depression	
Representation in the new government	
Slavery	

1

The Confederation Era

| MAIN IDEA | WHY IT MATTERS NOW | TERMS & NAMES |

MAIN IDEA

...icles of Confederation were ...ak to govern the nation after ...r ended.

WHY IT MATTERS NOW

The weakness of the Articles of Confederation led to the writing of the U.S. Constitution.

TERMS & NAMES

Wilderness Road
republic
Articles of Confederation

Land Ordinance of 1785
Northwest Territory
Northwest Ordinance
Shays's Rebellion

ONE AMERICAN'S STORY

In 1775, Daniel Boone and 30 woodsmen cut a road over the Appalachian Mountains into Kentucky. After about 250 miles, they arrived in a meadow along the banks of the Kentucky River. Felix Walker, a member of Boone's party, described what they saw.

A VOICE FROM THE PAST

On entering the plain we were permitted to view a very interesting and romantic sight. A number of buffaloes . . . between two and three hundred, made off. . . . Such a sight some of us never saw before, nor perhaps ever may again.

Felix Walker, quoted in *The Life and Adventures of Daniel Boone*

In the late 1700s, most Americans thought of Kentucky as the wild frontier. Some, like Boone, looked at the frontier and saw a world of opportunity. Exploring and governing these lands was one of the many challenges facing the new government of the United States.

Early travel to Kentucky is shown in this detail of *Daniel Boone Escorting Settlers Through the Cumberland Gap* (1851–1852) by Geo... Caleb Bingham.

Moving West

The trail into Kentucky that Daniel Boone helped build was called the **Wilderness Road**. This road was not easy to travel. It was too narrow for carts or wagons, but it became the main road into Kentucky. The settlers came on foot or on horseback. Settlers were drawn to Kentucky's rich river valleys, where few Native Americans lived. But some Native Americans, such as the Shawnee, did live, hunt, and fish in the area.

Tensions between Native Americans and settlers led to violent confrontations. But the settlers did not stop coming. By the early 1790s, about 100,000 Americans lived there. While settlers headed into the Western territories, the people in the East began to create new state governments.

Taking Notes

Use your chart to take notes about th... western lands and postwar depression

Problems	
Western lands	
Postwar depression	
Representation in the new government	
Slavery	

New State Governments

Once the American colonies declared independence, each of the states set out to create its own government. The framers, or creators, of the state constitutions did not want to destroy the political systems that they had had as colonies. They simply wanted to make those systems more democratic. Some states experimented with creating separate branches of government, giving different powers to different branches. By creating separate branches, Americans hoped to prevent the government from becoming too powerful.

Some states included a bill of rights in their constitutions as a way to keep the government under control. The idea of a bill of rights came from the English Bill of Rights of 1689. This was a list of rights that the government guaranteed to English citizens.

Although not all the states had a bill of rights, all of them did have a republican form of government. In a **republic,** the people choose representatives to govern them.

The Articles of Confederation

While the states were setting up their governments, Americans also discussed the form of their national government. During the Revolutionary War, Americans realized that they needed to unite to win the war against Britain. As Silas Deane, a diplomat from Connecticut, wrote, "United we stand, divided we fall."

In 1776, the Continental Congress began to develop a plan for a national government. Congress agreed that the government should be a republic. But the delegates disagreed about whether each state should have one vote or voting should be based on population. They also disagreed about whether the national government or the individual states should control the lands west of the Appalachians.

The Continental Congress eventually arrived at a final plan, called the **Articles of Confederation.** In the Articles, the national government had few powers, because many Americans were afraid that a strong government would lead to tyranny, or oppressive rule. The national government was run by a Confederation Congress. Each state had only one vote in the Congress. The national government had the power to wage war, make peace, sign treaties, and issue money.

But the Articles left most important powers to the states. These powers included the authority to set taxes and enforce national laws. The Articles proposed to leave the states in control of the lands west of the Appalachian Mountains.

"United we stand, divided we fall."

Silas Deane

Background

Two states, Connecticut and Rhode Island, kept their old colonial charters as their constitutions. The other 11 states wrote new constitu

Reading

A. Reading a Map Look at the map on page to see which states claimed territories in the West.

The Continental Congress passed the Articles of Confederation in November 1777. It then sent the Articles to the states for ratification, or approval. By July 1778, eight states had ratified the Articles. But some of the small states that did not have Western land claims refused to sign.

These states felt that unless the Western lands were placed under the control of the national government, they would be at a disadvantage. The states with Western lands could sell them to pay off debts left from the Revolution. But states without lands would have difficulty paying off the high war debts.

Over the next three years, all the states gave up their claims to Western lands. This led the small states to ratify the Articles. In 1781, Maryland became the 13th state to accept the Articles. As a result, the United States finally had an official government.

ding History
ding Main
Why did
ates with-
Western land
s want the
states to
p their
?

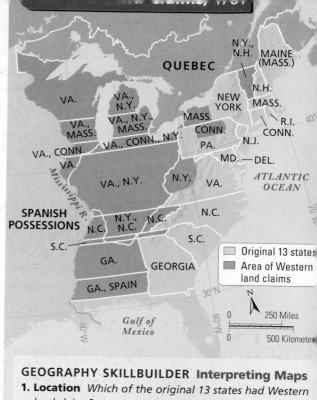

round
ng to the
est
ce, Native
ans were
eated
nd their
ere not
ken
em.

GEOGRAPHY SKILLBUILDER Interpreting Maps
1. **Location** Which of the original 13 states had Western land claims?
2. **Location** To what geographic feature did the Western land claims extend?

The Northwest Ordinance

One of the most important questions that the Confederation Congress faced was what to do with the Western lands that it now controlled. Congress passed important laws on how to divide and govern these lands—the Land Ordinance of 1785 and the Northwest Ordinance (1787). (See Geography in History on pages 226–227.)

The **Land Ordinance of 1785** called for surveyors to stake out six-mile-square plots, called townships, in the Western lands. These lands later became known as the **Northwest Territory**. The Northwest Territory included land that formed the states of Ohio, Indiana, Michigan, Illinois, and Wisconsin and part of Minnesota.

The **Northwest Ordinance** (1787) described how the Northwest Territory was to be governed. As the territory grew in population, it would gain rights to self-government. When there were 5,000 free males in an area, men who owned at least 50 acres of land could elect an assembly. When there were 60,000 people, they could apply to become a new state.

The Northwest Ordinance also set conditions for settlement in the Northwest Territory and outlined the settlers' rights. Slavery was outlawed, and the rivers were to be open to navigation by all. Freedom of religion and trial by jury were guaranteed.

The Northwest Ordinance was important because it set a pattern for the orderly growth of the United States. As the nation grew, it followed this pattern in territories added after the Northwest Territory.

Weaknesses of the Articles

Aside from its handling of land issues, however, the Confederation Congress had few successes. By the end of the Revolutionary War, the United States faced serious problems, and the Confederation Congress did not have enough power to solve them.

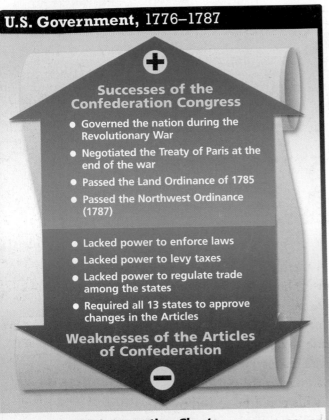

U.S. Government, 1776–1787

➕ Successes of the Confederation Congress

- Governed the nation during the Revolutionary War
- Negotiated the Treaty of Paris at the end of the war
- Passed the Land Ordinance of 1785
- Passed the Northwest Ordinance (1787)

- Lacked power to enforce laws
- Lacked power to levy taxes
- Lacked power to regulate trade among the states
- Required all 13 states to approve changes in the Articles

➖ Weaknesses of the Articles of Confederation

SKILLBUILDER Interpreting Charts

1. What do you think was the greatest success of the Confederation Congress?
2. What do you think was the greatest weakness of the Articles of Confederation?

Debt was a critical problem for the government. Congress had borrowed large sums to pay for the Revolutionary War. Much of that money was owed to soldiers of its own army. Upset at not being paid, several hundred soldiers surrounded the Pennsylvania State House where Congress was meeting in June 1783. The soldiers threatened the legislators, thrusting their bayonets through the windows. The delegates were forced to flee the city. The event was a clear sign of Congress's weakness.

Even if Congress wanted to pay the soldiers, it did not have the power to levy taxes. The national government depended on the states to send money to Congress. But the states sent very little money.

Congress was not alone in facing economic crises. People throughout the nation faced hard times. In Massachusetts, the economy was so bad that people rose up in arms against the government.

Reading **Hi**
C. Analyzing
Causes How
debt cause
lems for the
government
under the
Articles of
Confederati

Shays's Rebellion

In the mid-1780s, Massachusetts faced economic problems, as did other states. People had little money, but the state continued to levy high taxes. The average family owed $200 in taxes per year—more money than most farmers made. Many Massachusetts farmers fell deeply into debt. Debt laws at the time were strict. Anyone who could not repay his debts would have his property auctioned off. If the auction didn't raise enough money to settle the debts, the debtor could be put in jail. In western Massachusetts, many jails were packed with debtors.

Farmers asked the Massachusetts legislature to provide debt relief. But the legislature refused—and the farmers rebelled. One of the leaders of the rebellion was a Revolutionary War veteran named Daniel Shays. He commanded a group of about 1,500 men.

In January 1787, Shays and his men marched on a federal arsenal, a place to store weapons. The arsenal was defended by 900 soldiers from the state militia. The militia quickly defeated Shays's men. But even though the militia put down **Shays's Rebellion,** as the uprising came to be known, the farmers won the sympathy of many people. America's leaders realized that an armed uprising of common farmers spelled danger for the nation.

Some leaders hoped that the nation's ills could be solved by strengthening the national government. In the next section, you'll read how Americans held a convention to change the Articles of Confederation.

Shays's rebels take over a Massachusetts courthouse. A stone marker rests on the spot of the rebellion.

ground
8, Daniel
was
ned for
ions.

---

tion ❶ Assessment

Terms & Names

**plain the
gnificance of:**
ilderness Road
public
rticles of
onfederation
nd Ordinance
1785
orthwest Territory
orthwest
rdinance
ays's Rebellion

2. Using Graphics

Use a diagram like the one below to list some of the challenges Americans faced in shaping a new government.

Which challenge do you think was the toughest? Why?

3. Main Ideas

a. What issues affected the Western territories between 1775 and 1787?

b. What were three successes of the Continental Congress?

c. What were the strengths and weaknesses of the Articles of Confederation?

4. Critical Thinking

Forming and Supporting Opinions Which side would you have supported during Shays's Rebellion—the farmers or the officials who called out the militia? Why?

THINK ABOUT
• the farmers' problems
• the farmers' march on the arsenal
• the job of the government

VITY OPTIONS

CIVICS

EOGRAPHY

Write an **opinion article** about how the United States should govern the Western territories or draw a **map** showing how you would have divided the lands.

The Northwest Territory

The Northwest Territory was officially known as "the Territory Northwest of the River Ohio." In the mid-1780s, Congress decided to sell the land in the territory to settlers. The sale of land solved two problems. First, it provided cash for the government. Second, it increased American control over the land.

The Land Ordinance of 1785 outlined how the land in the Northwest Territory would be divided. Congress split the land into grids with clearly defined boundaries. It created townships that could be divided into sections, as shown on the map below. Each township was six miles by six miles. This was an improvement over earlier methods of setting boundaries. Previously, people had used rocks, trees, or other landmarks to set boundaries. There had been constant fights over disputed claims.

TOWNSHIP,

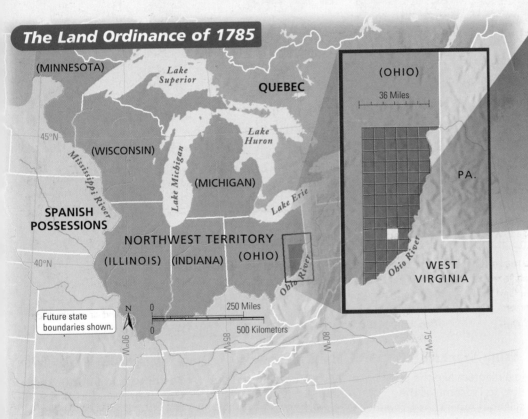

The Land Ordinance of 1785

36	30	24	18
35	29	23	17
34	28	22	16
33	27	21	15
32	26	20	14
31	25	19	13

Each township sections. Each s one square mil

ARTIFACT FILE

The Theodolite The theodolite is a surveying tool. It consists of a telescope that can be moved from side to side and up and down. A theodolite measures angles and determines alignment. These functions are necessary for land surveyors to establish accurate boundaries for land claims.

Township Map
Congress reserved several plots (outlined on map) for special purposes. A few were set aside for later sale to raise money for the government. One plot was reserved to support a local school.

e first things settlers needed were
od and shelter. Cutting trees
ovided fields for crops and wood for
cabins. The first crop most farmers
nted was corn. Even if the land was
t fully cleared of trees, farmers
nted corn between the stumps.

2 A shortage of labor meant that a
farmer working alone was doing well
if he cleared several acres a year. As a
result, few farms were completely
fenced in, and forest covered most of
the property. Hogs were allowed to
find food in the woods. Farmers
collected apples from trees and used
sap to make syrup.

3 Over time, families planted fruits and
vegetables. Cattle raising also became
more common. Beef cattle supplied
families with meat. Dairy cattle
provided milk. Families could sell extra
fruits, vegetables, and dairy products,
such as butter and cheese.

CONNECT TO GEOGRAPHY

1. **Region** What was the land in
   the Northwest Territory like
   before Americans settled there?
2. **Human-Environment
   Interaction** How did American
   settlers affect the landscape in
   the territory?

   G See Geography
   Handbook, pages 4–5.

CONNECT TO HISTORY

3. **Making Inferences** Why did
   so many people buy land in the
   new territory?

Line Field Trip

io Historical Society
d in Columbus, Ohio. It
s a Web site called Ohio
Central that includes
ion on the Ohio portion
rthwest Territory.

about the Northwest Territory . . .

ESEARCH LINKS
ASSZONE.COM

Creating the Constitution

MAIN IDEA	WHY IT MATTERS NOW	TERMS & NAMES
The states sent delegates to a convention to solve the problems of the Articles of Confederation.	The Constitutional Convention formed the plan of government that the United States still has today.	Constitutional Convention James Madison Virginia Plan New Jersey Great Com Three-Fifth Compron

ONE AMERICAN'S STORY

On May 15, 1787, Virginia Governor Edmund Randolph arrived in Philadelphia. The young nation faced lawlessness, as Shays's Rebellion had shown. Now delegates from throughout the states were coming to Philadelphia to discuss reforming the government. Early in the convention Randolph rose to speak.

A VOICE FROM THE PAST

Let us not be afraid to view with a steady eye the [dangers] with which we are surrounded. . . . Are we not on the eve of [a civil] war, which is only to be prevented by the hopes from this convention?

Edmund Randolph, quoted in *Edmund Randolph: A Biography*

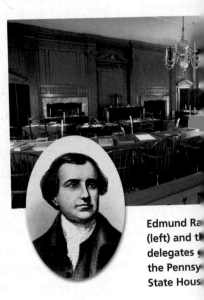

Edmund Ra (left) and t delegates the Pennsy State Hous

Over the next four months, the delegates debated how best to keep the United States from falling apart. In this section, you will read about the Convention of 1787 and the creation of the U.S. Constitution.

Taking Notes

Use your chart to take notes about the new government and slavery.

roblems	
Western lands	
ostwar depression	
Representation in the new government	
slavery	

A Constitutional Convention Is Called

In 1786, a series of events began that would eventually lead to a new form of government for the United States. In September of that year, delegates from five states met in Annapolis, Maryland, to discuss ways to promote trade among their states. At the time, most states placed high taxes on goods from other states. The delegates believed that creating national trade laws would help the economies of all the states.

Making such changes required amending the Articles of Confederation, because the national government had been granted no power to regulate trade among the states. The Annapolis delegates, led by Alexander Hamilton of New York, called for the states to send representatives to

Philadelphia the following May to discuss such changes.

At first, many Americans doubted that the national government needed strengthening. But news of Shays's Rebellion in late 1786 and early 1787 quickly changed many people's minds. Fearing that rebellion might spread, 12 states sent delegates to the meeting in Philadelphia in the summer of 1787. Only Rhode Island refused to participate.

The Convention's Delegates

The 55 delegates to the **Constitutional Convention,** as the Philadelphia meeting became known, were a very impressive group. About half were lawyers. Others were planters, merchants, and doctors. Three-fourths of them had been representatives in the Continental Congress. Many had been members of their state legislatures and had helped write their state constitutions. Along with other leaders of the time, these delegates are called the Founders, or Founding Fathers, of the United States.

America's most famous men were at the Constitutional Convention. George Washington, the hero of the Revolution, came out of retirement for the meeting. Benjamin Franklin, the famous scientist and statesman, lent his wit and wisdom to the convention. One of the ablest delegates was **James Madison.** Madison had read more than a hundred books on government in preparation for the meeting. When Thomas Jefferson, serving as ambassador to France, read the list of delegates, he wrote, "It is really an assembly of demigods."

Not everyone was at the Constitutional Convention. Thomas Jefferson and John Adams were overseas at their diplomatic posts. But they wrote home to encourage the delegates. Others had a less positive outlook on the convention. For example, Patrick Henry, who had been elected as a delegate from Virginia, refused to attend. He said he "smelled a rat in Philadelphia, tending toward monarchy."

Also, the convention did not reflect the diverse U.S. population of the 1780s. There were no Native Americans, African Americans, or women among the delegates. The nation's early leaders did not consider these groups of people to be citizens and did not invite any of them to attend. However, the framework of government the Founders established is the very one that would eventually provide full rights and responsibilities to all Americans.

The Delegates Assemble

Most of the delegates arrived at the Constitutional Convention without a clear idea of what to expect. Some thought they would only draft

ground
e Island did
nd dele-
because it
that a
national
ment
force
e to repay
r debts on
lt terms.

ngHistory
uating
ell do the
eristics of
nders
s models
virtue?

JAMES MADISON

1751–1836

James Madison was a short, soft-spoken man, but he may have made the greatest contribution of any of the Founders at the Constitutional Convention. He took thorough notes of the convention's proceedings. His notes are the most detailed picture we have of the debates and drama of the convention.

But Madison did not just observe the convention. He was perhaps the most important participant. One of the other delegates called him "the best informed Man of any point in debate." Madison was so important that he earned the title "Father of the Constitution."

How did Madison contribute to the Constitutional Convention?

amendments to the Articles of Confederation. Others thought they would design an entirely new plan for the government. But they all agreed that the government should protect people's rights.

Back in 1776, many Americans thought that government was the main threat to people's rights. But by 1787, many realized that the people often came into conflict and needed a government that could maintain order. As a result, the government had to be strong enough to protect people's rights but not too strong to be controlled. Madison later wrote about this problem.

A VOICE FROM THE PAST

If men were angels, no government would be necessary. If angels were to govern men, neither external nor internal controls on government would be necessary. In framing a government which is to be administered by men over men, the great difficulty lies in this: you must first enable the government to control the governed; and in the next place oblige it [the government] to control itself.

James Madison, *The Federalist* "Number 51"

This was the challenge that faced the delegates: how to set up a strong but limited federal government. By May 25, 1787, at least two delegates from each of seven states had arrived in Philadelphia. With 29 delegates in attendance, the convention was officially under way.

The Convention Begins

The first order of business was to elect a president for the convention. Robert Morris of Pennsylvania nominated George Washington. No American was more respected or admired than Washington. Every delegate voted for him. Washington's quiet and dignified leadership set a solemn and serious tone for the convention.

At their next meeting, the delegates decided on the rules for the convention. They wanted to be able to consider all ideas and to be able to change sides in any debate. They did not want to be pressured by the politics of the day. For these reasons, they decided that their discussions would remain secret. To ensure privacy, the windows in their meeting room were kept shut even though it was summer. Guards were posted outside the door. Whenever the door was opened, the delegates stopped talking. With the secrecy rule approved, they got down to business.

The Virginia Plan

On May 29, the delegates began the real work of designing a new national government. Presiding over the convention, George Washington

Reading **Hi**
B. Using Pri
Sources
According t
Madison, w
the central
lem in fram
governmen

Reading
C. Making
Decisions
agree with
Founders'
sion to ke
conventio
secret? W
why not?

The delegates at the Constitutional Convention debated the Constitution intensely.

recognized Edmund Randolph as the first speaker. Randolph offered a plan for a whole new government. The plan became known as the **Virginia Plan.** Madison, Randolph, and the other Virginia delegates had drawn up the plan while they waited for the convention to open.

The Virginia Plan proposed a government that would have three branches. The first branch of government was the legislature, which made the laws. The second branch was the executive, which enforced the laws. The third branch was the judiciary, which interpreted the laws.

The Virginia Plan proposed a legislature with two houses. In both houses, the number of representatives from each state would be based on the state's population or its wealth. The legislature would have the power to levy taxes, regulate commerce, and make laws "in all cases where the separate states are incompetent [unable]."

The Virginia Plan led to weeks of debate. Because they had larger populations, larger states supported the plan. It would give them greater representation in the legislature. The smaller states opposed this plan. They worried that the larger states would end up ruling the others. Delaware delegate John Dickinson voiced the concerns of the small states.

> "If men were angels, no government would be necessary."
> James Madison

*ng***History**
marizing
was the
a Plan?

A VOICE FROM THE PAST

Some of the members from the small states wish for two branches in the general legislature and are friends to a good [strong] national government; but we would sooner submit [give in] to a foreign power than submit to be deprived, in both branches of the legislature, of an equal suffrage [vote], and thereby be thrown under the domination of the larger states.

John Dickinson, quoted in *Mr. Madison's Constitution*

The Great Compromise

In response to the Virginia Plan, New Jersey delegate William Paterson presented an alternative on June 15. The **New Jersey Plan** called for a legislature with only one house. In it, each state would have one vote. In providing equal representation to each state, the New Jersey Plan was similar to the Articles of Confederation.

Even though the New Jersey Plan gave the legislature the power to regulate trade and to raise money by taxing foreign goods, it did not offer the broad powers proposed by the Virginia Plan. The delegates

The Great Compromise

VIRGINIA PLAN

- The legislative branch would have two houses.
- Both houses in the legislature would assign representatives according to state population or wealth.

NEW JERSEY PLAN

- The legislature would have one house.
- Each state would have one vote in the legislature.

THE GREAT COMPROMISE

- The Senate would give each state equal representation.

  The legislature would have two houses.
- The House of Representatives would have representation according to state population.

SKILLBUILDER Interpreting Charts

1. *Which plan appealed more to the small states?*
2. *Did the Great Compromise include more of what the large states wanted or more of what the small states wanted?*

voted on these two plans on June 19. The Virginia Plan won and became the framework for drafting the Constitution.

During the rest of June, the delegates argued over representation in the legislature. Emotions ran high as the delegates struggled for a solution. In desperation, the delegates selected a committee to work out a compromise in early July. The committee offered the **Great Compromise**. (Some people also refer to it as the Connecticut Compromise.)

To satisfy the smaller states, each state would have an equal number of votes in the Senate. To satisfy the larger states, the committee set representation in the House of Representatives according to state populations. More than a week of arguing followed the introduction of the plan, but on July 16, 1787, the convention passed it.

Backgrou
Roger Sher
Connecticut
widely cred
with propo
the Great
Compromis

Slavery and the Constitution

Because representation in the House of Representatives would be based on the population of each state, the delegates had to decide who would be counted in that population. The Southern states had many more slaves than the Northern states. Southerners wanted the slaves to be counted as part of the general population for representation but not for taxation. Northerners argued that slaves were not citizens and should not be counted for representation but should be counted for taxation.

On this issue, the delegates reached another compromise, known as the **Three-Fifths Compromise**. Under this compromise, three-fifths of the slave population would be counted when setting direct taxes on the states. This three-fifths ratio also would be used to determine representation in the legislature.

The delegates had another heated debate about the slave trade. Slavery had already been outlawed in several Northern states. All of the Northern states and several of the Southern states had banned the

ding**History**

rming and
orting

ions Did the
ates do the
thing in
eing to the
-Fifths
romise?
in.

importation of slaves. Many Northerners wanted to see this ban extended to the rest of the nation. But Southern slaveholders strongly disagreed. The delegates from South Carolina and Georgia stated that they would never accept any plan "unless their right to import slaves be untouched." Again, the delegates settled on a compromise. On August 29, they agreed that Congress could not ban the slave trade until 1808.

Regulating Trade

Aside from delaying any ban on the slave trade, the Constitution placed few limits on Congress's power "to regulate commerce with foreign nations, and among the several states, and with the Indian tribes." Most delegates were glad that Congress would regulate—and even promote—commerce. After all, commercial problems were the main cause of the Annapolis Convention in 1786. Southerners, however, succeeded in banning Congress from taxing exports because Southern economies depended on exports. The commerce clause also showed the shadowy status that Native Americans had under the Constitution. They were neither foreign nations nor part of the separate states.

The Constitutional Convention continued to meet into September. On Saturday, September 15, 1787, the delegates voted their support for the Constitution in its final form. On Sunday, it was written out on four sheets of thick parchment. On Monday, all but three delegates signed the Constitution. It was then sent, with a letter signed by George Washington, to the Confederation Congress, which sent it to the states for ratification, or approval. In the next section, you will read about the debate over ratification.

Now and then

PRESERVING THE CONSTITUTION

The National Archives is responsible for preserving the 200-year-old sheets of parchment on which the original Constitution was first written.

The Archives stores the document in an airtight glass case enclosed in a 55-ton vault of steel and concrete. Every few years, scientists examine the pages with the latest technology. For the last examination in 1995, they used fiber-optic light sources and computer-guided electronic cameras designed for space exploration.

---

ion ② Assessment

erms & Names

plain the
gnificance of:
nstitutional
nvention
mes Madison
rginia Plan
w Jersey Plan
eat Compromise
ree-Fifths
mpromise

2. Using Graphics

Use a chart like the one below to take notes on the contributions made by the leading delegates at the Constitutional Convention.

Delegate	Contribution

3. Main Ideas

a. What was the relationship between the Annapolis Convention and the Constitutional Convention?

b. What is the significance of the date 1787?

c. How did the Constitutional Convention reach a compromise on the issue of slavery?

4. Critical Thinking

Analyzing Points of View
How did the delegates at the convention differ on the issue of representation in the new government?

THINK ABOUT

• the large states and the small states
• the Virginia Plan
• the New Jersey Plan
• the Great Compromise

VITY OPTIONS

CHNOLOGY

ART

Think about the Three-Fifths Compromise. Make an **audio recording** of a speech or draw a **political cartoon** that expresses your views on the issue.

3

Ratifying the Constitution

MAIN IDEA	WHY IT MATTERS NOW	TERMS & NAMES
Americans across the nation debated whether the Constitution would produce the best government.	American liberties today are protected by the U.S. Constitution, including the Bill of Rights.	federalism Federalists Antifederalists	*The Federa...* George Ma... Bill of Righ...

ONE AMERICAN'S STORY

In 1788, in Hartford, Connecticut, 168 delegates met to decide whether their state should ratify the U.S. Constitution. Samuel Huntington, Connecticut's governor, addressed the assembly.

> *A VOICE FROM THE PAST*
>
> This is a new event in the history of mankind. Heretofore, most governments have been formed by tyrants and imposed on mankind by force. Never before did a people, . . . meet together by their representatives and . . . frame for themselves a system of government.
>
> **Samuel Huntington,** quoted in *Original Meanings*

Samuel Hu...

In this section, you will learn about the ratification of the Constitution.

Taking Notes

Use your chart to take notes about the new government.

oblems	
estern lands	
ostwar depression	
presentation in the w government	
avery	

Federalists and Antifederalists

By the time the convention in Connecticut opened, Americans had already been debating the new Constitution for months. The document had been printed in newspapers and handed out in pamphlets across the United States. The framers of the Constitution knew that the document would cause controversy. They immediately began to campaign for ratification, or approval, of the Constitution.

The framers suspected that people might be afraid the Constitution would take too much power away from the states. To address this fear, the framers explained that the Constitution was based on federalism. **Federalism** is a system of government in which power is shared between the central (or federal) government and the states. Linking themselves to the idea of federalism, the people who supported the Constitution took the name **Federalists.**

People who opposed the Constitution were called **Antifederalists.** They thought the Constitution took too much power away from the states and did not guarantee rights for the people. Some were afraid that a strong president might be declared king. Others thought the Senate might turn into a powerful aristocracy. In either case, the liberties won at great cost during the Revolution might be lost.

Antifederalists published their views about the Constitution in newspapers and pamphlets. They used logical arguments to convince people to oppose the Constitution. But they also tried to stir people's emotions by charging that it would destroy American liberties. As one Antifederalist wrote, "After so recent a triumph over British despots [oppressive rulers], . . . it is truly astonishing that a set of men among ourselves should have had the effrontery [nerve] to attempt the destruction of our liberties."

The Federalist Papers

The Federalists did not sit still while the Antifederalists attacked the Constitution. They wrote essays to answer the Antifederalists' attacks. The best known of the Federalist essays are **_The Federalist_ papers**. These essays first appeared as letters in New York newspapers. They were later published together in a book called _The Federalist_.

Three well-known politicians wrote _The Federalist_ papers—James Madison, Alexander Hamilton, and John Jay, the secretary of foreign affairs for the Confederation Congress. Like the Antifederalists, the Federalists appealed to reason and emotion. In _The Federalist_ papers, Hamilton described why people should support ratification.

A VOICE FROM THE PAST

Yes, my countrymen, . . . I am clearly of opinion it is in your interest to adopt it [the Constitution]. I am convinced that this is the safest course for your liberty, your dignity, and your happiness.

Alexander Hamilton, _The Federalist_ "Number 1"

John Jay

Federalists and Antifederalists

FEDERALISTS	ANTIFEDERALISTS
• Supported removing some powers from the states and giving more powers to the national government	• Wanted important political powers to remain with the states
• Favored dividing powers among different branches of government	• Wanted the legislative branch to have more power than the executive
• Proposed a single person to lead the executive branch	• Feared that a strong executive might become a king or tyrant
	• Believed a bill of rights needed to be added to the Constitution to protect people's rights

SKILLBUILDER Interpreting Charts
1. _Which group wanted a stronger central government?_
2. _If you had been alive in 1787, would you have been a Federalist or an Antifederalist?_

George Mason

The Federalists had an important advantage over the Antifederalists. Most of the newspapers supported the Constitution, giving the Federalists more publicity than the Antifederalists. Even so, there was strong opposition to ratification in Massachusetts, North Carolina, Rhode Island, New York, and Virginia. If some of these states failed to ratify the Constitution, the United States might not survive.

The Battle for Ratification

The first four state conventions to ratify the Constitution were held in December 1787. It was a good month for the Federalists. Delaware, New Jersey, and Pennsylvania voted for ratification. In January 1788, Georgia and Connecticut ratified the Constitution. Massachusetts joined these states in early February.

By late June, nine states had voted to ratify the Constitution. That meant that the document was now officially ratified. But New York and Virginia had not yet cast their votes. There were many powerful Antifederalists in both of those states. Without Virginia, the new government would lack the support of the largest state. Without New York, the nation would be separated into two parts geographically.

Virginia's convention opened the first week in June. The patriot Patrick Henry fought against ratification. **George Mason,** perhaps the most influential Virginian aside from Washington, also was opposed to it. Mason had been a delegate to the Constitutional Convention in Philadelphia, but he had refused to sign the final document. Both Henry and Mason would not consider voting for the Constitution until a bill of rights was added. A bill of rights is a set of rules that defines people's rights.

James Madison was also at Virginia's convention. He suggested that Virginia follow Massachusetts's lead and ratify the Constitution, and he recommended the addition of a bill of rights. With the addition of a bill of rights likely, Virginia ratified the Constitution at the end of June.

Reading
B. Drawing Conclusion did the lac bill of right endanger t Constitutio

The news of Virginia's vote arrived while the New York convention was in debate. The Antifederalists had outnumbered the Federalists when the convention had begun. But with the news of Virginia's ratification, New Yorkers decided to join the Union. New York also called for a bill of rights.

It was another year before North Carolina ratified the Constitution. In 1790, Rhode Island became the last state to ratify it. By then, the new Congress had already written a bill of rights and submitted it to the states for approval.

The Bill of Rights

At the same time that seven of the states ratified the Constitution, they asked that it be amended to include a bill of rights. Supporters of a bill of rights hoped that it would set forth the rights of all Americans. They believed it was needed to protect people against the power of the national government.

Madison, who was elected to the new Congress in the winter of 1789, took up the cause. He proposed a set of changes to the Constitution. Congress edited Madison's list and proposed placing the amendments at the end of the Constitution in a separate section.

The amendments went to the states for ratification. As with the Constitution, three-quarters of the states had to ratify the amendments for them to take effect. With Virginia's vote in 1791, ten of the amendments were ratified and became law. These ten amendments to the U.S. Constitution became known as the **Bill of Rights**. (See the Constitution Handbook, pages 266-268.)

The passage of the Bill of Rights was one of the first acts of the new government. In the next chapter, you will read about other issues that faced the new government.

America's HERITAGE

RELIGIOUS FREEDOM

Freedom of religion was an important part of the First Amendment. Jefferson and Madison believed that government enforcement of religious laws was the source of much social conflict. They supported freedom of religion as a way to prevent such conflict.

Even before Madison wrote the Bill of Rights, he worked to ensure religious liberty in Virginia. In 1786, he helped pass the Virginia Statute for Religious Freedom, originally written by Jefferson in 1777.

---

ion 3 Assessment

Terms & Names

Explain the significance of:

deralism
deralists
ntifederalists
e Federalist pers
eorge Mason
l of Rights

2. Using Graphics

Use a diagram like the one below to compare and contrast the Federalists and the Antifederalists.

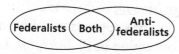

Federalists · Both · Antifederalists

Which group do you think made the stronger argument about ratification? Why?

3. Main Ideas

a. What were Patrick Henry's and George Mason's views on ratification?

b. How did the Federalists and the Antifederalists try to convince people to take their sides in the debate over the Constitution?

c. What was the significance of the Bill of Rights?

4. Critical Thinking

Recognizing Propaganda Reread the quotation by Hamilton on page 235. Is it an example of propaganda? Why or why not?

THINK ABOUT

- Hamilton's use of the word *countrymen*
- Hamilton's reference to liberty, dignity, and happiness

TIVITY OPTIONS

SPEECH
NGUAGE ARTS

Review the major arguments for and against ratification of the Constitution. Hold a **press conference** or write a **news report** on the ratification debate.

The Federalist "Number 51"

Setting the Stage James Madison wrote 29 essays in *The Federalist* papers to argue in favor of ratifying the Constitution. In *The Federalist* "Number 5 Madison explains how the government set up by the Constitution will prote the rights of the people by weakening the power of any interest, or group, to dominate the government. **See Primary Source Explorer**

It is of great importance in a republic not only to guard the society against oppression of its rulers, but to guard one part of the society against the i tice of the other part. Different interests necessarily exist in different cl of citizens. If a majority be united by a common interest, the rights o minority will be insecure. There are but two methods of providing agains evil: the one by creating a will in the community independent of the m ity—that is, of the society itself; the other, by **comprehending**[1] in the sc so many separate descriptions of citizens as will render an unjust combin of a majority of the whole very improbable, if not **impracticable**.[2] . . .

Whilst[3] all authority in it will be derived from and dependent on the ety, the society itself will be broken into so many parts, interests and c of citizens, that the rights of individuals, or of the minority, will be in danger from interested combinations of the majority. In a free govern the security for civil rights must be the same as that for religious righ consists in the one case in the multiplicity of interests, and in the other **multiplicity of sects**.[4] . . .

In the extended republic of the United States, and among the great v of interests, parties, and sects which it embraces, a **coalition**[5] of a major the whole society could seldom take place on any other principles than of justice and the general good. . . .

It is no less certain than it is important . . . that the larger the society vided it lie within a practicable sphere, the more duly capable it will self-government. And happily for the republican cause, the pract sphere may be carried to a very great extent by a **judicious modification** mixture of the *federal principle*.

—*James M*

A CLOSER LOOK

MINORITY RIGHTS

In the 1700s, people feared that democratic majorities could turn into mobs that would violate other people's rights. Madison had to explain how the Constitution would prevent this.

1. What two methods does Madison suggest a society can use to protect minority rights?

A CLOSER LOOK

REPUBLICS IN LARGE SOCIETIES

For centuries, people believed that only small societies could be republics. But Madison argues that large societies are more likely to remain republics.

2. Why does Madison believe that a large republic is likely to protect justice?

1. **comprehending:** understanding.
2. **impracticable:** not practical or realistic.
3. **whilst:** while.
4. **multiplicity of sects:** large number of groups.
5. **coalition:** alliance groups.
6. **judicious modific** careful change.

Objections to the Constitution

Setting the Stage George Mason was one of the leading Antifederalists. "Objections to the Constitution of Government Formed by the Convention," listed his reasons for opposing ratification. Above all, he feared that Constitution created a government that would destroy democracy in the young nation. **See Primary Source Explorer**

There is no Declaration of Rights; and the Laws of the general Government being **paramount**[1] to the Laws and Constitutions of the several States, the Declaration of Rights in the separate States are no Security. Nor are the people secured even in the Enjoyment of the Benefits of the common-Law. . . .

In the House of Representatives, there is not the Substance, but the Shadow only of Representation; which can never produce proper Information in the Legislature, or inspire Confidence in the People; the Laws will therefore be generally made by Men little concern'd in, and **unacquainted**[2] with their Effects and Consequences.

The Senate have the Power of altering all Money-Bills, and of originating Appropriations of Money and the **Sallerys**[3] of the Officers of their own Appointment in **Conjunction**[4] with the President of the United States; altho' they are not the Representatives of the People, or **amenable**[5] to them. . . .

The President of the United States has the unrestrained Power of granting Pardon for Treason; which may be sometimes exercised to screen from Punishment those whom he had secretly **instigated**[6] to commit the Crime, and thereby prevent a Discovery of his own Guilt.

This Government will **commence**[7] in a moderate **Aristocracy**;[8] it is at present impossible to foresee whether it will, in [its] Operation, produce a **Monarchy**,[9] or a corrupt oppressive Aristocracy; it will most probably vibrate some Years between the two, and then terminate in the one or the other.

—*George Mason*

1. **paramount:** most important.
2. **unacquainted:** not familiar.
3. **Sallerys:** salaries.
4. **conjunction:** joining.
5. **amenable:** agreeable.
6. **instigated:** caused.
7. **commence:** begin.
8. **aristocracy:** rule by a few, usually nobles.
9. **monarchy:** rule by one, usually a king.

Interactive Primary Sources Assessment

1. Main Ideas

Why does Madison believe that a society broken into many parts will not endanger minority rights?

What does Mason argue might happen if the president has the power to pardon people?

For each writer, what is one example of a fact and one example of an opinion?

2. Critical Thinking

Drawing Conclusions Who do you think makes the stronger argument? Explain your reasons.

THINK ABOUT
• what you know about the history of the United States
• the evidence used by each writer

VISUAL SUMMARY

Confederation to Constitution

Articles of Confederation

★
1777
Continental Congress passes the Articles of Confederation.

★
1777–1781
States debate ratification of the Articles of Confederation.

★
1781
Articles of Confederation go into effect.

★
1786
Annapolis Convention is held.

★
1786–1787
Shays's Rebellion occurs.

★
1787
Constitutional Convention is held in Philadelphia.

★
1788
U.S. Constitution is ratified.

★
1789
Government created by the new Constitution takes power.

★
1791
Bill of Rights is added to the Constitution.

Constitution

Bill of Rights

TERMS & NAMES

Briefly explain the significance of each of the following.

1. republic
2. Articles of Confederation
3. Northwest Ordinance
4. Shays's Rebellion
5. Constitutional Convention
6. James Madison
7. Great Compromise
8. Federalists
9. George Mason
10. Bill of Rights

REVIEW QUESTIONS

The Confederation Era (pages 221–227)

1. What is the Wilderness Road, and where did it lead?
2. What problems did the Confederation Congress successfully address?
3. What powers did the government have under the Articles of Confederation?
4. How did Shays's Rebellion affect people's views on the Articles of Confederation?

Creating the Constitution (pages 228–233)

5. What groups of people were not represented at the Constitutional Convention?
6. What were some things the delegates agreed on at the convention?
7. What compromises did the delegates make during the convention?

Ratifying the Constitution (pages 234–239)

8. What is federalism?
9. Why were Virginia and New York important in the battle for ratification of the Constitution?
10. Why did some states think that it was necessary to add a bill of rights to the Constitution?

CRITICAL THINKING

1. USING YOUR NOTES: SOLVING PROBLEMS

Problems	Solutions
Western lands	
Postwar depression	
Representation in the new government	
Slavery	

Using your completed chart, answer the questions below.

a. What were the major proble facing the nation during the Confederation Era?

b. How well did the nation solv these problems? Explain.

2. ANALYZING LEADERSHIP

Think about the leaders discusse this chapter. Based on their acti which leader do you think mad the greatest contribution to the Constitutional Convention? Wh

3. THEME: DEMOCRATIC IDEA

How do the Articles of Confed eration and the Constitution e carry out democratic ideals?

4. APPLYING CITIZENSHIP SK

Do you think the Founders we right to make the compromise they did in the Constitution or issues of representation and sl ery? What might have happen they had not compromised?

5. RECOGNIZING EFFECTS

How might U.S. history be diff if Virginia had refused to ratif Constitution? If New York had refused? If both had refused?

Interact *with* Histor

How did your ideas about how would form a government cha after reading this chapter?

se the map and your knowledge of U.S. history to
swer questions 1 and 2.

dditional Test Practice, pp. S1–S33.

Ratification in Middle States, 1790

- ■ Federalist majority
- ■ Antifederalist majority
- □ Evenly divided
- □ Sparsely populated

NEW YORK

PENNSYLVANIA

New York

Philadelphia

NEW JERSEY

ATLANTIC OCEAN

DELAWARE

N
0   100 Miles
0   200 Kilometers

Source: *American Heritage Pictorial Atlas of United States History*

In which two states did the Federalists have statewide majorities?

A. Delaware and New Jersey

B. Delaware and New York

C. New Jersey and Pennsylvania

D. New York and Pennsylvania

2. Which of the following is true?

A. Most of New York supported the Federalists.

B. Most of Pennsylvania supported the Antifederalists.

C. Philadelphia supported the Federalists.

D. New Jersey supported both positions equally.

This quotation from John Dickinson describes his view of the Virginia Plan. Use the quotation and your knowledge of U.S. history to answer question 3.

PRIMARY SOURCE

Some of the members from the small states wish for two branches in the general legislature and are friends to a good [strong] national government; but we would sooner submit [give in] to a foreign power than submit to be deprived, in both branches of the legislature, of an equal suffrage [vote], and thereby be thrown under the domination of the larger states.

John Dickinson, quoted in *Mr. Madison's Constitution*

3. Which statement best summarizes his concern?

A. Large states should have more votes.

B. Small states should have more votes.

C. All states should have equal votes.

D. The states should not have any votes.

TEST PRACTICE
CLASSZONE.COM

ERNATIVE ASSESSMENT

✍ WRITING ABOUT HISTORY

ose you are a reporter covering the Constitutional
ention. Write an **article** to inform readers about
irginia Plan and the New Jersey Plan.

nduct research about both plans in the library.

ote delegates in your article.

ke your article objective.

OPERATIVE LEARNING

with a group to stage a debate between a
alist and an Antifederalist. In preparation,
rch arguments on each side of these issues:

representation of people in Congress

strength of the president and Senate

need for a bill of rights

INTEGRATED TECHNOLOGY

DOING INTERNET RESEARCH

Conduct research to acquire biographical information about one of the following people highlighted in this chapter: Daniel Boone, John Jay, William Paterson, or George Mason.

- On the Internet, locate Web sites that include details about the person's early life, family life, education, accomplishments, and historical significance.

- Take notes from your Internet sources, keeping track of the addresses of Web sites you find to be most informative. Then write a short biography about the person you chose.

For more about these individuals . . .

INTERNET ACTIVITY
CLASSZONE.COM

The Living Constitution

The Framers of the Constitution created a flexible plan for governing the United States far into the future. They also described ways to allow changes in the Constitution. For over 200 years, the Constitution has guided the American people. It remains a "living document." The Constitution still thrives, in part, because it echoes the principles the delegates valued. Each generation of Americans renews the meaning of the Constitution's timeless ideas. These two pages show you some ways in which the Constitution has shaped events in American history. **See Primary Source Explorer**

"In framing a system which we wish to last for ages, we should not lose sight of the changes which ages will produce."

—JAMES MADISON, CONSTITUTIONAL CONVENTION

1787

Delegates in Philadelphia sign the Constitution.

1965

Civil rights leaders protest to end the violation of their constitutional rights. Dr. Martin Luther King, Jr., Coretta Scott King, and others march from Selma toward Montgomery, Alabama, to gain voting rights.

1971

The 26th Amendment to the Constitution gives young people "18 years of age or older" the right to vote.

981

Supreme Court ecision rules that ongress can exclude omen from the aft. Still, many omen who have ined the armed rces have served combat.

HOW TO READ THE CONSTITUTION

The complete text of the Constitution of the United States begins on page 248. The main column has the actual text. Some of the spellings and punctuation have been updated for easier reading. Headings and subheadings have been added to the Constitution to help you find specific topics. Those parts of the Constitution that are no longer in use have been crossed out. "A Closer Look" notes and charts will help you understand issues related to the Constitution.

The New York Times

National Edition

Midwest: Mostly sunny, breezy and seasonable in the Great Lakes area and Ohio Valley. Becoming very warm after a cold start in the western Plains. Weather map is on page A6.

e News 'it to Print'

SATURDAY, FEBRUARY 13, 1999

Printed in Chicago   ONE DOLLAR

VIII . . . . No. 51,432   Copyright © 1999 The New York Times

LINTON ACQUITTED DECISIVELY: NO MAJORITY FOR EITHER CHARGE

CENSURE IS BARRED

But Rebuke From Both Sides of Aisle Dilutes President's Victory

ident Says He Is Sorry nd Seeks Reconciliation

By JAMES BENNET and JOHN M. BRODER

Two hours after the Senate voted yesterday, President Clinton spoke in the Rose Garden of the White House.

he Fallout Of the Trial

1999

The Senate tries President Bill Clinton for the impeachment charges brought against him by the House of Representatives. As required by the Constitution, the Senate needs a two-thirds majority vote to convict him. This rule saves his presidency.

Seven Principles of the Constitution

The Framers of the Constitution constructed a new system of government. Seven principles supported their efforts. To picture how these principles work, imagine seven building blocks. Together they form the foundation of the United States Constitution. In the pages that follow, you will find the definitions and main ideas of the principles shown in the graphic below.

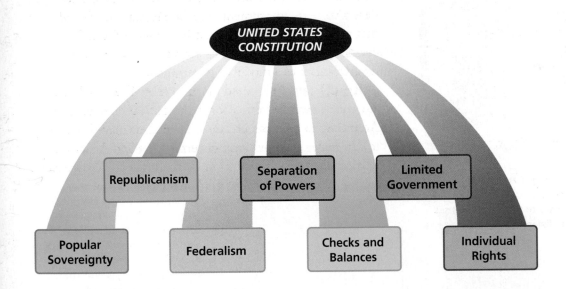

UNITED STATES CONSTITUTION

Republicanism

Separation of Powers

Limited Government

Popular Sovereignty

Federalism

Checks and Balances

Individual Rights

1 Popular Sovereignty
Who Gives the Government Its Power?

"We the people of the United States . . . establish this Constitution for the United States of America." These words from the Preamble, or introduction, to the Constitution clearly spell out the source of the government's power. The Constitution rests on the idea of **popular sovereignty**—a government in which the people rule. As the nation changed and grew, popular sovereignty took on new meaning. A broader range of Americans shared in the power to govern themselves.

In 1987, Americans gathered in Washington, D.C., to celebrate the 200th anniversary of the Constitution. The banner proudly displays that the power to govern belongs to the people.

② Republicanism
How Are People's Views Represented in Government?

The Framers of the Constitution wanted the people to have a voice in government. Yet the Framers also feared that public opinion might stand in the way of sound decision making. To solve this problem, they looked to republicanism as a model of government.

Republicanism is based on this belief: The people exercise their power by voting for their political representatives. According to the Framers, these lawmakers played the key role in making a republican government work. Article 4, Section 4, of the Constitution also calls for every state to have a "republican form of government."

In a republican government, voting citizens make their voices heard at the polls. The power of the ballot prompts candidates to listen to people's concerns.

Federalism
How Is Power Shared?

The Framers wanted the states and the nation to become partners in governing. To build cooperation, the Framers turned to federalism. **Federalism** is a system of government in which power is divided between a central government and smaller political units, such as states. Before the Civil War, federalism in the United States was closely related to dual sovereignty, the idea that the federal government and the states each had exclusive power over their own spheres.

The Framers used federalism to structure the Constitution. The Constitution assigns certain powers to the national government. These are *delegated powers.* Powers kept by the states are *reserved powers.* Powers shared or exercised by national and state governments are known as *concurrent powers.*

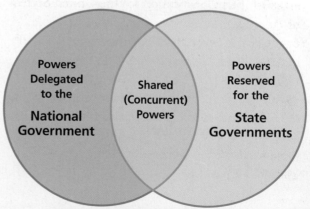

Federalism

Powers Delegated to the **National Government**

Shared (Concurrent) Powers

Powers Reserved for the **State Governments**

The overlapping spheres of power bind the American people together.

4 Separation of Powers
How Is Power Divided?

The Framers were concerned that too much power might fall into the hands of a single group. To avoid this problem, they built the idea of **separation of powers** into the Constitution. This principle means the division of basic government roles into branches. No one branch is given all the power. Articles 1, 2, and 3 of the Constitution detail how powers are split among the three branches.

Separation of Powers

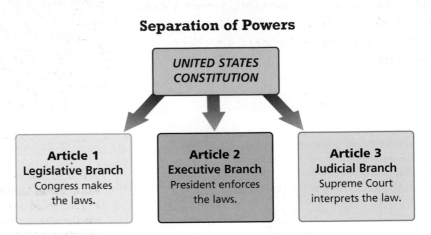

UNITED STATES CONSTITUTION

Article 1
Legislative Branch
Congress makes the laws.

Article 2
Executive Branch
President enforces the laws.

Article 3
Judicial Branch
Supreme Court interprets the law.

5 Checks and Balances
How Is Power Evenly Distributed?

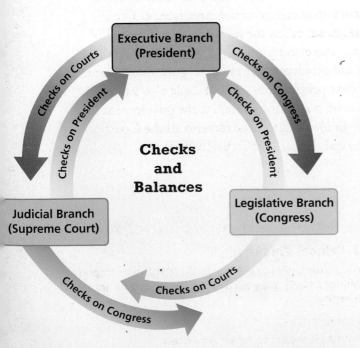

Checks and Balances

Executive Branch (President)

Checks on Courts

Checks on President

Checks on Congress

Checks on President

Judicial Branch (Supreme Court)

Legislative Branch (Congress)

Checks on Courts

Checks on Congress

Baron de Montesquieu, an 18th-century French thinker, wrote, "Power should be a check to pow His comment refers to the principle of **checks a balances**. Each branch of government can exerc checks, or controls, over the other branches. Tho the branches of government are separate, they re one another to perform the work of government

The Framers included a system of checks an balances in the Constitution to help make sure t the branches work together fairly. For example, Congress can pass laws. Yet the president can ch this power by refusing to sign a law into action. turn, the Supreme Court can declare that a law, passed by Congress and signed by the president, violates the Constitution.

Limited Government
How Is Abuse of Power Prevented?

The Framers restricted the power of government. Article 1, Section 9, of the Constitution lists the powers denied to the Congress. Article 1, Section 10, forbids the states to take certain actions.

The principle of <u>limited government</u> is also closely related to the "rule of law": In the American government everyone, citizens and powerful leaders alike, must obey the law. Individuals or groups cannot twist or bypass the law to serve their own interests.

'I AM THE LAW!'

In this political cartoon, President Richard Nixon shakes his fist as he defies the "rule of law." Faced with charges of violating the Constitution, Nixon resigned as president in 1974.

...ts exercise their right to protest. ...rge the community to protect the ...ment.

7 Individual Rights
How Are Personal Freedoms Protected?

The first ten amendments to the Constitution shield people from an overly powerful government. These amendments are called the Bill of Rights. The Bill of Rights guarantees certain **individual rights,** or personal liberties and privileges. For example, government cannot control what people write or say. People also have the right to meet peacefully and to ask the government to correct a problem. Later amendments to the Constitution also advanced the cause of individual rights.

...ssment: Principles of the Constitution

...ain Ideas

...What are the seven principles of government?

...ow does the Constitution reflect the principle of ...ration of powers?

...hy did the Framers include a system of checks and ...nces in the Constitution?

2. Critical Thinking

Forming Opinions How do the rights and responsibilities of U.S. citizenship reflect American national identity?

THINK ABOUT
• what it means to be an American
• the rights and responsibilities of U.S. citizens

The Constitution of the United States

See Primary
Source Explorer

*" In 1787, I was
not included in that
'We the people.'
… But through the
process of amendment,
interpretation,
and court decision,
I have finally
been included in
'We the people.'"*

—BARBARA JORDAN, 1974
The first African-American
congresswoman from the
South (Texas)

Preamble. *Purpose of the Constitution*

We the people of the United States, in order to for
more perfect Union, establish justice, insure dome
tranquility, provide for the common defense, prom
the general welfare, and secure the blessings of lib
to ourselves and our posterity, do ordain and estab
this Constitution for the United States of America

A CLOSER LOOK Goals of the Preamble

PREAMBLE	EXPLANATION	EXAMPLES
"Form a more perfect Union"	Create a nation in which states work together	• U.S. Postal System • U.S. coins, paper mon
"Establish justice"	Make laws and set up courts that are fair	• Court system • Jury system
"Insure domestic tranquility"	Keep peace within the country	• National Guard • Federal marshals
"Provide for the common defense"	Safeguard the country against attack	• Army • Navy
"Promote the general welfare"	Contribute to the happiness and well-being of all the people	• Birth certificate • Marriage license
"Secure the blessings of liberty to ourselves and our posterity"	Make sure future citizens remain free	• Commission on Civil Ri • National Council on Disability

SKILLBUILDER Interpreting Charts
1. *Which goal of the Preamble do you think is most important? Why?*
2. *How does the Preamble reflect the principle of popular sovereignty?*

...ticle 1. *The Legislature*

...IN IDEA The main role of Congress, the legislative branch, is to make laws. ...gress is made up of two houses—the Senate and the House of Representatives. ...didates for each house must meet certain requirements. Congress performs ...cific duties, also called delegated powers.

...Y IT MATTERS NOW Representatives in Congress still voice the views and ...cerns of the people.

...tion 1. Congress All legislative powers herein granted shall be ...d in a Congress of the United States, which shall consist of a Senate ...House of Representatives.

...tion 2. The House of Representatives

...ections The House of Representatives shall be composed of members ...en every second year by the people of the several states, and the ...ors in each state shall have the qualifications requisite for electors of the ...numerous branch of the state legislature.

...ualifications No person shall be a Representative who shall not have ...ned to the age of twenty-five years, and been seven years a citizen of ...nited States, and who shall not, when elected, be an inhabitant of that ...in which he shall be chosen.

...umber of Representatives Representatives and direct taxes shall be ...tioned among the several states which may be included within this ...n, according to their respective numbers, which shall be determined by ...g to the whole number of free persons, including those bound to ...e for a term of years, and excluding Indians not taxed, three-fifths of all ...Persons. The actual **enumeration** shall be made within three years after ...rst meeting of the Congress of the United States, and within every ...quent term of ten years, in such manner as they shall by law direct. The ...er of Representatives shall not exceed one for every thirty thousand, ...ch state shall have at least one Representative; and until such enumer- ...shall be made, the state of New Hampshire shall be entitled to choose ...Massachusetts eight, Rhode Island and Providence Plantations one, ...ecticut five, New York six, New Jersey four, Pennsylvania eight, ...are one, Maryland six, Virginia ten, North Carolina five, South ...na five, and Georgia three.

...ancies When vacancies happen in the representation from any state, the ...ive authority thereof shall issue writs of election to fill such vacancies.

...icers and Impeachment The House of Representatives shall choose ...peaker and other officers; and shall have the sole power of **impeachment.**

A CLOSER LOOK

ELECTIONS

Representatives are elected every two years. There are no limits on the number of terms a person can serve.

1. What do you think are the advantages of holding frequent elections of representatives?

A CLOSER LOOK

REPRESENTATION

Some delegates, such as Gouverneur Morris, thought that representation should be based on wealth as well as population. Others, such as James Wilson, thought representation should be based on population only. Ultimately, the delegates voted against including wealth as a basis for apportioning representatives.

2. How do you think the United States would be different today if representation were based on wealth?

Section 3. The Senate

1. **Numbers** The Senate of the United States shall be composed of Senators from each state, ~~chosen by the legislature thereof,~~ for six years; each Senator shall have one vote.

2. **Classifying Terms** Immediately after they shall be assembled in co quence of the first election, they shall be divided as equally as may be three classes. The seats of the Senators of the first class shall be vacated a expiration of the second year, of the second class at the expiration o fourth year, and of the third class at the expiration of the sixth year, so one-third may be chosen every second year; ~~and if vacancies happen by ignation, or otherwise, during the recess of the legislature of any state executive thereof may make temporary appointments until the next me of the legislature, which shall then fill such vacancies.~~

3. **Qualifications** No person shall be a Senator who shall not have att to the age of thirty years, and been nine years a citizen of the United S and who shall not, when elected, be an inhabitant of that state for whi shall be chosen.

A CLOSER LOOK Federal Office Terms and Requirements

POSITION	TERM	MINIMUM AGE	RESIDENCY	CITIZENSH
Representative	2 years	25	state in which elected	7 years
Senator	6 years	30	state in which elected	9 years
President	4 years	35	14 years in the U.S.	natural-born
Supreme Court Justice	unlimited	none	none	none

SKILLBUILDER **Interpreting Charts**
Why do you think the term and qualifications for a senator are more demanding than for a representative?

4. **Role of Vice-President** The Vice-President of the United States sh President of the Senate, but shall have no vote, unless they be equally div

5. **Officers** The Senate shall choose their other officers, and also a Pre **pro tempore**, in the absence of the Vice-President, or when he shall ex the office of President of the United States.

6. **Impeachment Trials** The Senate shall have the sole power all impeachments. When sitting for that purpose, they shall be or or affirmation. When the President of the United States is trie Chief Justice shall preside: and no person shall be convicted without th currence of two-thirds of the members present.

7. **Punishment for Impeachment** Judgment in cases of impeachmen not extend further than to removal from office, and disqualification t and enjoy any office of honor, trust or profit under the United States; l party convicted shall nevertheless be liable and subject to **indictmen** judgment and punishment, according to law.

Section 4. Congressional Elections

Regulations The times, places and manner of holding elections for Senators and Representatives shall be prescribed in each state by the legislature thereof; but the Congress may at any time by law make or alter such regulations, except as to the places of choosing Senators.

Sessions The Congress shall assemble at least once in every year, ~~and such meeting shall be on the first Monday in December, unless they shall by law appoint a different day.~~

Section 5. Rules and Procedures

Quorum Each house shall be the judge of the elections, returns and qualifications of its own members, and a majority of each shall constitute a **quorum** to do business; but a smaller number may adjourn from day to day, and may be authorized to compel the attendance of absent members, in such manner, and under such penalties as each house may provide.

Rules and Conduct Each house may determine the rules of its proceedings, punish its members for disorderly behavior, and, with the concurrence of two-thirds, expel a member.

Congressional Records Each house shall keep a journal of its proceedings and from time to time publish the same, excepting such parts as may in their judgment require secrecy; and the yeas and nays of the members of either house on any question shall, at the desire of one-fifth of those present, be entered on the journal.

Adjournment Neither house, during the session of Congress, shall, without the consent of the other, adjourn for more than three days, nor to any other place than that in which the two houses shall be sitting.

Section 6. Payment and Privileges

Salary The Senators and Representatives shall receive a compensation for their services, to be ascertained by law, and paid out of the treasury of the United States. They shall in all cases, except treason, felony and breach of the peace, be privileged from arrest during their attendance at the session of their respective houses, and in going to and returning from the same; and for any speech or debate in either house, they shall not be questioned in any other place.

Restrictions No Senator or Representative shall, during the time for which he was elected, be appointed to any civil office under the authority of the United States, which shall have been created, or the emoluments whereof shall have been increased during such time; and no person holding any office under the United States, shall be a member of either house during his continuance in office.

A CLOSER LOOK

SENATE RULES

Senate rules allow for debate on the floor. Using a tactic called filibustering, senators give long speeches to block the passage of a bill. Senator Strom Thurmond holds the filibustering record—24 hours, 18 minutes.

4. Why might a senator choose filibustering as a tactic to block a bill?

A CLOSER LOOK

SALARIES

Senators and representatives are paid $136,700 a year. The Speaker of the House is paid $175,400—the same as the vice-president.

5. How do the salaries of members of Congress compare to those of adults you know?

Section 7. How a Bill Becomes a Law

1. Tax Bills All bills for raising <u>revenue</u> shall originate in the Hous[e] Representatives; but the Senate may propose or concur with amendmen[ts] on other Bills.

2. Lawmaking Process Every bill which shall have passed the Hous[e] Representatives and the Senate, shall, before it become a law, be presente[d] the President of the United States; if he approves he shall sign it, but i[f] he shall return it, with his objections to that house in which it shall have [orig]inated, who shall enter the objections at large on their journal, and pro[ceed] to reconsider it. If after such reconsideration two-thirds of that house [shall] agree to pass the bill, it shall be sent, together with the objections, t[o the] other house, by which it shall likewise be reconsidered, and if approve[d by] two-thirds of that house, it shall become a law. But in all such cases the [votes] of both houses shall be determined by yeas and nays, and the names o[f the] persons voting for and against the bill shall be entered on the journal of [each] house respectively. If any bill shall not be returned by the President w[ithin] ten days (Sundays excepted) after it shall have been presented to him [the] same shall be a law, in like manner as if he had signed it, unless the Con[gress] by their adjournment prevent its return, in which case it shall not be a [law.]

3. Role of the President Every order, resolution, or vote to which concurrence of the Senate and House of Representatives may be nece[ssary] (except on a question of adjournment) shall be presented to the Pres[ident] of the United States; and before the same shall take effect, shall be app[roved] by him, or being disapproved by him, shall be repassed by two-thirds [of the] Senate and House of Representatives, according to the rules and limita[tions] prescribed in the case of a bill.

A CLOSER LOOK How a Bill Becomes a Law

Introduction

The House introduces a bill and refers it to a committee.

The Senate introduces a bill and refers it to a committee.

Committee Action

The House committee may approve, rewrite, or kill the bill.

The Senate committee may approve, rewrite, or kill the bill.

Floor Action

The House debates and votes on its version of the bill.

The Senate debates and votes on its version of the bill.

House and Senate committ[ee] members work out the diff[erences] between the two versions.

:tion 8. Powers Granted to Congress

axation The Congress shall have power to lay and collect taxes, duties, osts and excises, to pay the debts and provide for the common defense general welfare of the United States; but all duties, imposts and excises be uniform throughout the United States;

redit To borrow money on the credit of the United States;

ommerce To regulate commerce with foreign nations, and among the ral states, and with the Indian tribes;

aturalization, Bankruptcy To establish a uniform rule of **naturalization,** uniform laws on the subject of bankruptcies throughout the United States;

oney To coin money, regulate the value thereof, and of foreign coin, and ie standard of weights and measures;

ounterfeiting To provide for the punishment of counterfeiting the ities and current coin of the United States;

ost Office To establish post offices and post roads;

itents, Copyrights To promote the progress of science and useful arts, curing for limited times to authors and inventors the exclusive right to respective writings and discoveries;

deral Courts To constitute **tribunals** inferior to the Supreme Court;

nternational Law To define and punish piracies and **felonies** nitted on the high seas, and offenses against the law of nations;

Var To declare war, grant letters of marque and reprisal, and make rules erning captures on land and water;

rmy To raise and support armies, but no **appropriation** of money to ise shall be for a longer term than two years;

avy To provide and maintain a navy;

A CLOSER LOOK

REGULATING COMMERCE

Commerce can also apply to travelers crossing state lines. Congress's power to regulate the movement of people from state to state paved the way for the Civil Rights Act of 1964. This act included fair treatment of interstate travelers. People of all races can use public places, such as hotels and bus stations.

6. To what other areas might the commerce clause apply?

A CLOSER LOOK

DECLARING WAR

Only Congress can declare war. Yet in the following "undeclared" wars, Congress bowed to the president's power to take military action and send troops overseas: Korean War (1950–1953), Vietnam War (1957–1975), Persian Gulf War (1991), and Kosovo crisis (1999).

7. Why do you think the Constitution sets limits on the president's war-making powers?

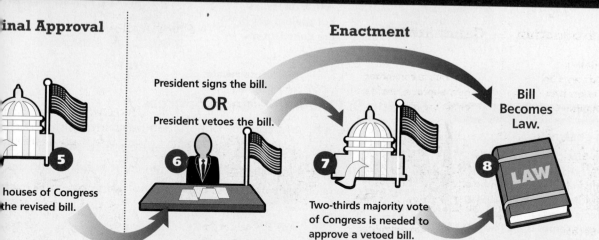

inal Approval

Enactment

President signs the bill.

OR

President vetoes the bill.

Bill Becomes Law.

houses of Congress ie revised bill.

Two-thirds majority vote of Congress is needed to approve a vetoed bill.

SKILLBUILDER Interpreting Charts

1. *How can a president block a bill?*
2. *What examples of checks and balances are shown in the chart?*

14. Regulation of Armed Forces To make rules for the government regulation of the land and naval forces;

15. Militia To provide for calling forth the **militia** to execute the laws of Union, suppress insurrections and repel invasions;

16. Regulations for Militia To provide for organizing, arming, and d plining the militia, and for governing such part of them as may be empl in the service of the United States, reserving to the states respectively appointment of the officers, and the authority of training the militia acc ing to the discipline prescribed by Congress;

17. District of Columbia To exercise exclusive legislation in all cases w soever, over such district (not exceeding ten miles square) as may, by ce of particular states, and the acceptance of Congress, become the seat o government of the United States, and to exercise like authority over all p purchased by the consent of the legislature of the state in which the shall be, for the erection of forts, magazines, arsenals, dockyards, and needful buildings;—and

18. Elastic Clause To make all laws which shall be necessary and prope carrying into execution the foregoing powers, and all other powers veste this Constitution in the government of the United States, or in any de ment or officer thereof.

A CLOSER LOOK The Elastic Clause

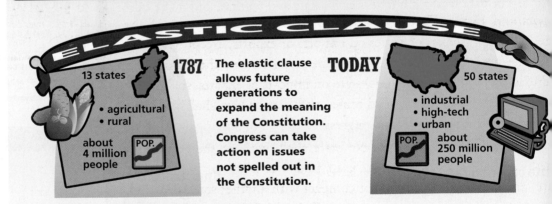

ELASTIC CLAUSE

1787
13 states
• agricultural
• rural
about 4 million people
POP.

The elastic clause allows future generations to expand the meaning of the Constitution. Congress can take action on issues not spelled out in the Constitution.

TODAY
50 states
• industrial
• high-tech
• urban
POP. about 250 million people

A CLOSER LOOK

HABEAS CORPUS

A writ of habeas corpus is a legal order. It protects people from being held in prison or jail without formal charges of a crime. In 1992, the Supreme Court recognized that "habeas corpus is the [basic] instrument for safeguarding individual freedom."

8. How does habeas corpus help ensure fairness and justice?

Section 9. Powers Denied Congress

~~1. Slave Trade The migration or importation of such persons as any states now existing shall think proper to admit, shall not be proh by the Congress prior to the year one thousand eight hundred and eig a tax or duty may be imposed on such importation, not exceeding ten for each person.~~

2. Habeas Corpus The privilege of the writ of habeas corpus shall suspended, unless when in cases of rebellion or invasion the public safet require it.

...legal Punishment No **bill of attainder** or **ex post facto law** shall be passed.

...irect Taxes No capitation, ~~or other direct,~~ tax shall be laid, ~~unless in~~ ~~...ortion to the census or enumeration herein before directed to be taken.~~

...xport Taxes No tax or duty shall be laid on articles exported from ...state.

...o Favorites No preference shall be given by any regulation of commerce or ...ue to the ports of one state over those of another: nor shall vessels bound ...from, one state be obliged to enter, clear, or pay duties in another.

...blic Money No money shall be drawn from the treasury, but in conse-...ce of appropriations made by law; and a regular statement and account ...e receipts and expenditures of all public money shall be published from ...to time.

...tles of Nobility No title of nobility shall be granted by the United ...s: and no person holding any office of profit or trust under them shall, ...ut the consent of the Congress, accept of any present, emolument, ..., or title, of any kind whatever, from any king, prince, or foreign state.

...tion 10. Powers Denied the States

...strictions No state shall enter into any treaty, alliance, or confedera-...grant letters of marque and reprisal; coin money; emit bills of credit; ...anything but gold and silver coin a **tender** in payment of debts; pass ...ill of attainder, ex post facto law, or law impairing the obligation of con-..., or grant any title of nobility.

...port and Export Taxes No state shall, without the consent of the ...ress, lay any imposts or duties on imports or exports, except what may ...solutely necessary for executing its inspection laws; and the net produce ...duties and imposts, laid by any state on imports or exports, shall be for ...se of the treasury of the United States; and all such laws shall be subject ...e revision and control of the Congress.

...cetime and War Restraints No state shall, without the consent of ...ress, lay any duty of tonnage, keep troops or ships of war in time ...ce, enter into any agreement or compact with another state, or with a ...n power, or engage in war, unless actually invaded, or in such imminent ...r as will not admit of delay.

A CLOSER LOOK

DIRECT TAX

In 1913, the 16th Amendment allowed Congress to collect an income tax—a direct tax on the amount of money a person earns. Americans today pay much more in taxes than their ancestors would have imagined.

9. Why do you think the issue of taxes is so important to people?

A CLOSER LOOK

TITLES OF NOBILITY

The Framers disapproved of titles of nobility. The list of grievances in the Declaration of Independence included numerous examples of King George III's abuses of power. Symbols of these abuses included English titles of nobility, such as "king," "queen," and "duke." The Framers said clearly that there would be no such titles in the new republic.

10. How do TV news reporters address members of Congress and the president?

...cle 1 Assessment

...ain Ideas

...hat is the main job of the legislative branch?

...hat role does the vice-president of the United States ...in the Senate?

...hy are there more members in the House of ...esentatives than the Senate?

...hat is one of the powers denied to Congress?

2. Critical Thinking

Drawing Conclusions How does Article 1 show that the Constitution is a clearly defined yet flexible document?

THINK ABOUT
• the powers of Congress
• the "elastic clause"

VOCABULARY

natural-born citizen a citizen born in the United States or a U.S. commonwealth, or to parents who are U.S. citizens living outside the country

affirmation a statement declaring that something is true

Article 2. *The Executive*

> **MAIN IDEA** The president and vice-president are the leaders of the execu branch. Their main role is to enforce the laws. The president commands the mili and makes foreign treaties with the Senate's approval.
>
> **WHY IT MATTERS NOW** As the United States has become a world power, authority of the president has also expanded.

Section 1. The Presidency

1. Terms of Office The executive power shall be vested in a President o United States of America. He shall hold his office during the term of years, and, together with the Vice-President, chosen for the same terr elected, as follows:

2. Electoral College Each state shall appoint, in such manner as Legislature thereof may direct, a number of electors, equal to the whole ber of Senators and Representatives to which the State may be entitled i Congress; but no Senator or Representative, or person holding an office of or profit under the United States, shall be appointed an elector.

A CLOSER LOOK Electoral College *(based on 2000 Census)*

American voters do not choose their president directly. Members of a group called the electoral college actually elect the president. Each state has electors. Together they form the electoral college. In most states, the winner takes all. Except for Maine and Nebraska, all the electoral votes of a state go to one set of candidates.

number of electors for each state = total number of its senators and representatives

WA 11 · OR 7 · MT 3 · ID 4 · WY 3 · ND 3 · SD 3 · MN 10 · WI 10 · MI 17 · NH 4 · VT 3 · ME 4 · NY 31 · MA 1 · RI 4 · CT 7 · NV 5 · UT 5 · CO 9 · NE 5 · IA 7 · IL 21 · IN 11 · OH 20 · WV 5 · PA 21 · NJ 1 · DE 3 · DC 3 · MD · CA 55 · AZ 10 · NM 5 · KS 6 · MO 11 · KY 8 · VA 13 · TN 11 · NC 15 · SC 8 · OK 7 · AR 6 · MS 6 · AL 9 · GA 15 · HI 4 · TX 34 · LA 9 · FL 27 · AK 3

SKILLBUILDER Interpreting Maps

1. *How many electoral votes does your state have?*
2. *In which states would a presidential candidate campaign most heavily? Why?*

~~**3. Former Method of Electing President** The electors shall meet in respective states, and vote by ballot for two persons, of whom one a shall not be an inhabitant of the same state with themselves. And they make a list of all the persons voted for, and of the number of votes for which list they shall sign and certify, and transmit sealed to the seat government of the United States, directed to the President of the S The President of the Senate shall, in the presence of the Senate and I of Representatives, open all the certificates, and the votes shall th counted. The person having the greatest number of votes shall b~~

dent, if such number be a majority
he whole number of electors
inted; and if there be more than
who have such majority, and have
equal number of votes, then the
se of Representatives shall imme-
ly choose by ballot one of them for
dent; and if no person have a
rity, then from the five highest on
ist the said House shall in like
er choose the President. But in
sing the President, the votes shall
ken by States, the representation
each state having one vote; a
am for this purpose shall consist
member or members from two-

s of the states, and a majority of all the states shall be necessary to a
e. In every case, after the choice of the President, the person having the
st number of votes of the electors shall be the Vice-President. But if
should remain two or more who have equal votes, the Senate shall
se from them by ballot the Vice-President.

ection Day The Congress may determine the time of choosing the
rs, and the day on which they shall give their votes, which day shall be
ame throughout the United States.

ualifications No person except a **natural-born citizen,** or a citizen of
nited States at the time of the adoption of this Constitution, shall be
le to the office of President; neither shall any person be eligible to that
who shall not have attained to the age of thirty-five years, and been
en years a resident within the United States.

ccession In case of the removal of the President from office, or of his
, resignation, or inability to discharge the powers and duties of the said
, the same shall devolve on the Vice-President, and the Congress may
provide for the case of removal, death, resignation or inability, both of
resident and Vice-President, declaring what officer shall then act as
ent, and such officer shall act accordingly, until the disability be
ed, or a President shall be elected.

ary The President shall, at stated times, receive for his services, a com-
ion, which shall neither be increased nor diminished during the period
nich he shall have been elected, and he shall not receive within that
any other emolument from the United States, or any of them.

h of Office Before he enter on the execution of his office, he shall take
lowing oath or **affirmation:**—"I do solemnly swear (or affirm) that I
ithfully execute the office of President of the United States, and will to
st of my ability, preserve, protect and defend the Constitution of the
l States."

Commander in Chief

As a military leader, President Abraham Lincoln meets with his generals during the Civil War.

Chief Executive

Like a business executive, the president solves problems and makes key decisions. President John F. Kennedy is shown in the oval office in 1962.

Chief Diplomat and Chief of State

As a foreign policy maker, President Richard M. Nixon visits the People's Republic of China in 1972.

Legislative Leader

President Lyndon Johnson signs the Civil Rights Act of 1964. All modern presidents have legislative programs they want Congress to pass.

Head of a Political Party

President Ronald Reagan rallies support at the 1984 Republican Convention. By this time, Reagan had put together a strong bloc of voters who supported the Republican Party's policies. During his presidency (1981–1989), Reagan helped build new unity among party members.

~~tion~~ 2. Powers of the President

~~M~~ilitary Powers The President shall be commander in chief of the Army ~~and~~ Navy of the United States, and of the militia of the several states, when ~~calle~~d into the actual service of the United States; he may require the opin-~~ion, i~~n writing, of the principal officer in each of the executive departments, ~~on~~ any subject relating to the duties of their respective offices, and he shall ~~have~~ power to grant **reprieves** and pardons for offenses against the United ~~State~~s, except in cases of impeachment.

~~Tr~~eaties, Appointments He shall have power, by and with the advice and ~~cons~~ent of the Senate, to make treaties, provided two-thirds of the Senators ~~prese~~nt concur; and he shall nominate, and by and with the advice and con-~~sent~~ of the Senate, shall appoint ambassadors, other public ministers and ~~consu~~ls, judges of the Supreme Court, and all other officers of the United ~~State~~s, whose appointments are not herein otherwise provided for, and which ~~shall~~ be established by law; but the Congress may by law vest the appoint-~~ment~~ of such inferior officers, as they think proper, in the President alone, in ~~the co~~urts of law, or in the heads of departments.

~~Vac~~ancies The President shall have power to fill up all vacancies that may ~~happe~~n during the recess of the Senate, by granting commissions which shall ~~expire~~ at the end of their next session.

~~Sect~~ion 3. Presidential Duties
He shall from time to time give ~~the~~ Congress information of the State of the Union, and recommend ~~to th~~eir consideration such measures as he shall judge necessary and ~~expedi~~ent; he may, on extraordinary occasions, **convene** both houses, or ~~either~~ of them, and in case of disagreement between them, with respect ~~to the~~ time of adjournment, he may adjourn them to such time as he shall ~~think~~ proper; he shall receive ambassadors and other public ministers; he ~~shall t~~ake care that the laws be faithfully executed, and shall commission ~~all the~~ officers of the United States.

~~Secti~~on 4. Impeachment
The President, Vice-President and all ~~civil o~~fficers of the United States shall be removed from office on ~~impea~~chment for, and conviction of, treason, bribery, or other high crimes ~~and m~~isdemeanors.

VOCABULARY

reprieves delays or cancellations of punishment

convene call together

misdemeanors violations of the law

A CLOSER LOOK

SUPREME COURT APPOINTMENTS

Recent presidents have used their power of appointment to add minorities and women to the Supreme Court. In 1967, President Lyndon Johnson appointed the first African-American justice, Thurgood Marshall. In 1981, President Ronald Reagan appointed the first woman, Sandra Day O'Connor.

12. What do you think influences a president's choice for a Supreme Court justice?

A CLOSER LOOK

STATE OF THE UNION

Major TV networks broadcast the State of the Union address to the whole nation. In this yearly message, the president urges Congress to achieve certain lawmaking goals. The president's speech also must gain the attention of TV viewers.

13. Why is the president's power to persuade an important political skill?

~~M~~ain Ideas

~~W~~hat is the chief purpose of the executive branch?

~~Wh~~at are the requirements for becoming president?

~~Ho~~w does the Constitution limit the president's power ~~to ma~~ke appointments and treaties?

2. Critical Thinking

Analyzing Issues Why do you think the Constitution states that the president must seek approval from the Senate for most political appointments and treaties?

THINK ABOUT
• the abuse of power
• the will of the voters

Article 3. *The Judiciary*

MAIN IDEA The judicial branch interprets the laws. This branch includes Supreme Court, the highest court in the nation, and other federal courts.

WHY IT MATTERS NOW Supreme Court rulings can shape government poli on hotly debated issues.

Section 1. Federal Courts and Judges
The judicial power c United States shall be vested in one Supreme Court, and in such **inferior c** as the Congress may from time to time ordain and establish. The judges, of the Supreme and inferior courts, shall hold their offices during good be ior, and shall, at stated times, receive for their services a compensation, v shall not be diminished during their continuance in office.

Section 2. The Courts' Authority

1. General Authority The judicial power shall extend to all cases, in la equity, arising under this Constitution, the laws of the United States treaties made, or which shall be made, under their authority;—to all affecting ambassadors, other public ministers and consuls;—to all ca admiralty and maritime jurisdiction;—to controversies to which the U States shall be a party;—to controversies between two or more sta between a state and citizens of another state;—between citizens of dif states;—between citizens of the same state claiming lands under gra different states, and between a state, or the citizens thereof, and f states, citizens or subjects.

A CLOSER LOOK Judicial Review

Judicial review allows the Supreme Court and other federal courts to play a key role in lawmaking. The judges examine a law or government activity. They then decide whether it violates the Constitution. The Supreme Court established this important right in the case of *Marbury* v. *Madison* (1803). (See Chapter 10.)

2. Supreme Court In all cases affecting ambassadors, other public m and consuls, and those in which a state shall be party, the Supreme shall have original jurisdiction. In all the other cases before mention Supreme Court shall have **appellate** jurisdiction, both as to law and fa such exceptions, and under such regulations, as the Congress shall m

CHECKS ON COURTS
- Appoints federal judges
- Can grant reprieves and pardons for federal crimes

Executive Branch (President)

CHECKS ON CONGRESS
- Can veto acts of Congress
- Can call special sessions of Congress
- Can suggest laws and send messages to Congress

CHECKS ON PRESIDENT
- Can impeach and remove the president
- Can override veto
- Controls spending of money
- Senate can refuse to confirm presidential appointments and to ratify treaties

CHECKS ON PRESIDENT
- Can declare executive acts unconstitutional
- Judges, appointed for life, are free from executive control

Judicial Branch (Supreme Court)

CHECKS ON CONGRESS
- Judicial review—Can declare acts of Congress unconstitutional

Legislative Branch (Congress)

CHECKS ON COURT
- Can impeach and remove federal judges
- Establishes lower federal courts
- Can refuse to confirm judicial appointments

LLBUILDER **Interpreting Charts**

/hy is judicial review an important action of the Supreme Court?

/hich check do you think is most powerful? Why?

al by Jury The trial of all crimes, except in cases of impeachment, shall
jury; and such trial shall be held in the state where the said crimes shall
been committed; but when not committed within any state, the trial
be at such place or places as the Congress may by law have directed.

ion 3. Treason

nition Treason against the United States shall consist only in levying
ainst them, or in adhering to their enemies, giving them aid and com-
Jo person shall be convicted of treason unless on the testimony of two
ses to the same overt act, or on confession in open court.

ishment The Congress shall have power to declare the punishment
son, but no attainder of treason shall work corruption of blood, or
ure except during the life of the person attained.

le 3 Assessment

ain Ideas

hat is the main purpose of the judicial branch?

hat is judicial review?

hat are two kinds of cases that can begin in the
me Court?

2. Critical Thinking

Drawing Conclusions Why might the Supreme Court
feel less political pressure than Congress in making judgments about the Constitution?

THINK ABOUT
- the appointment of Supreme Court justices
- Congress members' obligation to voters

immunities legal protections

suffrage right to vote

A CLOSER LOOK Federalism

Americans live under both national and state governments.

NATIONAL POWERS
- Maintain military
- Declare war
- Establish postal system
- Set standards for weights and measures
- Protect copyrights and patents

SHARED POWERS
- Collect taxes
- Establish courts
- Regulate interstate commerce
- Regulate banks
- Borrow money
- Provide for the general welfare
- Punish criminals

STATE POWERS
- Establish local governments
- Set up schools
- Regulate state commerce
- Make regulations for marriage
- Establish and regulate corporations

SKILLBUILDER Interpreting Charts

What do you think is the purpose of dividing the powers between national and state governments?

Article 4. *Relations Among States*

MAIN IDEA States must honor one another's laws, records, and court ruling

WHY IT MATTERS NOW Article 4 promotes cooperation, equality, and fair treatment of citizens from all the states.

Section 1. State Acts and Records Full faith and credit sh given in each state to the public acts, records, and judicial proceedi every other state. And the Congress may by general laws prescrib manner in which such acts, records and proceedings shall be prove the effect thereof.

Section 2. Rights of Citizens

1. Citizenship The citizens of each state shall be entitled to all pri and **immunities** of citizens in the several states.

2. Extradition A person charged in any state with treason, felony, or crime, who shall flee from justice, and be found in another state on demand of the executive authority of the state from which he f delivered up, to be removed to the state having jurisdiction of the

3. Fugitive Slaves No person held to service or labor in one state, the laws thereof, escaping into another, shall, in consequence of any law ulation therein, be discharged from such service or labor, but shall be de up on claim of the party to whom such service or labor may be due.

EXTRADITION

Persons charged with serious crimes cannot escape punishment by fleeing to another state. They must be returned to the first state and stand trial there.

16. Why do you think the Framers included the power of extradition?

tion 3. New States

Admission New states may be admitted by the Congress into this Union; no new state shall be formed or erected within the jurisdiction of any other state; nor any state be formed by the junction of two or more states, or parts of states, without the consent of the legislatures of the states concerned as well as of the Congress.

Congressional Authority The Congress shall have power to dispose of and make all needful rules and regulations respecting the territory or other property belonging to the United States; and nothing in this Constitution shall be so construed as to prejudice any claims of the United States, or of any particular state.

tion 4. Guarantees to the States

The United States shall guarantee to every state in this Union a republican form of government, and shall protect each of them against invasion; and on application of the legislature, or of the executive (when the legislature cannot be convened) against domestic violence.

icle 5. *Amending the Constitution*

IN IDEA The Constitution can be amended, or formally changed.

WHY IT MATTERS NOW The amendment process allows the Constitution to adapt to modern times.

The Congress, whenever two-thirds of both houses shall deem it necessary, shall propose amendments to this Constitution, or, on the application of the legislatures of two-thirds of the several states, shall call a convention for proposing amendments, which, in either case, shall be valid to all intents and purposes, as part of this Constitution, when ratified by the legislatures of three-fourths of the several states, or by conventions in three-fourths thereof, as the one or the other mode of ratification may be proposed by the Congress; ~~provided that no amendment which may be made prior to the year one thousand eight hundred and eight shall in any manner affect the first and fourth clauses in the ninth section of the first article;~~ and that no state, without its consent, shall be deprived of its equal **suffrage** in the Senate.

A CLOSER LOOK

ADMISSION TO STATEHOOD

In 1998, Puerto Ricans voted against their island becoming the 51st state. A lawyer in Puerto Rico summed up a main reason: "Puerto Ricans want to have ties to the U. S., but they want to protect their language and culture." Also, as a U.S. commonwealth, Puerto Rico makes its own laws and handles its own finances.

17. Do you think Puerto Rico should become a state? Why or why not?

CLOSER LOOK **Process for Amending the Constitution**

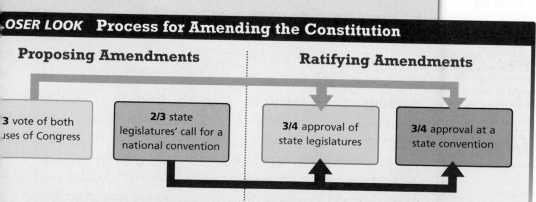

Proposing Amendments		Ratifying Amendments	
2/3 vote of both houses of Congress	2/3 state legislatures' call for a national convention	3/4 approval of state legislatures	3/4 approval at a state convention

SKILLBUILDER Interpreting Charts

Why do you think more votes are needed to ratify an amendment than to propose one?

A CLOSER LOOK

PAYING DEBTS

The U.S. government agreed to pay all debts held under the Articles of Confederation. For example, the United States still owed money from the costs of the Revolutionary War.

18. What problems might arise in a country that has a huge national debt?

Article 6. *Supremacy of the National Governme*

MAIN IDEA The Constitution, national laws, and treaties are the supreme highest, law of the land. All government officials must promise to support Constitution.

WHY IT MATTERS NOW The authority of federal laws over state laws h keep the nation unified.

Section 1. Valid Debts All debts contracted and engagem entered into, before the adoption of this Constitution, shall be as against the United States under this Constitution, as under Confederation.

Section 2. Supreme Law This Constitution, and the laws o United States which shall be made in pursuance thereof; and all tre made, or which shall be made, under the authority of the United S shall be the supreme law of the land; and the judges in every state sh bound thereby, anything in the constitution or laws of any state t contrary notwithstanding.

A CLOSER LOOK

In 1957, the "supreme law of the land" was put to a test. The governor of Arkansas defied a Supreme Court order. The Court ruled that African-American students could go to all-white public schools. President Dwight D. Eisenhower then sent federal troops to protect the first African-American students to enroll in Central High School in Little Rock, Arkansas.

Section 3. Loyalty to Constitution The Senators and sentatives before mentioned, and the members of the several state l tures, and all executive and judicial officers, both of the United Sta of the several states, shall be bound by oath or affirmation to suppo Constitution; but no religious test shall ever be required as a qualif to any office or public trust under the United States.

REDEUNT SATURNIA REGNA.

On the erection of the Eleventh PILLAR of the great National DOME, we beg leave most sincerely to felicitate " OUR DEAR COUNTRY "

Rise it will.

The foundation good—it may yet be SAVED.

The FEDERAL EDIFICE.

...ticle 7. Ratification

...AIN IDEA Nine of the 13 states had to ratify, or approve, the Constitution ...re it could go into effect.

...Y IT MATTERS NOW The approval of the Constitution launched a new plan ...overnment still followed today.

...ratification of the conventions of nine states shall be sufficient for the ...lishment of this Constitution between the states so ratifying the same. ... in convention by the **unanimous consent** of the states present, the sev- ...nth day of September in the year of our Lord one thousand seven hundred ...ighty-seven and of the independence of the United States of America the ...h. In witness whereof we have hereunto subscribed our names.

...ge Washington—President
...eputy from Virginia

...Hampshire: *John Langdon,*
...las Gilman

...achusetts: *Nathaniel Gorham,*
...King

...ecticut: *William Samuel Johnson,*
...Sherman

...York: *Alexander Hamilton*

...Jersey: *William Livingston,*
...Brearley, William Paterson,*
...han Dayton

...ylvania: *Benjamin Franklin,*
...s Mifflin, Robert Morris, George*
...r, Thomas FitzSimons, Jared*
...ll, James Wilson, Gouverneur Morris*

Delaware: *George Read, Gunning Bedford, Jr., John Dickinson, Richard Bassett, Jacob Broom*

Maryland: *James McHenry, Dan of St. Thomas Jenifer, Daniel Carroll*

Virginia: *John Blair, James Madison, Jr.*

North Carolina: *William Blount, Richard Dobbs Spaight, Hugh Williamson*

South Carolina: *John Rutledge, Charles Cotesworth Pinckney, Charles Pinckney, Pierce Butler*

Georgia: *William Few, Abraham Baldwin*

A CLOSER LOOK

THE SIGNERS

The 39 men who signed the Constitution were wealthy and well-educated. About half of them were trained in law. Others were doctors, merchants, bankers, and slaveholding planters. Missing from the list of signatures are the names of African Americans, Native Americans, and women. These groups reflected the varied population of the United States in the 1780s.

19. How do you think the absence of these groups affected the decisions made in creating the Constitution?

...cles 4–7 Assessment

...ain Ideas

...hat rights does Article 4 guarantee to citizens if they ... other states in the nation?

...hat are two ways of proposing an amendment to ...onstitution?

...at makes up "the supreme law of the land"?

2. Critical Thinking

Forming and Supporting Opinions Should the Framers of the Constitution have allowed the people to vote directly for ratification of the Constitution? Why or why not?

THINK ABOUT

- the idea that the government belongs to the people
- the general public's ability to make sound political decisions

The Bill of Rights and Amendments 11–27

In 1787, Thomas Jefferson sent James Madison a letter about the Constitution. Jefferson wrote, "I will now add what I do not like . . . [there is no] bill of rights." He explained his reasons: "A bill of rights is what the people are entitled to against every government on earth . . . and what no just government should refuse." Jefferson's disapproval is not surprising. In writing the Declaration of Independence, he spelled out basic individual rights that cannot be taken way. These are "life, liberty, and the pursuit of happiness." The Declaration states that governments are formed to protect these rights.

Several states approved the Constitution only if a list of guaranteed freedoms was added. While serving in the nation's first Congress, James Madison helped draft the Bill of Rights. In 1791, these first ten amendments became part of the Constitution.

AMENDMENTS 1–10. *The Bill of Rights*

MAIN IDEA The Bill of Rights protects citizens from government interference

WHY IT MATTERS NOW Issues related to the Bill of Rights are still being app tested, and interpreted.

AMENDMENT 1. Religious and Political Freedom (179

Congress shall make no law respecting an establishment of religio prohibiting the free exercise thereof; or **abridging** the freedom of spee of the press; or the right of the people peaceably to assemble, and to pe the Government for a redress of grievances.

A CLOSER LOOK The Five Freedoms

Freedom of Religion
Right to worship

Freedom of Speech
Right to state ideas

Freedom of the Press
Right to publish ideas

Freedom of Assembly
Right to meet peacefully in groups

Freedom to Petition
Right to protest the government

SKILLBUILDER Interpreting Charts
1. *Why is freedom of speech and the press important in a democratic society?*
2. *What impact has religious freedom had on the American way of life?*

AMENDMENT 2. Right to Bear Arms (1791) A well-regulated ...tia, being necessary to the security of a free state, the right of the ...ple to keep and bear arms, shall not be infringed.

AMENDMENT 3. Quartering Troops (1791) No soldier shall, in ...e of peace be **quartered** in any house, without the consent of the ...er, nor in time of war, but in a manner to be prescribed by law.

AMENDMENT 4. Search and Seizure (1791) The right of the ...ple to be secure in their persons, houses, papers, and effects, against ...easonable searches and seizures, shall not be violated, and no warrants ...l issue, but upon probable cause, supported by oath or affirmation, ...particularly describing the place to be searched, and the persons or ...gs to be seized.

AMENDMENT 5. Rights of Accused Persons (1791) No per-...shall be held to answer for a capital, or otherwise infamous crime, ...ss on a presentment or indictment of a Grand Jury, except in cases ...g in the land or naval forces, or in the militia, when in actual service ...me of war or public danger; nor shall any person be subject for ...ame offense to be twice put in jeopardy of life or limb; nor shall be ...pelled in any criminal case to be a witness against himself, nor be ...ved of life, liberty, or property, without **due process of law;** nor shall ...te property be taken for public use, without just compensation.

AMENDMENT 6. Right to a Speedy, Public Trial (1791)
...l criminal prosecutions, the accused shall enjoy the right to a speedy ...public trial, by an impartial jury of the State and district wherein the ...e shall have been committed, which district shall have been previ-...ascertained by law, and to be informed of the nature and cause of ...ccusation; to be confronted with the witnesses against him; to have ...ulsory process for obtaining witnesses in his favor, and to have the ...ance of **counsel** for his defense.

A CLOSER LOOK

SEARCHES

Metal detectors at airports search passengers. Airline workers search all carry-on luggage. Do these actions violate the 4th Amendment? The courts say no. They have cited many situations that allow for searches without a warrant, or written order. A person's right to privacy is balanced against the government's need to prevent crime.

20. What does the right to privacy mean to you at home and at school?

A CLOSER LOOK

In 1966, the Supreme Court made a decision based on the 5th and 6th Amendments. The warnings outlined in this ruling are often called "Miranda rights." Miranda rights protect suspects from giving forced confessions. Police must read these rights to a suspect they are questioning. For example:
• "You have the right to remain silent."
• "Anything that you say can and will be used against you in a court of law."
• "You have the right to an attorney."

A CLOSER LOOK

Protesters such as the young woman at left claim that the death penalty violates the 8th Amendment, which protects people against "cruel and unusual punishment." Supporters (above) believe that the death penalty is a justly deserved punishment.

A CLOSER LOOK

STATES' POWERS

The 10th Amendment gives the states reserved powers. Any powers not clearly given to the national government by the U.S. Constitution or denied to the states in Article I, Section 10, belong to the states. State constitutions sometimes assume authority in unexpected areas. For example, California's constitution sets rules for governing the use of fishing nets.

21. What are some common areas in which states have authority?

AMENDMENT 7. Trial by Jury in Civil Cases (1791) In at **common law,** where the value in controversy shall exceed twenty lars, the right of trial by jury shall be preserved, and no fact tried by a shall be otherwise reexamined in any court of the United States, according to the rules of the common law.

AMENDMENT 8. Limits of Fines and Punishments (1 Excessive **bail** shall not be required, nor excessive fines imposed, nor and unusual punishments inflicted.

AMENDMENT 9. Rights of People (1791) The enumer in the Constitution of certain rights shall not be construed to de disparage others retained by the people.

► **AMENDMENT 10. Powers of States and People (1791)** powers not delegated to the United States by the Constitution, no hibited by it to the States, are reserved to the States respectively, the people.

Bill of Rights Assessment

1. Main Ideas

a. Which amendment protects your privacy?

b. Which amendments guarantee fair legal treatment?

c. Which amendment prevents the federal government from taking powers away from the states and the people?

2. Critical Thinking

Forming and Supporting Opinions The 4th, 5th, 7th, and 8th Amendments protect innocent people accused of crimes. Do you think these five amendmen also favor the rights of actual criminals? Explain.

THINK ABOUT

• criminals who go free if valuable evidence is foun after their trials
• criminals released on bail

AIN IDEA The Constitution has adapted to social changes and historical trends.
HY IT MATTERS NOW Amendments 11–27 show that the Constitution is a
ng document.

ENDMENT 11. Lawsuits Against States (1798)

d by Congress March 4, 1794. Ratified February 7, 1795. Proclaimed 1798.
Article 3, Section 2, of the Constitution was modified by Amendment 11.

Judicial power of the United States shall not be construed to extend to any
in law or **equity**, commenced or prosecuted against one of the United
s by citizens of another state, or by citizens or subjects of any foreign state.

ENDMENT 12. Election of Executives (1804)

d by Congress December 9, 1803. Ratified June 15, 1804.
Part of Article 2, Section 1, of the Constitution was replaced by the 12th Amendment.

electors shall meet in their respective states and vote by ballot for
dent and Vice-President, one of whom, at least, shall not be an inhabi-
of the same state with themselves; they shall name in their ballots the
n voted for as President, and in distinct ballots the person voted for as
-President, and they shall make distinct lists of all persons voted for as
dent, and of all persons voted for as Vice-President, and of the number
tes for each, which lists they shall sign and certify, and transmit sealed
e seat of the government of the United States, directed to the President
e Senate;—the President of the Senate shall, in the presence of the
e and House of Representatives, open all the certificates and the votes
then be counted;—the person having the greatest number of votes for
dent, shall be the President, if such number be a majority of the whole
er of electors appointed; and if no person have such majority, then from
ersons having the highest numbers not exceeding three on the list of
voted for as President, the House of Representatives shall choose
diately, by ballot, the President. But in choosing the President, the votes
e taken by states, the representation from each state having one vote; a
m for this purpose shall consist of a member or members from two-
of the states, and a majority of all the states shall be necessary to a
e. And if the House of Representatives shall not choose a President
ever the right of choice shall devolve upon them, ~~before the fourth day~~
~~rch next following,~~ then the Vice-President shall act as President, as in
se of the death or other constitutional disability of the President. The
a having the greatest number of votes as Vice-President, shall be the
President, if such number be a majority of the whole number of
rs appointed, and if no person have a majority, then from the two
t numbers on the list, the Senate shall choose the Vice-President; a
m for the purpose shall consist of two-thirds of the whole number of
rs, and a majority of the whole number shall be necessary to a choice.
person constitutionally ineligible to the office of President shall be
e to that of Vice-President of the United States.

VOCABULARY

common law a system of law developed in England, based on customs and previous court decisions

bail money paid by arrested persons to guarantee they will return for trial

equity a system of justice not covered under common law

A CLOSER LOOK

SEPARATE BALLOTS

The presidential election of 1800 ended in a tie between Thomas Jefferson and Aaron Burr. At this time, the candidate with the most votes became president. The runner-up became vice-president. The 12th Amendment calls for separate ballots for the president and vice-president. The vice-president is specifically elected to the office, rather than being the presidential candidate with the second-most votes.

22. Why do you think it's important for a presidential election to result in a clear-cut winner?

AMENDMENT 13. Slavery Abolished (1865)

Passed by Congress January 31, 1865. Ratified December 6, 1865.

Note: A portion of Article 4, Section 2, of the Constitution was superseded b 13th Amendment.

Section 1. Neither slavery nor involuntary **servitude,** except as a pu ment for crime whereof the party shall have been duly convicted, exist within the United States, or any place subject to their jurisdicti

Section 2. Congress shall have power to enforce this article by appr ate legislation.

AMENDMENT 14. Civil Rights (1868)

Passed by Congress June 13, 1866. Ratified July 9, 1868.

Note: Article 1, Section 2, of the Constitution was modified by Section 2 of the Amendment.

Section 1. All persons born or **naturalized** in the United States, and ject to the jurisdiction thereof, are citizens of the United States and c state wherein they reside. No state shall make or enforce any law v shall abridge the privileges or immunities of citizens of the United S nor shall any state deprive any person of life, liberty, or property, wi due process of law; nor deny to any person within its jurisdiction the protection of the laws.

Section 2. Representatives shall be apportioned among the several according to their respective numbers, counting the whole number o sons in each state, excluding Indians not taxed. But when the right t at any election for the choice of electors for President and Vice-Presid the United States, Representatives in Congress, the executive and ju officers of a state, or the members of the legislature thereof, is denied of the male inhabitants of such state, being twenty-one years of age, ar izens of the United States, or in any way abridged, except for partici in rebellion, or other crime, the basis of representation therein sh reduced in the proportion whi number of such male citizens bear to the whole number of citizens twenty-one years of such state.

tion 3. No person shall be a Senator or Representative in Congress, or tor of President and Vice-President, or hold any office, civil or military, er the United States, or under any state, who, having previously taken an , as a member of Congress, or as an officer of the United States, or as a ber of any state legislature, or as an executive or judicial officer of any , to support the Constitution of the United States, shall have engaged in **rrection** or rebellion against the same, or given aid or comfort to the nies thereof. But Congress may, by a vote of two-thirds of each house, ve such disability.

ion 4. The validity of the public debt of the United States, authorized w, including debts incurred for payment of pensions and **bounties** for ces in suppressing insurrection or rebellion, shall not be questioned. But er the United States nor any state shall assume or pay any debt or ation incurred in aid of insurrection or rebellion against the United s, or any claim for the loss or emancipation of any slave; but all such , obligations and claims shall be held illegal and void.

ion 5. The Congress shall have power to enforce, by appropriate legis- , the provisions of this article.

ENDMENT 15. Right to Vote (1870)

d by Congress February 26, 1869. Ratified February 3, 1870.

ion 1. The right of citizens of the United States to vote shall not be d or abridged by the United States or by any state on account of race, , or previous condition of servitude.

on 2. The Congress shall have power to enforce this article by priate legislation.

A CLOSER LOOK

VOTING RIGHTS

The Voting Rights Act of 1965 extended the 15th Amendment. To qualify as voters, African Americans were no longer required to take tests proving that they could read and write. Also, federal examiners could help register voters. As a result, the number of African-American voters rose sharply.

23. What effect do you think the Voting Rights Act had on candidates running for office?

CLOSER LOOK Reconstruction Amendments

13th, 14th, and 15th Amendments are often called the Reconstruction Amendments. were passed after the Civil War during the government's attempt to rebuild the n and to grant rights to recently freed African Americans.

Amendment 13	Amendment 14	Amendment 15

1865	1868	1870
Ended slavery in the United States	• Defined national and state citizenship • Protected citizens' rights • Promised "equal protection of the laws"	• Designed to protect African Americans' voting rights

LLBUILDER Interpreting Charts

t problems did these amendments try to solve?

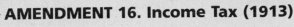

A CLOSER LOOK

INCOME TAX

People below the poverty level, as defined by the federal government, do not have to pay income tax. In 1997, the poverty level for a family of four was $16,400 per year. About 13.3 percent of all Americans were considered poor in 1997.

24. Why do you think people below the poverty level do not pay any income tax?

AMENDMENT 16. Income Tax (1913)

Passed by Congress July 12, 1909. Ratified February 3, 1913.

Note: Article 1, Section 9, of the Constitution was modified by the 16th Amendment.

The Congress shall have power to lay and collect taxes on incomes, f whatever source derived, without apportionment among the several st and without regard to any census or enumeration.

AMENDMENT 17. Direct Election of Senators (1913)

Passed by Congress May 13, 1912. Ratified April 8, 1913.

Note: Article 1, Section 3, of the Constitution was modified by the 17th Amendm

Section 1. The Senate of the United States shall be composed of two Sen from each state, elected by the people thereof, for six years; and each Ser shall have one vote. The electors in each state shall have the qualifications uisite for electors of the most numerous branch of the state legislatures.

Section 2. When vacancies happen in the representation of any state in Senate, the executive authority of such state shall issue writs of election such vacancies: Provided, that the legislature of any state may empowe executive thereof to make temporary appointments until the people fi vacancies by election as the legislature may direct.

Section 3. This amendment shall not be so construed as to affec election or term of any Senator chosen before it becomes valid as pa the Constitution.

AMENDMENT 18. Prohibition (1919)

Passed by Congress December 18, 1917. Ratified January 16, 1919. Repealed b 21st Amendment.

Section 1. After one year from the ratification of this article the manufa sale, or transportation of intoxicating liquors within, the importation th into, or the exportation thereof from the United States and all territory ject to the jurisdiction thereof for beverage purposes is hereby prohibite

Section 2. The Congress an several states shall have cc rent power to enforce this by appropriate legislation.

Section 3. This article sh inoperative unless it shall been ratified as an amendm the Constitution by the le tures of the several states, a vided in the Constitution, seven years from the date submission hereof to the by the Congress.

A CLOSER LOOK

Under Prohibition, people broke the law if they made, sold, or shipped alcoholic beverages. Powerful crime gangs turned selling illegal liquor into a big business. This photo shows federal agents getting ready to smash containers of illegal whiskey. The 21st Amendment ended Prohibition.

A CLOSER LOOK

At left, marchers campaign for the 19th Amendment—woman suffrage. Since winning the right to vote in 1920, women have slowly gained political power. Pictured below are Congress members who belong to the Congressional Caucus for Women's Issues.

ENDMENT 19. Woman Suffrage (1920)

d by Congress June 4, 1919. Ratified August 18, 1920.

on 1. The right of citizens of the United States to vote shall not be d or abridged by the United States or by any state on account of sex.

on 2. Congress shall have power to enforce this article by appropriate ation.

ENDMENT 20. "Lame Duck" Sessions (1933)

d by Congress March 2, 1932. Ratified January 23, 1933.

Article 1, Section 4, of the Constitution was modified by Section 2 of this amend- In addition, a portion of the 12th Amendment was superseded by Section 3.

on 1. The terms of the President and Vice-President shall end at noon e 20th day of January, and the terms of Senators and Representatives at on the 3rd day of January, of the years in which such terms would have l if this article had not been ratified; and the terms of their successors hen begin.

on 2. The Congress shall assemble at least once in every year, and such ng shall begin at noon on the 3rd day of January, unless they shall by ppoint a different day.

on 3. If, at the time fixed for the beginning of the term of the ent, the President elect shall have died, the Vice-President elect shall e President. If a President shall not have been chosen before the time or the beginning of his term, or if the President elect shall have failed alify, then the Vice-President elect shall act as President until a ent shall have qualified; and the Congress may by law provide for the herein neither a President elect nor a Vice-President elect shall have

A CLOSER LOOK

THE EQUAL RIGHTS AMENDMENT

In 1920, the 19th Amendment took effect, guaranteeing women the right to vote. Nevertheless, many women have continued to face discrimination in the United States. In 1923, the National Women's Party supported the passage of an equal rights amendment to protect women. Congress did not pass such an amendment until 1972. In 1982, however, the amendment died after it failed to be ratified by enough states to be added to the Constitution.

25. Why do you think the 19th Amendment failed to create equality for women?

qualified, declaring who shall then act as President, or the manner in w one who is to act shall be selected, and such person shall act according a President or Vice-President shall have qualified.

Section 4. The Congress may by law provide for the case of the death o of the persons from whom the House of Representatives may choc President whenever the right of choice shall have devolved upon them, for the case of the death of any of the persons from whom the Senate choose a Vice-President whenever the right of choice shall have deve upon them.

Section 5. Sections 1 and 2 shall take effect on the 15th day of Octobe lowing the ratification of this article.

Section 6. This article shall be **inoperative** unless it shall have been ra as an amendment to the Constitution by the legislatures of three-fourt the several states within seven years from the date of its submission.

AMENDMENT 21. Repeal of Prohibition (1933)

Passed by Congress February 20, 1933. Ratified December 5, 1933.

Section 1. The eighteenth article of amendment to the Constitution United States is hereby repealed.

Section 2. The transportation or importation into any state, territo possession of the United States for delivery or use therein of intoxic liquors, in violation of the laws thereof, is hereby prohibited.

Section 3. This article shall be inoperative unless it shall have been ra as an amendment to the Constitution by conventions in the several sta provided in the Constitution, within seven years from the date of the mission hereof to the states by the Congress.

AMENDMENT 22. Limit on Presidential Terms (1951)

Passed by Congress March 21, 1947. Ratified February 27, 1951.

Section 1. No person shall be elected to the office of the President than twice, and no person who has held the office of President, or ac President, for more than two years of a term to which some other perso elected President shall be elected to the office of the President more once. But this article shall not apply to any person holding the off President when this article was proposed by the Congress, and shall ne vent any person who may be holding the office of President, or act President, during the term within which this article becomes ope from holding the office of President or acting as President durin remainder of such term.

Section 2. This article shall be inoperative unless it shall have bee ified as an amendment to the Constitution by the legislatures of fourths of the several states within seven years from the date submission to the states by the Congress.

AMENDMENT 23. Voting in District of Columbia (1961)

Passed by Congress June 17, 1960. Ratified March 29, 1961.

Section 1. The district constituting the seat of government of the United States shall appoint in such manner as Congress may direct: a number of electors of President and Vice-President equal to the whole number of Senators and Representatives in Congress to which the district would be entitled if it were a state, but in no event more than the least populous state; they shall be in addition to those appointed by the states, but they shall be considered, for the purposes of the election of President and Vice-President, to be electors appointed by a state; and they shall meet in the district and perform such duties as provided by the twelfth article of amendment.

Section 2. The Congress shall have power to enforce this article by appropriate legislation.

AMENDMENT 24. Abolition of Poll Taxes (1964)

Passed by Congress August 27, 1962. Ratified January 23, 1964.

Section 1. The right of citizens of the United States to vote in any primary or other election for President or Vice-President, for electors for President or Vice-President, or for Senator or Representative in Congress, shall not be denied or abridged by the United States or any state by reason of failure to pay any poll tax or other tax.

Section 2. The Congress shall have power to enforce this article by appropriate legislation.

AMENDMENT 25. Presidential Disability, Succession (1967)

Passed by Congress July 6, 1965. Ratified February 10, 1967.

Article 2, Section 1, of the Constitution was affected by the 25th Amendment.

Section 1. In case of the removal of the President from office or of his death or resignation, the Vice-President shall become President.

Section 2. Whenever there is a vacancy in the office of the Vice-President, the President shall nominate a Vice-President who shall take office upon confirmation by a majority vote of both houses of Congress.

Section 3. Whenever the President transmits to the President pro tempore of the Senate and the Speaker of the House of Representatives his written declaration that he is unable to discharge the powers and duties of his office, and until he transmits to them a written declaration to the contrary, such powers and duties shall be discharged by the Vice-President as Acting President.

A CLOSER LOOK

POLL TAX

The poll tax was aimed at preventing African Americans from exercising their rights. Many could not afford to pay this fee required for voting.

26. How do you think the 24th Amendment affected elections?

A CLOSER LOOK

PRESIDENTIAL DISABILITY

President John F. Kennedy's death in 1963 signaled the need for the 25th Amendment. The Constitution did not explain what to do in the case of a disabled president. James Reston, a writer for *The New York Times,* summed up the problem: Suppose Kennedy was "strong enough to survive [the bullet wounds], but too weak to govern." The 25th Amendment provides for an orderly transfer of power.

27. What do you think can happen in a country where the rules for succession are not clear?

SUCCESSION

Who takes over if a president dies in office or is unable to serve? The top five in the line of succession follow:

- vice-president
- speaker of the house
- president pro tempore of the Senate
- secretary of state
- secretary of the treasury

28. Why should voters know the views of the vice-president?

Section 4. Whenever the Vice-President and a majority of either the pr pal officers of the executive departments or of such other body as Cong may by law provide, transmit to the President pro tempore of the Senate the Speaker of the House of Representatives their written declaration tha President is unable to discharge the powers and duties of his office, the V President shall immediately assume the powers and duties of the offic Acting President. Thereafter, when the President transmits to the Presi pro tempore of the Senate and the Speaker of the House of Representa his written declaration that no inability exists, he shall resume the powers duties of his office unless the Vice-President and a majority of either the cipal officers of the executive department[s] or of such other body as Con may by law provide, transmit within four days to the President pro tem of the Senate and the Speaker of the House of Representatives their wr declaration that the President is unable to discharge the powers and duti his office. Thereupon Congress shall decide the issue, assembling w forty-eight hours for that purpose if not in session. If the Congress, w twenty-one days after receipt of the latter written declaration, or, if Con is not in session, within twenty-one days after Congress is required to as ble, determines by two thirds vote of both houses that the President is u to discharge the powers and duties of his office, the Vice-President shall tinue to discharge the same as Acting President; otherwise, the President resume the powers and duties of his office.

A CLOSER LOOK Amendments Time Line *1791–1992*

Use the key below to help you categorize the amendments.

- ■ **Voting Rights**
- ■ **Social Changes**
- ■ **Overturned Supreme Court Decisions**
- ■ **Election Procedures and Conditions of Office**

Bill of Rights
Amendments 1–10
1791

1790

Amendment 15
1870
Stops national and state governments from denying the vote based on race.

Amendment 13
1865
Bans slavery.

Amendment 11
1798
Protects state from lawsuits filed by citizens of other states or countries.

Amendment 12
1804
Requires separate electoral ballots for president and vice-president.

Amendment 14
1868
Defines American citizenship and citizens' rights.

ENDMENT 26. 18-year-old Vote (1971)

d by Congress March 23, 1971. Ratified July 1, 1971.

Amendment 14, Section 2, of the Constitution was modified by Section 1 of the Amendment.

ion 1. The right of citizens of the United States, who are eighteen years e or older, to vote shall not be denied or abridged by the United States any state on account of age.

ion 2. The Congress shall have power to enforce this article by appro- e legislation.

ENDMENT 27. Congressional Pay (1992)

d by Congress September 25, 1789. Ratified May 7, 1992.

aw, varying the compensation for the services of the Senators and esentatives, shall take effect, until an election of Representatives shall intervened.

endments 11–27 Assessment

Main Ideas

Vhich amendments affected the office of president?

Vhich pair of amendments shows the failure of laws olve a social problem?

Vhich amendments corrected unfair treatment ard African Americans and women?

2. Critical Thinking

Summarizing What is the purpose of amending the Constitution?

THINK ABOUT

• the purpose of the Constitution
• problems and issues that Americans have faced throughout U.S. history

---

Amendment 23
1961
Gives citizens of Washington, D.C., right to vote in presidential elections.

Amendment 19
1920
Extends the vote to women.

Amendment 24
1964
Bans poll taxes.

ment 18
1919
ts making,
d shipping
beverages.

Amendment 21
1933
Repeals
Amendment 18.

Amendment 26
1971
Gives 18-year-olds right to vote in federal and state elections.

2000

Amendment 16
1913
Allows Congress to tax incomes.

Amendment 20
1933
Changes date for starting new Congress and inaugurating new president.

Amendment 25
1967
Sets procedures for presidential succession.

Amendment 27
1992
Limits ability of Congress to increase its pay.

Amendment 17
1913
Establishes direct election of U.S. senators.

Amendment 22
1951
Limits terms president can serve to two.

VISUAL SUMMARY

The Constitution of the United States

Preamble

WE THE PEOPLE

Article 1 Article 2 Article 3

The Branches of Government

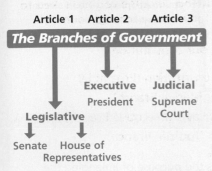

Executive
President

Judicial
Supreme
Court

Legislative

Senate   House of
Representatives

Article 4 Article 6

The Federal System

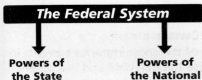

Powers of
the State

Powers of
the National
Government

"Supreme law
of the land"

Article 5

Amending the Constitution

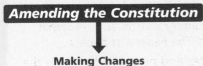

Making Changes

Bill of Rights

Amendments 1–10

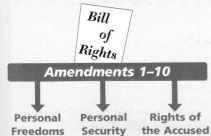

Personal
Freedoms

Personal
Security

Rights of
the Accused

Amendments 11–27

The living Constitution changes with the times.

VOCABULARY

Briefly explain the significance of each of the following.

1. electors
2. impeachment
3. naturalization
4. felonies
5. bill of attainder
6. ex post facto law
7. suffrage
8. due process of law
9. servitude
10. primary

SEVEN PRINCIPLES OF THE CONSTITUTION

Make a chart like the one shown. Then fill it in with a definition of each principle and an example from the Constitution.

Principle	Definition	Example
1. popular sovereignty		
2. republicanism		
3. federalism		
4. separation of powers		
5. checks and balances		
6. limited government		
7. individual rights		

REVIEW QUESTIONS

Article 1 (pages 249–255)

1. What are the requirements for becoming a member of the House of Representatives and the Senate?
2. What are two military powers granted to Congress?

Article 2 (pages 256–259)

3. How does the electoral college choose the president?
4. What are three powers of the president?

Article 3 (pages 260–261)

5. What are the two most important powers of the federal courts?

Articles 4–7 (pages 262–265)

6. How can the Constitution be changed?
7. If a state law and a federal law conflict, which law must be obeyed?
8. How was the Constitution ratified?

Bill of Rights and Amendments 11–27 (pages 266–277)

9. What five freedoms are guaranteed in the First Amendment?
10. Which amendments extend voting rights to a broader range of Amer

CRITICAL THINKING

DRAWING CONCLUSIONS

[two-]column chart, summarize the processes for [chan]ging the Constitution. Then use your completed [char]t to answer the questions below.

[P]roposing Amendments	Ratifying Amendments
	1.
	2.

[W]hat role can citizens play in proposing amendments?
[W]hat do you think are the main reasons for [ch]anging the Constitution?

MAKING INFERENCES

[Expla]in how the "elastic clause" in Article 1 gives [Cong]ress the authority to take action on other issues [unkn]own to the Framers of the Constitution.

ANALYZING LEADERSHIP

[Thin]k about the president's roles described in the [Const]itution. What qualities does a president need to [succe]ed as a leader in so many different areas?

RECOGNIZING EFFECTS

[How] would you describe the impact of the 14th, 15th, [and 1]6th Amendments on life in the United States?

APPLYING CITIZENSHIP

[Suppo]se you and your family go on a road trip [acros]s several states. According to Article 4 of the [Const]itution, what citizens' rights do you have in the [state]s you are visiting?

HISTORY SKILLS

INTERPRETING PRIMARY SOURCES

[In 19]37, President Franklin D. Roosevelt gave a speech [on t]he radio. He used interesting comparisons to [expla]in how the government works.

[Roosevelt des]cribed the American form of government as a [three]-horse team provided by the Constitution to the [Ame]rican people so that their field might be plowed.
[The]three horses are, of course, the three branches of [gove]rnment—the Congress, the Executive, and the [Cour]ts. . . . It is the American people themselves who [are in] the driver's seat. It is the American people [them]selves who want the furrow plowed.

[Frank]lin D. Roosevelt, Radio Address

[How] does Roosevelt describe the separation of powers?
[How] does Roosevelt explain popular sovereignty?

ALTERNATIVE ASSESSMENT

1. INTERDISCIPLINARY ACTIVITY: Government

Creating a Database Review the grievances against King George III listed in the Declaration of Independence. Then create a database that shows how specific sections of the U.S. Constitution addressed those grievances. Write a brief summary stating how well the Constitution addressed the grievances.

2. COOPERATIVE LEARNING ACTIVITY

Drafting a Constitution Imagine you are asked to write a constitution for a newly formed country. Working with a group, use the outline below to organize and write your constitution.

I. Purpose of the Constitution (Preamble)
II. Making Laws (Legislative Branch)
III. Carrying Out the Laws (Executive Branch)
IV. Making Laws Fair (Judicial Branch)
V. Choosing Leaders
VI. Citizens' Rights (Bill of Rights)

3. 💿 PRIMARY SOURCE EXPLORER

Making a Learning Center Creating the U.S. Constitution was one of the most important events in the nation's history. Use the CD-ROM and the library to collect information on different topics related to the Constitution.

Create a learning center featuring the suggestions below.

- Find biographies and portraits of the Framers.
- Collect important primary sources such as James Madison's notes and *The Federalist* papers.
- Gather recent pictures and news articles about the Congress, the president, the Supreme Court, and the Bill of Rights.

4. HISTORY PORTFOLIO

Review your draft of the constitution you wrote for the assessment activity. Choose one of these options below.

Option 1 Use comments made by your teacher or classmates to improve your work.

Option 2 Illustrate your constitution. Add your work to your history portfolio.

Additional Test Practice,
pp. S1–S33

TEST PRACTICE
CLASSZONE.COM

The Role of the Citizen

Citizens of the United States enjoy many basic rights and freedoms. Freedom of speech and religion are examples. These rights are guaranteed by the Constitution, the Bill of Rights, and other amendments to the Constitution. Along with these rights, however, come responsibilities. Obeying rules and laws, voting, and serving on juries are some examples.

Active citizenship is not limited to adults. Younger citizens can help their communities become better places. The following pages will help you to learn about your rights and responsibilities. Knowing them will help you to become an active and involved citizen of your community, state, and nation.

In this book you will find examples of active citizenship by young people like yourself. **Look for the Citizenship Today features.**

Citizen → KNOW YOUR RIGHTS → BE RESPONSIBLE → STAY INFORMED → MAKE GOOD DECISIONS → PARTICIPATE IN YOUR COMMUNITY → **Mo Citi**

President John F. Kennedy urged all Americans to become active citizens and work to improve their communities.

The weather was sunny but cold on January 20, 1961—the day that F. Kennedy became the 35th president of the United States. In his speech as president, he urged all Americans to serve their country. then, Kennedy's words have inspired millions of Americans to be more active citizens.

> *"Ask not what your country can do for you—ask what you can do for your country!"*
>
> —JOHN F. KENNEDY

What Is a Citizen?

A citizen is a legal member of a nation and pledges loyalty to nation. A citizen has certain guaranteed rights, protections, and resp bilities. A citizen is a member of a community and wants to mak good place to live.

Today in the United States there are a number of ways to beco citizen. The most familiar are citizenship by birth and citizensh naturalization. All citizens have the right to equal protection the law.

CITIZENSHIP BY BIRTH A child born in the United States is a citizen by birth. Children born to U.S. citizens traveling or living outside the country, such as military personnel, are citizens. Even children born in the United States to parents who are not citizens of the United States are considered U.S. citizens. These children have dual citizenship. This means they are citizens of two countries—both the United States and the country of their parents' citizenship. At the age of 18, the child may choose one of the countries for permanent citizenship.

CITIZENSHIP BY NATURALIZATION A person who is not a citizen of the United States may become one through a process called naturalization. The steps in this process are shown below. To become a naturalized citizen, a person must meet certain requirements.

- Be at least 18 years old. Children under the age of 18 automatically become naturalized citizens when their parents do.
- Enter the United States legally.
- Live in the United States for at least five years immediately prior to application.
- Read, write, and speak English.
- Show knowledge of American history and government.

See Citizenship Today: Becoming a Citizen, p. 427

Steps in the Naturalization Process

1. File an application.
2. Take an examination.
3. File a legal petition for naturalization.
4. Appear at a court hearing.
5. Take an oath of allegiance.

Hundreds of people become new citizens at a single ceremony in San Antonio, Texas.

What Are Your Rights?

Citizens of the United States are guaranteed rights by the U.S. Constitution, state constitutions, and state and federal laws. All citizens have three kinds of rights: basic freedoms, protection from unfair government actions, and equal treatment under the law.

Citizens' basic rights and freedoms are sometimes called **civil rights**. Some of these rights are personal, and others are political.

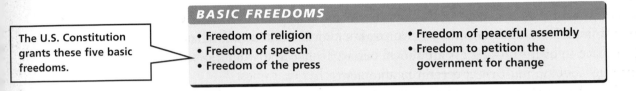

The U.S. Constitution grants these five basic freedoms.

BASIC FREEDOMS

- Freedom of religion
- Freedom of speech
- Freedom of the press
- Freedom of peaceful assembly
- Freedom to petition the government for change

The second category of rights is intended to protect citizens from unfair government actions.

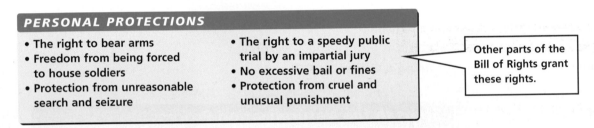

PERSONAL PROTECTIONS

- The right to bear arms
- Freedom from being forced to house soldiers
- Protection from unreasonable search and seizure
- The right to a speedy public trial by an impartial jury
- No excessive bail or fines
- Protection from cruel and unusual punishment

Other parts of the Bill of Rights grant these rights.

The third category is the right to equal treatment under the law. The government cannot treat one individual or group differently from another.

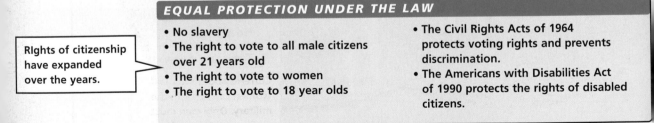

Rights of citizenship have expanded over the years.

EQUAL PROTECTION UNDER THE LAW

- No slavery
- The right to vote to all male citizens over 21 years old
- The right to vote to women
- The right to vote to 18 year olds
- The Civil Rights Acts of 1964 protects voting rights and prevents discrimination.
- The Americans with Disabilities Act of 1990 protects the rights of disabled citizens.

LIMITS TO RIGHTS The rights guaranteed to citizens have sensible limits. For example, the right to free speech does not allow a person to falsely shout, "Fire!" at a crowded concert. The government may place limits on certain rights to protect national security or to provide equal opportunities for all citizens. And rights come with responsibilities.

What Are Your Responsibilities?

For American democracy to work, citizens must carry out important responsibilities. There are two kinds of responsibilities—personal and civic. Personal responsibilities include taking care of yourself, helping your family, knowing right from wrong, and behaving in a respectful way.

Civic responsibilities are those that involve your government and community. They include obeying rules and laws, serving on juries, paying taxes, and defending your country when called upon. One of the most important responsibilities is voting. When you turn 18, you will have that right.

As a young person, you can be a good citizen in a number of ways. You might work with other people in your community to make it a fair and just place to live. Working for a political party or writing to your elected officials about issues that concern you are some other examples.

The chart below shows how responsibilities change with a citizen's age. Notice that all citizens share the responsibility to obey the laws of their communities.

See Citizenship Today: Obeying Rules and Laws, p. 300

sponsibilities of a Citizen

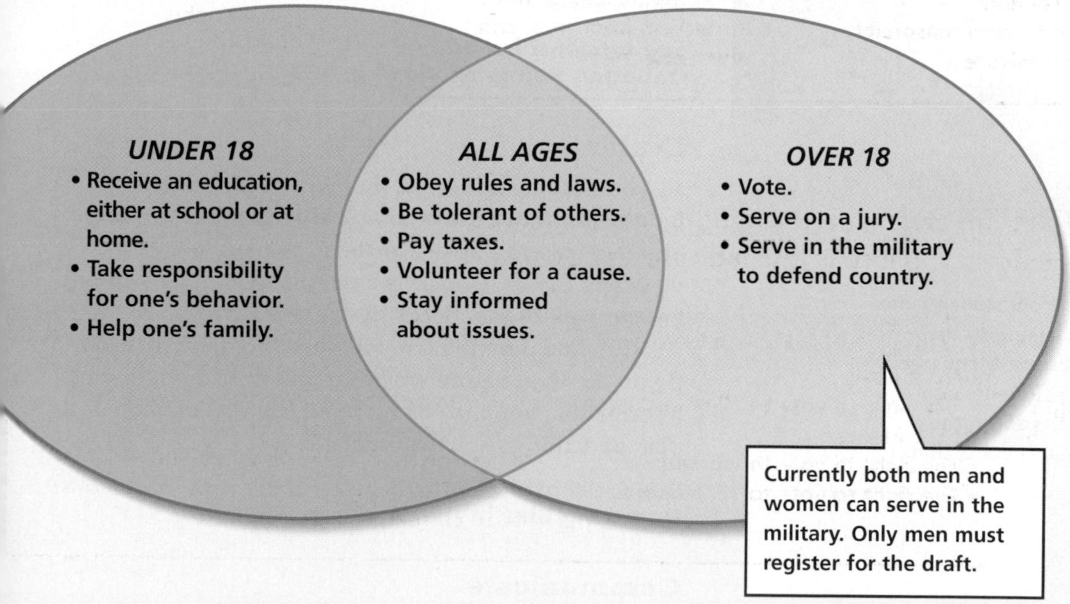

UNDER 18
- Receive an education, either at school or at home.
- Take responsibility for one's behavior.
- Help one's family.

ALL AGES
- Obey rules and laws.
- Be tolerant of others.
- Pay taxes.
- Volunteer for a cause.
- Stay informed about issues.

OVER 18
- Vote.
- Serve on a jury.
- Serve in the military to defend country.

Currently both men and women can serve in the military. Only men must register for the draft.

ZENSHIP ACTIVITIES

terview a recently naturalized citizen. Ask about e test he or she took to become a U.S. citizen. rite a report of your findings.

2. Using newspapers or magazines, find examples of citizens using their unalienable rights or practicing responsible citizenship. Cut out five articles to illustrate the points. Mount them and write a one-sentence explanation of each article.

Building Citizenship Skills

Good citizenship skills include **staying informed, solving problems** or **making decisions,** and **taking action.** Every citizen can find ways to build citizenship skills. By showing respect for the law and for the rights of others in your daily life, you promote democracy. You can also work to change conditions in your community to make sure all citizens experience freedom and justice.

How Do You Stay Informed?

Americans can sometimes feel that they have access to too much information. It may seem overwhelming. Even so, you should stay informed on issues that affect your life. Staying informed gives you the information you need to make wise decisions and helps you find ways to solve problems.

These Texas middle school students are staying informed by talking to their Texas state representative. Many public officials enjoy having students visit and ask them questions about their jobs, and about issues students think are important.

Watch, Listen, and Read

The first step in practicing good citizenship is to know how to find information that you need.

Sources of information include broadcast and print media and the Internet. Public officials and civic organizations are also good sources for additional information. Remember as you are reading to evaluate your sources.

**See Citizenship Today:
Debating Points of View, p. 469**

Evaluate

As you become informed, you will need to make judgments about the accuracy of your news sources. You must also be aware of those sources' points of view and biases. (A bias is a judgment formed without knowing all of the facts.)

You should determine if you need more information. If you do, then decide where to find it. After gathering information, you may be ready to form an opinion or a plan of action to solve a problem.

**See Citizenship Today:
Detecting Bias in the Media, p. 664**

Communicate

To bring about change in their communities, active citizens may need to contact public officials. In today's world, making contact is easy.

You can reach most public officials by telephone, voice mail, fax, or letter. Many public officials also have Internet pages or e-mail that encourages input from the public.

**See Citizenship Today:
Writing to Government Officials, p. 776**

How Do You Make Wise Decisions?

Civic life involves making important decisions. As a voter, whom should you vote for? As a juror, should you find the defendant guilty or not guilty? As an informed citizen, should you support or oppose a proposed government action? Unlike decisions about which video to rent, civic decisions cannot be made by a process as easy as tossing a coin. Instead, you should use a problem-solving approach like the one shown in the chart below. Decision making won't always proceed directly from step to step. Sometimes it's necessary to backtrack a little. For example, you may get to the "Analyze the Information" step and realize that you don't have enough information to analyze. Then you can go back a step and gather more information.

blem-Solving and Decision-Making Process

Problem-solving and decision-making involves many steps. This diagram shows you how to take those steps. Notice that you may have to repeat some steps depending on the information you gather.

EVALUATE THE SOLUTION
Review the results of putting your solution into action. Did the solution work? Do you need to adjust the solution in some way?

IMPLEMENT THE SOLUTION
Take action or plan to take action on a chosen solution.

CHOOSE A SOLUTION
Choose the solution you believe will best solve the problem and help you reach your goal.

CONSIDER OPTIONS
Think of as many ways as possible to solve the problem. Don't be afraid to include ideas that others might think are unacceptable.

ANALYZE THE INFORMATION
Look at the information and determine what it reveals about solving the problem.

GATHER INFORMATION
Get to know the basics of the problem. Find out as much as possible about the issues.

IFY THE PROBLEM
what the main issues
d what your goal is.

Students working on an environmental project are gathering and analyzing information to help them make decisions.

How Do You Participate in Your Community?

Across the country many young people have come up with ways to make their communities better places to live. Thirteen-year-old Aubyn Burnside of Hickory, North Carolina, is just one example. Aubyn felt sorry for foster children she saw moving their belongings in plastic trash bags. She founded Suitcases for Kids. This program provides used luggage for foster children who are moving from one home to another. Her program has been adopted by other young people in several states. Below are some ways in which you can participate in your community.

See Citizenship Today: Community Service, p. 612

Students participate in a rally to promote safety in their school.

Find a Cause

How can you become involved in your commu[n]? First, select a community problem or issue that interests you. Some ideas from other young people include starting a support group for children with cancer, publishing a neighborhoo[d] newspaper with children's stories and art, and putting on performances to entertain people in shelters and hospitals.

Develop Solutions

Once you have found a cause on which you w[ant] to work, develop a plan for solving the proble[m]. Use the decision-making or problem-solving sk[ills] you have learned to find ways to approach the problem. You may want to involve other peop[le] in your activities.

Follow Through

Solving problems takes time. You'll need to be patient in developing a plan. You can show leadership in working with your group by following through on meetings you set up and plans you make. When you finally solve the problem, you will feel proud of your accomplishments.

CITIZENSHIP ACTIVITIES

1. Use the telephone directory to make a list of names, addresses, and phone numbers of public officials or organizations that could provide information about solving problems in your community.

2. Copy the steps in the problem-solving and decision-making diagram and show how you followed them [to] solve a problem or make a decision. Be sure to clear[ly] state the problem and the final decision.

...acticing Citizenship Skills

...have learned that good citizenship involves three skills: staying ...med, solving problems, and taking action. Below are some activi- ...o help you improve your citizenship skills. By practicing these skills ...an work to make a difference in your own life and in the lives of ...e in your community.

...izen → KNOW YOUR RIGHTS → BE RESPONSIBLE → STAY INFORMED → MAKE GOOD DECISIONS → PARTICIPATE IN YOUR COMMUNITY → **Model Citizen**

...TIZENSHIP ACTIVITIES

...y Informed

...ATE A PAMPHLET OR ...RUITING COMMERCIAL

...your school counselors or ...e to your state department ...ducation to get information ...tate-run colleges, universities, ...chnical schools. Use this ...rmation to create a brochure ...ecruiting commercial ...ving these schools and the ...rent programs and degrees ...offer.

...P IN MIND

...t's there for me? It may ...you think about what areas ...ents are interested in and ...want to pursue in later life.

...re is it? You may want to ...a map showing where the ...ols are located in your state.

...can I afford it? Students ...t want to know if financial ...available to attend the ...ols you have featured.

Make Wise Decisions

CREATE A GAME BOARD OR SKIT

Study the decision-making diagram on page 285. With a small group, develop a skit that explains the steps in problem solving. Present your skit to younger students in your school. As an alternative, create a game board that would help younger students understand the steps in making a decision.

KEEP IN MIND

What do children this age understand? Be sure to create a skit or game at an age-appropriate level.

What kinds of decisions do younger students make? Think about the kinds of decisions that the viewers of your skit or players of the game might make.

How can I make it interesting? Use visual aids to help students understand the steps in decision making.

Take Action

CREATE A BULLETIN BOARD FOR YOUR CLASS

Do some research on the Internet or consult the yellow pages under "Social Services" to find the names of organizations that have volunteer opportunities for young people. Call or write for more information. Then create a bulletin board for your class showing groups that would like volunteer help.

KEEP IN MIND

What kinds of jobs are they? You may want to list the types of skills or jobs volunteer groups are looking for.

How old do I have to be? Some groups may be looking for younger volunteers; others may need older persons.

How do I get there? How easy is it to get to the volunteer group's location?

The Early Republic

"Our country! May she always be in the right; but our country, right or wrong."

—Stephen Decatur

Known as "Old Ironsides," the U.S.S. *Constitution* won more battles than any other early American warship. Today it rests in Boston Harbor.

CHAPTER 9

Launching a New Republic 1789–1800

George Washington's first cabinet. Left to right: Secretary of War Henry Knox, Secretary of State Thomas Jefferson, Attorney General Edmund Randolph, Secretary of the Treasury Alexander Hamilton, and President George Washington.

1789
George Washington inaugurated as president.

1791
The first Bank of the United States is established.

1792
Washington reelected president.

USA
World — 1789

1789
French Revolution begins.

1791
Slaves revolt in Santo Domingo.

1793
French execu Terro

The year is 1789, and George Washington has been inaugurated as the first president of the United States. It quickly becomes obvious to you and to others that the president will need help. He chooses people with different talents and experience to help him govern.

What kind of person would you choose to help you govern?

What Do You Think?

- Why might you want people with different viewpoints in your government?
- What do you think your biggest challenges would be?

RESEARCH LINKS
CLASSZONE.COM

Visit the Chapter 9 links for more information about the new republic.

1796
John Adams elected president.

1798
Alien and Sedition Acts

1800
Thomas Jefferson elected president.

1800

1797
Britain appoints Richard Wellesley Governor-General of India.

1798
French Expedition to Egypt

1800
Napoleon becomes First Consul of France.

Reading Strategy: Identifying and Solving P

What Do You Know?

What do you think of when you hear the words *democracy* and *republic?* Why do you think the citizens and leaders of the new country wanted to establish a republic governed by laws?

Think About
- the experience of the colonists under British rule
- the effect of the Revolutionary War and the period immediately after the war
- your responses to the Interact with History about choosing people to govern (see page 291)

This early American flag has 13
representing the original 13 co

What Do You Want to Know?

 What questions do you have about the people who created the U.S. government? Record your questions in your notebook before you read the chapter.

Identifying and Solving Problems

As you read history, try to identify problems in past times and the solutions that people came with to solve their problems. A graphic organizer such as the chart below can help you to ke track of problems and their solutions. In the middle of the chart, four headings categorize th major issues faced by the young nation. Copy the chart into your notebook and then record lems and the proposed solutions in each category.

 See Skillbuilder Handbook, page R18.

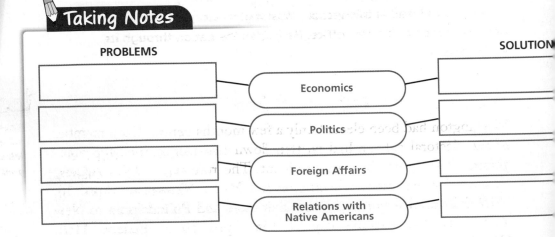

Taking Notes

PROBLEMS

SOLUTION

Economics

Politics

Foreign Affairs

Relations with
Native Americans

Washington's Presidency

MAIN IDEA	WHY IT MATTERS NOW	TERMS & NAMES
sident and the Congress o set up the new nent.	The strength of the U.S. today is due to the decisions of the Founders about how to organize the government.	inaugurate · cabinet Federal Judiciary Act · tariff

ONE AMERICAN'S STORY

Charles Thomson had served as secretary of the Continental Congress in 1774. Now, on April 14, 1789, he came to Mount Vernon in Virginia with a letter for George Washington. Washington knew the reason for the visit. Thomson's letter was to tell him that he had been elected the nation's first president. Before giving Washington the letter, Thomson made a short speech.

Charles Thomson delivers the letter to Washington announcing his election as president.

A VOICE FROM THE PAST

I have now Sir to inform you that . . . your patriotism and your readiness to sacrifice . . . private enjoyments to preserve the liberty and promote the happiness of your Country [convinced the Congress that you would accept] this important Office to which you are called not only by the unanimous votes of the Electors but by the voice of America.

Charles Thomson, quoted in Washington's Papers, Library of Congress

As you will read in this section, Washington accepted the honor and the burden of his new office. He guided the nation through its early years.

Washington Takes Office

Washington had been elected only a few months before. Each member of the electoral college had written down two names. The top vote-getter, Washington, became president. The runner-up, John Adams, became vice-president. Washington left Mount Vernon on April 16, 1789. He traveled north through Baltimore and Philadelphia to New York City, the nation's capital. On April 30 at Federal Hall, Washington was **inaugurated,** or sworn in, as president. John Adams of Massachusetts was his vice-president.

✏️ **Taking Notes**

Use your chart to take notes about Washington's presidency.

Economics

Politics

Foreign Affairs

Relations with Native Americans

As the nation's first president, Washington faced a difficult task. He knew that all eyes would be on him. His every action as president would set a precedent—an example that would become standard practice. People argued over what to call him. Some, including John Adams, suggested "His Excellency" or "His Highness." Others argued that such titles would suggest that he was a king. The debate tied up Congress for a month. Finally, "Mr. President" was agreed upon. Congress had to settle other differences about how the new government should be run.

Reading His
A. Making
Inferences V
were people
concerned a
how to addr
the presiden

Setting Up the Courts

The writers of the Constitution had left many matters to be decided by Congress. For example, the Constitution created a Supreme Court but left it to Congress to decide the number of justices. Leaders also argued about how much power the Supreme Court should have. One reason for disagreement was that the states already had their own courts. How would authority be divided between the state and federal courts?

To create a court system, Congress passed the **Federal Judiciary Act** of 1789. This act gave the Supreme Court six members: a chief justice, or judge, and five associate justices. Over time, that number has grown to nine. The act also provided for other lower, less powerful federal courts. Washington appointed John Jay, the prominent New York lawyer and diplomat, as chief justice.

Vocabular
judiciary: sy
of courts ar
judges

Now and then

THE PRESIDENT'S CABINET

The president's cabinet has more than tripled in size since it began with the secretaries of state, war, and treasury, and the attorney general. As the nation has faced new challenges, the government has added new departments. In 1977, concerns about oil shortages led to the creation of the Department of Energy. The Department of Veterans' Affairs was added in 1989. Today the cabinet (shown below) includes the heads of 14 departments.

Washington's Cabinet

The Constitution also gave Congress the task of creating departments to help the president lead the nation. The president had the power to appoint the heads of these departments, who were to assist the president with the many issues and problems he had to face. These heads of departments became his **cabinet**.

The Congress created three departments. In his first major task as president, Washington chose talented people to run them. For secretary of war, he picked Henry Knox, a trusted general during the Revolution. It was Knox's job to oversee the nation's defenses. For secretary of state, Washington chose Thomas Jefferson. He had been serving as U.S. minister to France. The State Department oversaw relations between the United States and other countries. Washington turned to the brilliant Alexander Hamilton to be the secretary of the treasury. Hamilton had to manage the government's money. The secretary's ties to the president began during the war when he had served as one of Washington's aides. To advise the

government on legal matters, Washington picked Edmund Randolph as attorney general.

These department heads and the attorney general made up Washington's cabinet. The Constitution made no mention of a cabinet. However, Washington began the practice of calling his department heads together to advise him.

Economic Problems

As secretary of the treasury, Alexander Hamilton faced the task of straightening out the nation's finances. First of all, the new government needed to pay its war debts. During the Revolution, the United States had borrowed millions of dollars from France, the Netherlands, and Spain. Within the United States, merchants and other private citizens had loaned money to the government. State governments also had wartime debts to pay back. By 1789, the national debt totaled more than $52 million.

Most government leaders agreed that the nation must repay its debts to win the respect of both foreign nations and its own citizens. Hamilton saw that the new nation must assure other countries that it was responsible about money. These nations would do business with the United States if they saw that the country would pay its debts. If the nation failed to do so, no country would lend it money in the future.

Hamilton came up with a financial plan that reflected his belief in a strong central government. He thought the power of the national government should be stronger than that of the state governments. Hamilton also believed that government should encourage business and industry. He sought the support

ᵍHistory
ng
ces Why
nerchants
nufacturers
a strong
govern-

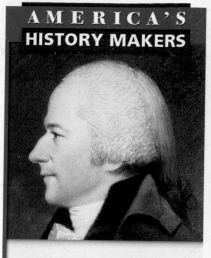

ALEXANDER HAMILTON
1755?–1804

Alexander Hamilton was born into poverty in the British West Indies. When he was ten years old, the young Alexander went to work as a clerk. He so impressed his employers that they helped to send him to school at King's College (now Columbia University) in New York.

During the Revolutionary War, he became an aide to General Washington. Hamilton moved up quickly in the army and later in political life. Although of humble origins, Hamilton had little faith in the common people and put his trust in the wealthy and educated to govern.

Why is it odd that Hamilton distrusted the common people to govern?

of the nation's wealthy merchants and manufacturers. He thought that the nation's prosperity depended on them. The government owed money to many of these rich men. By paying them back, Hamilton hoped to win their support for the new government.

Hamilton's Financial Plan

In 1790, Hamilton presented his plan to Congress. He proposed three steps to improve the nation's finances.

1. paying off all war debts
2. raising government revenues
3. creating a national bank

Hamilton wanted the federal government to pay off the war debts of the states. However, sectional differences arose over repayment of state debts. Virginia, Georgia, and many other Southern states had already repaid their debts and did not like being asked to help Northern states pay theirs.

Hamilton asked Thomas Jefferson of Virginia to help him gain Southern support. They reached a compromise. In exchange for Southern support of the plan, Northerners agreed to place the new nation's capital in the South. The location chosen was on the Potomac River between Virginia and Maryland.

The secretary of the treasury favored tariffs. A **tariff** is a tax on imported goods. It serves two purposes: raising money for the government and encouraging the growth of American industry. The government placed the highest tariffs on foreign goods—such as shoes and textiles—that Americans bought in great quantities. This ensured a steady flow of income to the government. In addition, since tariffs made foreign goods more expensive, they encouraged people to buy American goods.

Hamilton also called for the creation of a national bank. Such a bank would meet many needs. It would give the government a safe place to keep

Economics *in* History

How Banks Work

Why did Hamilton want to create a national bank? He believed that such a bank could help the economy of the new nation. It would create a partnership between the federal government and American business.

Let's say you deposited money into a bank account. Then you went back another day to withdraw some of the money. What happened in the meantime? Did the money just sit in the bank until you wanted it back? No—the bank used your money, and in doing so, helped fuel economic growth. In this way, money flows in a circular path from people like you into the general economy and back to you again. In the process, money can create goods and services, jobs, and profits, as the diagram explains.

CONNECT TO HISTORY
1. **Analyzing Points of Vie**
   Do you think that the pec
   who feared a strong centr
   government supported
   Hamilton's idea of a natio
   bank? Why or why not?

   See Skillbuilder Handboo
   page R9.

CONNECT TO TODAY
2. **Making Inferences** Hov
   banks make money?

For more about banking . . .

RESEARCH LINKS
CLASSZONE.COM

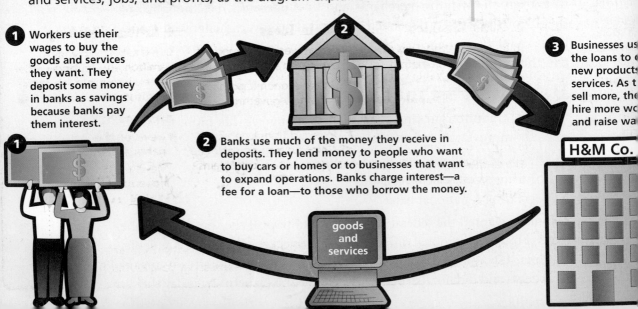

1. Workers use their wages to buy the goods and services they want. They deposit some money in banks as savings because banks pay them interest.

2. Banks use much of the money they receive in deposits. They lend money to people who want to buy cars or homes or to businesses that want to expand operations. Banks charge interest—a fee for a loan—to those who borrow the money.

3. Businesses us the loans to new products services. As t sell more, the hire more wc and raise wa

H&M Co.

goods and services

money. It would also make loans to businesses and government. Most important, it would issue bank notes—paper money that could be used as currency. Overall, Hamilton's plan would strengthen the central government. However, this worried Jefferson and Madison.

bulary

ncy: money

Interpreting the Constitution

Jefferson and Madison believed that the Constitution discouraged the concentration of power in the federal government. The Constitution's writers had tried to make the document general enough so that it would be flexible. As a result, disagreements sometimes arose over the document's meaning.

Two of the first
U.S. coins, 1792

The debate over Hamilton's plan for a national bank exposed differences about how to interpret the Constitution. Madison and Jefferson argued that the Constitution did not give the government the power to set up a bank. They believed in the strict construction—narrow or strict interpretation—of the Constitution. They stated that the government has only those powers that the Constitution clearly says it has. Therefore, since the Constitution does not mention a national bank, the government cannot create one.

Hamilton disagreed. He favored a loose construction—broad or flexible interpretation—of the Constitution. Pointing to the elastic clause in the document, he argued that the bank was "necessary and proper" to carry out the government's duties. (See The Living Constitution, page 254.) According to this view, when the Constitution grants a power to Congress, it also grants Congress the "necessary and proper" means to carry out that power. Jefferson and Hamilton argued their positions to Washington. Hamilton won, and the Bank of the United States was set up in 1791. The president, meanwhile, was dealing with other challenges at home and abroad, which you will read about in Section 2.

*ing*History

trasting
s the
lifference
en strict
ose
etations of
nstitution?

---

erms & Names

lain the
gnificance of:

augurate

deral Judiciary Act

binet

riff

2. Using Graphics

In a chart, list members of Washington's cabinet and their responsibilities.

Cabinet member	Responsibilities

Which cabinet member had the greatest responsibilities? Explain.

3. Main Ideas

a. What was the purpose of Washington's cabinet?

b. What economic problems did the new government face?

c. How did Hamilton's financial plan attempt to solve the nation's economic problems?

4. Critical Thinking

Contrasting How did Hamilton and Jefferson differ in their interpretation of the Constitution?

THINK ABOUT

• views on the national bank

• views on the role of government

VITY OPTIONS

GUAGE ARTS

ART

Imagine you oppose or support Hamilton's plan for the nation's finances. Write a **letter to the editor** or draw a **political cartoon** expressing your opinion.

2

Challenges to the New Government

MAIN IDEA	WHY IT MATTERS NOW	TERMS & NAMES
Washington established central authority at home and avoided war with European powers.	Washington's policies at home and abroad set an example for later presidents.	Battle of Fallen Timbers Treaty of Greenville Whiskey Rebellion French R neutral Jay's Tre Pinckney

ONE AMERICAN'S STORY

In the West, American settlers met fierce resistance from Native Americans. Chief Little Turtle of the Miami tribe of Ohio had won decisive victories against U.S. troops.

In 1793, the Miami again faced attack by American forces. Little Turtle warned his people about the troops led by General Anthony Wayne.

> **A VOICE FROM THE PAST**
>
> We have beaten the enemy twice under different commanders. . . . The Americans are now led by a chief [Wayne] who never sleeps. . . . We have not been able to surprise him. Think well of it. . . . It would be prudent [wise] to listen to his offers of peace.
>
> **Little Turtle,** quoted in *The Life and Times of Little Turtle*

General An
Wayne neg
with a Mia
chief.

While the council members weighed Little Turtle's warning, President Washington was making plans to secure—guard or protect—the western borders of the new nation.

Securing the Northwest Territory

As a general, Washington had skillfully waged war. As the nation's president, however, he saw that the country needed peace in order to prosper. But in spite of his desire for peace, he considered military action as trouble brewed in the Trans-Appalachian West, the land between the Appalachian Mountains and the Mississippi River. The 1783 Treaty of Paris had attempted to resolve the claims. The source of the trouble was competing claims for these lands. Some years later, however, Spain, Britain, the United States, and Native Americans claimed parts of the area as their own.

Spain held much of North America west of the Mississippi. It also claimed Florida and the port of New Orleans at the mouth of the

Taking Notes

Use your chart to take notes about challenges to the new government.

- Economics
- Politics
- Foreign Affairs
- Relations with Native Americans

Mississippi. For American settlers in the West, this port was key to trade. They carried their goods to market by flatboat down the Mississippi to New Orleans. They took Spanish threats to close the port very seriously. The Spanish also stirred up trouble between the white settlers and the Creeks, Choctaws, and other Native American groups in the Southeast.

The strongest resistance to white settlement came from Native Americans in the Northwest Territory. This territory was bordered by the Ohio River to the south and Canada to the north. Native Americans in that territory hoped to join together to form an independent Native American nation. In violation of the Treaty of Paris, the British still held forts north of the Ohio River. The British supported Native Americans in order to maintain their access to fur in these territories. Eventually, Native Americans and white settlers clashed over the Northwest Territory.

Battle of Fallen Timbers

Believing the Northwest Territory was critical to the security and growth of the new nation, Washington sent troops to the Ohio Valley. As you read in One American's Story, this first federal army took a beating from warriors led by Little Turtle in 1790. The chief's force came from many tribes, including the Shawnee, Ottawa, and Chippewa, who joined in a confederation to defeat the federal army.

After a second defeat in 1791 of an army headed by General Arthur St. Clair, Washington ordered another army west. This time Anthony Wayne, known as "Mad Anthony" for his reckless courage, was at its head.

The other chiefs ignored Little Turtle's advice to negotiate. They replaced him with a less able leader. Expecting British help, Native American warriors gathered at British-held Fort Miami. On August 20, 1794, a fighting force of around 2,000 Native Americans clashed with Wayne's troops. The site was covered with trees that had been struck down by a storm. The Native Americans were defeated in what became known as the **Battle of Fallen Timbers**.

...ding**History**

...king
...nces What
...tations
...t the Native
...icans have
...f the British
...e tribes
...into
...ct with
...settlers?

The Battle of Fallen Timbers memorial sculpture below shows two American soldiers and a Native American.

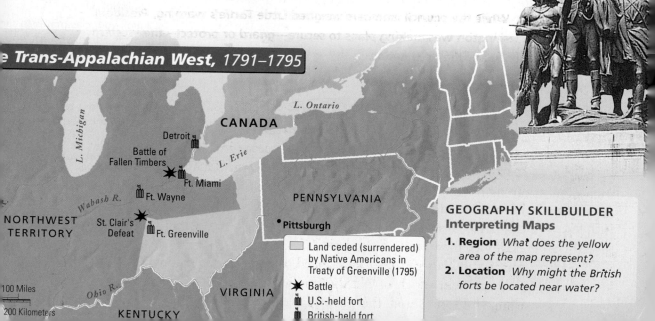

e Trans-Appalachian West, *1791–1795*

L. Michigan

L. Ontario

CANADA

L. Erie

Detroit

Battle of Fallen Timbers

Ft. Miami

Wabash R.

Ft. Wayne

PENNSYLVANIA

NORTHWEST TERRITORY

St. Clair's Defeat

Ft. Greenville

• Pittsburgh

100 Miles
200 Kilometers

Ohio R.

VIRGINIA

KENTUCKY

Land ceded (surrendered) by Native Americans in Treaty of Greenville (1795)

★ Battle

U.S.-held fort

British-held fort

GEOGRAPHY SKILLBUILDER
Interpreting Maps
1. **Region** *What does the yellow area of the map represent?*
2. **Location** *Why might the British forts be located near water?*

The Native Americans retreated to Fort Miami. The British, not wanting war with the United States, refused to help them. The Battle of Fallen Timbers crushed Native American hopes of keeping their land in the Northwest Territory. Twelve tribes signed the **Treaty of Greenville** in 1795. They agreed to cede, or surrender, much of present-day Ohio and Indiana to the U.S. government.

The Whiskey Rebellion

Not long after the Battle of Fallen Timbers, Washington put another army into the field. The conflict arose over the government's tax on whiskey, part of Hamilton's financial plan. From Pennsylvania to Georgia, outraged farmers resisted the tax. For them, whiskey—and the grain it was made from—were important products.

Because of poor roads, backcountry farmers had trouble getting their grain to market. Crops such as wheat and rye were more easily carried to market in liquid form, so farmers made their grain into whiskey. A farmer's horse could haul only two bushels of rye but could carry two barrels of rye whiskey. This was an amount equal to 24 bushels of the grain. In addition, their customers paid more for whiskey than grain. With little cash to buy goods, let alone pay the tax, farmers often traded whiskey for salt, sugar, and other goods. The farmers used whiskey as money to get whatever supplies they needed.

Reading His

B. Reading a
Use the map
page 299 to
which two st
to the south
bordered the
land ceded b
Native Ameri

CITIZENSHIP TODAY

Obeying Rules and Laws

As the Whiskey Rebellion shows, since the earliest days of the republic our government has made laws and punished those who broke them. These laws affect not only adult citizens, but young people as well.

Today, for example, communities across the country are trying to control the problem of juvenile crime by imposing curfews on young people. These laws require minors to be off the streets after a certain time, often ten or eleven at night. Penalties can be harsh. In certain communities, minors who break curfew laws can be detained, and their parents can be fined.

People who favor curfews believe such laws cut crime. Those who oppose curfews think such limits are the responsibility of parents and not the government.

Why Should You Obe
Rules and Laws?

1. What are some argument
   favor of curfew laws? Wh
   arguments against them?
   a list of each.

2. Poll your classmates to se
   many agree with each pos

3. Write an essay expressing
   opinion on this issue.

4. Brainstorm changes or
   adaptations to curfew law
   you think would make the
   more flexible.

See Citizenship
Handbook, page 283.

For more about young people an
the law . . .

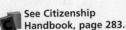

RESEARCH LINKS
CLASSZONE.COM

In the summer of 1794, a group of farmers in western Pennsylvania staged the **Whiskey Rebellion** against the tax. One armed group beat up a tax collector, coated him with tar and feathers, and stole his horse. Others threatened an armed attack on Pittsburgh.

Washington, urged on by Hamilton, was prepared to enforce the tax and crush the Whiskey Rebellion. They feared that not to act might undermine the new government and weaken its authority. Hamilton condemned the rebels for resisting the law.

> ## *"Such a resistance is treason."*
> Alexander Hamilton

A VOICE FROM THE PAST

Such a resistance is treason against society, against liberty, against everything that ought to be dear to a free, enlightened, and prudent people. To tolerate it were to abandon your most precious interests. Not to subdue it were to tolerate it.

Alexander Hamilton, *The Works of Alexander Hamilton*

In October 1794, General Henry Lee, with Hamilton at his side, led an army of 13,000 soldiers into western Pennsylvania to put down the uprising. As news of the army's approach spread, the rebels fled. After much effort, federal troops rounded up 20 barefoot, ragged prisoners. Washington had proved his point. He had shown that the government had the power and the will to enforce its laws. Meanwhile, events in Europe gave Washington a different kind of challenge.

The French Revolution

In 1789, a financial crisis led the French people to rebel against their government. Inspired by the American Revolution, the French revolutionaries demanded liberty and equality. At first, Americans supported the **French Revolution**. By 1792, however, the revolution had become very violent. Thousands of French citizens were massacred. Then, in 1793, Louis XVI, the king of France, was executed.

Other European monarchs believed the revolution threatened their own thrones. France soon declared war on Britain, Holland, and Spain. Britain led the fight against France.

The war between France and Britain put the United States in an awkward position. France had been America's ally in the Revolution against the British.

Connections TO WORLD HISTORY

EYEWITNESS TO REVOLUTION

In 1789, an American citizen with a strange first name, Gouverneur Morris, went to Paris as a private business agent. Three years later, President Washington appointed him U.S. minister to France. An eyewitness to the French Revolution, Morris kept a detailed record of what he saw, including the execution of the king and queen by guillotine, as shown below.

Here is part of a letter he wrote on October 18, 1793:

"Terror is the order of the Day. . . . The Queen was executed the Day before yesterday. Insulted during her Trial and reviled in her last Moments, she behav'd with Dignity throughout."

A 1778 treaty still bound the two nations together. In addition, many saw France's revolution as proof that the American cause had been just. Jefferson felt that a move to crush the French Revolution was an attack on liberty everywhere. Hamilton, though, pointed out that Britain was the United States' most important trading partner, and British trade was too important to risk war.

In April 1793, Washington declared that the United States would remain **neutral,** not siding with one country or the other. He stated that the nation would be "friendly and impartial" to both sides. Congress then passed a law forbidding the United States to help either side.

Remaining Neutral

Britain made it hard for the United States to remain neutral. Late in 1792, the British began seizing the cargoes of American ships carrying goods from the French West Indies.

Washington sent Chief Justice John Jay to England for talks about the seizure of U.S. ships. Jay also hoped to persuade the British to give up their forts on the Northwest frontier. During the talks in 1794, news came of the U.S. victory at the Battle of Fallen Timbers. Fearing another entanglement, the British agreed to leave the Ohio Valley by 1796. In **Jay's Treaty,** the British also agreed to pay damages for U.S. vessels they had seized. Jay failed, however, to open up the profitable British West Indies trade to Americans. Because of this, Jay's Treaty was unpopular.

Like Jay, Thomas Pinckney helped the United States reduce tensions along the frontier. In 1795, **Pinckney's Treaty** with Spain gave Americans the right to travel freely on the Mississippi River. It also gave them the right to store goods at the port of New Orleans without paying customs duties. In addition, Spain accepted the 31st parallel as the northern boundary of Florida and the southern boundary of the United States.

Meanwhile, more American settlers moved west. As you will read in the next section, change was coming back east as Washington stepped down.

Reading **Hi**
C. Drawing
Conclusions
What sort o
obligation t
France did t
wartime alli
and treaty c
1778 create

Reading **H**
D. Evaluati
What were
of the adva
to the new
of remainir
neutral?

Section 2 Assessment

1. Terms & Names

Explain the significance of:
- Battle of Fallen Timbers
- Treaty of Greenville
- Whiskey Rebellion
- French Revolution
- neutral
- Jay's Treaty
- Pinckney's Treaty

2. Using Graphics

Use a chart to record U.S. responses to various challenges.

Challenge	Response
From Spain	
From Britain	
From France	

Which challenge seemed greatest? Why?

3. Main Ideas

a. What military and other actions secured the West for the United States?

b. Why did Washington consider it important to put down the Whiskey Rebellion?

c. How did the French Revolution create problems for the United States?

4. Critical Thinking

Drawing Conclusions
Why was neutrality a dif policy for the United Sta to maintain?

THINK ABOUT
- ties with France
- ties with Britain
- restrictions on trade

ACTIVITY OPTIONS

GEOGRAPHY

ART

Make a **map** that describes the Battle of Fallen Timbers, or draw a **scene** from that battle.

3

The Federalists in Charge

MAIN IDEA	WHY IT MATTERS NOW	TERMS & NAMES
...t between Hamilton and ...n led to the growth of ...l parties.	The two-party system is still a major feature of politics in the United States.	foreign policy Alien and Sedition Acts political party states' rights XYZ Affair

ONE AMERICAN'S STORY

In 1796, President George Washington decided that two terms in office was enough. But as he left office, he feared the growth of political parties would split the nation into enemy camps. In 1796, he wrote a final address to the nation.

This painting portrays Mount Vernon in 1792.

A VOICE FROM THE PAST

Let me now . . . warn you . . . against the [harmful] effects of the spirit of party. . . . This spirit, unfortunately . . . exists in different shapes in all governments . . . but in those of the popular form, it is seen in its greatest rankness and is truly their worst enemy.

George Washington, Farewell Address

In his address, Washington warned of the dangers of political division, or what he termed "the spirit of party." As you will see in this section, few people took his advice.

Washington Retires

Washington had come to the presidency greatly admired by the American people. Throughout his eight years in office (1789–1797), he had tried to serve as a symbol of national unity. In large part, he succeeded. During his second term, however, opponents of Jay's Treaty led attacks on the president. Thomas Paine called Washington "treacherous in private friendship . . . and a hypocrite in public life" because he failed to support the French Revolution.

Washington saw such attacks as the outcome of political disagreements. In his farewell address, he warned that such differences could weaken the nation. Despite his advice, political parties became a part of American politics.

Taking Notes

Use your chart to take notes about the Federalists and the establishment of a two-party system.

- Economics
- Politics
- Foreign Affairs
- Relations with Native Americans

Americans listened more closely to Washington's parting advice on **foreign policy**—relations with the governments of other countries. He urged the nation's leaders to remain neutral and "steer clear of permanent alliances with any portion of the foreign world." He warned that agreements with foreign nations might work against U.S. interests. His advice served to guide U.S. foreign policy into the twentieth century.

Growth of Political Parties

Despite Washington's warning against political parties, Americans were deeply divided over how the nation should be run. During Washington's first term (1789–1792), Hamilton and Jefferson had hotly debated the direction the new nation should take. Then Jefferson returned to Virginia in 1793. During Washington's second term, Madison took Jefferson's place in the debates with Hamilton.

Both sides disagreed on how to interpret the Constitution and on economic policy. Hamilton favored the British government and opposed the French Revolution. Jefferson and Madison were the opposite. Hamilton fought for a strong central government. Jefferson and Madison feared such a government might lead to tyranny. They had different visions of what the nation should become. Hamilton wanted a United States in which trade, manufacturing, and cities grew. Jefferson and Madison pictured a rural nation of planters and farmers.

These differences on foreign and domestic policy led to the nation's first political parties. A **political party** is a group of people that tries to promote its ideas and influence government. It also backs candidates for office. Together, Jefferson and Madison founded the Democratic-Republican Party. The party name reflected their strong belief in democracy and the republican system. Their ideas drew farmers and workers to the new party. Hamilton and his friends formed the Federalist Party. Many Northern merchants and manufacturers became Federalists.

Reading **H**
A. Summari
What were
major belie
each party?

The First Political Parties	
FEDERALISTS	**DEMOCRATIC-REPUBLICANS**
Strong national government	Limited national government
Fear of mob rule	Fear of rule by one person or a powerful few
Loose construction (interpretation) of the Constitution	Strict construction (interpretation) of the Constitution
Favored national bank	Opposed national bank
Economy based on manufacturing and shipping	Economy based on farming
Supporters: lawyers, merchants, manufacturers, clergy	Supporters: farmers, tradespeople

SKILLBUILDER Interpreting Charts
1. *Which economic interests were served by the Federalists?*
2. *Which party favored a ruling elite? Which put more trust in the common people?*

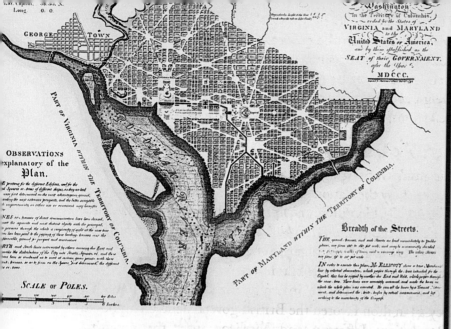

WASHINGTON, D.C., AND BENJAMIN BANNEKER

Benjamin Banneker was a free African-American farmer. He was a self-taught mathematician and astronomer. He also wrote an almanac (see below). He was named to the survey commission appointed to lay out the boundaries of the nation's new capital. Working with chief planner Pierre L'Enfant, Banneker helped to decide where the White House and Capitol would be located. Their final design is shown at the left.

John Adams Takes Office

In 1796, the United States held its first elections in which political parties competed. The Federalists picked Washington's vice-president, John Adams, as their candidate for president. An experienced public servant, Adams had been a leader during the Revolution and at the Continental Congress. He had also been a diplomat in France, the Netherlands, and Britain before serving with Washington. The Democratic-Republicans chose Jefferson.

In the electoral college, Adams received 71 votes and Jefferson 68. The Constitution stated that the runner-up should become vice-president. Therefore, the country had a Federalist president and a Democratic-Republican vice-president. Adams became president in 1797. His chief rival, Jefferson, entered office as his vice-president. In 1800, Adams became the first president to govern from the nation's new capital city, Washington, D.C.

Problems with France

When Washington left office in 1797, relations between France and the United States were tense. With Britain and France still at war, the French began seizing U.S. ships to prevent them from trading with the British. Within the year, the French had looted more than 300 U.S. ships.

Although some Federalists called for war with France, Adams hoped talks would restore calm. To this end, he sent Charles Pinckney, Elbridge Gerry, and John Marshall to Paris. Arriving there, they requested a meeting with the French minister of foreign affairs. For weeks, they were

American newspapers fueled public anger over the XYZ Affair by publishing editorials and cartoons like this one. Here the five-man group ruling France demands money at dagger point from the three Americans. The American diplomats respond, "Cease bawling, monster! We will not give you sixpence!"

What attitude does the cartoonist have toward France's role in this affair? How can you tell?

ignored. Then three French agents—later referred to as X, Y, and Z—took the Americans aside to tell them the minister would hold talks. However, the talks would occur only if the Americans agreed to loan France $10 million and to pay the minister a bribe of $250,000. The Americans refused. "No, no, not a sixpence," Pinckney shot back.

Adams received a full report of what became known as the <u>XYZ Affair</u>. After Congress and an outraged public learned of it, the press turned Pinckney's words into a popular slogan: "Millions for defense, not one cent for tribute!" In 1798, Congress canceled its treaties with France and allowed U.S. ships to seize French vessels. Congress also set aside money to expand the navy and the army.

Reading **H**
B. Drawing Conclusion did the XYZ Affair show young nati growing confidence

The Alien and Sedition Acts

The conflict with France made Adams and the Federalists popular with the public. Many Democratic-Republicans, however, were sympathetic to France. One Democratic-Republican newspaper called Adams "the blasted tyrant of America." In turn, Federalists labeled Democratic-Republicans "democrats, mobcrats, and other kinds of rats."

Angered by criticism in a time of crisis, Adams blamed the Democratic-Republican newspapers and new immigrants. Many of the immigrants were Democratic-Republicans. To silence their critics, the Federalist Congress passed the **Alien and Sedition Acts** in 1798. These acts targeted aliens—immigrants who were not yet citizens. One act increased the waiting period for becoming a U.S. citizen from 5 to 14 years. Other acts gave the president the power to arrest disloyal aliens or order them out of the country during wartime. A fourth act outlawed sedition, saying or writing anything false or harmful about the government.

With these acts, the Federalists clamped down on freedom of speech and the press. About 25 Democratic-Republican newspaper editors were

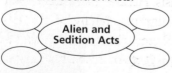

ding **History**

aking
ences How
t the theory
ates' rights
rmine the
ral
rnment?

charged under this act, and 10 were convicted of expressing opinions damaging to the government. A Vermont congressman, Matthew Lyon, was also locked up for saying that the president should be sent "to a mad house." The voters re-elected Lyon while he was in jail.

The Democratic-Republicans, led by Jefferson and Madison, searched for a way to fight the Alien and Sedition Acts. They found it in a theory called **states' rights**. According to this theory, states had rights that the federal government could not violate. Jefferson and Madison wrote resolutions (or statements) passed by the Kentucky and Virginia legislatures in 1798 and 1799. In the Kentucky Resolutions, Jefferson proposed nullification, the idea that a state could nullify a federal law within the state. In the Virginia Resolutions, Madison said a state could interpose, or place, itself between the federal government and its citizens. These resolutions declared that the Alien and Sedition Acts violated the Constitution. No other states supported Kentucky and Virginia. However, within two years the Democratic-Republicans won control of Congress, and they either repealed the Alien and Sedition Acts or let them expire between 1800 and 1802.

Peace with France

While Federalists and Democratic-Republicans battled at home, the United States made peace with France. Although war fever was high, Adams reopened talks with France. This time the two sides quickly signed the Convention of 1800, an agreement to stop all naval attacks. This treaty cleared the way for U.S. and French ships to sail the ocean in peace.

Adams's actions made him enemies among the Federalists. Despite this, he spoke proudly of having saved the nation from bloodshed. "I desire no other inscription over my gravestone than: 'Here lies John Adams, who took upon himself the responsibility of the peace with France in the year 1800.'" Adams lost the presidential election of 1800 to Thomas Jefferson. You will read more about Jefferson in the next chapter.

:tion **3** Assessment

Terms & Names

plain the
ignificance of:
oreign policy
political party
KYZ Affair
Alien and
edition Acts
tates' rights

2. Using Graphics

Use a cluster diagram to review details about the Alien and Sedition Acts.

Alien and Sedition Acts

What was the worst effect of the Alien and Sedition Acts? Why?

3. Main Ideas

a. What two pieces of advice did Washington give in his Farewell Address?

b. What led to the rise of political parties?

c. Why did Congress pass the Alien and Sedition Acts? How did Kentucky and Virginia respond?

4. Critical Thinking

Evaluating Do you think Washington's warning about political parties was good advice? Explain.

THINK ABOUT
• roles of political parties
• advantages of parties
• disadvantages of parties

TIVITY OPTIONS

ECHNOLOGY

SPEECH

Read more about Benjamin Banneker. Plan part of a **video presentation** on him or present **dramatic readings** of excerpts from the almanac he wrote.

TERMS & NAMES

Briefly explain the significance of each of the following.

1. inaugurate
2. cabinet
3. tariff
4. Battle of Fallen Timbers
5. Whiskey Rebellion
6. neutral
7. foreign policy
8. political party
9. Alien and Sedition Acts
10. states' rights

REVIEW QUESTIONS

Washington's Presidency (pages 293–297)

1. What questions about the judiciary were left open by the Constitution? How were they answered?
2. What financial problems did the new nation face?
3. How did Hamilton and Jefferson interpret the Constitution differently?

Challenges to the New Government (pages 298–302)

4. What did Washington do to secure the West?
5. What were the major arguments regarding taxation under the new government?
6. Why did Washington favor neutrality in the conflict between France and Britain?
7. What problems did the Jay and Pinckney treaties address?

The Federalists in Charge (pages 303–307)

8. Why did Washington oppose political parties?
9. What was the XYZ Affair?
10. Why did Federalists pass the Alien and Sedition Acts? How did Republicans respond?

CRITICAL THINKING

1. USING YOUR NOTES: IDENTIFYING AND SOLVING PROBLEMS

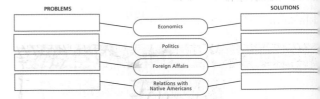

PROBLEMS | SOLUTIONS
- Economics
- Politics
- Foreign Affairs
- Relations with Native Americans

Using your completed chart, answer the questions.

a. What were the problems that characterized the Federalist era?

b. What do the solutions to these problems reveal about the characteristics of the era?

2. ANALYZING LEADERSHIP

How did Washington's efforts to serve as a symbol national unity help the new nation?

3. APPLYING CITIZENSHIP SKILLS

How might the farmers in the Whiskey Rebellion ha expressed their disapproval of the whiskey tax whil staying within the law?

4. THEME: DEMOCRATIC IDEALS

Did the formation of political parties make the nat more or less democratic?

Interact with History

How did the challenges of setting up a governmer that you discussed before you read the chapter co pare with the actual challenges you read about?

VISUAL SUMMARY

The First Presidents

WASHINGTON PRESIDENCY 1789–1797

Strong Government
- Cabinet
- Judiciary

Remaining Neutral
- Jay's Treaty
- Pinckney's Treaty

Secure the West
- Battle of Fallen Timbers
- Treaty of Greenville

ADAMS PRESIDENCY 1797–1801

Federalists vs. Democratic-Republicans
- Differed over Constitution
- Disagreed on national bank

Problems with Fr
- XYZ Affair
- Convention of 1

se the chart and your knowledge of U.S. history to
nswer questions 1 and 2.

dditional Test Practice, pp. S1–S33.

Financial Problems, *1789–1791*

DEBTS	EXPENSES	INCOME
$77,230,000 = total public debt	$4,270,000 budget to run government	$4,400,000 from duties or taxes imposed on imported and exported goods

Source: *Historical Statistics of the United States*

How much money did the government owe during
the period shown on the chart?

A. $4,270,000

B. $4,400,000

C. $77,000,000

D. $77,230,000

2. What could the government do to increase
income?

   A. decrease duties and taxes

   B. increase duties and taxes

   C. increase the national budget

   D. pay off the public debt

This quotation from George Washington's Farewell
Address is a warning to future leaders. Use this
quotation and your knowledge of U.S. history to
answer question 3.

PRIMARY SOURCE

Let me now . . . warn you . . . against the [harmful]
effects of the spirit of party. . . . This spirit,
unfortunately . . . exists in different shapes in all
governments . . . but in those of the popular form,
it is seen in its greatest rankness and is truly their
worst enemy.

George Washington, Farewell Address

3. What danger was Washington warning Americans
about in his Farewell Address?

   A. foreign governments

   B. Antifederalists

   C. political parties

   D. taxation

TEST PRACTICE
CLASSZONE.COM

ERNATIVE ASSESSMENT

✍ WRITING ABOUT HISTORY

ine that you are a U.S. citizen during the French
ution. Write a **letter** to the secretary of state giv-
easons why you think the United States should
he French, aid the British, or remain neutral.

e library resources to research the different sides.

e your research to persuade the secretary of state
your point of view.

OPERATIVE LEARNING

with other students to research the Alien and
on Acts and the positions taken by both political
es. Consider these questions: Were the acts consti-
al or an abuse of basic rights? Should criticism of
overnment be allowed in a time of possible war?
e two group members to debate the Federalist
emocratic-Republican positions.

INTEGRATED TECHNOLOGY

CREATING A CAMPAIGN COMMERCIAL

Create a 30-second television commercial for either
John Adams, the Federalist party candidate, or Thomas
Jefferson, the Democratic-Republican party candidate.

- On the Internet, find information about your candidate that shows why he is a good choice.

- Locate at least two pictures that reveal different
  images of the candidate. Also, use the Internet to
  find suitable background music for the commercial.

- Use your resource materials to create a 30-second
  campaign commercial.

For more about the 1796 election . . .

INTERNET ACTIVITY
CLASSZONE.COM

CHAPTER 10

The Jefferson Era 1800–1816

ection 1
efferson akes Office

ection 2
he ouisiana urchase nd xploration

ection 3
roblems vith oreign owers

ection 4
he War f 1812

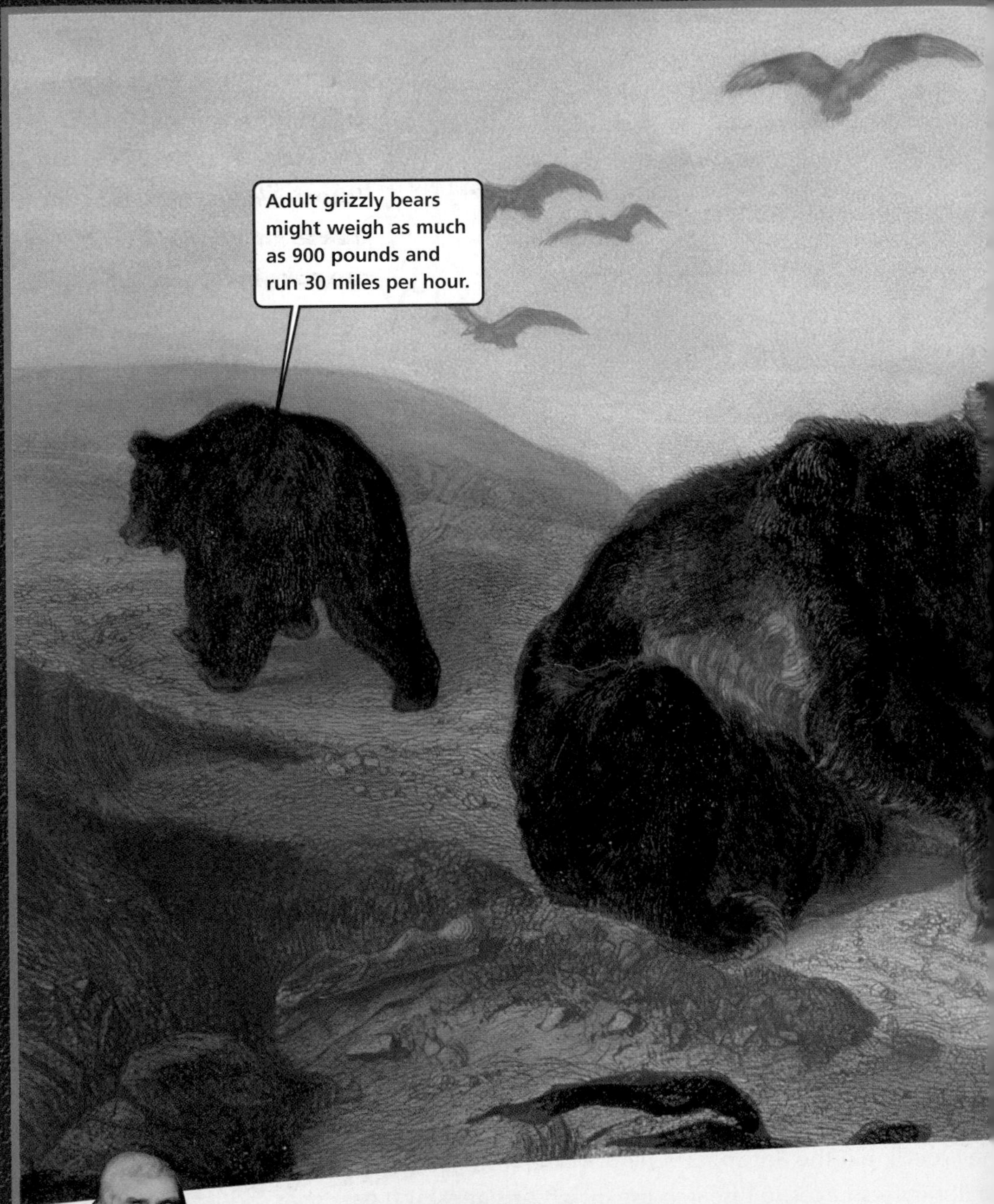
Adult grizzly bears might weigh as much as 900 pounds and run 30 miles per hour.

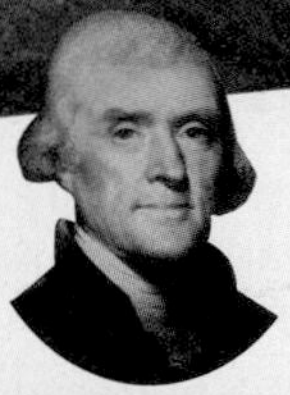

USA

1801
Thomas Jefferson is elected president.

1803
Louisiana Purchase is made.

1804
Jefferson is reelected.
Lewis and Clark expedition begins.

Emb

1800

World

1801
Tripoli declares war on the United States.

1803
Europe's Napoleonic wars resume after brief peace.

1805
British win at Trafalgar.
French win at Austerlitz.

You have been chosen to participate in an expedition to the West in the early 1800s. You are excited and curious, but also a little scared. You know that you will see and experience many new things. But you know there are risks involved, too.

What dangers will you face on an expedition west?

In the early 1800s, it took about 20 seconds to load and fire a gun.

What Do You Think?

- Notice the land features in these scenes. What problems might they hold for an explorer?
- What other people might you meet on the expedition?

RESEARCH LINKS
CLASSZONE.COM

Visit the Chapter 10 links for more information about the Jefferson Era.

1811
Battle of Tippecanoe is fought.

1812
War of 1812 begins.

1814
British attack Washington, D.C.

1815
Battle of New Orleans is fought.

1816

1810
Father Hidalgo calls for Mexican independence.

1814
Napoleon is defeated and exiled to Elba.

1815
Napoleon returns and is defeated at Waterloo.

Reading Strategy: Summarizing

What Do You Know?

What parts of the United States today were not part of the country in 1800? What should leaders consider before they buy land for their countries?

Think About

- where the money for the purchase will come from
- what should be done if people already live on the land
- your responses to the Interact with History about facing dangers on an expedition west (see page 311)

United States in 1800

Unit
State
181

What Do You Want to Know?

What details do you need to help you understand the nation's expansion in the early 1800s? Make a list of information you need in your notebook before you read the chapter.

Summarizing

When you study history, it is important to clearly understand what you read. One way to achieve a clear understanding is to summarize. When you summarize, you restate what y have read into fewer words, stating only the main ideas and essential details. It is import to use your own words in a summary. Use the chart below to record your summaries of th main ideas and essential details in Chapter 10.

S See Skillbuilder Handbook, page R2.

Taking Notes

The Jefferson Era
Summaries
Main Idea: Thomas Jefferson is elected president. **Details:** Jefferson replaces Federalist policies with his own but has problems with the judiciary.
Main Idea: **Details:**
Main Idea: **Details:**
Main Idea: **Details:**

Jefferson Takes Office

MAIN IDEA	WHY IT MATTERS NOW	TERMS & NAMES
...efferson became president in ...s party replaced Federalist ...ns with its own.	Today's Democratic Party traces its roots to the party of Jefferson, the Democratic-Republicans.	radical Judiciary Act of 1801 John Marshall *Marbury* v. *Madison* unconstitutional judicial review

ONE AMERICAN'S STORY

In the election of 1800, backers of John Adams and Thomas Jefferson fought for their candidates with nasty personal attacks. For instance, James Callender warned voters not to reelect President John Adams.

A VOICE FROM THE PAST

In the fall of 1796 . . . the country fell into a more dangerous juncture than almost any the old confederation ever endured. The tardiness and timidity of Mr. Washington were succeeded by the rancour [bitterness] and insolence [arrogance] of Mr. Adams. . . . Think what you have been, what you are, and what, under [Adams], you are likely to become.

James Callender, quoted in *American Aurora*

In the presidential election of 1800, Thomas Jefferson was the candidate of the Democratic-Republican Party. John Adams represented the Federalists.

Adams's defenders were just as vicious. Yet, in spite of the campaign's nastiness, the election ended with a peaceful transfer of power from one party to another. The 1800 election was a contest between two parties with different ideas about the role of government.

The Election of 1800

The two parties contesting the election of 1800 were the Federalists, led by President John Adams, and the Democratic-Republicans, represented by Thomas Jefferson. Each party believed that the other was endangering the Constitution and the American republic.

The Democratic-Republicans thought they were saving the nation from monarchy and oppression. They argued, again and again, that the Alien and Sedition Acts supported by the Federalists violated the Bill of Rights. (See pages 306–307.) The Federalists thought that the nation was about to be ruined by **radicals**—people who take extreme political positions. They remembered the violence of the French Revolution, in which radicals executed thousands in the name of liberty.

✏️ **Taking Notes**

Use your chart to take notes about Jefferson's presidency.

The Jefferson Era
Summaries
Main Idea: . Details:
Main Idea: Details:
Main Idea: Details:
Main Idea: Details:

When election day came, the Democratic-Republicans won the presidency. Jefferson received 73 votes in the electoral college, and Adams earned 65. But there was a problem. Aaron Burr, whom the Democratic-Republicans wanted as vice president, also received 73 votes.

Background
In 1804, the
Twelfth
Amendment
solved this p
lem by creat
separate ball
for president
vice presiden

Breaking the Tie

According to the Constitution, the House of Representatives had to choose between Burr and Jefferson. The Democratic-Republicans clearly intended for Jefferson to be president. However, the new House of Representatives, dominated by Jefferson's party, would not take office for some months. Federalists still held a majority in the House, and their votes would decide the winner.

The Federalists were divided. Some feared Jefferson so much that they decided to back Burr. Others, such as Alexander Hamilton, considered Burr an unreliable man and urged the election of Jefferson. Hamilton did not like Jefferson, but he believed that Jefferson would do more for the good of the nation than Burr. "If there be a man in the world I ought to hate," he said, "it is Jefferson. . . . But the public good must be [more important than] every private consideration."

Over a period of seven days, the House voted 35 times without determining a winner. Finally, two weeks before the inauguration, Alexander Hamilton's friend James A. Bayard persuaded several Federalists not to vote for Burr. On the thirty-sixth ballot, Jefferson was elected president. Aaron Burr, who became vice president, would never forget Hamilton's insults.

People were overjoyed by Jefferson's election. A Philadelphia newspaper reported that bells rang, guns fired, dogs barked, cats meowed, and children cried over the news of Jefferson's victory.

Reading Hi
A. Analyzin
Points of Vi
Why did
Hamilton th
that Jefferso
was the bet
choice for
president?

STRANGE *but* True

HAMILTON-BURR DUEL

In 1804, the Democratic-Republicans replaced Aaron Burr as their candidate for vice president. Burr then decided to run for governor of New York.

Alexander Hamilton questioned Burr's fitness for public office. He wrote that Burr was a "dangerous man . . . who ought not to be trusted with the reins of government."

Burr lost the election. Furious, he challenged Hamilton to a duel. Hamilton went to the duel but resolved not to fire. Burr, however, shot Hamilton, who died the next day.

The Talented Jefferson

In over 200 years, the United States has had more than 40 presidents. Many of them were great leaders. But no president has ever matched Thomas Jefferson in the variety of his achievements.

Jefferson's talents went beyond politics. He was still a young lawyer when he became interested in the architecture of classical Greece and Rome. The look of our nation's capital today reflects that interest. When Washington, D.C., was being built during the 1790s, Jefferson advised its architects and designers.

Jefferson's passion for classical styles can also be seen in his plan of Monticello, his Virginia home. For this elegant mansion, Jefferson designed storm windows, a seven-day clock, and a dumbwaiter—a small elevator that brought bottles of wine from the cellar.

Jefferson was a skilled violinist, horseman, amateur scientist, and a devoted reader, too. His book collection later became the core of the Library of Congress. After his election, Jefferson applied his many talents and ideas to the government of the United States.

Jefferson's Philosophy

The new president had strong opinions about what kind of country the United States ought to be. But his first order of business was to calm the nation's political quarrels.

ing **History**
*n*marizing
*l*id Thomas
*s*on try to
*t*he nation
*n*e was
d?

One way Jefferson tried to unite Americans was by promoting a common way of life. He wanted the United States to remain a nation of small independent farmers. Such a nation, he believed, would uphold the strong morals and democratic values that he associated with country living. He hoped that the enormous amount of available land would prevent Americans from crowding into cities, as people had in Europe.

As president, Jefferson behaved more like a gentleman farmer than a privileged politician. Instead of riding in a fancy carriage to his inauguration, Jefferson walked the two blocks from his boarding house to the Capitol. Though his chef served elegant meals, the president's guests ate at round tables so that no one could sit at the head of the table.

To the end, Jefferson refused to elevate himself because of his office. For his tombstone, he chose this simple epitaph: "Here was buried

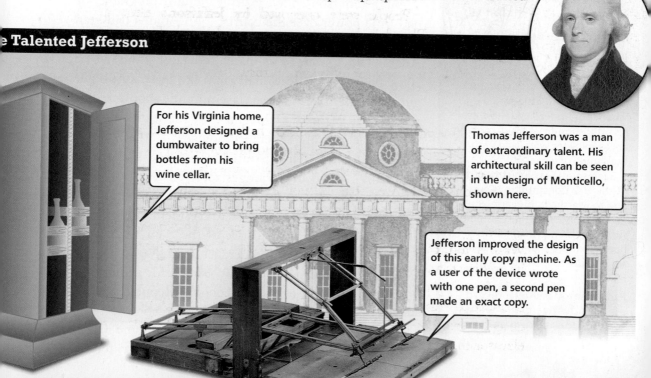

e **Talented Jefferson**

For his Virginia home, Jefferson designed a dumbwaiter to bring bottles from his wine cellar.

Thomas Jefferson was a man of extraordinary talent. His architectural skill can be seen in the design of Monticello, shown here.

Jefferson improved the design of this early copy machine. As a user of the device wrote with one pen, a second pen made an exact copy.

Thomas Jefferson, author of the Declaration of American Independence, of the statute of Virginia for religious freedom, and father of the University of Virginia." Jefferson chose not to list his presidency. His belief in a modest role for the central government is reflected in the changes he made during his presidency.

Undoing Federalist Programs

Jefferson believed that the federal government should have less power than it had had under the Federalists. During his term of office, he sought to end many Federalist programs.

At the president's urging, Congress—now controlled by Democratic-Republicans—allowed the Alien and Sedition Acts to end. Jefferson then released prisoners convicted under the acts—among them, James Callender. Congress also ended many taxes, including the unpopular whiskey tax. Because the loss of tax revenue lowered the government's income, Jefferson reduced the number of federal employees to cut costs. He also reduced the size of the military.

Jefferson next made changes to the Federalists' financial policies. Alexander Hamilton had created a system that depended on a certain amount of public debt. He believed that people who were owed money by their government would make sure the government was run properly. But Jefferson opposed public debt. He used revenues from tariffs and land sales to reduce the amount of money owed by the government.

Marshall and the Judiciary

Though Jefferson ended many Federalist programs, he had little power over the courts. John Adams had seen to that with the **Judiciary Act of 1801**. Under this act, Adams had appointed as many Federalist judges as he could between the election of 1800 and Jefferson's inauguration in 1801. These last-minute appointments meant that the new Democratic-Republican president would face a firmly Federalist judiciary.

Jefferson often felt frustrated by Federalist control of the courts. Yet because judges received their appointments for life, the president could do little.

Before he left office in 1801, President Adams also appointed a new Chief Justice of the Supreme Court. He chose a 45-year-old Federalist, **John Marshall**. He guessed that Marshall would be around for a long time to check the power of the Democratic-Republicans. He was right. Marshall served as Chief Justice for over three decades. Under Marshall, the Supreme Court upheld federal authority and strengthened federal

Backgroun
In addition t
founding th
University of
Virginia in 1
Jefferson
designed its
buildings an
supervised t
construction

Reading H
C. Analyzir
Causes Wh
the Federa
retain a gr
deal of po
even after
were defe
the Demo
Republican

courts. One of the most important decisions of the Marshall Court was **_Marbury v. Madison_** (1803).

Marbury v. Madison

William Marbury was one of Adams's last-minute appointments. Adams had named him as a justice of the peace for the District of Columbia.

Marbury was supposed to be installed in his position by Secretary of State James Madison. When Madison refused to give him the job, Marbury sued. The case went to the Supreme Court, which ruled that the law under which Marbury sued was **unconstitutional**— that is, it contradicted the law of the Constitution.

Although the Court denied Marbury's claim, it did establish the principle of **judicial review**. This principle states that the Supreme Court has the final say in interpreting the Constitution. In his decision, Marshall declared, "It is emphatically the province and duty of the Judicial Department to say what the law is." If the Supreme Court decides that a law violates the Constitution, then that law cannot be put into effect.

Jefferson and Madison were angry when Marshall seized this new power for the Supreme Court, but they could hardly fight his decision. After all, he had decided _Marbury_ v. _Madison_ in their favor.

By establishing judicial review, Marshall helped to create a lasting balance among the three branches of government. The strength of this balance would be tested as the United States grew. In the next section, you will read about a period of great national growth.

THE SUPREME COURT TODAY

The principle of judicial review is still a major force in American society. In June 1999, the Supreme Court used this power to restrict the ability of the federal government to enforce its laws in the 50 states.

In one case, _Alden_ v. _Maine_, the Court ruled that employees of a state government cannot sue their state even when the state violates federal labor laws—such as those that set guidelines for overtime wages.

**bulary
ce of the
e:** a low-
official with
ed authority,
ding the
r to per-
marriages

Section 1 Assessment

Terms & Names

Explain the significance of:
- radical
- Judiciary Act of 1801
- John Marshall
- Marbury v. Madison
- unconstitutional
- judicial review

2. Using Graphics

Use a chart like the one below to list some of the changes made by Jefferson and his party.

Changes made by Democratic-Republicans
1.

What branch of government gave Jefferson trouble?

3. Main Ideas

a. How was the tie between Jefferson and Burr settled after the election of 1800?

b. In what ways did Jefferson's talents reach beyond politics?

c. How did the opinions of Jefferson and Hamilton regarding the public debt differ?

4. Critical Thinking

Making Generalizations
How was Thomas Jefferson's philosophy reflected in his personal life?

THINK ABOUT
- how he behaved after being elected
- how he felt about his presidency later in life

ACTIVITY OPTIONS

TECHNOLOGY

ART

Read more about Thomas Jefferson. Design Jefferson's **Internet home page** showing his inventions or create a **model** of a building he designed.

2

The Louisiana Purchase and Exploration

MAIN IDEA	WHY IT MATTERS NOW	TERMS & NAMES
Jefferson purchased the Louisiana Territory in 1803 and doubled the size of the United States.	Thirteen more states were eventually organized on the land acquired by the Louisiana Purchase.	Louisiana Purchase, Meriwether Lewis, William Clark, Lewis and expeditio, Sacagawea, Zebulon Pi

ONE AMERICAN'S STORY

In 1790, Captain Robert Gray became the first American to sail around the world. Two years later, Gray explored a harbor in what is now Washington state. New England merchants like Captain Gray had to sail all the way around South America to reach the profitable trading regions of the Oregon Country. (See the map on page 320.) In spite of the long trip, merchants from Boston soon began to appear there frequently.

Gray's explorations helped to establish U.S. claims to the Pacific Northwest. In this section, you will learn how a lucky land purchase and a daring expedition further hastened westward expansion.

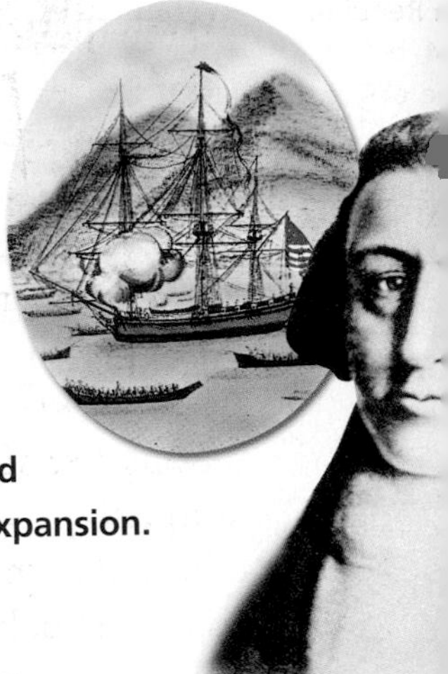

Robert Gra
his ship Co
on trading
to the Nort
and China.

Taking Notes

Jse your chart to take notes about the exploration of the West.

The Jefferson Era
nmaries
in Idea: Details:
in Idea: Details:
in Idea: Details:
in Idea: Details:

The West in 1800

In 1800, when Americans talked about the "West," they meant the area between the Appalachian Mountains and the Mississippi River. Thousands of settlers were moving westward across the Appalachians to settle in this region. Many moved onto land long inhabited by Native Americans. Even so, several U.S. territories soon declared statehood. Kentucky and Tennessee had become states by 1800, and Ohio entered the union in 1803.

Although the Mississippi River was the western border of the United States, there was a great deal of activity further west. In 1800, France and Spain were negotiating for ownership of the Louisiana Territory—the vast region between the Mississippi River and the Rocky Mountains.

The Pacific coast region and the Oregon Country, as you read in One American's Story, also attracted increasing attention. In California, Spain had a chain of 21 missions stretching from San Diego to San Francisco. Starting just north of San Francisco, Russian settlements dotted the Pacific coast all the way to Alaska. Great Britain also claimed land in the region.

ding History

ading a
Use the
on page 320
d the loca-
of New
ns.

As the number of Westerners grew, so did their political influence. A vital issue for many settlers was the use of the Mississippi River. Farmers and merchants used the river to move their products to the port of New Orleans, and from there to east coast markets. Threats to the free navigation of the Mississippi and the use of the port at New Orleans brought America to the brink of war.

Napoleon and New Orleans

"There is on the globe one single spot the possessor of which is our natural and habitual enemy," President Jefferson wrote. That spot was New Orleans. This strategic port was originally claimed by France. After losing the French and Indian War, France turned over the Louisiana Territory—including New Orleans—to Spain. But in a secret treaty in 1800, Spain returned Louisiana and the port to France's powerful leader, Napoleon. Now Napoleon planned to colonize the American territory.

ground
9,
eon was
the top
l of the
Republic.
4, he
e emperor.

In 1802, these developments nearly resulted in war. Just before turning Louisiana over to France, Spain closed New Orleans to American shipping. Angry Westerners called for war against both Spain and France. To avoid hostilities, Jefferson offered to buy New Orleans from France. He received a surprising offer back. The French asked if the United States wanted to buy all of the Louisiana Territory—a tract of land even larger than the United States at that time.

The Louisiana Purchase

A number of factors may have led Napoleon to make his surprising offer. He was probably alarmed by America's fierce determination to keep the port of New Orleans open. Also, his enthusiasm for a colony in America may have been lessened by events in a French colony in the West Indies. There, a revolt led by Toussaint L'Ouverture (too•SAN loo•vehr•TOOR) had resulted in disastrous losses for the French. Another factor was France's costly war against Britain. America's money may have been more valuable to Napoleon than its land.

ng History

ing
ces Why
ferson pur-
ouisiana
ough the
ution said
about
sident's
buy land?

Jefferson was thrilled by Napoleon's offer. However, the Constitution said nothing about the president's right to buy land. This troubled Jefferson, who believed in the strict interpretation of the Constitution. But he also believed in a republic of small farmers, and that required land. So, on April 30, 1803, the **Louisiana Purchase** was approved for $15 million—about three cents per acre. The purchase doubled the size of the United States. At the time, Americans knew little about the territory. But that would soon change.

Connections TO WORLD HISTORY

TOUSSAINT L'OUVERTURE

Toussaint L'Ouverture was born in Hispaniola, an island in the West Indies once colonized by both France and Spain. In 1791, L'Ouverture helped to lead a slave revolt against the French-controlled part of Hispaniola. A natural leader, L'Ouverture won admiration when he preached harmony between former slaves and planters.

In 1801, L'Ouverture overran the Spanish part of the island. He then freed all the slaves and put himself in charge of the entire island.

Hoping to regain their territory, the French invaded in 1802. They arrested L'Ouverture but failed to end the rebellion.

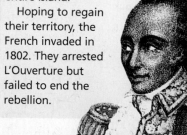

Lewis and Clark Explore

Since 1802, Thomas Jefferson had planned an expedition to explore the Louisiana country. Now that the Louisiana Purchase had been made, learning about the territory became even more important.

Jefferson chose a young officer, Captain **Meriwether Lewis,** to lead the expedition. In Jefferson's map-lined study, the two men eagerly planned the trip. Lewis turned to his old friend, Lieutenant **William Clark,** to select and oversee a volunteer force, which they called the Corps of Discovery. Clark was a skilled mapmaker and outdoorsman and proved to be a natural leader. The Corps of Discovery soon became known as the **Lewis and Clark expedition.**

Clark was accompanied by York, his African-American slave. York's hunting skills won him many admirers among the Native Americans met by the explorers. The first black man that many Indians had ever seen, York became something of a celebrity among them.

Lewis and Clark set out in the summer of 1803. By winter, they reached St. Louis. Located on the western bank of the Mississippi River, St. Louis would soon become the gateway to the West. But in 1803, the city was a sleepy town with just 180 houses. Lewis and Clark spent the winter at St. Louis and waited for the ceremony that would mark the transfer of Louisiana to the United States. In March 1804, the American flag flew over St. Louis for the first time.

Vocabulary
corps (kor): a number of p acting toget for a similar purpose

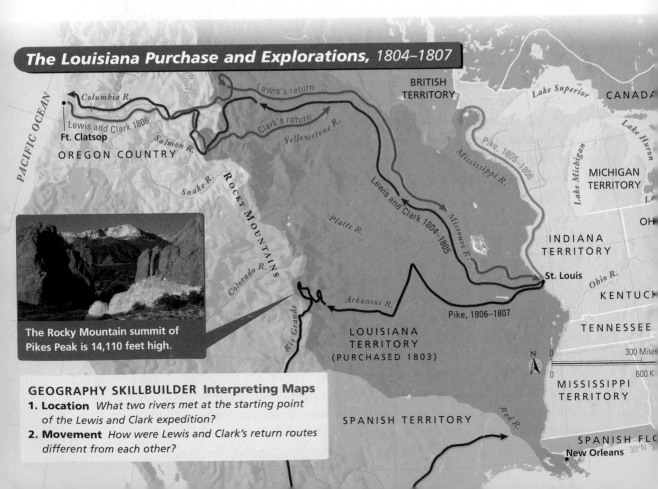

The Louisiana Purchase and Explorations, *1804–1807*

The Rocky Mountain summit of Pikes Peak is 14,110 feet high.

BRITISH TERRITORY

CANADA

Lake Superior

Lake Huron

Lake Michigan

MICHIGAN TERRITORY

Columbia R.

Lewis's return

Lewis and Clark 1806

Ft. Clatsop

OREGON COUNTRY

PACIFIC OCEAN

Salmon R.

Snake R.

Clark's return

Yellowstone R.

Pike, 1805–1806

Mississippi R.

ROCKY MOUNTAINS

Lewis and Clark 1804–1805

Platte R.

Missouri R.

INDIANA TERRITORY

OH

Colorado R.

St. Louis

Ohio R.

KENTUCKY

Rio Grande

Arkansas R.

Pike, 1806–1807

TENNESSEE

LOUISIANA TERRITORY (PURCHASED 1803)

300 Miles

600 K

MISSISSIPPI TERRITORY

SPANISH TERRITORY

Red R.

SPANISH FL

New Orleans 30°N

GEOGRAPHY SKILLBUILDER Interpreting Maps
1. **Location** *What two rivers met at the starting point of the Lewis and Clark expedition?*
2. **Movement** *How were Lewis and Clark's return routes different from each other?*

MERIWETHER LEWIS
1774–1809

Meriwether Lewis was well qualified for the first overland expedition to the Pacific Northwest. In Virginia, he had become an expert hunter. From 1801 to 1803, he worked for President Jefferson, who had him trained in geography, mineralogy, and astronomy.

The journals Lewis kept tell what the West was like in the early 1800s and are still exciting to read. In one entry, dated September 17, 1804, Lewis describes the "immense herds of Buffaloe, deer Elk and Antelopes which we saw in every direction feeding on the hills and plains."

WILLIAM CLARK
1770–1838

William Clark was an army friend of Meriwether Lewis. Lewis personally chose him to be co-captain of the Corps of Discovery.

Clark's experience in his state militia and the U.S. Army had taught him how to build forts, draw maps, and lead expeditions through enemy territory.

He had less formal training than Lewis, but with his six feet of height and muscular build, he was a more rugged explorer.

Clark's leadership skills smoothed disputes. Also, his artistic skills made the expedition's maps and drawings both accurate and beautiful.

What were the different skills of Lewis and Clark that qualified them as co-leaders of the expedition?

Up the Missouri River

ing History

king
nces Why
wis and
travel on
issouri

The explorers, who numbered about 40, set out from St. Louis in May of 1804. They headed up the Missouri River in one shallow-bottomed river-boat and two pirogues—canoes made from hollowed-out tree trunks. They had instructions from President Jefferson to explore the river and hoped to find a water route across the continent. Lewis and Clark were also told to establish good relations with Native Americans and describe the landscape, plants, and animals they saw.

The explorers inched up the Missouri. The first afternoon, they traveled only about three miles. Sometimes the men had to pull, rather than row or sail, their boats against the current. In late October, they reached the Mandan Indian villages in what is now North Dakota.

The explorers built a small fort and spent the winter with the friendly Mandan. There, they also met British and French-Canadian trappers and traders. They were not happy to see the Americans. They suspected that the Americans would soon compete with them for the rich trade in beaver furs—and they were right.

In the spring of 1805, the expedition set out again. A French trapper, his 17-year-old-wife, **Sacagawea** (SAK•uh•juh•WEE•uh), and their baby went with them. Sacagawea was a Shoshone woman whose language skills and knowledge of geography would be of great value to Lewis and Clark—especially when they reached the area where she was born.

On to the Pacific Ocean

On their way west, the expedition had to stop at the Great Falls of the Missouri. Lewis called this ten-mile-long series of waterfalls "the grandest sight I ever beheld." He described his approach to the falls.

A VOICE FROM THE PAST

I had proceeded on this course about two miles . . . whin my ears were saluted with the agreeable sound of a fall of water and advancing a little further I saw the spray arrise above the plain like a collumn of smoke. . . . (It) soon began to make a roaring too tremendous to be mistaken for any cause short of the great falls of the Missouri.

Meriwether Lewis, quoted in *Undaunted Courage*

Lewis and Clark kept beautiful journals that provided priceless information about the West.

To get around the Great Falls, the explorers had to carry their boats and heavy supplies for 18 miles. They built wheels from cottonwood trees to move the boats. Even with wheels, the trek took nearly two weeks. Rattlesnakes, bears, and even a hailstorm slowed their steps.

As they approached the Rocky Mountains, Sacagawea excitedly pointed out Shoshone lands. Eager to make contact with the tribe, Lewis and a small party made their way overland. Lewis soon found the Shoshone, whose chief recognized Sacagawea as his sister. The chief traded horses to Lewis and Clark, and the Shoshone helped them cross the Rocky Mountains.

The explorers then journeyed to the mighty Columbia River, which leads to the Pacific Ocean. In November 1805, Clark wrote in his journal, "Ocian in view! O! The joy." They soon arrived at the Pacific Coast. There, they spent a rain-soaked winter before returning to St. Louis the following year.

The Lewis and Clark expedition brought back a wealth of scientific and geographic information. Though they learned that an all-water route across the continent did not exist, Americans received an exciting report of what lay to the west.

Reading **Hi**
D. Finding M
Ideas Why v
the Lewis an
Clark exped
valuable?

Pike's Expedition

Lewis and Clark explored the northern part of the Louisiana Purchase. In 1806, an expedition led by **Zebulon Pike** left St. Louis on a southerly route. (Refer to the map on page 320.) Pike's mission was to find the sources of the Arkansas and Red rivers. The Red River formed a boundary between Spanish territory and Louisiana.

Pike's party of two dozen men headed westward across the Great Plains. When they reached the Arkansas River, they followed it toward the Rocky Mountains. From 150 miles away, Pike spied the Rocky Mountain peak that would later bear his name—Pikes Peak. However, he failed in his attempt to climb it. Then they turned south, hoping that they would eventually run into the Red River. Instead, they ran into the

Backgrou
The previou
year, Pike h
led a 5,000-
expedition
search for t
source of t
Mississippi

► **1. Accurate maps**
Lewis and Clark and Pike produced the first good maps of the Louisiana Territory. Later travelers would use these maps to make their way west.

► **2. Growth of fur trade**
Exploration boosted interest in the fur trade. Hunters and trappers would add to the knowledge of the West.

► **3. Mistaken view of Great Plains**
Pike inaccurately described the treeless Great Plains as a desert. This led many Americans to believe that the Plains were useless for farming.

SKILLBUILDER Interpreting Charts
Why might Pike's description of the Great Plains have led to the idea that Native Americans east of the Mississippi should be moved there?

Compass used by
Lewis and Clark

ulary
ande:
h for
er

Rio Grande, which was in Spanish territory. There, they were arrested by Spanish troops.

The explorers returned to the United States after being released by Spanish officials in 1807. Though Pike and his men never explored the Red River, they did bring back valuable descriptions of the Great Plains and the Rio Grande River Valley.

The Effects of Exploration

The first American explorers of the West brought back tales of adventure as well as scientific and geographical information. As the chart above shows, this information would have long-lasting effects.

Early in Jefferson's presidency, events at home occupied much of the new president's time. In the next section, you will learn about foreign affairs during the same time period.

ion **2** Assessment

erms & Names

lain the
gnificance of:

uisiana Purchase
eriwether Lewis
lliam Clark
wis and Clark
pedition
cagawea
oulon Pike

2. Using Graphics

Use a chart like the one below to record the factors that might have led Napoleon to sell the Louisiana Territory.

Causes

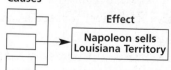

Effect

**Napoleon sells
Louisiana Territory**

3. Main Ideas

a. What groups might dispute European land claims in the West?

b. Why was New Orleans important to Americans?

c. How did Sacagawea help Lewis and Clark?

4. Critical Thinking

Recognizing Effects What were some of the effects of the explorations of the West in the 1800s?

THINK ABOUT

• how other people might use the information brought back by the explorers

• the economic effects of the expedition

VITY OPTIONS

LD HISTORY

OGRAPHY

Read more about New Orleans. Make an illustrated **time line** of the French, Spanish, and U.S. ownership of the city or create a **map** of its port.

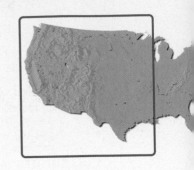

Native Americans on the Explorers' Route

When Thomas Jefferson bought the Louisiana Territory, Native Americans had already been living in that area for thousands of years. Before Lewis and Clark began their trip, Jefferson instructed them to deal with Native Americans in a peaceful manner and to make it clear that the United States wished to be "friendly and useful to them." On their journey, Lewis and Clark met almost 50 different tribes.

Sacagawea
In 1805, the explorers arrived in Shoshone territory near the Rocky Mountains. A Shoshone chief, Cameahwait, confirmed that there was no all-water route to the Pacific. Later, when Cameahwait recognized Sacagawea as his sister, he agreed to sell the explorers the horses they needed to cross the mountains.

❶ Oto
In 1804, Lewis and Clark met the
a buffalo-hunting people. This w
the first formal meeting of U.S.
representatives with western Na
Americans. Lewis told the Oto th
they were "children" of a new g
"father"—President Thomas Jeff

ARTIFACT FILE

Buffalo Robe Pictured to the right is a section of a Mandan buffalo robe. On it, a Mandan painted a battle scene between the Mandan and the Sioux.

Chinook
Columbia R.
Palouse
Blackfoot
Nez
Perce
Atsina
Lewis's return
Mandan ②

Lewis and Clark 1806
Umatilla
Walla-
Walla
Flatheads
Clark's return
Northern
Cheyenne

Yakima
Bannock
Teton ③
Sioux

Shoshone
Southern
Cheyenne

ROCKY MOUNTAINS

Pawnee
Oto ①

Kansa

Mississippi R.
50°N

Mandan ②

Lewis and Clark 1804–1805
Missouri R.

40°N

St. Louis

250 Miles

500 Kilometers

30°N

Gulf of Mexico

120°W

andan
...boring tribes as well as exploring
...eans relied on the mainstay of
...an culture—corn. The Mandan
...afted beautiful leatherwork
...ottery. Lewis and Clark spent an
...winter with the Mandan.

③ Teton Sioux
Upon meeting the Teton Sioux, Lewis
and Clark showed off an air gun.
Known for their aggressiveness, the
Teton already viewed the Americans
as competitors for trade in this region.
As a result, confrontation marked
Lewis and Clark's visit.

CONNECT TO GEOGRAPHY
1. **Place** What fort was built
   where the Columbia River
   empties into the Pacific Ocean?
2. **Location** In what mountain
   range did the Shoshone tribe
   live?

G See Geography
   Handbook, page 4.

CONNECT TO HISTORY
3. **Forming Opinions** What do
   you think the Native Americans
   that Lewis and Clark met
   thought about the explorers?

-Line Field Trip

...eabody Museum in Cambridge,
...husetts, holds an important collection
...ve American artifacts. This rain hat was
...y Chinook whalers of the Northwest.
...nook made these water-repellent hats
...edar bark and bear grass.

...e about Native American artifacts . . .

RESEARCH LINKS
CLASSZONE.COM

Problems with Foreign Powers

MAIN IDEA	**WHY IT MATTERS NOW**	**TERMS & NAMES**
Jefferson tried to avoid involvement in the problems of other nations.	British interference with the affairs of the United States led to the War of 1812.	impressment Embargo Act of 1807	Tecumseh War Hawk

ONE AMERICAN'S STORY

In 1804, the United States was at war with Tripoli, a state on the North African coast. The war was the result of repeated attacks on American merchant ships by African pirates. U.S. Navy Lieutenant Stephen Decatur was sent to destroy the U.S. warship *Philadelphia*—which had been captured by Tripoli—so that it could not be used by the enemy.

Decatur set fire to the *Philadelphia* and then escaped under enemy fire with only one man wounded. Decatur later issued this rallying cry for all Americans.

A VOICE FROM THE PAST

Our country! In her [relationships] with foreign nations may she always be in the right; but our country, right or wrong.

Stephen Decatur, 1816

The conflict with Tripoli showed how hard it was for the United States to stay out of foreign affairs while its citizens participated so heavily in overseas trade. In this section, you will learn how President Jefferson handled problems with other nations.

Stephen D
struggles i
to-hand cc
with Africa

Taking Notes

Use your chart to take notes about problems with foreign powers.

The Jefferson Era
mmaries
ain Idea:
tails:
ain Idea:
tails:
ain Idea:
tails:
ain Idea:
tails:

Jefferson's Foreign Policy

When Thomas Jefferson took office in 1801, he wanted to focus on domestic concerns. In his inaugural address, he noted that America was "kindly separated by nature and a wide ocean from the exterminating havoc [wars] of one quarter of the globe." He advised the United States to seek the friendship of all nations, but to enter into "entangling alliances with none."

However, the president's desire to keep the United States separated from other nations and their problems was doomed to fail. For one thing, American merchants were busily engaged in trade all over the world. For another, the Louisiana Purchase and the Lewis and Clark expedition were about to open the country to westward expansion. Expansion would bring Americans into closer contact with people from other nations who had already established settlements in the West.

Finally, the United States had little control over the actions of foreign nations—as North African interference with U.S. shipping had shown. Staying out of the ongoing conflict between France and England would be just as difficult.

ding **History**

alyzing
es Why was
d for the
d States
oid other
ns' problems?

Problems with France and England

For a long time, the United States managed not to get involved in the European wars that followed the French Revolution. At times, the nation even benefited from the conflict. Busy with affairs in Europe, France sold the Louisiana Territory to the United States. And American shippers eagerly took over the trade interrupted by the war.

By 1805, however, the British began to clamp down on U.S. shipping. They did not want Americans to provide their enemies with food and supplies. After the United States threatened to take action, the British decided to set up a partial blockade. This would only allow some American ships to bring provisions to Europe.

This partial blockade angered France, which enacted its own laws to control foreign shipping. These changes put American merchants in a difficult position. If they obeyed the British rules, their ships could be seized by the French. If they obeyed the French rules, their ships could be seized by the British.

Britain also interfered with U.S. trade by the **impressment,** or kidnapping, of American sailors to work on British ships. Between 1803 and 1812, the British impressed about 6,000 American sailors.

One of the most famous incidents occurred in 1807. The British ship *Leopard* attacked an American naval ship, the *Chesapeake,* off the coast of Virginia. Three Americans lost their lives in the battle. The attack aroused widespread anger. Had Congress been in session, America might have declared war. But Jefferson, who had been re-elected in 1804, decided against it. One critic, furious at the president's caution, called Jefferson a "dish of skim milk curdling at the head of our nation."

British officers seize an American sailor at gunpoint.

Trade as a Weapon

Instead of declaring war, Jefferson asked Congress to pass legislation that would stop all foreign trade. "Peaceable coercion," as the president described his policy, would prevent further bloodshed.

lary
: the
of
someone
a
vay by
ressure
ts

In December, Congress passed the **Embargo Act of 1807**. Now American ships were no longer allowed to sail to foreign ports. The act also closed American ports to British ships.

Jefferson's policy was a disaster. It was more harmful to the United States than to the British and French. American farmers and merchants were especially hard hit. Southern and Western farmers, for example, lost important markets for their grain, cotton, and tobacco. Shippers lost income, and many chose to violate the embargo by making false claims about where they were going. One New Englander said the embargo was like "cutting one's throat to cure the nosebleed."

The embargo became a major issue in the election of 1808. Jefferson's old friend James Madison won the election. By the time he took office, Congress had already repealed the embargo.

Madison's solution to the problem was a law that allowed merchants to trade with any country except France and Britain. Trade with these countries would start again when they agreed to respect U.S. ships. But this law proved no more effective than the embargo.

Reading **His**
B. Recognizi
Effects Wha
were the res
of the Emba
Act?

Tecumseh and Native American Unity

British interference with American shipping and impressment of U.S. citizens made Americans furious. They also were angered by Britain's actions in the Northwest. Many settlers believed that the British were stirring up Native American resistance to frontier settlements.

Since the Battle of Fallen Timbers in 1794 (see page 299), Native Americans continued to lose their land. Thousands of white settlers had swarmed into Ohio and then into Indiana.

Tecumseh, a Shawnee chief, vowed to stop the loss of Native American land. He believed that the reason Native Americans continued to lose their land was because they were separated into many different tribes. He concluded that Native Americans had to do what white Americans had done: unite. Events in 1809 proved him right.

That September, William Henry Harrison, governor of the Indiana Territory, signed the Treaty of Fort Wayne with chiefs of the Miami, Delaware, and Potawatomi tribes. They agreed to sell over three million acres of land. But Tecumseh declared the treaty meaningless.

The Shawnee chief Tecumseh led Native American resistance to white rule in the Ohio River Valley.

Reading l
C. Forming
Opinions
did Tecum
declare th
of Fort Wa
meaningle

A VOICE FROM THE PAST

[Whites] have taken upon themselves to say this [land] belongs to the Miamis, this to the Delawares and so on. But the Great Spirit intended [Native American land] to be the common property of all the tribes, [and it cannot] be sold without the consent of all.

Tecumseh, quoted in *Tecumseh and the Quest for Indian Leadership*

After the Treaty of Fort Wayne, many Native Americans began to answer Tecumseh's call for unity. But his efforts ultimately failed. In November 1811, while Tecumseh was away recruiting tribes for his alliance, the Shawnee were defeated by Harrison's forces at the Battle of

Tippecanoe. It was a severe set-back for Tecumseh's movement.

War Hawks

After the battle of Tippecanoe, Tecumseh and his warriors found a warm welcome with the British in Canada. At that point, the Native Americans and the British became allies. Tecumseh's welcome in Canada raised even higher the anti-British feelings in the West.

Leaders such as Congressman Henry Clay of Kentucky angrily demanded war against Britain. Westerners who called for war were known as **War Hawks**. They wanted British aid to Native Americans stopped, and they wanted the British out of Canada. Conquering Canada would open up a vast new empire for Americans.

Other Americans sought war because of the British violations of American rights at sea. Future president Andrew Jackson said hostilities were necessary "for the protection of our maritime citizens impressed on board British ships of war," and to "open a market for the productions of our soil."

Urged on by Jackson and the War Hawks, Congress declared war on Britain on June 18, 1812. In the next section, you will read about the second—and final—war between the United States and Great Britain.

Causes of the War of 1812

Impressment of U.S. Citizens

Interference with American shipping

British support of Native-American resistance

WAR

SKILLBUILDER Interpreting Charts
Which cause of the War of 1812 was not related to activities on the sea?

bulary
: a person
favors the
f military
to carry out
ɡn policy

---

tion **3** Assessment

Terms & Names

plain the
gnificance of:
npressment
mbargo Act
f 1807
ecumseh
Var Hawk

2. Using Graphics

Use a chart like the one below to record the effects of Jefferson's Embargo Act.

Causes | **Embargo Act**

Effects | ☐ ☐

Why didn't the act work?

3. Main Ideas

a. How did the British and French interfere with American shipping?

b. How did Jefferson respond to the interference?

c. Why did the War Hawks favor war?

4. Critical Thinking

Analyzing Points of View
Why did Tecumseh think it was important for Native Americans to unite?

THINK ABOUT
• what he learned about white men
• what Native Americans would lose if they did not act together

IVITY OPTIONS

ART
SPEECH

Do research on the Battle of Tippecanoe. Draw a **comic strip story** of the battle or hold a **press conference** to describe the battle's outcome.

4

The War of 1812

Angered by Britain's interference in the nation's affairs, the United States went to war.

The War of 1812 showed that the United States was willing and able to protect its national interests.

Oliver Hazard Perry

Battle of the Thames

Francis Sco Key

Treaty of G

ONE AMERICAN'S STORY

The war between the United States and Britain had begun in 1812. Two years later, British troops were marching toward Washington, D.C. Dolley Madison, the president's wife, stayed behind until the last minute to save important historical objects from the White House.

A VOICE FROM THE PAST

I have had [a wagon] filled with . . . the most valuable portable articles belonging to the house. . . . I insist on waiting until the large picture of General Washington is secured.

Dolley Madison, from a letter sent to her sister

When the British troops arrived in the city, they set fire to many public buildings, including the White House and the Capitol. You will learn about other events of the War of 1812 in this section.

Taking Notes

Use your chart to take notes about the War of 1812.

The Jefferson Era		
nmaries		
in Idea: .		
ails:		
in Idea:		
ails:		
in Idea:		
ails:		
in Idea:		
ails:		

The War Begins

Britain did not really want a war with the United States because it was already involved in another war with France. To try to avoid war, the British announced that they would no longer interfere with American shipping. But the slow mails of the day prevented this news from reaching the United States until weeks after June 18th, when Congress approved Madison's request for a declaration of war.

The War of 1812 had two main phases. From 1812 to 1814, Britain concentrated on its war against France. It devoted little energy to the conflict in North America, although it did send ships to blockade the American coast. The second phase of the war began after the British defeated France in April 1814. With their European war nearly at an end, the British could turn their complete attention to the United States.

Before B
set fire t
presiden
Dolley M
saved pr
historica

The United States military was weak when the war was declared. Democratic-Republicans had reduced the size of the armed forces. When the war began, the Navy had only about 16 ships. The army had fewer than 7,000 men. These men were poorly trained and equipped, and were often led by inexperienced officers. A young Virginia army officer complained that the older officers were victims of "sloth, ignorance, or habits of [excessive] drinking."

The First Phase of the War

In spite of its small size, the United States Navy rose to the challenge. Its warships were the fastest afloat. American naval officers had gained valuable experience fighting pirates in the Mediterranean Sea. Early in the war, before the British blockaded the coast, ships such as the *Constitution* and the *United States* won stirring victories. These victories on the high seas boosted American confidence.

The most important U.S. naval victory took place on Lake Erie. In the winter of 1812-1813, the Americans had begun to build a fleet on the shores of Lake Erie. **Oliver Hazard Perry,** an experienced officer, took charge of this infant fleet. In September 1813, the small British force on the lake set out to attack the American ships. Commodore Perry, who had predicted that this would be "the most important day of my life," sailed out to meet the enemy. Perry's ship, the *Lawrence,* flew a banner declaring, "Don't give up the ship."

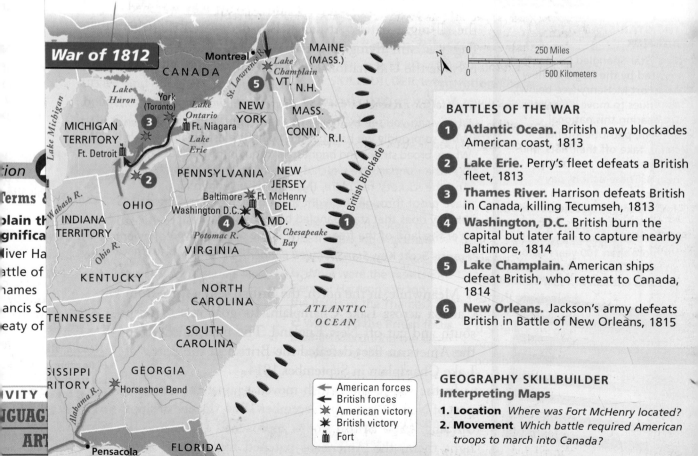

War of 1812

American forces →
British forces →
✳ American victory
✳ British victory
🏰 Fort

0 ——— 250 Miles
0 ——— 500 Kilometers

BATTLES OF THE WAR

1 Atlantic Ocean. British navy blockades American coast, 1813

2 Lake Erie. Perry's fleet defeats a British fleet, 1813

3 Thames River. Harrison defeats British in Canada, killing Tecumseh, 1813

4 Washington, D.C. British burn the capital but later fail to capture nearby Baltimore, 1814

5 Lake Champlain. American ships defeat British, who retreat to Canada, 1814

6 New Orleans. Jackson's army defeats British in Battle of New Orleans, 1815

GEOGRAPHY SKILLBUILDER
Interpreting Maps

1. Location Where was Fort McHenry located?

2. Movement Which battle required American troops to march into Canada?

A1

THE
BAN
The "
inspir
over
contir
On he
anthe
stand
put tr
heart
respe
and t

Fr
enjoy
for m
an ac
natio

Robert Fulton made the steamboat a commercial success.

The steam locomotive helped build U.S. industry.

The telegraph could quickly send messeges over great distances.

This Currier and Ives print, *Progress of the Century*, shows some inventions of the 1800s.

1807
Robert Fulton launches a steamboat on the Hudson River.

1808
Congress bans the African slave trade.

1812
War of 1812 disrupts U.S. shipping.

1816
James Monroe is elected President.

USA World 1800

1804
Haiti wins independence from France.

1815
Napoleon defeated at Waterloo.

Peru and M
gain independe
from S

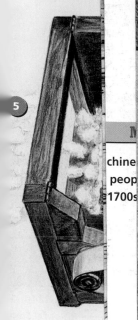

5

The rotery printing press was made for high volume printing.

ing History
ding a
Use the
n page 350
cotton-
g areas

ing History
ognizing
What
did the
gin have
South?

Interact *with* History

From 1790 to 1840, you have seen an explosion of new inventions. These include the cotton gin, the steamboat, the steel plow, and the telegraph. You have also seen neighbors leave their farms to run machines in new factories. You sense that the country is changing.

How will new inventions change your country?

What Do You Think?

- What would it mean to be able to grow more grain and cotton?
- What would it mean to communicate and travel more quickly?
- How might it feel to do factory work instead of farm work?

RESEARCH LINKS
CLASSZONE.COM
Visit the Chapter 11 links for more information about the growing nation.

1831
Nat Turner leads slave rebellion in Virginia.

1838
Frederick Douglass flees to New York City to escape slavery.

1844
Telegraph line connects Washington, D.C., and Baltimore.

1844

1833
Slavery is abolished in British Empire.

1839
Louis Daguerre is recognized for his photographic process.

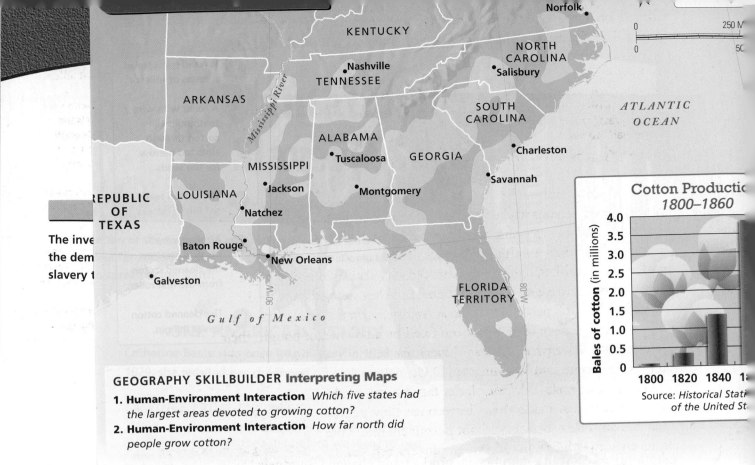

$1,000. After 1808, when it became illegal to import Africans for use as slaves, the trading of slaves already in the country increased.

The expansion of slavery had a major impact on the South's economy. But its effect on the people living there was even greater.

Slavery Divides the South

Slavery divided white Southerners into those who held slaves and those who did not. Slaveholders with large plantations were the wealthiest and most powerful people in the South, but they were relatively few in number. Only about one-third of white families owned slaves in 1840. Of these slave-owning families, only about one-tenth had large plantations with 20 or more slaves.

Most white Southern farmers owned few or no slaves. Still, many supported slavery anyway. They worked their small farms themselves and hoped to buy slaves someday, which would allow them to raise more cotton and earn more money. For both small farmers and large planters, slavery had become necessary for increasing profits.

African Americans in the South

Slavery also divided black Southerners into those who were enslaved and those who were free. Enslaved African Americans formed about one-third of the South's population in 1840. About half of them

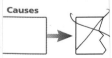
Reading
C. Analyzin
Points of Vi
Why did m
white farm
without sl
support sla

worked on large plantations with white overseers. Decades later, a former slave described the routine in an interview.

Not all slaves faced the back-breaking conditions of plantations. In cities, enslaved persons worked as domestic servants, skilled craftsmen, factory hands, and day laborers. Sometimes they were hired out and allowed to keep part of their earnings. Frederick Douglass, an African-American speaker and publisher, once commented, "A city slave is almost a freeman, compared with a slave on the plantation." But they were still enslaved.

In 1840, about 8 percent of African Americans in the South were free. They had either been born free, been freed by an owner, or bought their own freedom. Many free African Americans in the South lived in cities such as Baltimore and Washington, D.C.

Though not enslaved, free blacks faced many problems. Some states made them leave once they gained their freedom. Most states did not permit them to vote or receive an education. Many employers refused to hire them. But their biggest threat was the possibility of being captured and sold into slavery.

Finding Strength in Religion

An African-American culture had emerged on plantations by the early 1800s. Slaves relied on that culture—with its strong religious convictions, close personal bonds, and abundance of music—to help them endure the brutal conditions of plantation life.

Some slaveholders tried to use religion to make slaves accept their treatment. White ministers stressed such Bible passages as "Servants, obey your masters." But enslaved people took their own messages from the Bible. They were particularly inspired by the story of Moses leading the Hebrews out of bondage in Egypt.

Enslaved people expressed their religious beliefs in **spirituals,** religious folk songs. Spirituals often contained coded messages about a planned escape or an owner's unexpected return. African-American spirituals later influenced blues, jazz, and other forms of American music.

Detail of *Plantation Burial,* (1860), John Antrobus.

ng **History**

trasting
as plan-
slavery
nt from
in cities?

g **History**

ng
es Why
nslaved
Americans
red by the
story
s?

Families Under Slavery

Perhaps the cruelest part of slavery was the sale of family members away from one another. Although some slaveholders would not part mothers from children, many did, causing unforgettable grief. When enslaved people ran away, it was often to escape separation or to see family again.

When slave families could manage to be together, they took comfort in their family life. They married, though their marriages were not legally recognized. They tried to raise children, despite interference from owners. Most slave children lived with their mothers, who tried to protect them from punishment. Parents who lived on other plantations often stole away to visit their children, even at the cost of a whipping. Frederick Douglass recalled visits from his mother, who lived 12 miles away.

Reading H
F. Recogniz
Effects Ho
slavery har
family life?

A VOICE FROM THE PAST

I do not recollect of [remember] ever seeing my mother by the light of day. She was with me in the night. She would lie down with me, and get me to sleep, but long before I waked she was gone.

Frederick Douglass, *Narrative of the Life of Frederick Douglass*

Douglass's mother resisted slavery by the simple act of visiting her child. Douglass later rebelled by escaping to the North. Other enslaved people rebelled in more violent ways.

A slave auction threatens to split a family apart.

Slave Rebellions

Armed rebellion was an extreme form of resistance to slavery. Gabriel Prosser planned an attack on Richmond, Virginia, in 1800. In 1822, Denmark Vesey planned a revolt in Charleston, South Carolina. Both plots were betrayed, and the leaders were hanged.

The most famous rebellion was led by **Nat Turner** in Virginia in 1831. On August 21, Turner and 70 followers killed 55 white men, women, and children. Later, witnesses claimed that he spoke these words.

> ### A VOICE FROM THE PAST
>
> We do not go forth for the sake of blood and carnage; . . . Remember that ours is not a war for robbery, . . . it is a struggle for freedom.
>
> **Nat Turner,** quoted in *Nat Turner,* by Terry Bisson

Most of Turner's men were captured when their ammunition ran out, and 16 were killed. When Turner was caught, he was tried and hanged.

Turner's rebellion spread fear in the South. Whites killed more than 200 African Americans in revenge. State legislatures passed harsh laws that kept free blacks and slaves from having weapons or buying liquor. Slaves could not hold religious services unless whites were present. Postmasters stopped delivering antislavery publications.

After Turner's rebellion, the grip of slavery grew even tighter in the South. Tension over slavery increased between the South and the North, as you will see in the next section.

ng **History**

gnizing
How did *ner's* rebel-*ect* white *rners?*

AMERICA'S **HISTORY MAKERS**

NAT TURNER
1800–1831

Nat Turner was born on a plantation in Virginia. As a child, Turner learned to read and write. He became an enthusiastic reader of the Bible. Slaves gathered in forest clearings to listen to his powerful sermons. Turner believed that God wanted him to free the slaves, even if by armed rebellion. He defended the justice of his cause in what came to be known as *Confessions of Nat Turner,* which he dictated to a white lawyer before his execution.

How did Turner justify his rebellion?

---

ion ❷ **Assessment**

Terms & Names
plain the gnificance of:
- Whitney
- **tton gin**
- **irituals**
- **at Turner**

2. Using Graphics

In a chart like the one below, note facts about each group of Southerners.

Group	Facts
slaveholding whites	
nonslaveholding whites	
enslaved blacks	
free blacks	

Why do you think many free blacks lived in cities?

3. Main Ideas

a. How did the cotton gin lead to the spread of slavery?

b. How was life different for plantation slaves, city slaves, and free blacks in the South?

c. What were three ways that enslaved people resisted slavery?

4. Critical Thinking

Forming Opinions How do you think slave rebellions affected the institution of slavery?

THINK ABOUT
- Nat Turner's reasons for rebelling
- the reaction of white Southerners and slave owners to Turner's rebellion

VITY OPTIONS

IGUAGE ARTS

SPEECH

Write a **book report** on a slave narrative, or perform an **oral interpretation** of a passage from one.

③ Nationalism and Sectionalism

MAIN IDEA	WHY IT MATTERS NOW	TERMS & NAMES
Patriotic pride united the states, but tension between the North and South emerged.	The tension led to the Civil War, and regional differences can still be found in the United States today.	nationalism Henry Clay American System Erie Canal

TERMS & NAMES (continued): James Mo[...] sectionalis[...] Missouri C[...] Monroe D[...]

ONE AMERICAN'S STORY

The War of 1812 sent a wave of nationalist feeling through the United States. **Nationalism** is a feeling of pride, loyalty, and protectiveness toward your country. Representative **Henry Clay,** from Kentucky, was a strong nationalist. After the war, President James Madison supported Clay's plan to strengthen the country and unify its regions.

A VOICE FROM THE PAST

Every nation should anxiously endeavor to establish its absolute independence, and consequently be able to feed and clothe and defend itself. If it rely upon a foreign supply that may be cut off . . . it cannot be independent.

Henry Clay, quoted in *The Annals of America*

In this section, you will learn how nationalism affected U.S. economic growth and foreign policy. You'll also see how Americans were beginning to be torn between the interests of their own regions and those of the country as a whole.

Henry Clay

Taking Notes

Use your chart to take notes about nationalism and sectionalism.

Causes

Nationalism Unites the Country

In 1815, President Madison presented a plan to Congress for making the United States economically self-sufficient. In other words, the country would prosper and grow by itself, without foreign products or foreign markets.

The plan—which Henry Clay promoted as the **American System**—included three main actions.

1. **Establish a protective tariff,** a tax on imported goods that protects a nation's businesses from foreign competition. Congress passed a tariff in 1816. It made European goods more expensive and encouraged Americans to buy cheaper American-made products.

*ing*History

cognizing
s How
d the three
of the
ican System
o make
ountry self-
ent?

2. **Establish a national bank** that would promote a single currency, making trade easier. (Most regional banks issued their own money.) In 1816, Congress set up the second Bank of the United States.

3. **Improve the country's transportation systems,** which were important for a strong economy. Poor roads made transportation slow and costly.

Roads and Canals Link Cities

Representative John C. Calhoun of South Carolina also called for better transportation systems. "Let us bind the Republic together with a perfect system of roads and canals," he declared in 1817. Earlier, in 1806, Congress had funded a road from Cumberland, Maryland, to Wheeling, Virginia. By 1841, the National Road, designed as the country's main east-west route, had been extended to Vandalia, Illinois.

Water transportation improved, too, with the building of canals. In fact, the period from 1825 to 1850 is often called the Age of Canals. Completed in 1825, the massive **Erie Canal** created a water route between New York City and Buffalo, New York. The canal opened the upper Ohio Valley and the Great Lakes region to settlement and trade. It also fueled nationalism by unifying these two sections of the country.

The Erie Canal allowed farm products from the Great Lakes region to flow east and people and manufactured goods from the East to flow

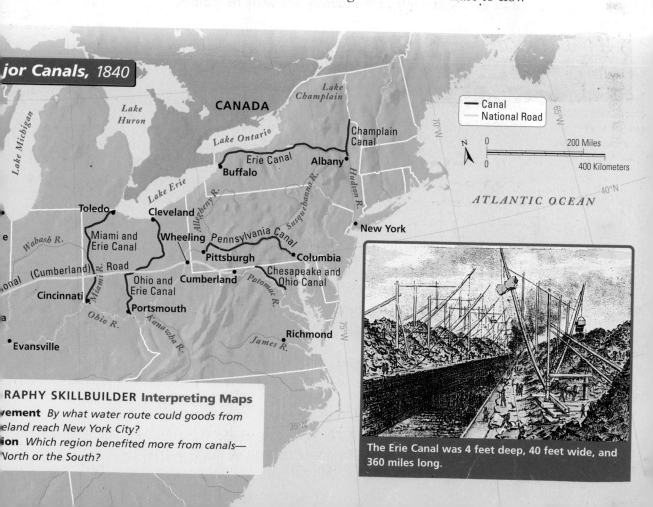

jor Canals, 1840

Legend:
— Canal
— National Road

The Erie Canal was 4 feet deep, 40 feet wide, and 360 miles long.

RAPHY SKILLBUILDER Interpreting Maps

ement By what water route could goods from *eland* reach New York City?

ion Which region benefited more from canals— *North* or the South?

west. Trade stimulated by the canal helped New York City become the nation's largest city. Between 1820 and 1830, its population swelled from less than 125,000 to more than 200,000.

Around the 1830s, the nation began to use steam-powered trains for transportation. In 1830, only about 30 miles of track existed in the United States. But by 1850, the number had climbed to 9,000 miles. Improvements in rail travel led to a decline in the use of canals.

The Era of Good Feelings

As nationalist feelings spread, people slowly shifted their loyalty away from state governments and more toward the federal government. Democratic-Republican **James Monroe** won the presidency in 1816 with a large majority of electoral votes. The Federalist Party provided little opposition to Monroe and soon disappeared. Political differences gave way to what one Boston newspaper called the Era of Good Feelings.

During the Monroe administration, several landmark Supreme Court decisions promoted national unity by strengthening the federal government. For example, in *McCulloch* v. *Maryland* (1819), the state of Maryland wanted to tax its branch of the national bank. If this tax were allowed, the states could claim to have power over the federal government. The Court upheld federal authority by ruling that a state could not tax a national bank.

James Monroe

Backgroun
Maryland a
argued tha
Congress ha
power to cr
the bank, b
the Court r
that it did
such power

A VOICE FROM THE PAST

The States have no power, by taxation or otherwise, to retard, impede, burden, or in any manner control the operations of the constitutional laws enacted by Congress.

Chief Justice John Marshall, *McCulloch* v. *Maryland* (1819)

Another Court decision that strengthened the federal government was *Gibbons* v. *Ogden* (1824). Two steamship operators fought over shipping rights on the Hudson River in New York and New Jersey. The Court ruled that interstate commerce could be regulated only by the federal government, not the state governments.

Reading
B. Finding
Ideas Hov
the Suprer
Court stre
the federa
governme

The Supreme Court under John Marshall clearly stated important powers of the federal government. A stronger federal government reflected a growing nationalist spirit.

Settling National Boundaries

This nationalist spirit also made U.S. leaders want to define and expand the country's borders. To do this, they had to reach agreements with Britain and Spain.

Two agreements improved relations between the United States and Britain. The Rush-Bagot Agreement (1817) limited each side's naval

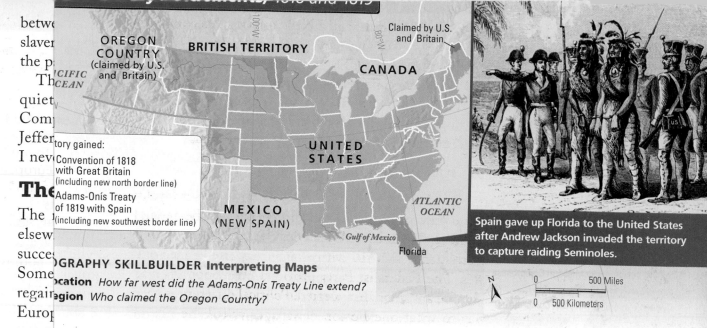

Territory gained:
Convention of 1818
with Great Britain
(including new north border line)
Adams-Onís Treaty
of 1819 with Spain
(including new southwest border line)

Spain gave up Florida to the United States
after Andrew Jackson invaded the territory
to capture raiding Seminoles.

GEOGRAPHY SKILLBUILDER Interpreting Maps
Location How far west did the Adams-Onís Treaty Line extend?
Region Who claimed the Oregon Country?

forces on the Great Lakes. In the Convention of 1818, the two countries set the 49th parallel as the U.S.-Canadian border as far west as the Rocky Mountains.

But U.S. relations with Spain were tense. The two nations disagreed on the boundaries of the Louisiana Purchase and the ownership of West Florida. Meanwhile, pirates and runaway slaves used Spanish-held East Florida as a refuge. In addition, the Seminoles of East Florida raided white settlements in Georgia to reclaim lost lands.

In 1817, President Monroe ordered General Andrew Jackson to stop the Seminole raids, but not to confront the Spanish. Jackson followed the Seminoles into Spanish territory and then claimed the Floridas for the United States.

Monroe ordered Jackson to withdraw but gave Spain a choice. It could either police the Floridas or turn them over to the United States. In the Adams-Onís Treaty of 1819, Spain handed Florida to the United States and gave up claims to the Oregon Country. The map above shows boundaries drawn and territories gained in 1818 and 1819.

Sectional Tensions Increase

At the same time nationalism was unifying the country, sectionalism was threatening to drive it apart. **Sectionalism** is loyalty to the interests of your own region or section of the country, rather than to the nation as a whole. Economic changes had created some divisions within the United States. As you have seen, white Southerners were relying more on cotton and slavery. In the Northeast, wealth was based on manufacturing and trade. In the West, settlers wanted cheap land and good transportation. The interests of these sections were often in conflict.

Sectionalism became a major issue when Missouri applied for statehood in 1817. People living in Missouri wanted to allow slavery in their state. At the time, the United States consisted of 11 slave states and 11

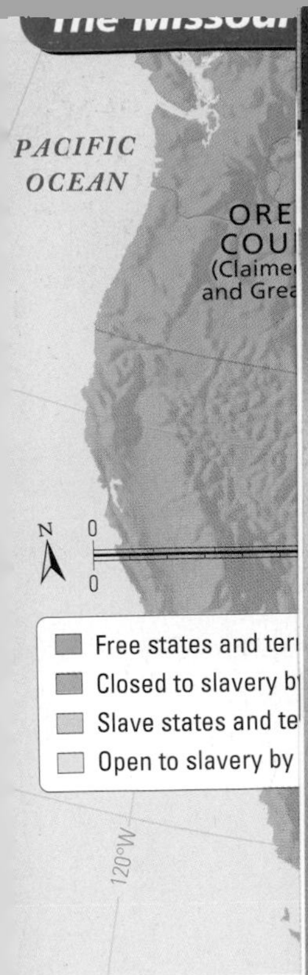
The Missouri
PACIFIC
OCEAN
ORE
COU
(Claime
and Grea
N
0
0
Free states and ter
Closed to slavery b
Slave states and te
Open to slavery by
120°W

GEOGRAPHY SK

1. **Location** *At wh*
2. **Region** *What te Compromise?*

UNIT 4

1810 – 1860

A Changing Nation

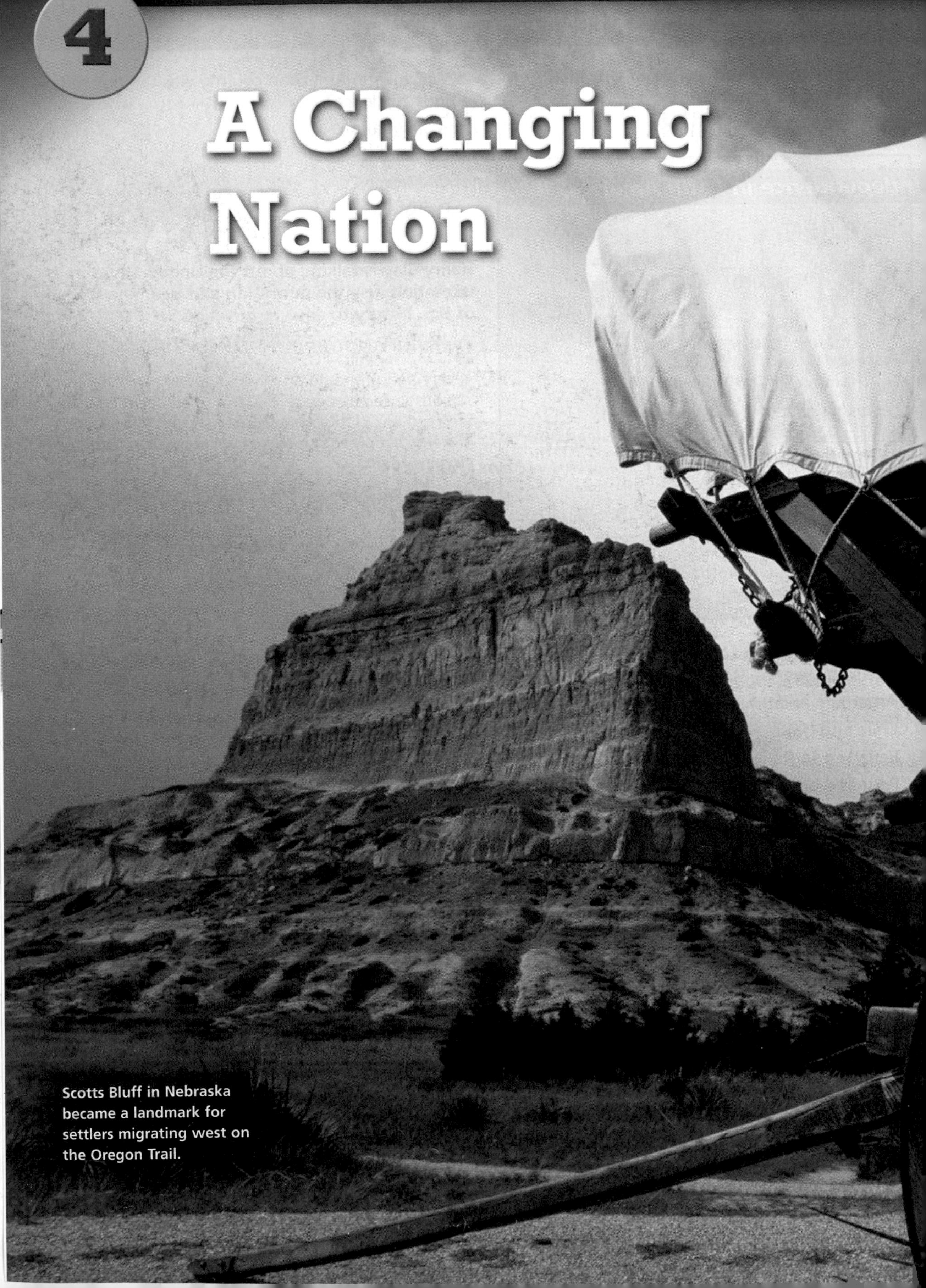

Scotts Bluff in Nebraska became a landmark for settlers migrating west on the Oregon Trail.

"Our manifest destiny is to overspread the continent."

—John L. O'Sullivan

Reading Strategy: Finding Main Ideas

What Do You Know?

What do you already know about the issues that faced the nation in the first half of the 19th century? How did presidents before Jackson deal with problems?

Think About
- what you have learned about Andrew Jackson from books and movies
- how American life is affected by the actions of a president, by conflicts among different parts of the country, and by the will of the people
- your responses to the Interact with History about qualities that make a strong leader (see page 367)

President Andrew Jackson's time in of influential, it has been called the Age

What Do You Want to Know?

 What questions do you have about Jackson and his presidency? Record them in your notebook before reading the chapter.

Finding Main Ideas

To make it easier for you to understand what you read, learn to find the main idea of ea paragraph, topic heading, and section. Remember that the supporting details help expla the main ideas. On the chart below, write down the main ideas about the political, eco- nomic, and social changes during Jackson's presidency.

 See Skillbuilder Handbook, page R5.

Taking Notes

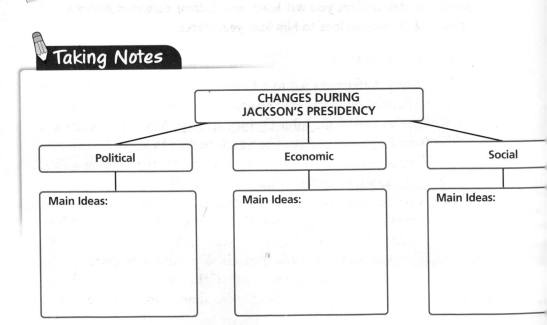

CHANGES DURING JACKSON'S PRESIDENCY

Political	Economic	Social
Main Ideas:	Main Ideas:	Main Ideas:

1

Politics of the People

MAIN IDEA	WHY IT MATTERS NOW	TERMS & NAMES
ackson's election to the y in 1828 brought a new pular democracy.	Jackson's use of presidential powers laid the foundation of the modern presidency.	John Quincy Adams Jacksonian democracy Andrew Jackson spoils system

ONE AMERICAN'S STORY

For 40 years, Margaret Bayard Smith and her husband, a government official, were central figures in the political and social life of Washington. In 1824, Smith described how John Quincy Adams reacted to his election as president.

A VOICE FROM THE PAST

When the news of his election was communicated to Mr. Adams by the Committee . . . the sweat rolled down his face—he shook from head to foot and was so agitated that he could scarcely stand or speak.

Margaret Bayard Smith, *The First Forty Years of Washington Society*

Margaret Bayard Smith wrote about life in the nation's capital in the first half of the 19th century.

Adams had reason to be shaken by his election. It had been hotly contested, and he knew that he would face much opposition as he tried to govern. In this section, you will learn how Adams defeated Andrew Jackson in 1824, only to lose to him four years later.

The Election of 1824

In 1824, regional differences led to a fierce fight over the presidency. The Democratic-Republican Party split apart, with four men hoping to replace James Monroe as president. **John Quincy Adams,** Monroe's secretary of state, was New England's choice. The South backed William Crawford of Georgia. Westerners supported Henry Clay, the "Great Compromiser," and **Andrew Jackson,** a former military hero from Tennessee.

Jackson won the most popular votes. But he did not receive a majority of electoral votes. According to the Constitution, if no person wins a majority of electoral votes, the House of Representatives must choose the president. The selection was made from the top three vote getters.

Clay had come in fourth and was out of the running. In the House vote, he threw his support to Adams, who then won. Because Adams

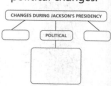

Taking Notes

Use your chart to take notes about political changes.

CHANGES DURING JACKSON'S PRESIDENCY

POLITICAL

JOHN QUINCY ADAMS
1767–1848

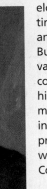

John Quincy Adams was born into wealth and social position. He was the son of President John Adams. Like his father, he had a sharp mind, spoke eloquently, worked tirelessly in public service, and had high principles. But he was sometimes vain, and unwilling to compromise. This made him unpopular with many people and often ineffective. After his presidency, he served with distinction in Congress.

ANDREW JACKSON
1767–1845

Andrew Jackson was the son of a poor farm couple from South Carolina. Orphaned by age 14, he was a wild and reckless youth.

Jackson moved on to become a successful lawyer and plantation owner in Tennessee. But his quick temper still got him into brawls and duels. Bullets in his body from two duels frequently caused him pain.

Jackson's humble background and reputation for toughness endeared him to voters. They considered him one of their own.

Why do you think Jackson was popular but Adams was not?

later named Clay as his secretary of state, Jackson's supporters claimed that Adams gained the presidency by making a deal with Clay. Charges of a "corrupt bargain" followed Adams throughout his term.

Adams had many plans for his presidency. He wanted to build roads and canals, aid education and science, and regulate the use of natural resources. But Congress, led by Jackson supporters, defeated his proposals.

Jacksonian Democracy

Jackson felt that the 1824 election had been stolen from him—that the will of the people had been ignored. Jackson and his supporters were outraged. He immediately set to work to gain the presidency in 1828.

For the next four years, the split in the Democratic-Republican Party between the supporters of Jackson and of Adams grew wider. Jackson claimed to represent the "common man." He said Adams represented a group of privileged, wealthy Easterners. This division eventually created two parties. The Democrats came from among the Jackson supporters, while the National Republicans grew out of the Adams camp.

The election of 1828 again matched Jackson against Adams. It was a bitter campaign—both sides made vicious personal attacks. Even Jackson's wife, Rachel, became a target. During the campaign, Jackson crusaded against control of the government by the wealthy. He promised to look out for the interests of common people. He also promoted the concept of majority rule. The idea of spreading political power to all the people and ensuring majority rule became known as **Jacksonian democracy**.

Actually, the process of spreading political power had begun before Jackson ran for office. When Jefferson was president in the early 1800s,

*Reading*His

A. Analyzing
Causes Wha
the main rea
John Quincy
Adams was r
effective as
president?

additional people had gained the right to vote as states reduced restrictions on who could vote. Before, for example, only those who owned property or paid taxes could vote in many states. This easing of voting restrictions increased the number of voters. But voting was still limited to adult white males.

The expansion of voting rights helped Jackson achieve an overwhelming win in the 1828 presidential election. Jackson's triumph was hailed as a victory for common people. Large numbers of Western farmers as well as workers in the nation's cities supported him. Their vote put an end to the idea that the government should be controlled by an educated elite. Now, the common people would be governed by one of their own. (See chart "Changes in Ideas About Democracy," page 373.)

ing History

ognizing
s What
made
n's appeal
"common
especially
tant in the
on of 1828?

The People's President

Jackson's humble background, and his reputation as a war hero, helped make him president. Many saw his rise above hardship as a real American success story. He was the first president not from an aristocratic Massachusetts or Virginia family, and the first from the West.

Jackson indeed had had a hard life. His father died shortly before his birth, and Jackson grew up on a frontier farm in South Carolina. At 13, he joined the militia with his older brother to fight in the Revolutionary War. In 1781, they were taken prisoner by the British. While captive, he allegedly refused when commanded to shine an officer's boots. The officer struck Jackson with a sword, leaving scars on his hand and head. Later, Jackson's mother obtained her sons' release from a military prison, where they had become ill with smallpox. Jackson's brother died, but his mother nursed Jackson back to health. A short time later, she also died. Jackson's experiences during the Revolution left him with a lifelong hatred of the British.

After the war, Jackson moved to the Tennessee frontier. In 1784, he began to study law. He built a successful legal practice and also bought and sold land. Jackson then purchased a plantation near Nashville and ran successfully for Congress. After the War of 1812 broke out, he was appointed a general in the army. At the Battle of New Orleans in 1815, Jackson soundly defeated the British even though his troops were greatly outnumbered. He became a national war hero. He earned the nickname "Old Hickory," after a soldier claimed that he was "tough as hickory."

Jackson Takes Office

Jackson's success in the presidential election of 1828 came at a high price. Shortly after he won, his wife, Rachel, died of a heart attack. Jackson believed that the campaign attacks on her reputation had killed her. She was a private woman who preferred a quiet life. In fact, she had

Jackson usually wore this miniature oil portrait of his beloved wife, Rachel, around his neck.

said that she would "rather be a doorkeeper in the house of God than . . . live in that palace at Washington." Margaret Bayard Smith described Rachel's importance to Jackson, saying she "not only made him a happier, but a better man."

Jackson looked thin, pale, and sad at his inauguration on March 4, 1829. But the capital was full of joy and excitement. Thousands of people were there. Senator Daniel Webster wrote about the inauguration.

A VOICE FROM THE PAST

I have never seen such a crowd before. Persons have come five hundred miles to see General Jackson, and they really seem to think that the country has been rescued from some dreadful danger.

Daniel Webster, *Correspondence*

Reading **Hi**

C. Drawing Conclusions did Jackson's supporters r with such er siasm at his inauguration

At the inauguration ceremony, the crowd shouted, waved, applauded, and saluted its hero. He bowed low to the people in turn. A throng followed Jackson to the White House reception. One person described the crowd as containing "all sorts of people, from the highest and most polished, down to the most vulgar and gross in the nation."

The crowd grew rowdy. People broke china and glasses as they grabbed for the food and drinks. The pushing and shoving finally drove the new president to flee the White House. As Supreme Court Justice Joseph Story observed, "The reign of King Mob seemed triumphant."

CITIZENSHIP TODAY

Exercising the Vote

During the Age of Jackson, rules on who could vote were eased. This increased the number of voters. But voting was still limited to adult white males. Over the years, other groups gained the right to vote, including African Americans, women, and Native Americans. Today's elections are open to all citizens aged 18 and over.

Future voters can practice casting their votes in mock, or pretend, elections. The National Student/Parent Mock Election teaches students to be informed voters. Mock presidential elections attract coverage by the media. Television stations may even broadcast live from schools, interviewing student voters.

Students register to vote in a mock election.

One high school student, Charlie Tran from San Jose, California, said, "Students seem to catch the important political events surrounding them. Some students are taking their views . . . to a new level by campaigning for the candidate they support."

How Do You Set Up a Mock Election?

1. Choose issues and candida and then set up a mock election in your classroom could focus on the nation state, or local level.)

2. Create the materials of ar election, such as the pollir place, ballots, and posters

3. Campaign for the candida or the issues you support.

4. Conduct the voting.

5. Prepare mock media repo the election's outcome. Yo may want to interview vo

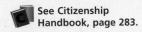

See Citizenship Handbook, page 283.

For more about citizenship and vo

RESEARCH LINKS CLASSZONE.COM

Changes in Ideas About Democracy

JEFFERSONIAN DEMOCRACY	JACKSONIAN DEMOCRACY
government for the people by capable, well-educated leaders	government by the people
democracy in political life	democracy in social, economic, and political life
championed the cause of the farmer in a mainly agricultural society	championed the cause of the farmer and the laborer in an agricultural and industrial society
limited government	limited government, but with a strong president

SKILLBUILDER Interpreting Charts
1. *What do you think was the most important change in democracy?*
2. *Did Jefferson or Jackson exercise more power?*

A New Political Era Begins

Jackson's inauguration began a new political era. In his campaign, he had promised to reform government. He started by replacing many government officials with his supporters. This practice of giving government jobs to political backers became known as the **spoils system**. The name comes from a statement that "to the victor belong the spoils [possessions] of the enemy." Jackson's opponents charged that the practice was corrupt. But he defended it, noting that it broke up one group's hold on government.

As president, Jackson would face three major issues—the status of Native Americans, the rights of the states, and the role of the Bank of the United States. In the next section, you will learn how Jackson's policies affected Native Americans.

⓵ Assessment

Terms & Names

plain the gnificance of:
ohn Quincy Adams
ndrew Jackson
acksonian emocracy
poils system

2. Using Graphics

Use a chart to identify important biographical information about Andrew Jackson.

Life of Andrew Jackson	
Youthful life	
Road to Congress	
War hero	
Appeal to voters	

3. Main Ideas

a. How did Andrew Jackson react to the election of 1824? Why?

b. What factors helped Jackson win the presidency in 1828?

c. What was the effect of expanding voting rights?

4. Critical Thinking

Analyzing Points of View
What are reasons for and against the spoils system?

THINK ABOUT
• the effects of giving government workers lifetime jobs
• the effects of rewarding political supporters

IVITY OPTIONS

EOGRAPHY
MATH

Find out which states Jackson and Adams won in the 1828 election. Show the results on a **map** or **chart** that includes vote totals and percentages.

2

Jackson's Policy Toward Native Americans

MAIN IDEA	WHY IT MATTERS NOW	TERMS & NAMES
During Jackson's presidency, Native Americans were forced to move west of the Mississippi River.	This forced removal forever changed the lives of Native Americans in the United States.	Sequoya Indian Removal Act	Indian Terri Trail of Tea Osceola

ONE AMERICAN'S STORY

In 1821, a brilliant Cherokee named <u>Sequoya</u> (sih KWOY uh) invented a writing system for the Cherokee language. Using this simple system, the Cherokees soon learned to read and write. A traveler in 1828 marveled at how many Cherokees had learned to read and write without schools or even paper and pens.

> *A VOICE FROM THE PAST*
>
> I frequently saw as I rode from place to place, Cherokee letters painted or cut on the trees by the roadside, on fences, houses, and often on pieces of bark or board, lying about the houses.
>
> **Anonymous traveler,** quoted in the *Advocate*

Sequoya hoped that by gaining literacy—the ability to read and write—his people could share the power of whites and keep their independence. But even Sequoya's invention could not save the Cherokees from the upheaval to come. In this section, you will learn about President Jackson's policy toward Native Americans and its effects.

Sequoya in
writing sys
86 characte
shown here
Cherokee la

Native Americans in the Southeast

Since the 1600s, white settlers had pushed Native Americans westward as they took more and more of their land. However, there were still many Native Americans in the East in the early 1800s. Some whites hoped that the Native Americans could adapt to the white people's way of life. Others wanted the Native Americans to move. They believed this was the only way to avoid conflict over land. Also, many whites felt that Native Americans were "uncivilized" and did not want to live near them.

By the 1820s, about 100,000 Native Americans remained east of the Mississippi River. The majority were in the Southeast. The major tribes

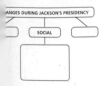

Taking Notes

Jse your chart to
ake notes about
ocial changes.

ANGES DURING JACKSON'S PRESIDENCY

SOCIAL

ding History

ading a
Use the map
ge 376 to
e Native
ican lands
Southeast.

were the Cherokee, Chickasaw, Choctaw, Creek, and Seminole. Whites called them the Five Civilized Tribes because they had adopted many aspects of white culture. They held large areas of land in Georgia, the Carolinas, Alabama, Mississippi, and Tennessee.

The Cherokee Nation

More than any other Southeastern tribe, the Cherokee had adopted white customs, including their way of dressing. Cherokees owned prosperous farms and cattle ranches. Some even had slaves. From Sequoya, they acquired a written language, and they published their own newspaper, the *Cherokee Phoenix*. Some of their children attended missionary schools. In 1827, the Cherokees drew up a constitution based on the U.S. Constitution and founded the Cherokee Nation.

A year after the Cherokees adopted their constitution, gold was discovered on their land in Georgia. Now, not only settlers but also miners wanted these lands. The discovery of gold increased demands by whites to move the Cherokees. The federal government responded with a plan to remove all Native Americans from the Southeast.

Jackson's Removal Policy

Andrew Jackson had long supported a policy of moving Native Americans west of the Mississippi. He first dealt with the Southeastern tribes after the War of 1812. The federal government ordered Jackson, then acting as Indian treaty commissioner, to make treaties with the Native Americans of the region. Through these treaties forced on the tribes, the government gained large tracts of land.

Jackson believed that the government had the right to regulate where Native Americans could live. He viewed them as conquered subjects who lived within the borders of the United States. He thought that Native Americans had one of two choices. They could adopt white culture and become citizens of the United States. Or they could move into the Western territories. They could not, however, have their own governments within the nation's borders.

After the discovery of gold, whites began to move onto Cherokee land. Georgia and other Southern states passed laws that gave them the right to take over Native American lands. When the Cherokee and other tribes protested, Jackson supported the states.

To solve the problem, Jackson asked Congress to pass a law that would require Native Americans to either move west or submit to state laws. Many Americans objected to Jackson's proposal. Massachusetts congressman Edward Everett opposed removing Native Americans against their will to a distant land. There, he said, they would face "the

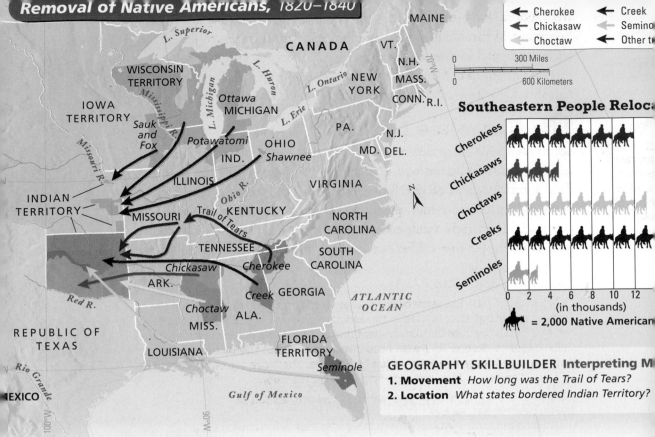

Southeastern People Reloca:

Cherokees	Chickasaws	Choctaws	Creeks	Seminoles

0   2   4   6   8   10   12
(in thousands)

= 2,000 Native American

GEOGRAPHY SKILLBUILDER Interpreting M
1. **Movement** How long was the Trail of Tears?
2. **Location** What states bordered Indian Territory?

perils and hardships of a wilderness." Religious groups such as the Quakers also opposed forced removal of Native Americans. After heated debate, Congress passed the **Indian Removal Act** in 1830. The act called for the government to negotiate treaties that would require Native Americans to relocate west.

Jackson immediately set out to enforce the law. He thought his policy was "just and liberal" and would allow Native Americans to keep their way of life. Instead, his policy caused much hardship and forever changed relations between whites and Native Americans.

Reading **H**
B. Drawing Conclusions What were sons for an against the Removal Ac

The Trail of Tears

As whites invaded their homelands, many Native Americans saw no other choice but to sign treaties exchanging their land for land in the West. Under the treaties, Native Americans would be moved to an area that covered what is now Oklahoma and parts of Kansas and Nebraska. This area came to be called **Indian Territory.**

Beginning in the fall of 1831, the Choctaw and other Southeast tribes were removed from their lands and relocated to Indian Territory. The Cherokees, however, first appealed to the U.S. Supreme Court to protect their land from being seized by Georgia. In 1832, the Court, led by Chief Justice John Marshall, ruled that only the federal government, not the states, could make laws governing the Cherokees. This ruling meant that the Georgia laws did not apply to the Cherokee Nation. However, both Georgia and President Jackson ignored the Supreme Court. Jackson said, "John Marshall has made his decision. . . . Now let him enforce it."

A small group of Cherokees gave up and signed a treaty to move west. But the majority of the Cherokees, led by John Ross, opposed the treaty. Jackson refused to negotiate with these Cherokees.

In 1838, federal troops commanded by General Winfield Scott rounded up about 16,000 Cherokees and forced them into camps. Soldiers took people from their homes with nothing but the clothes on their backs. Over the fall and winter of 1838–1839, these Cherokees set out on the long journey west. Forced to march in the cold, rain, and snow without adequate clothing, many grew weak and ill. One-fourth died. The dead included John Ross's wife. One soldier never forgot what he witnessed on the trail.

*ding***History**
cognizing
ts What
ened to
herokees
esult of
dian
val Act?

A VOICE FROM THE PAST

Murder is murder and somebody must answer, somebody must explain the streams of blood that flowed in the Indian country in . . . 1838. Somebody must explain the four-thousand silent graves that mark the trail of the Cherokees to their exile. I wish I could forget it all, but the picture of six-hundred and forty-five wagons lumbering over the frozen ground with their Cargo of suffering humanity still lingers in my memory.

John G. Burnett, quoted in *The Native Americans,* edited by Betty and Ian Ballantine

This harsh journey of the Cherokee from their homeland to Indian Territory became known as the **Trail of Tears.**

HISTORY *through* ART

In 1838, the Cherokees left their homeland by wagon, horse, donkey, and foot, forced to travel hundreds of miles along the Trail of Tears. This painting is by Robert Lindneux, a 20th-century artist.

How does this portrayal of the Trail of Tears reflect continuity and change in 19th-century American life?

Native American Resistance

Osceola led the Seminoles in their fight against removal.

Not all the Cherokees moved west in 1838. That fall, soldiers had rounded up an old Cherokee farmer named Tsali and his family, including his grown sons. On the way to the stockade, they fought the soldiers. A soldier was killed before Tsali fled with his family to the Great Smoky Mountains in North Carolina. There they found other Cherokees. The U.S. Army sent a message to Tsali. If he and his sons would give themselves up, the others could remain. They surrendered, and all except the youngest son were shot. Their sacrifice allowed some Cherokees to stay in their homeland.

Other Southeast tribes also resisted relocation. In 1835, the Seminoles refused to leave Florida. This refusal led to the Second Seminole War. One elderly Seminole explained why he could not leave: "If suddenly we tear our hearts from the homes around which they are twined [wrapped around], our heart strings will snap."

One of the most important leaders in the war was **Osceola** (AHS ee OH luh). Hiding in the Everglades, Osceola and his band used surprise attacks to defeat the U.S. Army in many battles. In 1837, Osceola was tricked into capture when he came to peace talks during a truce. He later died in prison. But the Seminoles continued to fight. Some went deeper into the Everglades, where their descendants live today. Others moved west. The Second Seminole War ended in 1842.

Some tribes north of the Ohio River also resisted relocation. The Shawnee, Ottawa, Potawatomi, Sauk, and Fox were removed to Indian Territory. But in 1832, a Sauk chief named Black Hawk led a band of Sauk and Fox back to their lands in Illinois. In the Black Hawk War, the Illinois militia and the U.S. Army crushed the uprising.

In the next section, you will learn about other issues Jackson faced, especially increasing tensions between various sections of the country.

Backgroun
The Semino
fought thre
wars agains
U.S. govern
between 18
and 1858, v
their resista
ended.

Section 2 Assessment

1. Terms & Names

Explain the significance of:
- Sequoya
- Indian Removal Act
- Indian Territory
- Trail of Tears
- Osceola

2. Using Graphics

Use a chart to list the reasons for Jackson's Native American removal policy.

Reasons Native Americans Were Forced West		
Economic	Political	Social

What do you think was the main reason?

3. Main Ideas

a. How did President Jackson justify the Indian Removal Act?

b. In what ways did Native Americans resist the Indian Removal Act?

c. What were the consequences of the Indian Removal Act?

4. Critical Thinking

Recognizing Effects
What were some econom
effects of the Indian Rem
Act on Native Americans?
On whites?

THINK ABOUT
- what the Native Americans lost
- what the white settlers gained

ACTIVITY OPTIONS

GEOGRAPHY

MATH

Use the map on page 376 to estimate the distance traveled by each of the five Southeastern tribes. Show your calculation on a **map** or **chart**.

Conflicts Over States' Rights

MAIN IDEA	WHY IT MATTERS NOW	TERMS & NAMES
...truggled to keep Southern ...m breaking away from the ...er the issue of tariffs.	Disputes about states' rights and federal power remain important in national politics.	John C. Calhoun Tariff of Abominations doctrine of nullification
		Webster-Hayne debate Daniel Webster secession

ONE AMERICAN'S STORY

Raised in South Carolina, **John C. Calhoun** was elected to the U.S. Congress at the age of 28. He soon became one of its leaders. Calhoun supported the need for a strong central government and also spoke out against sectionalism.

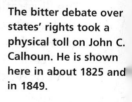

A VOICE FROM THE PAST

What is necessary for the common good may apparently be opposed to the interest of particular sections. It must be submitted to [accepted] as the condition of our [nation's] greatness.

John C. Calhoun, quoted in *John C. Calhoun: American Portrait* by Margaret L. Coit

But Calhoun's concern for the economic and political well-being of his home state of South Carolina, and the South in general, later caused him to change his beliefs. He became a champion of states' rights.

In this section, you will learn how two strong-willed men—Calhoun and Jackson—came in conflict over the issue of states' rights.

The bitter debate over states' rights took a physical toll on John C. Calhoun. He is shown here in about 1825 and in 1849.

Rising Sectional Differences

Andrew Jackson had taken office in 1829. At the time, the country was being pulled apart by conflicts among its three main sections—the Northeast, the South, and the West. Legislators from these regions were arguing over three major economic issues: the sale of public lands, internal improvements, and tariffs.

The federal government had acquired vast areas of land through conquests, treaties, and purchases. It raised money partly by selling these public lands. However, Northeasterners did not want public lands in the West to be sold at low prices. The cheap land would attract workers who were needed in the factories of the Northeast. But Westerners wanted

Taking Notes

Use your chart to take notes about political changes.

CHANGES DURING JACKSON'S PRESIDENCY

POLITICAL

Prosperity and Panic

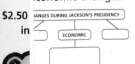

MAIN IDEA	WHY IT MATTERS NOW	TERMS & NAMES
Jackson's policies caused the economy to collapse after he left office and affected the next election.	The condition of the economy continues to affect the outcomes of presidential elections.	inflation depression Martin Van Buren Whig Party Panic of 1837 William He... John Tyler

ONE AMERICAN'S STORY

Nicholas Biddle was the president of the powerful Second Bank of the United States—the bank that Andrew Jackson believed to be corrupt. Jackson declared war on Biddle and the bank. But Biddle felt sure of his political power.

A VOICE FROM THE PAST

I have always deplored making the Bank a [political] question, but since the President will have it so, he must pay the penalty of his own rashness. . . . [M]y hope is that it will contribute to relieve the country of the domination of these miserable [Jackson] people.

Nicholas Biddle, from a letter to Henry Clay dated August 1, 1832

In this section, you will read about Jackson's war on the bank.

Mr. Biddle's Bank

The Second Bank of the United States was the most powerful bank in the country. It held government funds and issued money. As its president, Nicholas Biddle set policies that controlled the nation's money supply.

Although the bank was run efficiently, Jackson had many reasons to dislike it. For one thing, he had come to distrust banks after losing money in financial deals early in his career. He also thought the bank had too much power. The bank made loans to members of Congress, and Biddle openly boasted that he could influence Congress. In addition, Jackson felt the bank's lending policies favored wealthy clients and hurt the average person.

To operate, the bank had to have a charter, or a written grant, from the federal government. In 1832, Biddle asked Congress to renew the bank's charter, even though it would not expire until 1836. Because 1832 was an election year, he thought Jackson would agree to renewal rather than risk angering its supporters. But Jackson took the risk.

Nicholas Bi...
the preside...
powerful S...
Bank of the...
States, loca...
Philadelphi...

Ec

Taking Notes

Use your chart to make notes about economic changes.

CHANGES DURING JACKSON'S PRESIDENCY

ECONOMIC

$2.50 in

$3.00 in

Jackson's War on the Bank

When Congress voted to renew the bank's charter, Jackson vetoed the renewal. In a strongly worded message to Congress, Jackson claimed the bank was unconstitutional. He said the bank was a monopoly that favored the few at the expense of the many. The Supreme Court earlier had ruled that the bank was constitutional. But Jackson claimed elected officials had to judge the constitutionality of a law for themselves. They did not need to rely on the Supreme Court. His veto message also contained this attack on the bank.

A VOICE FROM THE PAST

It is to be regretted that the rich and powerful too often bend the acts of government to their selfish purposes. . . . Distinctions in society will always exist under every just government. . . . [B]ut when the laws undertake to . . . make the rich richer and the potent more powerful, the humble members of society . . . have a right to complain of the injustice of their Government.

Andrew Jackson, veto message, July 10, 1832

Jackson's war on the bank became the main issue in the presidential campaign of 1832. The National Republican Party and its candidate, Henry Clay, called Jackson a tyrant. They said he wanted too much power as president. The Democrats portrayed Jackson as a defender of the people. When he won reelection, Jackson took it as a sign that the public approved his war on the bank.

In his second term, Jackson set out to destroy the bank before its charter ended in 1836. He had government funds deposited in state banks, which opponents called Jackson's "pet banks." Biddle fought back by making it harder for people to borrow money. He hoped the resulting economic troubles would force Jackson to return government deposits to the bank. Instead, the people rallied to Jackson's position. Eventually, the bank went out of business. Jackson had won the war, but the economy would be a victim.

bulary
poly: a
any or
with com-
control
a product
vice

ingHistory
lyzing
of View
easons did
n have for
g to
the
Bank of
ited States?

son Fights the Second Bank

political cartoon, Jackson fights the many-
monster—the Second Bank of the United
and its branches—with a cane labeled "VETO."

esident Jackson

ne labeled
"ETO"

cholas Biddle

ce-President
n Buren

Prosperity Becomes Panic

Most of the nation prospered during Jackson's last years in office. Because it was easier to borrow money, people took out loans to buy public lands, and the economy boomed. But the "pet banks" issued too much paper money. The rise in the money supply made each dollar worth less. As a result, prices rose. **Inflation,** which is an increase in prices and decrease in the value of money, was the outcome. To fight inflation, Jackson issued an order that required people to pay in gold or silver for public lands.

Jackson left office proud of the nation's prosperity. But it was a puffed-up prosperity. Like a balloon, it had little substance. Because of Jackson's popularity, his vice-president, **Martin Van Buren,** was elected president in 1836. Within a few months after Van Buren took office, a panic—a widespread fear about the state of the economy—spread throughout the country. It became known as the **Panic of 1837.**

People took their paper money to the banks and demanded gold or silver in exchange. The banks quickly ran out of gold and silver. When the government tried to get its money from the state banks, the banks could not pay. The banks defaulted, or went out of business. A **depression,** or severe economic slump, followed.

The depression caused much hardship. Because people had little money, manufacturers no longer had customers for their goods. Almost 90 percent of factories in the East closed in 1837. Jobless workers had no way of buying food or paying rent. People went hungry. They lived in shelters or on the streets, where many froze in the winter. Every section of the country suffered, but the depression hit hardest in the cities. Farmers were hurt less because they could at least grow their own food. The depression affected politics, too.

Reading **H**
B. Recogniz
Effects Wh
were the sh
term and lc
term effect
Jackson's w
the bank?

The Rise of the Whig Party

In the depths of the depression, Senators Henry Clay and Daniel Webster argued that the government needed to help the economy. Van Buren disagreed. He believed that the economy would improve if left alone. He argued that "the less government interferes with private pursuits the better for the general prosperity." Many Americans blamed Van Buren for the Panic, though he had taken office only weeks before it started. The continuing depression made it almost impossible for him to win reelection in 1840.

Van Buren faced a new political party in that election. During Jackson's war on the national bank, Clay, Webster, and other Jackson opponents had formed the **Whig Party**. It was named after a British party that opposed royal power. The Whigs opposed the concentration of power in the chief executive—whom they mockingly called "King Andrew" Jackson. In 1840, the Whigs chose **William Henry Harrison** of Ohio to run for president and **John Tyler** of Virginia to run for vice-president.

*ing*History
king
nces Why
e Whigs
to nomi-
candidate
arrison,
id not have
political

The Whigs nominated Harrison largely because of his military record and his lack of strong political views. Harrison had led the army that defeated the Shawnees in 1811 at the Battle of Tippecanoe. He also had been a hero during the War of 1812. The Whigs made the most of Harrison's military record and his nickname, "Old Tippecanoe." The phrase "Tippecanoe and Tyler too" became the Whig election slogan.

The Election of 1840

During the 1840 election campaign, the Whigs emphasized personalities more than issues. They tried to appeal to the common people, as Andrew Jackson had done. Harrison was the son of a Virginia plantation owner. However, because he had settled on a farm in Ohio, the Whigs said Harrison was a true Westerner. They used symbols of the frontier, such as a log cabin, to represent Harrison. The Whigs contrasted Harrison with the wealthy Van Buren. Harrison won in a close election.

At his inauguration, the 68-year-old president spoke for nearly two hours in cold March weather with no hat or coat. Later, he was caught in the rain. He came down with a cold that developed into pneumonia. On April 4, 1841, one month after being inaugurated, Harrison died—the first president to die in office. Vice-President Tyler became president.

The election of 1840 showed the importance of the West in American politics. In the next chapter, you'll learn more about the lure of the West and the westward expansion of the United States.

ion **4** *Assessment*

Terms & Names

lain the
 gnificance of:
flation
artin Van Buren
nic of 1837
pression
hig Party
lliam Henry
rrison
n Tyler

2. Using Graphics

Use a diagram to list the events that led to the closing of the Second Bank of the United States.

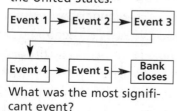

What was the most significant event?

3. Main Ideas

a. Why did Jackson declare war on the Second Bank of the United States?

b. How did Jackson kill the bank?

c. What role did Jackson's popularity play in the elections of 1836 and 1840?

4. Critical Thinking

Comparing What strategy did the Whig Party use in the 1840 election?

THINK ABOUT

- how Harrison was portrayed
- what group of voters it was trying to attract

VITY OPTIONS

GUAGE ARTS

ART

Imagine yourself as a presidential candidate in 1840. Focusing on the economy as an issue, write a campaign **slogan** or create a **banner** to rally support.

TERMS & NAMES

Briefly explain the significance of each of the following.

1. John Quincy Adams
2. Jacksonian democracy
3. spoils system
4. Sequoya
5. Indian Removal Act
6. Trail of Tears
7. secession
8. inflation
9. depression
10. Whig Party

REVIEW QUESTIONS

Politics of the People (pages 369–373)

1. How was Jackson different from earlier presidents?
2. How did Jackson appeal to voters in his election campaign of 1828?

Jackson's Policy Toward Native Americans (pages 374–378)

3. What were Georgia's policies toward Native Americans?
4. What was Jackson's position on Native Americans in the United States?
5. How did the Indian Removal Act affect Native Americans?

Conflicts over States' Rights (pages 379–383)

6. How did the issue of tariffs divide the country?
7. Why did nullification threaten the nation?
8. How was the nullification crisis resolved?

Prosperity and Panic (pages 384–387)

9. Why did Jackson oppose the Second Bank of the United States?
10. What were the effects of Jackson's war on the bank?

CRITICAL THINKING

1. USING YOUR NOTES: FINDING MAIN IDEAS

Use your completed chart to answer the questions.

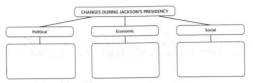

CHANGES DURING JACKSON'S PRESIDENCY

Political | Economic | Social

a. What do you think was the most positive chang of the Jackson era? Explain.
b. What was the most negative change? Explain.
c. Based on these changes, how would you describ the characteristics of the Jackson era?

2. ANALYZING LEADERSHIP

What was the basis of Andrew Jackson's power as president?

3. APPLYING CITIZENSHIP SKILLS

How did the majority of voters in the presidential elections of 1828 and 1840 exercise their vote in a similar way?

4. THEME: ECONOMICS IN HISTORY

Based on its economic effects, was Jackson's decis to end the national bank a good one? Explain.

5. MAKING INFERENCES

In what ways did Andrew Jackson's policy toward Native Americans reflect bias?

Interact *with* History

Now that you have read the chapter, do you thin qualities that made Jackson a strong military lead made him a good president? Explain your answe

VISUAL SUMMARY

Major Issues of Jackson's Presidency

POLICY TOWARD NATIVE AMERICANS	CONFLICT OVER STATES' RIGHTS	WAR ON BANK OF THE UNITED STATES
White settlers wanted Native American lands.	Sectional differences developed.	Second Bank of the United States economic and political power.
Jackson proposed Indian Removal Act of 1830.	Jackson supported strong central government.	Jackson opposed bank and vetoed renewal of its charter.
Thousands of Native Americans removed to Indian Territory.	South Carolina threatened to secede over tariff issue, but compromise reached.	Bank driven out of business, but Jackson's policies eventually led to inflation and depression.

Use the graph and your knowledge of U.S. history to answer questions 1 and 2.

Additional Test Practice, pp. S1–S33.

Voter Participation, 1824 & 1828 Elections

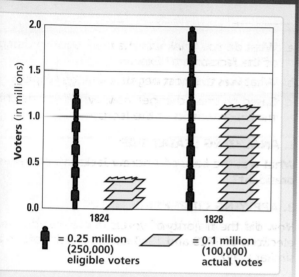

= 0.25 million
(250,000)
eligible voters

= 0.1 million
(100,000)
actual votes

Source: *Historical Statistics of the United States*

What does the red body figure represent on the graph?

A. .01 million eligible voters

B. .25 million eligible voters

C. .01 million actual voters

D. .25 million actual voters

2. Approximately what percentage of eligible voters cast their ballots in 1828?

A. 15 percent

B. 30 percent

C. 60 percent

D. 90 percent

In this speech Daniel Webster is speaking out against nullification. Use the quotation and your knowledge of U.S. history to answer question 3.

PRIMARY SOURCE

When my eyes shall be turned to behold for the last time the sun in heaven, may I not see him shining on the broken and dishonored fragments of a once glorious Union. . . . Liberty and Union, now and forever, one and inseparable!

Daniel Webster, a speech in the U.S. Senate, January 26, 1830

3. Which sentence sums up Webster's point of view?

A. A divided Union would be an impressive sight.

B. Webster has much to do before he dies.

C. Environmental protection laws are important.

D. A strong federal government is best for all states.

TEST PRACTICE
CLASSZONE.COM

ALTERNATIVE ASSESSMENT

WRITING ABOUT HISTORY

Write an **editorial** to convince voters to select the Whig candidate in 1840, William Henry Harrison. Focus on the beliefs and image of the Whig party as well as the personal characteristics of Harrison.

A good editorial supports an opinion with facts.

Read editorials from a local newspaper to become familiar with the persuasive language.

COOPERATIVE LEARNING

Working in a small group, help plan and write a proposal outlining a solution to the problems between settlers and Native Americans in the southeast in the early 1800s. List ideas and identify their positives and negatives. Divide the tasks of outlining, writing, editing, and presenting your plan to the class.

INTEGRATED TECHNOLOGY

DESIGNING A POLITICAL CAMPAIGN WEB SITE

Plan a Web site for candidate Andrew Jackson for the 1828 presidential campaign. Use the Internet and library resources to locate information about Jackson's personal and political life.

- Design the Web site to include biographical facts and photographs.

- Locate quotations from speeches and other primary sources. Include them to present Jackson's views on the major issues surrounding the campaign.

- Locate appropriate links for visitors to the Web site.

For more about Andrew Jackson . . .

INTERNET ACTIVITY
CLASSZONE.COM

Manifest Destiny 1810–1853

The inside of this wagon is only 4 feet by 10 feet—smaller than a modern minivan.

1821
Stephen Austin settles in Texas.

1824
Jedediah Smith finds South Pass.

An
ele

USA
World 1810

1815
Napoleon defeated at Waterloo.

1821
Mexico gains independence from Spain.

canvas roof with patch

kerosene lamp

butter churn

spinning wheel

chest of silverware

The year is 1844, and you live on a small rocky farm in Massachusetts. Your family has decided to move to Oregon to gain cheap, fertile land. Your father says this move will make your family better off—and give you a better future.

What might you gain or lose by going west?

What Do You Think?

- What do you think daily life on the trail west might be like?
- What might be the greatest obstacles that you face?
- Notice the necessities packed in this crowded wagon. What might have been left behind?

RESEARCH LINKS
CLASSZONE.COM

Visit the Chapter 13 links for more information about the westward movement.

1836
Martin Van Buren is elected president.

1841
John Tyler becomes president.

1844
James Polk is elected president.

1847
Mormons migrate to Utah.

1848
Zachary Taylor is elected president.

1853
United States makes Gadsden Purchase.

1853

1839
Opium War fought in China.

1840
Benito Juárez leads reform movement in Mexico.

1847
Liberia, established by a former American slave, proclaimed an independent nation.

Reading Strategy: Categorizing Information

What Do You Know?

What do you think of when you hear the phrase "the West"?
Who do you think moved west in the early 1800s?
What do you think drew them to the West?

Think About
- what you've learned about the West from movies or travel
- reasons that people move to new places today
- your responses to the Interact with History about going West (see page 391)

What Do You Want to Know?

What questions do you have about the westword movement of the 1800s? Write those questions in your notebook before you read the chapter.

Wagons, like the one in this m
photograph, carried many sett

Categorizing Information

To help you understand and remember historical information, learn to categorize. Categorizing means organizing information into groups. The chart below will help yo categorize the information in this chapter about the westward movement. Use the ch to categorize information about what groups went west, why they went, and what events brought each territory into the United States.

See Skillbuilder Handbook, page R6.

Taking Notes

	Types of people who traveled there	Why they went there	Key events that brought the territory into the United States
New Mexico			
Utah			
Oregon			
Texas			
California			

Trails West

MAIN IDEA	WHY IT MATTERS NOW	TERMS & NAMES

usands of settlers followed trails ough the West to gain land and a nce to make a fortune.

This migration brought Americans to the territories that became New Mexico, Oregon, and Utah.

Jedediah Smith
mountain man
Jim Beckwourth
land speculator

Santa Fe Trail
Oregon Trail
Mormon
Brigham Young

ONE AMERICAN'S STORY

The mountain man <u>Jedediah Smith</u> was leading an expedition to find a route through the Rocky Mountains when a grizzly bear attacked. The bear seized Smith's head in its mouth, shredded his face, and partially tore off one ear. Smith's men chased the bear away. Jim Clyman recalled the scene.

Jedediah Smith

A VOICE FROM THE PAST

I asked [Smith] what was best. He said, "One or two go for water and if you have a needle and thread get it out and sew up my wounds around my head." . . . I told him I could do nothing for his ear. "Oh, you must try to stitch it up some way or other," said he. Then I put in my needle and stitched it through and through.

Jim Clyman, quoted in *The West,* by Geoffrey C. Ward

Ten days after this attack, Jedediah Smith was ready to continue exploring. Smith was one of the daring fur trappers and explorers known as <u>mountain men</u>. The mountain men opened up the West by discovering the best trails through the Rockies. In this section, you will learn about the trails—and why pioneers followed them west.

Mountain Men and the Rendezvous

Mountain men spent most of the year alone, trapping small animals such as beavers. Easterners wanted beaver furs to make the men's hats that were in fashion at the time. To obtain furs, mountain men roamed the Great Plains and the Far West, the regions between the Mississippi River and the Pacific Ocean, and set traps in icy mountain streams.

Because of their adventures, mountain men such as Jedediah Smith and <u>Jim Beckwourth</u> became famous as rugged loners. However, they were not as independent as the legends have portrayed them. Instead, they were connected economically to the businessmen who bought their furs.

Taking Notes

Use your chart to take notes about New Mexico, Oregon, and Utah.

	Types of people who traveled there
New Mexico	
Utah	
Oregon	
Texas	
California	

One businessman, William Henry Ashley, created a trading arrangement called the rendezvous system. Under this system, individual trappers came to a pre-arranged site for a rendezvous with traders from the east. The trappers bought supplies from those traders and paid them in furs. The rendezvous took place every summer from 1825 to 1840. In that year, silk hats replaced beaver hats as the fashion, and the fur trade died out.

Mountain Men Open the West

During the height of the fur trade, mountain men worked some streams so heavily that they killed off the animals. This forced the trappers to search for new streams where beaver lived. The mountain men's explorations provided Americans with some of the earliest firsthand knowledge of the Far West. This knowledge, and the trails the mountain men blazed, made it possible for later pioneers to move west.

For example, thousands of pioneers used South Pass, the wide valley through the Rockies that Jedediah Smith had publicized. Smith learned of this pass, in present-day Wyoming, from Native Americans. Unlike the high northern passes used by Lewis and Clark, South Pass was low, so snow did not block it as often as it blocked higher passes. Also, because South Pass was wide and less steep, wagon trails could run through it.

Smith wrote to his brother that he wanted to help people in need: "It is for this that I go for days without eating, and am pretty well satisfied if I can gather a few roots, a few snails, . . . a piece of horseflesh, or a fine roasted dog."

Reading **Hi**
A. Reading
Map Find S
Pass on the
on page 39!
Notice whic
trails used t
pass.

The Lure of the West

Few of the people who went west shared Smith's noble motive. To many, the West with its vast stretches of land offered a golden chance to make money. The Louisiana Purchase had doubled the size of the United States, and some Americans wanted to take the land away from Native Americans who inhabited this territory.

People called **land speculators** bought huge areas of land. To speculate means to buy something in the hope that it will increase in value. If land value did go up, speculators divided their land holdings into smaller sections. They made great profits by selling those sections to the thousands of settlers who dreamed of owning their own farms.

Manufacturers and merchants soon followed the settlers west. They hoped to earn money by making and selling items that farmers needed. Other people made the trip to find jobs or to escape people to whom they owed money.

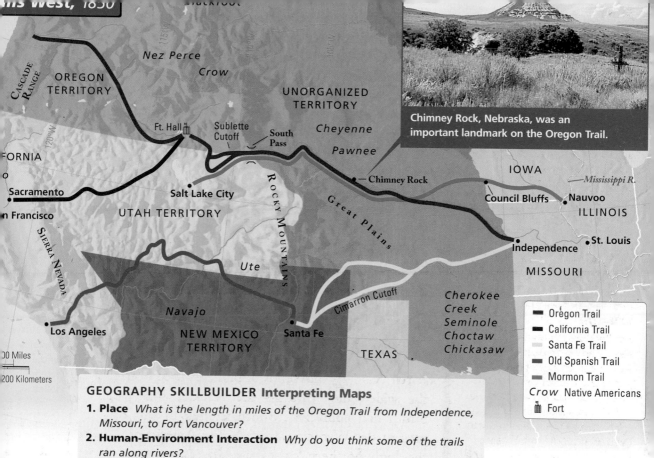

Chimney Rock, Nebraska, was an
important landmark on the Oregon Trail.

Legend:
- ▬ Oregon Trail
- ▬ California Trail
- ▬ Santa Fe Trail
- ▬ Old Spanish Trail
- ▬ Mormon Trail
- *Crow* Native Americans
- 🏛 Fort

GEOGRAPHY SKILLBUILDER Interpreting Maps

1. **Place** *What is the length in miles of the Oregon Trail from Independence, Missouri, to Fort Vancouver?*
2. **Human-Environment Interaction** *Why do you think some of the trails ran along rivers?*

The Trail to Santa Fe

Traders also traveled west in search of markets. After Mexico gained independence from Spain in 1821, it opened its borders to American traders, whom Spain had kept out. In response, the Missouri trader William Becknell set out with hardware, cloth, and china for Santa Fe, capital of the Mexican province of New Mexico. By doing so, he opened the **Santa Fe Trail,** which led from Missouri to Santa Fe. Once in Santa Fe, he made a large profit because the New Mexicans were eager for new merchandise.

When Becknell returned to Missouri weeks later, a curious crowd met him. One man picked up one of Becknell's bags and slit it open with a knife. As gold and silver coins spilled onto the street, the onlookers gasped. The news spread that New Mexico was a place where traders could become rich.

The following spring, Becknell headed to Santa Fe again. This time he loaded his trade goods into covered wagons, which Westerners called prairie schooners. Their billowing white canvas tops made them look like schooners, or sailing ships.

Becknell could not haul wagons over the mountain pass he had used on his first trip to Santa Fe. Instead, he found a cutoff, a shortcut that avoided steep slopes but passed through a deadly desert to the south. As his traders crossed the burning sands, they ran out of water. Crazed by

*ng***History**
ing
ces What
think
Missourians
decide to
r seeing
ll's
?

thirst, they lopped off mules' ears and killed their dogs to drink the animals' blood. Finally, the men found a stream. The water saved them from death, and they reached Santa Fe.

Becknell returned home with another huge profit. Before long, hundreds of traders and prairie schooners braved the cutoff to make the 800-mile journey from Missouri to New Mexico each year.

Oregon Fever

Hundreds of settlers also began migrating west on the **Oregon Trail,** which ran from Independence, Missouri, to the Oregon Territory. The first whites to cross the continent to Oregon were missionaries, such as Marcus and Narcissa Whitman in 1836. At that time, the United States and Britain were locked in an argument about which country owned Oregon. To the Whitmans' great disappointment, they made few converts among the Native Americans. However, their glowing reports of Oregon's rich land began to attract other American settlers.

Amazing stories spread about Oregon. The sun always shone there. Wheat grew as tall as a man. One tale claimed that pigs were "running about, . . . round and fat, and already cooked, with knives and forks sticking in them so you can cut off a slice whenever you are hungry."

Such stories tempted many people to make the 2,000-mile journey to Oregon. In 1843, nearly 1,000 people traveled from Missouri to Oregon. The next year, twice as many came. "The Oregon Fever has broken out," observed a Boston newspaper, "and is now raging."

One Family Heads West

The experiences of the Sager family show how difficult the trail could be. In 1844, Henry Sager, his wife, and six children left Missouri to find cheap, fertile land in Oregon. They had already moved four times in the past four years. Henry's daughter Catherine explained her family's moves.

> ### A VOICE FROM THE PAST
>
> Father was one of those restless men who are not content to remain in one place long at a time. . . . [He] had been talking of going to Texas. But mother, hearing much said about the healthfulness of Oregon, preferred to go there.
>
> **Catherine Sager,** quoted in *The West*, by Geoffrey C. Ward

The Oregon Trail was dangerous, so pioneers joined wagon trains. They knew their survival would depend on cooperation. Before setting out, the wagon train members agreed on rules and elected leaders to enforce them.

Even so, life on the trail was full of hardship. The Sagers had barely begun the trip when Mrs. Sager gave birth to her seventh child. Two months later, nine-year-old Catherine fell under a moving wagon, which crushed her left leg. Later, "camp fever" killed both of the Sager parents.

Even though the Sager parents had died, the other families in the train cooperated to help the Sager orphans make it to Oregon. There, the Whitmans agreed to adopt them. When Narcissa met them, Catherine recalled, "We thought as we shyly looked at her that she was the prettiest woman we had ever seen."

ding **History**
ding Main
What
ulties did
ies like the
s face?

The Mormon Trail

While most pioneers went west in search of wealth, one group migrated for religious reasons. The **Mormons,** who settled Utah, were members of the Church of Jesus Christ of Latter-Day Saints. Joseph Smith had founded this church in upstate New York in 1830. The Mormons lived in close communities, worked hard, shared their goods, and prospered.

The Mormons, though, also made enemies. Some people reacted angrily to the Mormons' teachings. They saw the Mormon practice of polygamy—allowing a man to have more than one wife at a time—as immoral. Others objected to their holding property in common.

ding **History**
alyzing
s Why did
am Young
he Mormons
h?

In 1844, an anti-Mormon mob in Illinois killed Smith. **Brigham Young,** the next Mormon leader, moved his people out of the United States. His destination was Utah, then part of Mexico. In this desolate region, he hoped his people would be left to follow their faith in peace.

In 1847, about 1,600 Mormons followed part of the Oregon Trail to Utah. There they built a new settlement by the Great Salt Lake. Because Utah has little rainfall, the Mormons had to work together to build dams and canals. These structures captured water in the hills and carried it to the farms in the valleys below. Through teamwork, they made their desert homeland bloom.

In the meantime, changes were taking place in Texas. As you will read in Section 2, Americans had been moving into that Mexican territory, too.

tion **1** **Assessment**

Terms & Names

plain **the**
ignificance of:
edediah Smith
mountain man
im Beckwourth
and speculator
anta Fe Trail
regon Trail
Mormon
righam Young

2. Using Graphics

Use a cluster diagram like the one shown to review details about the trails west.

Which trail would you have wanted to travel? Why?

3. Main Ideas

a. How did the mountain men open up the West for later settlement?

b. What are two examples of pioneer groups who used cooperation to overcome hardship?

c. What economic and social forces drew people to the West?

4. Critical Thinking

Drawing Conclusions Of all the hardships faced by people who went west, what do you think was the worst? Explain.

THINK ABOUT
• the mountain men
• William Becknell
• the Sagers
• the Mormons

IVITY **OPTIONS**

NGUAGE ARTS
ART

Research a pioneer from this section and either write a **letter** from his or her point of view to a friend or illustrate a **journal entry** with sights from your journey.

Survive the Oregon Trail!

You are part of a wagon train heading west on the Oregon Trail. During your journey, you will cross endless flat prairies and mountains that climb more steeply than a staircase. You will suffer through blazing heat and icy snowstorms. Food is scarce in the land you travel through—and human settlements are even more scarce.

COOPERATIVE LEARNING On this page are three challenges you will face on your journey. Working with a small group, create a solution for each challenge. To help your group work together, assign a task to each group member. You will find helpful information in the Data File. Be prepared to present your solutions to the class.

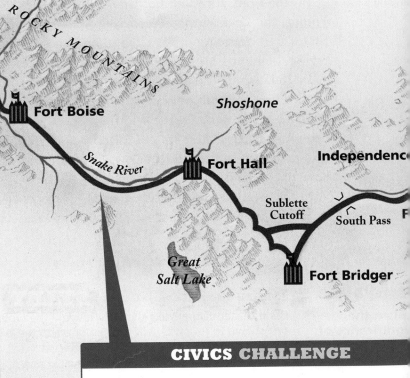

Fort Vancouver

Columbia River

Fort Walla Walla

Oregon City

Nez Perce

END

ROCKY MOUNTAINS

Fort Boise

Shoshone

Snake River

Fort Hall

Independence

Sublette Cutoff

South Pass

Great Salt Lake

Fort Bridger

SCIENCE CHALLENGE

"The most terrible mountains"

One pioneer called the Rockies "the most terrible mountains for steepness." Your oxen have struggled for hours to pull your wagon up a steep slope. Now you have to go down the other side without crashing—and wagon wheels have no brakes. How will you slow your descent? Use the Data File for help. Present your ideas using one of these options:

- Write instructions for climbing and descending the mountain.
- Illustrate your solution in a how-to diagram.

CIVICS CHALLENGE

"A thieving scoundrel"

You wake one morning to the sound of shouting. One of the men in the wagon train has been caught stealing another family's ox—to replace an ox that died from drinking bad water. The wagon train leader asks you to help decide how to punish the thief. Present your decision using one of these options:

- As a group, role-play a discussion of what the punishment should be.
- Write an explanation of a punishment to the wagon train leader.

The Journey

Distance: 2,000 miles

Length: 4–6 months

Average daily distance: 12–15 miles

Best time to travel: April–September

The Wagon

Size of box: 4 x 10 feet

Load: 1,600–2,500 pounds

Oxen needed per wagon: 4–8

Animals Taken

oxen, horses, dairy cows, cattle, chickens, mules, pigs, dogs, cats

Food Supplies

flour, corn meal, salt, baking soda, sugar, crackers, dried beans, rice, dried fruit, bacon, coffee, vinegar

Cooking Equipment

Dutch oven, large kettle, frying pan, bread pan, coffee grinder, rolling pin, tin cups and plates, water kegs, knives, spoons

Other Equipment

bedding, spare wagon parts, tar, rope, chains, pulleys, tools, fishing poles, guns, ammunition, matches, soap, medicines

Trail Hazards

Worst discomforts: heat, cold, wind, rain, dust, mud, mosquitoes, hunger, thirst

Biggest killer: disease

Most common accidents: shooting, drowning, crushing by wagon wheels, injuries from animals

For more about the Oregon Trail . . .

RESEARCH LINKS
CLASSZONE.COM

HEALTH CHALLENGE

"A grand blow-out"

n July 4, your wagon train stops near
dependence Rock for "a grand blow-out" to
elebrate your progress. Each family will bring
dish to the party. What will you cook that is
sty and nutritious? You might use supplies from
ur wagon and berries or animals from the area.
ook at the Data File for help. Present your
noice using one of these options:

Draw a picture of your dish and describe it.

Write an original recipe.

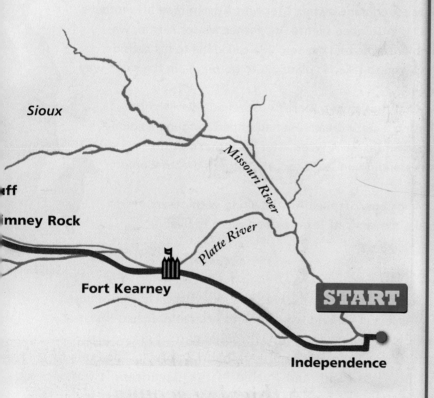

Sioux

Missouri River

ff

mney Rock

Platte River

Fort Kearney

START

Independence

ACTIVITY WRAP-UP

esent to the class Using the model shown here, ask and
swer questions about geographic patterns in the West.
oose the best questions to present to the class.

2

The Texas Revolution

MAIN IDEA	WHY IT MATTERS NOW	TERMS & NAMES
American and Tejano citizens led Texas to independence from Mexico.	The diverse culture of Texas has developed from the contributions of many different groups.	Stephen Austin William Tra[...] Tejano Juan Seguí[...] Antonio López de Santa Anna Battle of th[...] Lone Star R[...] Sam Houston

ONE AMERICAN'S STORY

Son of a bankrupt Missouri mine owner, **Stephen Austin** read his mother's letter, written in 1821, in stunned silence. His father, Moses Austin, was dead. In his last moments, she told her son, "He called me to his bedside, . . . he begged me to tell you to take his place . . . to go on . . . in the same way he would have done."

Stephen knew what that meant. Moses Austin had spent the last years of his life chasing a crazy dream. He had hoped to found a colony for Americans in Spanish Texas. A week after his father's death, Stephen Austin was standing on Texas soil. His father's dream would become his destiny.

This section explains how Stephen Austin, along with others, worked hard to make the lands of Texas a good place to live.

Stephen Au[...]

aking Notes

se your chart to
ke notes about
xas.

	Types of people who traveled there
Mexico	
n	
nia	

Spanish Texas

The Spanish land called *Tejas* (Tay•HAHS) bordered the United States territory called Louisiana. The land was rich and desirable. It had forests in the east, rich soil for growing corn and cotton, and great grassy plains for grazing animals. It also had rivers leading to natural ports on the Gulf of Mexico. It was home to Plains and Pueblo Native Americans. Even though *Tejas* was a state in the Spanish colony of New Spain, it had few Spanish settlers. Around 1819, Spanish soldiers drove off Americans trying to claim those lands as a part of the Louisiana Purchase.

In 1821, only about 4,000 *Tejanos* (Tay•HAH•nohs) lived in Texas. *Tejanos* are people of Spanish heritage who consider Texas their home. The Comanche, Apache, and other tribes fought fiercely against Spanish settlement of Texas. The Spanish officials wanted many more settlers to move to Texas. They hoped that new colonists would help to defend against Native Americans and Americans who illegally sneaked into Texas.

abulary

resarios:
iduals who
ed to recruit
ers for the

To attract more people to Texas, the Spanish government offered huge tracts of land to *empresarios*. But they were unable to attract Spanish settlers. So, when Moses Austin asked for permission to start a colony in Texas, Spain agreed. Austin was promised a large section of land. He had to agree that settlers on his land had to follow Spanish laws.

Mexican Independence Changes Texas

Shortly after Stephen Austin arrived in Texas in 1821, Mexico successfully gained its independence from Spain. *Tejas* was now a part of Mexico. With the change in government, the Spanish land grant given to Austin's father was worthless. Stephen Austin traveled to Mexico City to persuade the new Mexican government to let him start his colony. It took him almost a year to get permission. And the Mexican government would consent only if the new settlers agreed to become Mexican citizens and members of the Roman Catholic Church.

Between 1821 and 1827, Austin attracted 297 families to his new settlement. These original Texas settler families are known as the "Old Three Hundred." He demanded evidence that each family head was moral, worked hard, and did not drink. So law-abiding were his colonists that Austin could write to a new settler, "You will be astonished to see all our houses with no other fastening than a wooden pin or door latch."

The success of Austin's colony attracted more land speculators and settlers to Texas from the United States. Some were looking for a new life, some were escaping from the law, and others were looking for a chance to grow rich. By 1830, the population had swelled to about 30,000, with Americans outnumbering the *Tejanos* six to one.

Rising Tensions in Texas

ling History

r alyzing
s Why was
growing
n between
icans and
s?

As more and more Americans settled in Texas, tensions between them and the *Tejanos* increased. Used to governing themselves, Americans resented following Mexican laws. Since few Americans spoke Spanish, they were unhappy that all official documents had to be in that language. Slave owners were especially upset when Mexico outlawed slavery in 1829. They wanted to maintain slavery so they could grow cotton. Austin persuaded the government to allow slave owners to keep their slaves.

On the other hand, the *Tejanos* found the Americans difficult to live with, too. *Tejanos* thought that the Americans believed they were superior and deserved special privileges. The Americans seemed unwilling to adapt to Mexican laws.

EAST!

Emigrants who are desirious of assisting Texas at this important crisis of he affairs may have a free passage and equipments, by applying at the NEW-YORK and PHILADELPHIA HOTEL, On the Old Levee, near the Blue Stores.

Now is the time to ensure a fortune in Land: To all who remain in Texas during the War will be allowed 1280 Acres. To all who remain Six Months, 640 Acres. To all who remain Three Months, 320 Acres. And as Colonists, 4600 Acres for a family and 1470 Acres for a Single Man.

New Orleans, April 23d, 1836.

UNITED STATES

MEXICO

COAHUILA AND TEXAS (1824)

Gulf of Mexico

Posters such as the one above encouraged Americans from the East to settle in Texas. Some people scrawled G.T.T. on their doors to indicate they had "gone to Texas."

3

The War with Mexico

MAIN IDEA	WHY IT MATTERS NOW	TERMS & NAMES
The United States expanded its territory westward to stretch from the Atlantic to the Pacific coast.	Today, one-third of all Americans live in the areas added to the United States in 1848.	James K. Polk Winfield manifest destiny Treaty of Zachary Taylor Hidalgo Bear Flag Revolt Mexican

ONE AMERICAN'S STORY

Henry Clay sneered, "Who is **James K. Polk**?" Clay had just learned the name of the man nominated by Democrats to run against him for president in 1844. "A mistake!" answered Washington insiders.

News of Polk's nomination was flashed to the capital by the newly invented telegraph machine. People were convinced that the machine didn't work. How could the Democrats choose Polk? A joke!

Polk was America's first "dark horse," a candidate who received unexpected support. The Democrats had nominated this little-known man only when they could not agree on anyone else.

Still, Polk wasn't a complete nobody. He had been governor of Tennessee and served seven terms in Congress. Polk was committed to national expansion. He vowed to annex Texas and take over Oregon.

When the votes were counted, James Knox Polk became the 11th president of the United States. As you will read in this section, after his election Polk looked for ways to expand the nation.

James Po

Taking Notes

Use your chart to take notes about Oregon, New Mexico, and California.

	Types of people who traveled there
v Mexico	
h	
gon	
as	
fornia	

Americans Support Manifest Destiny

The abundance of land in the West seemed to hold great promise for Americans. Although populated with Native Americans and Mexicans, those lands were viewed by white settlers as unoccupied. Many Americans wanted to settle those lands themselves, and they worried about competition from other nations. Mexico occupied the southwest lands, and Britain shared the northwest Oregon Territory with the United States. Many Americans believed that the United States was destined to stretch across the continent from the Atlantic Ocean to the Pacific Ocean. In 1845, a newspaper editor named John O'Sullivan gave a name to that belief.

A VOICE FROM THE PAST

Our manifest destiny [is] to overspread and possess the whole of the continent which Providence [God] has given us for the development of the great experiment of liberty and . . . self-government.

John O'Sullivan, *United States Magazine and Democratic Review*

ing **History**

nwing
usions

were the
ves and
lives of the
f manifest
y?

John O'Sullivan used the word *manifest* to mean clear or obvious. The word *destiny* means events sure to happen. Therefore, **manifest destiny** suggested that expansion was not only good but bound to happen—even if it meant pushing Mexicans and Native Americans out of the way. After Polk's election in 1844, manifest destiny became government policy.

The term "manifest destiny" was new, but the idea was not. By the 1840s, thousands of Americans had moved into the Oregon Territory. Since 1818, Oregon had been occupied jointly by the United States and Britain. In his campaign, Polk had talked of taking over all of Oregon. "Fifty-four forty or fight!" screamed one of his slogans. The parallel of 54° 40′ N latitude was the northern boundary of the shared Oregon Territory.

Rather than fight for all of Oregon, however, Polk settled for half. In 1846, the United States and Great Britain agreed to divide Oregon at the 49th parallel. This agreement extended the boundary line already drawn between Canada and the United States. Today this line still serves as the border between much of the United States and Canada.

Oregon, 1846
- British territory under 1846 treaty
- U. S. territory under 1846 treaty

"Our manifest destiny [is] to . . . possess the whole of the continent."
John O'Sullivan

Troubles with Mexico

Polk had good reason for avoiding war with Britain over Oregon. By 1846, he had much bigger troubles brewing with Mexico over Texas.

In 1845, Congress admitted Texas as a slave state, in spite of Northern objections to the spread of slavery. However, Mexico still claimed Texas as its own. Mexico angrily viewed this annexation as an act of war. To make matters worse, Texas and Mexico could not agree on the official border between them. Texas claimed the Rio Grande, a river south of San Antonio, as its southern boundary. Mexico insisted on the Nueces (noo•AY•sis) River as the border of Texas. The difference in the distance between the two rivers was more than 100 miles at some points. Many thousands of miles of territory were at stake.

Mexico said it would fight to defend its claim. Hoping to settle the dispute peacefully, Polk sent John Slidell, a Spanish-speaking

ing **History**

ding a Map
e map on
08 to find
ations of
puted
between
nd Mexico.

ambassador, to offer Mexico $25 million for Texas, California, and New Mexico. But Slidell's diplomacy failed.

Believing that the American people supported his expansion plans, Polk wanted to force the issue with Mexico. He purposely ordered General **Zachary Taylor** to station troops on the northern bank of the Rio Grande. This river bank was part of the disputed territory. Viewing this as an act of war, Mexico moved an army into place on the southern bank. On April 25, 1846, a Mexican cavalry unit crossed the Rio Grande. They ambushed an American patrol and killed or wounded 16 American soldiers.

When news of the attack reached Washington, Polk sent a rousing war message to Congress, saying, "Mexico has invaded our territory and shed American blood upon American soil." Two days later, Congress declared war. The War with Mexico had begun. Thousands of volunteers, mostly from western states, rushed to enlist in the army. Santa Anna, who was president of Mexico, built up the Mexican army.

However, Americans had mixed reactions to Polk's call for war. Illinois representative Abraham Lincoln questioned the truthfulness of the president's message and the need to declare war. Northeasterners questioned the justice of men dying in such a war. Slavery became an issue in the debates over the war. Southerners saw expansion into Texas as an opportunity to extend slavery and to increase their power in Congress. To

Reading **Hi**
C. Analyzin
Causes How
the War wit
Mexico star

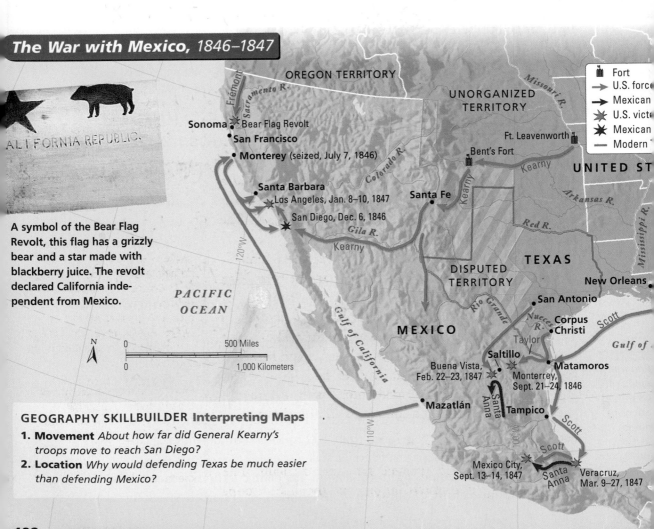

The War with Mexico, 1846–1847

A symbol of the Bear Flag Revolt, this flag has a grizzly bear and a star made with blackberry juice. The revolt declared California independent from Mexico.

GEOGRAPHY SKILLBUILDER Interpreting Maps
1. **Movement** *About how far did General Kearny's troops move to reach San Diego?*
2. **Location** *Why would defending Texas be much easier than defending Mexico?*

prevent this from happening, antislavery representatives introduced a bill to prohibit slavery in any lands taken from Mexico. Frederick Douglass, the abolitionist, summarized the arguments.

Despite opposition, the United States plunged into war. In May 1846, General Taylor led troops into Mexico. Many Americans thought it would be easy to defeat the Mexicans, and the war would end quickly.

Capturing New Mexico and California

Not long after the war began, General Stephen Kearny (KAHR•nee)— a U.S. Army officer—and his men left Fort Leavenworth, Kansas, with orders to occupy New Mexico. Then they were to continue west to California. As his troops marched along the Santa Fe Trail, they sang songs like this one.

Six weeks and 650 hot and rugged miles later, Kearny's army entered New Mexico. Using persuasion instead of force, he convinced the Mexican troops that he meant to withdraw. This allowed him to take New Mexico without firing a shot. Then Kearny and a small force of soldiers marched on toward California, which had only 8,000 to 12,000 Mexican residents. The remaining force moved south toward Mexico.

In California, Americans led by the explorer John C. Frémont rebelled against Mexican rule in the **Bear Flag Revolt.** They arrested the Mexican commander of Northern California and raised a crude flag showing a grizzly bear sketched in blackberry juice. The rebels declared California independent of Mexico and named it the Republic of California. In the fall, U.S. troops reached California and joined forces with the rebels. Within weeks, Americans controlled all of California.

The Invasion of Mexico

The defeat of Mexico proved far more difficult. The Mexican army was much larger, but the U.S. troops

ing History
king
nces
oes this
upport the
f manifest
y?

STRANGE *but* True

SANTA ANNA'S LOST LEG

Santa Anna lost his left leg in a battle with the French. In 1842, he held a funeral for his severed limb. On that day, church and political officials followed the dictator's leg through the streets of Mexico City to its final resting place—an urn placed on a column.

Two years later, an angry mob broke the urn and threw the leg away. The leg was rescued by a loyal soldier who took it home and hid it.

Thirty years later, that soldier visited Santa Anna and returned the bones of his long-lost leg.

Mexican army was much larger, but the U.S. troops were led by well-trained officers. American forces invaded Mexico from two directions.

General Taylor battled his way south from Texas toward the city of Monterrey in northern Mexico. On February 22, 1847, his 4,800 troops met General Santa Anna's 15,000 Mexican soldiers near a ranch called Buena Vista. After the first day of fighting, Santa Anna sent Taylor a note offering him a chance to surrender. Taylor declined. At the end of the second bloody day of fighting, Santa Anna reported that "both armies have been cut to pieces." However, it was Santa Anna who retreated after the Battle of Buena Vista. The war in the north of Mexico was over.

In southern Mexico, fighting continued. A second force led by General **Winfield Scott** landed at Veracruz on the Gulf of Mexico and battled inland toward Mexico City. Outside the capital, Scott met fierce resistance at the castle of Chapultepec (chuh•POOL•tuh•pek). About 1,000 soldiers and 100 young military cadets bravely defended the fortress. Despite their determined resistance, Mexico City fell to Scott in September 1847. As he watched, a Mexican officer sighed and said, "God is a Yankee."

Backgroun
General Wir
Scott had be
a national h
during the V
of 1812.

The Mexican Cession

On February 2, 1848, the war officially ended with the **Treaty of Guadalupe Hidalgo** (gwah•duh•LOOP•ay hih•DAHL•go). In this treaty, Mexico recognized that Texas was part of the United States, and the

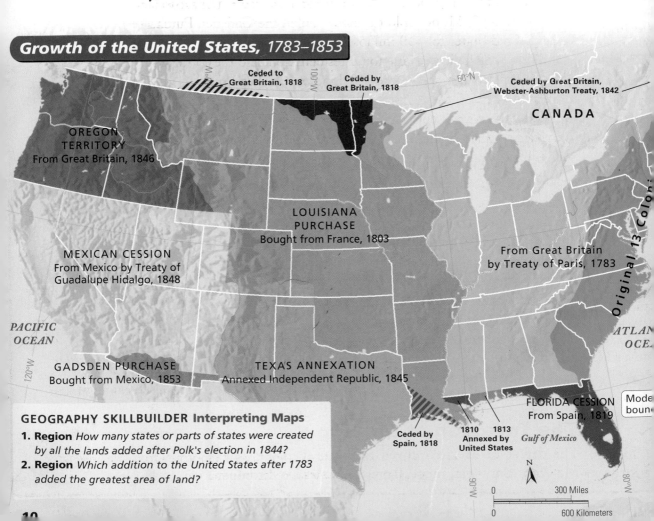

Growth of the United States, *1783–1853*

Ceded to Great Britain, 1818

Ceded by Great Britain, 1818

Ceded by Great Britain, Webster-Ashburton Treaty, 1842

CANADA

OREGON TERRITORY
From Great Britain, 1846

LOUISIANA PURCHASE
Bought from France, 1803

MEXICAN CESSION
From Mexico by Treaty of Guadalupe Hidalgo, 1848

From Great Britain by Treaty of Paris, 1783

Original 13 Coloni

PACIFIC OCEAN

GADSDEN PURCHASE
Bought from Mexico, 1853

TEXAS ANNEXATION
Annexed Independent Republic, 1845

FLORIDA CESSION
From Spain, 1819

ATLAN
OCE

Mode
boun

Ceded by Spain, 1818

1810
Annexed by United States

1813

Gulf of Mexico

GEOGRAPHY SKILLBUILDER Interpreting Maps
1. **Region** *How many states or parts of states were created by all the lands added after Polk's election in 1844?*
2. **Region** *Which addition to the United States after 1783 added the greatest area of land?*

N

0   300 Miles

0   600 Kilometers

ding **History**

ding Main

What were
hree main
of the
of the
v of
alupe
go?

Rio Grande was the border between the nations. Mexico also ceded, or gave up, a vast region known as the **Mexican Cession.** This area included the present-day states of California, Nevada, Utah, most of Arizona, and parts of New Mexico, Colorado, and Wyoming. Together with Texas, this land amounted to almost one-half of Mexico. The loss was a bitter defeat for Mexico, particularly because many Mexicans felt that the United States had provoked the war in the hope of gaining Mexican territory.

In return, the United States agreed to pay Mexico $15 million. The United States would also pay the $3.25 million of claims U.S. citizens had against Mexico. Finally, it also promised to protect the approximately 80,000 Mexicans living in Texas and the Mexican Cession.

Mexicans living in the United States saw the conquest of their land differently. Suddenly they were a minority in a nation with a strange language, culture, and legal system. At the same time, they would make important contributions to their new country. They taught new settlers how to develop the land for farming, ranching, and mining. A rich new culture resulted from the blend of many cultures in the Mexican Cession.

ing **History**

king
nces
lid the
l States
large price
e Gadsden
se?

"From Sea to Shining Sea"

The last bit of territory added to the continental United States was a strip of land across what is now southern New Mexico and Arizona. The government wanted the land as a location for a southern transcontinental railroad. In 1853, Mexico sold the land—called the Gadsden Purchase—to the United States for $10 million.

On July 4, 1848, in Washington, President Polk laid the cornerstone of a monument to honor George Washington. In Washington's day, the western border of the United States was the Mississippi River. The United States in 1848 now stretched "from sea to shining sea." In August, Polk learned that gold had been found in California. In the next section, you will read about the California gold rush.

tion **3** Assessment

Terms & Names

plain the
gnificance of:
mes K. Polk
anifest destiny
achary Taylor
ear Flag Revolt
infield Scott
eaty of
uadalupe
dalgo
exican Cession

2. Using Graphics

Review the chapter
and find five key events
to place on a time line
as shown.

War with Mexico

| event | event | event |

1846 ———————— 1848

| event | event |

3. Main Ideas

a. How did the acquisitions of Oregon and the Mexican Cession relate to the idea of manifest destiny?

b. Why were some people opposed to the War with Mexico?

c. What does the phrase "sea to shining sea" mean?

4. Critical Thinking

Comparing Compare the different ways land was acquired by the United States in the period of manifest destiny from 1844 to 1853.

THINK ABOUT

• the acquisition of the Oregon Territory
• lands in the Southwest

IVITY OPTIONS

MATH

EOGRAPHY

In an almanac, find the current population of the states formed from the Mexican Cession. Create a **graph** or a **map** to display the information.

The California Gold Rush

MAIN IDEA	WHY IT MATTERS NOW	TERMS & NAMES
Gold was found in California, and thousands rushed to that territory. California quickly became a state.	The gold rush made California grow rapidly and helped bring about California's cultural diversity.	forty-niner John Sut *Californio* James M Mariano Vallejo Californi

ONE AMERICAN'S STORY

Luzena Wilson said of the year 1849, "The gold excitement spread like wildfire." The year before, James Marshall had discovered gold in California. Luzena's husband decided to become a <u>forty-niner</u>—someone who went to California to find gold, starting in 1849.

Most forty-niners left their families behind, but Luzena traveled to California with her husband. She soon discovered that women—and their homemaking skills—were rare in California. Shortly after she arrived, a miner offered her five dollars for the biscuits she was baking. Shocked, she just stared at him. He quickly doubled his offer and paid in gold. Luzena realized she could make money by feeding miners, so she opened a hotel.

In this section, you will read about the forty-niners like the Wilsons and what their mining experiences were like. You will also discover how the gold rush boosted California's economy and changed the nation's history.

This woma
carrying fo
miners, jus
Luzena Wi

Taking Notes

se your chart to
ake notes about
alifornia.

	Types of people who traveled there
Mexico	
on	
s	
ornia	

California Before the Rush

Before the forty-niners came, California was populated by as many as 150,000 Native Americans and 8,000 to 12,000 *Californios*—settlers of Spanish or Mexican descent. Most *Californios* lived on huge cattle ranches. They had acquired their estates when the Mexican government took away the land that once belonged to the California missions.

One important *Californio* was **Mariano Vallejo** (mah•RYAH•noh vah•YEH•hoh). A member of one of the oldest Spanish families in America, he owned 250,000 acres of land. Proudly describing the accomplishments of the *Californios*, Vallejo wrote, "We were the pioneers of the Pacific coast . . . while General Washington was carrying on the war of the Revolution." Vallejo himself had been the commander of Northern California when it belonged to Mexico.

bulary

gration:
ovement
ople into a
ry or region
e they were
orn

When Mexico owned California, its government feared American immigration and rarely gave land to foreigners. But **John Sutter**, a Swiss immigrant, was one exception. Dressed in a secondhand French army uniform, Sutter had visited the Mexican governor in 1839. A charming man, Sutter persuaded the governor to grant him 50,000 acres in the unsettled Sacramento Valley. Sutter built a fort on his land and dreamed of creating his own personal empire based on agriculture.

In 1848, Sutter sent a carpenter named **James Marshall** to build a sawmill on the nearby American River. One day Marshall inspected the canal that brought water to Sutter's Mill. He later said, "My eye was caught by a glimpse of something shining. . . . I reached my hand down and picked it up; it made my heart thump for I felt certain it was gold."

Rush for Gold

News of Marshall's thrilling discovery spread rapidly. From all over California, people raced to the American River—starting the **California gold rush**. A gold rush occurs when large numbers of people move to a site where gold has been found. Throughout history, people have valued gold because it is scarce, beautiful, easy to shape, and resistant to tarnish.

Miners soon found gold in other streams flowing out of the Sierra Nevada Mountains. Colonel R. B. Mason, the military governor of California, estimated that the region held enough gold to "pay the cost of the present war with Mexico a hundred times over." He sent this news to Washington with a box of gold dust as proof.

The following year thousands of gold seekers set out to make their fortunes. A forty-niner who wished to reach California from the East had a choice of three routes, all of them dangerous:

*ng*History

egorizing
vere the
different
f trans-
on that
took to
California?

1. Sail 18,000 miles around South America and up the Pacific coast—suffering from storms, seasickness, and spoiled food.
2. Sail to the narrow Isthmus of Panama, cross overland (and risk catching a deadly tropical disease), and then sail to California.
3. Travel the trails across North America— braving rivers, prairies, mountains, and all the hardships of the trail.

Because the adventure was so difficult, most gold seekers were young men. "A gray beard is almost as rare as a petticoat," observed one miner. Luzena Wilson said that during the six months she lived in the mining city of Sacramento, she saw only two other women.

HISTORY *through*ART

Clipper ship companies used advertising cards such as this one to convince Easterners that their line provided the fastest, most pleasant voyages.

How has the artist tried to project a positive image for sailing west?

112 DAYS TO
SAN FRANCISCO.
MERCHANTS' EXPRESS LINE OF CLIPPER SHIPS.
Dispatching the Greatest Number of Vessels !
SMALLEST, CHEAPEST AND FASTEST VESSEL NOW UP !

THE MAGNIFICENT OUT-AND-OUT CLIPPER SHIP
WHITE SWALLOW
BUNKER, Commander, is now rapidly loading at PIER 16 E. R.
This splendid vessel, having made *very short passages*, and delivered her cargo in *unexceptionable order*, has established a reputation that will ensure immediate dispatch.
RANDOLPH M. COOLEY, 88 Wall Street,
Agents in San Francisco, Messrs. DE WITT, KITTLE & Co.
(FOSTINE BUILDING.)
NESBITT & CO., PRINTERS.

Life in the Mining Camps

The mining camps had colorful names like Mad Mule Gulch, Hangtown, and Coyote Diggings. They began as rows of tents along the streams flowing out of the Sierra Nevada. Gradually, the tents gave way to rough wooden buildings that housed stores and saloons.

Mining camps could be dangerous. One woman who lived in the region wrote about camp violence.

A VOICE FROM THE PAST

In the short space of twenty-four days, we have had murders, fearful accidents, bloody deaths, a mob, whippings, a hanging, . . . and a fatal duel.

Louise Clappe, quoted in *Frontier Women*

The mining life was hard for other reasons. Camp gossip told of miners who grew rich overnight by finding eight-pound nuggets, but in reality, such easy pickings were rare. Miners spent their days standing knee-deep in icy streams, where they sifted through tons of mud and sand to find small amounts of gold. Exhaustion, poor food, and disease all damaged the miners' health.

Not only was acquiring gold brutally difficult, but the miners had to pay outrageously high prices for basic supplies. In addition, gamblers and con artists swarmed into the camps to swindle the miners of their money. As a result, few miners grew rich.

Miners from Around the World

About two-thirds of the forty-niners were Americans. Most of these were white men—many from New England. However, Native Americans, free blacks, and enslaved African Americans also worked the mines.

Thousands of experienced miners came from Sonora in Mexico. Other foreign miners came from Europe, South America, Australia, and China. Most of the Chinese miners were peasant farmers who fled from a region that had suffered several crop failures. By the end of 1851, one of every ten immigrants was Chinese.

Used to backbreaking labor in their homeland, the Chinese proved to be patient miners. They would take over sites that American miners had abandoned because the easy gold was gone. Through steady, hard work, the Chinese made these "played-out" sites yield profits. American miners resented the success of the Chinese and were suspicious of their different foods, dress, and customs. As the numbers of Chinese miners grew, American anger toward them also increased.

Reading **H**
B. Making Inferences
do you thin
in the minl
camps was
rough?

Reading **H**
**C. Analyzir
Causes** Wl
some Ame
resent Chir
miners?

Surface Mining

Gold is found in cracks, called veins, in the earth's rocky crust. As mountains and other outcrops of rock erode, the gold veins come to the surface. The gold breaks apart into nuggets, flakes, and dust. Flood waters then wash it downhill into stream beds. To mine this surface gold, forty-niners had to use tools designed to separate it from the mud and sand around it. American miners learned some technology from Mexicans who came from the mining region of Sonora.

Miners shoveled dirt into the sluice. The rushing water carried lightweight materials along with it. Heavy gold sank to the bottom and was trapped between the ridges.

A sluice was a series of long boxes with ridges on the bottom. Water ran through the sluice, which angled downward.

Although this photograph shows American and Chinese miners working together, in many places Americans chased the Chinese away.

...an miners introduced the use ...pan. A miner would fill a ...ith dirt and water. Then he ... swirl the pan. Water ...d over the sides, carrying ...eight minerals with it. Gold ...in the bottom.

CONNECT TO HISTORY

1. **Drawing Conclusions**
Which mining method could be used by an individual miner and which needed a group of miners? Explain your answer.

S See Skillbuilder Handbook, page R13.

CONNECT TO TODAY

2. **Researching** How is gold mined today?

For more about the California gold rush . . .

Conflicts Among Miners

A mixture of greed, anger, and prejudice caused some miners to cheat others. For example, I. B. Gilman promised to free an enslaved African American named Tom if he saved enough gold. For more than a year, Tom mined for himself after each day's work was done. When he finally had $1,000, Gilman gave him a paper saying he was free. The next day, the paper suspiciously disappeared. Even though Tom was certain he had been robbed, he couldn't prove it. He had to work for another year before Gilman would free him.

Once the easy-to-find gold was gone, American miners began to force Native Americans and foreigners such as Mexicans and Chinese out of the gold fields to reduce competition. This practice increased after California became a state in 1850. One of the first acts of the California state legislature was to pass the Foreign Miners Tax, which imposed a tax of $20 a month on miners from other countries. That was more than most could afford to pay. As the tax collectors arrived in the camps, most foreigners left.

Reading **H**
D. Analyzin
Causes How
did the stat
governmen
make minir
harder for
foreigners?

Driven from the mines, the Chinese opened shops, restaurants, and laundries. So many Chinese owned businesses in San Francisco that their neighborhood was called Chinatown, a name it still goes by today.

The Impact of the Gold Rush

By 1852, the gold rush was over. While it lasted, about 250,000 people flooded into California. This huge migration caused economic growth that changed California permanently. The port city of San Francisco grew to become a center of banking, manufacturing, shipping, and trade. Its population exploded from around 400 in 1845 to 35,000 in 1850. Sacramento became the center of a productive farming region.

However, the gold rush ruined many *Californios*. The newcomers did not respect *Californios*, their customs, or their legal rights. In many cases,

CAUSE AND EFFECT: U.S. Expansion, 1846–1853

CAUSE	EFFECT
Westward trails move thousands to new territories.	▶ Oregon Territory acquired by the United States.
Austin and others colonize Texas.	▶ Texas Revolution
United States annexes Texas.	▶ War with Mexico
Mexican Cession acquired by the United States.	▶ United States expands "sea to sea."
Transcontinental railroad route needed.	▶ Gadsden Purchase
Thousands of gold seekers rush to California.	▶ California becomes a state.

SKILLBUILDER Interpreting Charts
1. *Which two causes are related to transportation?*
2. *Which cause fulfilled the nation's "manifest destiny"?*

ling History

cognizing
s What
t did the
rush have
e people
ived in
rnia before
rty-niners
?

Americans seized their property. For example, Mariano Vallejo lost all but 300 acres of his huge estate. Even so, their Spanish heritage became an important part of California culture.

Native Americans suffered even more. Thousands of them died from diseases brought by the newcomers. The miners hunted down and killed thousands more. The reason was the Anglo-American belief that Native Americans stood in the way of progress. By 1870, California's Native American population had fallen from 150,000 to only about 58,000.

A final effect of the gold rush was that by 1849 California had enough people to apply for statehood. Skipping the territorial stage, California applied to Congress for admission to the Union and was admitted as a free state in 1850. Although its constitution outlawed slavery, it did not grant African Americans the vote.

Mariano Vallejo, unhappy that *Californio* culture was ignored in the new American California, named his home "Tear of the Mountain."

For some people, California's statehood proved to be the opportunity of a lifetime. The enslaved woman Nancy Gooch gained her freedom because of the law against slavery. She then worked as a cook and washerwoman until she saved enough money to buy the freedom of her son and daughter-in-law in Missouri. Nancy Gooch's family moved to California to join her. Eventually, they became so prosperous that they bought Sutter's sawmill, where the gold rush first started.

On a national level, California's statehood created turmoil. Before 1850, there was an equal number of free states and slave states. Southerners feared that because the statehood of California made free states outnumber slave states, Northerners might use their majority to abolish slavery. As Chapter 18 explains, conflict over this issue threatened the survival of the Union.

tion 4 Assessment

Terms & Names

plain the
gnificance of:
rty-niner
alifornio
ariano Vallejo
hn Sutter
mes Marshall
alifornia gold rush

2. Using Graphics

Use a chart like the one shown to review and record hardships faced by the forty-niners.

HARDSHIPS	
In the camps	
At work mining	

Which hardships would you have found most difficult?

3. Main Ideas

a. How did the California gold rush get started?

b. Why didn't many forty-niners become rich?

c. How did women and people of different racial, ethnic, or national groups contribute to the California gold rush?

4. Critical Thinking

Recognizing Effects
What were some of the effects of the California gold rush?

THINK ABOUT
- changes in San Francisco
- California's bid for statehood

IVITY OPTIONS

**SCIENCE
ECHNOLOGY**

Research the hazards of mining gold and either plan a **science exhibit** or give an **electronic presentation.**

VISUAL SUMMARY

Manifest Destiny

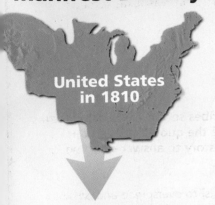

United States in 1810

Trails West

Mountain men and traders opened trails in the Far West. Pioneers then went west to gain land, wealth, or religious freedom.

The Texas Revolution

Americans moved into the Mexican territory of Texas. Conflicts led those Americans to revolt, and Texas gained independence.

The War with Mexico

President Polk wanted to expand the nation. He negotiated to gain Oregon. The United States fought Mexico to gain much of the Southwest.

The California Gold Rush

The discovery of gold lured thousands of people to California. California's economy and population grew, resulting in statehood.

United States in 1853

TERMS & NAMES

Briefly explain the significance of each of the following.

1. mountain man
2. Oregon Trail
3. Stephen Austin
4. *Tejano*
5. Antonio López de Santa Anna
6. manifest destiny
7. Bear Flag Revolt
8. Mexican Cession
9. forty-niner
10. California gold rush

REVIEW QUESTIONS

Trails West (pages 393–399)

1. What were three reasons why people moved west?
2. What were the three main trails that led to the West?
3. How did the Mormons make the land in Utah productive?

The Texas Revolution (pages 400–405)

4. Why were Texans unhappy with Mexican rule?
5. Why were the battles of the Alamo and San Jacinto important to the Texas Revolution?

The War with Mexico (pages 406–411)

6. What areas did the United States gain as a result of Americans' belief in manifest destiny?
7. How is the Bear Flag Revolt related to the War with Mexico?
8. What lands did the United States acquire as a result of the Treaty of Guadalupe Hidalgo?

The California Gold Rush (pages 412–417)

9. Who were four groups of people who became forty-niners?
10. What were three ways California changed because of the gold rush?

CRITICAL THINKING

1. USING YOUR NOTES: CATEGORIZING INFORMATION

	Types of people who traveled there	Why they went there	Key events that allow to take ownership of
New Mexico			
Utah			
Oregon			
Texas			
California			

Using your completed chart, answer the questions below.

a. In what ways were the reaso people went west similar?
b. Which of the five regions list on your chart entered the U States peacefully?
c. Which event added the mos territory to the United State

2. ANALYZING LEADERSHIP

Think about the leaders discuss in this chapter. What character did they have that made them good leaders?

3. THEME: EXPANSION

How did the idea of manifest tiny help bring about the expa sion of the United States?

4. DRAWING CONCLUSIONS

How did the War with Mexico the California gold rush contri to the cultural diversity of the United States?

5. APPLYING CITIZENSHIP SK

What were the different view-points that people held about War with Mexico?

Interact with Histor

Based on this chapter, what do think you would have gained lost by going west?

e the map and your knowledge of U.S. history to
;wer questions 1 and 2.

ditional Test Practice, pp. S1-S33.

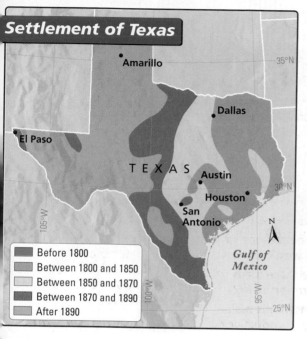

Settlement of Texas

- Amarillo
- Dallas
- El Paso
- T E X A S Austin
- Houston
- San Antonio
- 35°N
- 30°N
- 25°N
- 105°W
- 100°W
- 95°W
- N

Gulf of Mexico

- Before 1800
- Between 1800 and 1850
- Between 1850 and 1870
- Between 1870 and 1890
- After 1890

he area around which city in Texas was settled
rst?

. Houston

. Dallas

. San Antonio

. El Paso

2. In what general direction was Texas settled?

  A. north to south

  B. east to west

  C. west to east

  D. south to north

John O'Sullivan describes settling the United States in this quotation. Use the quotation and your knowledge of U.S. history to answer question 3.

PRIMARY SOURCE

Our manifest destiny[is] to overspread and possess the whole of the continent which Providence has given us for the development of the great experiment of liberty and . . . self-government.

John O'Sullivan, *United States Magazine and Democratic Review*

3. The passage supports which of the following points of view?

  A. Continental expansion by the United States is bound to happen.

  B. Continental expansion is limited by self-government.

  C. The claims of other countries to the same territory must be respected.

  D. Expansion across the entire continent will require some limits on liberty.

TEST PRACTICE
CLASSZONE.COM

RNATIVE ASSESSMENT

WRITING ABOUT HISTORY

e that you are a reporter for a newspaper in
rn California in 1849. Write a **news article** about
covery of gold. The article should follow the
rganization of a news article by answering the
ns *Who? What? Where? When? And How?*

an research your article by looking in books
t the California gold rush, in general histories
ifornia, and on the Internet.

PERATIVE LEARNING

ith a group of three or four other students to
 panel discussion that explores the different
ints surrounding the Mexican War. Research
es toward the war. Then outline and participate
anel discussion for the class.

INTEGRATED TECHNOLOGY ACTIVITY

DOING INTERNET RESEARCH

Life on the wagon trains was not like life "back east."

- On the Internet or in other sources, find primary sources about life on the wagon trains, such as letters, diaries, journals, newspaper articles, and books.

- Once you have collected a number of primary sources, present your findings to your class.

INTERNET ACTIVITY
CLASSZONE.COM

The poverty and overcrowding of the urban slums is the focus of this sketch.

Children found simple ways of entertaining themselves.

1828
Noah Webster publishes the *American Dictionary of the English Language.*

1829
David Walker prints *Appeal*, a pamphlet urging slaves to revolt.

USA
World   1820

1824
The British Parliament makes trade unions illegal.

1827
Ludwig van Beethoven dies.

1829
Louis Braille invents a raised type that allows blind people to read.

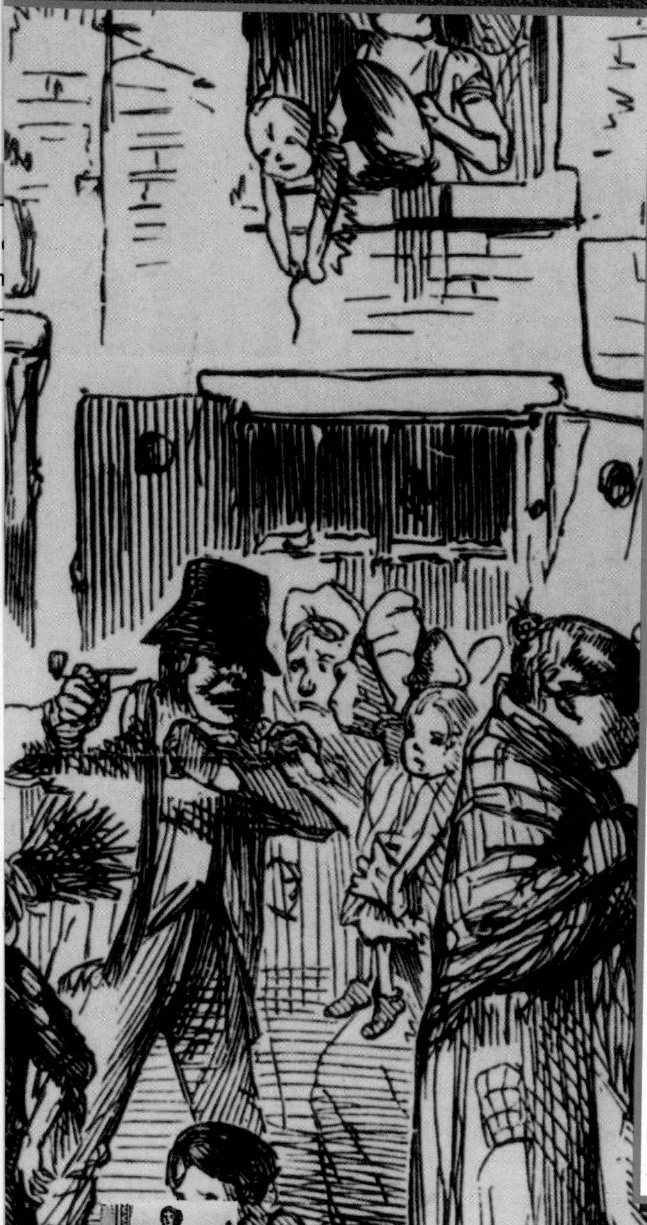

Interact *with* History

You are a writer who moves to New York in the mid-1800s. A newspaper hires you to write about reform. One day, you hear a speaker call for the end of slavery. Another day you talk to a factory worker whose pay has been cut. In the city, you see great poverty and suffering.

What reforms do you think will most benefit American society?

What Do You Think?

- **How might you persuade Americans to change life in the city?**
- **Should reform come about through new laws or through individual actions?**

RESEARCH LINKS
CLASSZONE.COM

Visit the Chapter 14 links for more information about the changing nation.

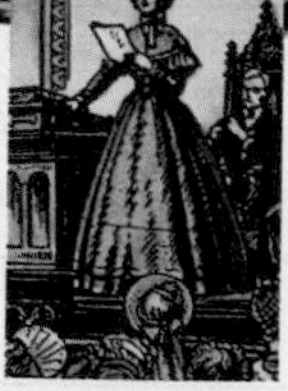

343
asks
etts
e to
e of
y ill.

1845
and's potato
ails, causing
famine.
ands flee to
America.

1848
The Seneca Falls Convention demands women's rights.

1848
A revolution in Germany fails. Some Germans move to America.

1851
Maine passes a law banning the sale of alcohol.

1854
Brazil's first railway opens.

1860

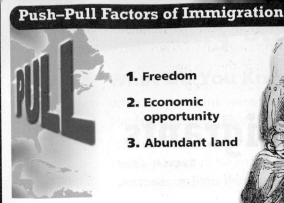

Push–Pull Factors of Immigration

PULL

1. **Freedom**
2. **Economic opportunity**
3. **Abundant land**

PUSH

1. **Population growth**
2. **Agricultural changes**
3. **Crop failures**
4. **Industrial Revolution**
5. **Religious and political turmoil**

push-pull factors. These forces push people out of their native lands and pull them toward a new place. **Push factors** included the following:

1. **Population growth.** Better food and sanitation caused Europe's population to boom after 1750, and the land became overcrowded.
2. **Agricultural changes.** As Europe's population grew, so did cities. Landowners wanted to make money selling food to those cities. New methods made it more efficient to farm large areas of land than to rent small plots to tenants. So landlords forced tenants off the land.
3. **Crop failures.** Poor harvests made it difficult for small farmers to pay their debts. Some of these farmers chose to start over in America. Crop failures also led to hunger, causing people to emigrate.
4. **Industrial Revolution.** Goods produced in factories became cheaper than goods produced by artisans. Suddenly out of work, some artisans took factory jobs. Others emigrated.
5. **Religious and political turmoil.** To escape religious persecution, Quakers fled Norway and Jews left Germany. Also, many Germans came to America after a revolution in Germany failed in 1848.

Immigrants chose the United States because of three main **pull factors**:

1. **Freedom.** As Gjert Hovland wrote, "Everyone has the freedom to practice the teaching and religion he prefers."
2. **Economic opportunity.** Immigrants sought a land where they could support their families and have a better future. Immigration often rose during times of U.S. prosperity and fell during hard times.
3. **Abundant land.** The acquisition of the Louisiana Purchase and the Mexican Cession gave the United States millions more acres of land. To land-starved Europeans, America was a land of opportunity.

Scandinavians Seek Land

Public land in America was sold for $1.25 an acre, which lured thousands of Scandinavians. At first, their governments tried to keep them at home. A Swedish law of 1768 restricted the right to emigrate. But growing poverty in Scandinavia caused officials to cancel this law in 1840.

Scandinavian clergymen also tried to halt the emigration. At first, they warned their church members against leaving the homeland. Eventually, though, the preachers realized their words had little effect. Some of them even went to America themselves.

Vocabular
tenant: ren

Vocabular
artisan: ski
worker

Reading
A. Solving
Problems
of the pus
tors were
lems. Whic
factors we
tions to w
problems?

ding History

aking
ences Why
ou think
dinavians
ed to places
felt familiar?

In the United States, Scandinavians chose regions that felt familiar. Many settled in the Midwest, especially Minnesota and Wisconsin. These states had lakes, forests, and cold winters like their homelands. A high proportion of Scandinavian immigrants became farmers.

Germans Pursue Economic Opportunity

Like the Scandinavians, many Germans moved to the Midwest. Germans especially liked Wisconsin because the climate allowed them to grow their traditional crop of oats. Some moved to Milwaukee, Wisconsin, because the Catholic bishop there was German. (In the 1800s, German Christian immigrants included both Catholics and Protestants.)

Germans also settled in Texas. In New Braunfels, a group of German nobles bought land and sold it in parcels to German immigrants. The town had to survive poor harvests and conflicts with Native Americans, but it eventually prospered. Germans also founded Fredericksburg, Texas, which still retains its German culture today.

Immigrants from Germany settled in cities as well as on farms or the frontier. German artisans opened businesses as bakers, butchers, carpenters, printers, shoemakers, and tailors. Many German immigrants achieved great success. For instance, in 1853 John Jacob Bausch and Henry Lomb started a firm to make eyeglasses and other lenses. Their company became the world's largest lens maker.

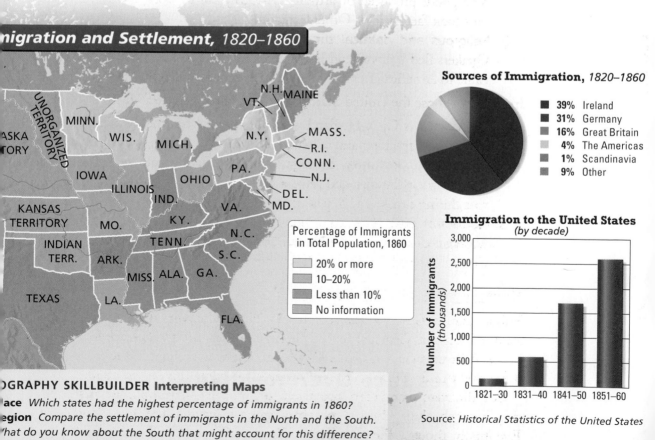

nigration and Settlement, *1820–1860*

Sources of Immigration, *1820–1860*

- 39% Ireland
- 31% Germany
- 16% Great Britain
- 4% The Americas
- 1% Scandinavia
- 9% Other

Percentage of Immigrants in Total Population, 1860

- 20% or more
- 10–20%
- Less than 10%
- No information

Immigration to the United States
(by decade)

Number of Immigrants (thousands): 3,000 / 2,500 / 2,000 / 1,500 / 1,000 / 500 / 0

1821–30   1831–40   1841–50   1851–60

Source: *Historical Statistics of the United States*

GRAPHY SKILLBUILDER Interpreting Maps

ace Which states had the highest percentage of immigrants in 1860?
egion Compare the settlement of immigrants in the North and the South.
hat do you know about the South that might account for this difference?

Some German immigrants were Jews. Many of them worked as traveling salespeople. They brought pins, needles, pots—and news—to frontier homes and mining camps. In time, some opened their own general stores. Other Jews settled in cities, where many found success.

For example, Alexander Rothschild worked as a grocer upon arriving in Hartford, Connecticut, in the 1840s. By 1851, he ran a popular hotel.

The Germans were the largest immigrant group of the 1800s and strongly influenced American culture. Many things we think of as originating in America came from Germany—the Christmas tree, gymnasiums, kindergartens, and the hamburger and frankfurter.

daily life

IMMIGRANT CULTURE

To maintain their culture, immigrants continued many of their traditional activities in the United States. For example, German culture is rich in music. German immigrants put together marching bands, symphony orchestras, and choruses.

In Ireland, many of the Irish had poured their energy into defying the British. This gave them experience with political organization. As a result, Irish immigrants became active in U.S. politics, especially in the cities.

Background
The hamburg
and frankfurt
are named aft
the German c
Hamburg and
Frankfurt am
Main.

The Irish Flee Hunger

Most Irish immigrants were Catholic. Protestant Britain had ruled Ireland for centuries—and controlled the Catholic majority by denying them rights. Irish Catholics could not vote, hold office, own land, or go to school. Because of the poverty produced by Britain's rule, some Irish came to America in the early 1800s.

Then, in 1845, a disease attacked Ireland's main food crop, the potato, causing a severe food shortage called a **famine**. The Irish Potato Famine killed 1 million people and forced many to emigrate. By 1854, between 1.5 and 2 million Irish had fled their homeland.

In America, Irish farmers became city-dwellers. Arriving with little or no savings, many of these immigrants had to settle in the port cities where their ships had docked. By 1850, the Irish made up one-fourth of the population of Boston, New York, Philadelphia, and Baltimore.

The uneducated Irish immigrants arrived with few skills and had to take low-paying, back-breaking jobs. Irish women took in washing or worked as servants. The men built canals and railroads across America. So many Irishmen died doing this dangerous work that people said there was "an Irishman buried under every [railroad] tie." In 1841, British novelist Charles Dickens observed the huts in which railroad workers lived.

Reading His
C. Drawing
Conclusions
did the effe
British rule n
it hard for Ir
immigrants
America to
good jobs?

A VOICE FROM THE PAST

The best were poor protection from the weather; the worst let in the wind and rain through the wide breaches in the roofs of sodden grass and in the walls of mud; some had neither door nor window; some had nearly fallen down.

Charles Dickens, quoted in *To Seek America*

The Irish competed with free blacks for the jobs that nobody else wanted. Both groups had few other choices in America in the 1800s.

U.S. Cities Face Overcrowding

Immigrants like the Irish and Germans flocked to American cities. So did native-born Americans, who hoped for the chance to make a better living. Between 1800 and 1830, New York's population jumped from 60,489 to 202,589. St. Louis doubled its population every nine years. Cincinnati grew even faster, doubling every seven years.

Rapid urban growth brought problems. Not enough housing existed for all the newcomers. Greedy landlords profited from the housing shortage by squeezing large apartment buildings onto small lots. Using every inch of space for rooms, these cramped living quarters lacked sunlight and fresh air. Their outdoor toilets overflowed, spreading disease. In such depressing urban neighborhoods, crime flourished.

American cities were unprepared to tackle these problems. In fact, before 1845, New York City had no public police force. Until the 1860s, it had only a volunteer fire department. And in 1857, the rapidly growing city had only 138 miles of sewers for 500 miles of streets.

Most immigrant groups set up aid societies to help newcomers from their country. Many city politicians also offered to assist immigrants in exchange for votes. The politicians set up organizations to help new arrivals find housing and work.

...ding History
...entifying
...ems What
...ems were
...cians trying
...ve by offer-
...o help new
...grants?

Some Americans Oppose Immigration

Some native-born Americans feared that immigrants were too foreign to learn American ways. Others feared that immigrants might come to outnumber natives. As a result, immigrants faced anger and prejudice. **Prejudice** is a negative opinion that is not based on facts. For example,

---

...TIZENSHIP TODAY

...Becoming a Citizen

...lost immigrants who came to America in the 1800s shared one ...hing: an appreciation for the nation's values and laws. As a result, ...any chose to become U.S. citizens.

This trend continues today. In recent decades, more than half a ...illion Vietnamese have immigrated to the United States. Many ...ecame citizens of their new country. One of them was Lam Ton, ...ho is a successful restaurant owner in Chicago. Ton viewed U.S. ...tizenship as both a privilege and a duty. ...We have to stick to this country and help ...do better," he said.

...Each year, immigrants from around ...e world are sworn in as U.S. citizens ...Citizenship Day, September 17. But ...st they must pass a test on English, ...e U.S. political system, and the ...hts and duties of citizenship.

...is young immigrant proudly holds
...his certificate of citizenship.

How Does Someone Become a Citizen?

1. In a small group, discuss what questions you would ask those seeking to become U.S. citizens.

2. Create a citizenship test using your questions.

3. Have another group take the test and record their scores.

4. Use the McDougal Littell Internet site to link to the actual U.S. citizenship test. Compare it to your test.

See Citizenship Handbook, page 281.

For more about becoming a U.S. citizen . . .

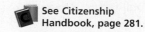

RESEARCH LINKS
CLASSZONE.COM

In 1844, a riot took place between Catholics and non-Catholics in Philadelphia. Several people were killed.

some Protestants in the 1800s believed that Catholics threatened democracy. Those Protestants feared that the Pope, the head of the Roman Catholic Church, was plotting to overthrow democracy in America.

Native-born Americans who wanted to eliminate foreign influence called themselves **nativists.** Some nativists refused to hire immigrants and put up signs like "No Irish need apply." In cities like New York and Boston, nativists formed a secret society. Members promised not to vote for any Catholics or immigrants running for political office. If asked about their secret group, they said, "I know nothing about it."

In the 1850s, nativists started a political party. Because of the members' answers to questions about their party, it was called the Know-Nothing Party. It wanted to ban Catholics and the foreign-born from holding office. It also called for a cut in immigration and a 21-year wait to become an American citizen. The Know-Nothings did elect six governors. But they disappeared quickly as a national party. Their northern and southern branches couldn't agree on the issue of slavery.

In spite of such barriers as prejudice, the immigrants of the 1800s had a strong impact on American culture. Writers and artists of the 1800s also shaped American culture. Section 2 discusses their influence.

Background Protestants feared the Po because in m European co tries, the Cat Church work closely with ruling monar

Section ❶ Assessment

1. Terms & Names

Explain the significance of:
- emigrant
- immigrant
- steerage
- push-pull factor
- famine
- prejudice
- nativist

2. Using Graphics

Use a cluster diagram like the one below to record details about immigration, such as which groups came, where they settled, and how they influenced America.

Immigration

3. Main Ideas

a. What were the push-pull factors that led to immigration?

b. How did the arrival of so many immigrants affect U.S. cities?

c. What was the Know-Nothing Party, and what was its point of view about immigration?

4. Critical Thinking

Analyzing Causes How the rapid increase in immigration cause conflict?

THINK ABOUT

- why Irish immigrants an free blacks competed fo jobs
- the growth of cities and the problems it created
- the prejudices of nativis
- religious differences

ACTIVITY OPTIONS

TECHNOLOGY

ART

Plan a **multimedia presentation** or design a **Web page** that shows immigrants the advantages of settling in the United States.

American Literature and Art

MAIN IDEA	WHY IT MATTERS NOW	TERMS & NAMES
by nature and democratic writers and artists produced America's greatest works.	Nineteenth-century writers such as Hawthorne and Thoreau laid the foundation for American literature.	romanticism transcendentalism Hudson River school civil disobedience

ONE AMERICAN'S STORY

Washington Irving wrote some of the first stories to describe America. For example, "Rip Van Winkle" tells of a man in New York State. Rip wakes up after a 20-year nap to find many changes. He goes to the inn, which once had a picture of King George on its sign.

> **A VOICE FROM THE PAST**
>
> The red coat was changed for one of blue and buff, a sword was held in the hand instead of a sceptre [staff of authority], the head was decorated with a cocked hat, and underneath was painted in large characters, GENERAL WASHINGTON.
>
> **Washington Irving,** "Rip Van Winkle"

In another Irving tale, "The Legend of Sleepy Hollow," a spooky creature chases a teacher.

While Rip slept, the Americans had fought and won their revolution!

Irving's work helped to win European respect for American writing for the first time. This section discusses other individuals of the 1800s who created uniquely American literature and art.

Writing About America

Irving and other writers were influenced by a style of European art called **romanticism**. It stressed the individual, imagination, creativity, and emotion. It drew inspiration from nature. American writers turned their interest in nature into a celebration of the American wilderness.

Many books featured the wilderness. James Fenimore Cooper wrote five novels about the dramatic adventures of wilderness scout Natty Bumppo. One that remains popular is *The Last of the Mohicans.* Francis Parkman wrote a travel book, *The Oregon Trail,* about the frontier trail.

Taking Notes

Use your chart to take notes about the influence of writers.

	How People
Immigrants	
Writers	
Reformers	
Abolitionists	
Women	

HISTORY *through*ART

Asher Durand was a founder of the Hudson River school of painting. His best-known work, *Kindred Spirits,* was painted in 1849. This romantic work shows two artists inspired by a beautiful landscape. The figures in the painting are Durand's friends, the poet William Cullen Bryant and the painter Thomas Cole.

Compare this painting to the one on page 180. Is the style different? If so, how?

In addition, writers began to use a more American style. A teacher and lawyer named Noah Webster gave guidelines to that style in his *American Dictionary of the English Language.* Webster first published his dictionary in 1828. He later revised it in 1840. The dictionary gave American, not British, spellings and included American slang.

Other writers besides Irving celebrated America's past. Henry Wadsworth Longfellow wrote many poems that retold stories from history. For example, "Paul Revere's Ride" depicted the Revolutionary hero's ride to warn of a British attack. Generations of students memorized lines from the poem, such as, "One if by land, and two if by sea; / And I on the opposite shore will be."

Creating American Art

European styles continued to influence American artists, but some took these styles in new directions. One group of painters influenced by romanticism worked near the Hudson River in New York State. **Hudson River school** artists painted lush natural landscapes. Several members of this school went west for a change of scenery. For example, Albert Bierstadt took several trips to America's mountainous West. He produced huge paintings that convey the majesty of the American landscape. (See page 310.)

kground
National
ubon Society,
se goal is the
ection of
life today, is
ed for John
es Audubon.

Other artists also went west. John James Audubon came to the United States from France at age 18. Traveling across the continent, Audubon sketched the birds and animals of his adopted country.

Enslaved African Americans also contributed to American art. They made beautiful baskets, quilts, and pottery. Most of these slaves remained anonymous, but one did not. David Drake worked in a South Carolina pottery factory and signed the pottery he created. He was the only factory worker to do so.

Following One's Conscience

By the 1840s, Americans took new pride in their emerging culture. Ralph Waldo Emerson, a New England writer, encouraged this pride. He urged Americans to cast off European influence and develop their own beliefs. His advice was to learn about life from self-examination and from nature as well as books.

Emerson's student, Henry David Thoreau, followed that advice. In 1845, Thoreau moved to a simple cabin he had built by Walden Pond near the town of Concord, Massachusetts. Thoreau furnished it with only a bed, a table, a desk, and three chairs. He wrote about his life in the woods in *Walden*. Thoreau said that people should live by their own individual standards.

> *"No law can be sacred to me but that of my nature."*
> **Ralph Waldo Emerson**

ding**History**
aking
ences What
ou think it
s to "hear
erent
mer"?

A VOICE FROM THE PAST

If a man does not keep pace with his companions, perhaps it is because he hears a different drummer. Let him step to the music which he hears, however measured or far away.

Henry David Thoreau, *Walden*

Emerson and Thoreau belonged to a group of thinkers with a new philosophy called **transcendentalism**. It taught that the spiritual world is more important than the physical world. It also taught that people can find the truth within themselves—through feeling and intuition.

Because Thoreau believed in the importance of individual conscience, he urged people not to obey laws they considered unjust. Instead of protesting with violence, they should peacefully refuse to obey those laws. This form of protest is called **civil disobedience**. For example, Thoreau did not want to support the U.S. government, which allowed slavery and fought the War with Mexico. Instead of paying taxes that helped to finance the war, Thoreau went to jail.

Another New England transcendentalist, Margaret Fuller, also called for change. In her magazine, *The Dial*, and in her book, *Woman in the Nineteenth Century*, Fuller argued for women's rights.

Connections TO LITERATURE

"CIVIL DISOBEDIENCE"

In his essay "Civil Disobedience," Thoreau wrote that "Under a government which imprisons any unjustly the true place for a just man is also a prison."

Thoreau did land in prison when he refused to pay his taxes. According to legend, Emerson visited Thoreau in jail and asked, "Why are you here?" Thoreau replied, "Why are you not here?"

In the 20th century, Mohandas K. Gandhi of India and Martin Luther King, Jr., of the United States both used civil disobedience to fight injustice.

Exploring the Human Heart

Like Thoreau, other writers broke with tradition. In 1855, poet Walt Whitman published *Leaves of Grass,* a book that changed American poetry. His bold, unrhymed poems praised ordinary people. Emily Dickinson lived in her family's home almost her entire life. She wrote poems on small pieces of paper that she sewed into booklets. Her subjects include God, nature, love, and death. Most of her 1,775 poems were published only after her death. Both Whitman and Dickinson shaped modern poetry by experimenting with language.

Fiction writers of the 1800s also shaped American literature. Edgar Allan Poe wrote terrifying tales that influence today's horror story writers. He also wrote the first detective story, "The Murders in the Rue Morgue."

Nathaniel Hawthorne depicted love, guilt, and revenge during Puritan times in *The Scarlet Letter.* The novel shows that harsh judgment without mercy can lead to tragedy. Hawthorne may have learned that lesson from his family history. One of his ancestors condemned people at the Salem witchcraft trials.

Herman Melville won fame by writing thrilling novels about his experiences as a sailor. In 1851, Melville published his masterpiece, *Moby Dick.* This novel tells about a man's destructive desire to kill a white whale. Although the novel was not popular when it was published, it is widely read now. Several movie versions exist.

These fiction writers portrayed the harmful effects of cruel actions. Other people thought that individuals could alter society for good. Section 3 describes those reformers.

*Reading*His

B. Recognizin Effects How did Poe influ the fiction th people read today?

Section 2 Assessment

1. Terms & Names

Explain the significance of:
- romanticism
- Hudson River school
- transcendentalism
- civil disobedience

2. Using Graphics

Use a chart like the one below to list important individual writers and artists. For each one, name or describe one of his or her works.

Writer or artist	His or her work

Which one would you like to learn more about? Why?

3. Main Ideas

a. What was romanticism and how did Americans adapt it?

b. What is civil disobedience and what did Thoreau do that is an example of it?

c. How did the writers of the mid-1800s shape modern literature?

4. Critical Thinking

Evaluating Why do you think the literature and art the mid-1800s are still valu

THINK ABOUT
- the way they feature U. history and culture
- their universal themes— themes that relate to al people in all time perio
- the way they reflect changes happening at th time

ACTIVITY OPTIONS

ART
TECHNOLOGY

Choose an American painting, sketch it, and make it into a **jigsaw puzzle;** or make an **audio recording** of a museum guide's description of it.

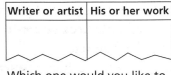

Reforming American Society

MAIN IDEA	WHY IT MATTERS NOW	TERMS & NAMES
...mid-1800s, several reform ...ents worked to improve ...n education and society.	Several laws and institutions, such as public schools, date back to this period.	revival Second Great Awakening temperance movement	labor union strike Horace Mann Dorothea Dix

ONE AMERICAN'S STORY

Anne Newport Royall wrote about America's growing interest in religion. She also described a preacher at a Tennessee **revival**, or meeting to reawaken religious faith.

A VOICE FROM THE PAST

His text was, "He that hath ears to hear, let him hear." The people must have been deaf indeed that could not have heard him. . . . He began low but soon bawled to deafening. He spit in his hands, rubbed them against each other, and then would smite them together, till he made the woods ring.

Anne Newport Royall, *Letters from Alabama*

This revival meeting took place during the Second Great Awakening.

Section 3 explains how, in the mid-1800s, many individuals called on Americans to reform, or to improve themselves and their society.

A Spirit of Revival

The renewal of religious faith in the 1790s and early 1800s is called the **Second Great Awakening**. Revivalist preachers said that anyone could choose salvation. This appealed to equality-loving Americans. Revivals spread quickly across the frontier. Settlers eagerly awaited the visits of preachers like Peter Cartwright. At the age of 16, Cartwright had given up a life of gambling and joined a Methodist Church. He became a minister and spent more than 60 years preaching on the frontier.

The revival also traveled to Eastern cities. There, former lawyer Charles Grandison Finney held large revival meetings. He preached that "all sin consists in selfishness" and that religious faith led people to help others. Such teaching helped awaken a spirit of reform. Americans began to believe that they could act to make things better.

Taking Notes

Use your chart to take notes about the influence of reformers.

	How People
Immigrants	
Writers	
Reformers	
Abolitionists	
Women	

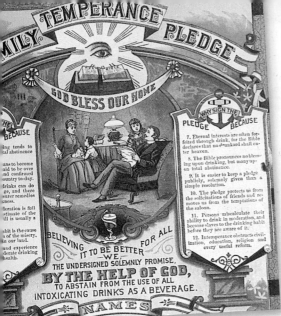

Temperance Societies

Led by churches, some Americans began the **temperance movement,** which is a campaign to stop the drinking of alcohol. Heavy drinking was common in the early 1800s. Some workers spent most of their wages on alcohol—leaving their families without enough money to live on. As a result, many women joined the temperance movement. "There is no reform in which women can act better or more appropriately than temperance," said Mary C. Vaughan.

Some temperance workers handed out pamphlets urging people to stop drinking. Others produced dramas, such as one entitled *The Drunkard,* to dramatize the evils of alcohol. In addition, temperance speakers traveled widely, asking people to sign a pledge to give up alcohol. By 1838, a million people had signed.

Temperance also won the support of business owners. Industry needed workers who could keep schedules and run machines. Alcohol made it hard for workers to do either. New England businessman Neal Dow led the fight to make it illegal to sell alcohol. In 1851, Maine banned the sale of liquor. By 1855, 13 other states passed similar laws. But many people opposed these laws, and most were repealed. Still, the movement to ban alcohol remained strong, even into the 20th century.

Temperance pledges often displayed inspiring pictures and mottoes.

Reading **Hi**
A. Evaluatin
How did the
perance mo
ment affect
developmer
drama?

Vocabulary
repeal: to ca

Fighting for Workers' Rights

As business owners tried to improve workers' habits, workers called for improvements in working conditions. Factory work was noisy, boring, and unsafe. In the 1830s, American workers began to organize.

The young women mill workers in Lowell, Massachusetts, started a labor union. A **labor union** is a group of workers who band together to seek better working conditions. In 1836, the mill owners raised the rent of the company-owned boarding houses where the women lived. About 1,500 women went on **strike,** stopping work to demand better conditions. Eleven-year-old Harriet Hanson helped lead the strikers.

A VOICE FROM THE PAST

I . . . started on ahead, saying, . . . "I don't care what you do, I am going to turn out, whether anyone else does or not," and I marched out, and was followed by the others. As I looked back at the long line that followed me, I was more proud than I have ever been since.

Harriet Hanson, quoted in *A People's History of the United States*

Other workers called for shorter hours and higher wages. In 1835 and 1836, 140 strikes took place in the eastern United States. Then the Panic of 1837 brought hard times. Jobs were scarce, and workers were afraid to cause trouble. The young labor movement fell apart. Even so, workers achieved a few goals. For example, in 1840 President Martin Van Buren ordered a ten-hour workday for government workers.

ground
dent Van
n's order
ced the
week from
60 hours.

Improving Education

In the 1830s, Americans also began to demand better schools. In 1837, Massachusetts set up the first state board of education in the United States. Its head was **Horace Mann**. Mann called public education "the great equalizer." He also argued that "education creates or develops new treasures—treasures never before possessed or dreamed of by any one." By 1850, many Northern states had opened public elementary schools.

Boston opened the first public high school in 1821. A few other Northern cities followed suit. In addition, churches and other groups founded hundreds of private colleges in the following decades. Many were located in states carved from the Northwest Territory. These included Antioch and Oberlin Colleges in Ohio, the University of Notre Dame in Indiana, and Northwestern University in Illinois.

Women could not attend most colleges. One exception was Oberlin. It was the first college to accept women as well as men. In 1849, English immigrant Elizabeth Blackwell became the first woman to earn a medical degree in the United States. Despite such individual efforts, it was rare for a woman to attend college until the late 1800s.

African Americans also faced obstacles to getting an education. This was especially true in the South. There, teaching an enslaved person to read had been illegal since the Nat Turner Rebellion in 1831. Enslaved African Americans who tried to learn were brutally punished. Even in the North, most public schools barred African-American children.

Mary Jane Patterson was the first African-American woman to earn a college degree. She graduated from Oberlin in 1862 and went on to work as a teacher.

ding History
king
ences
do you
women
frican
icans had a
time getting
ucation?

Few colleges accepted African Americans. Those that did often took only one or two blacks at a time. The first African American to receive a college degree was Alexander Twilight in 1823. John Russwurm received one in 1826 and later began the first African-American newspaper.

Caring for the Needy

As some people promoted education, others tried to improve society's care for its weakest members. In 1841, **Dorothea Dix**, a reformer from Boston, was teaching Sunday school at a women's jail. She discovered some women who were locked in cold, filthy cells

HORACE MANN
1796–1859

Horace Mann once said in a speech to students, "Be ashamed to die until you have won some victory for humanity." Mann had no reason to be ashamed. As a child, he knew poverty and hardship. He educated himself and later fought for public education for other people.

Toward the end of his life, Mann became president of Antioch College. It committed itself to education for both men and women and equal rights for African Americans.

DOROTHEA DIX
1802–1887

At the age of 12, Dorothea Dix left an unhappy home to go live with her grandparents in Boston. Just two years later, she began teaching little children.

In 1841, Dix saw the harsh treatment of mentally ill women. Society frowned upon women traveling alone, but Dix defied custom. She went by train to several places where the mentally ill were housed.

Dix wrote a report about her research. (See page 438.) That report changed the care of the mentally ill.

How might their backgrounds have motivated Dorothea Dix and Horace Mann to become leaders in reform movements?

simply because they were mentally ill. Visiting other jails, Dix learned that the mentally ill often received no treatment. Instead, they were chained and beaten. Dix pleaded with the Massachusetts Legislature to improve the care of the mentally ill. Later, she traveled all over the United States on behalf of the mentally ill. Her efforts led to the building of 32 new hospitals.

Some reformers worked to improve life for people with other disabilities. Thomas H. Gallaudet started the first American school for deaf children in 1817. Samuel G. Howe founded the Perkins School for the Blind in Boston in the 1830s.

Reformers also tried to improve prisons. In the early 1800s, debtors, lifelong criminals, and child offenders were put in the same cells. Reformers demanded that children go to special jails. They also called for the rehabilitation of adult prisoners. Rehabilitation means preparing people to live useful lives after their release from prison.

Reading **His**
C. Recognizin
Effects How
reformers ch
the treatmen
the mentally
the disabled,
prisoners?

Spreading Ideas Through Print

During this period of reform, Americans began to receive more information about how they should lead their lives. In the 1830s, cheaper newsprint and the invention of the steam-driven press lowered the price of a newspaper to a penny. Average Americans could afford to buy the "penny papers." Penny papers were also popular because, in addition to serious news, they published gripping stories of fires and crimes.

Hundreds of new magazines also appeared. One was the *Ladies' Magazine*. Its editor was Sarah Hale, a widow who used writing to support her family. The magazine advocated education for women. It also suggested that men and women were responsible for different, but equally important, areas of life. The magazine taught that a woman's area was the home and the world of "human ties." A man's area was politics and the business of earning a living for his family. Later, Hale edited *Godey's Lady's Book*, which published poems and stories as well as articles.

Creating Ideal Communities

While magazines sought to tell people how to live and reform movements tried to change society, some individuals decided to start over. They aimed to build an ideal society, called a utopia.

Two attempts at utopias were New Harmony, Indiana, and Brook Farm, Massachusetts. In both, residents received food and other necessities of life in exchange for work. However, both utopias experienced conflicts and financial difficulties. They ended after only a few years.

Religious belief led to some utopias. For example, the Shakers followed the beliefs of Ann Lee. She preached that people should lead holy lives in communities that demonstrate God's love to the world. When a person became a Shaker, he or she vowed not to marry or have children. Shakers shared their goods with each other, believed that men and women are equal, and refused to fight for any reason. Shakers set up communities in New York, New England, and on the frontier.

People called them *Shakers* because they shook with emotion during church services. Otherwise, Shaker life was calm. Shakers farmed and built simple furniture in styles that remain popular today. The childless Shakers depended on converts and adopting children to keep their communities going. In the 1840s, the Shakers had 6,000 members—their highest number. In 1999, only seven Shakers remained.

In the 1840s and 1850s, reform found a new direction. Many individuals began to try to win rights for two oppressed groups—women and enslaved persons. Section 4 discusses these efforts.

ing **History**

ming and
rting

ns Why
think it
ard for
s to
d? Give
s.

---

ion ❸ *Assessment*

erms & Names

plain the
gnificance of:
vival
cond Great
wakening
mperance
ovement
bor union
rike
orace Mann
orothea Dix

2. Using Graphics

Create a chart like the one below. Use it to list problems identified by reformers and their solutions to them.

Problem	Reformer's Solution

3. Main Ideas

a. How did the Second Great Awakening influence the reform movement?

b. How did labor unions try to force business owners to improve working conditions?

c. What were women's contributions to the reform movement?

4. Critical Thinking

Recognizing Effects What was the long-term impact of the reform movement that took place in the mid-1800s?

THINK ABOUT

• the changes reformers made in education, temperance, prisons, and the care of the disabled

• which of those changes are still in effect today

IVITY OPTIONS

SPEECH

CIVICS

Think of a modern problem that is similar to an issue discussed in this section. Give a **speech** or write a **letter** to a government official suggesting a reform.

Report to the Massachusetts Legislature

Setting the Stage After traveling to several places where the mental
were kept, Dorothea Dix wrote a report describing the conditions she
discovered. In 1843, she presented her report to lawmakers to alert the
to the horrible treatment of the mentally ill. This report has been calle
"first piece of social research ever conducted in America." An excerpt
from Dorothea Dix's report follows. **See Primary Source Explorer**

Report to the Massachusetts Legislature

Gentlemen: . . . I come to present the strong claims of suffering huma
come to place before the Legislature of Massachusetts the condition
miserable, the desolate, the outcast. I come as the **advocate**[1] of helpless
gotten, insane, and idiotic men and women; of beings sunk to a cond
from which the most unconcerned would start with real horror; of b
wretched in our prisons, and more wretched in our **almshouses**.[2]

I must confine myself to a few examples, but am ready to furnish othe
more complete details, if required.

I proceed, gentlemen, briefly to call your attention to the *present* st
insane persons confined within this **Commonwealth**,[3] in *cages, closets,*
stalls, pens! Chained, naked, beaten with rods, and *lashed* into obedience.

I offer the following extracts from my notebook and journal.

Springfield: In the jail, one lunatic woman, furiously mad, a state **pau**
improperly situated, both in regard to the prisoners, the keepers, and h
It is a case of extreme self-forgetfulness and oblivion to all the decenc
life, to describe which would be to repeat only the grossest scenes.
much worse since leaving Worcester. In the almshouse of the same tow
woman apparently only needing **judicious**[5] care and some well-c
employment to make it unnecessary to confine her in solitude in a
unfurnished room. Her appeals for employment and companionshi
most touching, but the mistress replied "she had no time to attend to

Lincoln: A woman in a cage. *Medford:* One idiotic subject chained, an
in a close stall for seventeen years. *Pepperell:* One often doubly chained,
and foot; another violent; several peaceable now. *Brookfield:* One man
comfortable. *Granville:* One often closely confined, now losing the use

A CLOSER LOOK

ADVOCATE OF THE HELPLESS

In earlier times, the term *idiotic* did
not mean stupid. It was used to
describe someone who was mentally retarded.

**1. For what groups of people is
Dix pleading for help?**

A CLOSER LOOK

JUDICIOUS CARE

Dix describes a woman who needs
only some care and a useful task
to do.

**2. What did the woman's keeper
say when Dix pointed that out?**

1. **advocate:** a person who
   pleads another person's
   cause.
2. **almshouses:** homes for
   poor people.
3. **Commonwealth:** one of
   four U.S. states whose
   constitution uses this term
   to describe their form of
   self-government; in this
   case, Massachusetts.
4. **pauper:** a person v
   lives on the state's
5. **judicious:** wise and
   careful.

s from want of exercise. *Charlemont:* One man caged. *Savoy:* One man
d. *Lenox:* Two in the jail, against whose unfit condition there the jailer
ests.

dham: The insane **disadvantageously**[6] placed in the jail. In the
shouse, two females in stalls, situated in the main building, lie in wooden
ks filled with straw; always shut up. One of these subjects is supposed
ble. The overseers of the poor have declined giving her a trial at the hos-
., as I was informed, on account of expense.

sides the above, I have seen many who, part of the year, are chained or
d. The use of cages is all but universal. Hardly a town but can refer to
e not distant period of using them; chains are less common; **negligences**[7]
uent; willful abuse less frequent than sufferings proceeding from igno-
e, or want of consideration. I encountered during the last three months
y poor creatures wandering reckless and unprotected through the coun-
. . . But I cannot **particularize**.[8] In traversing the state, I have found hun-
s of insane persons in every variety of circumstance and condition, many
se situation could not and need not be improved; a less number, but that
large, whose lives are the saddest pictures of human suffering and
adation.

ve a few illustrations; but description fades before reality. . . .

n of Massachusetts, I beg, I implore, I demand pity and protection for
e of my suffering, outraged sex. . . . Become the benefactors of your race,
ust guardians of the solemn rights you hold in trust. Raise up the fallen,
or[9] the desolate, restore the outcast, defend the helpless, and for your
ual and great reward receive the benediction, "Well done, good and faith-
ervants, become rulers over many things!"

advantageously:
mfully.

gligences: careless
ons.

8. **particularize:** to name
   in detail.

9. **succor:** to give help
   during a time of need.

---

eractive Primary Source Assessment

Main Ideas

On what evidence did Dorothea Dix base her report
out "suffering humanity"?

How were the mentally ill treated in Massachusetts?

Who did Dorothea Dix ask to help to improve the care
the mentally ill?

2. Critical Thinking

Evaluating Dix succeeded in convincing the legislature
to provide funds for new hospitals. What do you think
made her report so persuasive?

THINK ABOUT

• the details included in the report
• how Dix got the information to write her report
• the techniques you would use to persuade someone

4

Abolition and Women's Rights

MAIN IDEA

The spread of democracy led to calls for freedom for slaves and more rights for women.

WHY IT MATTERS NOW

The abolitionists and women reformers of this time inspired 20th–century reformers.

TERMS & NAMES

abolition
Frederick Douglass
Sojourner Truth
Underground Railroad
Harriet Tubmar
Elizabeth Cady
Seneca Falls Convention
suffrage

ONE AMERICAN'S STORY

African-American poet Frances Ellen Watkins Harper often wrote about the suffering of enslaved persons, such as enslaved mothers.

A VOICE FROM THE PAST

They tear him from her circling arms,
Her last and fond embrace.
Oh! never more may her sad eyes
Gaze on his mournful face.

No marvel, then, these bitter shrieks
Disturb the listening air:
She is a mother, and her heart
Is breaking in despair.

Frances Ellen Watkins Harper, "The Slave Mother"

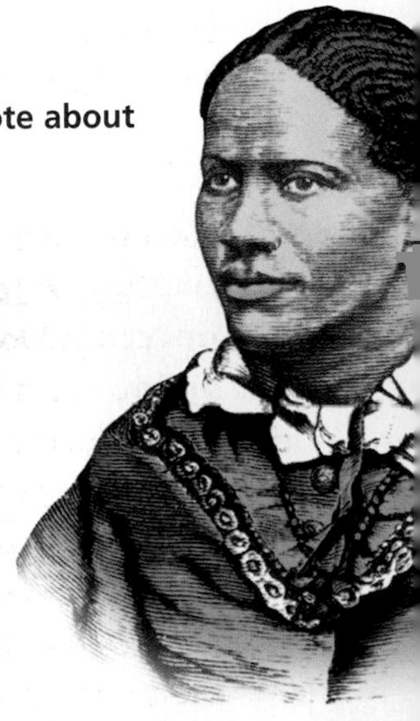

Frances
Watkins
impress
audienc
her spe
ability
called f

As this section explains, many individuals in the mid-1800s demanded equal rights for African Americans and women.

Taking Notes

se your chart to ke notes about the fluence of aboli- onists and women.

	How People
grants	
ers	
rmers	
itionists	
nen	

Abolitionists Call for Ending Slavery

Abolition, the movement to end slavery, began in the late 1700s. By 1804, most Northern states had outlawed slavery. In 1807, Congress banned the importation of African slaves into the United States. Abolitionists then began to demand a law ending slavery in the South.

David Walker, a free African American in Boston, printed a pamphlet in 1829 urging slaves to revolt. Copies of the pamphlet appeared in the South. This angered slaveholders. Shortly afterward, Walker died mysteriously.

A few Northern whites also fought slavery. In 1831, William Lloyd Garrison began to publish an abolitionist newspaper, *The Liberator,* in

Boston. Of his antislavery stand, he wrote, "I will not retreat a single inch—AND I WILL BE HEARD." Many people hated his views. In 1834, a furious mob in Boston grabbed Garrison and dragged him toward a park to hang him. The mayor stepped in and saved his life.

Two famous abolitionists were Southerners who had grown up on a plantation. Sisters Sarah and Angelina Grimké believed that slavery was morally wrong. They moved north and joined an antislavery society. At the time, women were not supposed to lecture in public. But the Grimkés lectured against slavery anyway. Theodore Weld, Angelina's husband, was also an abolitionist. He led a campaign to send antislavery petitions to Congress. Proslavery congressmen passed gag rules to prevent the reading of those petitions in Congress.

John Quincy Adams ignored the gag rules and read the petitions. He also introduced an amendment to abolish slavery. Proslavery congressmen tried to stop him. Such efforts, however, only weakened the proslavery cause by showing them to be opponents of free speech. Adams also defended a group of Africans who had rebelled on the slave ship *Amistad*. He successfully argued their case before the U.S. Supreme Court in 1841, and in 1842, the Africans returned home.

Eyewitnesses to Slavery

Two moving abolitionist speakers, **Frederick Douglass** and **Sojourner Truth,** spoke from their own experience of slavery. Douglass's courage and talent at public speaking won him a career as a lecturer for the Massachusetts Anti-Slavery Society. Poet James Russell Lowell said of him, "The very look and bearing of Douglass are an irresistible logic against the oppression of his race."

People who opposed abolition spread rumors that the brilliant speaker could never have been a slave. To prove them wrong, in 1845 Douglass published an autobiography that vividly narrated his slave experiences. Afterwards, he feared recapture by his owner, so he left America for a two-year speaking tour of Great Britain and Ireland. When Douglass returned, he bought his freedom. He began to publish an antislavery newspaper.

Sojourner Truth also began life enslaved. Originally named Isabella, Sojourner Truth was born in New York State. In 1827, she fled her owners and went to live with Quakers, who set her free. They also helped her win a court battle to recover her young son. He had been sold illegally into slavery in the South. A devout Christian, Truth changed her name in 1843 to reflect her life's work: to sojourn (or stay temporarily in a place) and "declare the truth to the people." Speaking for abolition, she drew huge crowds throughout the North.

ing **History**
awing
usions How
d the
é sisters'
round help
as aboli-
: speakers?

ng **History**
paring
ere
ck
ss and
er Truth
as
nists?

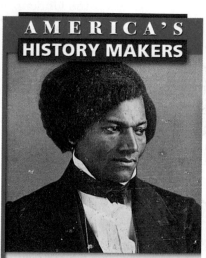

AMERICA'S HISTORY MAKERS

FREDERICK DOUGLASS
1817–1895

Douglass, born Frederick Bailey, was the son of a black mother and a white father. When he was eight, his owner sent him to be a servant for the Auld family. Mrs. Auld defied state law and taught young Frederick to read.

At the age of 16, Douglass returned to the plantation as a field hand. He endured so many whippings he later wrote, "I was seldom free from a sore back."

In 1838, he escaped to the North by hopping a train with a borrowed pass. To avoid recapture, he changed his last name.

How did Mrs. Auld unknowingly help Douglass become an abolitionist leader? Explain.

The Underground Railroad

Some abolitionists wanted to do more than campaign for laws ending slavery. Some brave people helped slaves escape to freedom along the Underground Railroad. Neither underground nor a railroad, the **Underground Railroad** was actually an aboveground series of escape routes from the South to the North. On these routes, runaway slaves traveled on foot. They also took wagons, boats, and trains.

Some enslaved persons found more unusual routes to freedom. For example, Henry Brown persuaded a white carpenter named Samuel A. Smith to pack him in a wooden box and ship him to Philadelphia. The box was only two and one half feet deep, two feet wide, and three feet long. It bore the label "This side up with care." Despite the label, Brown spent several miserable hours traveling head down. At the end of about 24 hours, Henry "Box" Brown climbed out of his box a free man in Philadelphia. Brown eventually made his way to Boston and worked on the Underground Railroad.

On the Underground Railroad, the runaways usually traveled by night and hid by day in places called stations. Stables, attics, and cellars all served as stations. At his home in Rochester, New York, Frederick Douglass hid up to 11 runaways at a time.

Harriet Tubman

The people who led the runaways to freedom were called conductors. One of the most famous conductors was **Harriet Tubman**. Born into slavery in Maryland, the 13-year-old Tubman once tried to save another slave from punishment. The angry overseer fractured Tubman's skull with a two-pound weight. She suffered fainting spells for the rest of her life but did not let that stop her from working for freedom. In 1849, Tubman learned that her owner was about to sell her. Instead, she escaped. She later described her feelings as she crossed into the free state of Pennsylvania: "I looked at my hands to see if I was the same person now that I was free. There was such a glory over everything."

After her escape, Harriet Tubman made 19 dangerous journeys to free enslaved persons. The tiny woman carried a pistol to frighten off slave hunters and medicine to quiet crying babies. Her enemies offered $40,000 for her capture, but no one caught her. "I never run my train off the track and I never lost a passenger," she proudly declared. Among the people she saved were her parents.

C. Reading
The map on
447 shows t
routes of th
Underground
Railroad. No
that most o
these route
to Canada.

Now and then

THE UNDERGROUND RAILROAD

In 1996, historian Anthony Cohen took six weeks to travel from Maryland to Canada. Cohen followed the paths runaway slaves had taken 150 years earlier. He is shown below arriving in Canada.

Cohen walked, sometimes as much as 37 miles in a day. He also hitched rides on trains and canal boats.

About those long-ago slaves fleeing toward the hope of freedom, Cohen said, "They had no choice. . . . Nobody would do this if they didn't have to."

Reading
D. Forming
Supporting
Opinions
do you thi
escaped sl
such as Br
Douglass,
Tubman ri
their lives
free other

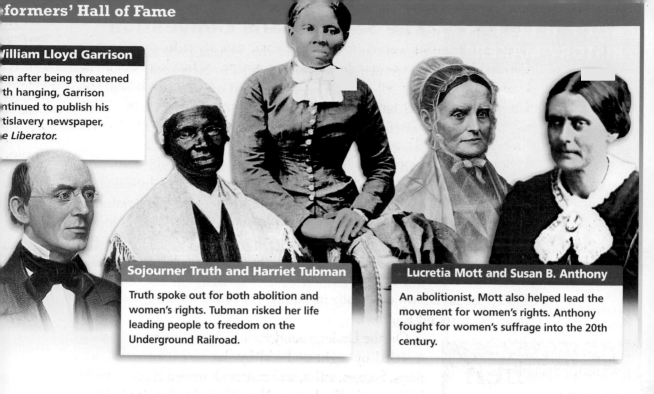

en after being threatened
th hanging, Garrison
ntinued to publish his
tislavery newspaper,
e *Liberator.*

Sojourner Truth and Harriet Tubman

Truth spoke out for both abolition and
women's rights. Tubman risked her life
leading people to freedom on the
Underground Railroad.

Lucretia Mott and Susan B. Anthony

An abolitionist, Mott also helped lead the
movement for women's rights. Anthony
fought for women's suffrage into the 20th
century.

Women Reformers Face Barriers

Other women besides the Grimké sisters and Sojourner Truth were abolitionists. Two of these were Lucretia Mott and **Elizabeth Cady Stanton**. Mott and Stanton were part of an American delegation that attended the World Anti-Slavery Convention in London in 1840. These women had much to say about their work. Yet when they tried to enter the convention, they were not allowed to do so. Men angrily claimed that it was not a woman's place to speak in public. Instead, the women had to sit silent behind a heavy curtain.

ulary
tion: a
that
nts a
group

To show his support, William Lloyd Garrison joined them. He said, "After battling so many long years for the liberties of African slaves, I can take no part in a convention that strikes down the most sacred rights of all women."

Stanton applauded Garrison for giving up his chance to speak on abolition, the cause for which he had fought so long. "It was a great act of self-sacrifice that should never be forgotten by women."

However, most people agreed with the men who said that women should stay out of public life. Women in the 1800s enjoyed few legal or political rights. They could not vote, sit on juries, or hold public office. Many laws treated women—especially married women—as children. Single women enjoyed some freedoms, such as being able to manage their own property. But in most states, a husband controlled any property his wife inherited and any wages she might earn.

As the convention ended, Stanton and Mott decided it was time to demand equality for women. They made up their minds to hold a convention for women's rights when they returned home.

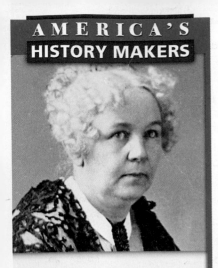

ELIZABETH CADY STANTON
1815–1902

Elizabeth Cady Stanton's first memory was the birth of a sister when she was four. So many people said, "What a pity it is she's a girl!" that Stanton felt sorry for the new baby. She later wrote, "I did not understand at that time that girls were considered an inferior order of beings."

When Stanton was 11, her only brother died. Her father said, "Oh, my daughter, I wish you were a boy!" That sealed Stanton's determination to prove that girls were just as important as boys.

How did Stanton's childhood experiences motivate her to help other people besides herself?

The Seneca Falls Convention

Stanton and Mott held the <u>Seneca Falls Convention</u> for women's rights in Seneca Falls, New York, on July 19 and 20, 1848. The convention attracted between 100 and 300 women and men, including Frederick Douglass.

Before the meeting opened, a small group of planners debated how to present their complaints. One woman read aloud the Declaration of Independence. This inspired the planners to write a document modeled on it. The women called their document the Declaration of Sentiments and Resolutions. Just as the Declaration of Independence said that "All men are created equal," the Declaration of Sentiments stated that "All men and women are created equal." It went on to list several complaints or resolutions. Then it concluded with a demand for rights.

A VOICE FROM THE PAST

Now, in view of this entire disenfranchisement [denying the right to vote] of one-half the people of this country, their social and religious degradation—in view of the unjust laws above mentioned, and because women do feel themselves aggrieved, oppressed, and fraudulently deprived of their most sacred rights, we insist that they have immediate admission to all the rights and privileges which belong to them as citizens of the United States.

Seneca Falls Declaration of Sentiments and Resolutions, 1848

Reading **H**
E. Using Pri
Sources W
the women
the Seneca
Convention
believe the
deserved ri
and privileg

Every resolution won unanimous approval from the group except **suffrage,** or the right to vote. Some argued that the public would laugh at women if they asked for the vote. But Elizabeth Cady Stanton and Frederick Douglass fought for the resolution. They argued that the right to vote would give women political power that would help them win other rights. The resolution for suffrage won by a slim margin.

The women's rights movement was ridiculed. In 1852, the *New York Herald* poked fun at women who wanted "to vote, and to hustle with the rowdies at the polls" and to be men's equals. The editorial questioned what would happen if a pregnant woman gave birth "on the floor of Congress, in a storm at sea, or in the raging tempest of battle."

Continued Calls for Women's Rights

In the mid-1800s, three women lent powerful voices to the growing women's movement. Sojourner Truth, Maria Mitchell, and Susan B. Anthony each offered a special talent.

In 1851, Sojourner Truth rose to speak at a convention for women's rights in Ohio. Some participants hissed their disapproval. Because Truth supported the controversial cause of abolition, they feared her appearance would make their own cause less popular. But Truth won applause with her speech that urged men to grant women their rights.

A VOICE FROM THE PAST

I have heard much about the sexes being equal. I can carry as much as any man, and can eat as much too, if I can get it. I am as strong as any man. . . . If you have woman's rights give it to her and you will feel better. You will have your own rights, and they won't be so much trouble.

Sojourner Truth, quoted by Marius Robinson, convention secretary

This drawing shows a husband and wife fighting over who will "wear the pants in the family"— that is, who will rule the household.

The scientist Maria Mitchell fought for women's equality by helping to found the Association for the Advancement of Women. Mitchell was an astronomer who discovered a comet in 1847. She became the first woman elected to the American Academy of Arts and Sciences.

Susan B. Anthony was a skilled organizer who worked in the temperance and antislavery movements. She built the women's movement into a national organization. Anthony argued that a woman must "have a purse [money] of her own." To this end, she supported laws that would give married women rights to their own property and wages. Mississippi passed the first such law in 1839. New York passed a property law in 1848 and a wages law in 1860. By 1865, 29 states had similar laws. (Anthony also fought for suffrage. See Chapter 22.)

But women's suffrage stayed out of reach until the 1900s, and the U.S. government did not fully abolish slavery until 1865. As you will read in the next chapter, the issue of slavery began to tear the nation apart in the mid-1800s.

Section 4 Assessment

1. Terms & Names

Explain the significance of:
abolition
Frederick Douglass
Sojourner Truth
Underground Railroad
Harriet Tubman
Elizabeth Cady Stanton
Seneca Falls Convention
suffrage

2. Using Graphics

On a time line like the one below, record significant individuals and events in the historical development of the abolition movement.

1807 ————————— 1865

Why does the time line end in 1865?

3. Main Ideas

a. Why were freedom of speech and freedom of the press important to the abolitionist movement?

b. What were Frederick Douglass's contributions to the abolitionist movement?

c. What were Elizabeth Cady Stanton's contributions to the women's rights movement?

4. Critical Thinking

Drawing Conclusions
Why do you think that many of the people who fought for abolition also fought for women's rights?

THINK ABOUT
• why they opposed slavery
• the social and economic position of women
• what the two causes had in common

ACTIVITY OPTIONS

TECHNOLOGY

DRAMA

With a partner, act out a meeting between a reformer from Section 3 and one from Section 4. **Videotape** their conversation or **perform** it for the class.

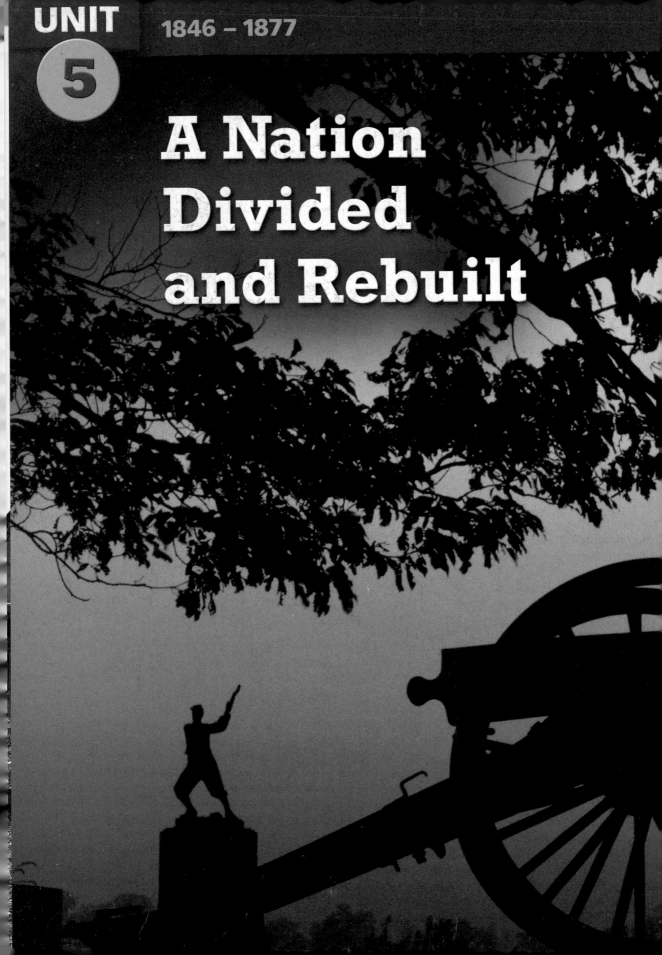

A Nation Divided and Rebuilt

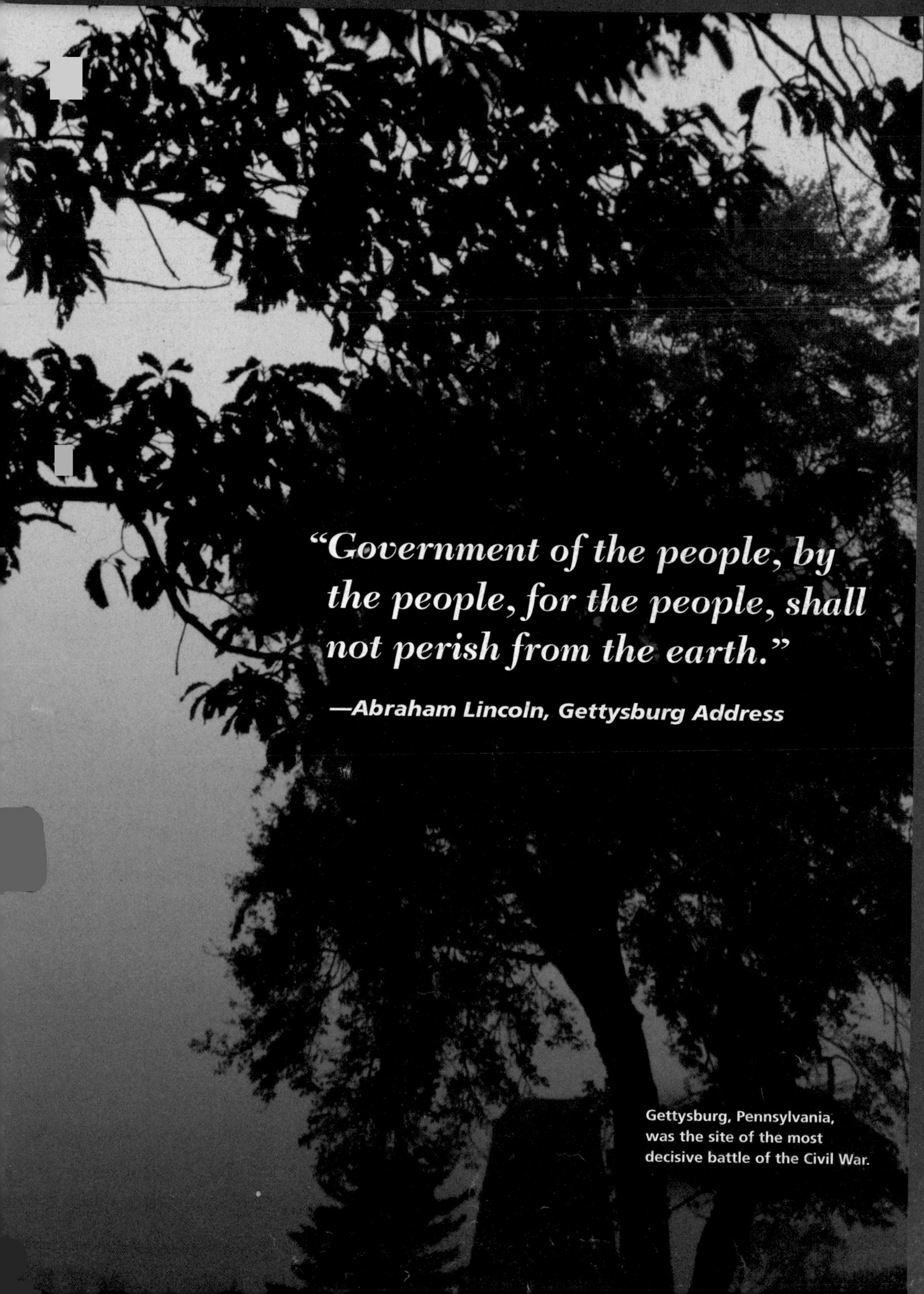

> "*Government of the people, by the people, for the people, shall not perish from the earth.*"
>
> **—Abraham Lincoln, Gettysburg Address**

Gettysburg, Pennsylvania, was the site of the most decisive battle of the Civil War.

Lincoln's eloquent speaking style often made him a crowd favorite.

Abraham Lincoln and Stephen A. Douglas debate the issue of slavery in the 1858 Senate campaign in Illinois.

1846
War with Mexico begins.

Wilmot Proviso is introduced.

1848
Zachary Taylor is elected president.

1850
President Taylor dies. Millard Fillmore becomes president.

Congress passes the Compromise of 1850.

1852
Uncle Tom's Cabin is published.

Franklin Pierce is elected president.

USA
World **1846**

1848
Rebellions erupt across Europe.

1850
Taiping Rebellion begins in China.

hough not allowed to
e, women clearly show
nterest in politics.

"WESTWARD THE
THE GIRLS LINK
THEIR N

You are a reporter following Abraham Lincoln and Stephen A. Douglas on the campaign trail in 1858. The issue of slavery is causing heated debates. Respectable men have turned to violence to settle their differences. You worry that soon this violence may affect the entire nation.

How would you keep the nation together?

What Do You Think?

- Why do you think people feel so strongly about slavery?

- Do you think debates, such as those between Lincoln and Douglas, could settle emotional issues without leading to violence?

RESEARCH LINKS
CLASSZONE.COM

Visit the Chapter 15 links for more information about pre-war tension.

1856
James Buchanan is elected president.

1857
Chief Justice Roger B. Taney delivers his opinion in the *Dred Scott* case.

1860
Abraham Lincoln is elected president.

1861
The Confederate States of America is formed.

1861

1856
War breaks out etween Britain and Persia.

1861
Czar Alexander II frees the serfs in Russia.

CHAPTER 15

Reading Strategy: Analyzing Causes

What Do You Know?

What do you think about when you hear the terms *slavery* and *abolition?* Why do you think the issue of slavery caused so much anger and resentment?

Think About

- what you've learned about differences between the North and the South from books, travel, television, or movies
- reasons people have violent conflicts today
- your responses to the Interact with History about keeping the nation together (see page 455)

What Do You Want to Know?

What questions do you have about the sectional crisis that led to the Civil War? Record them in your notebook before you read this chapter.

Slavery caused such strong emotio fights sometimes broke out betwe members of Congress.

Analyzing Causes

Analyzing causes means looking closely at events and describing why they happened. Th diagram below will help you analyze some of the causes of secession. Use the diagram t take notes on how each issue drove the North and the South farther apart.

 See Skillbuilder Handbook, page R11.

Taking Notes

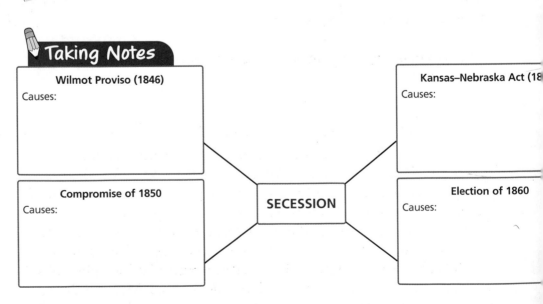

Wilmot Proviso (1846) Causes:	Kansas–Nebraska Act (18 Causes:
Compromise of 1850 Causes:	**SECESSION**	Election of 1860 Causes:

Growing Tensions Between North and South

MAIN IDEA	WHY IT MATTERS NOW	TERMS & NAMES
...ments between the North ...South, especially over the slavery, led to political conflict.	Regional differences can make national problems difficult to resolve.	Wilmot Proviso Free-Soil Party Henry Clay Daniel Webster Stephen A. Douglas Compromise of 1850

ONE EUROPEAN'S STORY

During the 1830s, a French government official named Alexis de Tocqueville [TOHK•vihl] traveled down the Ohio River. The river was the border between Ohio, a free state, and Kentucky, a slave state. Tocqueville noted what he saw on both sides of the river.

A VOICE FROM THE PAST

The State of Ohio is separated from Kentucky just by one river; on either side of it the soil is equally fertile, and the situation equally favourable, and yet everything is different. Here [on the Ohio side] a population devoured by feverish activity, trying every means to make its fortune. . . . There [on the Kentucky side] are people who make others work for them and show little compassion, a people without energy, mettle or the spirit of enterprise. . . . These differences cannot be attributed to any other cause but slavery.

Alexis de Tocqueville, *Journey to America*

Alexis de Tocqueville

In this section, you will read about the differences between the North and the South.

North and South Take Different Paths

As you read in Chapter 11, the economies of the North and the South developed differently in the early 1800s. Although both economies were mostly agricultural, the North began to develop more industry and commerce. By contrast, the Southern economy relied on plantation farming.

The growth of industry in the North helped lead to the rapid growth of Northern cities. Much of this population growth came from immigration. In addition, immigrants and Easterners moved west and built farms in the new states formed from the Northwest Territory. Most canals and railroads ran east and west, helping the Eastern and Midwestern states develop strong ties with each other.

Taking Notes

Use your chart to take notes about the Wilmot Proviso and the Compromise of 1850.

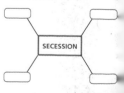

SECESSION

Economics *in* History

Trade

Trade is based on a simple idea. If you have something someone else needs or wants, and that person has something you need or want, you exchange, or trade, those two things. After the trade, you should both be better off than before.

The concept of trade works similarly for groups of people. For example, in the early 1800s, the South had few factories. Planters who wanted manufactured goods usually had to buy them from manufacturers in the North or in Europe. To have the cash to buy those goods, Southerners sold other goods, such as cotton, to the North and other countries. Each sold the goods they could produce in order to get money to buy the goods they could not make.

CONNECT TO HISTORY
1. Solving Problems What problem does trade help a country solve? How else co a country solve this problem

 See Skillbuilder Handbook, page R18.

CONNECT TO TODAY
2. Comparing What goods do Americans sell to other countries today? What goo do Americans buy from oth countries?

For more about trade . . .

RESEARCH LINKS
CLASSZONE.COM

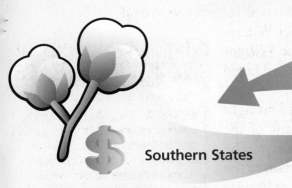

Northern States and Other Countries

Southern States

The South developed differently than the North. A few wealthy planters controlled Southern society. They made great profits from the labor of their slaves. Much of this profit came from trade. Planters relied on exports, especially cotton. Because these plantations were so profitable, planters invested in slaves instead of industry. As a result, the South developed little industry.

Most Southern whites were poor farmers who owned no slaves. But even many of the nonslaveholding whites supported slavery because it kept them off the bottom of society.

Antislavery and Racism

The issue of slavery caused tension between the North and the South. In the North, the antislavery movement had slowly been gaining strength since the 1830s. Abolitionists believed that slavery was unjust and should be abolished immediately. Many Northerners who opposed slavery took a less extreme position. Some Northern workers and immigrants opposed slavery because it was an economic threat to them. Because slaves did not work for pay, free workers feared that managers would employ slaves rather than them. Some workers were even afraid that the expansion of slavery might force workers into slavery to find jobs.

Despite their opposition to slavery, most Northerners, even abolitionists, were racist by modern standards. Many whites refused to go to

Reading **H**
A. Making
Generalizat
How did th
economies
North and
South diffe

school with, work with, or live near African Americans. In most states, even free African Americans could not vote.

When Northern attacks on slavery increased, slaveholders defended slavery. Most offered the openly racist argument that white people were superior to blacks. Many also claimed that slavery helped slaves by introducing them to Christianity, as well as providing them with food, clothing, and shelter throughout their lives. Slaveholders were determined to defend slavery and their way of life. In this way, the different ideas about slavery brought the North and the South into conflict.

The Wilmot Proviso

After the Missouri Compromise in 1820, political disagreements over slavery seemed to go away. But new disagreements arose with the outbreak of the War with Mexico in 1846. Many Northerners believed that Southerners wanted to take territory from Mexico in order to extend slavery. To prevent that, Representative David Wilmot of Pennsylvania proposed a bill, known as the **Wilmot Proviso,** to outlaw slavery in any territory the United States might acquire from the War with Mexico.

But slaveholders believed that Congress had no right to prevent them from bringing slaves into any of the territories. They viewed slaves as property. The Constitution, they claimed, gave equal protection to the property rights of all U.S. citizens. The Wilmot Proviso removed the right of slaveholders to take their slaves, which they regarded as property, anywhere in the United States or its territories. Southerners claimed that the bill was unconstitutional.

The Wilmot Proviso divided Congress along regional lines. The bill passed the House of Representatives. But Southerners prevented it from passing the Senate.

Even though the Wilmot Proviso never became law, it had important effects. It led to the creation of the **Free-Soil Party,** a political party dedicated to stopping the expansion of slavery. The party's slogan expressed its ideals—"Free Soil, Free Speech, Free Labor, and Free Men." The Free-Soil Party won more than ten seats in Congress in the election of 1848. More important, the party made slavery a key issue in national politics. Politicians could ignore slavery no longer.

Controversy over Territories

By 1848, the nation's leaders had begun to debate how to deal with slavery in the lands gained from the War with Mexico. The proposed addition of new states threatened the balance in Congress between North and South. The discovery of gold in California brought thousands of people into that territory. There would soon be enough people in California for it to apply for statehood. Most California residents wanted their state to

Connections TO WORLD HISTORY

EXPANDING SLAVERY

William Walker, a Tennessee-born adventurer, wanted to take over land in Central America. In 1855, he joined an army of Nicaraguan rebels and seized power. Walker declared himself president of Nicaragua in 1856. As president, he legalized slavery there.

Troops from nearby countries drove him from power in 1857. The actions of men like Walker helped to convince Northerners that slaveholders were intent on expanding slavery beyond the U.S. South.

be a free state. But this would tip the balance of power clearly in favor of the North. Southerners wanted to divide California in half, making the northern half a free state and the southern half a slave state.

In 1849, President Zachary Taylor—who opposed the extension of slavery—proposed that California submit a plan for statehood that year, without going through the territorial stage. Taylor's plan gave Southern slaveholders little time to move to California with their slaves.

In March 1850, California applied to be admitted as a free state. With California as a free state, slave states would become a minority in the Senate just as they were in the House. Jefferson Davis, a senator from Mississippi, warned, "For the first time, we are about permanently to destroy the balance of power between the sections."

The Compromise of 1850

California could not gain statehood, however, without the approval of Congress. And Congress was divided over the issue. Behind the scenes, statesmen sought compromise. Taking the lead was Senator **Henry Clay**

Backgroun
U.S. land ga
from the Wa
with Mexico
included all
parts of the
future state
of California
Nevada, Uta
Arizona, Ne
Mexico, and
Colorado.

This engraving dramatically portrays the Senate debate over the Compromise of 1850.

John C. Calhoun of Carolina opposed t Compromise of 185 believed the South no reason to comp on the issue of slav

Henry Clay led the Congress in creating compromises on several important issues during his long career.

Daniel Webster spoke eloquently in favor of the compromise.

of Kentucky. Clay had helped create the Missouri Compromise in 1820. Now Clay crafted a plan to settle the California problem.

ing History
ding a Map
at the map
ge 464 to
w the
romise of
ffected the
ries open
ery.

1. To please the North, California would be admitted as a free state, and the slave trade would be abolished in Washington, D.C.
2. To please the South, Congress would not pass laws regarding slavery for the rest of the territories won from Mexico, and Congress would pass a stronger law to help slaveholders recapture runaway slaves.

Many people on both sides felt they had to give up too much in this plan. But others were tired of the regional bickering. They wanted to hold the Union together. **Daniel Webster,** senator from Massachusetts, supported the compromise for the sake of the Union.

> *A VOICE FROM THE PAST*
>
> I wish to speak today, not as a Massachusetts man, nor as a Northern man, but as an American. . . . I speak today for the preservation of the Union. Hear me for my cause.
>
> **Daniel Webster,** quoted in *The Annals of America*

The job of winning passage of the plan fell to Senator **Stephen A. Douglas** of Illinois. By the end of September, Douglas succeeded, and the plan, now known as the **Compromise of 1850,** became law.

Some people celebrated the compromise, believing that it had saved the Union. But the compromise would not bring peace. In the next section, you will learn how sectional tensions continued to rise.

AMERICA'S HISTORY MAKERS

STEPHEN A. DOUGLAS
1813–1861

Stephen A. Douglas was one of the most powerful members of Congress in the mid-1800s. In fact, he was called the "Little Giant" because he commanded great respect even though he was only five feet four inches tall.

Perhaps the most important issue that Douglas faced during his career was the expansion of slavery into the territories. Douglas privately hated slavery. But he did not believe a debate on morality would do any good. He suggested that the people of each territory should decide whether or not to allow slavery.

What groups of Americans agreed with Douglas's position on slavery?

---

 ion 1 Assessment

Terms & Names

plain the *gnificance* of:
ilmot Proviso
ee-Soil Party
enry Clay
aniel Webster
ephen A. Douglas
ompromise of 1850

2. Using Graphics

Use a chart like the one below to explain the effects of each cause.

Causes	Effects
Abolitionism	
Wilmot Proviso	
California's application for statehood	

Which issue do you think most threatened national unity?

3. Main Ideas

a. What were two ways that the North and the South differed by the mid-1800s?

b. In what ways was racism common in both the North and the South?

c. How did the War with Mexico lead to conflict between the North and the South?

4. Critical Thinking

Comparing and Contrasting How was the Compromise of 1850 similar to and different from the Missouri Compromise?

THINK ABOUT

• the regional tensions at the time the compromises were proposed
• who proposed each bill
• the provisions of the bills

IVITY OPTIONS

ECHNOLOGY

SPEECH

Imagine you are a television news director. Plan a five-minute **documentary** or organize a **panel discussion** on the Compromise of 1850.

The Crisis Deepens

ONE AMERICAN'S STORY

Harriet Beecher Stowe was outraged when she heard about the part of the Compromise of 1850 that would help slaveholders recapture runaway slaves. She stated that the Christian men who passed this law "cannot know what slavery is."

Stowe's anger motivated her to write ***Uncle Tom's Cabin,*** a novel that portrayed slavery as brutal and immoral. In this section, you will learn how the Compromise of 1850 deepened the division between the North and the South.

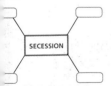
The Fugitive Slave Act

The 1850 law to help slaveholders recapture runaway slaves was called the **Fugitive Slave Act**. People accused of being fugitives under this law could be held without an arrest warrant. In addition, they had no right to a jury trial. Instead, a federal commissioner ruled on each case. The commissioner received five dollars for releasing the defendant and ten dollars for turning the defendant over to a slaveholder.

Southerners felt that the Fugitive Slave Act was justified because they considered slaves to be property. But Northerners resented the Fugitive Slave Act. It required Northerners to help recapture runaway slaves. It placed fines on people who would not cooperate and jail terms on people who helped the fugitives escape. In addition, Southern slave catchers roamed the North, sometimes capturing free African Americans.

The presence of slave catchers throughout the North brought home the issue of slavery to Northerners. They could no longer ignore the fact that, by supporting the Fugitive Slave Act, they played an important role in supporting slavery. They faced a moral choice. Should they

Harriet Bee

obey the law and support slavery, or should they break the law and oppose slavery?

Uncle Tom's Cabin

ling History
alyzing
s of View
did the play
Tom's
affect the
opment of
a in the
d States?

Stowe published *Uncle Tom's Cabin* in 1852. It dramatically portrayed the moral issues of slavery. In fact, a play based on the book increased the popularity of drama as well as abolitionism. The book's main character was Uncle Tom, a respected older slave. The plot centers on Tom's life under three owners. Two of the owners were kind, but the third was cruel. The novel includes dramatic scenes, such as the dangerous escape of a slave named Eliza and her baby across the Ohio River.

A VOICE FROM THE PAST

Eliza made her desperate retreat across the river just in the dusk of twilight. The gray mist of evening, rising slowly from the river, enveloped her as she disappeared up the bank, and the swollen current and floundering masses of ice presented a hopeless barrier between her and her pursuer.

Harriet Beecher Stowe, *Uncle Tom's Cabin*

Stowe's book was wildly popular in the North. But white Southerners believed the book falsely criticized the South and slavery.

The Kansas–Nebraska Act

While the Fugitive Slave Act and *Uncle Tom's Cabin* heightened the conflicts between the North and the South, the issue of slavery in the territories brought bloodshed to the West. In 1854, Senator Stephen A. Douglas of Illinois drafted a bill to organize territorial governments for the Nebraska Territory. He proposed that it be divided into two territories—Nebraska and Kansas.

To get Southern support for the bill, he suggested that the decision about whether to allow slavery in each of these territories be settled by popular sovereignty. **Popular sovereignty** is a system where the residents vote to decide an issue. If this bill passed, it would result in getting rid of the Missouri Compromise by

ground
ebraska
ry was part
Louisiana
se. It lay
of the
line, so
ssouri
omise
d slavery

In 1854, Bostonians protested the capture of an African American by federal marshals under the Fugitive Slave Act.

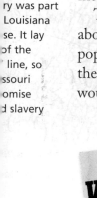

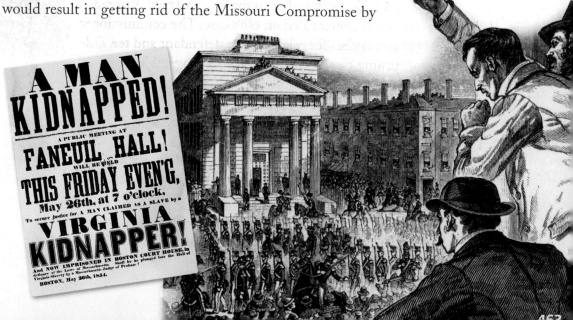

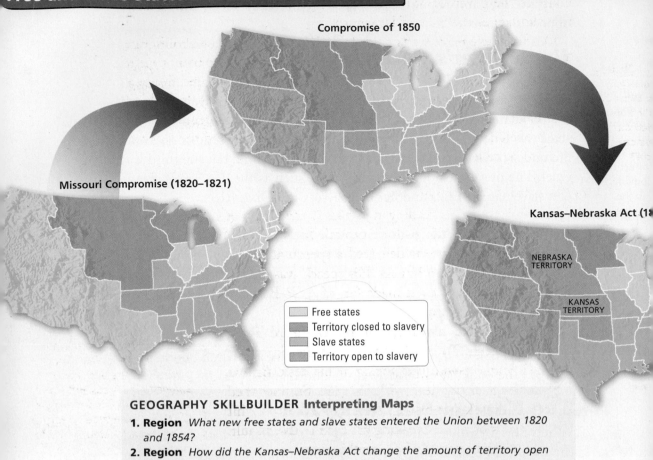

Compromise of 1850

Missouri Compromise (1820–1821)

Kansas–Nebraska Act (18

NEBRASKA
TERRITORY

KANSAS
TERRITORY

Free states
Territory closed to slavery
Slave states
Territory open to slavery

GEOGRAPHY SKILLBUILDER Interpreting Maps

1. **Region** *What new free states and slave states entered the Union between 1820 and 1854?*
2. **Region** *How did the Kansas–Nebraska Act change the amount of territory open to slavery?*

allowing people to vote for slavery in territories where the Missouri Compromise had banned it.

As Douglas hoped, Southerners applauded the repeal of the Missouri Compromise and supported the bill. Even though the bill angered opponents of slavery, it passed. It became known as the **Kansas–Nebraska Act**. Few people realized that the act would soon turn Kansas into a battleground over slavery.

"Bleeding Kansas"

Proslavery and antislavery settlers rushed into the Kansas Territory, just west of Missouri, to vote for the territorial legislature. At the time of the election in March 1855, there were more proslavery settlers than antislavery settlers in the territory. But the proslavery forces did not want to risk losing the election. Five thousand Missourians came and voted in the election illegally. As a result, the official Kansas legislature was packed with proslavery representatives.

Antislavery settlers boycotted the official government and formed a government of their own. With political authority in dispute, settlers on both sides armed themselves. In May, a proslavery mob attacked the town of Lawrence, Kansas. The attackers destroyed offices and the

Vocabula
boycott: r
to particip

house of the governor of the antislavery government. This attack came to be known as the Sack of Lawrence.

Onto this explosive scene came **John Brown,** an extreme abolitionist. To avenge the Sack of Lawrence, Brown and seven other men went to the cabins of several of his proslavery neighbors and murdered five people. This attack is known as the Pottawatomie Massacre, after the creek near where the victims were found. As news of the violence spread, civil war broke out in Kansas. It continued for three years, and the territory came to be called "Bleeding Kansas."

ing History
quencing
s What
s in Kansas
ded the
watomie
cre?

Violence in Congress

While violence was spreading in Kansas in the spring of 1856, blood was also being shed in the nation's capital. In late May, Senator Charles Sumner of Massachusetts delivered a speech attacking the proslavery forces in Kansas. His speech was packed with insults. Sumner even made fun of A. P. Butler, a senator from South Carolina.

Preston Brooks, a relative of Butler, heard about Sumner's speech. To defend Butler and the South, he attacked Sumner, who was sitting at his desk. Brooks hit Sumner over the head with his cane. Sumner tried to defend himself, but his legs were trapped. Brooks hit him 30 times or more, breaking his cane in the assault. (The painting on page 455 shows this event.)

Many Southerners cheered Brooks's defense of the South. But most Northerners were shocked at the violence in the Senate. "Bleeding Kansas" and "Bleeding Sumner" became rallying cries for antislavery Northerners and slogans for a new political party. In the next section, you will learn about the creation of the Republican Party.

STRANGE *but* True

PRESTON BROOKS'S CANE
Many Americans, Northerners and Southerners alike, were ashamed of the behavior of Sumner and Brooks. But sectional tensions were so high at the time that a large number of Southerners cheered Brooks for his actions.

A number of Brooks's supporters sent him new canes to replace the one he had broken while hitting Sumner on the head. Some of the canes were inscribed with mottoes such as "Hit Him Again."

---

tion 2 Assessment

Terms & Names

plain the
gnificance of:
arriet Beecher
owe
ncle Tom's Cabin
ugitive Slave Act
opular sovereignty
ansas–Nebraska
t
hn Brown

2. Using Graphics

Use a chart like the one below to compare Northern and Southern views of the issues listed.

Northern View	Issue	Southern View
	Fugitive Slave Act	
	Kansas–Nebraska Act	
	"Bleeding Kansas"	

3. Main Ideas

a. How did the book *Uncle Tom's Cabin* influence national politics?

b. Why was the Kansas–Nebraska Act so controversial?

c. What was the cause of "Bleeding Kansas"?

4. Critical Thinking

Solving Problems What would you have done to prevent the violence in Kansas?

THINK ABOUT
• the repeal of the Missouri Compromise
• popular sovereignty
• the actions of John Brown

VITY OPTIONS

TERATURE

ART

Read a chapter of *Uncle Tom's Cabin.* Write a **book review** or make a series of **drawings** illustrating the story.

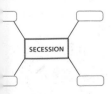

3

Slavery Dominates Politics

MAIN IDEA	WHY IT MATTERS NOW	TERMS & NAMES
Disagreement over slavery led to the formation of the Republican Party and heightened sectional tensions.	The Democrats and the Republicans are the major political parties of today.	Republican Party Roger B. T John C. Frémont Abraham James Buchanan Harpers Fe *Dred Scott* v. *Sandford*

ONE AMERICAN'S STORY

Joseph Warren, editor of the Detroit *Tribune,* wanted the antislavery parties of Michigan to join forces.

A VOICE FROM THE PAST

[A convention should be called] irrespective of the old party organizations, for the purpose of agreeing upon some plan of action that shall combine the whole anti-Nebraska, anti-slavery sentiment of the State, upon one ticket [set of candidates endorsed by a political party].

Detroit *Tribune,* quoted in *The Origins of the Republican Party*

On July 6, 1854, antislavery politicians from various parties met to form a new party and called themselves Republicans. In this section, you will learn why the Republican Party was formed and how it changed American politics in the 1850s.

This medal
early motto
Republican
also makes
Republican
to the antis
position of
Soil Party.

The Republican Party Forms

Taking Notes

Use your chart to take notes about the election of 1860.

SECESSION

The creation of the Republican Party grew out of the problems caused by the Kansas–Nebraska Act of 1854. The law immediately caused a political crisis for the Whig Party. Southern Whigs had supported the bill for the same reason that Northern Whigs had opposed it: the bill proposed to open new territories to slavery. There was no room for compromise, so the party split.

The Southern Whigs were destroyed by the split. A few joined the Democratic Party. But most searched for leaders who supported slavery and the Union. The Northern Whigs, however, joined with other opponents of slavery and formed the **Republican Party.**

The Republicans quickly gained strength in the North. "Bleeding Kansas" was the key to the Republican rise. Many people blamed the violence on the Democrats. With the 1856 elections nearing, the

Republicans believed that they had an excellent opportunity to gain seats in Congress and win the presidency.

The Republicans needed a strong presidential candidate in 1856 to strengthen their young party. They nominated **John C. Frémont.** Young and handsome, Frémont was a national hero for his explorations in the West, which earned him the nickname the "Pathfinder."

Republicans liked Frémont for a couple of reasons. He had spoken in favor of admitting both California and Kansas as free states. Also, he had little political experience and did not have a controversial record to defend. Even so, the Republican position on slavery was so unpopular in the South that Frémont's name did not appear on the ballot there.

ding **History**

mmarizing
did the
blicans nomi-
Frémont for
dent in 1856?

The Election of 1856

The Democrats nominated **James Buchanan** to run for the presidency in 1856. As minister to Great Britain, he had been in England since 1853 and had spoken neither for nor against the Kansas–Nebraska Act.

Buchanan took advantage of his absence from the country. He said little about slavery and claimed that his goal was to maintain the Union. Buchanan appealed to Southerners, to many people in the upper South and the border states, and to Northerners who were afraid that Frémont's election could tear the nation apart.

The American, or Know-Nothing, Party also nominated a presidential candidate in 1856. They chose Millard Fillmore, who had been president, following the death of Zachary Taylor, from 1850 until 1853. But the Know-Nothings were divided over slavery and had little strength.

The 1856 presidential election broke down into two separate races. In the North, it was Buchanan against Frémont. In the South, it was Buchanan against Fillmore. Buchanan won. He carried all the slave states except Maryland, where Fillmore claimed his only victory. Buchanan also won several Northern states.

Although he lost the election, Frémont won 11 Northern states. These results showed two things. First, the Republican Party was a major force in the North. Second, the nation was sharply split over slavery.

The Case of Dred Scott

The split in the country was made worse by the Supreme Court decision in the case of Dred Scott. Scott had been a slave in Missouri. His owner took him to live in territories where slavery was illegal. Then they returned to Missouri. After his owner's death, Scott sued for his freedom. He argued that he was a free man because he had lived in territories where slavery was illegal. His case, **_Dred Scott_ v. _Sandford_,** reached the Supreme Court in 1856.

Now and then

THIRD-PARTY CANDIDATES
American politics has usually been dominated by two parties. Most third-party candidates, such as the Republican Frémont in 1856, lose elections. Still, third parties are important. Women's right to vote, child labor laws, and the Social Security Act all began as third-party initiatives.

Modern third parties such as the Libertarian, Reform, and Green parties, continue to run candidates for office. In 1998, Reform Party candidate Jesse Ventura was elected governor of Minnesota. In the 2000 presidential election, Ralph Nader (below) ran for the Green Party and received nearly 3 million votes.

In 1857, the Court ruled against Scott. Chief Justice **Roger B. Taney** [TAW•nee] delivered his opinion in the case. In it, he said that Dred Scott was not a U.S. citizen. As a result, he could not sue in U.S. courts. Taney also ruled that Scott was bound by Missouri's slave code because he lived in Missouri. As a result, Scott's time in free territory did not matter in his case.

In addition, Taney argued that Congress could not ban slavery in the territories. To do so would violate the slaveholders' property rights, protected by the Fifth Amendment. In effect, Taney declared legislation such as the Missouri Compromise unconstitutional.

Southerners cheered the Court's decision. Many Northerners were outraged and looked to the Republican Party to halt the growing power of Southern slaveholders.

Reading His
B. Recognizi
Effects How
did Taney's
opinion affe
the Missouri
Compromise

Dred Scott (above) first sued for his freedom in 1846. The Supreme Court, led by Chief Justice Roger B. Taney (right), did not rule on the case until 1857.

Lincoln and Douglas Debate

After the *Dred Scott* decision, the Republicans charged that the Democrats wanted to legalize slavery not only in all U.S. territories but also in all the states. They used this charge to attack individual Democrats. Stephen A. Douglas, sponsor of the Kansas–Nebraska Act, was one of their main targets in 1858. That year, Illinois Republicans nominated **Abraham Lincoln** to challenge Douglas for his U.S. Senate seat. In his first campaign speech, Lincoln expressed the Northern fear that Southerners wanted to expand slavery to the entire nation. He set the stage for his argument by using a metaphor from the Bible.

A VOICE FROM THE PAST

"A house divided against itself cannot stand." I believe this government cannot endure, permanently half slave and half free. I do not expect the Union to be dissolved—I do not expect the house to fall—but I do expect it will cease to be divided. It will become all one thing, or all the other.

Abraham Lincoln, Springfield, Illinois, June 16, 1858

Later in the year, the two men held formal debates across Illinois. The Lincoln–Douglas debates are now seen as models of political debate. At the time, the debates allowed people to compare the short, stocky, well-dressed Douglas with the tall, thin, gawky Lincoln.

The two men squarely addressed the nation's most pressing issue: the expansion of slavery. For Lincoln, slavery was "a moral, a social and a political wrong." But he did not suggest abolishing slavery where it already existed. He argued only that slavery should not be expanded.

Douglas did not share Lincoln's belief that it was the national government's role to prevent the expansion of slavery. Instead, he argued

Debating Points of View

ebate has long been an important method of exploring public
sues. The Lincoln-Douglas debates drew crowds from all over Illinois
 hear Lincoln and Douglas discuss the issues of the day. Debates
ch as these can help people find out about candidates' views.

   Today, the National Forensic League (NFL) sponsors Lincoln-
ouglas Debates, competitions for high school students. Many judges,
ctors, news commentators, and talk show hosts began to develop
eir debating skills in such competitions.

   High school students can benefit from
arning to defend their positions in
ebates. One student explained
hat she learned from NFL
ebates. "I learned about
ow to think really fast
nd how to respond."

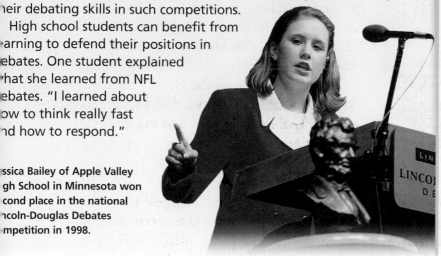

ssica Bailey of Apple Valley
gh School in Minnesota won
cond place in the national
ncoln-Douglas Debates
mpetition in 1998.

How Do You Debate an Issue?

1. Choose a debate opponent and an issue to debate. (One NFL topic for national competition was whether the federal government should establish an educational policy to increase academic achievement in secondary schools in the United States.)

2. Research the topic you chose.

3. Agree on a format for your debate—how many minutes for presentation, rebuttal, and closing.

4. Debate your opponent in front of the class.

5. Find out how many students in the audience agree with each side, then ask for their reasons.

See Citizenship Handbook, page 285.

For more about debating . . .

RESEARCH LINKS CLASSZONE.COM

that popular sovereignty was the best way to address the issue because it was the most democratic method to do so.

ing**History**

king
nces Why
popular
eignty and
pinion in
ed Scott
nconsistent?

   But popular sovereignty was a problem for Douglas. The Supreme Court decision in the *Dred Scott* case had made popular sovereignty unconstitutional. Why? It said that people could not vote to ban slavery, because doing so would take away slaveholders' property rights. In the debates, Lincoln asked Douglas if he thought people in a territory who were against slavery could legally prohibit it—despite the *Dred Scott* decision.

   Douglas replied that it did not matter what the Supreme Court might decide about slavery because "the people have the lawful means to introduce it or exclude it as they please." Douglas won reelection. Lincoln, despite his loss, became a national figure and strengthened his standing in the Republican Party.

John Brown Attacks Harpers Ferry

ulary
l: stock of
ns

In 1859, John Brown, who had murdered proslavery Kansans three years before, added to the sectional tensions. Brown had a plan. He wanted to inspire slaves to fight for their freedom. To do this, he planned to capture the weapons in the U.S. arsenal at **Harpers Ferry,** Virginia.

   On October 16, 1859, Brown and 18 followers—13 whites and 5 blacks—captured the Harpers Ferry arsenal. They killed four people in the raid. Brown then sent out the word to rally and arm local slaves.

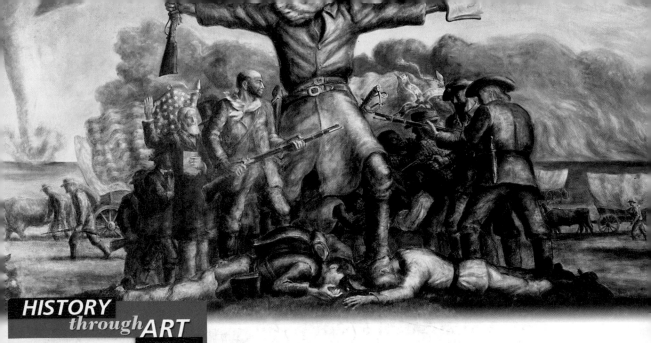

HISTORY through ART

John Steuart Curry painted *The Tragic Prelude* between 1937 and 1942. He shows a wild-eyed John Brown standing on the bodies of Civil War soldiers.

What do you think Curry's views were on John Brown's role in U.S. history?

But no slaves joined the fight. The U.S. Marines attacked Brown at Harpers Ferry. Some of his men escaped. But Brown and six others were captured, and ten men were killed.

Brown was then tried for murder and treason. He was convicted and sentenced to hang. On the day he was hanged, abolitionists tolled bells and fired guns in salute. Southerners were enraged by Brown's actions and horrified by Northern reactions to his death.

As the nation headed toward the election of 1860, the issue of slavery had raised sectional tensions to the breaking point. In the next section, you will read about the election of 1860 and its effect on the nation.

Section 3 Assessment

1. Terms & Names

Explain the significance of:
- Republican Party
- John C. Frémont
- James Buchanan
- *Dred Scott* v. *Sandford*
- Roger B. Taney
- Abraham Lincoln
- Harpers Ferry

2. Using Graphics

Use a chart like the one below to take notes on the major events discussed in this section.

Election of 1856	
Dred Scott v. *Sandford*	
Lincoln–Douglas debates	
Harpers Ferry	

3. Main Ideas

a. What issues led to the creation of the Republican Party?

b. What consequences did the *Dred Scott* decision have for free blacks?

c. How did John Brown's attack on Harpers Ferry increase tensions between the North and the South?

4. Critical Thinking

Identifying Facts and Opinions How did Lincoln and Douglas disagree about slavery? Which of their views were facts, and which were opinions?

THINK ABOUT
- Lincoln's speech at Springfield in 1858
- Douglas's support of popular sovereignty

ACTIVITY OPTIONS

MATH

GEOGRAPHY

Do research to find election returns from the 1856 presidential election. Make **graphs** or draw a **map** to illustrate the results.

4

Lincoln's Election and Southern Secession

ONE AMERICAN'S STORY

In 1860, most people assumed that William Seward of New York would win the Rebublican party's presidential nomination.

However, throughout the Republican convention, other candidates tried to win away Seward's delegates. Abraham Lincoln, a lesser-known candidate from Illinois, gained strength. The reporter Murat Halstead described the scene as Lincoln received the winning votes.

A VOICE FROM THE PAST

There was a moment's silence. The nerves of the thousands, which through the hours of suspense had been subjected to terrible tension, relaxed, and as deep breaths of relief were taken, there was a noise in the Wigwam [convention hall] like the rush of a great wind [just before] a storm—and in another breath, the storm was there. There were thousands cheering with the energy of insanity.

Murat Halstead, *Caucuses of 1860*

In 1860, the Republican delegates met in Chicago at a convention hall known as the Wigwam.

Having won the nomination, Lincoln could turn his attention to winning the general election. In this section, you will learn about the election of 1860 and its role in pushing the nation toward civil war.

Political Parties Splinter

In April, a few weeks before the Republicans nominated Abraham Lincoln, the Democrats held their convention in Charleston, South Carolina. Northern and Southern Democrats disagreed over what to say about slavery in the party's **platform,** or statement of beliefs.

The Southerners wanted the party to defend slavery in the platform.

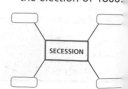

Taking Notes

Use your chart to take notes about the election of 1860.

SECESSION

But Northerners wanted the platform to support popular sovereignty as a way of deciding whether a territory became a free state or a slave state. The Northerners won the platform vote, causing 50 Southern delegates to walk out of the convention.

The remaining delegates tried to nominate a presidential candidate. Stephen A. Douglas was the leading contender, but the Southerners who stayed refused to back him because of his support for popular sovereignty. Douglas could not win enough votes to gain the nomination.

Finally, the Democrats gave up and decided to meet again in Baltimore in June to choose a candidate. But as the Baltimore convention opened, Northerners and Southerners remained at odds. This time, almost all the Southerners left the meeting.

With the Southerners gone, the Northern Democrats nominated Douglas. Meanwhile, the Southern Democrats decided to nominate their own candidate. They chose John Breckinridge of Kentucky, the current vice-president and a supporter of slavery.

As you read in One American's Story on page 471, the Republicans had already nominated Abraham Lincoln. In addition to Lincoln, Douglas, and Breckinridge, a candidate from a fourth party entered the race. This party was called the Constitutional Union Party, and its members had one aim—to preserve the Union. They nominated John Bell of Tennessee to run for president.

*Reading*His
A. Recognizi
Effects How
slavery affec
political par
in 1860?

The Election of 1860

The election of 1860 turned into two different races for the presidency, one in the North and one in the South. Lincoln and Douglas were the only candidates with much support in the North. Breckinridge and Bell competed for Southern votes.

Lincoln and Breckinridge were considered to have the most extreme views on slavery. Lincoln opposed the expansion of slavery into the territories. Breckinridge insisted that the federal government be required to protect slavery in any territory. Douglas and Bell were considered moderates because neither wanted the federal government to pass new laws on slavery.

The outcome of the election made it clear that the nation was tired of compromise. Lincoln defeated Douglas in the North. Breckinridge carried most of the South. Douglas and Bell managed to win only in the states between the North and the Deep South. Because the North had more people in it than the South, Lincoln won the election.

This cartoon of the long-legged Abe Lincoln shows him to be the fittest candidate in the 1860 presidential election.

A POLITICAL RACE

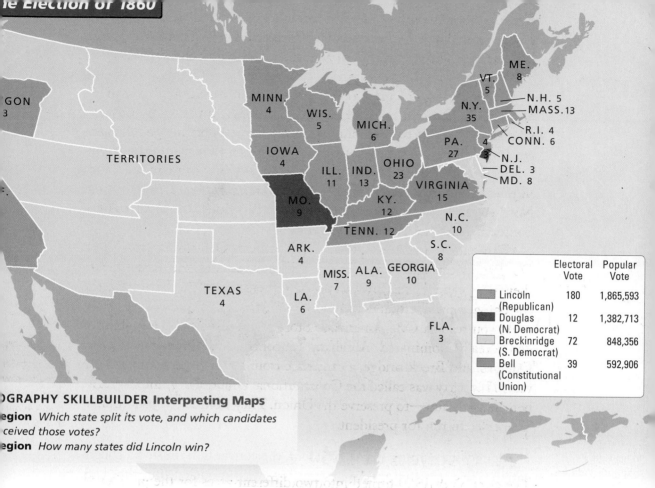

Region Which state split its vote, and which candidates received those votes?
Region How many states did Lincoln win?

Despite Lincoln's statements that he would do nothing to abolish slavery in the South, white Southerners did not trust him. Many were sure that he and the other Republicans would move to ban slavery. As a result, white Southerners saw the Republican victory as a threat to the Southern way of life.

Southern States Secede

Before the 1860 presidential election, many Southerners had warned that if Lincoln won, the Southern states would **secede,** or withdraw from the Union. Supporters of secession based their arguments on the idea of states' rights. They argued that the states had voluntarily joined the Union. Consequently, they claimed that the states also had the right to leave the Union.

On December 20, 1860, South Carolina became the first state to secede. Other states in the Deep South, where slave labor and cotton production were most common, also considered secession. During the next six weeks, Mississippi, Florida, Alabama, Georgia, Louisiana, and Texas joined South Carolina in secession.

In early February 1861, the states that had seceded met in Montgomery, Alabama. They formed the **Confederate States of America.** The convention named **Jefferson Davis** president of the Confederacy.

round
becoming
nt of the
eracy,
ad been
during
r with
and a
ator.

In his First Inaugural Address, Lincoln argued passionately for the North and the South to preserve the Union.

Along with naming Davis president, the convention drafted a constitution. The Confederate Constitution was modeled on the U.S. Constitution. But there were a few important differences. For example, the Confederate Constitution supported states' rights. It also protected slavery in the Confederacy, including any territories it might acquire.

Having formed its government, the Confederate states made plans to defend their separation from the Union. Some believed that war between the states could not be avoided. But everyone waited to see what the Union government would do in response.

The Union Responds to Secession

Northerners considered the secession of the Southern states to be unconstitutional. During his last months in office, President James Buchanan argued against secession. He believed that the states did not have the right to withdraw from the Union because the federal government, not the state governments, was sovereign. If secession were permitted, the Union would become weak, like a "rope of sand." He believed that the U.S. Constitution was framed to prevent such a thing from happening.

In addition to these issues, secession raised the issue of majority rule. Southerners complained that Northerners intended to use their majority to force the South to abolish slavery. But Northerners responded that Southerners simply did not want to live by the rules of democracy. They complained that Southerners were not willing to live with the election results. As Northern writer James Russell Lowell

Vocabular
sovereign:
supreme, s
governing
authority

wrote, "[The Southerners'] quarrel is not with the Republican Party, but with the theory of Democracy."

Efforts to Compromise Fail

With the states in the lower South forming a new government in Montgomery, Alabama, some people continued to seek compromise. Senator John J. Crittenden of Kentucky developed a compromise plan. The **Crittenden Plan** was presented to Congress in late February 1861, but it did not pass.

> ## "We must not be enemies."
> Abraham Lincoln

With the hopes for compromise fading, Americans waited for Lincoln's inauguration. What would the new president do about the crisis? On March 4, Lincoln took the oath of office and gave his First Inaugural Address. He assured the South that he had no intention of abolishing slavery there. But he spoke forcefully against secession. Then he ended his speech with an appeal to friendship.

A VOICE FROM THE PAST

*ing*History

*k*ing
*n*ces What
u think
n meant by
c chords of
ry"?

We are not enemies, but friends. We must not be enemies. Though passion may have strained, it must not break our bonds of affection. The mystic chords of memory, stretching from every battle-field and patriot grave, to every living heart and hearthstone, all over this broad land, will yet swell the chorus of the Union, when again touched, as surely they will be, by the better angels of our nature.

Abraham Lincoln, *First Inaugural Address*

Lincoln would not press the South. He wanted no invasion. But he would not abandon the government's property there. Several forts in the South, including Fort Sumter in South Carolina, were still in Union hands. These forts would soon need to be resupplied. Throughout March and into April, Northerners and Southerners waited anxiously to see what would happen next. You will find out in the next chapter.

---

4 **Assessment**

Terms & Names

plain the
gnificance of:
atform
cede
nfederate States
* America*
fferson Davis
ittenden Plan

2. Using Graphics

Use a time line to fill in the main events that occurred between April 1860 and March 1861.

April	June	Feb.
1860	1860	1861

May	Nov.	March
1860	1860	1861

Do you think secession could have been avoided? Why?

3. Main Ideas

a. Who were the candidates in the 1860 presidential election, and what policies did each candidate stand for?

b. Which states seceded right after Lincoln's election? How did they justify this action?

c. What attempts did the North and the South make to compromise? What were the results?

4. Critical Thinking

Analyzing Points of View
Do you think the Southern states seceded to protect slavery or states' rights?

THINK ABOUT
• the Southern view of the Fugitive Slave Act
• the Confederate Constitution
• slaveholders' views of the Republican Party

IVITY OPTIONS

SPEECH
ECHNOLOGY

Read Lincoln's First Inaugural Address. Deliver a section of the **speech** before the class or plan an **electronic presentation** about that day and Lincoln's message.

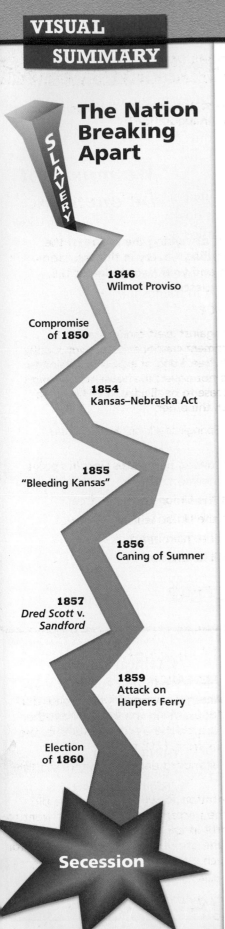

VISUAL SUMMARY

The Nation Breaking Apart

SLAVERY

1846 Wilmot Proviso

Compromise of 1850

1854 Kansas–Nebraska Act

1855 "Bleeding Kansas"

1856 Caning of Sumner

1857 *Dred Scott* v. *Sandford*

1859 Attack on Harpers Ferry

Election of 1860

Secession

TERMS & NAMES

Briefly explain the significance of each of the following.

1. Wilmot Proviso
2. Compromise of 1850
3. *Uncle Tom's Cabin*
4. popular sovereignty
5. Kansas–Nebraska Act
6. John Brown
7. John C. Frémont
8. *Dred Scott* v. *Sandford*
9. secede
10. Confederate States of America

REVIEW QUESTIONS

Growing Tensions Between North and South (pages 457–461)

1. How did the North and the South differ in the 1840s?
2. How did Southerners react to the Wilmot Proviso?
3. What was Stephen A. Douglas's role in passing the Compromise of 1850?

The Crisis Deepens (pages 462–465)

4. How did Northerners react to the Fugitive Slave Act?
5. Why did most Northerners and Southerners disagree about the Kansas–Nebraska Act?
6. How did "Bleeding Kansas" cause problems for Democrats?

Slavery Dominates Politics (pages 466–470)

7. What positions did Lincoln and Douglas take in their debates?
8. What was the result of John Brown's raid on Harpers Ferry?

Lincoln's Election and Southern Secession (pages 471–475)

9. What were the results of the election of 1860, and what did these results show?
10. How did Southerners justify secession?

CRITICAL THINKING

1. USING YOUR NOTES: ANALYZING CAUSES

Using your completed diagram, answer the questions below.

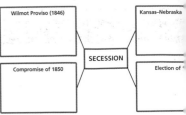

a. What did the Compromise o 1850 and the Kansas–Nebras Act have in common?
b. Which event do you think caused the most damage to the relationship between th North and the South? Expla

2. ANALYZING LEADERSHIP

Why were the nation's leaders 1860 unable to compromise lik the leaders in 1820 and 1850? Does their failure to comprom in 1860 mean that they were r as capable as earlier leaders?

3. APPLYING CITIZENSHIP SK

What alternatives did the state the lower South have to secess Which of these alternatives do you think would have been th best choice?

4. SOLVING PROBLEMS

How did slavery divide Americ in the 1850s?

5. THEME: DIVERSITY AND U

What could have been done in 1850s to prevent the Southern states from seceding? What di Americans have in common th could have overcome their dif ences over slavery?

Interact *with* Histo

Now that you have read abou sectional crisis of the 1850s, d think the solution you came u with at the start of the chapte would have helped keep the together? Explain.

e the map and your knowledge of U.S. history to
swer questions 1 and 2.

dditional Test Practice, pp. S1–S33.

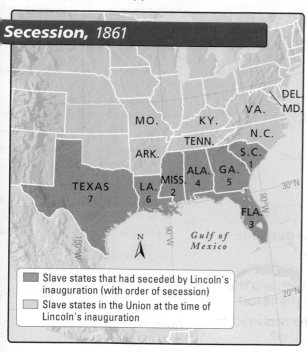

Secession, 1861

Slave states that had seceded by Lincoln's
inauguration (with order of secession)

Slave states in the Union at the time of
Lincoln's inauguration

Of the following states, which was the last to
secede before Lincoln's Inauguration?

A. South Carolina

B. Texas

C. Georgia

D. Louisiana

2. How many slave states were in the Union at the
time of Lincoln's inauguration?

A. 6

B. 7

C. 8

D. 9

**Abraham Lincoln is discussing the future of the
United States regarding slavery in this quotation.
Use the quotation and your knowledge of U.S.
history to answer question 3.**

PRIMARY SOURCE

"A house divided against itself cannot stand." I
believe this government cannot endure, permanently
half slave and half free. I do not expect the Union to
be dissolved—I do not expect the house to fall—but I
do expect it will cease to be divided. It will become
all one thing, or all the other.

Abraham Lincoln, Springfield, Illinois, June 16, 1858

3. Which of the following best states Lincoln's point
of view?

A. The states of the Union will be all free.

B. The states of the Union will be all slave.

C. The Union will remain intact.

D. The Union will be divided.

TEST PRACTICE
CLASSZONE.COM

ERNATIVE ASSESSMENT

✎ WRITING ABOUT HISTORY

ne you work for a popular magazine and have been
ed to write an **article** about one of the important
s in this chapter. You might choose such figures such
riet Beecher Stowe or Stephen A. Douglas.

ite a series of questions to ask this person.

library resources to see how he or she might
wer your questions.

OPERATIVE LEARNING

with a small group to research the Dred Scott
nd conduct a mock trial. In your research, look
formation about the roles of Taney, the other
s, Scott, and other major participants. After you
ct the trial, have your class decide on a verdict.

INTEGRATED TECHNOLOGY

DOING INTERNET RESEARCH

Political parties in America changed a great deal during the 1840s and 1850s. Using the Internet or other
library resources, research the election returns of the
presidential elections from 1848 to 1860.

- Use an online or standard encyclopedia to find the
  election results.

- Prepare a presentation for your class. Create pie
  charts to show the percentage of votes that went to
  each political party in each election. Or use bar
  graphs to show the growth in total popular vote for
  each party for each election.

For more about these elections . . .

INTERNET ACTIVITY
CLASSZONE.COM

The Civil War Begins 1861–1862

In this vivid engraving, South Carolina shore guns fire on Fort Sumter in Charleston's harbor.

March 4, 1861
Abraham Lincoln inaugurated as president.

April 12, 1861
Confederate forces fire on Fort Sumter.

July 21, 1861
First Battle of Bull Run (Manassas) occurs.

USA
World 1861

March, 1861
Italy unified under King Victor Emmanuel II.

May 13, 1861
Britain declares neutrality in American Civil War.

The battle rages in the harbor.

People watch the bombardment from their rooftops.

The date is April 12, 1861. You and other residents of Charleston, South Carolina, watch the bombardment of Fort Sumter by Confederate forces. This event signals the beginning of the Civil War—a war between factions or regions of the same country.

How might a civil war be worse than other wars?

What Do You Think?

• What social, political, and economic problems might be likely to occur in a civil war?

• What might happen when a civil war breaks out?

RESEARCH LINKS
CLASSZONE.COM

Visit the Chapter 16 links for more information about the beginning of the Civil War.

April 6, 1862
Battle of Shiloh takes place.

April 25, 1862
New Orleans falls to Union forces.

September 17, 1862
Battle of Antietam (Sharpsburg) occurs.

1862

ril 13, 1862
rance annexes
Cochin China
ern Vietnam).

May 5, 1862
French troops are defeated at Puebla, Mexico.

June 25, 1862
Imperial decree expels foreigners from Japan.

September, 1862
Bismarck becomes prime minister of Prussia.

Reading Strategy: Comparing and Contrastin

What Do You Know?

What do you think of when you hear the phrase *civil war*? What would it be like to fight in a war of brother against brother? Where and how did the Civil War begin?

Think About

- what a civil war is
- what you've learned about the Civil War from movies, television, and books
- reasons that countries threaten to break apart in today's world
- your responses to the Interact with History about how a civil war is worse than other wars (see page 479)

These are the Union flag (left) and a Confe flag (right).

What Do You Want to Know?

 What details do you need to help you understand the outbreak of the Civil War? Make list of those details in your notebook before you read the chapter.

Comparing and Contrasting

When you compare, you look for similarities between two or more objects, ideas, events people. When you contrast, you look for differences. Comparing and contrasting can be useful strategy for studying the two sides in a war. Use the chart shown here to compare and contrast the North and the South in the early years of the Civil War.

 See Skillbuilder Handbook, page R10.

Taking Notes

	North	South
Reasons for fighting		
Advantages		
Disadvantages		
Military strategy		
Battle victories		

War Erupts

ONE AMERICAN'S STORY

Like other South Carolinians, Emma Holmes got caught up in the passions that led her state to secede. In her diary, she wrote about South Carolina's attack on Fort Sumter, a federal fort in Charleston's harbor.

A VOICE FROM THE PAST

[A]t half past four this morning, the heavy booming of cannons woke the city from its slumbers. . . . Every body seems relieved that what has been so long dreaded has come at last and so confident of victory that they seem not to think of the danger of their friends. . . . With the telescope I saw the shots as they struck the fort and [saw] the masonry crumbling.

Emma Holmes, *The Diary of Emma Holmes 1861–1866*

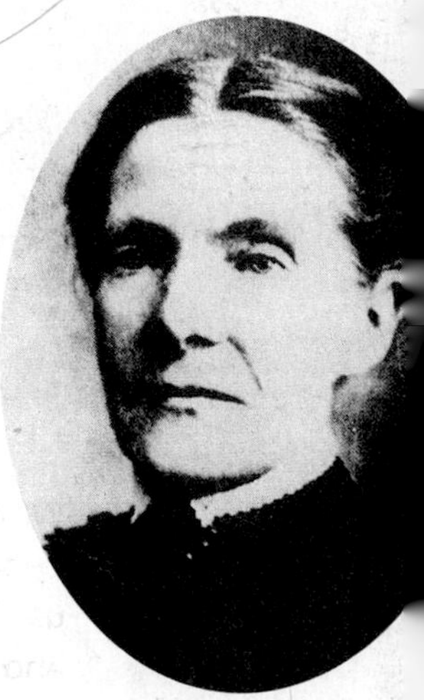

Many Southerners expected a short war that they would easily win. Northerners expected the same. In this section, you will learn how the war started, how the states divided, and how each side planned to win.

This photograph of Emma Holmes was taken in 1900.

First Shots at Fort Sumter

As they seceded from the Union (the states loyal to the United States of America during the Civil War), the Southern states took over most of the federal forts inside their borders. President Abraham Lincoln had to decide what to do about the forts that remained under federal control. Major Robert Anderson and his garrison held on to **Fort Sumter** in the harbor of Charleston, South Carolina, but they were running out of supplies.

If Lincoln supplied the garrison, he risked war. If he ordered the troops to leave the fort, he would be giving in to the rebels. Lincoln informed South Carolina that he was sending supply ships to Fort Sumter. Leaders of the Confederacy (the nation formed by Southern states in 1861) decided to prevent the federal government from holding onto the fort by attacking before the supply ships arrived.

Taking Notes

Use your chart to take notes about military strategies and the advantages and disadvantages for both sides.

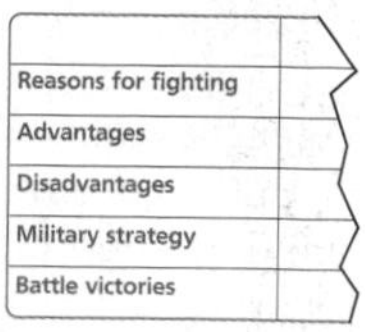

Reasons for fighting	
Advantages	
Disadvantages	
Military strategy	
Battle victories	

At 4:30 A.M. on Aril 12, 1861, shore guns opened fire on the island fort. For 34 hours, the Confederates fired shells into the fort until Anderson was forced to surrender. No one was killed, but the South's attack on Fort Sumter was the beginning of the Civil War.

Lincoln Calls Out the Militia

Two days after the surrender of Fort Sumter, President Lincoln asked the Union states to provide 75,000 militiamen for 90 days to put down the uprising in the South. Citizens of the North responded with enthusiasm to the call to arms. A New York woman wrote, "It seems as if we never were alive till now; never had a country till now."

In the upper South, however, state leaders responded with anger. The governor of Kentucky said that the state would "furnish no troops for the wicked purpose of subduing her sister Southern States." In the weeks that followed, Virginia, North Carolina, Tennessee, and Arkansas voted to join the Confederacy.

As each state seceded, volunteers rushed to enlist, just as citizens did in the North. A young Arkansas enlistee wrote, "So impatient did I become for starting that I felt like ten thousand pins were pricking me in every part of the body, and started off a week in advance of my brothers." Some feared the war would be over before they got the chance to fight.

With Virginia on its side, the Confederacy had a much better chance for victory. Virginia was wealthy and populous, and the Confederacy in May of 1861 moved its capital to Richmond. Virginia also was the home of **Robert E. Lee,** a talented military leader. When Virginia seceded, Lee resigned from the United States Army and joined the Confederacy. Although Lee opposed slavery and secession, he explained, "I cannot raise my hand against my birthplace, my home, my children." He eventually became the commanding general of the Army of Northern Virginia.

Choosing Sides

After Virginia seceded, both sides knew that the border states would play a key role in the war's outcome. The **border states**—Delaware, Maryland, Kentucky, and Missouri—were slave states that bordered states in which slavery was illegal. Because of their location and resources, the border states could tip the scales toward one side.

Keeping Maryland in the Union was important for the North. If Maryland seceded, then Washington, D.C., would be cut off from the Union. To hold on to the state, Lincoln ordered the arrest of Maryland lawmakers who backed the South. Union forces arrested 31 secessionist

Backgroun
The state mil
were armies
ordinary citiz
rather than p
fessional sol

Reading **Hi**
A. Comparir
Why might
zens in both
North and t
South have
eager to fig
the Civil Wa

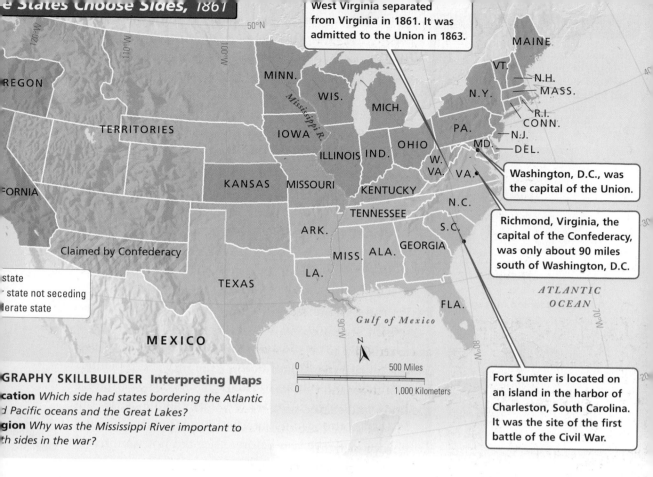

West Virginia separated from Virginia in 1861. It was admitted to the Union in 1863.

MAINE

VT.

N.H.

MASS.

R.I.

CONN.

N.J.

DEL.

MINN.

WIS.

MICH.

N.Y.

PA.

IOWA

OHIO

ILLINOIS IND.

W. VA.

VA.

MD.

Washington, D.C., was the capital of the Union.

REGON

TERRITORIES

KANSAS MISSOURI

KENTUCKY

N.C.

Richmond, Virginia, the capital of the Confederacy, was only about 90 miles south of Washington, D.C.

TENNESSEE

ARK.

S.C.

GEORGIA

MISS. ALA.

LA.

TEXAS

FLA.

ATLANTIC OCEAN

Claimed by Confederacy

state

state not seceding

erate state

MEXICO

Gulf of Mexico

0   500 Miles

0   1,000 Kilometers

Fort Sumter is located on an island in the harbor of Charleston, South Carolina. It was the site of the first battle of the Civil War.

GRAPHY SKILLBUILDER **Interpreting Maps**

cation *Which side had states bordering the Atlantic d Pacific oceans and the Great Lakes?*

gion *Why was the Mississippi River important to th sides in the war?*

members of the legislature. They were held for at least two months—after the election of a new legislature.

Kentucky was also important to both sides because of its rivers. For the Union, the rivers could provide an invasion route into the South. For the South, the rivers could provide a barrier. Kentuckians were deeply divided over secession. However, a Confederate invasion in 1861 prompted the state to stay in the Union.

Both Missouri and Delaware also stayed in the Union. In Virginia, federal troops helped a group of western counties break away. These counties formed the state of West Virginia and returned to the Union. In the end, 24 states made up the Union and 11 joined the Confederacy.

History

narizing

ere the

states crit-

he war's

e?

Strengths and Weaknesses

The Union had huge advantages in manpower and resources. The North had about 22 million people. The Confederacy had roughly 9 million, of whom about 3.5 million were slaves. About 85 percent of the nation's factories were located in the North. The North had more than double the railroad mileage of the South. Almost all the naval power and shipyards belonged to the North.

The Union's greatest asset, however, was President Abraham Lincoln. He developed into a remarkable leader. Lincoln convinced Northerners that democracy depended on preserving the Union.

The pie charts show the relative strength of the Union and the Confederacy in population and industry.

Total U.S. Population

29%   71%

■ Union   ■ Confederacy

Total U.S. Railroad Mileage

29%   71%

Total U.S. Manufacturing Plants

15%

85%

Total U.S. Industrial Workers

8%

92%

Source: *Encyclopedia Americana*

SKILLBUILDER
Interpreting Charts

1. *Which side had more resources?*
2. *How might the North's railways and factories have helped its armies?*

The Confederacy had some advantages, too. It began the war with able generals, such as Robert E. Lee. It also had the advantage of fighting a defensive war. This meant Northern supply lines would have to be stretched very far. In addition, soldiers defending their homes have more will to fight than invaders do.

The Confederate Strategy

At first, the Confederacy took a defensive position. It did not want to conquer the North—it only wanted to be independent. "All we ask is to be let alone," said Confederate President Jefferson Davis. Confederate leaders hoped the North would soon tire of the war and accept Southern independence.

The South also depended on **King Cotton** as a way to win foreign support. Cotton was king because Southern cotton was important in the world market. The South grew most of the cotton for Europe's textile mills. When the war broke out, Southern planters withheld cotton from the market. They hoped to force France and Britain to aid the Confederate cause. But in 1861, European nations had surplus cotton because of a big crop the year before. They did not want to get involved in the American war.

As the war heated up, the South soon moved away from its cautious plans. It began to take the offensive and try for big victories to wreck Northern morale.

The Union Strategy

The North wanted to bring the Southern states back into the Union. To do this, the North developed an offensive strategy based on General Winfield Scott's **Anaconda Plan.** This plan was designed to smother the South's economy like a giant anaconda snake squeezing its prey.

The plan called for a naval blockade of the South's coastline. In a **blockade,** armed forces prevent the transportation of goods or people into or out of an area. The plan also called for the Union to gain control of the Mississippi River. This would split the Confederacy in two.

One of the drawbacks of Scott's plan was that it would take time to work. But many people, eager for action, were calling for an immediate attack on Richmond, the Confederate capital. Lincoln ordered an invasion of Virginia in the summer of 1861.

*Reading*H
C. Supporti
Opinions *A*
beginning
Civil War, v
side would
have predi
win? Why?

Battle of Bull Run

To take Richmond, the Union army would first have to defeat the Confederate troops stationed at the town of Manassas, Virginia. This was a railway center southwest of Washington, D.C.

On July 21, 1861, Union forces commanded by General Irvin McDowell clashed with Confederate forces headed by General Pierre Beauregard near a little creek called Bull Run north of Manassas. In the North, this battle came to be known as the **First Battle of Bull Run**.

The Confederate
Army passes in
review before
General Pierre
Beauregard.

At one point in the battle, a Confederate officer rallied his troops by pointing his sword toward Southern General Thomas J. Jackson. The officer cried, "There is Jackson standing like a stone wall! Rally behind the Virginians!" From this incident, Jackson won the nickname "Stonewall" Jackson. His men held fast against the Union assault.

As fresh troops arrived, the Confederates equaled the Union forces in number and launched a countercharge. Attacking the Union line, they let out a blood-curdling scream. This scream, later called the "rebel yell," caused the Union troops to panic. They broke ranks and scattered.

The Confederate victory in the First Battle of Bull Run thrilled the South and shocked the North. Many in the South thought the war was won. The North realized it had underestimated its opponent. Lincoln sent the 90-day militias home and called for a real army of 500,000 volunteers for three years. In the next section, you will learn what army life was like.

---

tion ❶ Assessment

Terms & Names

plain the
gnificance of:

rt Sumter

bert E. Lee

rder state

ng Cotton

aconda Plan

ockade

rst Battle of
ll Run

2. Using Graphics

Use a Venn diagram to compare and contrast the strengths of the North and the South.

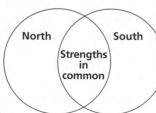

3. Main Ideas

a. How did citizens in the North and the South respond to the outbreak of the Civil War?

b. Why were the border states important to both sides in the Civil War?

c. What kind of military strategy did each side develop?

4. Critical Thinking

Comparing How was the South's situation in the Civil War similar to the situation of the Patriots in the Revolutionary War?

THINK ABOUT

• their reasons for fighting
• their opponents' strengths

IVITY OPTIONS

NGUAGE ARTS

ECHNOLOGY

Read an account of the First Battle of Bull Run. Use the information to write a **news article** or plan the battle's **home page** for the Internet.

Life in the Army

MAIN IDEA	WHY IT MATTERS NOW	TERMS & NAMES
Both Union and Confederate soldiers endured many hardships serving in the army during the Civil War.	The hardships endured led to long-lasting bitterness on both sides.	hygiene minié ball rifle ironclad

ONE AMERICAN'S STORY

In 1862, Peter Vredenburgh, Jr., answered President Lincoln's call for an additional 300,000 soldiers. Nearly 26 years old, Vredenburgh became a major in the 14th Regiment New Jersey Volunteer Infantry. Less than two months after joining the regiment, he wrote a letter urging his parents to keep his 18-year-old brother from enlisting.

> *A VOICE FROM THE PAST*
>
> I am glad that Jim has not joined any Regt. [regiment] and I hope he never will. I would not have him go for all my pay; it would be very improbable that we could both go through this war and come out unharmed. Let him come here and see the thousands with their arms and legs off, or if that won't do, let him go as I did the other day through the Frederick hospitals and see how little account a man's life and limbs are held in by others.
>
> **Major Peter Vredenburgh, Jr.,** quoted in *Upon the Tented Field*

Major Peter Vredenbur[gh], an officer i[n the] Union arm[y]

On September 19, 1864, Vredenburgh was killed in battle. In this section, you will learn more about other soldiers and what their experiences were like.

Taking Notes

Use your chart to take notes about the reasons for fighting the Civil War.

[re]asons for fighting
[ad]vantages
[di]sadvantages
[mi]litary strategy
[ba]ttle victories

Those Who Fought

Like Peter Vredenburgh, the majority of soldiers in the Civil War were between 18 and 30 years of age. But both the Confederate and Union armies had younger and older soldiers. Charles Carter Hay was just 11 years old when he joined an Alabama regiment. William Wilkins was 83 when he became one of the Pennsylvania Home Guards.

Farmers made up the largest group among Civil War soldiers. About half the soldiers on both sides came from farms. Having rarely traveled far from their fields, many viewed going off to war as an exciting adventure. Some rode a train for the first time.

Although the majority of soldiers in the war were born in the United States, immigrants from other countries also served. German and Irish immigrants made up the largest ethnic groups. One regiment from New York had soldiers who were born in 15 foreign countries. The commanding officer gave orders in seven languages.

At the beginning of the war, African Americans wanted to fight. They saw the war as a way to end slavery. However, neither the North nor the South accepted African Americans into their armies. As the war dragged on, the North finally took African Americans into its ranks. Native Americans served on both sides.

In all, about 2 million American soldiers served the Union, and fewer than 1 million served the Confederacy. The vast majority were volunteers. Why did so many Americans volunteer to fight? Many sought adventure and glory. Some sought an escape from the boredom of farm and factory work. Some signed up because their friends and neighbors were doing it. Others signed up for the recruitment money offered by both sides. Soldiers also fought because they were loyal to their country or state.

ing **History**
nmarizing
did most
the North
e South
out going
war?

Turning Civilians into Soldiers

After enlisting, a volunteer was sent to a nearby army camp for training. A typical camp looked like a sea of canvas tents. The tents were grouped by company, and each tent held from two to twenty men. In winter, the soldiers lived in log huts or in heavy tents positioned on a log base. In the Civil War, Confederate soldiers and soldiers in volunteer units in the Union Army elected their company officers. Both the Union and Confederate armies followed this practice.

A soldier in training followed a set schedule. A bugle or drum awakened the soldier at dawn. After roll call and breakfast, the soldier had the first of several drill sessions. In between drills and meals, soldiers performed guard duty, cut wood for the campfires, dug trenches for latrines (outdoor toilets), and cleaned up the camp.

Shortly after they came to camp, new recruits were given uniforms and equipment. Union soldiers wore blue uniforms, and Confederate soldiers wore gray or

daily *life*

DRILL SESSIONS

"The first thing in the morning is drill. Then drill, then drill again. Then drill, drill, a little more drill. Then drill, and lastly drill." That is the way one soldier described his day in camp.

A soldier in training might have as many as five drill sessions a day, each lasting up to two hours. The soldiers learned to stand straight and march in formation. They also learned to load and fire their guns. Shown drilling below are soldiers of the 22nd New York State Militia near Harpers Ferry, Virginia, in 1862.

yellowish-brown uniforms. Getting a uniform of the right size was a problem, however. On both sides, soldiers traded items to get clothing that fit properly.

Early in the war, Northern soldiers received clothing of very poor quality. Contractors took advantage of the government's need and supplied shoddy goods. Shoes made of imitation leather, for example, fell apart when they got wet. In the Confederacy, some states had trouble providing uniforms at all, while others had surpluses. Because the states did not always cooperate and share supplies, Confederate soldiers sometimes lacked shoes. Like soldiers in the Revolutionary War, they marched over frozen ground in bare feet. After battles, needy soldiers took coats, boots, and other clothing from the dead.

At the beginning of the war, most soldiers in army camps received plenty of food. Their rations included beef or salt pork, flour, vegetables, and coffee. But when they were in the field, the soldiers' diet became more limited. Some soldiers went hungry because supply trains could not reach them.

STRANGE *but* True

DEADLIER THAN BULLETS

"Look at our company—21 have died of disease, 18 have become so unhealthy as to be discharged, and only four have been killed in battle." So a Louisiana officer explained the high death rate in the Civil War.

More than twice as many men died of disease as died of battle wounds. Intestinal disorders, including typhoid fever, diarrhea, and dysentery, killed the most. Pneumonia, tuberculosis, and malaria killed many others. Bad water and food, poor diet, exposure to cold and rain, unsanitary conditions, and disease-carrying insects all contributed to the high rate of disease.

Hardships of Army Life

Civil War soldiers in the field were often wet, muddy, or cold from marching outdoors and living in crude shelters. Many camps were unsanitary and smelled from the odors of garbage and latrines. One Union soldier described a camp near Washington. In the camp, cattle were killed to provide the troops with meat.

A VOICE FROM THE PAST

The hides and [waste parts] of the [cattle] for miles upon miles around, under a sweltering sun and sultry showers, would gender such swarms of flies, armies of worms, blasts of stench and oceans of filth as to make life miserable.

William Keesy, quoted in *The Civil War Infantryman*

Not only were the camps filthy, but so were the soldiers. They often went weeks without bathing or washing their clothes. Their bodies, clothing, and bedding became infested with lice and fleas.

Poor **hygiene**—conditions and practices that promote health—resulted in widespread sickness. Most soldiers had chronic diarrhea or other intestinal disorders. These disorders were caused by contaminated water or food or by germ-carrying insects. People did not know that germs cause diseases. Doctors failed to wash their hands or their instruments. An observer described how surgeons "armed with long, bloody knives and saws, cut and sawed away with frightful rapidity, throwing the mangled limbs on a pile nearby as soon as removed."

Backgroun
Before unifc
became stan
ized, soldier
dressed in o
supplied fro
home. This c
confusion or
battlefield.

*Reading*H
B. Making
Inferences
changes co
have helpe
lower the s
of disease
soldiers?

: two years of t
le gained a dec
ther.

bulary
lties: num-
f people
or injured

In the
comm
defea
confid
Confe
McCle

ling History
wing
usions
A VC changes in
[S]oo ry technol-
stron ad an effect
of my e average
r? Why?
Gene

Lin
stalling
the We

Uni
That
civilia
egy of
strike
In F
ironcla
These
nearby
opene
could r
ple of l
panic.

The naval duel
between the
Union *Monitor* and
the Confederate
Merrimack (or
Virginia) took place
on March 9, 1862.

Changes in Military Technology

While camp life remained rough, military technology advanced. Improvements in the weapons of war had far-reaching effects. Battle tactics changed, and casualties soared.

Rifles that used minié balls contributed to the high casualty rate in the Civil War. A **rifle** is a gun with a grooved barrel that causes a bullet to spin through the air. This spin gives the bullet more distance and accuracy. The **minié ball** is a bullet with a hollow base. The bullet expands upon firing to fit the grooves in the barrel. Rifles with minié balls could shoot farther and more accurately than old-fashioned muskets. As a result, mounted charges and infantry assaults did not work as well. Defenders using rifles could shoot more of the attackers before they got close.

Ironclads, warships covered with iron, proved to be a vast improvement over wooden ships. In the first ironclad battle, the Confederate *Virginia* (originally named the *Merrimack*) battled the Union *Monitor* off the coast of Virginia in 1862. After hammering away for about four hours, the battle ended in a draw. (See page 492 for more information on ironclads.)

Despite new technology and tactics, neither side gained a decisive victory in the first two years of the war, as you will see in the next section.

Section 2 Assessment

1. Terms & Names

plain the
ignificance of:
ygiene
fle
ninié ball
onclad

2. Using Graphics

Complete the chart below.

The Typical Civil War Soldier	
Age	
Occupation	
Training	
Hardships	

Which hardship do you think would have been most difficult to endure? Why?

3. Main Ideas

a. How were the wartime experiences of Northern and Southern soldiers alike?

b. What factors contributed to the spread of disease among soldiers?

c. How did the use of the rifle and minié ball change combat tactics in the Civil War?

4. Critical Thinking

Forming and Supporting Opinions What were the motives that led individual soldiers to fight in the Civil War?

THINK ABOUT
• the multiple reasons that people had for enlisting
• what you consider valid reasons for fighting

ACTIVITY OPTIONS

LANGUAGE ARTS
ART

Imagine you are a soldier in the Civil War. Write a **letter** home to your parents about your experience or draw an **illustrated map** of your training camp.

The Civil War

Iro...

They m...
huge, h...
wooder...
ble me...

With...
rotating...
the old...
(or *Virg*...
waged...
begun.

The Battle of Shiloh

After Grant's river victories, Albert S. Johnston, Confederate commander on the Western front, ordered a retreat to Corinth, Mississippi. Grant followed. By early April, Grant's troops had reached Pittsburg Landing on the Tennessee River. There he waited for more troops from Nashville. Johnston, however, decided to attack before Grant gained reinforcements. Marching his troops north from Corinth on April 6, 1862, Johnston surprised the Union forces near Shiloh Church. The **Battle of Shiloh** in Tennessee turned into the fiercest fighting the Civil War had yet seen.

Commanders on each side rode into the thick of battle to rally their troops. One Union general, William Tecumseh Sherman, had three horses shot out from under him. General Johnston was killed, and the command passed to General Pierre Beauregard. By the end of the day, each side believed that dawn would bring victory.

That night, there was a terrible thunderstorm. Lightning lit up the battlefield, where dead and dying soldiers lay in water and mud. During the night, Union boats ran upriver to ferry fresh troops to Grant's camp. Grant then led an attack at dawn and forced the exhausted Southern troops to retreat.

The cost of the Union victory was staggering. Union casualties at Shiloh numbered over 13,000, about one-fourth of those who had fought. The Confederates lost nearly 11,000 out of 41,000 soldiers. Describing

Reading **H**

A. Contrast
How did Gr
differ from
McClellan a
military lea

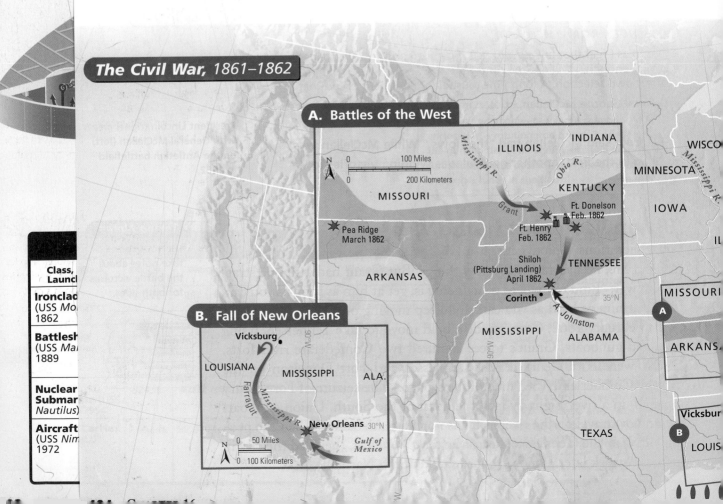

The Civil War, *1861–1862*

A. Battles of the West

INDIANA

ILLINOIS

WISCO

Mississippi R.

Ohio R.

0   100 Miles
0   200 Kilometers

MISSOURI

Grant

KENTUCKY

MINNESOTA

Mississippi R.

Ft. Donelson
Feb. 1862

IOWA

Ft. Henry
Feb. 1862

Pea Ridge
March 1862

ARKANSAS

Shiloh
(Pittsburg Landing)
April 1862

TENNESSEE

Corinth

35°N

MISSOURI

A. Johnston

A

IL

MISSISSIPPI

ALABAMA

ARKANS

B. Fall of New Orleans

Vicksburg

LOUISIANA

MISSISSIPPI

ALA.

Farragut

Mississippi R.

90°W

New Orleans

30°N

0   50 Miles
0   100 Kilometers

Gulf of Mexico

TEXAS

Vicksbur

B

LOUIS

the piles of mangled bodies, General Sherman wrote home, "The scenes on this field would have cured anybody of war." Congressmen criticized Grant for the high casualties and urged Lincoln to replace him. But Lincoln replied, "I can't spare this man—he fights."

The Fall of New Orleans

The spring of 1862 brought other bad news for the Confederacy. On April 25, a Union fleet led by David Farragut captured New Orleans, the largest city in the South. Rebel gunboats tried to ram the Union warships and succeeded in sinking one. Farragut's ships had to run through cannon fire and then dodge burning rafts in order to reach the city. Residents stood on the docks and cursed the Yankee invaders, but they were powerless to stop them.

The fall of New Orleans was a heavy blow to the South. Mary Chesnut of South Carolina, the wife of an aide to President Davis, wrote in her diary, "New Orleans gone—and with it the Confederacy. Are we not cut in two?" Indeed, after the victories of General Grant and Admiral Farragut, only a 150-mile stretch of the Mississippi remained in Southern hands. The Union was well on its way to achieving its goal of cutting the Confederacy in two. But guarding the remaining stretch of the river was the heavily armed Confederate fort at Vicksburg, Mississippi.

*ing***History**
ognizing
s Why
e fall of
Orleans
cant?

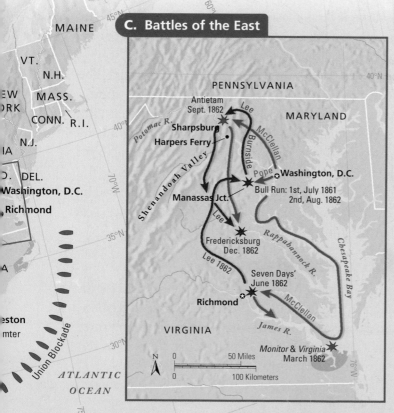

C. Battles of the East

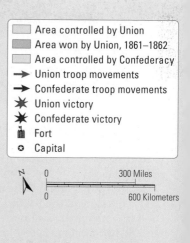

Area controlled by Union
Area won by Union, 1861–1862
Area controlled by Confederacy
→ Union troop movements
→ Confederate troop movements
✹ Union victory
✹ Confederate victory
🏛 Fort
✪ Capital

0   300 Miles
0   600 Kilometers

GEOGRAPHY SKILLBUILDER

1. **Location** *Where did most of the early Union victories take place? Where did early Confederate victories take place?*

2. **Region** *Why did much of the fighting take place in the Virginia-Maryland region?*

Lee Claims Victories in the East

Meanwhile, also in the spring of 1862, McClellan finally made his move to try to capture Richmond. He planned to attack the Confederate capital by way of a stretch of land between the York and James rivers. McClellan succeeded in bringing his troops within a few miles of Richmond.

But in June 1862, Robert E. Lee took charge of the Army of Northern Virginia and proceeded to turn the situation around. Lee sent Jeb Stuart and his **cavalry**—soldiers on horseback—to spy on McClellan. With about 1,000 men, Stuart rode around the whole Union army in a few days and reported its size back to Lee. Lee then attacked McClellan's army. The two sides clashed for a week, from June 25 to July 1, 1862, in what became known as the **Seven Days' Battles**. The Army of Northern Virginia suffered heavier losses, but it forced McClellan's army to retreat.

In late August, the Confederates won a second victory at Bull Run, and Union troops withdrew back to Washington. Within just a few months, Lee had ended the Union threat in Virginia.

Lee Invades the North

Riding a wave of victories, General Lee decided to invade the Union. He wrote to tell President Davis of his plan. Lee thought it was a crucial time, with the North at a low point. Without waiting for Davis's response, Lee crossed the Potomac with his army and invaded Maryland in early September 1862.

Lee had several reasons for taking the war to the North. He hoped a victory in the North might force Lincoln to talk peace. The invasion would give Virginia farmers a rest from war during the harvest season. The Confederates could plunder Northern farms for food.

Lee hoped the invasion would show that the Confederacy could indeed win the war, which might convince Europe to side with the South. By this time, both Britain and France were leaning toward recognizing the Confederacy as a separate nation. They were impressed by Lee's military successes, and their textile industry was now hurting from the lack of Southern cotton.

Bloody Antietam

Soon after invading Maryland, Lee drew up a plan for his campaign in the North. A Confederate officer accidentally left a copy of Lee's battle plans wrapped around three cigars at a campsite. When Union troops stopped to rest at the abandoned campsite, a Union soldier stumbled on the plans. The captured plans gave McClellan a chance to stop Lee and his army.

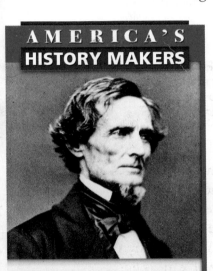

AMERICA'S HISTORY MAKERS

JEFFERSON DAVIS

1808–1889

Jefferson Davis expected to be given a military command when the Confederacy was formed in 1861. But Davis was chosen President of the Confederacy instead, which stunned and saddened him.

Because of his strong sense of duty and loyalty to the South, Davis accepted the unwelcome post. He had to immediately form a national government and prepare for war at the same time. Davis found it hard to compromise or accept disagreement with his opinions.

How do the qualities required in a military leader differ from those required in a political leader?

Reading **Hi**

C. Making Inferences H was Lee's ap ment fortun for the Sout

Reading **Hi**

D. Reading Use the map page 495 to low Lee's m ments into North.

McClellan went on the attack, though he moved slowly as always. On September 17, 1862, at Antietam Creek near Sharpsburg, Maryland, McClellan's army clashed with Lee's. The resulting **Battle of Antietam** was the bloodiest day in all of American history. A Confederate officer later described the battle.

Confederate artillery soldiers lie dead after the Battle of Antietam.

A VOICE FROM THE PAST

Again and again . . . by charges and counter-charges, this portion of the field was lost and recovered, until the green corn that grew upon it looked as if it had been struck by a storm of bloody hail. . . . From sheer exhaustion, both sides, like battered and bleeding athletes, seemed willing to rest.

John B. Gordon, quoted in *Voices of the Civil War*

After fighting all day, neither side had gained any ground by nightfall. The only difference was that about 25,000 men were dead or wounded. Lee, who lost as much as one-third of his fighting force, withdrew to Virginia. The cautious McClellan did not follow, missing a chance to finish off the crippled Southern army. Lincoln was so fed up that he fired McClellan in November, 1862. In the next chapter, you will learn about the historic action Lincoln took after the Battle of Antietam.

tion ❸ Assessment

Terms & Names	2. Using Graphics	3. Main Ideas	4. Critical Thinking
Explain the significance of:	Review the section and find five key events to place on a time line as shown.	**a.** Why were Union victories in the West and the fall of New Orleans significant to the Union cause?	**Making Inferences** What does Lee's invasion of the North suggest about his qualities as a general and a leader?

Explain the significance of:
• Ulysses S. Grant
• Battle of Shiloh
• cavalry
• Seven Days' Battles
• Battle of Antietam

a. Why were Union victories in the West and the fall of New Orleans significant to the Union cause?

b. Why did Lee go on the offensive against the North?

c. How did the South's fortunes change after Lee took command of the Army of Northern Virginia?

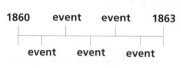

Which of these events do you think was most important?

Making Inferences What does Lee's invasion of the North suggest about his qualities as a general and a leader?

THINK ABOUT
• Lee's military skills and style
• the North's resources

ACTIVITY OPTIONS

GEOGRAPHY

ART

Develop a new military strategy for either the North or the South. Show your strategy on a **map** or in a **diagram** of troop movements.

CHAPTER 17

The Tide of War Turns 1863–1865

ction 1
e
ancipation
oclamation

ction 2
ar Affects
ciety

ction 3
e North
ns

ction 4
e Legacy
the War

Confederate and Union cavalry clash at Yellow Tavern, Virginia, on May 11, 1864.
The slight curve of the cavalry sword provided a better slashing motion when fighting on horseback.

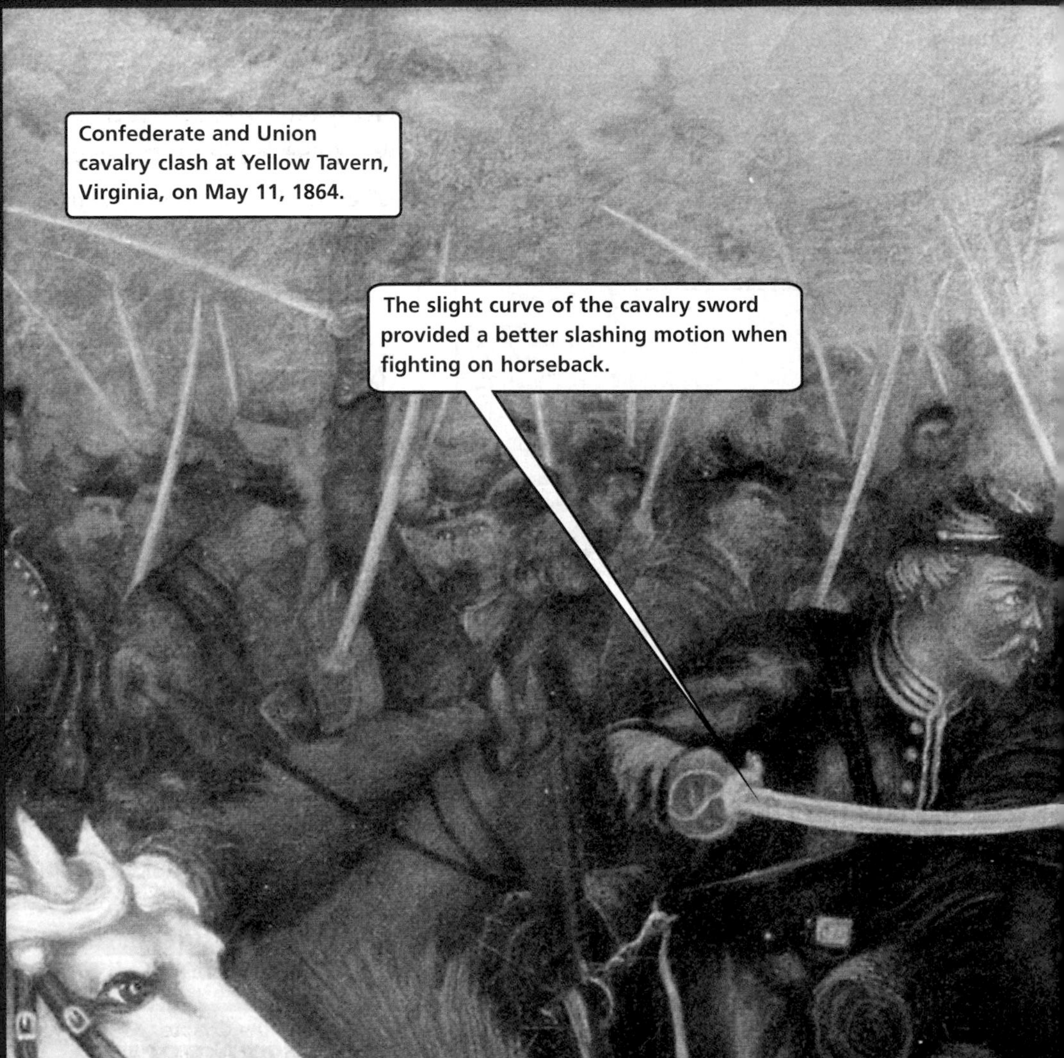

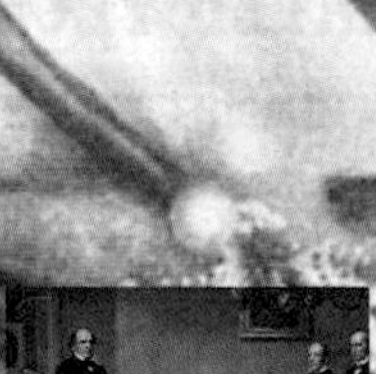

January 1863
Lincoln issues the Emancipation Proclamation after presenting it to his cabinet.

July 1863
Battle of Gettysburg takes place.

Union takes Vicksburg.

March 1864
Grant is put in charge of all Union armies.

USA
World
1863

January 1863
Polish nationalists revolt against Russian rule.

July 1863
Source of Nile River is found at Lake Victoria in present-day Uganda.

Archduk
A
emp

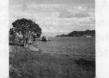

The Confederate uniforms were gray and the Union's were blue. The two sides are often referred to by these colors.

In 1863, you have been a Civil War soldier for two years. The life of a soldier is a hard one. The food is awful. Disease is common. Worst of all is the horrible violence and death. Often you feel the urge to run away and go home.

What would inspire you to keep fighting?

What Do You Think?

- What would you be willing to sacrifice for your country? What if your country fought for something you did not believe in?

- How would the attitudes of fellow soldiers influence your decision?

RESEARCH LINKS
CLASSZONE.COM

Visit the Chapter 17 links for more information about the Civil War.

April 1865
Union takes Richmond.
Lee surrenders at Appomattox Court House.
Lincoln is assassinated.

vember 1864
:oln is reelected.

1866

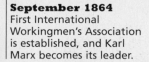

September 1864
First International Workingmen's Association is established, and Karl Marx becomes its leader.

September 1865
English officials arrest *Fenian* leaders of planned uprising in Ireland.

Reading Strategy: Comparing and Contrasti

What Do You Know?

What advantages and disadvantages did the North and the South have? Did particular individuals give either side an advantage during the Civil War?

Think About
- what qualities contribute to the success of military leaders
- the importance of obeying orders for soldiers even if it might mean death
- your responses to the Interact with History about what would inspire you to keep fighting (see page 502)

Robert E. Lee was the military genius at the head of the Confederate armies.

Ulysses S. Grant took of the Union armies i 1864.

What Do You Want to Know?

 What questions do you have about the later part of the Civil War and how it ended Make a list of those questions before you read the chapter.

Comparing and Contrasting

When you study historical events, it is important to compare and contrast the effects that events had on different individuals and groups. A single event might affect two groups of p ple in completely different ways. Use the chart below to compare and contrast the impact o events on the Union and the Confederacy in the later years of the Civil War.

S See Skillbuilder Handbook, page R10.

Taking Notes

	North	South
Emancipation Proclamation		
War's Impact		
Northern Victories in Battle		
Union Wins Civil War		

The Emancipation Proclamation

MAIN IDEA	WHY IT MATTERS NOW	TERMS & NAMES
, President Lincoln issued the pation Proclamation, which to change the war's course.	The Emancipation Proclamation was an important step in ending slavery in the United States.	Emancipation Proclamation · 54th Massachusetts Regiment

ONE AMERICAN'S STORY

During the Civil War, abolitionists like Frederick Douglass continued their bitter fight against slavery. Douglass urged President Lincoln to emancipate, or free, enslaved Americans.

A VOICE FROM THE PAST

To fight against slaveholders, without fighting against slavery, is but a half-hearted business, and paralyzes the hands engaged in it. . . . Fire must be met with water. . . . War for the destruction of liberty [by the South] must be met with war for the destruction of slavery.

Frederick Douglass, quoted in *Battle Cry of Freedom*

During the Civil War, Frederick Douglass urged President Lincoln to make the conflict a war against slavery.

Douglass pointed out that the Confederate war effort depended on slave labor. For both practical and moral reasons, Douglass said, Lincoln should free the slaves. In this section, you will learn how ending slavery became an important goal of the Civil War.

Calls for Emancipation

Throughout the war, abolitionists had been urging Lincoln to emancipate enslaved persons. Many criticized the president for being too cautious. Some even charged that Lincoln's lack of action aided the Confederate cause.

Still, Lincoln hesitated. He did not believe he had the power under the Constitution to abolish slavery where it already existed. Nor did he want to anger the four slave states that remained in the Union. He also knew that most Northern Democrats, and many Republicans, opposed emancipation.

Lincoln did not want the issue of slavery to divide the nation further than it already had. Although he disliked slavery, the president's first priority was to preserve the Union. "If I could save the Union without freeing

Taking Notes

Use your chart to take notes about the effects of the Emancipation Proclamation.

Emancipation Proclamation
War's Impact
Northern Victories in Battle
Union Wins Civil War

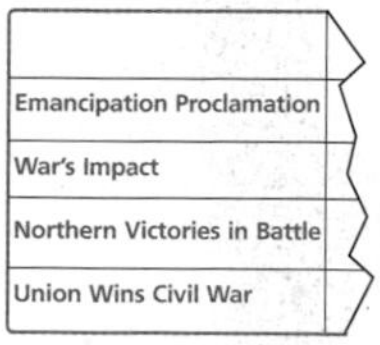

any slave I would do it," he declared. "If I could save it by freeing *all* the slaves I would do it; and if I could save it by freeing some and leaving others alone, I would also do that."

By the summer of 1862, however, Lincoln had decided in favor of emancipation. The war was taking a terrible toll. If freeing the slaves helped weaken the South, then he would do it. Lincoln waited, however, for a moment when he was in a position of strength. After General Lee's forces were stopped at Antietam, Lincoln decided to act.

The Emancipation Proclamation

On January 1, 1863, Lincoln issued the **Emancipation Proclamation,** which freed all slaves in Confederate territory. The proclamation had a tremendous impact on the public. However, it freed very few slaves. Most of the slaves that Lincoln intended to liberate lived in areas distant from the Union troops that could enforce his proclamation.

Background
In September
1862, Lincoln
issued an ear
proclamation
gave rebellio
states a chan
preserve slav
by rejoining
Union.

Lincoln presents the Emancipation Proclamation to his cabinet.

A VOICE FROM THE PAST

On the first day of January, in the year of our Lord one thousand eight hundred and sixty-three, all persons held as slaves within any State or designated part of a State, the people whereof shall then be in rebellion against the United States, shall be then, [thenceforth], and forever free.

Abraham Lincoln, from the *Emancipation Proclamation*

Why, critics charged, did Lincoln free slaves only in the South? The answer was in the Constitution. Because freeing Southern slaves weakened the Confederacy, the proclamation could be seen as a military action. As commander-in-chief, Lincoln had this authority. Yet the Constitution did not give the president the power to free slaves within the Union. But Lincoln did ask Congress to abolish slavery gradually throughout the land.

Reading **Hi**
A. Drawing Conclusions did Lincoln choose to lir his proclama mostly to re lious states?

Although the Emancipation Proclamation did not free many enslaved people at the time it was issued, it was important as a symbolic measure. For the North, the Civil War was no longer a limited war whose main goal was to preserve the Union. It was a war of liberation.

Response to the Proclamation

Abolitionists were thrilled that Lincoln had finally issued the Emancipation Proclamation. "We shout for joy that we live to record this righteous decree," wrote Frederick Douglass. Still, many believed the law should have gone further. They were upset that Lincoln had not freed *all* enslaved persons, including those in the border states.

ing **History**

nmarizing
did
ern
crats
e the
cipation
mation?

Other people in the North, especially Democrats, were angered by the president's decision. Northern Democrats, the majority of whom were against emancipating even Southern slaves, claimed that the proclamation would only make the war longer by continuing to anger the South. A newspaperman in Ohio called Lincoln's proclamation "monstrous, impudent, and heinous . . . insulting to God as to man."

Most Union soldiers, though, welcomed emancipation. One officer noted that, although few soldiers were abolitionists, most were happy "to destroy everything that . . . gives the rebels strength."

White Southerners reacted to the proclamation with rage. Although it had limited impact in areas outside the reach of Northern armies, many slaves began to run away to Union lines. At the same time that these slaves deprived the Confederacy of labor, they also began to provide the Union with soldiers.

African-American Soldiers

In addition to freeing slaves, the Emancipation Proclamation declared that African-American men willing to fight "will be received into the armed service of the United States."

Frederick Douglass had argued for the recruitment of African-American soldiers since the start of the war. He declared, "Once [you] let the black man get upon his person the brass letters, U.S. . . . there is no power on earth which can deny that he has earned the right to citizenship."

Before the proclamation, the federal government had discouraged the enlistment of African Americans, and only a few regiments were formed. After emancipation, African Americans rushed to join the army. By war's end, about 180,000 black soldiers wore the blue uniform of the Union army.

African-American soldiers were organized in all-black regiments, usually led by white officers. They were often given the worst jobs

Thousands of African Americans, such as these men of the 4th U.S. Colored Troops, fought for the Union during the Civil War.

"Who Would Be Free, Themselves Strike the Blow!"

$200

COLORED ME
Of Burlington Co.

NOW IS YOUR TIME

The Board of Freeholders of Burlington Co

$200 **CASH!** $200
$10 PER MONTH

GEO. SNYDER,

AFRICAN AMERICANS IN THE MILITARY

During the Civil War, no African-American soldier was promoted above the rank of captain. But times have changed. In 1989, General Colin Powell (shown below) was made a four-star general and named chairman of the Joint Chiefs of Staff—the highest position in the military.

General Powell's appointment was the climax of a long struggle to fully integrate American armed forces. From the Civil War through World War II, African-American soldiers were kept apart from white soldiers and denied equal rights. However, in 1948, President Harry Truman ended segregation in the armed forces. Today the American military is fully integrated.

to do and were paid less than white soldiers. Despite these obstacles, African-American soldiers showed great courage on the battlefield and wore their uniforms with pride. More than one regiment insisted on fighting without pay rather than accepting lower pay than the white soldiers.

The 54th Massachusetts

One unit that insisted on fighting without pay was the **54th Massachusetts Regiment,** one of the first African-American regiments organized in the North. The soldiers of the 54th—among whom were two sons of Frederick Douglass—soon made the regiment the most famous of the Civil War.

The 54th Massachusetts earned its greatest fame in July 1863, when it led a heroic attack on Fort Wagner in South Carolina. The soldiers' bravery at Fort Wagner made the 54th a household name in the North and increased African-American enlistment.

The soldiers of the 54th Massachusetts and other African-American regiments faced grave dangers if captured. Rather than take African Americans as prisoners, Confederate soldiers often shot them or returned them to slavery.

The war demanded great sacrifices, not only from soldiers and prisoners, but also from people back home. In the next section, you will read about the hardships that the Civil War placed on the civilian populations in both the North and the South.

Reading **Hi**
C. Identifyin
Facts How c
many black s
diers protest
when they v
offered lowe
pay than wh
soldiers?

Section 1 Assessment

1. Terms & Names

Explain the significance of:

• Emancipation Proclamation
• 54th Massachusetts Regiment

2. Using Graphics

Use a chart to record responses to the Emancipation Proclamation.

Responses to Proclamation

How did the proclamation change Northerners' views of the war?

3. Main Ideas

a. What was Lincoln's reason for not emancipating slaves when the war began?

b. Why was the immediate impact of the Emancipation Proclamation limited?

c. Why did black soldiers often face greater hardships than white soldiers?

4. Critical Thinking

Recognizing Effects Ho did the Emancipation Proclamation change the of African Americans in th war?

THINK ABOUT

• how the proclamation changed military policy
• the response of many Southern slaves to the proclamation

ACTIVITY OPTIONS

TECHNOLOGY
MUSIC

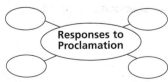

Do research on the 54th Massachusetts Regiment. Create a **Web site** for the regiment or write a **song** about the soldiers' heroism at Fort Wagner.

War Affects Society

MAIN IDEA	WHY IT MATTERS NOW	TERMS & NAMES	
l War caused social, ic, and political changes in th and the South.	Some changes, like the growth of industry, affected Americans long after the end of Civil War.	Copperhead conscription bounty	income tax greenback Clara Barton

ONE AMERICAN'S STORY

As the Civil War moved into its third year, the constant demand for men and resources began to take its toll back home. Sometimes, the hardships endured by civilians resulted in angry scenes. On April 3, 1863, a resident of Richmond, Virginia, named Agnes came upon a group of hungry women and children, who had gathered in front of the capitol. She described the scene as these women and children were joined by other people who were upset by the shortage of food.

A VOICE FROM THE PAST

The crowd now rapidly increased, and numbered, I am sure, more than a thousand women and children. It grew and grew until it reached the dignity of a mob—a bread riot.

Agnes, quoted in *Reminiscences of Peace and War*

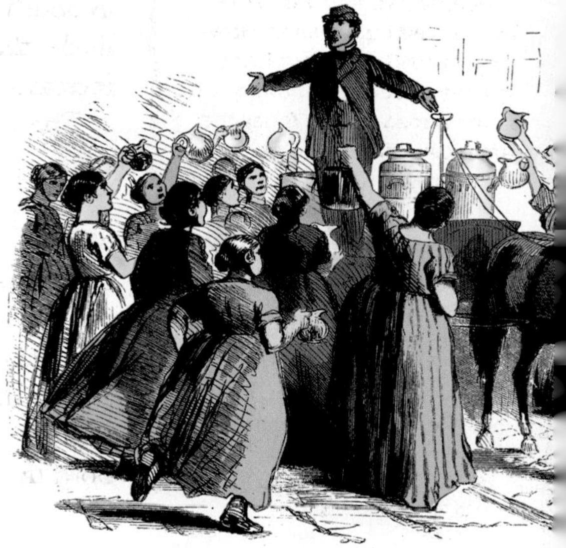

Food became scarce many places during Civil War. Here, wo demand milk for th hungry families.

The mob then went out of control. It broke into shops and stole food and other goods. Only the threat of force ended the riot. In this section, you will read more about hardships that the Civil War caused on the home front.

Taking Notes

Use your chart to take notes about the effects of the Civil War.

- Emancipation Proclamation
- War's Impact
- Northern Victories in Battle
- Union Wins Civil War

Disagreement About the War

In the spring of 1863, riots like the one in Richmond broke out in a number of Southern towns. Southerners were growing weary of the war and the constant sacrifices it demanded.

Confederate soldiers began to leave the army in increasing numbers. By the end of the year, the Confederate army had lost nearly 40 percent of its men. Some of these men were on leave, but many others were deserters.

In this political cartoon, the Union defends itself against "Copperheads." This was the name given to Northerners who sympathized with the South.

Faced with the difficulties of waging war, the Confederate states fell into disagreement. The same principle of states' rights that led them to break with the Union kept them from coordinating their war effort. As one Southern governor put it, "I am *still* a rebel . . . no matter who may be in power."

Disagreements over the conduct of the war also arose in the North. Lincoln's main opponents were the **Copperheads,** Northern Democrats who favored peace with the South. (A copperhead is a poisonous snake that strikes without warning.) Lincoln had protesters arrested. He also suspended the writ of habeas corpus, which prevents the government from holding citizens without a trial.

The Draft Laws

As the war dragged on, both the North and the South needed more soldiers. As a result, both sides passed laws of **conscription,** also known as the draft. These laws required men to serve in the military.

The Confederates had been drafting soldiers since the spring of 1862. By 1863, all able-bodied white men between the ages of 18 and 45 were required to join the army. However, there were a number of exceptions. Planters who owned 20 or more slaves could avoid military service. In addition, wealthy men could hire substitutes to serve in their place. By 1863, substitutes might cost as much as $6,000. The fact that wealthy men could avoid service caused poor Southerners to complain that it was a "rich man's war but a poor man's fight."

The Union draft law was passed in March 1863. Like the Confederacy, the Union allowed draftees to hire substitutes. However, the North also offered $300 **bounties,** or cash payments, to men who volunteered to serve. As a result, only a small percentage of men in the North were drafted. Most men volunteered and received the bounty.

Reading **H**
A. Drawing Conclusions were many diers dissat with the dr laws?

Even so, the draft was extremely unpopular. In July 1863, anger over the draft and simmering racial tensions led to the New York City draft riots. For four days, rioters destroyed property and attacked people on the streets. Over 100 people were killed—many of them African Americans.

Economic Effects of the War

Many people suffered economic hardship during the war. The suffering was severe in the South, where most battles were fought, but the North also experienced difficulties.

Food shortages were very common in the South, partly because so many farmers were fighting in the Confederate army. Moreover, food sometimes could not get to market because trains were now being used to carry war materials. The Confederate army also seized food and other supplies for its own needs.

Another problem, especially in the South, was inflation—an increase in price and decrease in the value of money. The average family food bill in the South increased from $6.65 a month in 1861 to $68 by mid–1863. Over the course of the war, prices rose 9,000 percent in the South.

Inflation in the North was much lower, but prices still rose faster than wages, making life harder for working people. Some people took advantage of wartime demand and sold goods for high prices.

Overall, though, war production boosted Northern industry and fueled the economy. In the short term, this gave the North an economic advantage over the South. In the long term, industry would begin to replace farming as the basis of the national economy.

During the war, the federal government passed two important economic measures. In 1861, it established the first **income tax**—a tax on earnings. The following year, the government issued a new paper currency, known as **greenbacks** because of their color. The new currency helped the Northern economy by ensuring that people had money to spend. It also helped the Union to pay for the war.

Some Southerners in the border states took advantage of the stronger Union economy by selling cotton to Northern traders, in violation of Confederate law. "Yankee gold," wrote one Confederate officer, "is fast accomplishing what Yankee arms could never achieve—the subjugation of our people."

Resistance by Slaves

Another factor that affected the South was the growing resistance from slaves. To hurt the Southern economy, slaves slowed their pace of work or stopped working altogether. Some carried out sabotage, destroying crops and farm equipment to hurt the plantation economy. When white

daily *life*

INFLATION IN THE SOUTH

During the Civil War, inflation caused hardship in the North and the South. But inflation was especially severe in the Confederacy, where prices could become outrageously high.

The food prices shown below are from 1864. Consider how many days it took a Confederate soldier to earn enough money to buy each of these foods.

$6.00
Dozen Eggs

$6.25
Pound of Butter

$10.00
Quart of Milk

$12.00
Pound of Coffee

$18.00

Confederate Soldier's Monthly Pay

planters fled advancing Union armies, slaves often refused to go along. They stayed behind, waiting for Union soldiers to free them.

Some enslaved people even rose up in rebellion against their overseers. More commonly, though, slaves ran away from plantations to join the Union forces as they pushed farther into Confederate territory. One Union officer described a common sight.

A VOICE FROM THE PAST

It was very touching to see the vast numbers of colored [African-American] women following after us with babies in their arms, and little ones like our Anna clinging to their tattered skirts. One poor creature, while nobody was looking, hid two boys, five years old, in a wagon, intending, I suppose that they should see the land of freedom if she couldn't.

Union officer, quoted in *The Civil War*

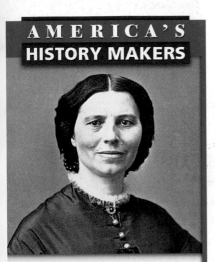

AMERICA'S HISTORY MAKERS

CLARA BARTON
1821–1912

Trained as a schoolteacher, <u>Clara Barton</u> was working for the government when the Civil War began. She organized a relief agency to help with the war effort. "While our soldiers stand and fight," she said, "I can stand and feed and nurse them."

She also made food for soldiers in camp and tended to the wounded and dying on the battlefield. At Antietam, she held a doctor's operating table steady as cannon shells burst all around them. The doctor called her "the angel of the battlefield." After the war, Barton founded the American Red Cross.

How did Clara Barton demonstrate her leadership abilities?

After Lincoln issued the Emancipation Proclamation, the number of slaves fleeing Southern plantations greatly increased. By the end of the war, as many as half a million had fled to Union lines.

Women Aid the War Effort

With so many men away at war, women in both the North and the South assumed increased responsibilities. Women plowed fields and ran farms and plantations. They also took over jobs in offices and factories that had previously been done only by men.

Other social changes came about because of the thousands of women who served on the front lines as volunteer workers and nurses. Susie King Taylor was an African-American woman who wrote an account of her experiences as a volunteer with an African-American regiment. She asked her readers to remember that "many lives were lost,—not men alone but noble women as well."

Relief agencies put women to work washing clothes, gathering supplies, and cooking food for soldiers. Also, nursing became a respectable profession for many women. By the end of the war, around 3,000 nurses had worked under the leadership of Dorothea Dix in Union hospitals. Southern women were also active as nurses and as volunteers on the front.

Women also played a key role as spies in both the North and the South. Harriet Tubman served as a spy for Union forces along the coast of South Carolina. The most famous Confederate spy was Belle Boyd. Although she was arrested six times, she continued her work through much of the war. At one point, she even sent messages from her jail cell by putting them in little rubber balls and tossing them out the window.

Reading **Hi**
C. Summari
How did wc
participate
Civil War?

Civil War Prison Camps

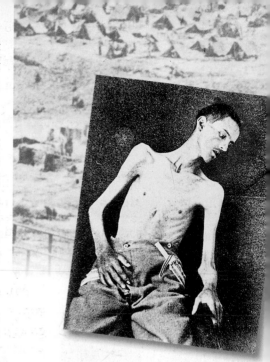

Women caught spying were thrown into jail, but soldiers captured in battle suffered far more. At prison camps in both the North and the South, prisoners of war faced terrible conditions.

One of the worst prison camps in the North was in Elmira, New York. Perhaps the harshest feature of a prisoner's life at the camp was the New York winter. One prisoner called Elmira "an excellent summer prison for southern soldiers, but an excellent place for them to find their graves in the winter." In just one year, more than 24 percent of Elmira's 12,121 prisoners died of sickness and exposure to severe weather.

Conditions were also horrible in the South. The camp with the worst reputation was at Andersonville, Georgia. Built to hold 10,000 prisoners, at one point it housed 33,000. Inmates had little shelter from the heat or cold. Most slept in holes scratched in the dirt. Drinking water came from one tiny creek that also served as a sewer. As many as 100 men per day died at Andersonville from starvation, disease, and exposure.

People who saw the camps were shocked by the condition of the soldiers. The poet Walt Whitman—who served as a Union nurse—described a group of soldiers who returned from a prison camp. He exclaimed, "Can those be *men?* . . . are they not really mummied, dwindled corpses?"

Around 50,000 men died in Civil War prison camps. But this number was dwarfed by the number of dead on the battlefronts and even more from disease in army camps. In the next section, you will read about the bloody battles that led to the end of the Civil War.

The terrible conditions at Civil War prison camps caused much suffering and death.

---

tion 2 Assessment

Terms & Names

plain the gnificance of:

opperhead

onscription

ounty

come tax

reenback

ara Barton

2. Using Graphics

Use a diagram like the one below to compare conditions in the North and South during the later years of war.

Conditions During the War

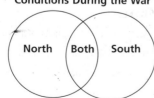

North | Both | South

3. Main Ideas

a. How did the South's principle of states' rights undermine the Confederate war effort?

b. How did the draft laws in the North and South differ?

c. What conditions at prison camps caused so many to suffer behind enemy lines?

4. Critical Thinking

Making Generalizations What economic changes took place during the Civil War?

THINK ABOUT

• the war's effect on prices

• industry and agriculture

• new economic measures begun by the government

IVITY OPTIONS

EOGRAPHY

SPEECH

Study Civil War prison camps. Make a **map** showing where they were located or give a **speech** explaining why prisoners should be treated better.

The North Wins

MAIN IDEA

Thanks to victories, beginning with Gettysburg and ending with Richmond, the Union survived.

WHY IT MATTERS NOW

If the Union had lost the war, the United States might look very different now.

TERMS & NAMES

Battle of Gettysburg
Pickett's Charge
Ulysses S. Grant
Robert E. Lee
Siege of V
William Te Sherma
Appomat House

ONE AMERICAN'S STORY

Joshua Lawrence Chamberlain left his job as a college professor and took command of troops from his home state of Maine. His description of the aftermath of one battle shows how soldiers got used to the war's violence.

A VOICE FROM THE PAST

It seemed best to [put] myself between two dead men among the many left there by earlier assaults, and to draw another crosswise for a pillow out of the trampled, blood-soaked sod, pulling the flap of his coat over my face to fend off the chilling winds, and still more chilling, the deep, many voiced moan [of the wounded] that overspread the field.

Joshua Lawrence Chamberlain, quoted in *The Civil War*

Chamberlain is best remembered for his courageous actions at the Battle of Gettysburg. In this section, you will read about that battle and others that led to the end of the Civil War.

Taking Notes

Use your chart to make notes about the military victories of the North.

The Road to Gettysburg

In September 1862, General McClellan stopped General Lee's Northern attack at the Battle of Antietam. But the cautious McClellan failed to finish off Lee's army, which retreated safely to Virginia.

President Lincoln, who was frustrated by McClellan, replaced him with Ambrose Burnside. But Burnside also proved to be a disappointment. At the Battle of Fredericksburg, Virginia, in December 1862, Burnside attacked Confederate troops who had dug trenches. The bloody result was 12,600 Union casualties. This disastrous attack led General Lee to remark, "It is well that war is so terrible—we should grow too fond of it!"

Lincoln replaced Burnside with General Joseph Hooker, who faced Lee the following May at Chancellorsville, Virginia. The result was yet another Union disaster. With half as many men as Hooker, Lee still managed to

In 1862, Jo Chamberla offered a y travel with study lang Europe. He fight for th instead.

cut the Union forces to pieces. However, the South paid a high price for its victory. As General "Stonewall" Jackson returned from a patrol on May 2, Confederate guards thought he was a Union soldier and shot him in the arm. Shortly after a surgeon amputated the arm, Jackson caught pneumonia. On May 10, Lee's prized general was dead.

In spite of Jackson's tragic death, Lee decided to head North once again. He hoped that a Confederate victory in Union territory would fuel Northern discontent with the war and bring calls for peace. He also hoped a Southern victory would lead European nations to give diplomatic recognition and aid to the Confederacy.

The Battle of Gettysburg

ling **History**

ading a
Use the and illustra-
on pages
15 to study sburg's
raphy.

In late June 1863, Lee crossed into southern Pennsylvania. The Confederates learned of a supply of shoes in the town of Gettysburg and went to investigate. There, on July 1, they ran into Union troops. Both sides called for reinforcements, and the **Battle of Gettysburg** was on.

The fighting raged for three days. On the rocky hills and fields around Gettysburg, 90,000 Union troops, under the command of General George Meade, clashed with 75,000 Confederates.

During the struggle, Union forces tried to hold their ground on Cemetery Ridge, just south of town, while rebel soldiers tried to dislodge them. At times, the air seemed full of bullets. "The balls were whizzing so thick," said one Texan, "that it looked like a man could hold out a hat and catch it full."

The turning point came on July 3, when Lee ordered General George Pickett to mount a direct attack on the middle of the Union line. It was a deadly mistake. Some 13,000 rebel troops charged up the ridge into heavy Union fire. One soldier recalled "bayonet thrusts, sabre strokes, pistol shots . . . men going down on their hands and knees, spinning round like tops . . . ghastly heaps of dead men."

ing **History**

king
ces Why Lincoln
een disap-
d after the victory at
burg?

Pickett's Charge, as this attack came to be known, was torn to pieces. The Confederates retreated and waited for a Union counterattack. But once again, Lincoln's generals failed to finish off Lee's army. The furious Lincoln wondered when he would find a general who would defeat Lee once and for all.

Even so, the Union rejoiced over the victory at Gettysburg. Lee's hopes for a Confederate victory in the North were crushed. The North had lost 23,000 men, but Southern losses were even greater. Over one-third of Lee's army, 28,000 men, lay dead or wounded. Sick at heart, Lee led his army back to Virginia.

America's HERITAGE

THE GETTYSBURG ADDRESS

On November 19, 1863, President Lincoln spoke at the dedication of a cemetery in Gettysburg for the 3,500 soldiers buried there. His speech was short, and few who heard it were impressed. Lincoln himself called it "a flat failure."

Even so, the Gettysburg Address has since been recognized as one of the greatest speeches of all time. In it, Lincoln declared that the nation was founded on "the proposition that all men are created equal." He ended with a plea to continue the fight for democracy so that "government of the people, by the people, for the people shall not perish from the earth."

See page 524 for the full text of the Gettysburg Address.

Battle of Gettysburg

A monument stands today near a ridge at the Gettysburg battle-field. Labeled the "High Water Mark of the Rebellion," it shows how far Confederate troops advanced against Union lines. There, on July 3, 1863, the South came closest to winning the Civil War.

The fighting began on July 1. When a Confederate force captured Gettysburg, Union defenders took up new positions in the hills south of town. The next day, Confederate troops attacked across a wheat field and peach orchard in an attempt to seize the hill called Little Round Top. But Union forces held their ground.

July 3 was the decisive day. Lee, having failed to crack the side of General Meade's Union line, attacked its center. In an assault that came to be known as Pickett's Charge, some 13,000 men charged uphill across an open field toward the Union lines along Cemetery Ridge. Union soldiers covered the field with rifle and cannon fire. "Pickett's Charge" was a Confederate disaster.

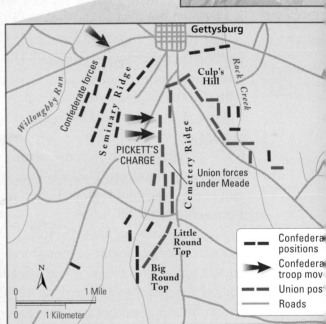

PENNSYLVANIA

• Gettysburg

Washington, D.C.

Gettysburg

Culp's Hill

Willoughby Run

Confederate forces

Seminary Ridge

Rock Creek

PICKETT'S CHARGE

Cemetery Ridge

Union forces under Meade

Little Round Top

Big Round Top

N

0 _____ 1 Mile
0 _____ 1 Kilometer

Confedera
positions

Confedera
troop mov

Union pos

Roads

Before beginning the charge named for him, Major General Pickett wrote to his fiancée, "My brave Virginians are to attack in front. Oh, may God in mercy help me."

ARTIFACT FILE

Soldiers' Diaries
Many Civil War soldiers wrote about their wartime experiences in personal diaries, such as this one belonging to Sergeant Alfred S. Rowe of Maryland.

MECHANICSVILLE
HANOVER
MANASSAS
CEDAR RUN
OX HILL
HARPERS FERRY
COLD HARBOR
FRAZIERS FARM

Regimental Flag Flags h
soldiers to identify the dif
sides during battle. Often,
regiment's flag would sho
names of battles it had fo
This flag, which belonged
the 28th North Carolina, v
captured at Pickett's Charg

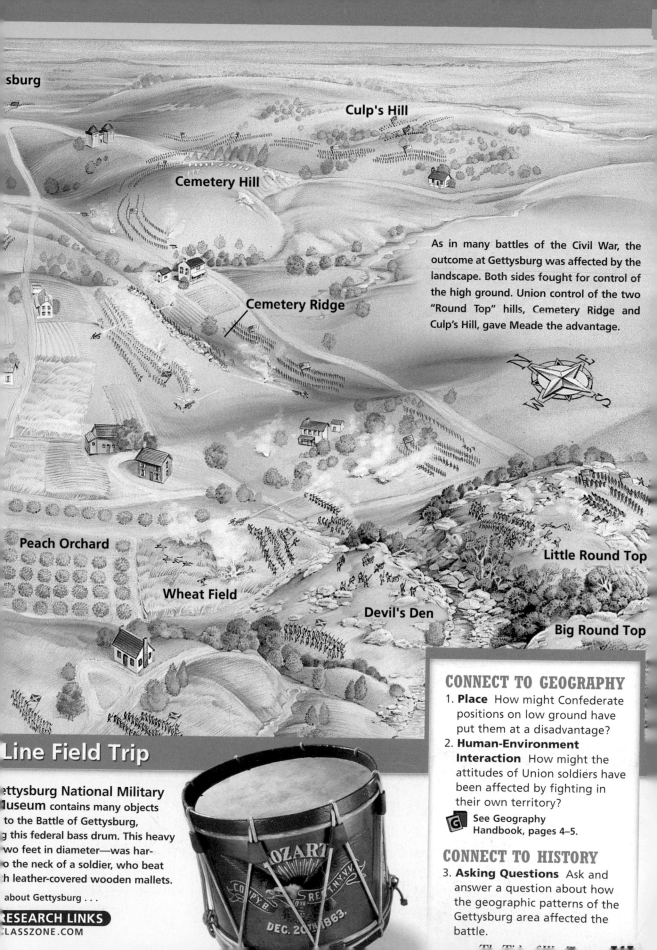

sburg

Culp's Hill

Cemetery Hill

Cemetery Ridge

As in many battles of the Civil War, the outcome at Gettysburg was affected by the landscape. Both sides fought for control of the high ground. Union control of the two "Round Top" hills, Cemetery Ridge and Culp's Hill, gave Meade the advantage.

Peach Orchard

Wheat Field

Devil's Den

Little Round Top

Big Round Top

Line Field Trip

ettysburg National Military useum contains many objects to the Battle of Gettysburg, g this federal bass drum. This heavy wo feet in diameter—was har- o the neck of a soldier, who beat h leather-covered wooden mallets.

about Gettysburg . . .

CONNECT TO GEOGRAPHY

1. **Place** How might Confederate positions on low ground have put them at a disadvantage?
2. **Human-Environment Interaction** How might the attitudes of Union soldiers have been affected by fighting in their own territory?

   See Geography Handbook, pages 4–5.

CONNECT TO HISTORY

3. **Asking Questions** Ask and answer a question about how the geographic patterns of the Gettysburg area affected the battle.

ULYSSES S. GRANT
1822–1885

General Ulysses S. Grant was an unlikely war hero. Although educated at West Point Military Academy, he was a poor student and showed little interest in an army career. With his quiet manner and rumpled uniform, he often failed to impress his fellow officers.

Yet on the battlefield, Grant proved to be a brilliant general. Highly focused and cool under fire, he won the first major Union victories of the war.

Grant was willing to fight Lee—even if the costs were high. He told his generals, "Wherever Lee goes, there you will go also."

ROBERT E. LEE
1807–1870

Robert E. Lee seemed destined for greatness. In his crisp uniform and trim, white beard, Lee was a dashing figure on the battlefield.

Born to a leading Virginia family, Lee was a top student at West Point and won praise for his actions in the Mexican War. General Winfield Scott called him "the very best soldier I have ever seen in the field."

Lee did not want to fight the Union, but he felt he had to stand by Virginia. "I did only what my duty demanded," Lee said. "I could have taken no other course without dishonor."

How did the tough decisions made by Grant and Lee affect the Civil War?

The Siege of Vicksburg

On July 4, 1863, the day after Pickett's Charge, the Union received more good news. In Mississippi, General Ulysses S. Grant had defeated Confederate troops at the **Siege of Vicksburg**.

The previous year, Grant had won important victories in the West that opened up the Mississippi River for travel deep into the South. Vicksburg was the last major Confederate stronghold on the river. Grant had begun his attack on Vicksburg in May 1863. But when his direct attacks failed, he settled in for a long siege. Grant's troops surrounded the city and prevented the delivery of food and supplies. Eventually, the Confederates ran out of food. In desperation, they ate mules, dogs, and even rats. Finally, after nearly a month and a half, they surrendered.

The Union victory fulfilled a major part of the Anaconda Plan. The North had taken New Orleans the previous spring. Now, with complete control over the Mississippi River, the South was split in two.

With the victories at Vicksburg and Gettysburg, the tide of war turned in favor of the North. Britain gave up all thought of supporting the South. And, in General Grant, President Lincoln found a man who was willing to fight General Lee.

Sherman's Total War

In March 1864, President Lincoln named General Grant commander of all the Union armies. Grant then developed a plan to defeat the Confederacy. He would pursue Lee's army in Virginia, while Union forces under General **William Tecumseh Sherman** pushed through the Deep South to Atlanta and the Atlantic coast.

Vocabulary
siege: the surrounding of a city, town, or fortress by an army trying to capture it

Background
The Anaconda Plan called for blockading Southern ports, taking control of the Mississippi, and capturing Richmond.

Battling southward from Tennessee, Sherman took Atlanta in September 1864. He then set out on a march to the sea, cutting a path of destruction up to 60 miles wide and 300 miles long through Georgia.

Sherman waged total war: a war not only against enemy troops, but against everything that supports the enemy. His troops tore up rail lines, destroyed crops, and burned and looted towns.

Sherman's triumph in Atlanta was important for Lincoln. In 1864, the president was running for reelection, but his prospects were not good. Northerners were tired of war, and Democrats—who had nominated George McClellan—stood a good chance of winning on an antiwar platform.

Sherman's success changed all that. Suddenly, Northerners could sense victory. Lincoln took 55 percent of the popular vote and won re-election. In his second inaugural speech, Lincoln hoped for a speedy end to the war: "With malice towards none; with charity for all; . . . let us strive on to finish the work we are in; to bind up the nation's wounds; . . . to do all which may achieve and cherish a just, and a lasting peace." (See page 525 for more of Lincoln's Second Inaugural Address.)

In December, Sherman took Savannah, Georgia. He then sent a telegram to Lincoln: "I beg to present you, as a Christmas gift, the city of Savannah, with 150 heavy guns and . . . about 25,000 bales of cotton."

*ing*History

wing
usions How
the politi-
uation in
orth have
different if
an had not
Atlanta?

> **"Let us strive . . . to bind up the nation's wounds."**
>
> Abraham Lincoln

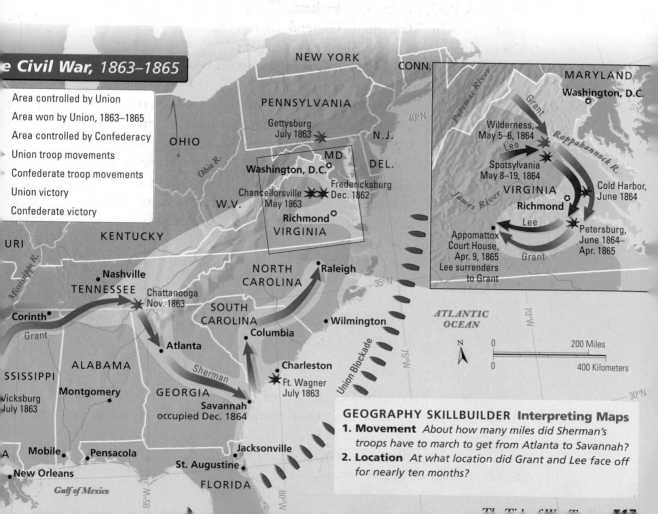

e Civil War, *1863–1865*

Area controlled by Union
Area won by Union, 1863–1865
Area controlled by Confederacy
Union troop movements
Confederate troop movements
Union victory
Confederate victory

NEW YORK
CONN.
MARYLAND
Washington, D.C.
PENNSYLVANIA
Gettysburg July 1863
40°N
N.J.
OHIO
MD.
DEL.
Washington, D.C.
Wilderness, May 5–6, 1864
Spotsylvania May 8–19, 1864
Cold Harbor, June 1864
VIRGINIA
Richmond
Fredericksburg Dec. 1862
Chancellorsville May 1863
W.V.
Richmond
VIRGINIA
Appomattox Court House, Apr. 9, 1865 Lee surrenders to Grant
Petersburg, June 1864– Apr. 1865
KENTUCKY
URI
Nashville
TENNESSEE
Chattanooga Nov. 1863
NORTH CAROLINA
Raleigh
35°N
Corinth
Grant
SOUTH CAROLINA
Wilmington
ATLANTIC OCEAN
70°W
Atlanta
Columbia
Charleston
Ft. Wagner July 1863
75°W
N
0   200 Miles
0   400 Kilometers
ALABAMA
Sherman
GEORGIA
Savannah occupied Dec. 1864
Union Blockade
SSISSIPPI
Montgomery
30°N
Vicksburg July 1863
Mobile
Pensacola
Jacksonville
St. Augustine
New Orleans
FLORIDA
Gulf of Mexico
80°W

GEOGRAPHY SKILLBUILDER Interpreting Maps
1. **Movement** *About how many miles did Sherman's troops have to march to get from Atlanta to Savannah?*
2. **Location** *At what location did Grant and Lee face off for nearly ten months?*

Grant's Virginia Campaign

Reading Hi
D. Reading
Map Use th
map on pag
to find the l
tions of the
major battle
Grant's Virg
campaign.

After taking Savannah, Sherman moved north through the Carolinas seeking to meet up with Grant's troops in Virginia. Since May 1864, Grant and his generals had been fighting savage battles against Lee's forces. In battle after battle, Grant would attack, rest, then attack again, all the while moving south toward Richmond.

At the Battle of the Wilderness in May 1864, Union and Confederate forces fought in a tangle of trees and brush so thick that they could barely see each other. Grant lost over 17,000 men, but he pushed on. "Whatever happens," he told Lincoln, "we will not retreat."

At Spotsylvania and Cold Harbor, the fighting continued. Again, the losses were staggering. Grant's attack in June, at Cold Harbor, cost him 7,000 men, most in the first few minutes of battle. Some Union troops were so sure they would die in battle that they pinned their names and addresses to their jackets so their bodies could be identified later.

In June 1864, Grant's armies arrived at Petersburg, just south of Richmond. Unable to break through the Confederate defenses, the Union forces dug trenches and settled in for a long siege. The two sides faced off for ten months.

In the end, though, Lee could not hold out. Grant was drawing a noose around Richmond. So Lee pulled out, leaving the Confederate capital undefended. The Union army marched into Richmond on April 3. One Richmond woman recalled, "Exactly at eight o'clock the Confederate flag that fluttered above the Capitol came

In 1861, Congress created the Medal of Honor to reward individual bravery in combat.

HISTORY *through* ART

This photograph shows Union officers before the Battle of the Wilderness. Next to the tree on the right is the photographer Mathew Brady. Photography was still a new art when the Civil War began. Brady's Civil War photos represent one of the first examples of photojournalism.

How might people's attitudes toward war be affected when they can see pictures from the front lines?

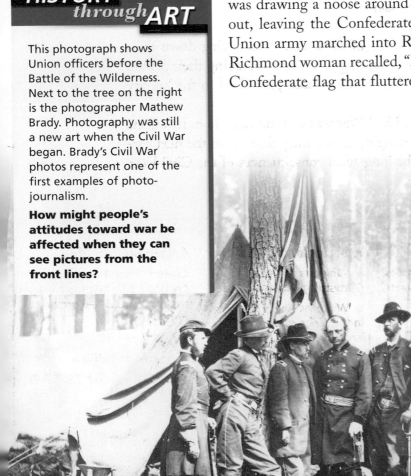

down and the Stars and Stripes were run up. . . . We covered our faces and cried aloud."

Surrender at Appomattox

From Richmond and Petersburg, Lee fled west, while Grant followed in pursuit. Lee wanted to continue fighting, but he knew that his situation was hopeless. He sent a message to General Grant that he was ready to surrender.

On April 9, 1865, Lee and Grant met in the small Virginia town of **Appomattox Court House** to arrange the surrender. Grant later wrote that his joy at that moment was mixed with sadness.

A VOICE FROM THE PAST

I felt like anything rather than rejoicing at the downfall of a foe who had fought so long and valiantly, and had suffered so much for a cause, though that cause was, I believe, one of the worst for which a people ever fought, and one for which there was the least excuse. I do not question, however, the sincerity of the great mass of those who were opposed to us.

Ulysses S. Grant, *Personal Memoirs*

Grant offered generous terms of surrender. After laying down their arms, the Confederates could return home in peace, taking their private possessions and horses with them. Grant also gave food to the hungry Confederate soldiers.

After four long years, the Civil War was coming to a close. Its effects would continue, however, changing the country forever. In the next section, you will learn about the long-term consequences of the Civil War.

STRANGE *but* True

WILMER MCLEAN

The first major battle of the Civil War was fought on the property of Wilmer McLean. McLean lived in Manassas, Virginia, the site of the Battle of Bull Run. After the battle, McLean decided to move to a more peaceful place. He chose the village of Appomattox Court House (see map on page 517).

When Lee made the decision to surrender in April 1865, he sent Colonel Charles Marshall to find a location for a meeting with Grant. Marshall stopped the first man he saw in the deserted streets of Appomattox Court House. It was Wilmer McLean. . . .

McLean reluctantly offered his home. Thus, the war that began in McLean's back yard ended in his parlor.

---

ion ③ Assessment

Terms & Names

Explain the significance of:
- Battle of Gettysburg
- Pickett's Charge
- Ulysses S. Grant
- Robert E. Lee
- Siege of Vicksburg
- William Tecumseh Sherman
- Appomattox Court House

2. Using Graphics

Use a time line like the one below to record key events from Section 3.

1862 ————————————— 1866

Which event is considered the turning point of the war?

3. Main Ideas

a. Why was the Battle of Gettysburg important?

b. Why was Northern success in the Siege of Vicksburg important?

c. How did Grant treat Confederate soldiers after the surrender at Appomattox Court House?

4. Critical Thinking

Contrasting How was the Civil War different from wars that Americans had previously fought?

THINK ABOUT
- the role of civilians
- Sherman's military strategy

ACTIVITY OPTIONS

GEOGRAPHY

LANGUAGE ARTS

Research the Siege of Vicksburg. Make a **topographic map** of the area or write an **article** describing the soldiers' hardships during the siege.

The Legacy of the War

ONE AMERICAN'S STORY

In the spring of 1864, a year before the end of the Civil War, the Union army was running out of cemetery space to bury its war dead. The secretary of war ordered Quartermaster General Montgomery Meigs to find a new site for a cemetery. Without hesitation, Meigs chose Robert E. Lee's plantation in Arlington, Virginia, just across the Potomac River from Washington, D.C.

Meig's decision to turn Lee's plantation into a Union cemetery was highly symbolic. The Union soldiers who died fighting Lee's army would be buried in Lee's front yard. That site became Arlington National Cemetery.

During the
the goverr
turned Rob
Lee's Virgi
plantation
graveyard.

Taking Notes

Use your chart to take notes about the effects of the Union's victory in the Civil War.

ancipation Proclamation
r's Impact
rthern Victories in Battle
ion Wins Civil War

Costs of the War

Many Northerners shared Montgomery Meigs's bitter feelings toward the South. At the same time, many Southerners felt great resentment toward the North. After the war, President Lincoln hoped to heal the nation and bring North and South together again. The generous terms of surrender offered to Lee were part of that effort. Hard feelings remained, however, in part because the costs of the war were so great.

The Civil War was the deadliest war in American history. In four years of fighting, approximately 620,000 soldiers died—360,000 for the Union and 260,000 for the Confederacy. Another 275,000 Union soldiers and 260,000 Confederate soldiers were wounded. Many suffered from their wounds for the rest of their lives.

Altogether, some 3,000,000 men served in the armies of the North and South—around 10 percent of the population. Along with the soldiers, many other Americans had their lives disrupted by the war.

ing **History**

ntrasting
did govern-
spending
g the Civil
ompare to
during previ-
ears?

The war also had great economic costs. Together, the North and South spent more than five times the amount spent by the government in the previous eight decades. Many years after the fighting was over, the federal government was still paying interest on loans taken out during the war.

The Thirteenth Amendment

One of the greatest effects of the war was the freeing of millions of enslaved persons. As the Union army moved through the South during and after the war, Union soldiers released African Americans from bondage. One of those released was Booker T. Washington, who later became a famous educator and reformer. He recalled the day a Union officer came to his plantation to read the Emancipation Proclamation.

A VOICE FROM THE PAST

After the reading we were told that we were all free, and could go when and where we pleased. My mother, who was standing by my side, leaned over and kissed her children, while tears of joy ran down her cheeks. She explained to us what it all meant, that this was the day for which she had been so long praying, but fearing that she would never live to see.

Booker T. Washington, quoted in his autobiography, *Up from Slavery*

ing **History**

king
nces Why
n amend-
needed to
nslaved
as even
he
ipation
mation?

The Emancipation Proclamation applied primarily to slaves in the Confederacy, however. Many African Americans in the border states were still enslaved. In 1864, with the war still under way, President Lincoln had approved of a constitutional amendment to end slavery entirely, but it failed to pass Congress.

In January 1865, Lincoln urged Congress to try again to end slavery. This time, the measure—known as the **Thirteenth Amendment**—passed. By year's end, 27 states, including eight in the South, had ratified the amendment. From that point on, slavery was banned in the United States.

Lincoln's Assassination

Lincoln did not live to see the end of slavery, however. Five days after Lee's surrender at Appomattox, the president and his wife went to see a play at Ford's Theatre in Washington, D.C. During the play, a Confederate supporter, **John Wilkes Booth**, crept into the balcony where the president sat and shot him in the back of the head. Booth then jumped over the railing and landed on the stage. Although he broke his leg in the leap, he managed to escape the theater.

CONNECTIONS TO MATH
Costs of the Civil War

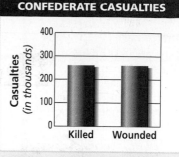

CONFEDERATE CASUALTIES

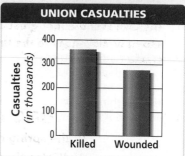

UNION CASUALTIES

Source: *World Book; Historical Statistics of the United States; The United States Civil War Center*

ECONOMIC COSTS

- Federal loans and taxes to finance the war totaled $2.6 billion.
- Federal debt on June 30, 1865, rose to $2.7 billion.
- Confederate debt ran over $700 million.
- Union inflation reached 182% in 1864 and 179% in 1865.
- Confederate inflation rose to 9,000% by the end of the war.

SKILLBUILDER
Interpreting Graphs
1. *About how many Confederate soldiers were killed in the Civil War?*
2. *Approximately how many soldiers were wounded in the war?*

That same evening, an accomplice of Booth stabbed Secretary of State William Seward, who later recovered. Another man was supposed to assassinate Vice-President Johnson, but he failed to carry out the attack.

Although Booth had managed to escape after shooting the president, Union troops found and killed him several days later. Soldiers also hunted down Booth's accomplices, whom they either hanged or imprisoned.

After Lincoln was shot, he was carried to a house across the street from the theater. The bullet in his brain could not be removed, however. The next morning, April 15, 1865, the president died. He was the first American president to be assassinated.

Lincoln's murder stunned the nation and caused intense grief. In Washington, D.C., people wept in the streets. One man who mourned the nation's loss was the poet Walt Whitman. In one poem, Whitman considered the president's legacy.

> **A VOICE FROM THE PAST**
> This dust was once the man,
> Gentle, plain, just and resolute, under whose cautious hand,
> Against the foulest crime in history known in any land or age,
> Was saved the Union of these States.
>
> **Walt Whitman,** *This Dust Was Once the Man*

The loss of Lincoln's vast experience and great political skills was a terrible setback for a people faced by the challenge of rebuilding their nation. In both the North and the South, life would never be the same after the Civil War.

Consequences of the War

In the North, the war changed the way people thought about the country. In fighting to defend the Union, people came to see the United States as a single nation rather than a collection of states. After 1865, people no longer said "the United States *are*" but "the United States *is.*"

The war also caused the national government to expand. Before the war, the government was relatively small and had limited powers. With the demands of war, however, the government grew larger and more powerful. Along with a new paper currency and income tax, the government established a new federal banking system. It also funded railroads, gave western land to settlers, and provided for state colleges. This growth of federal power continued long after the war was over.

The war also changed the Northern economy. New industries such as steel, petroleum, food processing, and manufacturing grew rapidly. By

CAUSE AND EFFECT: The Civil War, 1861–1865

CAUSES	IMMEDIATE EFFECTS
Conflict over slavery in territories	Abolition of slavery
Economic differences between North and South	Devastation of South
Failure of Congress to compromise	Reconstruction of South
	LONG-TERM EFFECTS
Election of Lincoln as president	Growth of industry
Secession of Southern states	Government more powerful
Firing on Fort Sumter	Nation reunited

SKILLBUILDER Interpreting Charts
1. *What military event is among the causes of the Civil War?*
2. *What effect did the Civil War have on the federal government?*

ground
people
called the
War the first
rn war
se of the
machines,
structiveness,
he effects
ilians, which
be repeated
r wars.

the late 1800s, industry had begun to replace farming as the basis of the national economy.

For the South, however, the war brought economic disaster. Farms and plantations were destroyed. About 40 percent of the South's livestock was killed. Fifty percent of its farm machinery was wrecked. Factories were also demolished, and thousands of miles of railroad tracks were torn up. Also gone was the labor system that the South had used—slavery.

Before the war, the South accounted for 30 percent of the nation's wealth. After the war it accounted for only 12 percent. These economic differences between the North and the South would last for decades.

The country faced difficult challenges after the war. How would the South be brought back into the Union, and how would four million former slaves be integrated into national life? You will read more about these challenges in the next chapter.

tion 4 Assessment

Terms & Names

plain the
ignificance of:
hirteenth
mendment
ohn Wilkes Booth

2. Using Graphics

Use a chart like the one below to record the social, economic, and political legacy of the Civil War.

Legacy of the Civil War

Society	Economy	Politics

Is the legacy of the Civil War still apparent today? How?

3. Main Ideas

a. What were some of the human costs of the Civil War?

b. What did the Thirteenth Amendment achieve?

c. What was the state of the Southern economy after the Civil War?

4. Critical Thinking

Making Inferences How do you think the assassination of President Lincoln affected the nation?

THINK ABOUT
• the reaction of ordinary citizens
• its impact on government

IVITY OPTIONS

MATH

ECHNOLOGY

Read about the postwar economy. Create a **database** on industry in the North or make a **storyboard** for a video on the problems in the South.

ANDREW JOHNSON
1808–1875

Andrew Johnson was a self-educated man whose strong will led to trouble with Congress.

As a former slaveholder from Tennessee, Johnson called for a mild program for bringing the South back into the Union. In particular, he let states decide whether to give voting rights to freed African Americans.

Johnson's policies led to a break with the Radical Republicans in Congress and, finally, to his impeachment trial (see page 537).

Why might Johnson have chosen not to punish the South?

had put him on the ticket in 1864 to help win support in the nation's border states. Johnson was a former slaveholder and, unlike Lincoln, a stubborn, unyielding man.

Johnson believed that Reconstruction was the job of the president, not Congress. His policies were based on Lincoln's goals. He insisted that the new state governments ratify the Thirteenth Amendment, which prohibited slavery. He also insisted that they accept the supreme power of the federal government.

Johnson offered amnesty, or official pardon, to most white Southerners. He promised to return their property. In return, they had to pledge loyalty to the United States. At first, the large plantation owners, top military officers, and ex-Confederate leaders were not included in this offer. But they, too, eventually won amnesty.

Rebuilding Brings Conflict

As the Southern states rebuilt, they set up new state governments that seemed very much like the old ones. Some states flatly refused to ratify the Thirteenth Amendment. "This is a white man's government," said the governor of South Carolina, "and intended for white men only."

The Southern states passed laws, known as **black codes,** which limited the freedom of former slaves. In Mississippi, for instance, one law said that African Americans had to have written proof of employment. Anyone without such proof could be put to work on a plantation. African Americans were forbidden to meet in unsupervised groups or carry guns. Because of such laws, many people in the North suspected that white Southerners were trying to bring back the "old South."

When Congress met in December 1865, its members refused to seat representatives from the South. Many of these Southern representatives had been Confederate leaders only months before.

Under the Constitution, Congress has the right to decide whether its members are qualified to hold office. So instead of admitting the Southerners, Congress set up a committee to study conditions in the South and decide whether the Southern states should be represented. By taking such action, Congress let the president know that it planned to play a role in Reconstruction.

Republicans outnumbered Democrats in both houses of Congress. Most Republicans were moderates who believed that the federal government should stay out of the affairs of individuals and the states.

The Radical Republicans, however, wanted the federal government to play an active role in remaking Southern politics and society. Led by Thaddeus Stevens and Massachusetts senator Charles Sumner, the

Background
Not all Confederate leaders were pardoned. Former Confederate president Jefferson Davis, for example, was imprisoned for two years awaiting trial for treason. But he was never tried.

Reading **History**
A. Analyzing Causes What was the main reason Southern states passed black codes?

Vocabulary
moderates: people opposed to extreme views

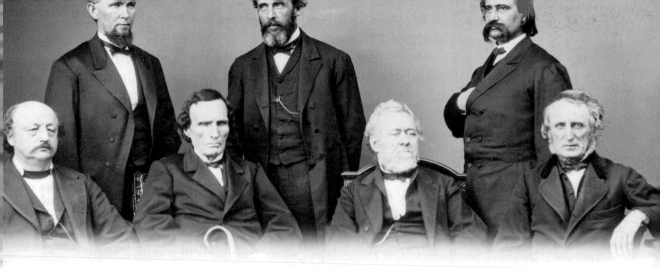

group also demanded full and equal citizenship for African Americans. Their aim was to destroy the South's old ruling class and turn the region into a place of small farms, free schools, respect for labor, and political equality for all citizens.

Radical Republicans pose for a formal portrait. Standing (left to right): James F. Wilson, George S. Boutwell, and John A. Logan. Seated: Benjamin F. Butler, Thaddeus Stevens, Thomas Williams, and John A. Bingham.

The Civil Rights Act

Urged on by the Radicals, Congress passed a bill promoting **civil rights**—those rights granted to all citizens. The Civil Rights Act of 1866 declared that all persons born in the United States (except Native Americans) were citizens. It also stated that all citizens were entitled to equal rights regardless of their race.

Republicans were shocked when President Johnson vetoed the bill. Johnson argued that federal protection of civil rights would lead "towards centralization" of the national government. He also insisted that making African Americans full citizens would "operate against the white race." Congress voted to override Johnson's veto. That is, two-thirds of the House and two-thirds of the Senate voted for the bill after the president's veto, and the bill became law.

The Fourteenth Amendment

*ling*History

king
nces How
e
eenth
dment
rage states
e African
cans the

Republicans were not satisfied with passing laws that ensured equal rights. They wanted equality to be protected by the Constitution itself. To achieve this goal, Congress proposed the **Fourteenth Amendment** in 1866. It stated that all people born in the United States were citizens and had the same rights. All citizens were to be granted "equal protection of the laws." However, the amendment did not establish black suffrage. Instead, it declared that any state that kept African Americans from voting would lose representatives in Congress. This meant that the Southern states would have less power if they did not grant black men the vote.

Johnson refused to support the amendment. So did every former Confederate state except Tennessee. This rejection outraged both moderate and Radical Republicans. As a result, the two groups agreed to join forces and passed the Reconstruction Acts of 1867. The passage of these

Rebuilding Richmond

You live in Richmond, Virginia, the capital of the Confederacy. It is 1865, and the South faces defeat in the Civil War. On April 2, Confederate officials set fire to supplies in Richmond to prevent the approaching Union army from using them. The fire spreads out of control and destroys downtown Richmond. The next day, Union troops march into the city and take command. You must now help rebuild the city.

COOPERATIVE LEARNING On this page are two challenges you face as a resident of Richmond. Working with a small group, decide how to solve one of these problems. Divide the work among the group members. You will find useful information in the Data File. Be prepared to present your solutions to the class.

This picture shows a street in Richmond before the fire.

ARTS CHALLENGE

"We want the burnt district of Richmond to . . . sit proudly again."

The smell of charred wood still floats in the breeze. However, spirit and determination fill the air. Warehouses are opening. Newly cleared streets bustle with activity. The rebuilding of Richmond has begun. How would you design one block of Richmond's new downtown business district? Use the Data File for help. Then present your plan using one of these options:

• Make a model of your new city block.
• Ask and answer questions about how buildings and services should be distributed on the model block.

CIVICS CHALLENGE

"Open robberies have been perpetrated."

...obberies and assaults are commonplace, especially ...t the burnt area of the downtown. Groups of ...phaned children also roam the city, picking pockets ...support themselves. Union military police suppos- ...ly protect the public. However, soldiers sometimes ...mmit crimes themselves. What would you do to ...prove public safety? Use the Data File for help. ...esent your ideas using one of these options:

Hold a town meeting to explore possible solutions.

Create a set of emergency laws, with plans for publicizing them.

THE BURNT DISTRICT

- about $30 million damage
- 20 city blocks destroyed, including 900 buildings

Destroyed Property
all banks, 20 law offices, 24 grocery stores, 36 merchant shops, 2 carriage factories, 2 paper mills, 7 book and stationery stores, 2 train depots, 3 bridges, a church, a machine shop, a tin shop, a pottery factory, several flour mills and printing offices

Surviving Property
capitol and city hall, residential areas, ironworks

EMERGENCY SERVICES

Union Army
- distributes 13,000 food rations
- provides medical help
- guards homes; patrols streets

American Union Commission
- hands out food tickets
- distributes 80,000 pounds of flour; feeds soup to 800 people a day
- provides garden seeds and sells shovels at cost to farmers

REBUILDING

April 1865
- rubble is cleared
- markets sell meat, fish, produce
- hotels and bakeries open
- one bridge is rebuilt

May 1865
- two banks open
- gas and telegraph service is restored
- river opens to steamboat traffic

Summer 1865
- horse-drawn buses operate
- city government is reinstated

Fall 1865
- ironworks reopens
- 100 buildings are now under construction

For more about Reconstruction . . .

RESEARCH LINKS
CLASSZONE.COM

ACTIVITY WRAP-UP

...eet as a group to review your responses to rebuilding ...hmond. Pick your most creative solution and present it to ...e class.

TERMS & NAMES

Briefly explain the significance of each of the following.

1. Reconstruction
2. Andrew Johnson
3. black codes
4. civil rights
5. Fourteenth Amendment
6. sharecropping
7. lynch
8. Fifteenth Amendment
9. Panic of 1873
10. Compromise of 1877

REVIEW QUESTIONS

Rebuilding the Union (pages 533–539)

1. What was the Freedmen's Bureau?
2. What were the main parts of President Johnson's Reconstruction plan?
3. Who were scalawags and carpetbaggers?
4. What reason did the House give for impeaching President Johnson?

Reconstruction and Daily Life (pages 540–544)

5. Why did Congress not pass a land-reform plan?
6. What new systems of labor developed in the South after the Civil War?
7. How did the Ku Klux Klan serve the Democratic Party?

End of Reconstruction (pages 545–549)

8. Why did the Fifteenth Amendment arouse anger in many women?
9. What caused an economic depression in the 1870s?
10. How did Supreme Court rulings during Reconstruction help weaken African Americans' civil rights?

CRITICAL THINKING

1. USING YOUR NOTES: IDENTIFYING AND SOLVING PROBLEMS

Problems		Solutions
Black codes	➤	
President Johnson	➤	
Education	➤	
Economy	➤	
Ku Klux Klan	➤	
Voting	➤	

Using your diagram, answer the following questic

a. What was the solution to the problem of educa African Americans?

b. What was the solution to the problem of Ku Kl Klan violence?

2. ANALYZING LEADERSHIP

Why might Reconstruction be considered a time i which the presidency was weak?

3. THEME: DEMOCRATIC IDEALS

How did the Fourteenth and Fifteenth amendmer promote greater equality for African Americans? were the amendments limited?

4. APPLYING CITIZENSHIP SKILLS

What were the different viewpoints of Elizabeth Stanton and Frances E. W. Harper regarding the Fifteenth Amendment's failure to give women an important right of citizenship—the right to vote?

5. ANALYZING CAUSES

What aspect of the Compromise of 1877 likely pl the greatest role in ending Reconstruction?

Interact with History

How did your solutions to rebuilding the nation pare with the actual solutions carried out?

VISUAL SUMMARY

Reconstruction

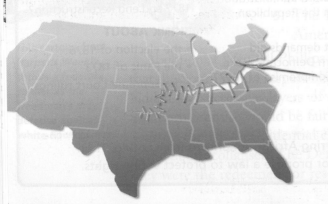

Rebuilding the Union

During Reconstruction, Congress decided how the Sou states would be readmitted to the Union and passed l to improve conditions for freed people.

Reconstruction and Daily Life

After slavery ended, freed African Americans reunited families, attended school, and began working for pay. Racist violence and lack of land slowed their progress.

End of Reconstruction

In the 1870s, hostile Supreme Court decisions, the Sou Democrats' return to power, and the withdrawal of fe troops from the South ended Reconstruction.

e the map and your knowledge of U.S. history to
swer questions 1 and 2.

ditional Test Practice, pp. S1–S33.

Election of 1876

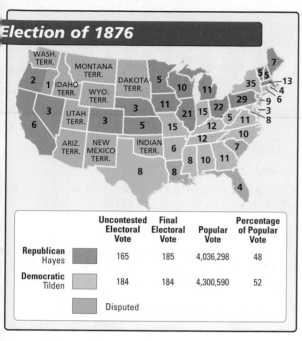

		Uncontested Electoral Vote	Final Electoral Vote	Popular Vote	Percentage of Popular Vote
Republican Hayes		165	185	4,036,298	48
Democratic Tilden		184	184	4,300,590	52
		Disputed			

n what region of the country were most of the
disputed votes located?

A. the North

B. the South

C. the Northeast

D. the Southwest

2. What regions voted mostly Republican?

   A. the North and East

   B. the South and East

   C. the South and West

   D. the North and West

**Robert B. Elliott gives his views of the civil rights bill
in this quotation. Use the quotation and your
knowledge of U.S. history to answer question 3.**

PRIMARY SOURCE

The passage of this bill will determine the civil status,
not only of the negro but of any other class of
citizens who may feel themselves discriminated
against. It will form the capstone of that temple
of liberty begun on this continent.

Robert B. Elliott, quoted in *The Glorious Failure*

3. This passage supports which point of view?

   A. African Americans would never gain freedom
without the passage of the civil rights bill.

   B. The passage of the civil rights bill would be
important to southern states only.

   C. The passage of the civil rights bill would help
any group subject to discrimination.

   D. Failure to pass the civil rights bill would mean
renewed war in the United States.

TEST PRACTICE
CLASSZONE.COM

ERNATIVE ASSESSMENT

WRITING ABOUT HISTORY

a **letter** to the editor of a newspaper stating
pinion of the freedmen's schools. You might
from the perspective of a plantation owner, or
that of a recently-freed African American.

library resources to research the schools.

port your opinion with facts from your research.

to persuade your reader to support your position.

OPERATIVE LEARNING

with two classmates to research sharecropping.
roup member can choose a different perspective
earch: a land owner; a white sharecropper, or an
n-American sharecropper. Explain how their per-
es differ from each other.

INTEGRATED TECHNOLOGY

PARTICIPATING IN A NET SIMULATION

Go to *NetSimulations: The Impeachment of Andrew
Johnson* at **classzone.com** to participate in the
impeachment trial of the president. You must evaluate
the evidence against President Johnson and vote to
retain or remove him from office.

- Use the simulation to learn about the impeachment
process, the conflicts between Congress and the
president, and the events that led to the trial.

- Answer questions in the Senator's Journal, and use
it to take notes.

- Before you cast your vote, carefully consider the
closing arguments of each attorney.

NET SIMULATION
CLASSZONE.COM

"Give me your tired, your poor,
Your huddled masses, yearning
to breathe free..."
—Emma Lazarus

European immigrants such as those
shown in this photograph (taken
around 1900) streamed into Ellis
Island at the turn of the century.

Growth in the West 1860–1900

A Nebraska "sodbuster" family takes time away from their chores to pose in front of their sod house.

Antlers left over from a successful hunt

1862
Congress passes the Homestead Act.

1864
Sand Creek Massacre

1867
The Grange is founded.

1876
Sitting Bull leads Native American warriors at the Battle of the Little Bighorn.

USA
World — 1860

1861
Serfs are freed in Russia.

1871
Franco-Prussian War ends.

1876
Japan recognizes Korean independence.

Interact *with* History

The windows in this sod house are a real luxury.

It is 1865, and the Civil War has just ended. You are drawn to the West by stories of gold, silver, fertile soil, and free land, and by tales of adventure and new opportunities. Yet you know there would be hardships and unknown dangers. Your life would never be the same.

How might your life change in the West?

What Do You Think?

- What might be some of the ways to make a living in the West?
- What do you think your daily life would be like in the West?
- What would be the biggest difference in your life?

RESEARCH LINKS
CLASSZONE.COM

Visit the Chapter 19 links for more information about the American West.

1884
Grover Cleveland is elected president.

1889
Oklahoma land rush begins.

1890
Wounded Knee Massacre

1891
Farmers organize the Populist Party.

1896
William McKinley is elected president.

1900

1885
African among ations.

1889
First Pan-American Conference is held.

1893
France takes over Indochina.

1900
Boxer Rebellion takes place in China.

Native Americans Fight to Survive

MAIN IDEA	WHY IT MATTERS NOW	TERMS & NAMES
The Native Americans of the Great Plains fought to maintain their way of life as settlers poured onto their lands.	The taking of their lands led to social and economic problems for Native Americans that continue to this day.	reservation Sand Creek Massacre Sitting Bull George A. Custer	Battle of t Bighorn Wounded Massacre Dawes Act

ONE AMERICAN'S STORY

Buffalo Bird Woman was a Hidatsa who lived almost 100 years. She was born in 1840. As a child, she and her family made their home along the Missouri River. Later the federal government forced her family onto a reservation. A **reservation** is land set aside for Native American tribes.

The federal government attempted to "Americanize" Native American children, including Buffalo Bird Woman, by sending them away to boarding schools. But Buffalo Bird Woman struggled to hold on to Hidatsa customs. As an old woman, she looked back on her early years.

A VOICE FROM THE PAST

Sometimes at evening I sit, looking out on the . . . Missouri [River]. . . . In the shadows I seem . . . to see our Indian village, with smoke curling upward from the earth lodges; and in the river's roar I hear the yells of the warriors, the laughter of . . . children as of old.

Buffalo Bird Woman, quoted in *Native American Testimony,* edited by Peter Nabokov

As white settlers claimed Native American lands, Plains peoples fought a losing battle to save not only their homes but their way of life.

Buffalo B

Taking Notes

Use your chart to take notes about Native Americans.

Many diverse people settled the West!

Native American Life on the Plains

Before the arrival of Europeans in the 1500s, most Plains tribes lived in villages along rivers and streams. The women tended crops of beans, corn, and squash. The men hunted deer and elk and in the summer stalked the vast buffalo herds that inhabited the Plains.

In the early 1540s, the Spanish brought the first horses to the Great Plains. The arrival of horses changed the way of life of the Plains people. They quickly became expert riders. By the late 1700s, most Plains tribes kept their own herds of horses. Mounted on horseback, hunters traveled far from their villages seeking buffalo.

The buffalo was central to the life of Plains tribes. Its meat became the chief food in their diet, while its skins served as portable shelters called tepees. Plains women turned buffalo hides into clothing, shoes, and blankets and used buffalo chips (dried manure) as cooking fuel. Bones and horns became tools and bowls. Over time, many Plains tribes developed a nomadic way of life tied to buffalo hunting.

A Clash of Cultures

When the federal government first forced Native American tribes of the Southeast to move west of the Mississippi in the 1830s, it settled them in Indian Territory. This territory was a huge area that included almost all of the land between the Missouri River and Oregon Territory. Most treaties made by the government with Native Americans promised that this land would remain theirs "as long as Grass grows or water runs."

Unfortunately, these treaty promises would be broken. Government policy was based on the belief that white settlers were not interested in the Plains. The land was considered too dry for farming. However, as wagon trains bound for Oregon and California crossed the Great Plains in the 1850s, some pioneers saw possibilities for farming and ranching on its grasslands. Soon white settlers moved onto the prairies.

These settlers pressured the federal government for more land. They also wanted protection from Native Americans in the area. In 1851, the government responded by calling the Sioux, Cheyenne, Arapaho, and

abulary

adic:
dering from
e to place

dingHistory

nalyzing
es What
the major
e of conflict
een white
rs and
e Americans?

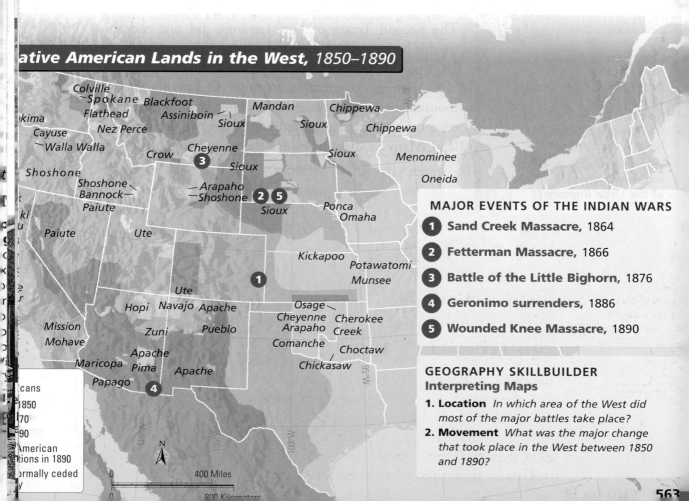

Native American Lands in the West, 1850–1890

Colville
Spokane Blackfoot
Flathead Assiniboin
kima
Cayuse Nez Perce
Walla Walla
Crow
Shoshone
Shoshone
Bannock
Paiute
Paiute Ute
Mission
Mohave Zuni
Maricopa Apache
Pima
Papago

Mandan Chippewa
Sioux
Sioux Chippewa
Cheyenne Sioux Menominee
Sioux Oneida
Arapaho
Shoshone
Sioux
Ponca
Omaha
Kickapoo
Potawatomi
Munsee
Hopi Navajo Apache Osage
Pueblo Cheyenne Cherokee
Arapaho Creek
Comanche Choctaw
Apache Chickasaw

MAJOR EVENTS OF THE INDIAN WARS

1 **Sand Creek Massacre,** 1864

2 **Fetterman Massacre,** 1866

3 **Battle of the Little Bighorn,** 1876

4 **Geronimo surrenders,** 1886

5 **Wounded Knee Massacre,** 1890

GEOGRAPHY SKILLBUILDER
Interpreting Maps

1. **Location** In which area of the West did most of the major battles take place?

2. **Movement** What was the major change that took place in the West between 1850 and 1890?

cans
1850
70
90
American
ions in 1890
rmally ceded

N

0   400 Miles

0   800 Kilometers

At the turn of the century, industrial strikes for better conditions often erupted in violence, as this illustration shows.

Most of the workers have only bricks, stones, or sticks for weapons.

There were no laws protecting children from dangerous work or long hours.

1863
Two companies begin to build a transcontinental railroad across the United States.

1879
Thomas Edison invents a practical lightbulb.

1882
Thomas Edison installs electric lights in New York City.

USA
World   1860

1869
Suez Canal opens in Egypt.

The year is 1894. You work in a factory that is unheated and badly lit. The machine that you operate is dangerous. The economy is doing poorly, so the factory has cut your wages. Some of your coworkers have gone out on strike. They want better pay and working conditions.

Would you join the strike? Why or why not?

What Do You Think?

- What are some risks you would be taking if you join the strike?

- What might you gain if you take part in the strike?

- What other methods might you use to persuade your employer to meet your demands?

RESEARCH LINKS
CLASSZONE.COM

Visit the Chapter 20 links for more information about U.S. industry.

1892
Grover Cleveland is elected president for the second time.

1894
Pullman Strike halts rail traffic across the nation.

1901
Oil drillers discover a huge oil field in Texas.

1905
Supreme Court overturns a New York law establishing a 60-hour workweek for bakers.

1914

...world's tallest ...ure to date, ...ffel Tower in ...is built of iron.

1896
The Italian engineer Guglielmo Marconi patents the radio.

1904
Russia finishes building the first Trans-Siberian railway across Asia.

Reading Strategy: Analyzing Causes and Effe

What Do You Know?

Do you know of any businesses that started back in the 1800s? How do businesses grow?

Think About

- businesses that you see in your community
- businesses that are advertised on television, in magazines or newspapers, or on the Internet
- your responses to the Interact with History about conflict with workers (see page 583)

What Do You Want to Know?

 What facts and details would help you understand how a nation of small businesses became a nation of giant corporations? In your notebook, list the facts and details you hope to learn from this chapter.

Business leader John D. Rockefeller is shown as a weal† king. Notice which industries a the "jewels in his crown."

Analyzing Causes and Effects

The conditions or actions that lead to a historical event are its causes. The consequences an event are its effects. As you read the chapter, look for the causes and effects of indus† and railroad growth. Causes include geographical factors and actions by individuals and government. Effects include both benefits and problems. Use the diagram below to record both causes and effects.

S See Skillbuilder Handbook, page R11.

Taking Notes

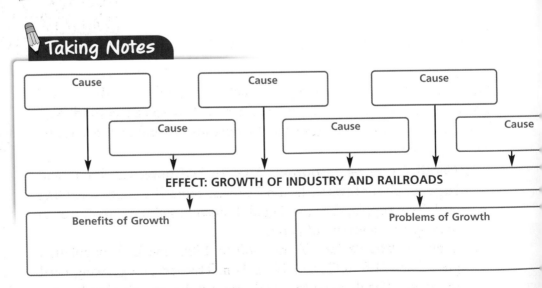

Cause	Cause	Cause
Cause	Cause	Cause

EFFECT: GROWTH OF INDUSTRY AND RAILROADS

Benefits of Growth

Problems of Growth

The Growth of Industry

ONE AMERICAN'S STORY

In the 1850s, most Americans lit their homes with oil lamps. They could have used kerosene, an oil made from coal, but it was expensive. Then, in 1855, a chemist reported that kerosene could be made more cheaply from an oily liquid called **petroleum**. However, people didn't know how to obtain petroleum from underground. They just gathered it slowly when it seeped to the surface.

In 1857, Edwin Drake visited a site in Pennsylvania where petroleum oozed to the surface.

Drake began drilling in 1859. He struck oil in August. This event launched the oil industry—one of many new industries that developed in the late 1800s, as this section explains.

The wooden structure is Drake's first oil well.

The Industrial Revolution Continues

Throughout the 1800s, factory production expanded in the United States. By the Civil War, factory production had spread beyond New England textiles to other regions and industries. Several factors encouraged this growth.

1. **Plentiful natural resources.** America had immense forests and large supplies of water. It also had vast mineral wealth, including coal, iron, copper, silver, and gold. Industry used these resources to manufacture a variety of goods.
2. **Growing population.** From 1860 to 1900, the U.S. population grew from 31.5 million to 76 million. This led to a growing need for goods. The demand for goods spurred the growth of industry.

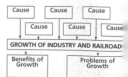

Taking Notes

Use your chart to take notes about the growth of industry.

Cause	Cause	Cause

	Cause	Cause	Cause

GROWTH OF INDUSTRY AND RAILROAD

Benefits of Growth	Problems of Growth

3. **Improved transportation.** In the early 1800s, steamboats, canals, and railroads made it possible to ship items long distances more quickly. Railroad building boomed after the Civil War. As shipping raw materials and finished goods to markets became even easier, industry grew.

4. **High immigration.** Between 1860 and 1900, about 14 million people immigrated to the United States. Many of them knew specialized trades, such as metalworking. Such knowledge was valuable to industries. In addition, unskilled immigrants supplied the labor that growing industry needed.

5. **New inventions.** New machines and improved processes helped industry produce goods more efficiently. Inventors applied for patents for the machines or processes they invented. A **patent** is a government document giving an inventor the exclusive right to make and sell his or her invention for a specific number of years.

6. **Investment capital.** When the economy was thriving, many businesses made large profits. Hoping to share in those profits, banks and wealthy people lent businesses money. The businesses used this capital to build factories and buy equipment.

7. **Government assistance.** State and federal governments used tariffs, land grants, and subsidies to help businesses grow.

Background
Some of the
canals were
because of H
Clay's Ameri
System. (See
Chapter 11.)

Vocabulary
capital: mor
and propert
used in a bu

The Business Cycle

American industry did not grow at a steady pace; it experienced ups and downs. This pattern of good and bad times is called the **business cycle**. During good times, called booms, people buy more, and some invest in business. As a result, industries and businesses grow. During bad times, called busts, spending and investing decrease. Industries lay off workers and make fewer goods. Businesses may shrink—or even close. Such a period of low economic activity is a depression.

America experienced depressions in 1837 and 1857. Both were eventually followed by periods of strong economic growth. In the late 1800s, there were two harsh depressions, also called panics. The depression of 1873 lasted five years. At its height, three million people were out of work. During the depression that began in 1893, thousands of businesses failed, including more than 300 railroads.

The Business Cycle

Peak

Peak (high point)

Contraction (decrease)

Expansion (growth)

Expansion

Trough (low point)

Change in volume of what businesses produce

Passage of time

SKILLBUILDER Interpreting Charts
1. *How does the amount of goods produced at the peak compare to the amount at the trough?*
2. *Are all peaks equally prosperous? Explain.*

Reading B
A. Recogni
Effects Ho
you think
depression
affect ordi
people?

Even with these economic highs and lows, industries in the United States grew tremendously between 1860 and 1900. Overall, the amount of manufactured goods increased six times during these years.

Steel: The Backbone of Industry

The steel industry contributed to America's industrial growth. Before the mid-1800s, steel was very expensive to manufacture because the steel-making process used huge amounts of coal. In the 1850s, William Kelly in the United States and Henry Bessemer in England independently developed a new process for making steel. It used less than one-seventh of the coal that the older process used. This new manufacturing technique was called the **Bessemer steel process**.

Because the Bessemer process cut the cost of steel, the nation's steel output increased 500 times between 1867 and 1900. Industry began to make many products out of steel instead of iron. These products included plows, barbed wire, nails, and beams for buildings. But the main use of steel throughout the late 1800s was for rails for the expanding railroads. (See Section 2.)

Edison and Electricity

Another industry that grew during the late 1800s was the electric-power industry. By the 1870s, inventors had designed efficient generators. A **generator** is a machine that produces electric current. As a result, people grew eager to tap the power of electricity.

The inventor who found the most ways to use electricity was **Thomas Edison**. In 1876, he opened a laboratory in Menlo Park, New Jersey. He employed many assistants, whom he organized into teams to do research. Edison's laboratory invented so many things that Edison received more than 1,000 U.S. patents, more than any other individual inventor.

Edison would start with an idea for a possible invention. Then he would work hard to make that idea a reality—even if problems arose.

A VOICE FROM THE PAST

It has been just so in all my inventions. The first step is an intuition—and comes with a burst, *then* difficulties arise. . . . "Bugs"—as such little faults and difficulties are called—show themselves and months of anxious watching, study and labor are requisite [needed] before commercial success—or failure—is certainly reached.

Thomas Edison, quoted in *Edison* by Matthew Josephson

Edison's most famous invention was practical electric lighting. Other inventors had already created electric lights, but they were too bright and

*ing***History**
wing
usions
industries
ted from
eel
cts
oned here?

*ng***History**
ing Main
According
on, is
ng easy?

No. 174,465.   Patented March 7, 18

T. A. EDISON.
Electric-Lamp.

Thomas A. Edison

Imagine life without being able to burn lights 24 hours a day. Or without movies and recorded music. Edison invented not only the light bulb but also the phonograph and a moving-picture viewer.

Alexander Graham Bell

As a teacher of the deaf, Bell experimented to learn how vowel sounds are produced. This led to his interest in the electrical transmission of speech.

flickery for home use. Edison figured out how to make a safe, steady light bulb. He also invented a system to deliver electricity to buildings.

By 1882, he had installed electric lighting in a half-mile-square area of New York City. Electric lighting quickly replaced gaslights. By the late 1880s, Edison's factory produced about a million light bulbs a year.

Bell and the Telephone

Electricity played a role in communications devices invented during the 1800s. In 1835, Samuel Morse developed the telegraph. It allowed people to use electrical impulses to send messages over long distances.

The next step in communications was the telephone, invented by **Alexander Graham Bell.** He was a Scottish immigrant who taught deaf students in Boston. At night, Bell and his assistant, Thomas Watson, tried to invent a device to transmit human speech using electricity.

After years of experiments, Bell succeeded. One day in March 1876, he was adjusting the transmitter in the laboratory in his apartment. Watson was in another room with the receiver. The two doors between the rooms were shut. According to Watson's memoirs, Bell accidentally spilled acid on himself and said, "Mr. Watson, come here. I want you." Watson rushed down the hall. He burst into the laboratory, exclaiming that he had heard and understood Bell's words through the receiver.

Bell showed his telephone at the **Centennial Exhibition** in June 1876. That was an exhibition in Philadelphia to celebrate America's 100th birthday. There, several of the world's leading scientists and the emperor of Brazil saw his demonstration. Afterward, they declared, "Here is the greatest marvel ever achieved in electrical science."

Inventions Change Industry

The telephone industry grew rapidly. By 1880, more than 50,000 telephones had been sold. The invention of the switchboard allowed more and more people to connect into a telephone network. Women commonly worked in the new job of switchboard operator.

The typewriter also opened jobs for women. Christopher Latham Sholes helped invent the first practical typewriter in 1867. He also

Reading **H**
D. Analyzin
Points of V
Why do you
think the
scientists sa
about the
telephone?

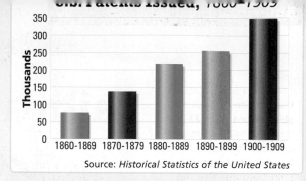

Source: *Historical Statistics of the United States*

Jan Matzeliger

mmigrant from Dutch
na, Matzeliger worked
shoe factory. To reduce
time needed to fasten
leather to the sole by
d, he invented a
hine to do the job. It
ased production by
0 percent!

SKILLBUILDER Interpreting Graphs

1. *How many more patents were issued from 1900 to 1909 than from 1860 to 1869?*
2. *Was this a time of increasing or decreasing inventiveness?*

improved the machine and sold his rights to it to a manufacturer who began to make typewriters in the 1870s.

The sewing machine also changed American life. Elias Howe first patented it in 1846. In the next few years, the sewing machine received many design improvements. Isaac Singer patented a sewing machine in 1851 and continued to improve it. It became a bestseller and led to a new industry. In factories, people produced ready-made clothes. Instead of being fitted to each buyer, clothes came in standard sizes and popular styles. Increasingly, people bought clothes instead of making their own.

Other inventors helped industry advance. African-American inventor Granville T. Woods patented devices to improve telephone and tele-graph systems. Margaret Knight invented machines for the packaging and shoemaking industries and also improved motors and engines.

Of all the up-and-coming industries of the middle 1800s, one would have a larger impact on American life than any other. That was the rail-road industry. You will read about railroads in Section 2.

---

tion ❶ Assessment

Terms & Names	**2. Using Graphics**	**3. Main Ideas**	**4. Critical Thinking**
plain the **ignificance of:**	Use a cluster diagram like the one below to list some of the inventions of the late 1800s.	**a.** What factors contributed to industrial growth in the United States?	**Recognizing Effects** How did the inventions of the late 1800s make it easier to do business?

etroleum
patent
business cycle
Bessemer steel
process
generator
homas Edison
Alexander Graham
Bell
Centennial Exhibition

b. What is the business cycle?

c. What caused the steel-making industry to boom and why?

How has one of these inventions recently been improved?

THINK ABOUT

• electric generators and light bulbs
• the telephone
• the typewriter

TIVITY OPTIONS

SCIENCE
ECHNOLOGY

Choose an invention and learn more about it. Create a **display** explaining how it works or design a **Web page** linking to sites with more information.

Railroads Transform the Nation

MAIN IDEA	WHY IT MATTERS NOW	TERMS & NAMES
The railroads tied the nation together, speeded industrial growth, and changed U.S. life.	The railroad first made possible our modern system of shipping goods across the country.	transcontinental railroad standard time

ONE AMERICAN'S STORY

Ah Goong was one of thousands of Chinese workers on the Western railroads in the late 1800s. In some places, the workers had to blast rock from a cliff wall. The lightest Chinese were lowered in wicker baskets hundreds of feet to the blasting site. Years later, Ah Goong's granddaughter described her grandfather's job.

A VOICE FROM THE PAST

Swinging near the cliff, Ah Goong . . . dug holes, then inserted gunpowder and fuses. . . . The basketmen signaled one another to light the fuses. He struck match after match and dropped the burnt matches over the sides. At last his fuse caught; he waved, and the men above pulled hand over hand hauling him up, pulleys creaking.

Maxine Hong Kingston, *China Men*

This section discusses the building of the railroads.

Chinese immigrants—l at the lower left—help several railroads in the

aking Notes

e your chart to
e notes about
e growth of
lroads.

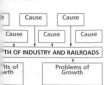

Deciding to Span the Continent

Americans had talked about building a **transcontinental railroad**—one that spanned the entire continent—for years. Such a railroad would encourage people to settle the West and develop its economy. In 1862, Congress passed a bill that called for two companies to build a transcontinental railroad across the center of the United States.

The Central Pacific, led by Leland Stanford, was to start in Sacramento, California, and build east. The Union Pacific was to start in Omaha, Nebraska, and build west. To build the railroad, these two companies had to raise large sums of money. The government lent them millions of dollars. It also gave them 20 square miles of public land for every mile of track they laid. The railroad companies could then sell the land to raise money.

With the guarantees of loans and land, the railroads attracted many investors. The Central Pacific began to lay its first track in 1863. The

Union Pacific laid its first rail in July 1865 (after the Civil War had ended).

Building the Railroad

The Central Pacific faced a labor shortage because most men preferred to try to strike it rich as miners. Desperate for workers, the Central Pacific's managers overcame the widespread prejudice against the Chinese and hired several dozen of them. The Chinese were small and weighed, on average, no more than 110 pounds. But they were efficient, fearless, and hard working.

They also followed their own customs, which led to an unexpected benefit for the railroad company. The Chinese drank tea instead of unboiled water, so they were sick less often than other workers. Pleased with the Chinese workers, the company brought more men over from China. At the peak of construction, more than 10,000 Chinese worked on the Central Pacific.

The Union Pacific hired workers from a variety of backgrounds. After the Civil War ended in 1865, former soldiers from both North and South flocked to work on the railroad. Freed slaves came, too. But one of the largest groups of Union Pacific workers was immigrants, many from Ireland.

Both railroads occasionally hired Native Americans. Washos, Shoshones, and Paiutes all assisted the race of the rails across the deserts of Nevada and Utah.

ground
g water
erms.

ing**History**
wing
sions Why
e Union
have a
supply of
rs?

ing**History**
ding a Map
the map on
92, find
ion Pacific
ntral
Railroads.
how they
t Omaha
amento.

Railroads Tie the Nation Together

Only short, undergrown trees dotted the vast open space. To the south shimmered the Great Salt Lake. In the east rose the bluish shapes of the Rocky Mountains. Across that space, from opposite directions, the workers of the Central Pacific and the Union Pacific toiled. By May 10, 1869, Central Pacific workers had laid 690 miles of track. Union Pacific workers had laid 1,086 miles. Only one span of track separated the two lines at their meeting point at Promontory, Utah.

Hundreds of railroad workers, managers, spectators, and journalists gathered on that cool, windy day to see the transcontinental railroad completed. Millions of Americans waited to hear the news by telegraph. A band played as a Chinese crew and an Irish crew laid the last rails. The last spike, a golden one, was set in place. First, the president of the Central Pacific raised a hammer to drive in the spike. After he swung the hammer down, the crowd roared with laughter. He had missed. The vice-president of the Union Pacific took a turn and also missed. But the telegraph operator couldn't see and had already sent the message: "done." People across the nation celebrated.

This golden spike united the Central Pacific and Union Pacific Railroads.

The Union Pacific-Central Pacific line was the first transcontinental railroad. By 1895, four more U.S. lines had been built across the continent. Between 1869 and 1890, the amount of money railroads earned carrying freight grew from $300 million to $734 million per year.

Railroad Time

The railroads changed America in a surprising way: they altered time. Before the railroads, each community determined its own time, based on calculations about the sun's travels. This system was called "solar time." Solar time caused problems for people who scheduled trains crossing several time zones and for travelers.

A VOICE FROM THE PAST

I have been annoyed and perplexed by the changes in the time schedules of connecting railroads. My watch could give me no information as to the arrival and departure of trains, nor of the time for meals.

John Rodgers, quoted in *Passage to Union*

To solve this problem, the railroad companies set up **standard time**. It was a system that divided the United States into four time zones. Although the plan went into effect on November 18, 1883, Congress did not adopt standard time until 1918. By then, most Americans saw its benefit because following schedules had become part of daily life.

Backgroun
Canada had
built a trans
tinental rail
so there we
altogether.

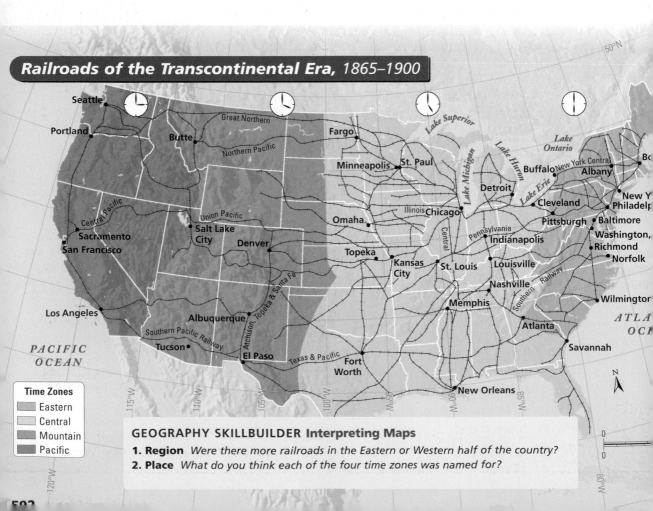

Railroads of the Transcontinental Era, *1865–1900*

Time Zones
- Eastern
- Central
- Mountain
- Pacific

GEOGRAPHY SKILLBUILDER Interpreting Maps
1. **Region** *Were there more railroads in the Eastern or Western half of the country?*
2. **Place** *What do you think each of the four time zones was named for?*

Economic and Social Changes

The railroads changed people's lives in many other important ways. They helped create modern America.

1. **Linked the economies of the West and East.** From the West, the railroads carried eastward raw materials such as lumber, livestock, and grain. Materials like these were processed in Midwestern cities such as Chicago and Cleveland. (See Geography in History on pages 598–599.) From Eastern cities, in turn, came manufactured goods, which were sold to Westerners.

2. **Helped people settle the West.** Railroads were lifelines for settlers. Trains brought them lumber, farm equipment, food, and other necessities and hauled their crops to market.

3. **Weakened the Native American hold on the West.** As Chapter 19 explained, the railroads carried hunters who killed off the herds of buffalo. They also brought settlers and miners who laid claim to Native American land.

4. **Gave people more control of the environment.** Before railroads, people lived mainly where there were waterways, such as rivers. Roads were primitive. Railroads made possible cities such as Denver, Colorado, which had no usable waterways.

Just as railroads changed life for many Americans in the late 1800s, so did big business. You will read about big business in Section 3.

ding **History**

aluating
h of these
changes do
hink were
ive, and
n were
tive?

Connections TO
ART & MUSIC

RAILROAD HEROES
Several American songs celebrate railroad heroes. One tells of Casey Jones, an engineer who saved lives. He slammed on the brakes as his train rounded a bend and plowed into a stalled freight train. He died but slowed the train enough to save his passengers.

Another song tells of a mythical worker named John Henry, shown below. This ballad celebrates an African American's strength in a track-laying race against a steam-driven machine.

John_ Hen_
John_ Hen_
2   3

---

ction **2** **Assessment**

Terms & Names

xplain the
ignificance of:
:ranscontinental
railroad
standard time

2. Using Graphics

Using a chart like the one below, record which groups of people helped build the transcontinental railroad.

Central Pacific	Union Pacific

Which group worked on both railroads?

3. Main Ideas

a. Why did the federal government want a transcontinental railroad built?

b. How did the government encourage the building of the railroad?

c. Why was standard time created?

4. Critical Thinking

Recognizing Effects
Which of the trends started by railroads are still part of the modern business world?

THINK ABOUT
• railroads' effect on time
• the way they linked the economy
• the way they changed where people settled

TIVITY OPTIONS

ART

TECHNOLOGY

You have been asked to honor those who built the transcontinental railroad. Design a **memorial** or create the opening screen of a **multimedia presentation**.

The Rise of Big Business

ONE AMERICAN'S STORY

In 1853, when Jay Gould was 17, he visited New York. Big-city wealth impressed Gould. After returning to his small hometown, he told a friend, "Crosby, I'm going to be rich. I've seen enough to realize what can be accomplished by means of riches, and I tell you I'm going to be rich."

Gould achieved his goal. By the time he died in 1892, he was worth $77 million. He made a lot of his money using methods that are illegal today—such as bribing officials and selling fake stock. Most of his deals involved railroads.

Jay Gould was a robber baron. A **robber baron** was a business leader who became wealthy through dishonest methods. This section discusses other business leaders and their companies.

Jay Gould us[ed] methods suc[h as] trickery and [...] reports to "b[...] his competit[ors]

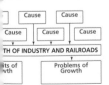
The Growth of Corporations

Until the late 1800s, most businesses were owned directly by one person or by a few partners. Then advances in technology made many business owners want to buy new equipment. One way to raise money to do so was to turn their businesses into corporations. A **corporation** is a business owned by investors who buy part of the company through shares of stock. A corporation has advantages over a privately owned business:

1. By selling stock, a corporation can raise large amounts of money.
2. A corporation has a special legal status and continues to exist after its founders die. Banks are more likely to lend a corporation money.
3. A corporation limits the risks to its investors, who do not have to pay off the corporation's debts.

In the late 1800s, few laws regulated corporations. This led to the growth of a few giant corporations that dominated American industry. The oil and steel industries are examples of this process.

The Oil and Steel Industries

As Section 1 explained, the oil and steel industries began to grow in the late 1800s. Two men dominated these industries. **John D. Rockefeller** led the oil industry, and **Andrew Carnegie** controlled the steel industry.

John D. Rockefeller built his first refinery in 1863. He decided that the best way to make money was to put his competitors out of business. A company that wipes out its competitors and controls an industry is a **monopoly.** Rockefeller bought other refineries. He made secret deals with railroads to carry his oil at a lower rate than his competitors' oil. He also built and purchased his own pipelines to carry oil.

Rockefeller's most famous move to end competition was to develop the trust in 1882. A **trust** is a legal body created to hold stock in many companies, often in the same industry. Rockefeller persuaded other oil companies to join his Standard Oil Trust. By 1880, the trust controlled 95 percent of all oil refining in the United States—and was able to set a high price for oil. The public had to pay that price because they couldn't buy oil from anyone else. As head of Standard Oil, Rockefeller earned millions of dollars. He also gained a reputation as a ruthless robber baron.

Businessmen in other industries began to follow Rockefeller's example. Trusts were formed in the sugar, cottonseed oil, and lead-mining industries. Many people felt that these monopolies were unfair and hurt the economy. But the government was slow to regulate them.

Rockefeller tried to control all the companies in his industry. By contrast, Andrew Carnegie tried to beat his competition in the steel industry

bulary
ery: a plant
ourifies oil

ling**History**

alyzing
s of View
do you
people
ght monop-
were
r?

AMERICA'S
HISTORY MAKERS

JOHN D. ROCKEFELLER
1839–1937

John D. Rockefeller was born to a poor family in upstate New York. From his mother, he learned the habit of frugality— he avoided unnecessary spending. "Willful waste makes woeful want" was a saying that Rockefeller's mother passed down to him.

By 1897, he had made millions and millions of dollars. Instead of keeping all that vast fortune for himself and his family, he spent the rest of his life donating money to several worthy causes.

ANDREW CARNEGIE
1835–1919

When Andrew Carnegie was 12, he and his family moved from Scotland to Pennsylvania. Carnegie's first job was in a cotton mill.

Later he worked in a telegraph office. There he was noticed by a railroad superintendent, who hired Carnegie as his assistant. Carnegie learned not only about running a big business but also about investing money. Eventually, he quit to start his own business.

Despite his fortune, Carnegie once wrote that none of his earnings gave him as much happiness as his first week's pay.

Compare the characters of Rockefeller and Carnegie. What do you think made each of them successful?

by making the best and cheapest product. To do so, he sought to control all the processes related to the manufacture of steel. He bought the mines that supplied his iron ore, and the ships and railroads that carried that ore to his mills. Carnegie's company dominated the U.S. steel industry from 1889 to 1901, when he sold it to J.P. Morgan, the nation's most prominent banker.

Rockefeller and Carnegie were multimillionaires. They also were both **philanthropists,** people who give large sums of money to charities. Rockefeller donated money to the University of Chicago and Rockefeller University in New York. Carnegie also gave money to universities, and he built hundreds of public libraries. During his life, Rockefeller gave away more than $500 million. Carnegie gave away more than $350 million.

The Gilded Age

The rags-to-riches stories of people such as Rockefeller and Carnegie inspired many Americans to believe that they too could grow rich. Stories like theirs also inspired writer Horatio Alger. He wrote popular stories about poor boys who worked hard and became quite successful.

Inspiring as these stories were, they hid an important truth. Most people who made millions of dollars had not been raised in poverty. Many belonged to the upper classes and had attended college. Most began their careers with the advantage of money or family connections.

For the rich, the late 1800s was a time of fabulous wealth. Writers Mark Twain and Charles Warner named the era the **Gilded Age.** To

Reading **His**
B. Contrastin
How did the
methods tha
Carnegie an
Rockefeller
to eliminate
petition diffe

HISTORY *through* ART

Artist Eastman Johnson painted this portrait of Alfredrick Smith Hatch's family, one of the wealthiest families in America, in 1870–1871. It shows the family in their New York mansion. Notice the expensive furnishings.

Photographer Jessie Tarbox Beals shot this photograph of a poor family in a tenement in 1910. A tenement is an apartment house that is usually rundown and overcrowded. This family probably had only this tiny space.

How do these two images reflect continuity and change in American life during the Gilded Age?

gild is to coat an object with gold leaf. Gilded decorations were popular
during the era. But the name has a deeper meaning. Just as gold leaf can
disguise an object of lesser value, so did the wealth of a few people mask
society's problems, including corrupt politics and widespread poverty.

The South Remains Agricultural

One region that knew great poverty was the South. The Civil War had
left the South in ruins. Industry did grow in some Southern areas, such
as Birmingham, Alabama. Founded in 1871, Birmingham developed as
an iron- and steel-producing town. In addition, cotton mills opened
from southern Virginia to Alabama. Compared with the Northern economy, however, the Southern economy grew very slowly after the war.

Most of the South remained agricultural. As you have read, many
Southern landowners rented their land to sharecroppers who paid a large
portion of their crops as rent. Often sharecroppers had to buy their seed
and tools on credit. The price of cotton, the South's main crop, was very
low. Sharecroppers made little money from selling cotton and had difficulty paying what they owed. And because most sharecroppers had little education, merchants cheated them, increasing their debt.

*ding***History**

aking
ences What
rtune imply-
bout the
keeper?

A VOICE FROM THE PAST

My father once kept an account . . . of the things he "took up" at the store
as well as the storekeeper. When the accounts were footed [added] up at the
end of the year the thing became serious. The storekeeper had $150 more
against my father than appeared on the latter's book. . . . It is by this means
that [sharecroppers] are swindled and kept forever in debt.

T. Thomas Fortune, testimony to a Senate committee, 1883

At the same time that sharecroppers struggled to break free of debt,
workers in the industrial North also faced injustices. In the next section,
you will learn how labor unions tried to fight back.

---

ction **3** *Assessment*

Terms & Names

xplain the
significance of:
robber baron
corporation
John D. Rockefeller
Andrew Carnegie
monopoly
trust
philanthropist
Gilded Age

2. Using Graphics

Use a Venn diagram like the
one shown to compare and
contrast Rockefeller and
Carnegie.

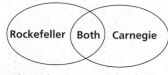

Whose business methods do
you agree with more?

3. Main Ideas

a. Why did the number of
corporations grow in the
late 1800s?

b. Who is an example of a
robber baron? Why?

c. Why was the South so
much less industrial than
the North?

4. Critical Thinking

**Forming and Supporting
Opinions** Do you think that
wealthy people have a duty
to become philanthropists?
Explain your opinion.

THINK ABOUT
• Carnegie and Rockefeller
• how most wealthy people
  gain their money
• the differences between
  the rich and the poor

TIVITY OPTIONS

MATH	In your local or school library, look up the business cycle. Create a **graph** of the
SPEECH	cycle for the last century or prepare an **oral report** to Congress on the trends.

Industry in the Midwest

The Midwest is the region around the Great Lakes and the Upper Mississippi Valley. The region saw explosive growth during the 1800s. The first wave came after 1825, when the Erie Canal linked the East with the Great Lakes region. The second wave, caused by investments in products related to the Civil War (1861–1865), saw a boom in mining, farming, forestry, and meat-packing. By 1890, 29 percent of the country's manufacturing employment was in the Midwest, and the next big wave of growth was just beginning. New industries included steel and steel products, such as train rails and skyscraper beams.

Transportation and resources spurred the region's growth. Coal, oil, iron ore, limestone, and lumber were abundant, and the land was fertile. Trains, rivers, and lakes connected the Midwest to markets in the East and South and brought in raw materials from the West. The map on page 599 shows the resources of the lower Great Lakes and how transportation by rail and water joined regions.

The industries of the Midwest used raw materials that came both from their own region and from other regions of the country. For example, the cattle in this photograph of the Chicago stockyards came by rail from the ranches of the West. In contrast, the logs being floated down the river came from the pine forests of Michigan and Wisconsin.

ARTIFACT FILE

A Quick Dinner Midwestern meat-packing companies advertised canned meats as a way to save time feeding a hungry family.

Affordable Housing People bega[n] build with wooden siding over a f[rame] of wooden two-by-fours. These ho[uses] were cheap and quick to construct[.]

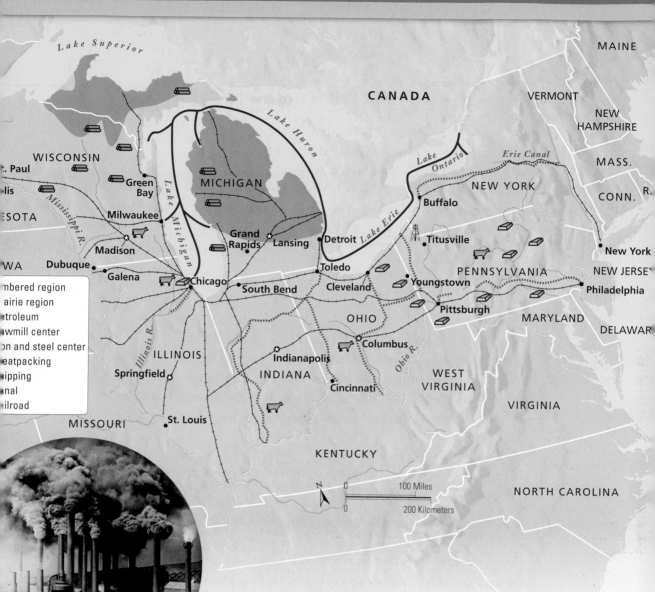

Lake Superior

CANADA

MAINE

VERMONT

NEW HAMPSHIRE

WISCONSIN

Lake Huron

MICHIGAN

Lake Ontario

Erie Canal

MASS.

.. Paul

Lake Michigan

NEW YORK

CONN. R.

.lis

Green Bay

Buffalo

...SOTA

Milwaukee

Lake Erie

New York

Madison

Grand Rapids

Lansing

Detroit

Titusville

NEW JERSE...

...WA

Dubuque

Galena

PENNSYLVANIA

NEW JERSE...

Chicago

South Bend

Toledo

Cleveland

Youngstown

Philadelphia

Mississippi R.

Illinois R.

ILLINOIS

OHIO

Pittsburgh

MARYLAND

DELAWAR...

Springfield

Indianapolis

Columbus

Ohio R.

WEST VIRGINIA

INDIANA

VIRGINIA

Cincinnati

MISSOURI

St. Louis

KENTUCKY

NORTH CAROLINA

N

0   100 Miles

0   200 Kilometers

...mbered region
...airie region
...troleum
...wmill center
...n and steel center
...eatpacking
...ipping
...nal
...ilroad

Iron ore from the Lake Superior region and coal from southern Illinois were used to manufacture steel.

-Line Field Trip

...hicago Historical Society
...ago, Illinois, contains photographs, ...ents, and artifacts such as this ...n Electric typewriter, made in 1900. ...riters enabled office workers to ...e neat, clean documents quickly.

...e about the Midwest . . .

CONNECT TO GEOGRAPHY

1. **Region** What advantages did the Midwest have that helped it become highly industrialized?

2. **Human-Environment Interaction** How did the development of railroads add to the region's advantages?

G See Geography Handbook, pages 4–5.

CONNECT TO HISTORY

3. **Analyzing Causes** Chicago was a big meatpacking center. Why do you think that industry chose to locate there?

Workers Organize

MAIN IDEA	WHY IT MATTERS NOW	TERMS & NAMES
To increase their ability to bargain with management, workers formed labor unions.	Many of the modern benefits that workers take for granted were won by early unions.	sweatshop Pullman St Knights of Labor Eugene V. socialism Samuel Go Haymarket affair American F of Labor (

ONE AMERICAN'S STORY

In 1867, Mary Harris Jones lost her husband and four children to yellow fever. Moving to Chicago, she started a dressmaking business. But the great Chicago fire of 1871 destroyed everything she owned. Instead of giving up in despair, Jones found a cause to fight for.

> *A VOICE FROM THE PAST*
>
> From the time of the Chicago fire I . . . decided to take an active part in the efforts of the working people to better the conditions under which they worked and lived.
>
> **Mary Harris Jones,** *Autobiography of Mother Jones*

Jones became an effective labor leader. Workers loved her so much that they called her Mother Jones. In this section, you will learn about the labor movement of the late 1800s.

Mother Jon
the love of
people by f
their rights.

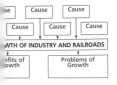

aking Notes

se your chart to
ke notes about
rganized labor.

GROWTH OF INDUSTRY AND RAILROADS

efits of
owth

Problems of
Growth

Workers Face Hardships

Business owners of the late 1800s wanted to keep their profits high, so they ran their factories as cheaply as possible. Some cut costs by requiring workers to buy their own tools or to bring coal to heat the factories. Others refused to buy safety equipment. For example, railroads would not buy air brakes or automatic train-car couplers. Because of this, 30,000 railroad workers were injured and 2,000 killed every year.

If a factory became too crowded, the owner rarely built a larger one. Instead, the owner sent part of the work to be done by smaller businesses that critics called sweatshops. **Sweatshops** were places where workers labored long hours under poor conditions for low wages. Often both children and adults worked there.

Factory and sweatshop workers did the same jobs, such as sewing collars or making buttonholes, all day long. They grew bored and did not

ground
managers
child labor
use children
unlikely to
st poor
tions and
ed for less
y than
s.

experience the satisfaction that came from making an entire product themselves. Further, both factory and sweatshop owners kept wages low. In the 1880s, the average weekly wage was less than $10. This barely paid a family's expenses. If a worker missed work due to illness or had any unexpected bills, the family went into debt. Workers began to feel that only other working people could understand their troubles.

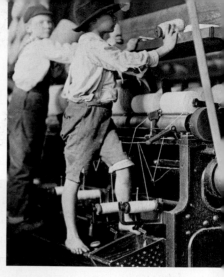

Child labor was common in the late 1800s, and as this boy's bare feet demonstrate, safety practices were rare.

A VOICE FROM THE PAST

They know what it is to bring up a family on ninety cents a day, to live on beans and corn meal week in and week out, to run in debt at the stores until you cannot get trusted [credit] any longer, to see the wife breaking down . . . , and the children growing sharp and fierce like wolves day after day because they don't get enough to eat.

A railroad worker, quoted in the *Philadelphia Inquirer*, July 23, 1877

bulary
iate: to dis-
omething in
to reach an
ment

So discontented workers joined together to try to improve their lives. They formed labor unions—groups of workers that negotiated with business owners to obtain better wages and working conditions.

Early Unions

As you read in Chapter 14, the first labor unions began in the mid-1800s but were unable to win many improvements for workers. After the Civil War, some unions started to form national organizations. One of these was the **Knights of Labor.** This was a loose federation of workers from all different trades. Unlike many labor organizations, the Knights allowed women and, after 1878, African-American workers to join their union. They inspired many people to support their cause.

Then, beginning in 1873, the United States fell into a serious economic depression. Over the next four years, millions of workers took pay cuts, and about one-fifth lost their jobs. In July 1877, the Baltimore and Ohio (B & O) Railroad declared a wage cut of 10 percent. The day the pay cut was to go into effect, B & O workers in Martinsburg, West Virginia, refused to run the trains. No labor union had called the

"[Working people] know what it is to bring up a family on ninety cents a day."
A railroad worker, 1877

strike. The workers themselves had stopped working on their own.

This work stoppage was the Railroad Strike of 1877. As the news spread, workers in many cities and in other industries joined in. This threw the country into turmoil. In several cities, state militias battled angry mobs. President Rutherford B. Hayes called out federal troops. Before the two-week strike ended, dozens of people were killed.

The strike did not prevent the railroad pay cut, but it showed how angry American workers had become. In 1884–1885, railroaders again went out on strike. This time they went on strike against the Union

ingHistory
lyzing
Why do
ink the
ent acted
the

Pacific and two other railroads. The strikers, who were members of the Knights of Labor, gained nationwide attention when they won their strike. Hundreds of thousands of new workers joined the union.

Union Setbacks

The growth of labor unions scared many business leaders. They blamed the labor movement on socialists and anarchists. Socialists believe in **socialism**. In that economic system, all members of a society are equal owners of all businesses—they share the work and the profits. Anarchists are far more extreme. They want to abolish all governments.

Business and government leaders feared that unions might spread such ideas, so they tried to break union power. In Chicago in 1886, the McCormick Harvester Company locked out striking union members and hired strikebreakers to replace them. On May 3, union members, strikebreakers, and police clashed. One union member was killed.

The next day, union leaders called a protest meeting at Haymarket Square. Held on a rainy evening, the rally was small. As police moved in to end the meeting, an unknown person threw a bomb. It killed 7 police and wounded about 60. The police then opened fire on the crowd, killing several people and wounding about a hundred. This conflict was called the **Haymarket affair**.

Afterward, the Chicago police arrested hundreds of union leaders, socialists, and anarchists. Opposition to unions increased. The membership in the Knights of Labor dropped rapidly—even though that wasn't the union that had called the meeting at Haymarket Square.

The Homestead and Pullman Strikes

Labor conflicts grew more bitter. In 1892, Andrew Carnegie reduced wages at his steel mills in Homestead, Pennsylvania, but the union refused to accept the cut. The company responded by locking out union workers from the mills and announcing that it would hire nonunion labor. The company also hired 300 armed guards. In response, the locked-out workers gathered weapons. The guards arrived on July 6, and a battle broke out that left ten people dead. The Pennsylvania state militia began to escort the nonunion workers to the mills. After four months, the strike collapsed, breaking the union.

Workers lost another dispute in 1894. In that depression year, many railroad companies went bankrupt. To stay in business, the Pullman Palace Car Company, which made railroad cars,

One night during the Pullman Strike, some 600 freight cars were burned.

Reading **His**
B. Recognizir
Effects Did t
action of the
bomber mak
seem more c
likely that ar
chists were
behind unio
activity? Exp

Reading **Hi**
C. Analyzing
Causes Why
it so difficul
early unions
win against
business?

cut workers' pay 25 percent. But Pullman did not lower the rent it charged workers to live in company housing. After their rent was deducted from the lower pay, many Pullman workers took home almost nothing.

The Pullman workers began the **Pullman Strike,** a strike which spread throughout the rail industry in 1894. When the Pullman Company refused to negotiate, American Railway Union president **Eugene V. Debs** called on all U.S. railroad workers to refuse to handle Pullman cars. Rail traffic in much of the country came to a halt. President Grover Cleveland called out federal troops, which ended the strike. Debs was put in jail.

Gompers Founds the AFL

Not all companies treated workers as harshly as Carnegie and Pullman did. For instance, in the 1880s, the soap company Procter & Gamble began to give its employees an extra half day off a week. It also began a profit-sharing plan, in which a company gives part of its profits to workers.

However, workers at most companies received low wages and few benefits. So in spite of the opposition to unions, the labor movement did not die. In 1886, labor leader **Samuel Gompers** helped found a new national organization of unions called the **American Federation of Labor (AFL).** Gompers served as AFL president for 37 years.

The AFL focused on improving working conditions. By using strikes, boycotts, and negotiation, the AFL won shorter working hours and better pay for workers. By 1904, it had about 1.7 million members.

In the next few decades, labor unions helped change the way all Americans worked. At the same time, city growth and immigration transformed America. You will read about that in Chapter 21.

ding **History**
entifying
lems What
lems did the
ry to solve?

Now and then

MODERN BENEFITS WON BY UNIONS

Today, many Americans work 40 hours per week—perhaps 9-to-5, Monday through Friday. Contrast this situation with the 10-to-12-hour days of most 19th-century workers. The 8-hour day was one benefit won by labor unions. Other benefits unions won include workers' compensation (insurance that pays for injuries received on the job), pensions, and paid vacation.

Unions continue to fight to improve the lives of working Americans. In recent years they have tried to increase benefits for part-time and temporary workers. They have also fought for safety standards to prevent injuries, such as carpal tunnel syndrome, which affects many workers who use computers.

---

tion **4** Assessment

Terms & Names

xplain the significance of:
*weatshop
Knights of Labor
ocialism
Haymarket affair
Pullman Strike
Eugene V. Debs
Samuel Gompers
American Federation of Labor (AFL)

2. Using Graphics

Review this section and find five key events to place on a time line like the one below.

1870   event   event   1910
|———|———|———|———|
     event   event   event

What individuals played significant roles in these events?

3. Main Ideas

a. What hardships did workers face in the late 1800s?

b. What happened to unions after the protest at Haymarket Square?

c. How did Carnegie's company break the union at the Homestead mills?

4. Critical Thinking

Drawing Conclusions In your opinion, was the government more supportive of unions or business in the late 1800s? Explain.

THINK ABOUT
• the Railroad Strike of 1877
• the Homestead Strike
• the Pullman Strike

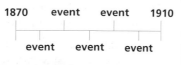

TIVITY OPTIONS

NGUAGE ARTS

ART

Decide whether unions should be encouraged. Write an **editorial** or create a **public message poster** expressing your opinion.

Crowds of people walk, work, and shop on Mulberry Street in New York's Lower East Side.

Vendors sel
assortment
and vegetal

1882
Congress passes
the Chinese
Exclusion Act.

1889
The first electric elevator is installed.

Jane Addams founds Hull House.

1888
Electric trolleys are set up
in Richmond, Virginia.

1892
Immigration center
opens on Ellis Island.

1893
Columbian Expos
opens in Chicago

USA
World 1880

1889
Brazil becomes a republic.

Barnum & Baily circus opens
in London.

1893
Karl Benz
invents
the modern
automobile.

East Coast cities like New York developed large immigrant neighborhoods.

Horse drawn carts are the most popular method for moving people and goods through the streets.

It is 1900, and you have decided to leave your native country. After a long and difficult voyage, you arrive in the United States. Now you need to find a new home and a job. You have to create a new life in a strange land.

How will you make a home in your new country?

What Do You Think?

- What caused you to leave your native country?
- What problems did you face on your voyage?
- What do you hope to find in the United States?

RESEARCH LINKS
CLASSZONE.COM

Visit the Chapter 21 links for more information about the changing American society.

1906
Earthquake and fire devastate San Francisco.

1909
National Association for the Advancement of Colored People (NAACP) is founded.

1914

1910
Mexican Revolution begins.

Reading Strategy: Categorizing Information

What Do You Know?

What do you think about when you hear the term *immigration?* Why do people move to different countries? What kinds of challenges might immigrants face in their new country?

Asia

Think About

- what you know about immigration from the experience of your family
- what would make you want to move away from your home
- your responses to the Interact with History about making a home in a new country (see page 607)

Latin America

What Do You Want to Know?

 What questions do you have about American life around 1900? Write them in your notebook before you read the chapter.

Categorizing Information

To help you make sense of what you read, learn to categorize. Categorizing means sorting information into groups. The chart below will help you take notes and categorize the changes in American life that occurred during the late 19th and early 20th centuries.

S See Skillbuilder Handbook, page R6.

 Taking Notes

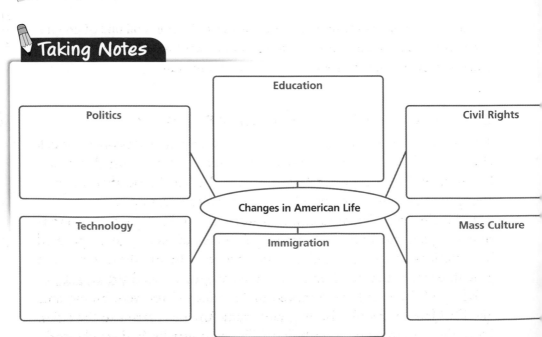

Education

Politics

Civil Rights

Changes in American Life

Technology

Mass Culture

Immigration

1

Cities Grow and Change

MAIN IDEA	WHY IT MATTERS NOW	TERMS & NAMES

MAIN IDEA

...alization and immigration ...American cities to grow

WHY IT MATTERS NOW

Modern American city life first emerged during this period.

TERMS & NAMES

urbanization   Jane Addams

tenement   Hull House

slum   political machine

social gospel   Tammany Hall

ONE AMERICAN'S STORY

Carl Jensen came to the United States from Denmark in 1906. Like most of the millions of immigrants who came to America around the turn of the century, he immediately began to look for work.

A VOICE FROM THE PAST

I wandered in search of work . . . waiting through rain and sleet and snow with gangs of longshoremen [dockworkers] to reach the boss before he finished picking the men he wanted. . . . Strong men crushed each other to the ground in their passion for work.

Carl Jensen, quoted in *A Sunday Between Wars*

Shipyards in growing ci... provided jobs for many Americans.

At the turn of the century, the promise of work drew millions of people like Carl Jensen from around the world to American cities. In this section, you will read about the rapid growth of American cities.

Industrialization Expands Cities

The Industrial Revolution, which had been changing how people worked, also changed *where* people worked. Since colonial days, most Americans had lived and worked in rural areas. But in the late 1800s, that began to change as more and more people moved to cities to find jobs.

Industries were drawn to cities because cities offered good transportation and plentiful workers. Increasing numbers of factory jobs appeared in America's cities, followed by more workers to fill those jobs. The growth of cities that resulted from these changes is called **urbanization**.

Many of the people who moved to American cities were immigrants like Carl Jensen. People also migrated from America's farms to the cities. Once there, even workers with few skills could usually find steady work.

Taking Notes

Use your chart to take notes about changes in technology and politics.

Changes in American Life

Modern cities depend on skyscrapers to increase the space for people to live and work. Steel, electricity, and elevators make skyscrapers possible.

1 STEEL FRAMES Steel beams can carry much more weight than brick or stone walls. The strength of the steel allows architects to design extremely tall buildings.

2 WINDOWS In skyscrapers, the outer walls do not support the weight of the building; the steel beams do. As a result, many skyscrapers have outer walls made of glass to allow sunlight inside.

3 ELEVATOR Tall buildings would be useless if people could not reach all of the floors. Elevators powered by electricity make such tall buildings practical.

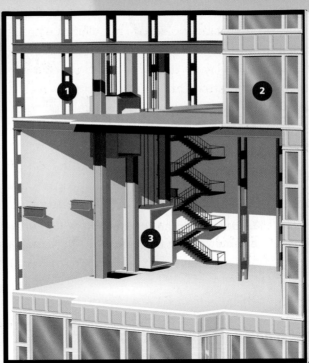

Technology Changes City Life

New technologies helped cities absorb the millions of people who flocked there. For example, new technologies made possible the construction of skyscrapers, buildings that looked tall enough to scrape the sky. Skyscrapers helped cities grow and made modern city life possible.

The elevator was a key invention for constructing tall buildings that could hold greater numbers of people. Before the 1860s, buildings rarely rose higher than four stories because it was hard for people to climb to the top. In 1889, the Otis Elevator Company installed the first electric elevator. Now buildings could be more than a few stories tall because people no longer had to walk up to the higher floors. As a result, buildings could hold more people.

The use of steel also helped to increase the height of buildings. In 1885, the Home Insurance Building in Chicago boasted an iron and steel skeleton that could hold the immense weight of the skyscraper's floors and walls. The building climbed to ten stories. Skyscrapers changed city skylines forever.

The Streetcar City

As electricity helped change the way people traveled inside buildings, it also changed how people traveled around cities. Before industrialization, people walked or used horse-drawn vehicles to travel over land. But by 1900, electric streetcars in American cities were carrying more than 5 billion passengers a year. Streetcars and trains changed the walking city into the streetcar city.

Reading **H**
A. Recogni
Effects Ho
industry an
technology
cities grow

Backgrou
Streetcars a
called trolle

In 1888, Richmond, Virginia, became the first American city to have a transportation system powered by electricity. Other cities soon installed their own electric streetcars. The streetcars could quickly carry people to work and play all over the city. Some cities, such as Chicago, moved their electric streetcars above the street level, creating elevated, or "el," lines. Other cities, like New York, placed their city rail lines in underground tunnels, making subways.

The streetcar city spread outward from the city's center in ways the walking city never could. The ability to live farther away from work helped new suburbs to develop around cities. Some people in the suburbs wanted to become part of the city they bordered. That way they also could be served by the city's transportation system. Largely due to public transportation, cities expanded. For example, in 1889, Chicago annexed several suburbs and more than doubled its population as well as its area.

ulary
to add

Urban Disasters and Slums

The concentration of people in cities increased the danger of disasters because people and buildings were packed closely together. For example, in 1906, a powerful earthquake rocked San Francisco. The tremors caused large fires to tear through the city. The central business district was destroyed. About 700 people died, and nearly $400 million in property was damaged. But natural disasters were not the only source of danger for the people of the cities. Poverty and disease also threatened their lives.

As people flocked to cities, overcrowding became a serious problem. It was especially serious for families who could not afford to buy a house. Such families usually lived in rented apartments or tenements. A **tenement** is an apartment house that is usually run-down and overcrowded.

Old buildings, landlord neglect, poor design, and little government control led to dangerous conditions in many tenements. Poor families who could not afford to rent a place of their own often needed to move in with other families. This resulted in severely overcrowded tenements. Inadequate garbage pick-up also caused problems. Tenants sometimes dumped their garbage into the narrow air shafts between tenements. There was little fresh air, and the smell was awful.

Many tenements had no running water. Residents had to collect water

gHistory
marizing
as it like
n a turn-
century
nt?

HISTORY *through* **ART**

This photograph by Lewis Hine shows a family of Italian immigrants in their cramped, decaying tenement in New York City in 1912. Often photographers, such as Hine, had their subjects pose for their pictures to create the strongest effect.

What effect do you think Hine wanted this photograph to have?

from a faucet on the street. The water could be heated for bathing. But it was often unsafe for drinking. Sewage flowed in open gutters and threatened to spread disease among tenement dwellers.

A neighborhood with such overcrowded, dangerous housing was called a **slum**. The most famous example was New York City's Lower East Side. But every city had slums. After visiting Chicago's slums, the British writer Rudyard Kipling wrote in disgust, "Having seen it [Chicago], I urgently desire never to see it again."

Reformers Attack Urban Problems

Many Americans were also disgusted by poverty and slums. Some people fought to reform, or create changes, that would solve these problems. They were known as urban reformers.

The social gospel movement provided one basis for these beliefs. The **social gospel** movement aimed to improve the lives of the poor. Led by Protestant ministers, the ideas of the movement were based on Christian values. The most important concerns of the social gospel movement were labor reforms, such as abolishing child labor. Some reformers inspired by the movement opened settlement houses. They helped the poor and immigrants improve their lives. Settlement houses offered services such as daycare, education, and health care to needy people in slum neighborhoods.

Reading **H**
C. Making Inferences did Christia values supp the social g movement

CITIZENSHIP TODAY

Community Service

Since the United States began, citizens have shared concerns about their communities. Many citizens, such as Jane Addams in 1889, have identified problems and proposed solutions to them.

In 1993, sixth-grader David Levitt asked his principal if the leftover food from the school cafeteria could be sent to a program to feed needy people. David was told that many restrictions prevented giving away the food.

Determined to get food to people who needed it, David talked to the school board, the state health department, and private companies to convince them to back his program. Today, more than 500,000 pounds of food from schools has been given to hungry people in the Seminole, Florida, area.

David Levitt carries supplies for his food pantry program.

How Do You Particip in Your Community?

1. In a small group, think about problems within yo community. Make a list o those problems.

2. Choose one problem to work on.

3. Gather information abou problem. Keep a log of your sources to use again

4. After you gather informa brainstorm solutions to th problem. Create a plan to out one solution.

5. Present the problem and your plan to the class.

See the Citizenship Handbook, page 286.

For more about community servic

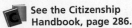
RESEARCH LINKS

CLASSZONE.COM

Many settlement house founders were educated middle-class women. **Jane Addams** founded Chicago's **Hull House** in 1889 with Ellen Gates Starr. Hull House soon became a model for other settlement houses, including New York's Henry Street Settlement House, which Lillian D. Wald established in 1889.

Political Machines Run Cities

Political machines were another type of organization that addressed the problems of the city. A **political machine** is an organization that influences enough votes to control a local government.

Political machines gained support by trading favors for votes. For example, machine bosses gave jobs or food to supporters. In return, supporters worked and voted for the machine. Political machines also did many illegal things. They broke rules to win elections. They accepted bribes to affect government actions.

The most famous political machine was **Tammany Hall** in New York City. It was led by William Marcy Tweed. Along with his greedy friends, "Boss" Tweed stole enormous amounts of money from the city.

Despite such corruption, political machines did a number of good things for cities. They built parks, sewers, schools, roads, and orphanages in many cities. In addition, machine politicians often helped immigrants get settled in the United States by helping them find jobs or homes. Many immigrants gratefully supported the political machine after this kind of help. In the next section, you will learn more about immigration.

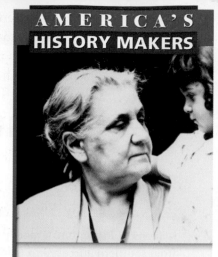

JANE ADDAMS
1860–1935
Jane Addams founded Hull House as an "effort to aid in the solution of the social and industrial problems which are [caused] by the modern conditions of life in a great city."

In addition to Hull House, Addams was active in many other areas. She fought for the passage of laws to protect women workers and outlaw child labor. She also worked to improve housing and public health. In 1931, she was awarded a share of the Nobel Peace Prize for her efforts.

Why did Jane Addams found Hull House?

g **History**

paring and *ting* How *ttlement* *and politi-* *hines simi-* *w were* *ferent?*

---

on 1 Assessment

erms & Names

lain the **gnificance of:**

banization
nement
m
cial gospel
he Addams
ll House
litical machine
mmany Hall

2. Using Graphics

Use a chart like the one below to show the causes and effects of urban growth.

Cause	Effect
Steel	
Elevators	
Streetcars	
Immigration	

3. Main Ideas

a. Why did immigrants and farmers settle in big cities at the end of the 19th century?

b. What are two inventions that made modern city life possible?

c. What urban problems did reformers try to solve?

4. Critical Thinking

Evaluating What were some of the advantages and disadvantages of machine politics?

THINK ABOUT
• the problems faced by immigrants and cities
• Tammany Hall and "Boss" Tweed

VITY OPTIONS

GUAGE ARTS
ART

It is 1900, and you have just moved to an American city. Write a **letter** to friends back home or draw a **picture** that describes your new home.

The New Immigrants

MAIN IDEA	WHY IT MATTERS NOW	TERMS & NAMES

Millions of immigrants—mostly from southern and eastern Europe—moved to the United States.

The new immigrants had an important role in shaping American culture in the 20th century.

new immigrants   melting
Ellis Island   assimila
Angel Island   Chinese
  Act

ONE AMERICAN'S STORY

In 1907, 10-year-old Edward Corsi left Italy to come to America. After two weeks at sea, he caught sight of the Statue of Liberty.

A VOICE FROM THE PAST

This symbol of America . . . inspired awe in the hopeful immigrants. Many older persons among us, burdened with a thousand memories of what they were leaving behind, had been openly weeping. . . . Now somehow steadied, I suppose, by the concreteness of the symbol of America's freedom, they dried their tears.

Edward Corsi, *In the Shadow of Liberty*

In this section, you will learn about the immigrants who came to the United States around 1900 and their effect on the nation.

The Statue
Liberty and
Island wer
of the first
many imm
saw of the
United Sta

Taking Notes

Use your chart to take notes about changes in immigration.

Changes in American Life

The New Immigrants

Until the 1890s, most immigrants to the United States had come from northern and western Europe. But after 1900, fewer northern Europeans immigrated, and more southern and eastern Europeans did. This later group of immigrants came to be known as the **new immigrants**. Southern Italy sent large numbers of immigrants. Many Jews from eastern Europe and Slavic peoples, such as Poles and Russians, also immigrated.

Ellis Island was the first stop for most immigrants from Europe. There, they were processed before they could enter the United States. First, they had to pass a physical examination. Those with serious health problems or diseases were sent home. Next, they were asked a series of questions: Name? Occupation? How much money do you have?

Slovenian immigrant Louis Adamic described the night he spent on Ellis Island. He and many other immigrants slept in a huge hall. Lacking a warm blanket, the young man "shivered, sleepless, all night, listening to snores" and dreams "in perhaps a dozen different languages."

5. Immigration, *1841–1900*

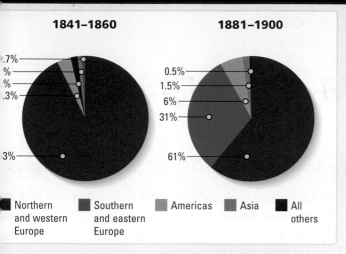

1841–1860

.7%
%
%
.3%

3%

1881–1900

0.5%
1.5%
6%
31%

61%

■ Northern and western Europe
■ Southern and eastern Europe
■ Americas
■ Asia
■ All others

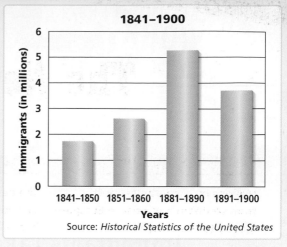

1841–1900

Immigrants (in millions)

Years: 1841–1850, 1851–1860, 1881–1890, 1891–1900

Source: *Historical Statistics of the United States*

SKILLBUILDER Interpreting Graphs

1. *About how many immigrants came to the United States from 1841 to 1860?*
2. *About how many southern and eastern European immigrants came to the United States from 1881 to 1900?*

While European immigrants passed through Ellis Island on the East Coast, Asians landed at **Angel Island** in San Francisco Bay. In Angel Island's filthy buildings, most Chinese immigrants were held for several weeks. One unhappy prisoner carved in the wall, "For what reason must I sit in jail? It is only because my country is weak and my family poor."

Many Mexican immigrants entered the United States through Texas. Jesús [heh•SOOS] Garza recalled how simple his journey was. "I paid my $8, passed my examination, then changed my Mexican coins for American money and went to San Antonio, Texas."

Settling in America

Immigrants settled where they could find jobs. Many found work in American factories. The immigrants contributed to the growth of cities such as New York, Boston, Philadelphia, Pittsburgh, and Chicago. About half of the new immigrants settled in four industrial states: Massachusetts, New York, Pennsylvania, and Illinois.

Once in America, newer immigrants looked for people from the same village in the old country to help them find jobs and housing. People with similar ethnic backgrounds often moved to the same neighborhoods. As a result, ethnic neighborhoods with names like "Little Italy" and "Chinatown" became common in American cities.

The immigrants living in these communities pooled money to build places of worship for their neighborhoods. They published newspapers in their native languages. They commonly supported political machines, often led by politicians who had also come from their country of origin. Such politicians could speak the native language and help new arrivals feel comfortable. Most importantly, politicians could help immigrants find jobs.

*ng***History**
tifying
ns How
migrants
reativity in
problems?

"I paid my $8 passed my examination . . . and wen to San Antonio."

Jesús Gar

Labor unions helped immigrants fit into American life. The various languages on the signs at this rally show the ethnic diversity in the labor movement.

Immigrants Take Tough Jobs

Immigrants took whatever jobs they could get. Many immigrants worked in Northern factories. As you read in Chapter 20, most factories offered low wages, long hours, and unsafe conditions. Many European immigrants who had settled in the East found jobs in sweatshops for about $10 a week. One observer of textile sweatshops noted, "The faces, hands, and arms to the elbows of everyone in the room are black with the color of the cloth on which they are working."

While European immigrants settled mostly in the East and Midwest, Asian immigrants settled mostly in the West. Many Chinese immigrants worked on the railroad. Others settled in Western cities where they set up businesses such as restaurants and stores. Large numbers of Japanese immigrants first came to Hawaii in 1885 to work on sugar plantations. Others settled on the mainland, where they fished, farmed, and worked in mines.

Immigrants from Mexico came to the Southwest. Mexican immigration increased after 1910 when revolution in that country forced people to flee. Growers and ranchers in California and Texas used the cheap labor Mexican immigrants offered. Owners of copper mines in Arizona hired Mexicans as well.

Reading **Hi**
B. Making Inferences What did a the immigr seem to hav in common

Becoming Americans

Some Americans have described the United States as a **melting pot,** or a place where cultures blend. The new immigrants blended into American society as earlier immigrants had. This process of blending into society is called **assimilation.** Most new immigrants were eager to assimilate. To do so, they studied English and how to be American citizens.

Many workers began to assimilate at work. Employers and labor unions both tried to "Americanize" immigrant workers by offering classes in citizenship and English. A Lithuanian worker explained that his labor union helped him learn to "read and speak and enjoy life like an American." He then became an interpreter for the union to help other Lithuanians become Americans.

At the same time the immigrants were learning about America, they were also *changing* America. Immigrants did not give up their cultures right away. Bits and pieces of immigrant languages, foods, and music worked their way into the rest of American culture.

Despite their efforts to assimilate, immigrants faced prejudice from native-born Americans. Many Protestants feared the arrival of Catholics and Jews. Other native-born Americans thought immigrants would not fit into democratic society because they would be controlled by political machines. Such prejudices led some native-born Americans to push for restrictions to reduce the numbers of new immigrants coming to America.

Restrictions on Immigration

Many native-born Americans also feared they would have to compete with immigrants for jobs. Immigrants were desperate for jobs and would often take work for lower wages in worse conditions than other Americans. Some Americans worried that there would not be enough jobs for everyone. These fears led to an upsurge in nativist opposition to immigration. In 1882, Congress began to pass laws to restrict immigration. They placed taxes on new immigrants and banned specific groups, such as beggars and people with diseases. Nonwhites faced deeper prejudice than European immigrants, and Asians faced some of the worst. In 1882, Congress passed the **Chinese Exclusion Act**. It banned Chinese immigration for ten years.

The Chinese Exclusion Act was not the only example of prejudice in America around 1900. As you will read in the next section, racial discrimination was common throughout the United States.

round
inese
on Act was
d in 1892.
, the ban
de perma-
was not
d until

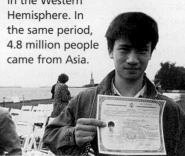

Now and then

LATE 20TH-CENTURY IMMIGRATION

Historians refer to the people who came to the United States around 1900 as the "new immigrants." But an even newer wave of immigrants has been coming to the United States since the 1980s.

From 1981 to 1996, nearly 13.5 million people immigrated to the United States. About 6.5 million came from other nations in the Western Hemisphere. In the same period, 4.8 million people came from Asia.

---

ion ② Assessment

erms & Names

lain the gnificance of:

ew immigrants
is Island
ngel Island
elting pot
similation
inese Exclusion
t

2. Using Graphics

Use a chart to take notes on immigrant experiences in the United States.

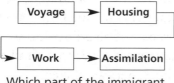

Which part of the immigrant experience was the most difficult?

3. Main Ideas

a. How were the new immigrants different from earlier immigrants?

b. How did immigrants support one another?

c. Why did nonwhite immigrants have a harder time assimilating than European immigrants did?

4. Critical Thinking

Making Generalizations
How well does the idea of the melting pot reflect U.S. immigration around 1900?

THINK ABOUT
• assimilation
• immigrant languages and cultures
• ethnic neighborhoods

VITY OPTIONS

MATH

EOGRAPHY

Research immigration to your city or state. Create a **spreadsheet** of this information or draw a **map** showing immigration routes.

from

Dragonwings

by Laurence Yep

In 1903, eight-year-old Moon Shadow makes the long journey from China to join his father in San Francisco. After living for a time in Chinatown, the two move into a white neighborhood where Moon Shadow's father takes a job as a handyman working for Miss Whitlaw, who runs a boarding house for elderly people. Moon Shadow makes friends with Miss Whitlaw's niece Robin. In April of 1906, their world is turned upside down. As Moon Shadow goes outside to fetch water from the pump, an earthquake hits San Francisco, endangering rich and poor, young and old, American and immigrant alike.

The morning was filled with that soft, gentle twilight of spring, when everything is filled with soft, dreamy colors and shapes; so when the earthquake hit, I did not believe it at first. It seemed like a nightmare where everything you take to be the rock-hard, solid basis for reality becomes unreal.

Wood and stone and brick and the very earth became fluidlike. The pail beneath the pump jumped and rattled like a spider dancing on a hot stove. The ground deliberately seemed to slide right out from under me. I landed on my back hard enough to drive the wind from my lungs. The whole world had become unglued. Our stable and Miss Whitlaw's house and the tenements to either side heaved and bobbed up and down, riding the ground like ships on a heavy sea. Down the alley mouth, I could see the cobblestone street **undulate**[1] and twist like a red-backed snake.

From inside our stable, I could hear the cups

and plates begin to rattle on their shelves, a equipment on Father's work table clattere rumbled **ominously**.[2]

Suddenly the door banged open and stumbled out with his clothes all in a bundl an earthquake, I think," he shouted. H washed his hair the night before and had n time to twist it into a **queue**,[3] so it hung his back long and black.

He looked around in the back yard. such a wide, open space that we were fair there. Certainly more safe than in the doorway of our stable. He got into his pan shirt and then his socks and boots.

"Do you think one of the mean drag doing all this?" I asked him.

"Maybe. Maybe not." Father had sat to stuff his feet into his boots. "Time to w about that later. Now you wait here."

He started to get to his feet when the s tremor shook and he fell forward flat on hi I heard the city bells ringing. They were ru no human hand—the earthquake ha shaken them in their steeples. The second was worse than the first. From all over ca immense wall of noise: of metal tearing, of crashing, of wood breaking free from wood and all. Everywhere, what man had built undone. I was looking at a tenement house right and it just seemed to shudder and the lapse. One moment there were solid w walls and the next moment it had fallen w cracking of wood and the tinkling of gla the screams of people inside.

---

1. **undulate:** to move like a wave.
2. **ominously:** threateningly.
3. **queue:** a long braid of hair hanging down the back.

Mercifully, for a moment, it was lost to view [i]e cloud of dust that rose up. The debris [?]l against Miss Whitlaw's fence and toppled [?] with a creak and a groan and a crash. I saw [a?]n sticking up from the mound of rubble [t]he hand was twisted at an impossible angle [?] the wrist. Coughing, Father pulled at my [?] Stay here now," he ordered and started for [?]Whitlaw's.

[I] turned. Her house was still standing, but [te]nement house to the left had partially col-[lapsed?]; the wall on our side and part of the front [b]ack had just fallen down, revealing the [apartme]nts within: the laundry hanging from [the] old brass beds, and a few lucky if aston-[ished?] people just looking out dazedly on what [had on]ce been walls. I could see Jack sitting up in [bed] with his two brothers. His mother and father [were] standing by the bed holding on to Maisie. [The] whole family crowded into a tiny two-[room] apartment. Then they were gone, disap-[pearin]g in a cloud of dust and debris as the walls [and flo]or collapsed. Father held me as I cried.

Miss Whitlaw came out onto her porch in [a ni]ghtdress and a shawl. She pulled the shawl [close]r about her shoulders. *"Are you all right?"*

["Y]es," Father said, patting me on the back.

"Aren't we, Moon Shadow?"

"Yes." I wiped my eyes on my sleeves.

"Is everyone okay inside?" Father asked Miss Whitlaw.

She nodded. We joined her on the porch and walked with her into her house. Robin was sitting on the stairs that led up to the second floor. She huddled up, looking no longer like the noisy, **boisterous**[4] girl I knew. The front door was open before her. She must have gone outside to look. *"Just about the whole street's gone."*

From up the stairs we could hear the **querulous**[5] old voices of the boarders demanding to know what had happened. Miss Whitlaw shouted up the stairs, "Everything's all right."

"Are you sure?" Father asked quietly.

Miss Whitlaw laughed. *"From top to bottom. Papa always built well. He said he wanted a house that could hold a herd of thundering elephants—that was what he always called Mama's folks. He never liked them much."*

"It's gone," Robin repeated. *"Just about the whole street's gone."*

"Oh, really now." Miss Whitlaw walked past Robin. We followed her out the front door to the front porch. Robin was right.

[bois]terous: loud, noisy.

5. **querulous:** complaining.

San Franciscans watch the destruction caused by the 1906 earthquake and the resulting fire.

CONNECT TO HISTORY

1. **Finding Main Ideas** How does the earthquake affect the neighborhood that Moon Shadow lives in?

    See Skillbuilder Handbook, page R5.

CONNECT TO TODAY

2. **Researching** What happened in San Francisco after the quake? Did it affect the immigrants differently than others?

For more about the San Francisco earthquake . . .

RESEARCH LINKS
CLASSZONE.COM

Segregation and Discrimination

3

MAIN IDEA	WHY IT MATTERS NOW	TERMS & NAMES
Racial discrimination ran through American society in the late 19th and early 20th centuries.	Modern American society continues to face the problems caused by racism and discrimination.	racial discrimination Jim Crow segregation *Plessy* v. *Ferguson*	Booker Washi... W. E. B. NAACP Ida B. V...

ONE AMERICAN'S STORY

African-American sisters Bessie and Sadie Delany grew up in North Carolina in the early 20th century. Almost 100 years later, they described their first taste of **racial discrimination**, different treatment on the basis of race.

> **A VOICE FROM THE PAST**
>
> We were about five and seven years old. . . . Mama and Papa used to take us to Pullen Park . . . and that particular day, the trolley driver told us to go to the back. We children objected loudly, because we always liked to sit in the front. . . . But Mama and Papa just gently told us to hush and took us to the back.
>
> **Sarah L. Delany and A. Elizabeth Delany,** *Having Our Say*

Bessie (left)
Sadie Delan...

As you will read in this section, racial discrimination was common throughout the United States.

Taking Notes

Use your chart to make notes about changes in civil rights.

Changes in American Life

Racism Causes Discrimination

As you read in earlier chapters, racist attitudes had been developing in America since the introduction of slavery. The low social rank held by slaves led many whites to believe that whites were superior to blacks. Most whites held similar attitudes toward Asians, Native Americans, and Latin Americans. Even most scientists of the day believed that whites were superior to nonwhites. However, no scientists believe this today.

Such attitudes led whites to discriminate against nonwhites across the country. The most obvious example of racial discrimination was in the South. Southern blacks had their first taste of political power during Reconstruction. (See Chapter 18.) But when Reconstruction ended in 1877, Southern states began to restrict African Americans' rights.

Segregation Expands in the South

One way for whites to weaken African-American political power was to restrict their voting rights. For example, Southern states passed laws that set up literacy, or reading, tests and poll taxes to prevent African Americans from voting. White officials made sure that blacks failed literacy tests by giving unfair exams. For example, white officials sometimes gave blacks tests written in Latin. Poll taxes kept many blacks from voting because they didn't have enough cash to pay the tax.

ing **History**
ognizing
s What was
urpose
d literacy
poll taxes,
randfather
s?

Such laws threatened to prevent poor whites from voting, too. To keep them from losing the vote, several Southern states added grandfather clauses to their constitutions. Grandfather clauses stated that a man could vote if he or an ancestor, such as a grandfather, had been eligible to vote before 1867. Before that date, most African Americans, free or enslaved, did not have the right to vote. Whites could use the grandfather clause to protect their voting rights. Blacks could not.

In addition to voting restrictions, African Americans faced Jim Crow laws. **Jim Crow** laws were meant to enforce **segregation,** or separation, of white and black people in public places. As a result, separate schools, trolley seats, and restrooms were common throughout the South.

Plessy v. Ferguson

African Americans resisted segregation, but they had little power to stop it. In 1892, Homer Plessy, an African American, sued a railroad company, arguing that segregated seating violated his Fourteenth Amendment right to "equal protection of the laws."

In 1896, the case of ***Plessy v. Ferguson*** reached the Supreme Court. The Court ruled against Plessy. It argued that "separate but equal" facilities did not violate the Fourteenth Amendment. This decision allowed Southern states to maintain segregated institutions.

ing **History**
ntifying
ms Why
policy of
rate but
" unfair?

But the separate facilities were not equal. White-controlled governments and companies allowed the facilities for African Americans to decay. African Americans would have to organize to fight for equality.

Segregation forced African Americans to use separate entrances from whites and to attend separate, usually inferior, schools like the one shown below.

African Americans Organize

Booker T. Washington was an early leader in the effort to achieve equality. He had been born into slavery. But after the Civil War, he became a teacher. In 1881, he founded the Tuskegee Institute in Alabama to help African Americans learn trades and gain economic strength. Washington hired talented teachers and scholars, such as George Washington Carver.

To gain white support for Tuskegee, Washington did not openly challenge segregation. As he said in an 1895 speech in Atlanta, in "purely social matters" whites and blacks "can be as separate as the fingers, yet one as the hand in all things essential to mutual progress."

However, some blacks disagreed with Washington's views. **W. E. B. Du Bois** (doo•BOYS) encouraged African Americans to reject segregation.

Backgroun
Carver made
important d
eries to imp
farming.

A VOICE FROM THE PAST

Is it possible . . . that nine millions of men can make effective progress in economic lines if they are deprived of political rights? . . . If history and reason give any distinct answer to these questions, it is an emphatic *No.*

W. E. B. Du Bois, *The Souls of Black Folk*

Reading Hi
C. Making
Inferences
what way d
Washington
Du Bois disa
about how
achieve Afri
American
progress?

In 1909, Du Bois and other reformers founded the National Association for the Advancement of Colored People, or the **NAACP**. The NAACP played a major role in ending segregation in the 20th century.

Violence in the South and North

Besides discrimination, African Americans in the South also faced violence. The Ku Klux Klan, which first appeared during Reconstruction, used violence to keep blacks from challenging segregation. More than 2,500 African Americans were lynched between 1885 and 1900.

Ida B. Wells, an African-American journalist from Memphis, led the fight against lynching. After three of her friends were lynched in 1892, she mounted an anti-lynching campaign in her newspaper. When whites called for Wells herself to be lynched, she moved to Chicago. But she continued her work against lynching. (See Interactive Primary Sources, page 624.)

Like Wells, many blacks moved north to escape discrimination. Public facilities there were not segregated by law. But Northern whites still discriminated against blacks. Blacks could not get housing in white neighborhoods and usually were denied good jobs. Anti-black feelings among whites sometimes led to violence. In 1908, whites in Springfield, Illinois, attacked blacks who had moved there. The whites lynched two blacks within a half mile of Abraham Lincoln's home.

AMERICA'S HISTORY MAKERS

W. E. B. DU BOIS

1868–1963

W. E. B. Du Bois grew up in a middle-class home. He went to college and earned his doctorate at Harvard. Du Bois became one of the most distinguished scholars of the 20th century.

Du Bois fought against segregation. He believed that the best way to end it would be to have educated African Americans lead the fight. He referred to this group of educated African Americans as the "Talented Tenth"—the most educated 10 percent of African Americans.

Why do you think Du Bois believed the Talented Tenth should lead the fight against segregation?

Racism in the West

Chinese immigrants who came to the West in the 1800s also faced severe discrimination. Chinese laborers received lower wages than whites for the same work. Sometimes, Chinese workers faced violence. In 1885, white workers in Rock Springs, Wyoming, refused to work in the same mine as Chinese workers. The whites stormed through the Chinese part of town, shooting Chinese people and burning buildings. During the attack, 28 Chinese people were killed and 15 were wounded.

The Workingmen's Party of California produced this anti-Chinese poster during the 1880s.

At the same time, Mexicans and African Americans who came to the American Southwest were forced into peonage (PEE•uh•nihj). In this system of labor, people are forced to work until they have paid off debts. Congress outlawed peonage in 1867, but some workers were still forced to work to repay debts. In 1911, the U.S. Supreme Court declared such labor to be the same as peonage. As a result, the Court struck down such forms of labor as a violation of the Thirteenth Amendment.

Despite the problems caused by racism, many Americans had new opportunities to enjoy their lives at the turn of the century. In the next section, you will learn about changes in people's daily lives.

round
irteenth
dment
d "involun-
rvitude"—
er term
very.

---

from *Crusade for Justice* (1892)

Setting the Stage Ida B. Wells was the editor of the *Free Speech and Headlight,* a small Baptist newspaper in Memphis, Tennessee. She used the paper to attack the evils of Jim Crow, especially lynching. In her autobiography, *Crusade for Justice,* she described the events that led to the lynching of three of her friends. **See Primary Source Explorer**

While I was thus carrying on the work of my newspaper . . . there cam[e] lynching in Memphis which changed the whole course of my life. . . .

Thomas Moss, Calvin McDowell, and Henry Stewart owned and oper[ated] grocery store. . . . There was already a grocery owned and operated by a [white] man who **hitherto**[1] had had a **monopoly**[2] on the trade of this thickly pop[ulated] colored suburb. Thomas's grocery changed all that, and he and his **asso[ciates]**[3] were made to feel that they were not welcome by the white grocer. . . .

About ten o'clock that [one Saturday] night, . . . shots rang out in the [back] room of the store. The men stationed there had seen several white men [com]ing through the rear door and fired on them without a moment's [warning.] Three of these men were wounded, and others fled and gave the alarm[.]

Sunday morning's paper came out with **lurid**[4] headlines telling how o[fficers] of the law had been wounded while in the **discharge**[5] of their duties. . . [The] same newspaper told of the arrest and jailing of the **proprietor**[6] of the [store] and many of the colored people. . . .

On Tuesday following, . . . a body of picked [white] men was admit[ted to] the jail. . . . This mob took out of their cells Thomas Moss, C[alvin] McDowell, and Henry Stewart. . . . They were loaded on a switch eng[ine of] the railroad which ran back of the jail, carried a mile north of the city [limits,] and horribly shot to death.

Although stunned by the events of that hectic week, the *Free Speech* [Wells's newspaper] felt that it must carry on. Its [lead article] for that week sai[d:]

The city of Memphis has demonstrated that neither character [nor] standing **avails**[7] the Negro if he dares to protect himself against the wh[ite] man or become his rival. There is nothing we can do about the lynch[ing] now, as we are out-numbered and without arms. The white mob co[uld] help itself to ammunition without pay, but the order was rigidly enfor[ced] against the selling of guns to Negroes. There is therefore only one th[ing] left that we can do; save our money and leave a town which will neit[her] protect our lives and property, nor give us a fair trial in the courts, [but] takes us out and murders us in cold blood when accused by white pers[ons.]

A CLOSER LOOK

ECONOMIC COMPETITION

Moss, McDowell, and Stewart were African Americans who opened a grocery store near a white-owned store in a black neighborhood.

1. Why might the opening of the black-owned grocery store lead to problems?

A CLOSER LOOK

LYNCHINGS

There was a sharp increase in the number of lynchings in the United States in the 1890s. From 1891 to 1900, more than 1,100 African Americans were lynched.

2. Why do you think the number of lynchings increased in this period?

A CLOSER LOOK

THE GREAT MIGRATION

Between 1890 and 1920, hundreds of thousands of African Americans left the South to escape racism. This movement is called the Great Migration.

3. Why does Wells's newspaper advise African Americans to move away in the wake of the lynching?

1. **hitherto:** until this time.
2. **monopoly:** exclusive control by one person or group.
3. **associates:** friends or partners.
4. **lurid:** causing shock or horror.
5. **discharge:** perform[ance] of duty.
6. **proprietor:** owne[r.]
7. **avails:** helps.

ike Country Pretty Much

ing the Stage Kee Low was a Chinese immigrant. He had come to
United States in 1876. He was interviewed in 1924 as part of a project
holars to create a "Survey of Race Relations." This is an excerpt from
interview. In it, Kee Low tells his story. Despite the racism,
ill "like country pretty much." **See Primary Source Explorer**

ved in San Francisco in 1876, 49 years ago. Come to San Francisco when
try one hundred years old. People treat Chinese rotten then. Don't blame
le much at that time. Chinese and European not educated as much then
day. More civilized today. People drive Chinese out of country. . . .

as living on the waterfront, and they told me to get out one day. Sunday
ning, they come together and drive Chinese out. . . . They want to get us
o San Francisco, to go on steamer, and we stayed on the **wharf**[1] all night,
they bring us little black coffee and little bread in morning. We pretty
gry. The last day, some of the citizens, Judge Greene, Judge Hanford,
ed States Attorney, nice fellow want to help us. . . . Judge Greene told
Chinese that those who wanted to stay and make good citizens could
and those who wanted to go could go. One half wanted to go, and one
wanted to stay. . . .

ere were so many around the streets that they had to have somebody to
ct these people. Some of the **hobos**[2] tried to make them go back to the
f, but volunteers tried to keep these fellows away. They **commenced**[3]
ting and kill one of them. So Chinese people get excited when gun begin
und, so they throw shoes, blankets and everything and run. I was uptown
lf. I didn't intend to go. I ran outside to see what happened because I was
cited. . . . Call up one or two friends of mine and tell them get killed, and
etter get out of the way. We run out in woods. Build fire. Pretty cold. I
friends, we got to protect ourselves. We got to get out of here.

A CLOSER LOOK

RACIST ATTITUDES

Some people believe that racism
is caused by ignorance.

**4. Why does Kee Low believe
that discrimination against the
Chinese was worse in the 1870s
than in the 1920s?**

A CLOSER LOOK

REASONS TO STAY

Despite the violence that they faced
for having Asian ancestry, half of
the Chinese with Kee Low wanted
to stay in the United States.

**5. Why do you think Asian-
Americans stayed in the United
States despite discrimination?**

arf: landing place for   2. **hobos:** homeless people.   3. **commenced:** began.
s.

eractive Primary Sources Assessment

Main Ideas

What do the accounts of Wells and Low have in
mmon?

How did the officers of the law behave differently in
e report by Low than in the one by Wells?

What conclusions do Wells and Low come to about
w someone should respond to discrimination?

2. Critical Thinking

Forming and Supporting Opinions Do you think
Wells and Low were right to flee racism? Why?

THINK ABOUT
- the causes of racism
- the threat of violence to Wells and Low

Society and Mass Culture

4

MAIN IDEA	WHY IT MATTERS NOW	TERMS & NAMES
Industrialization and new technologies created a mass culture in the United States.	Modern American mass culture had its beginnings during this period.	mass culture mail-ord Joseph Pulitzer leisure William Randolph vaudevi Hearst ragtime department store

ONE AMERICAN'S STORY

Mary Ellen Chase dreaded her first day of teaching, but she did her best to control the class.

> ### A VOICE FROM THE PAST
>
> I stormed up and down. . . . This pathetic pretense of courage, aided by the mad flourishing of my razor strop, brought forth . . . the expression of respectful fear on the faces of the young giants.
>
> **Mary Ellen Chase,** quoted in *The Good Old Days—They Were Terrible!*

Students wo
on their less
in this New Y
City classroo
in 1906.

In this section, you will learn how education helped create an American **mass culture**—a common culture experienced by large numbers of people.

aking Notes

e your chart to
ke notes about
anges in education
d mass culture.

Changes in American Life

Education and Publishing Grow

Immigration caused enormous growth in American schools. To teach citizenship and English to immigrants, new city and state laws required children to attend school. Between 1880 and 1920, the number of children attending school more than doubled. To serve the growing number of students, the number of public high schools increased from 2,526 in 1890 to 14,326 in 1920.

The growth of education increased American literacy. Reading became more popular. Americans read large numbers of novels. Dime novels were especially popular. They sold for ten cents each and told exciting tales of romance and adventure, often set in the West or on the high seas.

Americans also read more newspapers. Tough competition pushed newspaper publishers to try all sorts of gimmicks to outsell their rivals. For example, **Joseph Pulitzer,** owner of the *New York World,* and

William Randolph Hearst, owner of the *New York Morning Journal*, were fierce competitors. They filled the pages of their papers with spectacular stories. They also added special features, such as comics and sports.

Modern Advertising and New Products

Newspapers had a wide influence on American life, including the rise of modern advertising. Advertisers used images of celebrities in newspapers and magazines to tempt people to buy products. They advertised everything from cereal to jewelry to soap. Some ads played on people's fears. For example, advertisers might scare a young woman concerned about her appearance into buying a particular brand of face cream. Advertising was effective in turning brand names into household words.

Advertisements also helped people learn about new products. At the turn of the century, new inventions, such as the electric washing machine, promised to help people do their household chores more easily. Because women did most of these chores as well as most of the shopping, manufacturers marketed these new devices to women.

One of the places people could buy these—and many other—goods was in department stores. **Department stores** sold everything from clothing to furniture to hardware. The Chicago businessman Marshall Field discovered as a sales clerk that he could increase his sales by paying close attention to each woman customer. Field opened his own department store in downtown Chicago with the motto, "Give the lady what she wants."

People who did not live near a department store could order goods through the mail. Companies like Montgomery Ward and Sears Roebuck sent catalogs to customers. These **mail-order catalogs** included pictures and descriptions of merchandise. People could place their orders by mail, and the company would deliver the product. Richard Sears claimed that he sold 10,000 items a minute.

In 1896, the post office made it easier for people to receive goods through the mail by establishing a new delivery system. Rural free delivery brought packages directly to homes in rural areas. Now people in these areas could get the same goods as people in the cities.

ng **History**
marizing
developchanged
an methselling at
n of the
?

STRANGE *but* True

BICYCLES TO AIRPLANES

At the turn of the century, two bicycle mechanics invented a machine that would help advertisers and businessmen reach new customers. In 1892, Orville and Wilbur Wright opened a bicycle shop in Ohio. They used the profits to fund experiments in aeronautics, the construction of aircraft.

In 1903, the Wright brothers took a gasoline-powered airplane that they had designed to a sandy hill outside Kitty Hawk, North Carolina. On December 17 of that year, Orville made the first successful flight of a powered aircraft in history. By 1918, the U.S. Postal Service began airmail service that made it faster and easier for people to get goods.

Urban Parks and World's Fairs

Advertising and shopping were not the only daily activities changing at this time. **Leisure,** or free time, activities also changed. In cities, new parks provided people with entertainment. The increasing number of people working in factories and offices liked going to parks to get some sunshine and fresh air. Parks helped bring grass and trees back into city landscapes.

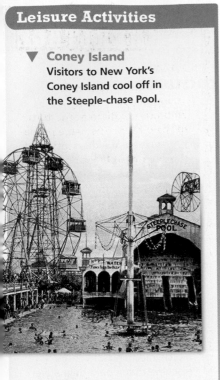

Central Park in New York City is the nation's best-known urban park. Opened in 1876, Central Park looked like the country. Trees and shrubs dotted its gently rolling landscape. Winding walkways let city dwellers imagine they were strolling in the woods. People could also ride bicycles and play sports in the park.

In addition to urban parks, amusement parks provided a place people could go for fun. The most famous amusement park was Coney Island in New York City. Completed in 1904, Coney Island had shops, food vendors, and exciting rides like roller coasters. One immigrant woman said Coney Island "is just like what I see when I dream of heaven!"

World's fairs provided another wildly popular form of entertainment for Americans. Between 1876 and 1916, several U.S. cities, including Philadelphia, Chicago, St. Louis, and San Francisco, hosted world's fairs. The fairs were designed to show off American technology. The 1876 fair in Philadelphia displayed Alexander Graham Bell's newly invented telephone. Millions of people attended these fairs. Nearly 10 million attended the Philadelphia fair alone. Visitors were drawn to foods, shows, and amusements. The historian Thomas Schlereth described the giant wheel built by George Ferris at the 1893 Chicago fair.

*Reading**H**

B. Compari **and Contra** What did u parks and v fairs have i common?

A VOICE FROM THE PAST

Chicago's answer to Paris's 1889 Eiffel Tower, Ferris's 264-foot bicycle wheel in the sky dominated the landscape. With thirty-six cars, each larger than a Pullman coach and capable of holding 60 people, the wheel, when fully loaded, rotated 2,160 people in the air.

Thomas Schlereth, *Victorian America*

Spectator Sports

During this time, spectator sports also became popular entertainment. Baseball, football, boxing, and many other sports drew thousands of people to fields and gyms around the country.

Baseball was the most popular sport. Summer games drew crowds of enthusiastic fans. By the 1890s, baseball had standardized rules and a published schedule of games. Racial discrimination kept African-American baseball players out of baseball's American and National Leagues. In order to compete, African Americans formed their own teams in the Negro American League and the Negro National League. (See Geography in History, pages 722–723.)

Going to the Show

In addition to sports, other forms of live entertainment attracted large audiences. **Vaudeville,** for example, featured a mixture of song, dance, and comedy. A show would have a series of acts leading up to an exciting end, which advertisers billed as the "wow finish."

New types of music also began to be heard. **Ragtime,** a blend of African-American songs and European musical forms, was an important new musical form. African-American composer Scott Joplin heard ragtime while he traveled through black communities from New Orleans to Chicago. Joplin's "Maple Leaf Rag," published in 1899, became a hit in the first decade of the 20th century.

Early in the 20th century, movies began to compete with live entertainment. The first movies were silent and were added as the final feature of a vaudeville show. Soon storefront theaters appeared that showed only movies. After 1905, these movie theaters were called nickelodeons because they charged just a nickel for admission.

Movies, music, sports, and advertising contributed to shaping modern American mass culture. People across the nation experienced many of these things. In the next chapter, you will learn about different nationwide changes—the reform movements of the Progressive era.

ing **History**
king
nces How
u think
s con-
ed to
culture?

Scott Joplin

---

tion **4** *Assessment*

Terms & Names

plain the
gnificance of:
ass culture
oseph Pulitzer
Villiam Randolph
earst
epartment store
ail-order catalog
isure
audeville
agtime

2. Using Graphics

Use a diagram like the one below to note the changes that created a mass culture at the turn of the century.

3. Main Ideas

a. What did dime novels and newspapers have in common?

b. How did new technologies change the way people bought goods?

c. What did visitors see at world's fairs?

4. Critical Thinking

Making Inferences Why did mass culture emerge during this period?

THINK ABOUT
• the impact of newspapers
• advertising and catalogs
• the development of leisure time

IVITY OPTIONS

ART
NGUAGE ARTS

Research a world's fair from the turn of the century. Then make a **poster** or write a **newspaper advertisement** that will attract people to the fair.

TERMS & NAMES

Briefly explain the significance of each of the following.

1. urbanization
2. Jane Addams
3. political machine
4. Ellis Island
5. assimilation
6. Jim Crow
7. *Plessy* v. *Ferguson*
8. W. E. B. Du Bois
9. Joseph Pulitzer
10. leisure

REVIEW QUESTIONS

Cities Grow and Change (pages 609–613)

1. How did public transportation change city life?
2. What dangers did urban overcrowding pose to tenement dwellers?
3. How did big-city political machines keep their power?

The New Immigrants (pages 614–619)

4. Where did most American immigrants come from around 1900?
5. How did immigrants enter the United States?
6. Why have some people described the United States as a melting pot?

Segregation and Discrimination (pages 620–625)

7. Why was *Plessy* v. *Ferguson* an important Supreme Court decision?
8. What did African-American leaders do to fight discrimination?

Society and Mass Culture (pages 626–629)

9. What is mass culture?
10. How did city parks improve city life?

CRITICAL THINKING

1. USING YOUR NOTES: CATEGORIZING INFORMATION

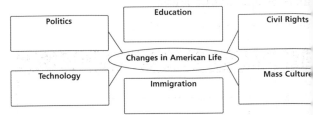

Using your completed chart, answer the questions be

a. What changes did increased immigration cause?
b. How did the growing popularity of spectator sp and movies help bring about mass culture?
c. Which changes helped immigrants assimilate int American life?

2. ANALYZING LEADERSHIP

Think about the actions of Booker T. Washington W. E. B. Du Bois. What approach did each take aga discrimination? Whose approach do you think was most likely to be effective?

3. THEME: DIVERSITY AND UNITY

How do you think the emergence of mass culture around 1900 affected immigrants and nonwhites?

4. APPLYING CITIZENSHIP SKILLS

What kinds of things prevented African American immigrants from having full citizenship? How did attempt to participate in American politics?

Interact *with* History

Have your ideas about how you'll make a home the United States changed after reading the cha

VISUAL SUMMARY

Changes in American Life

Cities Grow and Change

Industrialization caused American cities to grow.

The New Immigrants

Large numbers of immigrants, especially from southern and eastern Europe, came to the United States.

American Life Around 1900

Segregation and Discrimination

Racial and ethnic minorities faced discrimination across the country.

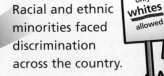

only **whites** allowed

Society and Mass Cultu

New leisure activities and culture emerged at this ti

e the graph and your knowledge of U.S. history
answer questions 1 and 2.

dITIONAL Test Practice, pp. S1–S33.

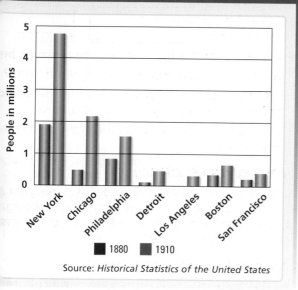

Growth of Cities, *1880–1910*

People in millions

5
4
3
2
1
0

New York Chicago Philadelphia Detroit Los Angeles Boston San Francisco

■ 1880 ■ 1910

Source: *Historical Statistics of the United States*

Which city's population increased by the greatest
amount between 1880 and 1910?

A. Boston

B. Chicago

C. New York

D. Philadelphia

2. For which city is no 1880 population information
provided?

A. Chicago

B. Detroit

C. Los Angeles

D. New York

This quotation from teacher Mary Ellen Chase is
about how she controlled a classroom. Use the quotation and your knowledge of U.S. history to
answer question 3.

PRIMARY SOURCE

I stormed up and down. . . . This pathetic pretense of
courage, aided by the mad flourishing of my razor
strop, brought forth . . . the expression of respectful
fear on the faces of the young giants.

Mary Ellen Chase, quoted in *The Good Old Days—They
Were Terrible!*

3. Based on this passage, which of the following best
states Mary Ellen Chase's view of what was important in a classroom?

A. fear and punishment

B. large classrooms

C. a physically-strong teacher

D. respect and discipline

TEST PRACTICE
CLASSZONE.COM

RNATIVE ASSESSMENT

WRITING ABOUT HISTORY

a **guide** for new immigrants coming to the
d States at the beginning of the 20th century.
ude information about life in the cities, job
ortunities, discrimination, and leisure activities.
ude icons or other illustrations where possible as
aid to people who are just learning English.

OPERATIVE LEARNING

with a few of your classmates to research city
built in the late 1800s and design your own
nclude sports fields, areas for rest, places for
and wildlife, and buildings for food and rest-
Divide responsibilities for researching and
ing the park.

INTEGRATED TECHNOLOGY

DOING INTERNET RESEARCH

Racial discrimination has been a tragic feature of
American history. Conduct research to create a
museum exhibit about discrimination and civil rights.

- Use the Internet to locate primary sources such as
  newspaper articles or autobiographies.

- Look for information on racial or ethnic groups that
  faced discrimination, as well as biographies of
  important civil rights leaders. Then prepare a presentation for your class that illustrates how beliefs
  and practices have changed.

For more about racial discrimination . . .

INTERNET ACTIVITY
CLASSZONE.COM

Create an Exhibit

In 1904 the Louisiana Purchase Exposition, better known as the St. Louis World's Fair, opened to great fanfare. The event celebrated the 100th anniversary of the U.S. purchase of the Louisiana Territory from France in 1803. Taking five years to plan and opening a year late, the fair focused on education and American technology. The automobile was among the most notable attractions at the fair. People from 63 countries and 43 states gathered in St. Louis.

People stroll down The Great Pike at the St. Louis World's Fair.

ACTIVITY Create an exhibit that reflects some aspect of technology at the end of the 19th century. Then make a classroom fair. Write an article about it and give a speech describing your favorite exhibit.

TOOLBOX

Each group will need:

bifold (type of poster board that folds open)	scissors
	pencils
poster board	glue
drawing paper	cardboard
markers	

STEP BY STEP

1 **Form groups.** Each group should consist of three or f... students. During the workshop, ea... group will be expected to:

- research technology and inventi... just prior to 1904
- design and create an exhibit for... classroom fair
- write a news report about the f...
- give a speech in praise of a favo... exhibit at the fair

2 **Research the fair.** Using ... chapter, books on the St. L... fair, or the Internet, find out wha... kinds of exhibits were displayed. A... research the technology and inven... of the time. Some themes of the f... massive exhibit halls are listed bel... Pick one theme on which to focus... Then brainstorm ideas for your ex... and choose the best one.

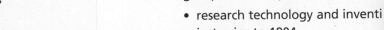

World's Fair Themes	
transportation	education
technology	the arts

The New York-to-St. Louis Automobile Parade arrives at the St. Louis World's Fair.

HELP DESK

For related information, see pages 627–628 in Chapter 21.

Researching Your Project
- *The Song of the Molimo* by Jane Cutler

For more about world's fairs . . .

RESEARCH LINKS CLASSZONE.COM

Design your exhibit. Think about what your [grou]p wants to create. Using draw[ing p]aper, sketch a design of the [exhi]bit in pencil. Next to your [sketc]h, list all the items you'll need [for th]e exhibit. Assign each person [in yo]ur group certain items to bring [for th]e next class period.

4 **Lay out your display.** Use the images and text you found to visually organize the three-panel display. Vary the size of the images, type-size of the text, and include color to make your layout clear and interesting. Remember to create a title.

Did You Know?
One vender at the fair had difficulty selling tea in the hot St. Louis summer. As a result, he began putting ice cubes in the tea, and sales of his "iced tea" soared.

Though there has been some controversy over who invented the ice-cream cone, the St. Louis World's Fair was the place it became popular. One story states that a vendor at the fair rolled a waffle into a cone-shaped holder when another vendor ran out of dishes. However, Italo Marchiony of New York City claimed to have been selling ice-cream cones since 1896.

A Machine for the New Century

REFLECT & ASSESS
- How did your group come up with its idea?
- How does your design fit into the theme of the St. Louis fair?
- What criteria did you use when judging the exhibits?

Create a mini St. Louis [World's] fair. Along with the other [group]s, arrange the exhibits around [the cla]ssroom. Walk around the room and look at the other groups' exhibits. Discuss with other groups how you created your exhibit.

[WRI]TE AND SPEAK

[Write] a newspaper article. Cover the fair as a journalist from [anoth]er city. Write an article about the classroom fair, describ[ing th]e atmosphere as well as the exhibits. Then give a speech [in prai]se of the outstanding exhibit of the fair.

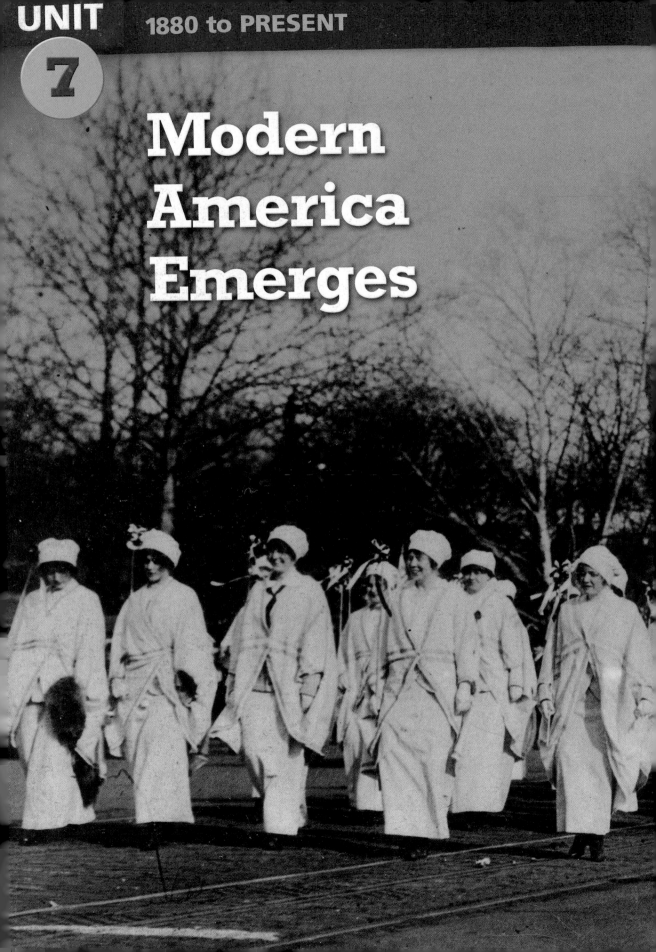

Modern America Emerges

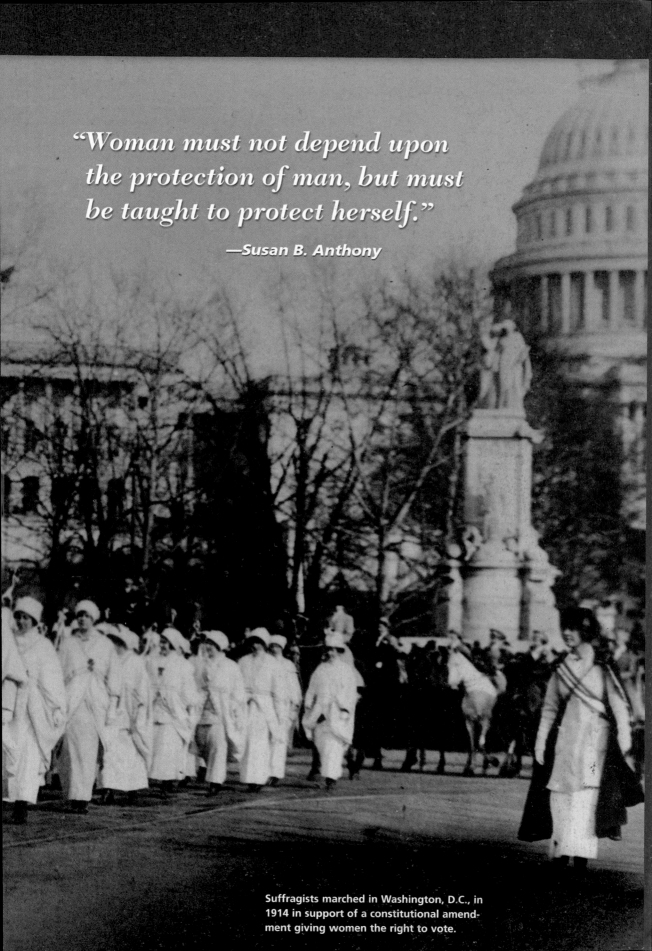

"Woman must not depend upon the protection of man, but must be taught to protect herself."

—Susan B. Anthony

Suffragists marched in Washington, D.C., in 1914 in support of a constitutional amendment giving women the right to vote.

The Progressive Era 1890–1920

A family earns money by making artificial flowers in its tenement.

1890
Congress passes Sherman Antitrust Act.

1896
William McKinley is elected president.

1901
McKinley is assassinated, and Theodore Roosevelt becomes president.

USA
World   1890

1890
German leader Bismarck is dismissed by Kaiser Wilhelm II.

1894
Uganda becomes a British protectorate.

1898
Marie Curie discovers radium.

1900
Boxer uprising against foreigners begins in China.

y in the
gutter.

It is 1901, and Theodore Roosevelt has suddenly become president. You and all Americans are counting on him to help end child labor, poverty, business abuses, and political corruption. You're anxious to see what actions the new president will take to address these problems.

How would you solve one of these problems?

What Do You Think?

- What problems do the photographs show?
- What qualities would a leader need to tackle such problems?
- What might be the cause of these problems?

RESEARCH LINKS
CLASSZONE.COM
Visit the Chapter 22 links for more information about the Progressive Era.

1908
d Taft is
esident.

ces the
mobile.

1912
Woodrow Wilson is elected president.

1913
17th Amendment provides for direct election of senators.

1919
18th Amendment outlaws alcohol.

1920
19th Amendment grants women the right to vote.

1920

1910
Union of South Africa is established.

1913
Gandhi, leader of Indian resistance movement, is arrested.

CHAPTER 24

World War I

1914–1920

Section 1
War Breaks Out in Europe

Section 2
America Joins the Fight

Section 3
Life on the Home Front

Section 4
The Legacy of World War I

This photograph shows a battlefield view of trench warfare during World War I.
The soldiers "go over the top" and charge the enemy lines.

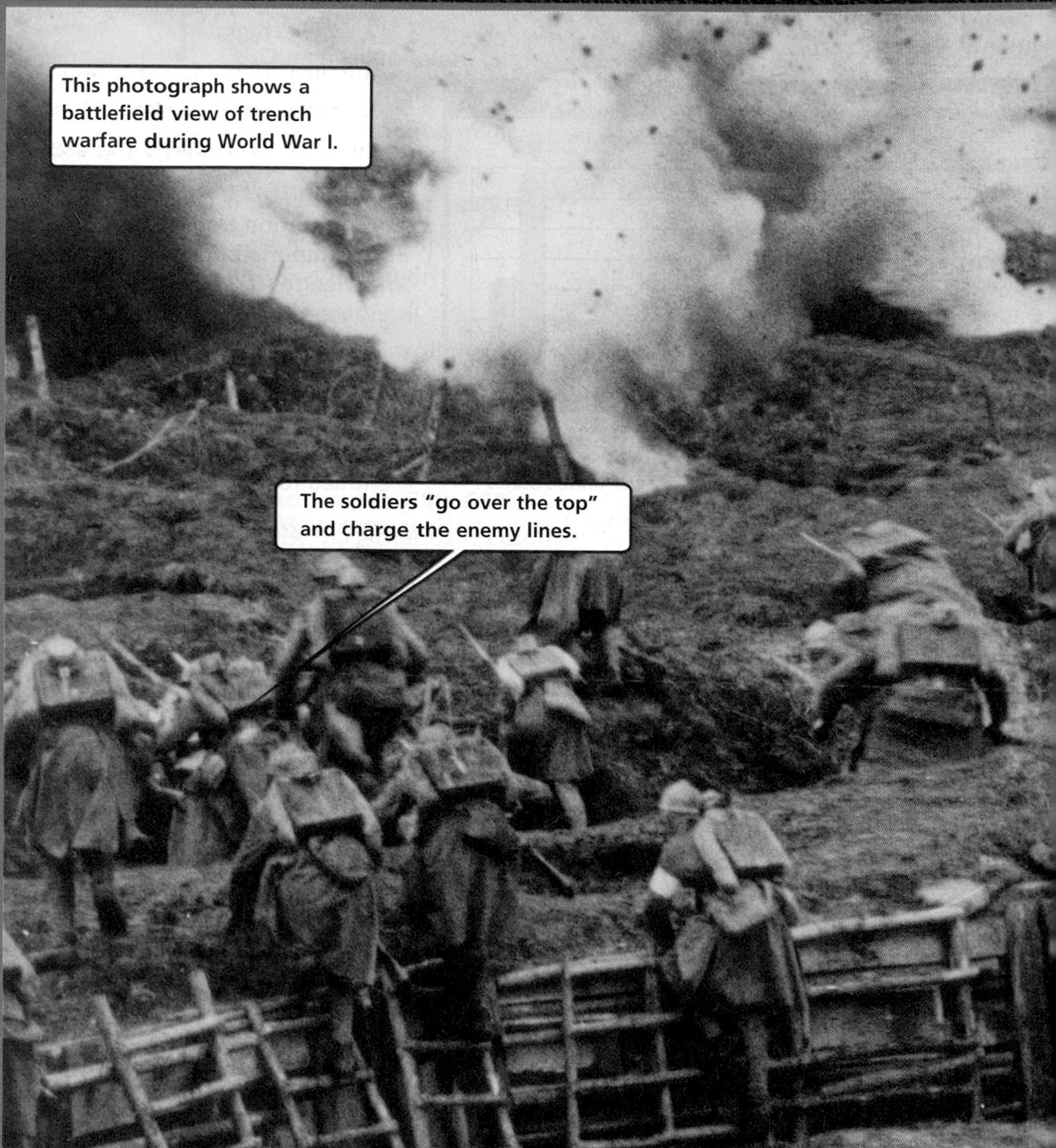

August 15, 1914
U.S.-built Panama Canal officially opens.

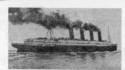

May 7, 1915
Many Americans die as a German U-boat sinks *Lusitania*.

Novem
Woo
reele

USA
World
1914

June 28, 1914
Austria-Hungary's Archduke Franz Ferdinand is assassinated, starting World War I.

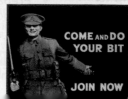

COME AND DO YOUR BIT
JOIN NOW

February–December, 1915
Allies and Central Powers clash at Gallipoli in the Ottoman Empire.

Novem
French,
Germans
losses a
of

The year is 1917, and the United States has been drawn into World War I. Each citizen is called upon to help the war effort. Some will join the American armed forces and go to fight in Europe. Others will work in factories at home, producing weapons and supplies. Even children will do their part.

How will you support the war effort?

What Do You Think?

- How can Americans at home help win the war?
- What might U.S. soldiers experience in Europe?
- How might being at war affect the country?

RESEARCH LINKS
CLASSZONE.COM
Visit the Chapter 24 links for more information about World War I.

...ound the ...g soldiers ...at ...ind.

2, 1917
...asks
...s to declare
...Germany.

I WANT YOU FOR U.S. ARMY
NEAREST RECRUITING STATION

January 8, 1918
President Wilson proposes League of Nations.

November 2, 1920
Warren G. Harding is elected president.

1920

March 3, 1918
Russia withdraws from the war.

November 11, 1918
The Allies defeat the Central Powers, ending World War I.

June 28, 1919
The Allies and Germany sign the Treaty of Versailles.

Reading Strategy: Recognizing Effects

What Do You Know?

What do you think of when you hear the phrase "world war"? What were the major countries in the war? Where did most of the fighting take place?

Think About

- what you've learned about World War I from movies or television
- reasons that millions of people might choose to risk their lives in a global conflict
- your responses to the Interact with History about supporting the war effort (see page 677)

This 1918 poster urged Ar not to waste food during

What Do You Want to Know?

What details do you need to help you understand what is involved in waging a world war? Make a list of these details in your notebook before you read the chapter.

Recognizing Effects

To help you make sense of what you read, learn to analyze the effects of important historical events. The chart below will help you analyze some of the effects of World War both on the world and on the United States. In each box, fill in a different effect. Add m boxes if you need to.

S See Skillbuilder Handbook, page R11.

Taking Notes

EFFECTS ON THE WORLD

EFFECTS ON THE UNITED STATE

World War I

War Breaks Out in Europe

MAIN IDEA	WHY IT MATTERS NOW	TERMS & NAMES
rld War I broke out, the ates eventually joined side.	This was the first time that the United States was involved in a European conflict.	militarism U-boat Central Powers Woodrow Wilson Allies neutrality trench warfare Zimmermann telegram

ONE AMERICAN'S STORY

In the late 1800s and early 1900s, European nations competed to expand their empires. Rivalry caused tension among these nations. In 1914, President Woodrow Wilson sent Colonel Edward M. House to study the situation.

House gave the president a troubling report. He compared Europe to an open keg of gunpowder that only needed a spark to explode. He was right. On June 28, 1914, a Serbian shot and killed Archduke Franz Ferdinand, the heir to the throne of Austria-Hungary. Soon Austria declared war on Serbia. The nations of Europe chose sides and the Great War, later called World War I, began.

Archduke Franz Ferdinand and his wife are murdered at Sarajevo on June 28, 1914.

Causes of World War I

A single action, the assassination of the archduke, started World War I. But the conflict had many underlying causes.

1. **Imperialism.** Britain, France, Germany, and Italy competed for colonies in Africa and Asia. Because it had fewer colonies than Britain and France, Germany felt it deserved more colonies to provide it with resources and buy its goods.

2. **Nationalism.** Europeans were very nationalistic, meaning that they had strong feelings of pride, loyalty, and protectiveness toward their own countries. They wanted to prove their nations were the best. They placed their countries' interests above all other concerns. In addition, some ethnic groups hoped to form their own separate nations and were willing to fight for such a cause.

3. **Militarism.** The belief that a nation needs a large military force is **militarism**. In the decades before the war, the major powers built up their armies and navies.

Taking Notes

Use your chart to take notes about the effects of World War I.

EFFECTS ON THE WORLD   EFFECTS ON 1 UNITED STAT

World War I

Allies
Central Powers
Neutral Nations

STEPS TO WORLD WAR I

1 **June 28** Archduke Franz Ferdinand is assassinated.

2 **July 28** Austria-Hungary declares war on Serbia.

3 **July 30** Russia (Serbia's ally) mobilizes armed forces.

4 **August 1** Germany (Austria-Hungary's ally) declares war on Russia.

5 **August 3** Germany declares war on France (Russia's ally) prepares to invade Belgium.

6 **August 4** Britain, having pledged to protect Belgium declares war on Germany.

7 **August 6** Austria-Hungary declares war on Russia.

8 **August 12** France and Britain declare war on Austria-Hungary.

NORWAY
SWEDEN
DENMARK
North Sea
Baltic Sea
GREAT BRITAIN
London
NETH.
BELG.
Berlin
GERMANY
Paris
LUXEMBOURG
Vienna
FRANCE
SWITZ.
AUSTRIA-HUNGARY
Sarajevo
ITALY
ROMANIA
MONTENEGRO
SERBIA
BULGARIA
Rome
ALBANIA
OTTOMAN EMPIRE
GREECE
Madrid
SPAIN
PORTUGAL
ATLANTIC OCEAN
Mediterranean Sea
SP. MOROCCO
RUSSIA
Black Sea
58°N

0   300 Miles
0   600 Kilometers

GEOGRAPHY SKILLBUILDER Interpreting Maps
1. **Location** *What neutral countries were landlocked in the heart of Europe?*
2. **Region** *Which country covered the greatest amount of land, including territory in both Europe and Asia?*

4. **Alliances** In 1914, a tangled network of competing alliances bound European nations together. An attack on one nation forced all its allies to come to its aid. Any small conflict could become a larger war.

European nations had divided into two opposing alliances. The **Central Powers** were made up of Austria-Hungary, Germany, the Ottoman Empire, and Bulgaria. They faced the Allied Powers, or **Allies,** consisting of Serbia, Russia, France, Great Britain, Italy, and seven other countries.

Stalemate in the Trenches

When the war began in August, most people on both sides assumed it would be over within a few months. With France as its goal, the German army invaded Belgium on August 4, 1914. Despite stiff resistance, the Germans fought their way west into France. They reached the Marne River about 40 miles from Paris. There the French, supported by the British, rallied and prepared to fight back. The First Battle of the Marne, in September 1914, stopped the German advance.

Instead of one side quickly defeating the other, the two sides stayed stuck in the mud for more than three years. The soldiers were fighting a new kind of battle, **trench warfare.** Troops huddled at the bottom of rat-infested trenches. They fired artillery and machine guns at each other. Lines of trenches stretched across France from the English Channel to the border with Switzerland. (See pages 684–685 for an

Backgrou
The Ottoma
Empire incl
modern-da
Turkey and

Reading **H**
A. Reading
Map On th
on page 68
the site of
first Battle
Marne.

Vocabular
trench: a lo
deep ditch
for protect

illustration of the trenches.) For more than three years, the battle lines remained almost unchanged. Neither side could win a clear victory.

In the trenches, soldiers faced the constant threat of sniper fire. Artillery shelling turned the area between the two opposing armies into a "no man's land" too dangerous to occupy. When soldiers left their trenches to attack enemy lines, they rushed into a hail of bullets and clouds of poison gas.

When battles did take place, they cost many thousands of lives, often without gaining an inch for either side. The Battle of the Somme (SAHM), between July and November 1916, resulted in more than 1.2 million casualties. British dead or wounded numbered over 400,000. German losses totaled over 600,000, and French nearly 200,000. Despite this, the Allies gained only about seven miles.

A War of New Technology

New technology raised the death toll. The tank, a British invention, smashed through barbed wire, crossed trenches, and cleared paths through no man's land. Soldiers also had machine guns that fired 600 bullets a minute. Poison gas, used by both sides, burned and blinded soldiers.

World War I was the first major conflict in which airplanes were used in combat. By 1917, fighter planes fought each other far above the clouds. Manfred von Richthofen, known as the Red Baron, was Germany's top ace. An ace was an aviator who had downed five or more enemy aircraft. Von Richthofen shot down over 80 enemy planes.

At sea, the Germans used submarines, which they called **U-boats,** to block trade. They were equipped with both guns and torpedoes. German U-boats sank over 11 million tons of Allied shipping.

ing **History**
*d*ing a Map
e site of
*t*tle of
*m*me on
p on
88.

*r*ound
was short
*n*dersea

w Technology of War

used effectively during World
I, these new weapons caused
casualties.

Airplane

Poison Gas

Machine Gun

Tank

681

EUROPE VIA LIVERPOOL
LUSITANIA
Fastest and Largest Steamer
now in Atlantic Service Sails
SATURDAY, MAY 1, 10 A. M.
Transylvania, Fri., May 7, 5 P.M.
Orduna, - - Tues., May 18, 10 A.M.
Tuscania, - - Fri., May 21, 5 P.M.
LUSITANIA, Sat., May 29, 10 A.M.
Transylvania, Fri., June 4, 5 P.M.

Gibraltar–Genoa–Naples–Piraeus
S.S. Carpathia, Thur., May 13, Noon
ROUND THE WORLD TOURS
Through bookings to all principal Ports
of the World.
Company's office, 21-24 State St., N. Y.

NOTICE!
TRAVELLERS intending to embark on the Atlantic voyage are reminded that a state of war exists between Germany and her allies and Great Britain and her allies; that the zone of war includes the waters adjacent to the British Isles; that, in accordance with formal notice given by the Imperial German Government, vessels flying the flag of Great Britain, or of any of her allies, are liable to destruction in those waters and that travellers sailing in the war zone on ships of Great Britain or her allies do so at their own risk.

IMPERIAL GERMAN EMBASSY
WASHINGTON, D. C., APRIL 22, 1915.

The British liner *Lusitania* is sunk off the Irish coast by a German submarine on May 7, 1915.

America's Path to War

When the war started in 1914, President <u>Woodrow Wilson</u> announced a policy of <u>neutrality,</u> refusing to take sides in the war. A popular song, "I Didn't Raise My Boy to Be a Soldier," expressed the antiwar sentiment of many Americans.

Over time, however, German attacks shifted public opinion to the Allied cause. In the fall of 1914, Britain set up a naval blockade of German ports, seizing all goods bound for Germany. In response, German submarines sank all Allied merchant ships they found off the British coast. In May 1915, a German U-boat torpedoed the British passenger ship *Lusitania,* killing 1,198 people, including 128 Americans. The sinking turned many Americans against Germany.

But President Wilson kept the United States neutral. He demanded that the German government halt unrestricted submarine warfare, and it agreed. In the election of 1916, the Democratic Party's campaign slogan, "He kept us out of war," appealed to voters. Wilson won reelection.

Desperate to defeat Britain, Germany resumed unrestricted submarine warfare at the end of January 1917. Its military leaders knew this action would bring the United States into the war. However, they hoped to win the war before the Americans arrived.

The next month, another blow to German-American relations came from the <u>Zimmermann telegram</u>. The telegram was discovered by the British, who passed it on to the Americans. In it, Arthur Zimmermann, the German foreign minister, told the German ambassador in Mexico to propose that Mexico join the Germans. In exchange, Germany would help Mexico get back its "lost" territories of Texas, New Mexico, and Arizona. Americans were furious.

Reading **H**
C. Making
Inferences
did the sink
of the *Lusit*
turn Ameri
against Ger

In March, German submarines sank three American ships. President Wilson asked for a declaration of war.

"The world must be made safe for democracy."
Woodrow Wilson

A VOICE FROM THE PAST

The world must be made safe for democracy. . . . We desire no conquest. . . . We are but one of the champions of the rights of mankind. We shall be satisfied when those rights have been made . . . secure.

Woodrow Wilson, message to Congress, April 2, 1917

Six senators and 50 representatives, including the first woman in Congress, Jeannette Rankin of Montana, voted against going to war. But the majority shared the president's commitment to join the Allies.

Revolution in Russia

Events in Russia made U.S. entry into the war more urgent for the Allies. By early 1915, the huge Russian army had been outfought by a smaller German army led by better-trained officers. In August 1915, Czar Nicholas II insisted on taking control of the troops himself. His poor leadership was blamed for more deaths. By 1917, food shortages led to riots, and soaring inflation led to strikes by angry workers in Russia.

In March 1917, Czar Nicholas II was forced to step down. A temporary government continued the unpopular war until November. In that month the Bolsheviks, a communist group led by Vladimir Ilich Lenin, took power. Communism is a political system in which the government owns key parts of the economy, and there is no private property.

Because the war had devastated Russia, Lenin at once began peace talks with Germany. In March 1918, Russia withdrew from the war by signing the Treaty of Brest-Litovsk. German troops could now turn from Russia to the Western front. The Allies urged American troops to come quickly, as you will read in the next section.

*ng***History**
lyzing
What led
to pull out
war?

tion 1 Assessment

Terms & Names
plain the
gnificance of:
ilitarism
entral Powers
llies
ench warfare
-boat
Voodrow Wilson
eutrality
mmermann
legram

2. Using Graphics

Write at least four events that brought the United States into World War I.

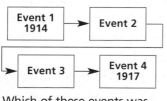

Event 1 1914 → Event 2

Event 3 → Event 4 1917

Which of these events was most important? Why?

3. Main Ideas

a. What were the long-term causes of World War I?

b. Why were Americans divided over the issue of remaining neutral?

c. Why was Russia's withdrawal from the war in 1917 a blow to Allies?

4. Critical Thinking

Analyzing Causes How did imperialism, nationalism, and militarism work to reinforce each other?

THINK ABOUT
• the goals of each
• how nationalism might encourage military buildup
• how nationalism contributed to the race for colonies

IVITY OPTIONS

SCIENCE
ART

Research one of the new weapons of World War I. Explain how it works using a **model,** or draw an illustrated **diagram** of a defense against the weapon.

Survive Trench Warfare

You are a platoon leader assigned to a section of the front in central France. You have 60 men under your command. Day and night, through constant rain, earthen trenches full of sticky mud serve as your only protection. Sometimes, you think, the cold, rain, mud, rats, and fatigue are tougher to endure than a German bombardment.

COOPERATIVE LEARNING On this page are two challenges you face as a soldier during World War I. Working with a small group, decide how to deal with each challenge. Choose an option, assign a task to each group member, and do the activity. You will find useful information in the Data File. Be prepared to present your solutions to the class.

PHYSICAL EDUCATION CHALLENGE

"They must have 20 or 30 pounds of mud on them."

Until now, no one thought the trenches would be a permanent part of this war. So you, like the other soldiers along the front, weren't trained to cope with heavy, thick mud, 70-pound backpacks, and the other demands of living and fighting in these conditions. You learned on the job. Now you've been ordered to contribute ideas for a training program that will prepare recruits for the trenches. Look at the Data File for help. Then present your ideas using one of these options:

• Design an exercise regimen to strengthen troops for the trenches.
• Write a booklet of survival tips based on your platoon's experiences.

THE TRENCHES

- Trenches covered about 450 miles between the North Sea and the Swiss border.
- In France, ten-foot-deep trenches were dug into the ground and topped with sandbag parapets.
- Inside was a fire step, a ledge two or three feet up from bottom of the trench, used by sentries or troops firing.
- The sides were held up by sandbags and timber.

A SOLDIER'S GEAR

60–75 pounds of gear, including blankets, waterproof ground-sheet, extra boots and occasionally waterproof gum boots, quilted coat, shovel for digging trenches, helmet, wire clippers, pail for rations, 2 quarts of water, 4 days' food, 200 cartridges, 6 hand grenades, gas mask, 3 pairs of socks, soap, toothbrush, bottle of whale oil, towel, rifle, bayonet

TRENCH FOOD

beef stew, corned beef, bread, hard biscuits, pork and beans, tins of jam, butter, sugar, tea

PROBLEMS

- **trench foot:** condition caused by feet staying wet 24 hours a day; feet swell, turn numb and blue; if not treated, gangrene sets in and feet must be amputated; helped by rubbing whale oil on feet, changing to dry socks three times daily
- **mud:** mud traps the wounded until some drown, clogs rifles and gear, weighs men down, causes trench walls to fall in
- **rats:** huge rats, as big as rabbits, infest the trenches

For more about trench warfare . . .

RESEARCH LINKS
CLASSZONE.COM

HEALTH CHALLENGE

"Your feet swell to two or three times . . . normal size."

You're worried about your men getting trench foot. You've heard horror stories about men whose feet swelled so much they couldn't pull off their boots. Some of these men developed gangrene and had their feet amputated. The key to preventing trench foot is staying dry. What will you do? Use the Data File for help. Then present your solution using one of these options:

- Come up with a way to keep the men's feet dry.
- Role-play a conversation with veteran soldiers about preventing trench foot.

ACTIVITY WRAP-UP

Present to the Class As a group, review your methods of surviving the trenches. Pick the most creative solution for each challenge, and present these solutions to the class.

America Joins the Fight

MAIN IDEA	WHY IT MATTERS NOW	TERMS & NAMES
U.S. forces helped the Allies win World War I.	For the first time, the United States asserted itself as a world power.	John J. Pershing American Expeditionary Force convoy system

TERMS & NAMES (continued): Second Bat of the Ma, Alvin York, armistice

ONE AMERICAN'S STORY

Eddie Rickenbacker was America's most famous flying ace. He was one of the first Americans to get a look at the trenches from the cockpit of an airplane.

A VOICE FROM THE PAST

[T]here appeared to be nothing below but these old battered ditches . . . and billions of shell holes. . . . [N]ot a tree, a fence . . . nothing but . . . ruin and desolation. The whole scene was appalling.

Eddie Rickenbacker, *Fighting the Flying Circus*

As you will read in this section, Rickenbacker and other U.S. soldiers helped the Allies win the war.

Taking Notes

Use your chart to take notes about the effects of America's entrance into World War I.

EFFECTS ON WORLD   EFFECTS ON THE UNITED STATES

World War I

Raising an Army and a Navy

The U.S. Army was not ready for war. American fighting forces consisted of fewer than 200,000 soldiers, many of them recent recruits. To meet its need for troops, the government began a draft. This system of choosing people for forced military service was first used during the Civil War. In May 1917, Congress passed the Selective Service Act. This act required all males between the ages of 21 and 30 to sign up for military service. By the end of 1918, nearly 3 million men had been drafted.

About 2 million American soldiers went to France. They served under General **John J. Pershing** as the **American Expeditionary Force,** or AEF. British commanders asked the U.S. government to have AEF troops join existing French and British combat units. Wilson refused. He believed that having "distinct and separate" American combat units would guarantee the United States a major role in the peace talks at war's end. Most U.S. troops fought separately, but some fought under Allied command.

An American crew advanc against Germ positions in

Close to 50,000 American women also served in World War I. Some volunteered for overseas duty with the American Red Cross. However, for the first time in American history, women also served in the military. The Navy, desperate for clerical workers, took about 12,000 female volunteers. The Marine Corps accepted 305 female recruits, known as Marinettes. Over 1,000 women went overseas for the Army. Nurses made up the largest group of females in the armed forces. However, women also acted as interpreters, operated switchboards, entertained troops, and drove ambulances for the AEF.

Around 400,000 African Americans served in the armed forces. More than half of them served in France. As they had at home, African-American troops overseas faced discrimination. However, it came from white American soldiers rather than from their European allies. At first, the Army refused to take black draftees. However, responding to pressure from African-American groups, the military eventually created two African-American combat divisions.

American Ships Make a Difference

In the first years of the war, German U-boat attacks on supply ships were a serious threat to the Allied war effort. American Rear Admiral William S. Sims convinced the Allies to adopt a system of protection. In a **convoy system,** a heavy guard of destroyers escorted merchant ships across the Atlantic in groups. Begun in May 1917, this strategy quickly reduced the loss rate.

Another American tactic gave the Allies added protection from the U-boat menace. Beginning in June 1918, the Allies laid a barrier of 70,000 mines in the North Sea. The 180-mile-long minefield made U-boat access to the North Atlantic almost impossible. Admiral Sims called the North Sea minefield "one of the wonders of the war."

ingHistory
ding Main
How did
n serve in
S. armed
?

ulary
hidden
ive devices

nvoy System

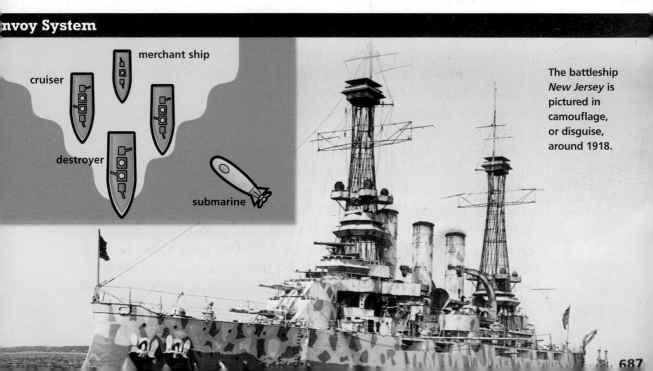

merchant ship
cruiser
destroyer
submarine

The battleship *New Jersey* is pictured in camouflage, or disguise, around 1918.

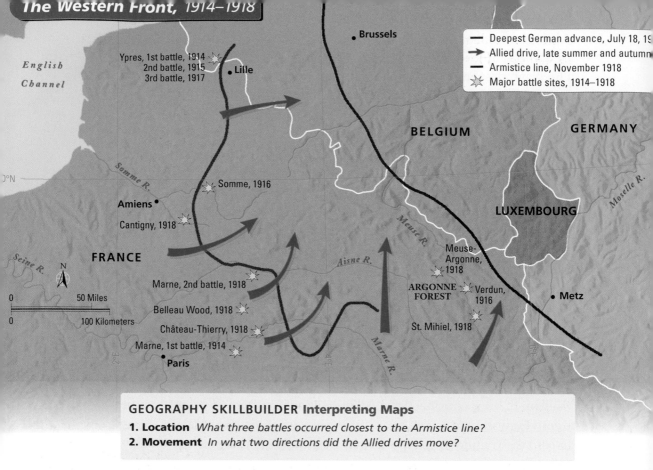

- — Deepest German advance, July 18, 19
- → Allied drive, late summer and autumn
- — Armistice line, November 1918
- ✳ Major battle sites, 1914–1918

English Channel

Ypres, 1st battle, 1914
2nd battle, 1915
3rd battle, 1917

Lille

Brussels

BELGIUM

GERMANY

Somme R.

Somme, 1916

Amiens

Cantigny, 1918

LUXEMBOURG

Moselle R.

Seine R.

FRANCE

Aisne R.

Meuse R.

Meuse-Argonne, 1918

Marne, 2nd battle, 1918

ARGONNE FOREST

Verdun, 1916

Metz

Belleau Wood, 1918

St. Mihiel, 1918

Château-Thierry, 1918

Marne, 1st battle, 1914

Marne R.

Paris

0   50 Miles
0   100 Kilometers

N

GEOGRAPHY SKILLBUILDER Interpreting Maps

1. **Location** *What three battles occurred closest to the Armistice line?*
2. **Movement** *In what two directions did the Allied drives move?*

American Troops Enter the War

By the time the first American troops arrived in France in June 1917, the Allies had been at war for almost three years. The small force of 14,000 Yanks boosted the morale of the battle-weary Allies. However, almost a year would pass before the bulk of the American troops landed in Europe.

After their Russian opponents withdrew from the war, the Germans and the other Central Powers prepared to finish the fight in France. In March 1918, the Germans launched an offensive to end the war before the Americans arrived in force. Within two months, they had smashed through the French lines, reaching the Marne River only 50 miles from Paris. Just in time, in May 1918, one million fresh American troops arrived ready for action.

On May 28, American soldiers attacked the French town of Cantigny (kahn•tee•NYEE), which was occupied by the Germans. The soldiers advanced into the town, blasting enemy soldiers out of trenches and dragging them from cellars. Within two hours, the Yanks had taken control of Cantigny. The American victory lifted Allied morale.

When the Germans moved against the town of Château-Thierry (shah•toh•tyeh•REE), the Americans held their ground. They helped the French stop the German advance. Encouraged by these successes, French General Ferdinand Foch, commander of the Allied forces, ordered General Pershing's American forces to retake Belleau (beh•LOH) Wood.

Backgroun
American so
were also ca
doughboys.
term was us
even during
Civil War.

This was a forest near the Marne River well defended by German troops. American soldiers succeeded, but at a fearful cost. One unit lost 380 of its 400 men. However, the Americans had proved themselves in combat.

Pushing the Germans Back

The **Second Battle of the Marne** in the summer of 1918 was the turning point of the war. It began with a German drive against the French line. During three days of heavy fighting, about 85,000 Americans helped the Allies halt the German advance. The Allies then took the initiative. They cut the enemy off from its supply lines and forced the Germans back.

For the rest of the war, the Allies advanced steadily. By early September, the Germans had lost all the territory they had gained since the spring. September 26, 1918, marked the beginning of the final Meuse-Argonne (myooz•ahr•GAHN) offensive. Around 1.2 million U.S. soldiers took part in a massive drive to push back the German line between the Argonne Forest and the Meuse River. The war's final battle left 26,000 Americans dead. But by November, the Germans were retreating.

The Meuse-Argonne offensive made a hero of American soldier **Alvin York.** At first, Tennessee-born Sergeant York seemed an unlikely candidate for military fame. Because of his religious beliefs, he tried unsuccessfully to avoid the draft. He refused to bear arms on religious grounds. An army captain convinced him to change his mind. In October 1918, in the Argonne Forest, York attacked German machine gunners, killing 25 of them. Other German soldiers surrendered, and York returned to the American lines with 132 captives.

Another American hero was pilot Eddie Rickenbacker. He won fame as the U.S. "ace of aces" for shooting down a total of 26 enemy planes. Just before the Meuse-Argonne offensive, he attacked seven German planes, sending two of them crashing to the ground. This action won him the Medal of Honor.

Four African-American combat units also received recognition for their battlefield valor. Fighting under French commanders, the 369th, 371st, and 372nd regiments (and part of the 370th) were awarded France's highest honor, the Croix de Guerre. The 369th spent more continuous time on the front lines than any other American unit. Although under intense fire for 191 days, it never lost a foot of ground.

ing **History**
ognizing
s What was
fect of the
e-Argonne
sive?

ing **History**
luating
was heroic
Sergeant

Connections TO LITERATURE

LITERATURE OF WORLD WAR I

Several notable American writers served in World War I. They included Ernest Hemingway, the poet E. E. Cummings, and John Dos Passos. Hemingway drove an ambulance for the Italian army. He put this experience into his war novel *A Farewell to Arms.* Cummings wrote of his time in France in *The Enormous Room.*

Dos Passos, who also worked as an ambulance driver, once explained what attracted him to the battlefront: "What was war like, we wanted to see with our own eyes. I wanted to see the show."

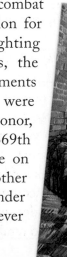

Americans were proud of the contribution their troops made to the war effort. They helped shift the balance in favor of the Allies.

Germany Stops Fighting

After the defeat of the Meuse-Argonne, General Erich Ludendorff advised the German government to seek peace. In early November, Germany's navy mutinied and its allies dropped out. On November 9, the Kaiser stepped down. Two days later Germany agreed to an **armistice,** an end to fighting. On November 11, 1918, at 11:00 A.M.—the 11th hour of the 11th day of the 11th month—all fighting ceased.

About 8.5 million soldiers died in the war, and about 21 million were wounded. Before he was killed in battle, one British soldier summed up the war's tragic costs.

Backgroun
For many ye
after the wa
Americans c
brated Armi
Day as a nat
holiday.

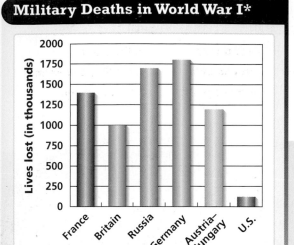

CONNECTIONS TO MATH
Military Deaths in World War I*

*Not all countries are listed.
Source: *Over There,* by Byron Farwell

SKILLBUILDER
Interpreting Graphs

1. *Which two nations on the chart suffered the most deaths?*
2. *U.S. deaths were about what percentage of combined French and British deaths?*

A VOICE FROM THE PAST

The sufferings of the men at the Front, of the wounded whose flesh and bodies are torn in a way you cannot conceive; the sorrow of those at home. . . . What a cruel and mad diversion of human activity!

William John Mason, quoted in *The Lost Generation of 1914*

Millions of civilians in Europe, Asia, and Africa also died in the war—from starvation and disease. In the next section, you will learn how the war affected U.S. civilians.

Section 2 Assessment

1. Terms & Names

Explain the significance of:
- John J. Pershing
- American Expeditionary Force
- convoy system
- Second Battle of the Marne
- Alvin York
- armistice

2. Using Graphics

Create a web to show how American groups or individuals helped fight the war.

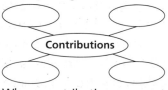

Contributions

Whose contribution was most surprising?

3. Main Ideas

a. Why did Wilson want U.S. forces to fight as a separate American combat unit?

b. What were two ways the U.S. Navy countered the U-boat threat?

c. Why was the Meuse-Argonne offensive a turning point in the war?

4. Critical Thinking

Recognizing Effects Ho important was America's entry into the war to the Allied cause?

THINK ABOUT
- the morale of Allied troo
- troop strength
- performance in battle

ACTIVITY OPTIONS

MUSIC
LANGUAGE ARTS

Make an **audiotape** of music or sounds that suggest the stages of the war, or write a **letter** in the voice of a soldier in the war.

Life on the Home Front

MAIN IDEA	WHY IT MATTERS NOW	TERMS & NAMES
equired sacrifice for s at home and changed life vays.	Some wartime changes were permanent, such as black migration to Northern cities.	war bonds propaganda Espionage Act	Sedition Act Oliver Wendell Holmes Great Migration

ONE AMERICAN'S STORY

On the home front, the war opened up new jobs for women. But when the war ended, female workers were laid off. Carrie Fearing wrote to her boss, hoping to keep her job.

A VOICE FROM THE PAST

We never took a soldier's place, a soldier would not do the work we did . . . such as sweeping, picking up waste and paper. . . . We . . . like our job very much and I hope you will . . . place us back at the shop.

Carrie Fearing, quoted in *Women, War, and Work*

In May 1918, these women worked in the Union Pacific Railroad freight yard in Cheyenne, Wyoming.

Like Fearing, many women were proud of the part they played in getting the country ready for war. In this section, you will learn more about wartime life at home.

Mobilizing for War

To prepare for war, the government needed money. World War I cost the United States $35.5 billion. Americans helped pay almost two-thirds of that amount by buying government war bonds. **War bonds** were low-interest loans by civilians to the government, meant to be repaid in a number of years. To sell the bonds, officials held Liberty Loan drives. Posters urged citizens to "Come Across or the Kaiser Will." Hollywood actors like Charlie Chaplin toured the country selling bonds to starstruck audiences.

Schoolchildren rolled bandages and collected tin cans, paper, toothpaste tubes, and apricot pits. The pits were burned and made into charcoal for gas mask filters. Some Boy Scout troops even sold war bonds. So that more food could be sent to soldiers, people planted "victory gardens" in backyards and vacant lots. Women's groups came together in homes and churches to knit socks and sweaters and sew hospital gowns.

Taking Notes

Use your chart to take notes about the effects of World War I on the home front.

EFFECTS ON THE WORLD

EFFECTS ON UNITED STAT

World War I

WOMEN!
HELP AMERICA'S SONS
WIN THE WAR

To persuade women to buy war bonds, this poster appealed to their love of family.

Patriotic citizens also saved food by observing wheatless Mondays and Wednesdays, when they ate no bread, and meatless Tuesdays. To save gas, they stopped their Sunday pleasure drives. The government limited civilian use of steel and other metals. Women donated their corsets with metal stays to scrap drives. Manufacturers stopped making tin toys for children and removed metal from caskets.

The war brought more government control of the economy. To produce needed war supplies, in 1917 President Wilson set up the War Industries Board. The board had great power. It managed the buying and distributing of war materials. It also set production goals and ordered construction of new factories. With the president's approval, the board also set prices. Another government agency, the National War Labor Board, settled conflicts between workers and factory owners.

To rally citizen support, Wilson created the Committee on Public Information. The committee's writers, artists, photographers, and film-makers produced **propaganda**, opinions expressed for the purpose of influencing the actions of others. The committee sold the war through posters, pamphlets, and movies. One popular pamphlet, "How the War Came to America," came out in Polish, German, Swedish, Bohemian, and Spanish. In movie houses, audiences watched such patriotic films as *Under Four Flags* and *Pershing's Crusaders*.

Intolerance and Suspicion

Patriotic propaganda did much to win support for the war. But its anti-German, anti-foreign focus also fueled prejudice. Suddenly people distrusted anything German. A number of towns with German names changed their names. Berlin, Maryland, became Brunswick. People called sauerkraut "liberty cabbage," and hamburger became "Salisbury steak." Owners of German shepherds took to calling their pets "police dogs."

On June 15, 1917, Congress passed the **Espionage Act**. The **Sedition Act** followed in May 1918. These laws set heavy fines and long prison terms for such antiwar activities as encouraging draft resisters. The laws made it illegal to criticize the war. U.S. courts tried more than 1,500 pacifists, socialists, and other war critics. Hundreds went to jail. Socialist Party leader Eugene Debs gave a speech arguing that the war was fought by poor workingmen for the profit of wealthy business owners. For this talk, a judge sentenced him to ten years in prison.

The government ignored complaints that the rights of Americans were being trampled. In the 1919 decision in *Schenck* v. *United States*, the Supreme Court upheld the Espionage Act. Schenck, convicted of

Reading **His**
A. Finding M
Ideas What
civilians aske
do for the w
effort?

Reading **Hi**
B. Recognizi
Effects How
war propaga
fuel prejudi

distributing pamphlets against the draft, had argued that the Espionage Act violated his right to free speech. Justice **Oliver Wendell Holmes** wrote the court's opinion.

Justice Holmes argued that free speech, guaranteed by the First Amendment, could be limited, especially in wartime.

New Jobs and the Great Migration

As soldiers went off to battle, the United States faced a labor shortage. Northern factories gearing up for war were suddenly willing to hire workers they had once rejected. Throughout the South, African Americans heeded the call. Between 1910 and 1920, about 500,000 African Americans moved north to such cities as New York, Chicago, Detroit, Cleveland, and St. Louis. This movement became known as the **Great Migration.** African Americans left to escape the bigotry, poverty, and racial violence of the South. They hoped for a better life in the North.

HISTORY *through***ART**

The Migration of the Negro, Panel No. 1 (1940–41), by Jacob Lawrence, shows three of the most common destinations for African Americans leaving the South.

How does Lawrence's painting reflect continuity and change in American life?

CHICAGO   NEW YORK   ST. LOUIS

New jobs were opening up in the American Southwest. These jobs were fueled by the growth of railroads and irrigated farming. A revolution was under way in Mexico, and the chaos led many Mexicans to flee across the border after 1910. Many immigrants settled in Texas, Arizona, Colorado, and California. Most became farm workers. During the war years, some went to Northern cities to take better-paying factory jobs.

The wartime labor shortage also meant new job choices for women. Women replaced male workers in steel mills, ammunition factories, and assembly lines. Women served as streetcar conductors and elevator operators. The war created few permanent openings for women, but their presence in these jobs gave the public a wider view of their abilities. Women's contributions during the war helped them win the vote.

Reading **His**
D. Recognizir
Effects Wha**t**
groups gaine**d**
new jobs as a
result of the

Now *and* then

THE FLU EPIDEMIC

In 1918, flu victims often came down with pneumonia and died within a week. Today, bacterial infections such as pneumonia resulting from the flu can be controlled with antibiotics.

The 1998 discovery of the frozen remains of a 1918 flu victim in an Alaskan cemetery may one day lead to a better understanding of the virus. Scientists have found a genetic link between the 1918 flu virus and swine flu, a virus first found in pigs. The Alaskan find may help scientists develop vaccines to protect against future flu outbreaks.

The Flu Epidemic of 1918

Another result of the war was a deadly flu epidemic that swept the globe in 1918. It killed more than 20 million people on six continents by the time it disappeared in 1919. It had no known cure. Spread around the world by soldiers, the virus took some 500,000 American lives. People tried desperately to protect themselves. Everywhere, schools and other public places shut down to limit the flu's spread.

In the army, more than a quarter of the soldiers caught the disease. In some AEF units, one-third of the troops died. Germans fell victim in even larger numbers than the Allies. World War I brought death and disease to millions. It would also have longer-term effects, as you will read in Section 4.

Section **3** Assessment

1. Terms & Names

Explain the significance of:
- war bonds
- propaganda
- Espionage Act
- Sedition Act
- Oliver Wendell Holmes
- Great Migration

2. Using Graphics

Make a chart like the one below to show reasons for wartime shifts in population.

	Shift	Reason(s)
African Americans		
Mexicans		

How similar were the two groups' reasons for moving?

3. Main Ideas

a. What were three ways American families could contribute to the war effort?

b. What was the purpose of the Espionage and Sedition Acts? What groups were most affected by them?

c. What kinds of new job opportunities did the war create for women and minorities?

4. Critical Thinking

Making Inferences Wha**t** were the positive and the negative consequences of American wartime propaganda?

THINK ABOUT
- contributions to war eff**ort**
- effect on opponents of war and on German-Americans

ACTIVITY OPTIONS

SPEECH

MATH

Deliver a **radio broadcast** on the importance of conserving food, or make a **calculation** of the amount of food your class wastes monthly.

The Legacy of World War I

MAIN IDEA	WHY IT MATTERS NOW	TERMS & NAMES
war, Americans were ver foreign policy and issues.	The war affected the role the United States played in the world during the rest of the century.	League of Nations reparations Fourteen Points Red Scare Treaty of Versailles Palmer raids

ONE AMERICAN'S STORY

Senator Henry Cabot Lodge opposed President Wilson's idea that the United States join the **League of Nations**—an organization set up to settle conflicts through negotiation. Lodge felt that joining such an alliance would require the United States to guarantee the freedom of other nations.

Senator Henry Cabot Lodge (1850–1924) opposed U.S. entry into the League of Nations.

> *A VOICE FROM THE PAST*
>
> If we guarantee any country . . . its independence . . . we must [keep] at any cost . . . our word. . . . I wish [the American people] carefully to consider . . . whether they are willing to have the youth of America ordered to war by other nations.
>
> **Henry Cabot Lodge,** speech to the Senate, February 28, 1919

Lodge's speech helped turn the public against the League. In this section, you will learn how the United States and Europe adjusted to the end of the war.

Wilson's Fourteen Points

In January 1918, ten months before the war ended, President Wilson told Congress his goals for peace. His speech became known as the **Fourteen Points** (see page 699). It called for smaller military forces, an end to secret treaties, freedom of the seas, free trade, and changes in national boundaries. Most of these changes gave independence to peoples that Austria-Hungary or the Ottoman Empire had ruled.

For Wilson, the fourteenth point mattered most. He called for an association of nations to peacefully settle disputes. This association was to become the League of Nations, which Republicans like Lodge opposed. Wilson firmly believed that acceptance of his Fourteen Points by the warring parties would bring about what he called a "peace without victory."

Taking Notes

Use your chart to take notes about the effects of World War I.

EFFECTS ON THE WORLD

EFFECTS ON T UNITED STATE

World War I

Massachusetts. They claimed they were innocent, but both were found guilty and executed. Their trial attracted worldwide attention.

Racial Tensions Increase

Americans also saw a rise in racial tensions after the war. Between 1910 and 1920, the Great Migration brought a half million African Americans to Northern cities. In the cities where African Americans had settled in large numbers, whites and blacks competed for factory jobs and housing.

On July 2, 1917, tensions erupted into a race riot in East St. Louis, Illinois. The trouble began when blacks were brought in to take the jobs of white union members who had gone on strike. A shooting incident touched off a full-scale riot.

Reading **His**
D. Analyzing Causes How the war contribute to rac tensions?

Two years later, African-American soldiers returning from the war found their social plight unchanged. They had fought to make the world "safe for democracy." At home, though, they were still second-class citizens.

Simmering resentments over housing, job competition, and segregation exploded during the summer of 1919. In 25 cities around the country, race riots flared. In Chicago, a black man swimming in Lake Michigan drifted into the white section of a beach. Whites stoned him until he drowned. Thirteen days of rioting followed. Before it ended, 38 people were dead.

Longing for "Normalcy"

By the time campaigning began for the 1920 election, Americans felt drained. Labor strikes, race riots, the Red Scare, and the fight over the Treaty of Versailles and the League of Nations had worn them out. Voters were ready for a break. Republican candidate Warren G. Harding of Ohio offered them one. His promise to "return to normalcy" appealed to voters. Harding won a landslide victory. In the next chapter, you will learn about American life after his election.

Section **4** *Assessment*

1. Terms & Names

Explain the significance of:
- League of Nations
- Fourteen Points
- Treaty of Versailles
- reparations
- Red Scare
- Palmer raids

2. Using Graphics

Create a diagram to examine the war's effects on Europe and America.

Effects of World War I	
Europe	United States

Which effects were positive and which were negative?

3. Main Ideas

a. Why did Germany resent the Treaty of Versailles?

b. Why did Lodge and other Republicans oppose joining the League of Nations?

c. What caused the Red Scare? Who was most affected by it?

4. Critical Thinking

Analyzing Points of Vie
Why was Wilson unable to get other powers to accept his goals for the peace conference?

THINK ABOUT
- conflicting goals
- practicality of Wilson's a
- attitudes of other natio toward U.S. contribution during the war

---

ACTIVITY OPTIONS

LANGUAGE ARTS

ART

Imagine that you work for a newspaper. Write an **editorial** about the Palmer raids, or draw a political **cartoon** about the raids.

The Fourteen Points

ting the Stage Nine months after the United States entered World
I, President Wilson delivered to Congress a statement of war aims.
statement became known as the "Fourteen Points." In the speech,
ident Wilson set forth 14 proposals for reducing the risk of war
he future. Numbers have been inserted to help identify the
points, as well as those omitted. **See Primary Source Explorer**

the peoples of the world are in effect partners . . . , and for our own part
ee very clearly that unless justice be done to others it will not be done to
he program of the world's peace, therefore, is our program; and that pro-
, . . . as we see it, is this:

Open **covenants**[1] of peace, openly arrived at, after which there shall be
rivate international understandings of any kind but diplomacy shall pro-
always frankly and in the public view.

Absolute freedom of navigation upon the seas . . . in peace and in war. . . .

The removal, so far as possible, of all economic barriers and the estab-
ent of an equality of trade conditions among all the nations. . . .

Adequate guarantees given and taken that national **armaments**[2] will be
ced. . . .

A free, open-minded, and absolutely impartial adjustment of all colonial
s, based upon . . . the principle that . . . the interests of the populations
erned must have equal weight with the . . . claims of the government
se title is to be determined.

13: These eight points deal with specific boundary changes.]

] A general association of nations must be formed under specific
nants for the purpose of affording mutual guarantees of political inde-
ence and territorial **integrity**[3] to great and small states alike.

—*Woodrow Wilson*

A CLOSER LOOK

THE VALUE OF OPENNESS

The first of Wilson's points
attempts to solve one of the problems that caused the outbreak of
World War I—agreements between
nations arrived at in secret.

**1. How might agreements
arrived at in public prevent
another world war?**

A CLOSER LOOK

BALANCING CLAIMS

Wilson frequently appeals to fairness, balance, and impartiality in
settling competing claims.

**2. What might be unusual about
a leader such as Wilson calling
for an impartial adjustment of
colonial claims?**

A CLOSER LOOK

LEAGUE OF NATIONS

Wilson proposes that nations join
a formal organization to protect
one another.

**3. Why did Wilson believe that
such an organization would
benefit the world?**

renants: binding
eements.

2. **armaments:** weapons
and supplies of war.

3. **integrity:** the condition
of being whole or
undivided; completeness.

eractive Primary Source Assessment

Main Ideas

Why should diplomacy avoid private dealings and pro-
d in public view?

How might equality of trade be important to keeping
peace?

What must nations join together to guarantee?

2. Critical Thinking

Evaluating The first five points address issues that
Wilson believed had caused the war. How successful do
you think Wilson's ideas have been in the rest of the
20th century?

THINK ABOUT

• other conflicts since World War I
• peacekeeping efforts around the world

TERMS & NAMES

Briefly explain the significance of each of the following.

1. militarism
2. Allies
3. trench warfare
4. Zimmermann telegram
5. American Expeditionary Force
6. convoy system
7. propaganda
8. Great Migration
9. Treaty of Versailles
10. Red Scare

REVIEW QUESTIONS

War Breaks Out in Europe (pages 679–685)

1. What were the sources of tension between the European powers that led to war?
2. Why did the United States at first remain neutral in the war between the Allies and the Central Powers?
3. What brought the United States into the war on the Allied side?

America Joins the Fight (pages 686–690)

4. How did the Allies fight the German U-boat threat?
5. How did U.S. entry into the war affect the Allies?
6. What led Germany to agree to an armistice?

Life on the Home Front (pages 691–694)

7. How did U.S. civilians aid the war effort?
8. How did Congress contribute to increased prejudice and intolerance on the home front?

The Legacy of World War I (pages 695–699)

9. How did Wilson's goals for the peace conference differ from those of his European allies?
10. Why did the Senate reject the Treaty of Versailles?

CRITICAL THINKING

1. USING YOUR NOTES: RECOGNIZING EFFECTS

Using your chart, answer the questions below.

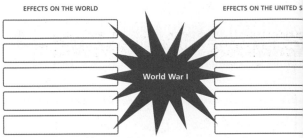

EFFECTS ON THE WORLD   EFFECTS ON THE UNITED S

World War I

a. Were the effects of the war greater in Europe or United States?
b. What political effects did the war have on the United States?
c. How did the war affect African-American civilian

2. APPLYING CITIZENSHIP SKILLS

Are limitations on freedom of speech justified by w Explain your opinion.

3. THEME: AMERICA IN THE WORLD

How did Wilson's view of the role the United State should play in world affairs compare with Theodor Roosevelt's view of America's role?

4. ANALYZING LEADERSHIP

Do you think Wilson's refusal to compromise to ge the Treaty of Versailles through Congress was a go decision? Why?

Interact *with* History

How accurately did you predict the ways in which American citizens might support the war effort?

VISUAL SUMMARY

World War I

USA

EUR

W

War Breaks Out in Europe

When the Allies and the Central Powers went to war in Europe, the United States reluctantly joined the Allies.

America Joins the Fight

Millions of U.S. soldiers and civilian volunteers went abroad and helped the Allies win the war.

Life on the Home Front

The war required Americans to sacrifice many things, even political freedoms. The war also brought new jobs.

The Legacy of World War I

The war broke up European empires and left lasting social changes in the United States.

Use the map and your knowledge of U.S. history to answer questions 1 and 2.

Additional Test Practice, pp. S1–S33.

Great Migration, 1910–1920

Northeast 201,000

Midwest 233,000

West Coast 16,000

← Movement of African Americans
201,000 Number of migrants

Source: *Historical Statistics of the United States*

1. How many African Americans migrated to the Northeast?
   A. 16,000
   B. 201,000
   C. 233,000
   D. 450,000

2. To which region did the fewest number of African Americans move?
   A. Northwest
   B. Northeast
   C. Midwest
   D. West Coast

This quotation from Senator Henry Cabot Lodge supports his opposition to the United States entering the League of Nations. Use the quotation and your knowledge of U.S. history to answer question 3.

PRIMARY SOURCE

If we guarantee any country . . . its independence . . . we must [keep] at any cost . . . our word. I wish [the American people] carefully to consider . . . whether they are willing to have the youth of America ordered to war by other nations.

Henry Cabot Lodge, speech to the Senate, February 28, 1919

3. What was Lodge's major opposition to U.S. entry into the League of Nations?
   A. The U.S. would have to pay the expenses.
   B. U.S. soldiers would have to fight foreign wars.
   C. The League of Nations would not be effective.
   D. Deals with a foreign country would lead to war.

TEST PRACTICE
CLASSZONE.COM

📝 **WRITING ABOUT HISTORY**

Write a **newspaper article** on the new technologies used in World War I. Choose one type of technology, such as airplanes, submarines, or tanks, and explain its use, advantages, and disadvantages.

- Look for and include primary sources from soldiers.
- Include a section on why you believe or do not believe that these new weapons are necessary.

COOPERATIVE LEARNING

Working in one of seven groups, research the conference that created the Treaty of Versailles. Your group will represent one of these nations: Germany, France, Britain, the United States, Italy, Japan, or Poland.

- Make a list of goals and issues you want discussed.
- Then choose a spokesperson to represent your group at a mock conference.

INTEGRATED TECHNOLOGY

DOING INTERNET RESEARCH

Research the posters that were used to influence public opinion during World War I. Use a search engine to find pictures of these posters on the Internet.

- View as many posters as possible.
- Print images of the two posters you find most interesting. Try to find some background information about the purpose and audience for each poster.
- Write your reactions to the posters including what actions you think the posters were trying to promote, how the posters made you feel, and how effective you think they were.

For more about World War I posters . . .

INTERNET ACTIVITY
CLASSZONE.COM

Campaign for Liberty Bonds

To rally Americans to support World War I, the government set up the Committee on Public Information (CPI). This agency called on creative individuals to join "the world's greatest adventure in advertising." Speakers gave patriotic speeches in theaters, hotels, and restaurants. Artists designed posters persuading Americans to buy Liberty Bonds. These loans to the government helped fund the war effort. Liberty Bonds were actually sold through four Liberty Loan drives in 1917 and 1918.

ACTIVITY Create a poster to help the government raise money for World War I. In addition, write and present a patriotic speech that wins public support of the war.

TOOLBOX

Each group will need:

poster board	drawing paper
colored markers	glue
pencils	scissors

STEP BY STEP

1 **Form an imaginary ad agency.** Meet with three o four other students to discuss you latest contract: The CPI has hired y agency to create a poster as part o nationwide campaign to sell Liber Bonds and promote World War I. Y group will:

- do research on Liberty Bonds
- design and create a poster advertising Liberty Bonds
- write and deliver a "pep talk" p suading people to buy Liberty Bo

2 **Research Liberty Bonds.** Look on the Internet, in t chapter, or in books about World V to find out more about Liberty Bo and to see actual posters. As you l over the posters, think about the ings the posters bring out. What images and words seem most pow or persuasive?

Posters such as this one appealed to patriotism and love of family to sell Liberty Bonds.

Choose a theme for your poster. Persuading people to buy Liberty Bonds means that you need to show that winning World [War] I is important. One way is to appeal to people's emotions. For example, the poster can appeal to their sense of fear, pride, or love of family.

Sketch out your idea. Write out a slogan and choose images based on the theme of your poster. Make sure your words and pictures communicate the same feeling and message. Draw an outline of the images and the letters. Then cut both the letters and images out. Be sure they're large enough to be seen from several yards away.

Create the poster. Decide where the art and writing will appear. Experiment with the arrangement of the art and the writing. Move them around. Do not overwhelm your viewers with too many images or too many words. Use vivid, patriotic colors for your poster.

Create a bulletin board display. [O]r tape your poster [to th]e wall, along with [the p]osters of the other [grou]ps. As you examine [the o]ther posters, com[pare] and contrast your [poste]r with the others.

[WR]ITE AND SPEAK

[Writ]e a patriotic speech. As a group, write a two-minute ["pep talk"] persuading people to buy Liberty Bonds and to sup[port] the soldiers fighting overseas. Include reasons why the war [is wo]rth fighting. Each group member should be prepared to [deliver] the speech, using the poster you made as a visual aid.

HELP DESK

For related information, see pages 691–692 in Chapter 24.

Researching Your Project
- *World War I* by Gail Stewart
- *Causes and Consequences of World War I* by Stewart Ross

For more about World War I . . .

RESEARCH LINKS
CLASSZONE.COM

Did You Know?
The CPI used about 75,000 lecturers. They gave around 755,190 speeches to about 300 million people in 5,000 towns.

Even children were moved by advertising slogans to help fund the war: "Lick a stamp and lick the kaiser." Children filled books with war stamps, each worth 25 cents. These stamps were then converted into government bonds.

Even President Wilson helped to raise money for the war effort. He sold wool from sheep raised on the White House lawn.

REFLECT & ASSESS
- **What aspects of your poster do you think will inspire people to buy Liberty Bonds?**
- **How well does your speech inspire patriotic feeling about the war?**
- **Which do you think is a more powerful means of persuasion—your poster or your speech?**

21st Century

1920 Warren G. Harding is elected president.	**1929** Stock market crash marks beginning of Great Depression.	**1932** Franklin D. Roosevelt is elected president.

1941
Japanese bomb Pearl Harbor, and U.S. enters World War II.

1945
Germany and Japan surrender, ending World War II.

USA World (1919)

1922
Benito Mussolini becomes prime minister of Italy.

1933
Adolf Hitler is appointed chancellor of Germany.

1937
Japan invades China.

1939
Germany invades Poland, setting off World War II.

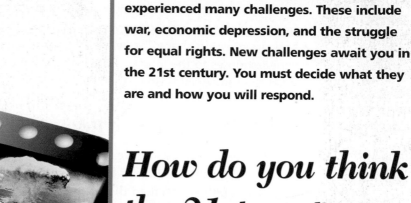

During the 20th century, the United States has experienced many challenges. These include war, economic depression, and the struggle for equal rights. New challenges await you in the 21st century. You must decide what they are and how you will respond.

How do you think the 21st century will differ from the 20th century?

What Do You Think?

- How will technology play a part in your life?
- What are your talents, and how could you use them to benefit yourself and society?

RESEARCH LINKS
CLASSZONE.COM
Visit the Chapter 6 links for more information about the American Revolution.

1972
President Nixon travels to China.

1980
Ronald Reagan is elected president.

2000
George W. Bush is elected president.

2001
The World Trade Center in New York City is attacked by terrorists.

present

1973
Arab nations and Israel fight in Yom Kippur War.

1989
Berlin Wall is torn down.

1991
The Soviet Union collapses.

Reading Strategy: Categorizing Information

What Do You know?

What do you think of when you hear the phrase "the Great Depression"? Who do you think fought in World War II? How can a war be a "Cold War"?

Think About
- what you've learned about any of these topics from movies, television, or travel
- how great events shape the lives of individuals
- your responses to the Interact with History about what the future holds (see page 705)

What Do You Want to Know?

 What questions do you have about great events of the 20th century? Record these questions in your notebook before you read the chapter.

In this political cartoon published in tl *Post* in the 1930s, Uncle Sam turns his

Categorizing Information

To help you make sense of what you read, learn to categorize. Categorizing means sorti information into groups. The chart below will help you to categorize the information in chapter. Use the chart to take notes on important political, economic, and social events selected decades of this century.

S See Skillbuilder Handbook, page R6.

Taking Notes

The 20th Century	Political Events	Economic Events	Social Events
1920–1939			
1940–1959			
1960–1979			
1980–1999			

Prosperity and the Great Depression

MAIN IDEA	WHY IT MATTERS NOW	TERMS & NAMES
ock market crash of 1929 and reat Depression led to Franklin osevelt's New Deal.	The New Deal increased the role of the federal government.	Warren G. Harding Great Depression Calvin Coolidge Franklin D. Roosevelt jazz New Deal Harlem Renaissance

ONE AMERICAN'S STORY

Louis Armstrong grew up in New Orleans. Armstrong often listened to jazz music played at funeral processions, dance halls, saloons, and lawn parties. He became a great jazz musician. In 1922, he accepted a job offer to play jazz with a Chicago band.

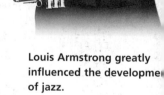

A VOICE FROM THE PAST

When I left New Orleans to go up North in 1922 the toughest Negro . . . his name is Slippers . . . he gave me a pep talk. . . . He loved the way I played those Blues. . . . When he found out that I was leaving to go to Chicago, he was the first one to congratulate me. . . . He said, "I love the way you blow that Quail." Of course he meant the cornet.

Louis Armstrong, quoted in *Louis: The Louis Armstrong Story*

Louis Armstrong greatly influenced the developme of jazz.

In this section, you will read about popular culture, the Harlem Renaissance, and the stock market crash of 1929.

The Roaring Twenties' Business Boom

By the start of the 1920s, Americans were turning away from progressive reforms. World War I was over. Americans were disappointed with the Treaty of Versailles. This, and the terrible human cost of the war, made them unwilling to fight "other people's wars." Now they wanted to help themselves. Americans were ready for a decade-long buying spree.

Earlier in the century, presidents like Roosevelt and Taft had sought to place tighter controls on business. Under presidents **Warren G. Harding** and **Calvin Coolidge,** the government put into practice pro-business policies. These policies made business growth easier and more profitable. President Coolidge came into office in 1923. He spoke for many when he said, "the chief business of the American people is business."

Taking Notes

Use your chart to take notes about events in the 1920s and 1930s.

The 20th Century	Political Events
1920–1930	
1940–1950	
1960–1970	
1980–1990	

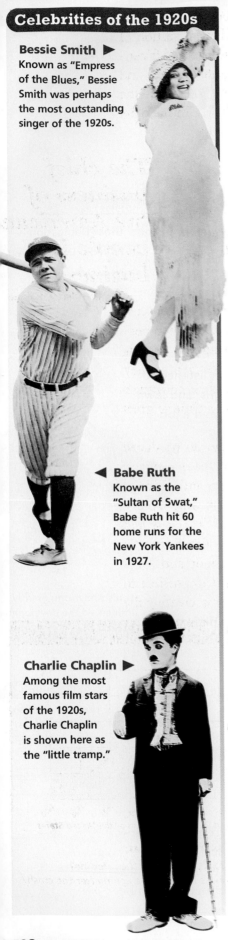

Giant business empires, such as the automobile industry, made the economy boom. Between 1920 and 1930, the number of cars in the United States almost tripled from about 8 million to 23 million. Car sales fueled demand for steel, oil, rubber, gasoline, and glass. Tourism thrived as more people took vacations by car. Improvements in methods of mass production made it possible to turn out products faster and more cheaply. As a result, prices fell for such goods as washing machines and refrigerators. At the same time, the nation's wealth grew. During the 1920s, the income of the average American rose by almost 40 percent. People had both more money to spend and more goods to buy.

The Rise of Popular Entertainment

After the sacrifices of World War I, Americans wanted to enjoy themselves. Radio, movies, and sports gained in popularity. Big-city dwellers flocked to nightclubs where they learned hot new dances like the Charleston and the shimmy. The 1920s also introduced more Americans to a musical form called **jazz.** The new jazz music sprang up in cities such as New Orleans and Chicago. It blended African and European musical traditions. Trumpeter Louis Armstrong and composer and bandleader Duke Ellington drew crowds to jazz clubs and speakeasies. Singer Bessie Smith, known as "Empress of the Blues," thrilled audiences wherever she performed.

Audiences for movies grew throughout the decade. Even small towns had a movie theater. In 1922, people bought tickets to see such stars as Clara Bow and Charlie Chaplin on the silent screen. In 1925, Chaplin charmed audiences with his portrayal of the "little tramp" in silent films such as *The Gold Rush.* Two years later, Al Jolson's *The Jazz Singer* became the first talking picture. By the end of the decade, more than 100 million people a year were packing movie theaters for talking pictures.

The growing popularity of radio helped put sports in the spotlight. Radio spread the fame of such teams as the New York Yankees and the Chicago Cubs. It made national heroes out of sports figures like Babe Ruth, who was baseball's home-run king. Baseball, boxing, and football all gained wider audiences.

In literature, such writers as Ernest Hemingway, F. Scott Fitzgerald, and Edna St. Vincent Millay were

Vocabular
speakeasie
places for i
sale and co
sumption o
alcoholic d
during the

able to capture the feelings of disillusionment and rebellion that some young people felt at the end of World War I. In the Harlem section of New York City, the 1920s were a time of great creativity for African-American artists. Writers such as Langston Hughes, Countée Cullen, and Zora Neale Hurston belonged to the cultural movement known as the **Harlem Renaissance.** Hughes used jazz rhythms and dialect in his writings to celebrate black urban life and to call for social change.

Stock Market Crash and Great Depression

During the 1920s, the stock market soared. Ordinary people saw buying stocks as a safe, quick way to get rich. Many ordinary people invested their life savings. Most did not understand the risks of investing. Many investors even borrowed money to buy shares. Then, in October 1929, the stock market crashed.

"The chief business of the American people is business."

President Coolidge

ground
ock market
ame on
er 29, 1929.
t day, the
of stocks
amatically.

ngHistory
lyzing
   Why did
anks shut
during the
sion?

The crash sparked a chain reaction. First, banks demanded that customers pay back the money they had borrowed to buy stock. When people could not repay these loans, the banks ran short of money. Fearing that banks would close, customers lined up to withdraw their money. Since banks rarely keep enough cash on hand to pay all their customers at once, many banks shut down. The **Great Depression,** a time of great economic hardship, had begun.

As banks failed or cut back on loans to businesses, factories produced fewer goods and therefore laid off workers. With more people out of work, spending declined. Businesses let more workers go and factories closed. By 1932, almost one-fourth of the nation's workers were jobless.

Everywhere, sales of farm products fell sharply. In the Midwest and Great Plains, farmers not only faced economic losses but also suffered a terrible drought that lasted for years. Poor farming methods and over-farming of the land led to massive soil erosion, making it impossible to grow crops. Winds carried away dry soil over millions of acres, creating the Dust Bowl. Thousands were forced to abandon their farms and leave the Great Plains.

Republican President Herbert Hoover took office early in 1929. When the stock market crashed in October 1929, he urged Americans to be patient. He warned that government programs would only make things worse. Relief, or government

ngHistory
narizing
vas
's attitude
govern-
tion?

aid to the hungry and homeless, would make Americans dependent on government handouts. In the 1932 election, they voted for a leader who promised another way.

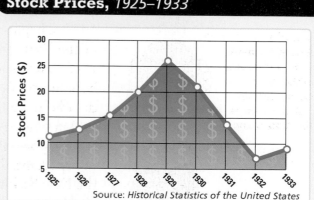

Stock Prices, 1925–1933

Stock Prices ($)

Source: *Historical Statistics of the United States*

SKILLBUILDER Interpreting Charts
1. *In what year did stock prices begin their decline?*
2. *In what year did prices begin to rise again after the crash?*

The Federal Arts Project was part of the New Deal. It commissioned murals for post offices and other public buildings. This mural, titled *Construction of a Dam,* was painted by William Gropper (1897–1977). It was painted in the Department of the Interior building in Washington, D.C.

What does the painting reveal about the value of work in a time of both economic depression and unemployment?

Roosevelt's New Deal

When Democrat <u>Franklin D. Roosevelt,</u> also known as FDR, took over as president, millions of families lacked food or shelter. People searched in garbage dumps for food or stood for hours in long lines for soup. Former business executives sold apples on streetcorners. Blaming Hoover for the hard times, the homeless called their camps consisting of tin-and-cardboard shacks "Hoovervilles." Roosevelt set out to restore hope and confidence both in government and in the American economy. His inaugural address expressed his optimism.

> **A VOICE FROM THE PAST**
>
> This great nation will endure as it has endured, will revive and will prosper. So, first of all, let me assert my firm belief that the only thing we have to fear is fear itself.
>
> **Franklin D. Roosevelt,** First Inaugural Address, March 4, 1933

Roosevelt promised immediate action, and he kept his word. His first target was the bank crisis. Calling for a "bank holiday," he ordered a brief shutdown of all banks. Federal officials went to work examining bank records. They decided which ones could reopen at once and which needed government help to do so. FDR's confidence persuaded Americans to put their money back into the banks.

With the public and Congress firmly supporting him, Roosevelt began a bold new program to end the Great Depression. It was called the <u>New Deal.</u> During a period known as the "Hundred Days," Congress passed with little debate almost all the bills the White House sent over. Even Republican lawmakers admired FDR's decisiveness.

Roosevelt's New Deal had three major goals, known as the "three R's":

1. **Relief programs** to help the hungry and jobless
2. **Recovery programs** to help agriculture and industry
3. **Reform of the economy** to ensure that a crisis like the Great Depression did not happen again

Not all of FDR's policies worked, and many angered business leaders because they led to higher taxes. Still, most Americans believed his policies were effective, and they reelected him to office in 1936.

Lasting New Deal Changes

The New Deal made lasting changes in American society and government. It increased the power of the federal government. It encouraged presidents and Congress to practice deficit spending during economic hard times. This means spending more money than the government raises in taxes. Many New Deal programs were financed by deficit spending. The New Deal created Social Security, unemployment insurance, and other federal programs to care for the elderly, jobless, and needy. Roosevelt believed in using the power of government to help those in need. Government-supported social programs were the centerpiece of the New Deal.

Full economic prosperity did not return until the United States entered World War II in 1941. Even so, the New Deal restored Americans' faith in democracy. In the decade ahead, Americans put their lives on the line to preserve democracy abroad.

*ing*History

nmarizing
were some
accom-
ents of the
Deal?

**AMERICA'S
HISTORY MAKERS**

FRANKLIN DELANO ROOSEVELT
1882–1945
A distant cousin of Theodore Roosevelt, Franklin D. Roosevelt became a New York state senator when he was 29. Later, he served as assistant secretary of the navy.

At the age of 39, FDR caught polio. For the rest of his life, he walked with braces or rode in a wheelchair (see below). Despite this, he continued in politics and was elected New York governor in 1928.

The public rarely saw photos revealing FDR's disability. Even so, many Americans sensed that he understood trouble. This quality helped him as a leader during the Depression.

How would an understanding of trouble help FDR to lead?

Terms & Names

plain the gnificance of:

Warren G. Harding
alvin Coolidge
zz
arlem Renaissance
reat Depression
ranklin D. Roosevelt
ew Deal

2. Using Graphics

Fill in the diagram with some causes of the Depression.

Which cause was most important? Why?

3. Main Ideas

a. How did the boom times of the 1920s lead to the stock market crash?

b. What happened to farm prices during the Great Depression?

c. What were the three goals of FDR's New Deal?

4. Critical Thinking

Making Inferences Why might the Great Depression have caused people to consider changes in the role of government?

THINK ABOUT
• aims of democracy
• fears sparked by the Depression
• attitudes toward government

Truman's anti-Soviet policy was called **containment**. It sought to contain, or stop, the Soviet Union from gaining influence outside its borders. Containment became the foundation of American foreign policy.

The Marshall Plan and the North Atlantic Treaty Organization (NATO) were key elements of containment. The Marshall Plan helped pay for Western and Southern Europe's recovery. Under the NATO agreement, Western allies formed a defense pact. The members pledged to protect one another in case of attack. The Soviet Union and its allies formed the Warsaw Pact.

The Korean War and McCarthyism

In 1949, the Communists led by Mao Zedong took power in China. In 1950, troops from Communist North Korea, supplied by the Soviet Union, invaded American-backed South Korea. U.S. troops made up most of a UN force commanded by General Douglas MacArthur. The UN force drove the North Koreans out of the South and back into North Korea.

Fighting continued after General Dwight D. Eisenhower became the new U.S. president in 1953. He soon arranged a truce that ended the three-year war. The national boundaries of the two Koreas had changed very little. However, the United States had shown that the free world would fight Communist aggression.

In the postwar United States, public fears of communism allowed Senator Joseph McCarthy of Wisconsin to gain great power. He claimed that hundreds of government workers were Communists or Communist supporters. His hunt for Communists ruined many lives. A new word—McCarthyism—described the use of unproven charges against opponents and innocent citizens. By 1954, however, the public had turned away in disgust from McCarthy. His power quickly faded.

Nuclear Threat and Superpower Conflicts

In 1945, the United States had dropped two atomic bombs on Japan to end World War II. Four years later, the Soviets built their own atomic bomb. A deadly arms race had begun. Both superpowers stockpiled nuclear weapons. By the end of the decade, both sides were developing missiles to carry bombs to each other's doorsteps.

Neither superpower wanted to risk an all-out war. Instead, they pursued their rivalry indirectly by supporting opposite sides in conflicts in the Third World. These were the poorer nations of Latin America, Asia, and Africa. One such conflict brought the superpowers to the brink of war. In Cuba, Fidel Castro led a revolution that brought a Communist government to power in 1959. Attempts by the United States to topple Castro failed.

This photograph shows a Soviet ship thought to be carrying nuclear missiles to Cuba.

Then, in 1962, President **John F. Kennedy** learned that the Soviets were supplying Cuba with missiles. U.S. navy ships blockaded the island. The threat of nuclear war seemed very real. The world waited to see if the Soviets would remove all missiles and missile bases from Cuba. Finally, the Soviet Union agreed to remove them.

By the 1960s, the superpowers were in a space race as well as an arms race. Americans were stunned in 1957 when the Soviets sent *Sputnik,* a man-made satellite, into orbit around the earth. Alarm deepened as a Soviet cosmonaut took the first manned space flight. Throughout the 1960s, the two nations raced to see who would be first to put a person on the moon. Americans cheered as Neil Armstrong and Buzz Aldrin made the first lunar landing in 1969.

In 1963, Kennedy was assassinated in Dallas, Texas. Kennedy's vice-president, **Lyndon B. Johnson,** succeeded him as president. Under Johnson, the United States became more deeply involved in conflict in the Southeast Asian countries of North and South Vietnam.

The U.S. flag is planted on the surface of the moon in July 1969.

War in Vietnam

In 1954, Vietnam was divided in two. The Communists controlled North Vietnam and the non-Communists controlled South Vietnam. The **Vietnam War** began in 1957 when Communist forces rebelled against the South Vietnamese government. American presidents Eisenhower, Kennedy, and Johnson all feared a Communist victory in South Vietnam. Experts argued that if South Vietnam fell to the Communists, other Southeast Asian nations would soon fall.

By 1968, more than 500,000 American troops were serving in Vietnam. U.S. planes dropped thousands of tons of bombs on North Vietnam. The large, well-equipped U.S. military faced a disciplined North Vietnamese force. Communist soldiers used hit-and-run guerrilla tactics. They sometimes relied on civilians for shelter and supplies. American soldiers won many battles, but they were stuck in an unwinnable war.

By 1968, the war had divided the United States. Strong criticism of Johnson's Vietnam policy contributed to his decision not to run for reelection. **Richard M. Nixon,** who was elected president in 1968, pledged to end the war. Over the next four years, he expanded the air war into neighboring Cambodia and Laos. At the same time, Nixon withdrew U.S. ground troops from South Vietnam. A 1973 ceasefire brought American troops home. Two years later, South Vietnam fell to the Communists. In 1976, the two Vietnams were united under Communist rule.

ing **History**
nmarizing
are some
oles of
oower
·?

ground
lea that if
ation fell to
ommunists,
s would
follow, was
the
ino theory."

daily *life*

THE "TELEVISION WAR"
The Vietnam War was the first "television war," broadcast each night on the evening news. Reports rarely showed actual battles, partly because much of the fighting occurred off and on and at night between small units.

Networks also tried to avoid gruesome scenes because they did not want to offend viewers. In addition, the networks agreed not to show any American dead or wounded so that their families would not recognize them on screen. Still, the images of war shocked viewers.

CAUSE AND EFFECT: The Cold War, 1945–1991

CAUSES		IMMEDIATE EFFECTS	LONG-TERM EFFE(...
Soviet domination of Eastern Europe	THE COLD WAR	Truman Doctrine and Marshall Plan	Arms race between United States and Soviet Union
Communist victory in China		East-West tension	Rivalry between United States and Soviet Union for world power
Distrust between United States and Soviet Union		Founding of NATO and Warsaw Pact	

SKILLBUILDER Interpreting Charts

1. *Which of the causes was not centered in Europe?*
2. *Which alliance was founded by the Soviet Union and its allies?*

Nixon as President

In the early 1970s, President Nixon took steps to improve relations with the Soviet Union and Communist China. In 1972, Nixon visited China. He reopened direct communication between the two nations after a 21-year break. After Nixon's visit to the Soviet Union, the superpowers signed an agreement limiting nuclear arms.

The **Watergate scandal** took up much of Nixon's second term as president. People who worked for Nixon carried out illegal activities. These included wiretapping telephones and breaking into the Democratic Party headquarters in the Watergate building in Washington, D.C. An investigation showed that Nixon had ordered his staff to cover up White House involvement in these crimes.

In 1974, a congressional committee wanted to impeach Nixon. Rather than face impeachment, Nixon resigned. He became the only U.S. president to do so. Gerald Ford succeeded Nixon as president and eventually pardoned him.

Foreign Policy of the 1970s and 1980s

Jimmy Carter won the 1976 presidential election, defeating Gerald Ford. He made human rights a cornerstone of his foreign policy. In 1977, Carter signed a treaty to turn the Panama Canal over to Panama in 2000. Carter also negotiated the Camp David Accords—a peace agreement between Egypt and Israel.

In 1979, the Soviet Union invaded Afghanistan to prop up a pro-Communist government. Ronald Reagan, who became president in 1980, took a tough stance toward the Soviet Union. Reagan increased U.S. defense spending and pledged to oppose communism in Central America. For several years, U.S.-Soviet relations became more tense.

By the late 1980s, however, U.S.-Soviet relations improved. A new Soviet leader, Mikhail Gorbachev, tried to reform the Soviet government and economy. Reagan and Gorbachev signed treaties agreeing to destroy some of their own nations' nuclear weapons.

Reading **Hi**
C. Summari
What were
Reagan's pc
toward the
Union?

Meanwhile, many people in Communist nations wanted more freedom. They overthrew Communist rulers and formed democratic governments. In 1991, Communist leaders also lost power in the Soviet Union. The country split into independent states. Russia remained the largest of these states. The collapse of the Soviet Union ended the Cold War.

New Threats to the United States

As the Soviet Union fell apart, the United States stood as the world's only superpower. But major issues still challenged the nation. In 1990, Iraq invaded Kuwait. President George H. W. Bush organized a coalition of nations to drive Iraq out of Kuwait. In 1991, the coalition defeated Iraq in the Persian Gulf War and freed Kuwait of Iraqi control.

Then, in 2001, Americans faced a more direct threat. On September 11, 2001, terrorists hijacked commercial airplanes and crashed them into the World Trade Center in New York City, the Pentagon, and in a Pennsylvania field. Within hours, both World Trade Center towers collapsed. In these attacks, nearly 3,000 people died.

President George W. Bush (George H. W. Bush's son) began a war against terrorism. In October 2001, the United States led a coalition attack on Afghanistan. The goal of the attack on Afghanistan was to break up the al-Qaeda terrorist network believed responsible for the September 11 attacks. And in March 2003, U.S. and British forces invaded Iraq. The goal of the war in Iraq was to prevent Iraq from supplying terrorists with weapons of mass destruction (WDM). (For more information on terrorism and the war in Iraq, see pages 732-737.)

Smoke billows from the World Trade Center buildings after the terrorist attack of September 11, 2001.

---

tion **3** *Assessment*

Terms & Names

plain the ignificance of:
Harry S. Truman
Cold War
ontainment
ohn F. Kennedy
yndon B. Johnson
Vietnam War
ichard M. Nixon
Watergate scandal

2. Using Graphics

Use a diagram to summarize America's Cold War policy.

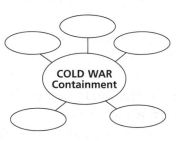

COLD WAR Containment

3. Main Ideas

a. How did the goals of the Soviet Union and the United States for Eastern Europe differ after World War II?

b. What were the space race and the arms race?

c. How did the breakup of the Soviet Union change U.S.-Soviet relations?

4. Critical Thinking

Comparing How were the Korean War and the Vietnam War similar and different?

THINK ABOUT
• American goals
• those who fought on each side
• the outcome of each struggle

IVITY OPTIONS

SPEECH

SCIENCE

Give an **oral presentation** on one scientific challenge of landing on the moon or create a **diagram** of the lunar module.

Life in America Since 1945

④

MAIN IDEA	WHY IT MATTERS NOW	TERMS & NAMES
Since World War II, civil rights, economic growth, and social change have dominated American life.	Prosperity, equality, and rapid change will remain important issues in the 21st century.	baby boom Dr. Martin Luther King, Jr.

Great Sc
counterc

ONE AMERICAN'S STORY

When World War II ended, Americans were eager to return to normal life. Newlyweds and young families were looking for a way out of crowded city apartments. Builder William J. Levitt had the answer. He built cheap houses using assembly-line methods. On New York's Long Island, Levitt built more than 17,000 homes in Levittown. It was America's first suburban housing development. Levitt liked to brag that his home building was helping to win the war against Communism. "No man who owns his own house and lot," he said, "can be a Communist. He has too much to do." As you will read, in the 1950s a home in the suburbs became a part of the American dream.

William J. L
builder of L
shown abov
aerial view

Taking Notes

se your chart to
ke notes about
ents in America
fter World War II.

20th Century	Political Events
~1930	
~1950	
~1970	
~1990	

Economic Boom and Baby Boom

After World War II, the U.S. economy boomed. The GI Bill offered returning soldiers schooling and job training. The Veterans Administration provided low-interest mortgages to home buyers. Rising demand for homes made possible the rapid growth of the suburbs. Other home builders were soon copying the building methods pioneered by Levitt. Car sales soared, too. Suburban families needed cars. They drove to work, to shopping centers, to movie theaters, and to restaurants.

During the late 1940s and the 1950s, the population grew rapidly. Americans were having more children, a trend known as the **baby boom.** Many people moved from the cities to the suburbs. They also moved from the Northeast to the sunbelt—the states of the South and the Southwest.

As Americans earned more, they spent more. Television appeared in almost every home. Americans eagerly bought the cars, electrical appliances, and other goods advertised on television and in magazines.

Not all Americans shared in the new prosperity, however. In the 1950s, African Americans and other minorities continued to face discrimination, as did working women. In rural areas and inner cities, many people struggled to survive.

The Civil Rights Movement

In the 1950s, reformers began to win legal victories to end segregation in the South. In 1954, in *Brown* v. *Board of Education of Topeka*, the Supreme Court ruled that segregated public schools were illegal. Two years later, after a black-led boycott of the Montgomery, Alabama, bus system, the Court ruled that segregated public transportation was against the law.

By the early 1960s, a young minister named **Dr. Martin Luther King, Jr.,** led a strong civil rights movement. Despite attacks by whites, the movement for equal rights remained largely nonviolent. At the 1963 March on Washington, King inspired more than 200,000 supporters with his words.

> *A VOICE FROM THE PAST*
>
> I have a dream that my four little children will one day live in a nation where they will not be judged by the color of their skin but by the content of their character. I have a dream today.
>
> **Martin Luther King, Jr., "I Have a Dream," August 28, 1963**

In 1964, President Johnson pushed a Civil Rights Act through Congress. It banned discrimination in employment and voter registration. It also banned discrimination in public places such as restaurants, motels, and gas stations. Four years later, the Fair Housing Act outlawed discrimination in housing. Many of these changes were inspired by the leadership of Dr. King. King's assassination in Memphis, Tennessee, on April 4, 1968, stunned the nation.

Laws now guarantee African Americans and other minority groups equal treatment. With a growing number of African Americans elected to local, state, and federal offices, they have a greater voice in government.

The Great Society

In 1964, President Lyndon B. Johnson convinced Congress to fund his War on Poverty. This effort created many government and private agencies to fight poverty. Some agencies provided job training. Others sent volunteers to teach in poor rural communities and rundown urban neighborhoods. Some programs funded part-time jobs for needy college students. Others offered preschool classes to give poor children a head

AMERICA'S HISTORY MAKERS

DR. MARTIN LUTHER KING, JR.
1929–1968

Dr. King (shown below) became leader of the Montgomery bus boycott. Fresh out of school, he had been in Montgomery about a year. But his courage and eloquence made him the perfect person to lead the movement.

King learned about nonviolence by studying religious writers and thinkers. He came to believe that only love could convert people to the side of justice. He described the power of nonviolent resisters: "We will soon wear you down by our capacity to suffer. So in winning . . . freedom . . . you will be changed also."

How might King's beliefs have supported his leadership of a nonviolent protest?

start on learning. In 1965, Johnson got Congress to set aside millions for health care for poor, elderly, and disabled people. These health-care programs were called Medicare and Medicaid.

Reducing poverty, extending civil rights, and expanding medical care were all parts of Johnson's plan for a better America. He called it the **Great Society**. Like FDR's New Deal, the Great Society reflected Johnson's belief that government can improve people's lives. Johnson's social programs were costly. However, they attempted to reduce the poverty rate during the 1960s. As the U.S. role in the Vietnam War grew, though, fewer dollars were directed to Great Society programs.

Rights for All

In the 1960s, minorities and women struggled for equal rights. Native Americans turned to the courts to fight for their land rights. They held protests highlighting the federal government's failure to honor treaties. One of the most outspoken Native American groups was the American Indian Movement (AIM).

In the early 1960s, César Chávez began organizing poorly paid Mexican-American farm workers in California. He led a five-year-long strike by grape pickers. Then Chávez formed the nation's first successful union of farm workers. It later became the United Farm Workers of America. Chávez's success inspired other Mexican Americans to work for change. In 1969–1970, they formed La Raza Unida—"the united people." This group worked to improve the lives of Mexican Americans and others.

In 1963, Betty Friedan wrote a best-selling book called *The Feminine Mystique*. This book led many women to rethink their roles. In 1966, Friedan and other activists founded the National Organization for Women (NOW). NOW and other women's groups such as Working Women and The American Association of University Women have worked to change laws that discriminate against women. They have helped to reform property rights and hiring. They continue working for equal pay and fair treatment in the workplace.

César Chávez organized the United Farm Workers of America during the 1960s.

Reading **His**
B. Comparing
and Contrast
What was sir
and differen
about the st
gles of vario
groups for th
rights?

Youth Protests and the Counterculture

No controversy was more heated than that over the Vietnam War. Opponents of the war argued that it was a civil war between Communists and non-Communists for control of Vietnam. They stated that the United States had no right to interfere. The war's supporters considered these opponents to be traitors who were undermining the war effort. Antiwar protests brought millions of Americans into the streets. Shouting matches and flag burnings followed. Some protests turned violent. Antiwar activists clashed with supporters of the war. At Ohio's Kent State University in 1970, National Guardsmen fired their weapons and killed four students.

Vietnam widened the gap between younger and older Americans. Differences in beliefs and values between generations eventually gave rise to the **counterculture.** These were groups of people seeking new ways of living. One of the central values for members of the counterculture was a concern for the environment. Environmentalists sought to protect the environment by fighting pollution of the country's natural resources. Some younger Americans had different values from those of the mainstream. "Hippies" emphasized the importance of love and freedom. They celebrated at music festivals such as the one at Woodstock, New York, in 1969. Critics such as President Nixon charged that hippies and antiwar protesters were tearing the nation apart. Many critics spoke out against the way young people questioned American values. Despite such concerns, in 1971 the Twenty-Sixth Amendment lowered the voting age to 18.

Protesters march in 1969 in opposition to the war in Vietnam.

Reagan, Bush, and Conservatism

Throughout the 1960s and 1970s, Democratic presidents such as Jimmy Carter had favored a strong role for government in the economy. They favored regulation of big business, support for organized labor, and public spending on the poor.

Ronald Reagan, a former movie actor and governor of California, was elected president in 1980, defeating Jimmy Carter. Reagan, a conservative Republican, wanted to reduce the role of government in American life. He sharply cut taxes and slashed spending on social programs for the poor. At the same time, he greatly increased military spending.

The tax cuts, coupled with heavy defense spending, caused the national debt to skyrocket. The government was borrowing more money to pay for spending than it was taking in through taxes. As a result, the national debt doubled in size from 1981 through 1986.

Reagan pushed pro-business economic policies. He abolished thousands of government regulations on business. After a recession in 1982, the economy sharply improved. A new wealthy class of young people emerged, whom reporters labeled "yuppies" (from "young urban professionals").

Reagan's successor, George Bush, shared his conservative outlook. In the early 1990s, after his successful management of the Persian Gulf War, Bush's popularity surged. However, when the country headed into a recession, Bush's approval ratings fell sharply. The causes of the weak economy included the nation's growing national debt, rising oil prices as a result of the Persian Gulf War, and shrinking factory production. In 1992, Bush lost his reelection bid to Democrat Bill Clinton, the governor of Arkansas.

ding **History**
mmarizing
are some
ples of how
an limited
le of gov-
ent in eco-
c affairs?

RE-ELECT
1984
REAGAN ★ BUSH

The Clinton Presidency

During his first term, Bill Clinton focused on domestic issues. To reduce the deficit, he supported tax increases and spending cuts. To fight crime, he pushed gun-control laws through Congress.

In 1994, the Democrats lost control of Congress to the Republicans. The new Congress pushed for deeper cuts in taxes and social programs than Clinton would support. A compromise led to deep cuts in some government social programs but protected some spending for education, welfare, and health care programs for the needy. The nation's strong economy helped Clinton win reelection in 1996.

Clinton's second term in office was marred by scandal. An investigation into Clinton's finances revealed that he had had an improper relationship with a White House intern. And he allegedly had lied about it under oath. The charges led to his impeachment in 1998. The Senate opened its trial of President Clinton in January 1999. Nearly a month later, the Senate acquitted him and Clinton remained in office.

(From left) Presidents Clinton, Bush, Reagan, Carter, and Ford at the funeral for President Nixon on April 27, 1994.

Reading **His**
D. Contrastin
What effect
the economy
have on the
tions of 1992
and 1996?

The Bush Presidency

In 2000, the nation held a presidential election to choose Clinton's successor. The Democrats nominated Vice-President Al Gore as their candidate. The Republicans chose Texas governor George W. Bush, the son of the former president.

The 2000 election was one of the closest in U.S. history. By the morning after Election Day, Gore held a narrow lead in the popular vote. However, he did not have enough electoral votes to claim the presidency. Bush led in Florida by a few hundred votes, which promised to give him enough electoral votes to win the election. For five weeks, the two campaigns fought legal battles over recounts of the Florida ballots. Finally, on December 12, the U.S. Supreme Court voted 5 to 4 to stop the recounts, ensuring that Bush would win the presidency.

Political opinion remained deeply divided through Bush's first term. While Bush's antiterrorism policies initially gained wide support, many Americans began to question his handling of the invasion of Iraq. In 2004, Massachusetts senator John Kerry challenged Bush. After both sides waged one of the most expensive campaigns in history, Bush was able to win a majority of the popular vote, but once again the electoral vote came down to one state. In Ohio, Bush held a lead of more than 130,000 votes, which would give him the state's 20 electoral votes and the presidency. After deciding that the uncounted absentee and paper ballots would not be enough to take the lead, Kerry conceded the race to Bush the day after the election.

Immigrants and the New Millennium

From 1981 to 1996, nearly 13.5 million legal immigrants came to the United States. These new immigrants increased U.S. diversity. Most of the immigrants who arrived in America during earlier periods had come from Europe. Nearly 85 percent of the most recent arrivals came from Latin America or Asia. The Census Bureau predicts that by 2020 the U.S. Hispanic population will increase from 12.5 percent to 17 percent. At the same time, the Asian population is expected to climb from 3.6 percent to nearly 6 percent.

While immigrants bring their culture to America, they also have embraced many American traditions. Most wear American clothes, adopt American customs, and learn English. Furthermore, they share with other Americans a belief in democracy and freedom.

Citizens of all races and backgrounds will play a vital role in shaping America. So will today's students. You have a part to play in helping the United States embrace people from every culture and land. You are the generation that will create the America of the future.

The American People

Origins of Immigrants, 1981–1996	Numbers of Immigrants*
1. Mexico	3,300,000
2. Philippines	840,000
3. China°	730,000
4. Vietnam	720,000
5. Dominican Republic	510,000
6. India	500,000
7. Korea	450,000
8. Soviet Union†	420,000
9. El Salvador	360,000
10. Jamaica	320,000

* Numbers rounded to nearest 10,000.
° China includes Taiwan.
† The Soviet Union broke apart in 1991. This figure includes the former Soviet republics.

Source: *U.S. Bureau of the Census*

SKILLBUILDER Interpreting Charts

1. *From which European countries were there still substantial numbers of immigrants in the 1980s and 1990s?*
2. *From what regions of the world do most recent immigrants come?*

Section 4 Assessment

1. Terms & Names

Explain the significance of:
- baby boom
- Dr. Martin Luther King, Jr.
- Great Society
- counterculture

2. Using Graphics

Use the chart to examine the aims of groups that protested in the 1960s.

	Goal	Success
African Americans		
Mexican Americans		
Native Americans		
Women		

3. Main Ideas

a. How did the civil rights movement of the 1960s lessen discrimination against African Americans?

b. What were the goals of President Johnson's Great Society programs?

c. How did Reagan attempt to reduce the role of government in American life?

4. Critical Thinking

Supporting Opinions Do any youth countercultures exist today? Why or why not?

THINK ABOUT
- music and the arts
- politics
- religion
- values

ACTIVITY OPTIONS

LANGUAGE ARTS

MATH

Find out about voters' attitudes toward politicians. Create a survey, conduct a poll, and either write a **report** or display your results in a **graph**.

Protecting the Environment

The nation has made great strides over the past several decades in taking better care of the environment. However, much work remains to be done. As the United States embarks on a new century, the country continues to face such controversial issues as global warming and the problems of water pollution and a growing amount of waste.

COOPERATIVE LEARNING You have recently joined a local organization whose goal is to find solutions to the environmental challenges that affect your community. On these pages are three challenges you face as a member of the organization. Working with a small group, decide how to deal with each challenge. Choose an option, assign a task to each group member, and do the activity. You will find useful information in the Data File. Present your solutions to the class.

ECONOMICS CHALLENGE

"from a feel-good issue to a bottom-line issue"

growing number of businesses have begun aking steps to curb the amount of trash they roduce. These companies have found that caling back on waste helps to save money. ow can you convince businesses in your ommunity to follow this trend? Use the ata File for help. Use one of these options:

Create an economic report showing companies ways they can cut back on waste while saving money.

Write a proposal outlining further ways companies can reduce waste.

ART CHALLENGE

"very troubled wate

In the decades after the Clean Water of 1972, many U.S. rivers became cle Recently, however, the government had to name more waterways as uns able for fishing or swimming.

The main pollutants include pesticid sewage runoff from large farms, run from city and suburban sewer system and chemical waste from mining. Ho can you alert people in your commu to these problems? Use the Data File help. Present your information using of these options:

• Design a poster showing one or m types of pollutants reaching a rive

• Create a graphic for town officials depicts the Data File information a contaminated rivers.

MATH CHALLENGE

"the seas would rise . . . and whole forest types could disappear"

lobal warming remains a pressing environmental problem. Many **ientists** believe that air pollutants create a ceiling that traps **eat** near the earth's surface. Foremost among the pollutants is **arbon dioxide**—which is generated by factories, automobiles, **nd** common household appliances. Encourage families to cut **ack** on their carbon dioxide output. Use the Data File for help. **resent** your information using one of these options:

Make a graph showing the yearly carbon dioxide output of **various** household items.

Write a report detailing ways in which a family could reduce **its** carbon dioxide output by 25 percent.

"Gentlemen, it's time we gave some serious thought to the effects of global warming."

ACTIVITY WRAP-UP

resent to the Class Meet as a group to review your responses to **various** environmental challenges. Pick the most creative solution **or** each challenge and present these solutions to the class.

Global Warming

Average U.S. Household's Yearly Output of Carbon Dioxide (in pounds):

Human respiration (2-6 persons)—1,950
Television—510
Range—933
Dishwasher—1,038
Lighting—1,045
Refrigerator—1,136
Dryer—1,177
Washer—1,199
Oil-fired water heater—4,476
Oil-fired space heater—12,958
Car—20,956

What's in Our Dirty Rivers

From a 1998 study: 36 percent of U.S. rivers are contaminated. Percentage of contaminated rivers affected by the following pollutants:

- Toxic chemicals—9%
- Waste and chemicals from mining—13%
- City/suburban run-off (trash, chemical fertilizers)—13%
- Treated sewage (nitrogen and phosphorus)—14%
- Silt and sediment (from construction projects)—37%
- Agriculture runoff (dirt, manure, chemical fertilizers)—70%

Corporate Conservation

- Colonial Pacific Leasing Corp. in Oregon cut $5,200 from its yearly electrical bill by using energy-efficient light bulbs.
- Stonyfield Farm Inc. in New Hampshire saved $60,000 one year by reducing the amount of plastic packaging on products.
- Mercer Color Corp. in Ohio made $8,000 one year by selling its waste for recycling.
- Xerox saves more than $200 million a year by reusing print and toner cartridges.

For more about conservation . . .

RESEARCH LINKS
CLASSZONE.COM

VISUAL SUMMARY

The United States Since 1919

1920s:
Prosperity; increased income and leisure

1930s:
Great Depression; New Deal; rise of dictators

1940s:
World War II; beginning of Cold War

1950s:
Prosperity; growth of suburbs; baby boom

1960s:
Civil rights movement; Vietnam War

1970s:
Détente; Vietnam War ends; Nixon resigns

1980s:
Soaring federal deficit; U.S.-Soviet relations improved

1990s:
Collapse of Soviet Union; prosperity

TERMS & NAMES

Briefly explain the significance of each of the following.

1. Great Depression
2. New Deal
3. fascism
4. World War II
5. Holocaust
6. Harry S. Truman
7. Cold War
8. containment
9. baby boom
10. Great Society

REVIEW QUESTIONS

Prosperity and the Great Depression (pages 707–711)

1. What role did the market crash play in the Great Depression?
2. What was the purpose of Roosevelt's bank holiday?
3. What problems did FDR's New Deal address?

The Rise of Dictators and World War II (pages 712–716)

4. How did Hitler and the Nazi Party gain the support of Germans in the 1930s?
5. How did the role of the United States in World War II change between 1939 and 1945?

The Cold War (pages 717–721)

6. What differences between the Soviet Union and the United States fueled the Cold War?
7. What strategies did the United States use to carry out its containment policy?
8. How did the end of the Cold War change the United States' role in world affairs?

Life in America Since 1945 (pages 722–729)

9. What methods did civil rights activists use?
10. How did the views of presidents Johnson and Reagan differ on the role of government?

CRITICAL THINKING

1. USING YOUR NOTES: CATEGORIZING INFORMATION

The 20th Century	Political Events	Economic Events	Social Events
1920–1930			
1940–1950			
1960–1970			
1980–1990			

Using your completed chart, answer the questions below.

a. What was an important polit event in the period 1940–195
b. What was an important socia event in the period 1960–197
c. What was an important economic event in the perioc 1980–1990?

2. APPLYING CITIZENSHIP SKI

How has the African-American struggle for civil rights changed since the 1960s?

3. THEME: AMERICA IN THE WORLD

As the world's most powerful nation, does the United States a special responsibility to interv in conflicts around the world? or why not?

4. ANALYZING LEADERSHIP

How do the leadership skills of president differ in times of war in times of peace and prosperit Explain your answer.

5. FORMING AND SUPPORTIN OPINIONS

Should the government's focus today be on domestic issues or c foreign affairs? Explain your ans

Interact with Histor

Now that you've read the chap what are some ways the 21st ce tury may be the same as and di ent from the 20th century? Exp your ideas.

se the map and your knowledge of U.S. history to
aswer questions 1 and 2.

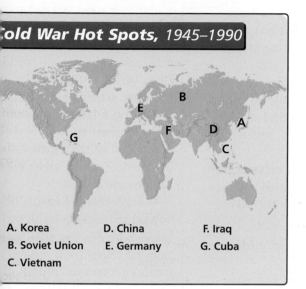

old War Hot Spots, *1945–1990*

A. Korea   D. China   F. Iraq
B. Soviet Union   E. Germany   G. Cuba
C. Vietnam

dditional Test Practice, pp. S1–S33.

Which Cold War hot spot was located in Europe?

A. Cuba
B. Germany
C. Korea
D. Iraq

2. What is the subject of this map?
  A. volcanic activity during the Cold War
  B. popular travel spots during the Cold War
  C. points of conflict during the Cold War
  D. places occupied by foreign armies during the Cold War

This quotation is from President Franklin D. Roosevelt's first inaugural address. It was delivered in 1933, during the Great Depression. Use the quotation and your knowledge of U.S. History to answer question 3.

PRIMARY SOURCE

This great nation will endure as it has endured, will revive and will prosper. So, first of all, let me assert my firm belief that the only thing we have to fear is fear itself.

Franklin D. Roosevelt, First Inaugural Address, March 4, 1933

3. What was Roosevelt trying to convey to Americans with this speech?
  A. a sense of reassurance
  B. a growing feeling of fear
  C. the worsening situation
  D. the humor of the situation

TEST PRACTICE
CLASSZONE.COM

ERNATIVE ASSESSMENT

WRITING ABOUT HISTORY

ometimes said that the 20th century will be remem-
d as the century of war. In other words, the thing
will be remembered most about the 20th century is
ars that were fought. Write a persuasive **essay** sup-
1g or opposing this position.

torials in newspapers and magazines from 1999
2000 discussing the past century might be helpful.
member to use specific examples to support your
e and persuade your reader of your position.

OPERATIVE LEARNING

ing in groups, make a list of social issues that con-
Americans today, such as education, pollution,
, or terrorism. Have each person research one issue
ebate which is most important in front of the class.

INTEGRATED TECHNOLOGY

DOING INTERNET RESEARCH

During the 1920s, there was a dramatic rise in popular entertainment. Using library resources and the Internet, find information about important celebrities of the time, such as Babe Ruth, Bessie Smith, or Charlie Chaplin.

- Find images of the celebrities and perhaps film clips or recordings of the celebrities.
- Include short biographies of the celebrities.
- Present your research to the class.

For more about celebrities of the 1920s . . .

INTERNET ACTIVITY
CLASSZONE.COM

The Attack: September 11, 2001

Terrorism is the use of violence against people or property to force changes in societies or governments. Acts of terrorism are not new. Throughout history, individuals and groups have used terror tactics to achieve political or social goals.

In recent decades, however, terrorist groups have carried out increasingly destructive and high-profile attacks. The growing threat of terrorism has caused many people to feel vulnerable and afraid. However, it also has prompted action from many nations, including the United States.

Many of the terrorist activities of the late 20th century occurred far from U.S. soil. As a result, most Americans felt safe from such violence. All that changed, however, on the morning of September 11, 2001.

A Surprise Strike

As the nation began another workday, 19 terrorists hijacked four airplanes heading from East Coast airports to California. The hijackers crashed two of the jets into the twin towers of the World Trade Center in New York City. They slammed a third plane into the Pentagon outside Washington, D.C. The fourth plane crashed into an empty field in Pennsylvania after passengers apparently fought the hijackers.

The attacks destroyed the World Trade Center and badly damaged a section of the Pentagon. In all, some 3,000 people died. Life for Americans would never be the same after that day. Before, most U.S. citizens viewed terrorism as something that happened in other countries. Now they knew it could happen on their soil as well.

Officials soon learned tha[t] responsible for the attacks w[ere] part of a largely Islamic terro[r] network known as al-Qaeda[.] Observers, including many Muslims, accuse al-Qaeda of preaching a false and extrem[e] form of Islam. Its members b[elieve,] among other things, that th[e] United States and other Wes[tern] nations are evil.

U.S. president George W. [Bush] vowed to hunt down all tho[se] responsible for the attacks. [In addi]tion, he called for a greater [inter]national effort to combat gl[obal] terrorism. "This battle will ta[ke] time and resolve," the presid[ent] declared. "But make no mist[ake] about it: we will win."

Securing the Nation

As the Bush Administration [began] its campaign against terrori[sm]

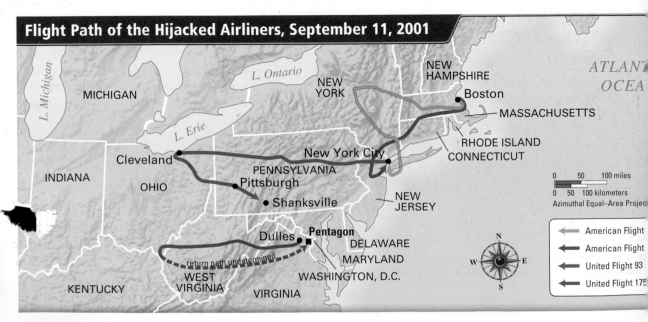

Flight Path of the Hijacked Airliners, September 11, 2001

ATLANTIC OCEAN

L. Michigan

MICHIGAN

L. Ontario

NEW YORK

NEW HAMPSHIRE

Boston

MASSACHUSETTS

L. Erie

Cleveland

New York City

RHODE ISLAND

CONNECTICUT

INDIANA

OHIO

PENNSYLVANIA

Pittsburgh

Shanksville

NEW JERSEY

Dulles   Pentagon

DELAWARE

return path undetermined

MARYLAND

WASHINGTON, D.C.

KENTUCKY

WEST VIRGINIA

VIRGINIA

0   50   100 miles
0   50   100 kilometers
Azimuthal Equal–Area Projec[tion]

← American Flight
← American Flight
← United Flight 93
← United Flight 175

sought to prevent any fur-
attacks on America. In
ober 2001, the president
ed into law the USA Patriot
The law gave the federal
ernment a broad range of
powers to strengthen nation-
curity.

he new law enabled officials
etain foreigners suspected of
orism for up to seven days
out charging them with a
e. Officials could also monitor
hone and Internet use by sus-
s, and prosecute terrorist
es without any time restric-
or limitations.

addition, the government
ted a new cabinet position,
Department of Homeland
rity, to coordinate national
rts against terrorism.
dent Bush named former
sylvania governor Tom
e as the first Secretary of
eland Security.

Underneath a U.S. flag posted amid the rubble of the World Trade Center, rescue workers search for survivors of the attack.

Some critics charged that a number of the government's new anti-terrorism measures violated people's civil rights. Supporters countered that occasionally limiting some civil liberties was justified in the name of greater national security.

The federal government also stepped in to ensure greater security at the nation's airports. The September 11 attacks had originated at several airports, with four hijackings occurring at nearly the same time. In November 2001, President Bush signed the Aviation and Transportation Security Act into law. The law put the federal government in charge of airport security. Before, individual airports had been responsible for security. The new law created a federal security force to inspect passengers and carry-on bags. It also required the screening of checked baggage.

While the September 11 attacks shook the United States, they also strengthened the nation's unity and resolve. In 2003, officials approved plans to rebuild on the World Trade Center site and construct a memorial. Meanwhile, the country has grown more unified as Americans recognize the need to stand together against terrorism.

ed bystanders look on as smoke billows from the twin towers of the World Trade
moments after an airplane slammed into each one.

Fighting Back

The attack against the United States on September 11, 2001, represented the single most deadly act of terrorism in modern history. By that time, however, few regions of the world had been spared from terrorist attacks. Today, America and other nations are responding to terrorism in a variety of ways.

The Rise of Terrorism

The problem of modern international terrorism first gained world attention during the 1972 Summer Olympic Games in Munich, Germany. Members of a Palestinian terrorist group killed two Israeli athletes and took nine others hostage. Five of the terrorists, all the hostages, and a police officer were later killed in a bloody gun battle.

Since then, terrorist activities have occurred across the globe. In Europe, the Irish Republican Army (IRA) used terrorist tactics for decades against Britain. The IRA has long opposed British control of Northern Ireland. Since 1998, the two sides have been working toward a peaceful solution to their conflict. In South America, a group known as the Shining Path terrorized the residents of Peru throughout the late 20th century. The group sought to overthrow the government and establish a Communist state.

Africa, too, has seen its share of terrorism. Groups belonging to the al-Qaeda terrorist organization operated in many African countries. Indeed, officials have linked several major attacks against U.S. facilities in Africa to al-Qaeda. In 1998, for example, bombings at the U.S. embassies in Kenya and Tanzania left more than 200 dead and 5,000 injured.

Most terrorists work in a similar way: targeting high profile events or crowded places where people normally feel safe. include such places as subway stations, bus stops, restaurants or shopping malls. Terrorists choose these spots carefully in order to gain the most attention and to achieve the highest of intimidation.

Terrorists use bullets and bombs as their main weapons. recent years, however, some terrorist groups have used biological and chemical agents in their attacks. These actions involve release of bacteria or poison gas into the air. Gas was the weapon of choice for a radical Japanese religious cult, Aum Shinrikyo. In 1995, cult members released sarin, a deadly nerve in subway stations in Tokyo. Twelve people were killed and more than 5,700 injured. The possibility of this type of terror particularly worrisome, because biochemical agents are relatively easy to acquire.

Terrorism: A Global Problem

PLACE	YEAR	EVENT
Munich, Germany	1972	Palestinians take Israeli hostages at Summer Olympics; hostages and terrorists die in gun battle with police
Beirut, Lebanon	1983	Terrorists detonate truck bomb at U.S. marine barracks, killing 241
Tokyo, Japan	1995	Religious extremists release lethal gas into subway stations killing 12 and injuring thousands
Omagh, Northern Ireland	1998	Faction of Irish Republican Army sets off car bomb, killing
Beslan, Russia	2004	Separatists from Chechnya take over a school and hold more than 1,000 people hostage; more than 300 people killed

unting Down
rrorists

t governments have adopted
ggressive approach to tracking
n and punishing terrorist
ps. This approach includes spy-
on the groups to gather infor-
on on membership and future
s. It also includes striking back
nly after a terrorist attack, even
e point of assassinating known
rist leaders.

nother approach that govern-
ts use is to make it more diffi-
for terrorists to act. This
ves eliminating a terrorist
p's source of funding.

dent Bush issued an executive
r freezing the U.S. assets of
ed terrorist organizations as
as various groups accused of
orting terrorism. President
asked other nations to freeze
assets as well. By the spring of
, the White House reported,
United States and other coun-
had blocked nearly $80 million
eged terrorist assets.

ttling al-Qaeda

e of the more aggressive
onses to terrorism, the United
s quickly took military action
nst those it held responsible for
eptember 11 attacks.

S. officials had determined
members of the al-Qaeda ter-
group had carried out the
lt under the direction of the
o's leader, Osama bin Laden.
aden was a Saudi Arabian mil-
ire who lived in Afghanistan.
rected his terrorist activities
r the protection of the coun-
extreme Islamic government,
n as the Taliban.

The United States
demanded that the Taliban
turn over bin Laden. The
Taliban refused. In October
2001, U.S. forces began
bombing Taliban air defenses, airfields, and command
centers. They also struck
numerous al-Qaeda training
camps. On the ground, the
United States provided assistance to rebel groups
opposed to the Taliban. By
December, the United States
had driven the Taliban from
power and severely weak-
ened the al-Qaeda network.
However, as of November
2004, Osama bin Laden was
still believed to be at large.

Osama bin Laden delivers a videotaped
message from a hidden location shortly after
the U.S.-led strikes against Afghanistan began.

Troops battling the Taliban in Afghanistan await transport by helicopter.

The War in Iraq

In the ongoing battle against terrorism, the United States confronted the leader of Iraq, Saddam Hussein. The longtime dictator had concerned the world community for years. During the 1980s, Hussein had used chemical weapons to put down a rebellion in his own country. In 1990, he had invaded neighboring Kuwait—only to be pushed back by a U.S.-led military effort. In light of such history, many viewed Hussein as an increasing threat to peace and stability in the world. As a result, the Bush Administration led an effort in early 2003 to remove Hussein from power.

The Path to War

One of the main concerns about Saddam Hussein was his possible development of so-called weapons of mass destruction. These are weapons that can kill large numbers of people. They include chemical and biological agents as well as nuclear devices.

Bowing to world pressure, Hussein allowed inspectors from the United Nations to search Iraq for such outlawed weapons. Some investigators, however, insisted that the Iraqis were not fully cooperating with the inspections.

U.S. and British officials soon threatened to use force to disarm Iraq. During his State of the Union address in January 2003, President Bush declared Hussein too great a threat to ignore in an age of increased terrorism. Reminding Americans of the September 11 attacks, Bush stated, "Imagine those 19 hijackers with other weapons and other plans—this time armed by Saddam Hussein. It would take one vial, one canister, one crate slipped into this country to bring a day of horror like none we have ever known. We will do every-

thing in our power to make sure that day never comes."

Operation Iraqi Freedom

In the months that followed, the UN Security Council debated what action to take. Some countries, such as France and Germany, called for letting the inspectors continue searching for weapons. British prime minister Tony Blair, however, accused the Iraqis of "deception and evasion" and insisted inspections would never work.

On March 17, President Bush gave Saddam Hussein and his top aides 48 hours to leave the country or face a military strike. The Iraqi leader refused. On March 19, a coalition led by the United States and Britain launched air strikes in and around the Iraqi capital, Baghdad. The next day, coalition forces marched into Iraq though Kuwait. The invasion of Iraq to remove Saddam Hussein, known as Operation Iraqi Freedom, had begun.

The military operation met with strong opposition from numerous countries. Russian

president Vladimir Putin claimed the invasion cou[ld] no way be justified." He a[nd] others criticized the policy [of] attacking a nation to preve[nt] from future misdeeds. U.S. [and] British officials, however, ar[gued] that they would not wait fo[r] Hussein to strike first.

As coalition troops march[ed] north to Baghdad, they me[t] ets of stiff resistance and er[?] in fierce fighting in several [?]ern cities. Meanwhile, coali[tion] forces parachuted into nort[h] Iraq and began moving sou[th] toward the capital city. By e[arly] April, Baghdad had fallen a[nd the] regime of Saddam Hussein collapsed. After less than fo[ur] weeks of fighting, the coali[tion] had won the war.

U.S. Army Specialist Shoshana [?] was one of several Americans h[eld] prisoner and eventually release[d ?] the war in Iraq.

...e regime of Saddam Hussein collapsed, statues of ...tator toppled.

established their own interim government several months after the war. The new governing body went to work creating a constitution and planning democratic elections.

Meanwhile, intelligence officials searched for clues of Saddam Hussein's whereabouts. The defeated dictator was captured near his hometown of Tikrit on December 13, 2003. Despite Hussein's capture, numerous U.S. troops had to remain behind to help maintain order and battle pockets of Iraqi insurgents—different groups made up of Hussein loyalists, followers of rebel Islamic clerics, and terrorists with links to al-Qaeda.

Finally, inspectors were not able to find any weapons of mass destruction in the months after major combat had ended. The governments of the United States and Britain issued reports in 2004 saying that pre-war intelligence regarding such weapons was flawed.

Despite the unresolved issues, coalition leaders declared the defeat of Saddam Hussein to be a victory for global security. In a post-war speech to U.S. troops aboard the aircraft carrier *USS Abraham Lincoln*, President Bush urged the world community to keep moving forward in its battle against terrorism. "We do not know the day of final victory, but we have seen the turning of the tide," declared the president. "No act of the terrorists will change our purpose, or weaken our resolve, or alter their fate. Their cause is lost. Free nations will press on to victory."

President George W. Bush and British prime minister Tony Blair stood together throughout the war.

...e Struggle ...ntinues

...te the coalition victory,
... work remained in Iraq.
...United States installed a
...dministrator, retired diplo-
... Paul Bremer, to help
...ee the rebuilding of the
...n. With the help of
...er and others, the Iraqis

...cial Report Assessment

...ain Ideas

...What steps did the U.S. government take to make ...he nation more secure after the attacks on ...eptember 11, 2001?

...Why did the United States take military action ...gainst the Taliban in Afghanistan?

...hat was the result of Operation Iraqi Freedom?

2. Critical Thinking

Analyzing Issues Is it important for the U.S. government to respect people's civil rights as it wages a war against terrorism? Why or why not?

THINK ABOUT

- what steps are necessary to protect the nation
- a government that grows too powerful

The Supreme Court

The task of the Supreme Court, according to Chief Justice John Marshall, is "to say what the law is." The Court reviews appeals decisions by lower courts. It judges whether federal laws or gove ment actions violate the Constitution. And it settles conflicts between state and federal laws.

By interpreting the law, the Supreme Court wields great pow for its decisions affect practically every aspect of life in the Unite States. In the following pages, you'll learn about some of the Supreme Court's landmark cases—decisions that altered the cou of history or brought major changes to American life.

"When we have examined . . . the Supreme Cou and the [rights] which it exercises, we shall read ly admit that a more imposing judicial power w never constituted by any people."

— ALEXIS DE TOCQUEVILLE, *DEMOCRACY IN AMERICA*

Chief Justice John Marshall established the principle of judicial review.

The development of steamships led to Supreme Court decisions on interstate commerce.

McCulloch v. *Maryland* decided if a state had the power to tax a federal agency.

180
Marbury v. *Madison*
Judicial Review

1819
McCulloch v. *Maryland*
Powers of Congress and States' Rights

1824
Gibbons v. *Ogden*
State Versus Federal Authority

1857
Dred Scott v. *Sandford*
Citizenship

1896
Plessy v. *Ferg*
Segregation

Landmark decisions on school desegregation helped give rise to the civil rights movement.

Opinions written by Justice Oliver Wendell Holmes, Jr., helped to set standards for free speech.

TABLE OF CONTENTS

BEFORE YOU READ

Think About It Why is there a need for a judicial authority "to say what the law is"? How might the history of the United States have been different if the Supreme Court had not taken on this role?

Find Out About It Use library resources or the Internet to find out what issues the Supreme Court is presently reviewing. How might the Court's decisions on these issues affect you?

For more information on the Supreme Court . . .

RESEARCH LINKS
CLASSZONE.COM

The Supreme Court has reviewed several affirmative-action cases in recent years.

k v. United States
n of Speech

1954
Brown v. Board of Education of Topeka
School Desegregation

1964
Reynolds v. Sims
One Person, One Vote

1978
Regents of the University of California v. Bakke
Affirmative Action

Marbury v. Madison (1803)

THE ISSUE Judicial Review

ORIGINS OF THE CASE In 1801, just before he left office, President Joh Adams appointed dozens of Federalists as judges. Most of these "midni justices" took their posts before Thomas Jefferson, Adams's Democratic-Republican successor, took office. Jefferson ordered his secretary of stat James Madison, to block the remaining appointees from taking their po One of these appointees, William Marbury, asked the Supreme Court to issue an order forcing Madison to recognize the appointments.

THE RULING The Court ruled that the law under which Marbury had a the Supreme Court to act was unconstitutional.

The Legal Arguments

Chief Justice John Marshall wrote the Court's opinion, stating tha Marbury had every right to receive his appointment. Further, Ma noted, the Judiciary Act of 1789 gave Marbury the right to file hi claim directly with the Supreme Court. But Marshall questioned whether the Court had the power to act. The answer, he argued, ed on the kinds of cases that could be argued directly in the Supr Court without first being heard by a lower court.

Article 3 of the Constitution clearly identified those cases that Court could hear directly. A case like Marbury's was not one of th The Judiciary Act, therefore, was at odds with the Constitution. V one should be upheld? Marshall's response was clear:

> . . . [T]he particular phraseology of the Constitution of the United St confirms and strengthens the principle . . . that a law repugnan the Constitution is void; and that *courts* . . . are bound by that instrument.

Since Section 13 of the Judiciary Act violated the Constitution, Marshall concluded, it could not be enforced. The Court, therefore, could not issue the order. With this decision, Marshall appeared to limit the powers of the Supreme Court. In fact, the decision increased the Court's power because it established the principle of judicial review. This holds that the courts—most notably the Supreme Court—have the power to decide if laws are unconstitutional.

William Marbury received his appointment as a reward for his loyal support of John Adams in the 1800 presidential election.

LEGAL *Sources*

U.S. CONSTITUTION/LEGISLATION

Article 3, Section 2 (1789)
"In all cases affecting ambassadors, other public ministers and consuls, and those in which a state shall be party, the Supreme Court shall have original jurisdiction. In all the other cases . . . the Supreme Court shall have appellate jurisdiction."

Judiciary Act, Section 13 (1789)
"The Supreme Court shall . . . have power to issue . . . writs of *mandamus,* in cases warranted by the principles and usages of law."

RELATED CASES

Fletcher v. Peck (1810)
For the first time, the Supreme Court ruled a state law unconstitutional.

Cohens v. Virginia (1821)
For the first time, the Court overturned a state court decision.

y Did It Matter Then?

principle of judicial review had been set down rlier state and lower federal court decisions. ever, Marshall did not refer to those cases in *ury.* Rather, he based his argument on logic. r a written constitution to have any value, hall stated, it is logical that any "legislative hat is] contrary to the Constitution is not

Only then could the Constitution be—as e VI calls it—"the supreme law of the land." then, decides that a law is invalid? Marshall red that this power rests only with the courts:

is, emphatically, the province and duty of the icial department to say what the law is. Those o apply the rule to particular cases must of cessity expound and interpret that rule. If [the nstitution and a law] conflict with each er, the courts must decide on the oper- on of each.

t only did the courts have ower, Marshall said, it 'the very essence of ial duty" for them ercise it.

Why Does It Matter Now?

Over the years, judicial review has become a cornerstone of American government. The principle plays a vital role in the system of checks and balances that limits the powers of each branch of the federal government. For example, since 1803 the Court has struck down more than 125 acts of Congress as unconstitutional.

The Court has cited *Marbury* more than 250 times to justify its decisions. In *Clinton* v. *Jones* (1997), for example, the Court found that presidents are not protected by the Constitution from lawsuits involving actions in their private lives. The Court supported this finding by pointing to its power "to say what the law is." More recently, in *United States* v. *Morrison* (2000), the Court ruled that Congress went beyond its constitutional bounds by basing a federal law banning violence against women on the Fourteenth Amendment and the Commerce Clause of the Constitution. The opinion pointed out that "ever since *Marbury* this Court has remained the ultimate [explainer] of the constitutional text."

John Marshall, a Federalist, was practically a "midnight justice." John Adams appointed him chief justice in January 1801, just two months before Thomas Jefferson took office.

NNECT TO HISTORY

laking Decisions Marshall was a Federalist, and any people expected him to act quickly on larbury's case. What do you think might have been e consequences if Marshall had found for larbury?

See Skillbuilder Handbook, page R14.

CONNECT TO TODAY

2. Researching Find a recent instance of a law or administrative action that was ruled unconstitutional by the Supreme Court. What were the Court's reasons for the ruling, and what impact did the decision have? Prepare a summary of your findings.

For more information on judicial review . . .

RESEARCH LINKS
CLASSZONE.COM

McCulloch v. Maryland
(1819)

THE ISSUES Balance of power between the federal and state governments

ORIGINS OF THE CASE The second Bank of the United States (BUS) wa established by an act of Congress in 1816. It set up branches nationwide But many states objected to the bank's policies and wanted to limit its (ations. In fact, Maryland set a tax on the currency issued by the Baltimo branch. The bank could avoid the tax by paying an annual fee of $15,00 However, James McCulloch, the branch cashier, refused to pay either the or the fee. The state sued McCulloch, and the Maryland courts ordered I to pay. McCulloch appealed the case to the Supreme Court.

THE RULING The Court ruled that Congress had the power to establish national bank and that the Maryland tax on that bank was unconstitutio

The Legal Arguments

The Court first addressed Maryland's argument that the act establi ing the BUS was unconstitutional. Chief Justice John Marshall wro that the Constitution listed the specific powers of Congress. These included collecting taxes, borrowing money, and regulating commerce. In addition, the Elastic Clause gave Congress the authority make all "necessary and proper" laws needed to exercise those po ers. Establishing a bank, he concluded, was necessary for Congress carry out its powers. The BUS, then, was constitutional.

Next, Marshall addressed whether Maryland had the power to t the BUS. Marshall acknowledged that the states had the power of ation. But he said:

> [T]he constitution and the laws made in pursuance thereof are supre ... they control the constitution and laws of the respective states, a cannot be controlled by them.

So, to give a state the power to tax a federal agency created unde the Constitution would turn the Supremacy Clause, Article 6, Secti 2, on its head. Further, Marshall observed, "the power to tax invol the power to destroy." If a state could tax one federal agency, it might tax others. This eventually "would defeat all the ends of go ernment." He added that the framers of the Constitution certainly not intend to make the national government subject to the states:

> [T]he States have no power, by taxation or otherwise, to retard, impe burden, or in any manner control, the operations of the constitutio laws enacted by Congress to carry [out its] powers.

The Maryland tax, therefore, was unconstitutional.

LEGAL Sources

U.S. CONSTITUTION/LEGISLATION

Article 1, Section 8 (1789)
"The Congress shall have the power to . . . make all laws which shall be necessary and proper for carrying into execution the [specific powers given to Congress]."

Article 6, Section 2 (1789)
"This Constitution, and the laws of the United States . . . shall be the supreme law of the land; . . . anything in the Constitution or laws of any state to the contrary notwithstanding."

RELATED CASES

Fletcher v. Peck (1810)
Noting that the Constitution was the supreme law of the land, the Supreme Court ruled a state law unconstitutional.

Gibbons v. Ogden (1824)
The Court ruled that the federal Congress—not the states—had the power to regulate interstate commerce.

y Did It Matter Then?

e time of the *McCulloch* case, there was con-
able debate over what powers Congress held.
e people took a very limited view. They sug-
d that Congress's powers should be restricted
ose named in the Constitution. Others point-
t that the Elastic Clause implied that
ress had much broader powers.
e *McCulloch* opinion followed this second
Marshall wrote:

t **the end be [lawful], let it be within the scope of**
e Constitution, and all means which are appropri-
e, which are plainly adapted to that end, which
not prohibited, but consist with the letter and
rit of the Constitution, are constitutional.

her words, Congress could exercise the pow-
considered appropriate to achieve its lawful
.

rshall's broad view of congressional power
gthened the federal government. And this
ger government reflected and encouraged
rowing nationalist spirit in the early 1800s.

Why Does It Matter Now?

Since Marshall's time, the United States has under-
gone many changes. Over the course of the 19th
and 20th centuries, the country has grown dramatically. The population has increased and
moved. In Marshall's day, the United States was
predominantly rural. Today, most people live in
urban areas, where economic and leisure activities
abound.

The economy of the United States, too, has
changed. The country has moved from an agricultural economy to one based on industry and, later,
service and information.

During this time, the federal government has
stretched its powers to meet the needs of the
ever-changing American society. Programs like
Franklin Roosevelt's New Deal and Lyndon
Johnson's Great Society came about through this
expanding of powers. Marshall's broad reading of
the Elastic Clause in the *McCulloch* opinion, in
large part, laid the groundwork for this growth in
the size and power of the federal government.

The Bank of the United States
had branches throughout the
country, including this one in
Philadelphia.

NNECT TO HISTORY

orming and Supporting Opinions Chief Justice
ohn Marshall considered the *McCulloch* decision the
most important that he made. Why do you think he
onsidered it such an important decision? Give
easons for your answer.

See Skillbuilder Handbook, page R17.

CONNECT TO TODAY

2. **Researching** One issue addressed in *McCulloch* was
states' rights and federal authority. Do research to
find a recent Supreme Court case that has dealt with
this issue. Write a paragraph describing the basis of
the case and the Court's decision.

For more information on states' rights and federal authority . . .

Plessy v. Ferguson (1896)

THE ISSUE Segregation

ORIGINS OF THE CASE By the 1890s, most Southern states had begun t[o] pass laws enforcing segregation—the separation of the races—in public pla[ces]. One Louisiana law called for "equal but separate accommodations for th[e] white and colored races" on trains. On June 7, 1892, Homer Plessy, who w[as] part African American, took a seat in a train car reserved for whites. Whe[n the] conductor told him to move, Plessy refused. Plessy was convicted of brea[k-]ing the "separate car" law. He appealed the case, saying that the law vio[lat-]ed his rights under the Thirteenth and Fourteenth amendments.

THE RULING The Court ruled that "separate but equal" facilities for bla[cks] and whites did not violate the Constitution.

LEGAL Sources

U.S. CONSTITUTION/LEGISLATION

Thirteenth Amendment (1865)
"Neither slavery nor involuntary servitude . . . shall exist within the United States, or any place subject to their jurisdiction."

Fourteenth Amendment (1868)
"No state shall make or enforce any law which shall abridge the privileges or immunities of citizens of the United States; nor shall any state deprive any person of life, liberty, or property, without due process of law; nor deny to any person within its jurisdiction the equal protection of the laws."

RELATED CASE

Cumming v. Board of Education of Richmond County (1899)
The Court ruled that because education is a local issue, the federal government could not stop school districts from having separate facilities for black and white students.

The Legal Arguments

The Court's opinion, written by Justice Henry Billings Brown, reje[cted] Plessy's appeal. Brown first answered Plessy's claim that the separa[te] car law created a relationship between whites and blacks similar t[o] that which existed under slavery. The Thirteenth Amendment simply ended the ownership of one person by another, Brown wrote. Louisiana's law did not reestablish this system of ownership.

Brown then turned to Plessy's claim that the Fourteenth Amendment was designed to ensure the equality of the races before the law. Brown wrote that the amendment "could not have been intended to abolish distinctions based on color." A law that treated the races differently did not brand one race as inferior. If a law made people feel inferior, it was because they chose to see it that way. Summing up, Brown stated:

> A [law] which implies merely a legal distinction between the white and colored races . . . has no tendency to destroy the legal equality of the two races.

Justice John Marshall Harlan strongly disagreed with the majority view. In a bitter dissent, he wrote that the "thin disguise" of separate but equal facilities would fool no one, "nor atone for the wrong this day done."

In his dissent, J[ustice] Harlan stated th[at] "our constitutio[n is] color-blind, and neither knows [nor] tolerates classe[s] among citizens.["]

Did It Matter Then?

was one of several cases in the late 1800s
ving the civil rights of African Americans. In
cases, the Court misread the Fourteenth
ndment and let stand state laws that denied
an Americans their rights. *Plessy* has come to
for all of these decisions because it said that
arate but equal" facilities for blacks and
es did not violate the Constitution.

hough the *Plessy* decision dealt only with
c transportation, state governments across
outh applied it to all areas of life. In time,
Crow" laws forced African Americans to use
ate restaurants, hotels, train cars, parks,
ls, and hospitals. Signs reading "For Colored
and "Whites Only" ruled everyday life in
outh for years to come.

Why Does It Matter Now?

After *Plessy,* many African Americans and some
whites looked for ways to fight segregation. Some
of these people helped to found the National
Association for the Advancement of Colored
People (NAACP).

Throughout the first half of the 20th century,
lawyers working for the NAACP chipped away at
segregation laws. Their greatest victory came in
1954, in *Brown* v. *Board of Education of Topeka.*
In this decision, the Supreme Court ruled that
separate educational facilities were "inherently
unequal" and, therefore, unconstitutional.
Southern state and local governments had used
the *Plessy* decision to build a system of legal
segregation. In the same way, civil rights workers
used the *Brown* ruling to dismantle it.

After the *Plessy* decision, signs designating separate facilities for whites and
African Americans became a common sight throughout the South.

NNECT TO HISTORY

rawing Conclusions Read the section of the
ourteenth Amendment reprinted in the "Legal
ources" section on page 748. Based on that
assage, what do you think "equal protection of the
aws" means? How does it apply to the *Plessy* case?

See Skillbuilder Handbook, page R13.

CONNECT TO TODAY

2. **Researching** Use library resources and the Internet
   to find information on Supreme Court cases that
   dealt with segregation. Present your findings in a
   three-column chart. Use "Case," "Brief Description of
   Issues Involved," and "Decision" as column headings.

For more information on segregation and the law . . .

RESEARCH LINKS
CLASSZONE.COM

Schenck v. United States (1919)

THE ISSUE Freedom of Speech

ORIGINS OF THE CASE In August 1917, Charles Schenck, a Socialist Par official, distributed several thousand antiwar leaflets throughout the cit Philadelphia. The leaflets called the draft a crime and urged people to v for the repeal of the Selective Service Act. Schenck was found guilty of lating the Espionage Act of 1917 and sentenced to prison. He appealed conviction, arguing that the language in the leaflets was protected by t First Amendment.

THE RULING The Court upheld the verdict against Schenck, noting tha leaflets presented "a clear and present danger" to the country during wartime.

LEGAL *Sources*

U.S. CONSTITUTION/LEGISLATION

First Amendment (1791)
"Congress shall make no law . . . abridging the freedom of speech, or of the press."

The Espionage Act (1917)
"[Anyone who] shall wilfully obstruct . . . the recruiting or enlistment service of the United States . . . shall be punished by . . . fine . . . or imprisonment . . . or both."

RELATED CASES

Debs v. United States (1919)
Upheld the conviction of Socialist Party leader Eugene V. Debs for violating the Espionage Act.

Frohwerk v. United States (1919)
Confirmed the guilty verdict against a newspaper publisher for printing articles opposing U. S. involvement in World War I.

Abrams v. United States (1919)
Upheld convictions of five people under the Espionage Act. Holmes dissented, arguing that their action did not present "a clear and imminent danger."

The Legal Arguments

Justice Oliver Wendell Holmes, Jr., wrote the Court's unanimous o ion. In ordinary times, Holmes noted, Schenck's claim of First Amendment rights might well be valid. "But the character of eve act depends upon the circumstances in which it is done," Holmes added. Schenck distributed the leaflets during wartime, when "m things that might be said in time of peace . . . will not be endure Holmes suggested that Schenck's "impassioned" appeal for peopl oppose the draft was just like someone "falsely shouting fire in a atre and causing a panic." The First Amendment certainly did not tect such behavior.

Holmes then went on to offer a guide for judging when speech is protected by the First Amendment:

> The question in every case is whether the words used are used in such circumstances and are of such a nature as to create a clear and present danger that they will bring about the . . . evils that Congress has a right to prevent.

Schenck's words, Holmes charged, did pose "a clear and present danger" to the United States war effort. Therefore, they did not merit protection under the First Amendment.

Justice Holmes's opinions in the Espionage Act cases set the standard for free speech.

Why Did It Matter Then?

Supreme Court decisions in *Schenck* and other
...nage Act cases considered the limits of free
...ch during wartime. In *Schenck,* Justice Holmes
...d that speech that presented "a clear and
...ent danger" to the country's well being was
...protected. As he looked at other cases, how-
... Holmes began to refine this view.

... *Frohwerk* v. *United States* (1919), decided
...a week after *Schenck,* the Court again upheld
...nviction under the Espionage Act. However,
...nes noted that anti-government speech
...ed during wartime is not always a crime.
... do not lose our right to condemn either
...ures or men because the country is at war,"
...rote.

...olmes broadened this statement in his dissent
...e majority opinion in *Abrams* v. *United States*
...9). The government's power to limit speech
...ng wartime undoubtedly is greater, he noted,
...ause war opens dangers that do not exist at
...r times." However, the basic principles of free
...ch are the same in war as in peace:

...is only the present dan-
...r of immediate evil or an
...tent to bring it about
...at warrants Congress in
...tting a limit to the
...pression of opinion.

...pinions, even ones
...nd hateful, should be
...d, Holmes concluded.

Why Does It Matter Now?

The Supreme Court has been asked to decide on
free speech issues dozens of times since *Schenck.*
In making these decisions, the Court has attempted to heed Justice Holmes's words and strike a
balance between protecting free speech and
maintaining political and social order.

Over the years, the Court has applied this balance test to free speech questions in many set-
tings, including schools. In *Tinker* v. *Des Moines
Independent Community School District* (1969),
the Court upheld students' right to protest in
school. However, the Court added that in certain
circumstances school officials might limit the exercise of such rights—if the students' actions disrupt
the work of the school, for example.

In two later cases, *Bethel School District No.
403* v. *Fraser* (1986) and *Hazelwood School
District* v. *Kuhlmeier* (1988), the Court felt that
such circumstances existed. In *Bethel,* the Court
upheld the suspension of a student who, during a
school assembly, gave a speech that included
inappropriate language. The Court ruled that the
school could punish behavior
that "interferes with the educational process." In *Hazelwood,* the Court ruled that
school officials could censor
the content of a student newspaper if it was "inconsistent
with [the school's] educational
mission."

During the Vietnam War, some Americans vigorously
challenged government policies.

...ONNECT TO HISTORY

...Making Inferences The Supreme Court decided
Schenck and other Espionage Act cases during the
...Red Scare. Do you think the timing of the cases
...nfluenced the Court's decisions? Why or why not?

See Skillbuilder Handbook, page R12.

CONNECT TO TODAY

2. Researching Working with a group of two or three
other students, identify and research recent court
cases involving free speech issues. Present your
findings in a brief oral report to the class.

For more information on free speech . . .

RESEARCH LINKS
CLASSZONE.COM

Brown v. Board of Education of Topeka (1954)

THE ISSUE School desegregation

ORIGINS OF THE CASE In September 1950, Oliver Brown tried to enroll h
seven-year-old daughter, Linda, at the neighborhood grade school. The sch
principal rejected Brown's request because Linda was an African American
The school was for white students only. Linda ended up attending a schoc
farther away from her home. Brown filed suit against the school board,
demanding that Linda be allowed to go to the neighborhood school. The
Supreme Court heard arguments in the *Brown* case in 1952 and 1953.

THE RULING A unanimous court ruled that segregation in education w;
unconstitutional.

LEGAL *Sources*

U.S. CONSTITUTION/LEGISLATION

Fourteenth Amendment (1868)
"No state shall . . . deprive
any person of life, liberty, or
property, without due process
of law; nor deny to any person
within its jurisdiction the equal
protection of the laws."

RELATED CASES

Plessy v. Ferguson (1896)
Upheld Louisiana laws that
segregated railroad passenger
cars according to race.
Established the doctrine of
"separate but equal."

**Brown v. Board of Education
of Topeka (May, 1955)**
Ordered that desegregation
take place "with all deliberate
speed." Often called "*Brown II.*"

The Legal Arguments

Chief Justice Earl Warren wrote the Court's decision. He began by
reviewing the history of the Fourteenth Amendment. Its equal
protection clause was the basis for the decision. The Court had
ruled in *Plessy* v. *Ferguson* (1896) that "separate but equal"
facilities for blacks and whites did not violate this amendment. However, Warren pointed out that *Plessy* involved
transportation, not education. He then stressed the
importance of education for society:

> It is doubtful that any child may reasonably be expect-
> ed to succeed in life if he is denied the
> opportunity of an education.

Warren went on to suggest that segregation denied
African-American children that opportunity. He
concluded with *Brown's* most famous statement:

> . . . [I]n the field of public education the doctrine of
> "separate but equal" has no place. Separate educational
> facilities are inherently unequal.

The Court expected whites in the South, where
segregation was dominant, to resist the ruling.
Therefore, it delayed orders on how to put the
decision into action for several months.

Thurgood Marshall was one of the team of
lawyers that represented Oliver Brown. In 1967,
Marshall became the first African American
appointed as a Supreme Court justice.

y Did It Matter Then?

ourteenth Amendment had guaranteed
an Americans equal rights as citizens. In the
800s, however, many Southern states passed
Crow" laws, which enforced separation of
aces in public places. In 1896, the Supreme
t upheld a "Jim Crow" law in *Plessy* v.
uson. In the Court's view, "separate but
l" rail cars did not violate the Fourteenth
ndment.

own, however, stated that segregated schools
ed African Americans the "equal protection
e laws" guaranteed by the Fourteenth
ndment. Segregation, therefore, had no
in school systems.

the Court expected, the decision met
sition. One Southern politician accused
ourt of "a flagrant abuse of judicial
er." Even after *Brown*
any school districts,
cularly in the South,
ged their feet on
gregation. Some 10
later, segregation
till the rule in most
nern school districts.
so, the impact of the
n decision on
rican society was
ense. It marked the
nning of the civil rights
ement, which you read
t in Chapter 29.

Why Does It Matter Now?

Throughout the 1960s and 1970s, the Supreme
Court continued to review the issue of school
segregation. In *Green* v. *New Kent County* (1968),
the Court called for the end of the dual school
system—one white and one black. This involved
integrating not only students, but also teachers,
support staff, and services.

In *Swann* v. *Charlotte-Mecklenburg Board of
Education* (1971), the Court ruled that busing
could be used to achieve school desegregation.
Later, in *Milliken* v. *Bradley* (1974), the Court ruled
that students might be bused between school districts to achieve this goal. However, this step could
be taken only in very exceptional circumstances.

In recent years, the Court has moved away from
enforcing desegregation. Still, the *Brown* decision
brought about far-reaching changes. The statement that separate facili-
ties are "inherently
unequal" proved a power-
ful weapon against segre-
gation in all areas of
American life. Indeed, the
Court's opinion in *Brown*
provided the basis for
most of the civil rights
laws passed in the late
1950s and 1960s.

The *Brown* decision was a front-page story in newspapers
across the United States.

NNECT TO HISTORY

Analyzing Points of View Chief Justice Earl
Warren wanted the *Brown* opinion to be unanimous.
He even pressured Justice Stanley Reed, a
outherner, not to file a dissenting opinion. Why
do you think Warren insisted that all the justices
gree to the *Brown* decision?

See Skillbuilder Handbook, page R9.

CONNECT TO TODAY

2. Researching Working with a group of two or three
other students, conduct research to find out about
efforts to desegregate another part of American
society, such as the military, the workplace, or colleges.
Report your findings to the class.

For more information on civil rights today . . .

RESEARCH LINKS
CLASSZONE.COM

Reynolds v. Sims (1964)

THE ISSUE One Person, One Vote

ORIGINS OF THE CASE Most state constitutions require a redrawing of
islative districts every 10 years, based on the latest U.S. Census figures. B
the 1960s, however, many states had not redrawn their districts for deca
For example, Alabama's last redrawing—in 1901—did not reflect the grea
population changes that had taken place. In 1962, a group of Alabama vo
ers sued to have their legislative map redrawn. When a federal court fou
for the voters, the Alabama state legislature appealed to the Supreme Co

THE RULING The Court firmly established the principle of "one person,
vote." It ruled that Alabama must redraw its legislative districts so that
district had about the same number of people.

LEGAL *Sources*

U.S. CONSTITUTION/LEGISLATION

Fourteenth Amendment (1868)
"No state shall . . . deprive any
person of life, liberty, or property, without due process of law;
nor deny to any person within
its jurisdiction the equal protection of the laws."

**Alabama Constitution, Article 9,
Section 198 (1901)**
"The members of the house of
representatives shall be apportioned by the legislature among
the several counties of the state,
according to the number of
inhabitants in them, respectively,
as ascertained by the decennial
census of the United States."

RELATED CASES

Baker v. Carr (1962)
Ruled that federal courts could
intervene in state legislative dis-
tricting issues.

Gray v. Sanders (1963)
Ruled that when counting votes
in primary elections, states
should follow the principle of
"one person, one vote."

The Legal Arguments

The Court's ruling, written by Chief Justice Earl
Warren, clearly stated the issue:

> The right to vote freely for the candidate of one's
> choice is of the essence of a democratic society,
> and any restrictions on that right strike at the
> heart of representative government.

Weakening the power of an individual's vote,
Warren added, was as much a restriction as
preventing that individual from voting.

"Legislators represent people, not trees or
acres," Warren continued. Population, therefore, had to be the determining factor in
redrawing legislative districts. Warren based his
argument squarely on the Fourteenth
Amendment:

Chief Justice Earl W
considered *Reynold*
Sims one of the mo
important opinions
had written.

> We hold that as a basic constitutional standard, the Equal Protect
> Clause requires that seats in . . . a . . . state legislature must be app
> tioned on a population basis. . . . [T]he Equal Protection Clause requ
> that a State make an honest and good faith effort to construct distr
> . . . as nearly of equal population as is practicable.

John Marshall Harlan—the grandson of the justice who wrote t
famous dissent to *Plessy* v. *Ferguson*—dissented. He claimed that t
Constitution did not give the Court the power to interfere in how
states decide on their legislative districts.

y Did It Matter Then?

...nolds was one of several voting rights cases
...the Court heard in the 1960s. In the first,
...er v. Carr (1962), the Court broke with past
...sions and said that federal courts had the
...er to make sure that states drew legislative
...icts fairly. A year later, in Gray v. Sanders
...3), the Court applied the principle of "one
...on, one vote" for the first time. The Court
...erved that the vote of someone living in one
...of a state should count as much as that of
...eone living in another part.

...Reynolds, the court extended the "one per-
...one vote" principle to the drawing of state
...slative districts. In time, the Reynolds ruling
...ed most states to draw new district bound-
...s. As a result, there was a shift in political
...ver in state legislatures. The number of state
...esentatives from cities, which had larger pop-
...ions, increased. In contrast, the number from
...l areas, where fewer people lived, declined.

Why Does It Matter Now?

During the 1990s, the Court faced a new redistricting issue. The Voting Rights Act of 1965 urged
states to increase minority representation in the
legislatures. To do so, many states created districts
where minorities made up a voting majority.
However, some white voters challenged these districts under the Fourteenth Amendment.

In several cases—Bush v. Vera (1996), for example—the Court ruled that such districts were unconstitutional. Since these districts were drawn solely
based on race, the Court said, they violated the
Fourteenth Amendment's equal protection clause.
In Lawyer v. Department of Justice (1997), the
Court upheld a Florida district drawn to include
several African-American communities. The Court
found that in this case, race was only one of several
factors used to draw district boundary lines.

After the U.S. Census of 2000, the states began
a new round of redistricting. As a result, the
Supreme Court probably will revisit this issue over
the next few years.

Representation in the Alabama State Legislature, 1962

COUNTY	POPULATION	NUMBER OF HOUSE REPRESENTATIVES
Bullock	13,462	2
Henry	15,286	2
Mobile	314,301	3
Jefferson	634,864	7

Source: U.S. Supreme Court, Reynolds v. Sims, 377 U.S. 533 (1964)

In 1962, the rural counties of Bullock
and Henry had less than one-thirtieth
of the population of the urban counties of Mobile and Jefferson. Even so,
they returned close to half as many
state representatives as did the two
urban counties.

CONNECT TO HISTORY

Finding Main Ideas Use library or Internet
resources to locate a copy of the majority opinion
in Reynolds v. Sims. Make a chart listing the main
idea and details for each part of the opinion. Make
a similar chart for Harlan's dissenting opinion in
this case.

See Skillbuilder Handbook, page R5.

CONNECT TO TODAY

2. **Researching** Conduct research to find news stories
about a recent Supreme Court decision on the issue
of redistricting. Write a summary of the background
of the case, the ruling the Court made, and the legal
reasoning behind that ruling.

For more information on the Supreme Court
and redistricting . . .

RESEARCH LINKS
CLASSZONE.COM

Regents of the University of California v. Bakke (1978

THE ISSUE Affirmative action

ORIGINS OF THE CASE In 1970, the medical school of the University of California at Davis adopted an "affirmative action" admissions policy. The policy set a quota calling for 16 percent of each year's incoming students be minority students. Allan Bakke, a white applicant, had better test scor and grades than most of the students accepted under the affirmative-actic plan. However, he was not admitted. Bakke sued, arguing that he had be rejected because of his race. The California Supreme Court ordered the sch to admit Bakke. The school appealed the case to the U.S. Supreme Court.

THE RULING The Court ruled that the school could use race as one of se eral factors in making admissions decisions but that setting racial quotas was unconstitutional.

LEGAL Sources

U.S. CONSTITUTION/LEGISLATION

Fourteenth Amendment (1868)
"No state shall . . . deprive any person of life, liberty, or property, without due process of law; nor deny to any person within its jurisdiction the equal protection of the laws."

Civil Rights Act, Title VI (1964)
"No person in the United States shall, on the ground of race, color, or national origin, be excluded from participation in . . . any program or activity receiving Federal financial assistance."

RELATED CASE

Fullilove v. Klutznick (1980)
The Court upheld the Public Works Employment Act of 1977, which required that minority-owned businesses receive 10 percent of all federal funds for public works projects.

The Legal Arguments

The Court upheld the California Supreme Court decision in a 5–4 v Four of the five majority justices maintained that holding a set nur ber of admission slots for minority students violated the Civil Right Act of 1964. The fifth justice, Justice Lewis Powell, noted that racia quotas violated the Fourteenth Amendment. Powell wrote:

> The guarantee of equal protection cannot mean one thing when appli to one individual and something else when applied to a person of anot er color. If both are not accorded the same protection, then it is not equ

However, the Court did not reject affirmative action completely. By different 5-4 majority, the Court ruled that race could be used as o of several factors in college admissions. Powell, who again provide the deciding vote, thought that race should be considered in order promote a "diverse student body."

Allan Bakke graduated from the University of California at Davis with a medical degree in 1982.

y Did It Matter Then?

:an Americans made many gains in civil rights
ng the 1950s and 1960s. President Lyndon
nson, however, thought more needed to be
e. He explained why:

*u do not take a person who for years has been
obbled by chains and . . . bring him up to the start-
g line of a race and then say, "you are free to
ompete with all the others" and still justly believe
at you have been completely fair.*

965, Johnson urged companies to increase the
g and promoting of minorities.

time, many businesses, colleges, and other
anizations set up affirmative-action programs.
everyone was happy with this development,
ever. Some whites felt that affirmative action
ounted to little more than "reverse discrimina-
." That is, they felt
they would be denied
or college places
ause of their race.
/ith the Bakke ruling,
Supreme Court took a
promise position on
mative-action pro-
ns. They were accept-
, the Court said, as
g as they did not use
t racial quotas.

Why Does It Matter Now?

Since *Bakke,* the Court has ruled on several affirmative-action cases. In *Metro Broadcasting* v.
Federal Communications Commission (1990), for
example, the Court upheld a policy that gave
preference to minority broadcasters. However, in
Adarand Constructors, Inc. v. *Peña* (1995), the
Court struck down a similar affirmative-action
program.

The standing of affirmative action in college
admissions is somewhat clearer, however. Some
states have abandoned the policy altogether. In
California, for example, voters approved a 1996
referendum banning the state's universities from
using affirmative action in admissions.

Washington voters passed a similar measure in
1998. These and other states are looking for new
ways to help minority students attend college. One
method—adopted by California,
Florida, and Texas—guarantees
admission to state universities
for the top students from each
high school graduating class.

The affirmative-action debate, at
times, has been quite bitter. Here,
supporters and opponents of
affirmative action confront each
other at a demonstration on the
campus of the University of
California at Berkeley.

ONNECT TO HISTORY

Making Inferences In the *Bakke* case, the Supreme
Court issued six separate opinions. Also, the voting
on the two issues in the case was 5-4. From this
information, what inferences can you draw on the
Court's attitudes on affirmative action?

See Skillbuilder Handbook, page R12.

CONNECT TO TODAY

2. **Researching** The state university system of
Michigan recently has faced court challenges to its
affirmative-action program. Track the progress of
these challenges and write a few paragraphs
comparing the arguments and court findings in
Michigan to those in the *Bakke* case.

For more information on affirmative action . . .

RESEARCH LINKS
CLASSZONE.COM

RAND McNALLY
World Atlas

CONTENTS

Complete Legend for Physical and Political Maps

Symbols

Lake

Salt Lake

Seasonal Lake

River

\ Waterfall

— Canal

△ Mountain Peak

▲ Highest Mountain Peak

Cities

■ Los Angeles — City over 1,000,000 population

▣ Calgary — City of 250,000 to 1,000,000 population

• Haifa — City under 250,000 population

✪ Paris — National Capital

★ Vancouver — Secondary Capital (State, Province, or Territory)

Type Styles Used to Name Features

CHINA — Country

ONTARIO — State, Province, or Territory

PUERTO RICO (U.S.) — Possession

ATLANTIC OCEAN — Ocean or Sea

Alps — Physical Feature

Borneo — Island

Boundaries

International Boundary

Secondary Boundary

Land Elevation and Water Depths

Land Elevation

Meters	Feet
3,000 and over	9,840 and over
2,000 - 3,000	6,560 - 9,840
500 - 2,000	1,640 - 6,560
200 - 500	656 - 1,640
0 - 200	0 - 656

Water Depth

Less than 200	Less than 656
200 - 2,000	656 - 6,560
Over 2,000	Over 6,560

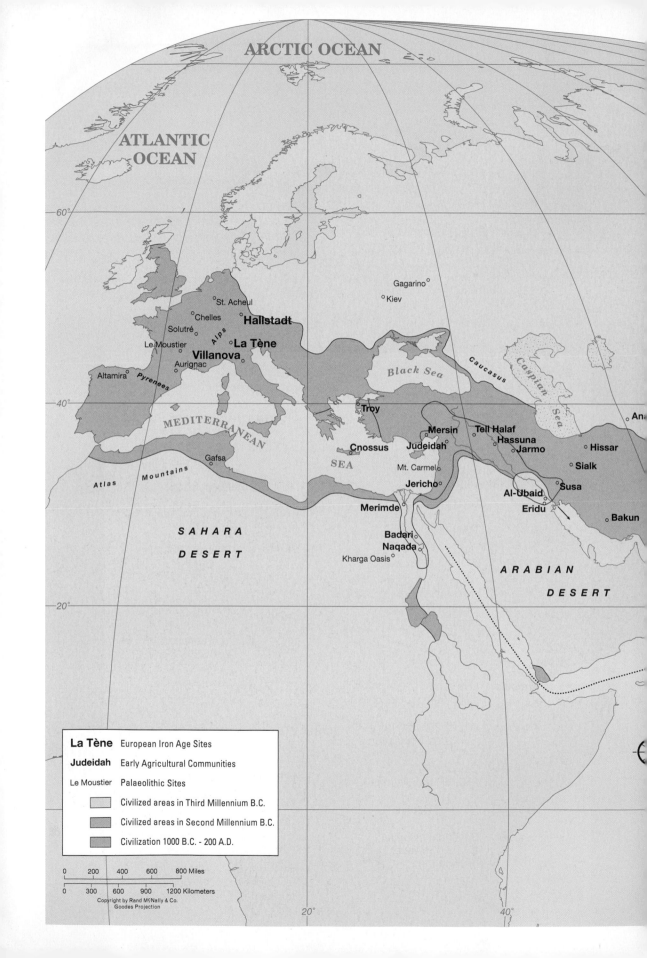

ARCTIC OCEAN

ATLANTIC
OCEAN

60°

Gagarino °
° Kiev

St. Acheul
° Chelles   Hallstadt
Solutré °
Le Moustier °   La Tène
          Villanova
Aurignac °

Altamira ° Pyrenees   Black Sea   Caucasus   Caspian Sea

40°   Troy   ° An

MEDITERRANEAN   Mersin   ° Tell Halaf
                              Cnossus   Judeidah   Hassuna
                                         °   ° Jarmo   ° Hissar
                    Gafsa   SEA   Mt. Carmel °   ° Sialk
Atlas   Mountains   Jericho °   Susa
                                    Merimde °   Al-Ubaid °   ° ° Bakun
                                                       Eridu °

SAHARA   Badari °
                                 Naqada °
DESERT   Kharga Oasis °   ARABIAN

                                                          DESERT
20°

La Tène   European Iron Age Sites

Judeidah   Early Agricultural Communities

Le Moustier Palaeolithic Sites

           Civilized areas in Third Millennium B.C.

           Civilized areas in Second Millennium B.C.

           Civilization 1000 B.C. - 200 A.D.

0   200   400   600   800 Miles

0   300   600   900   1200 Kilometers
Copyright by Rand McNally & Co.
Goodes Projection

20°   40°

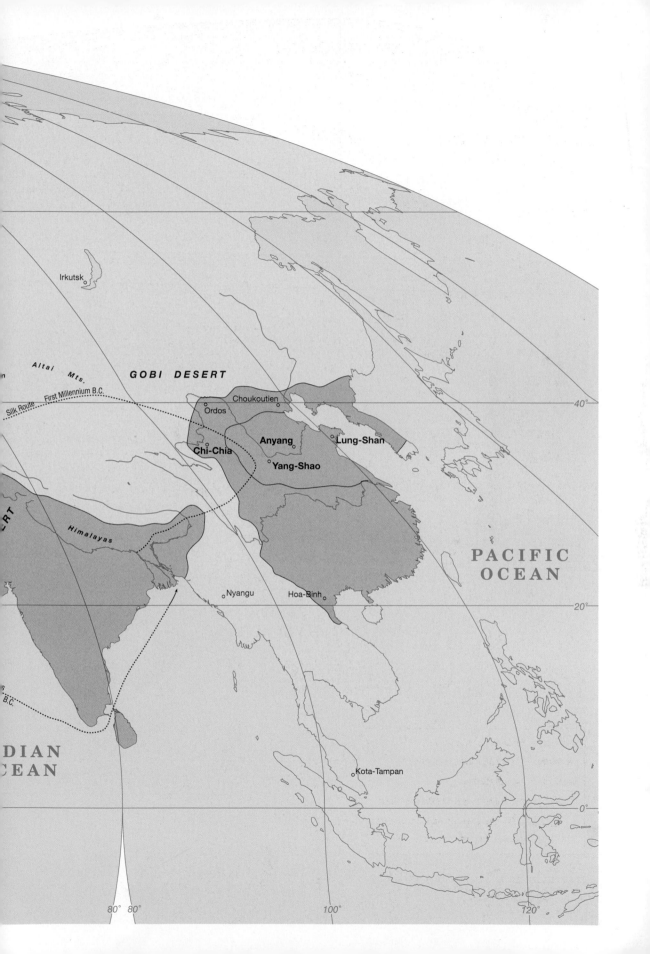

Irkutsk

Altai   Mts.
Silk Route   First Millennium B.C.
GOBI DESERT

Ordos   Choukoutien

Chi-Chia

Anyang   Lung-Shan

Yang-Shao

Himalayas

RT

Nyangu   Hoa-Binh

PACIFIC
OCEAN

DIAN
CEAN

B.C.

Kota-Tampan

40°

20°

0°

80° 80°   100°   120°

ARCTIC OCEAN

GREENLAND
(Den.)

Baffin
Bay

RUSSIA
ALASKA
Yukon (U.S.)
Anchorage

Hudson
Bay

C A N A D A

Aleutian Islands

Vancouver

Missouri

Newfoundland

Montréal
Ottawa

Chicago

UNITED STATES

New York
Washington D.C.

Azores
(Port.)

Colorado

Los Angeles

Mississippi

Houston

ATLANTIC

MIDWAY IS.
(U.S.)

Tropic of Cancer

MEXICO

Gulf of Mexico

BAHAMAS

Can.
Islar
(Sp

Hawaiian
Islands
(U.S)

Mexico City

CUBA

HAITI

DOM. REP.

PUERTO RICO (U.S.)

CAPE
VERDE

BELIZE

JAMAICA

Caribbean
Sea

PACIFIC

GUAT.
HOND.

GAI

EL. SAL.
NIC.

Caracas

TRINIDAD AND TOBAGO

GUINEA-B

COSTA
RICA

VENEZUELA

SIER

PANAMA

GUYANA

COLOMBIA

SURINAME
FRENCH GUIANA

Equator

ECUADOR

KIRIBATI

Galapagos Islands
(Ecuador)

Amazon

BRAZIL

PERU

O

SAMOA

OCEAN

Lima

AMERICAN
SAMOA

BOLIVIA

COOK
ISLANDS (N.Z.)

TONGA

FRENCH POLYNESIA

PARAGUAY

Rio de Janeiro

Tropic of Capricorn

Easter Island
(Chile)

ARGENTINA

URUGUAY

Santiago

Buenos
Aires

N

FALKLAND IS.
(U.K.)

South
Georgia
(U.K.)

0   1000   2000 Miles

0   1000   2000   3000 Kilometers
Copyright by Rand McNally & Co.
Robinson Projection

South
Orkney Is.
(U.K.)

Antarctic Circle

South
Shetland Is.
(U.K.)

Weddell
Sea

180   165   150   135   120   105   90   75   60   45

ARCTIC OCEAN

Franz Josef
Land

Novaya
Zemlya

RUSSIA

Yenisey

Lena

Bering

Sea

LAND
EST.
LAT.
A.
BELARUS

Volga
⊛ Moscow

Novosibirsk

Sea of Okhotsk

60°

UKRAINE

MOLD.

KAZAKHSTAN

ROM.

Black Sea

MONGOLIA

NORTH
KOREA

45°

BUL.

Sea of Japan

GEO.

Caspian Sea

UZBEKISTAN

KYAG.

REECE

ARM. AZER.

TURKMENISTAN

TAJIK.

CHINA

Beijing
⊛

SOUTH
KOREA

JAPAN

Tokyo

TURKEY

CYPRUS

SYRIA

LEB.

ISRAEL

IRAQ

JORDAN

KUWAIT

IRAN

AFGHANISTAN

Chang Jiang
(Yangtze)

Shanghai

PACIFIC

30°

n Sea

Cairo

QATAR

SAUDI

U.A.E.

EGYPT

ARABIA

OMAN

PAKISTAN

NEPAL

Ganges

BHU.

Kolkata
(Calcutta)

BNGL.

Guangzhou

TAIWAN

Tropic of Cancer

Mumbai
(Bombay)

INDIA

MYANMAR

LAOS

South China

NORTHERN
MARIANA ISLANDS
(U.S.)

WAKE ISLAND
(U.S.)

Nile

Red Sea

SUDAN

YEMEN

Arabian

Sea

Bay of

Bengal

THAILAND

Bangkok
⊛

CAMBODIA

VIETNAM

Sea

PHILIPPINES

GUAM (U.S.)

15°

Addis
Ababa
⊛

DJIBOUTI

SRI LANKA

OCEAN

NTRAL

RICAN

PUBLIC

ETHIOPIA

SOMALIA

PALAU

FED. STATES OF
MICRONESIA

ongo

UGANDA

KENYA

MALDIVES

BRUNEI

MARSHALL
ISLANDS

RWANDA

MALAYSIA

EM. REP.

BURUNDI

SINGAPORE

Borneo

New Guinea

SOLOMON
ISLANDS

F CONGO

TANZANIA

SEYCHELLES

Sumatra

PAPUA
NEW GUINEA

Equator

0°

Jakarta
⊛

INDONESIA

Java

EAST TIMOR

ZAMBIA

COMOROS

INDIAN

Darwin

15°

ZIMBABWE

MADAGASCAR

MAURITIUS

Coral Sea

VANUATU

BOTSWANA

REUNION
(Fr.)

NEW CALEDONIA
(Fr.)

FIJI

OCEAN

AUSTRALIA

Tropic of Capricorn

OUTH

SWAZILAND

Darling

Perth

Sydney

30°

FRICA

LESOTHO

Melbourne

Kerguelen
Islands
(Fr.)

NEW ZEALAND

Tasmania

Wellington ⊛

45°

60°

Antarctic Circle

75°

ARCTICA

45°   60°   75°   90°   120°   135°   150°   165°   180°

⊛ National Capital

• Major Cities

ARCTIC OCEAN

180° 165° 150° 135° 120° 105° 90° 75° 60° 45°

75°

Baffin
Island

Baffin
Bay

Greenland

Mt. McKinley △
20,320 Ft.
6,194m

Yukon

Mackenzie

Canadian Shield

Hudson
Bay

60°

Aleutian Islands

Newfoundland

Vancouver

NORTH
AMERICA

Rocky Mountains

Great Plains

St. Lawrence

45°

Azores

Los Angeles

Colorado

Mississippi

Appalachian Mts.

Washington D.C.

Cape Hatteras

ATLANTIC

Can.
Isla

30°

Midway Is.

Tropic of Cancer

Baja
California

Gulf of Mexico

Hawaiian
Islands

Yucatan
Peninsula

Cuba

Hispaniola

Puerto Rico

Cape
Verde
Islands

15°

Jamaica

Caribbean
Sea

Cape Ve

PACIFIC

OCEAN

Palmyra

Galapagos Islands

Orinoco

Trinidad

OCEAN

0°

Equator

Kiribati

OCEAN

Amazon

Amazon

SOUTH

Basin

Marquesas Is.

AMERICA

Andes

15°

Samoa
Islands

Mato Grosso
Plateau

Tonga
Is.

Cook
Islands

Tahiti

Tropic of Capricorn

Easter Island

Rio de Janeiro

Andes

Paraná

30°

△ Mt. Aconcagua
22,831 Ft.
6,959m

Buenos Aires

Archipiélago
Juan Fernández

N

Chatham Is.

45°

Patagonia

Falkland Is.

South
Georgia

0   1000   2000 Miles

0   1000   2000   3000 Kilometers

Copyright by Rand McNally & Co.
Robinson Projection

Tierra del Fuego

Cape Horn

South
Orkney Is.

60°

S

Antarctic Circle

South
Shetland Is.

Antarctic
Peninsula

Wedde
Sea

75°

Ross
Sea

Marie
Byrd
Land

△ Vinson Massif
16,066 Ft.
4,897m

180° 165° 150° 135° 120° 105° 90° 75° 60° 45°

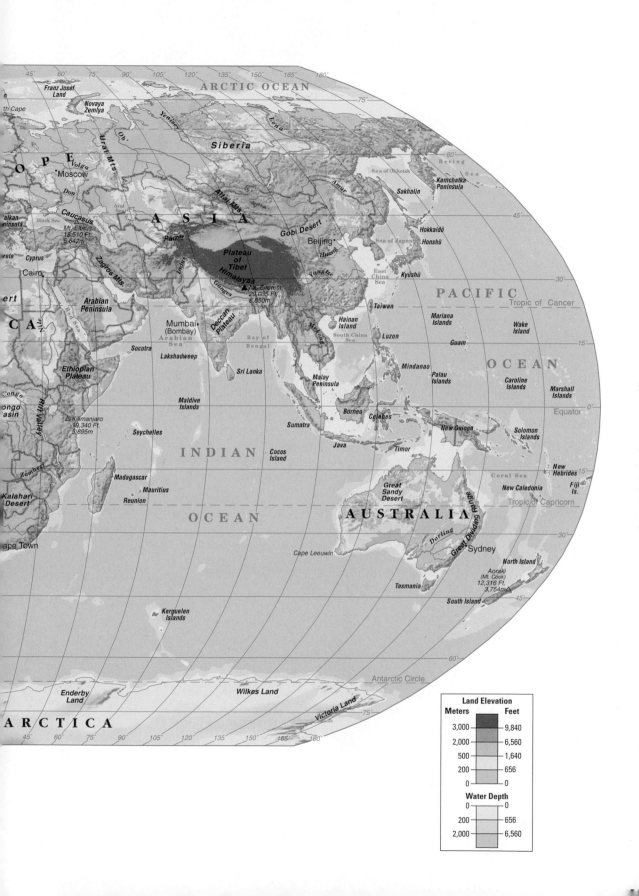

ARCTIC OCEAN

Franz Josef
Land

th Cape

Novaya
Zemlya

OPE

Volga
Moscow

Don

Ural Mts.

Ob'

Yenisey

Lena

Siberia

Bering
Sea

Sea of Okhotsk

Kamchatka
Peninsula

Sakhalin

A S I A

Aral
Sea

Black Sea

Caucasus

Mt. Elbrus
18,510 Ft.
5,642m

Pamir

Altai Mts.

Gobi Desert

Beijing

Amur

Hokkaidō

Honshū

Sea of Japan

alkan
ninsula

rete

Cyprus

Zagros Mts.

Plateau
of
Tibet

Himalayas

Huang

Yangtze

East
China
Sea

Kyūshū

PACIFIC

Cairo

Arabian
Peninsula

Indus

Ganges

Mt. Everest
29,035 Ft.
8,850m

Mekong

Taiwan

Tropic of Cancer

ert

CA

Nile

Red Sea

Mumbai
(Bombay)

Arabian
Sea

Deccan
Plateau

Bay of
Bengal

Hainan
Island

South China
Sea

Mariana
Islands

Wake
Island

Ethiopian
Plateau

Socotra

Lakshadweep

Sri Lanka

Luzon

Guam

OCEAN

Congo
asin

Rift Valley

△Kilimanjaro
19,340 Ft.
5,895m

Maldive
Islands

Seychelles

Maldive
Islands

Malay
Peninsula

Mindanao

Palau
Islands

Caroline
Islands

Marshall
Islands

Sumatra

Borneo

Celebes

New Guinea

Solomon
Islands

Equator

INDIAN

Cocos
Island

Java

Timor

Zambezi

Madagascar

Mauritius

Reunion

OCEAN

Great
Sandy
Desert

AUSTRALIA

Coral Sea

New Caledonia

New
Hebrides

Fiji
Is.

Kalahari
Desert

Tropic of Capricorn

ape Town

Cape Leeuwin

Darling

Great Dividing Range

Sydney

North Island

Kerguelen
Islands

Aoraki
(Mt. Cook)
12,316 Ft.
3,754m△

Tasmania

South Island

Antarctic Circle

Enderby
Land

Wilkes Land

Victoria Land

ARCTICA

Land Elevation		
Meters		Feet
3,000		9,840
2,000		6,560
500		1,640
200		656
0		0

Water Depth		
0		0
200		656
2,000		6,560

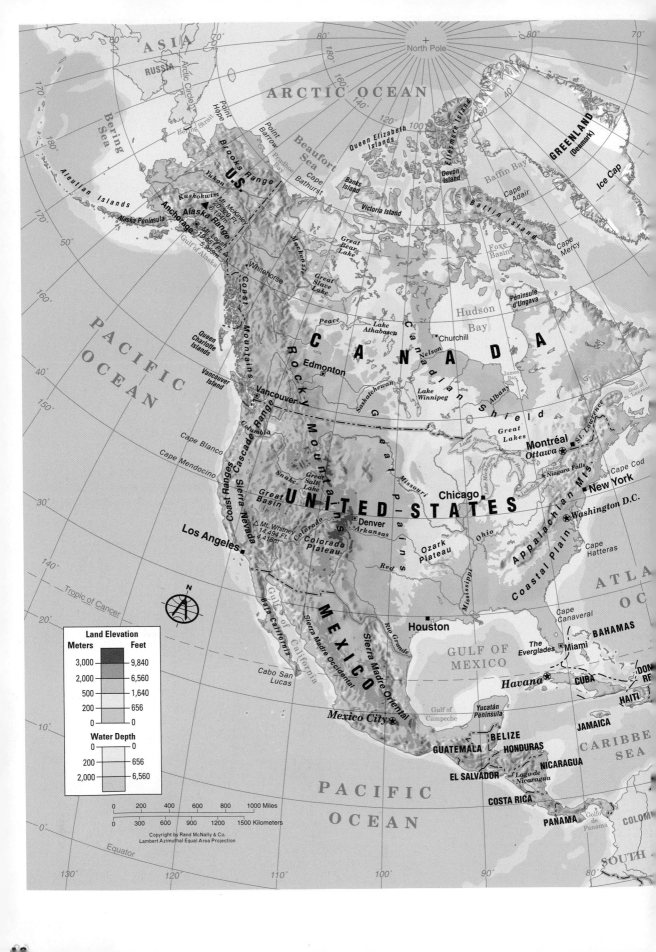

AMERICA

CUBA

DOMINICAN
REPUBLIC

HAITI

JAMAICA

PUERTO
RICO
(U.S.)

Greater Antilles

CARIBBEAN SEA

Lesser Antilles

BELIZE

Gulf of Honduras

HONDURAS

NICARAGUA

COSTA RICA

PANAMA

Gulf of
Panama

ATLANTIC
OCEAN

Cristóbal Colón Peak
18,948 Ft.
5,775m

Caracas

TRINIDAD AND
TOBAGO

Orinoco

Magdalena

Llanos

VENEZUELA

GUYANA

SURINAME

FRENCH
GUIANA

Cape Orange

Bogotá

COLOMBIA

agos
nds
c.)

ECUADOR

Chimborazo
20,703 Ft.
6,310m

Putumayo

Japurá

Amazon

Amazon

Basin

Manaus

Ilha de
Marajó

Belém

Equator

Juruá

Negro

Tapajós

Tocantins

Madeira

Selvas

BRAZIL

PERU

Andes

Ucayali

Mt. Huascaran
22,133 Ft.
6,746m

Lima

Lake
Titicaca

Mt. Illampu
21,066 Ft.
6,421m

Cordillera Oriental

BOLIVIA

Mato Grosso
Plateau

Recife

Serra do Espinhaço

Brasília

São Francisco

Mt. Sajama
21,463 Ft.
6,542m

Gran Chaco

PARAGUAY

Paraná

Atacama Desert

Isla San Ambrosio
(Chile)

Mt. Ojos del Salado
22,615 Ft.
6,893m

Andes

Paraná

São Paulo

Rio de
Janeiro

Tropic of Capricorn

of Capricorn

Isla San Felix
(Chile)

URUGUAY

Archipiélago
Juan Fernández
(Chile)

Santiago

CHILE

ARGENTINA

Mt. Aconcagua
22,831 Ft.
6,959m

Buenos
Aires

Río de la Plata

Pampas

CIFIC
EAN

Land Elevation

Meters		Feet
3,000		9,840
2,000		6,560
500		1,640
200		656
0		0

Water Depth

0		0
200		656
2,000		6,560

San Matías Gulf

Península Valdés

Chiloé

Patagonia

San Jorge Gulf

Point Medanoso

N

ATLANTIC
OCEAN

40°

Grand
Bay

West
Falkland

FALKLAND ISLANDS
(U.K.)

East
Falkland

Strait of Magellan

Tierra del
Fuego

Cape Horn

200 400 600 800 1000 Miles

300 600 900 1200 1500 Kilometers

Copyright by Rand McNally & Co.
Lambert Azimuthal Equal Area Projection

Drake Passage

South Shetland
Islands (U.K.)

South Orkney
Islands (U.K.)

South
Georgia
(U.K.)

South
Sandwich
Islands
(U.K.)

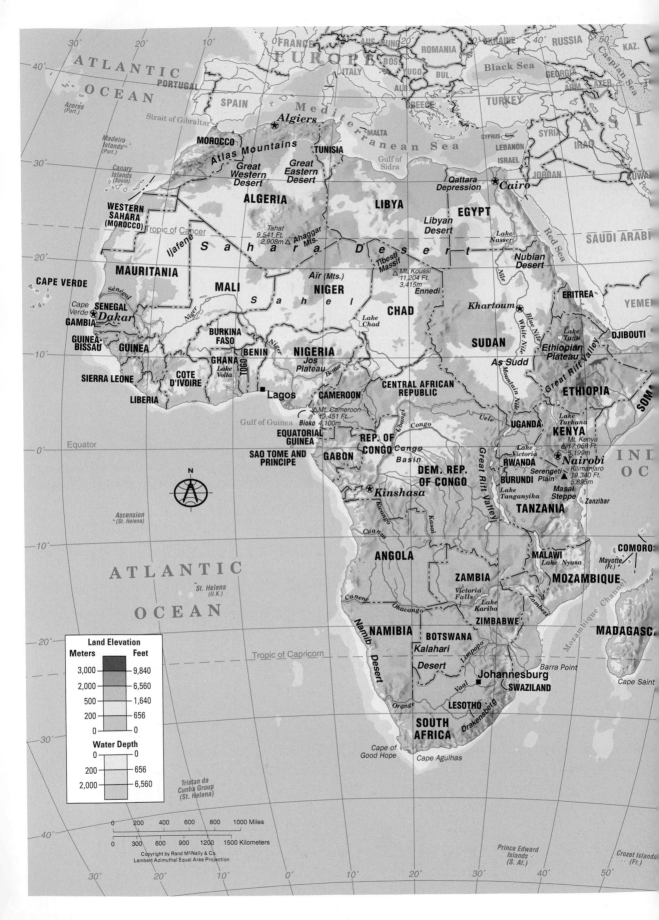

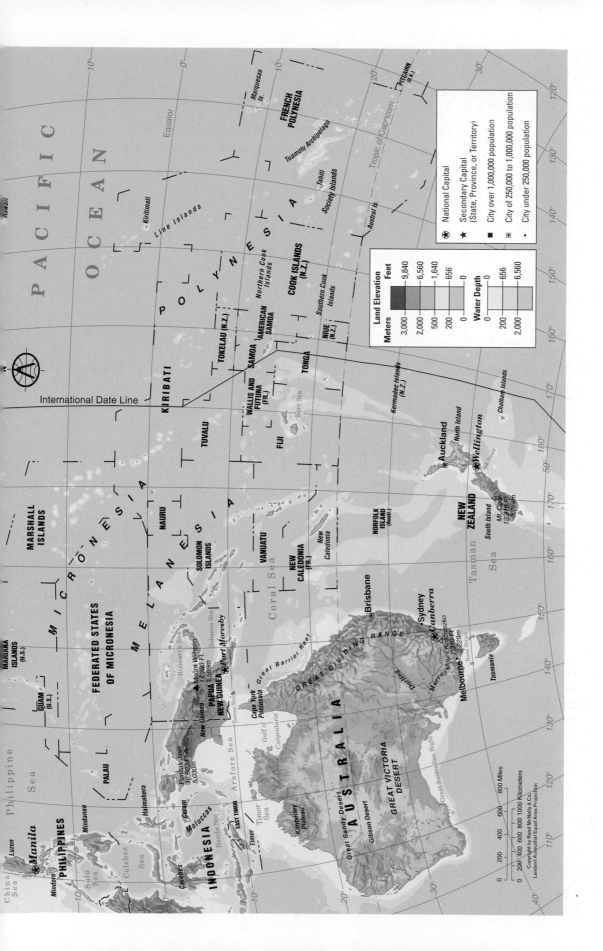

Land Elevation

Meters		Feet
3,000		9,840
2,000		6,560
500		1,640
200		656
0		0

Water Depth

0		0
200		656
2,000		6,560

N

0   100   200   300   400 Miles
0   200   400   600 Kilometers

Copyright by Rand McNally & Co.
Lambert Conformal Conic Projection

ICELAND

Horn

Surtsey

Fontur

Arctic Circle

NORWEGIAN
SEA

FAROE ISLANDS
(Den.)

Lofoten Islands

Scandina
Peninsu

NORWAY   SWEDE

Galdhøpiggen △
8,100 Ft.
2,469m

Glomma

Klaráliven

Dalö

Stockholm

Vänern   Vättern

ATLANTIC

OCEAN

Hebrides

Orkney
Islands

Grampian
Mts.

Cheviot
Hills

UNITED

KINGDOM

NORTH
SEA

Skagerrak

DENMARK

Norther

Bornholm
(Den.)

IRELAND

Irish
Sea

Great
Britain

St. George's Channel

Thames

London

NETHERLANDS

Elbe

Berlin ✪

Oder

GERMANY

English Channel

Strait of Dover

BELGIUM

Rhine

LUX.

CZECH
REPUBLIC

✪ Paris
Paris
Basin

Seine

Black
Forest

Bohemian
Forest

Danube

AUSTRIA

Loire

FRANCE

Saône

Jura

SWITZERLAND   LIECH.

A   l   p   s

Bay of Biscay

Cantabrian Mts.

Dordogne

Massif
Central

Mt. Blanc
15,771 Ft.
4,808m

Rhône

Po

Apennines

SLOVENIA

CROATIA

Doure

Iberian Mts.

Ebro

Pyrenees

ANDORRA

MONACO

SAN
MARINO

BOSNIA
HERZE

Dinaric Alps

ADRIATIC S

Lisbon ✪

PORTUGAL

Tagus

Iberian

Peninsula

SPAIN

Duero

Corsica
(Fr.)

Rome ✪

ITALY

Sierra Morena

Balearic Islands

Minorca

Ibiza   Majorca

Sardinia
(It.)

△ Vesuvius
4,190 Ft.
1,277m

Strait of Gibraltar

GIBRALTAR
(U.K.)

TYRRHENIAN
SEA

Algiers ⊛

MEDITERR

Mt. Etna
10,902 Ft.
3,323m △
Sicily

Io

MOROCCO

AFRICA

ALGERIA

TUNISIA

MALTA

ATLANTIC
OCEAN

ARCTI

Arctic Circle

Barents
Sea

IRELAND

FAEROE
ISLANDS
(Den.)

Novaya
Zemlya

UNITED
KINGDOM

London

NORWAY

SWEDEN

FINLAND

PORTUGAL

SPAIN

North Sea

DENMARK

Moscow

Ural Mountains

Ob

Sib

Lower

Yan
Pen

GIBRALTAR
(U.K.)

MOROCCO

ANDORRA

Monaco

FRANCE

GERMANY

POLAND

BELARUS

ESTONIA

LATVIA

LITH

Astana

KAZAKHSTAN

Lake
Balkh

AUSTRIA HUNGARY

SLOVAKIA

UKRAINE

Volga

ALGERIA

TUNISIA

ITALY

ROMANIA

BULGARIA

Black Sea

Caspian Depression

Aral
Sea

Astana

Syr Darya

Ishim

Tia

K2 (
28.2
8.6

ALBANIA

GREECE

Ankara

TURKEY

GEORGIA

Caucasus

Mount Ararat
16,940 ft.
5,165m

ARM.

AZER.

Caspian
Sea

Ust-Urt
Plateau

UZBEKISTAN

Amu Darya

KYRGYZSTAN

TAJIKISTAN

Pamirs

Hindu Kush

Mediterranean Sea

LIBYA

Cairo

EGYPT

Nile

N. CYPRUS

CYPRUS

LEBANON

ISRAEL

JORDAN

SYRIA

IRAQ

Euphrates

Tigris

Tehran

Zagros Mts.

Dasht-e Kavir

IRAN

Kara Kum
(Desert)

TURKMENISTAN

AFGHANISTAN

PAKISTAN

Indus

New
Delhi

Great
Indian
Desert

HIMA

Gang

CHAD

SUDAN

Sinai
Pen.

Red Sea

An-Nafud

SAUDI
ARABIA

Arabian
Peninsula

KUWAIT

Persian Gulf

BAHRAIN
QATAR

U.A.E.

Gulf of
Oman

OMAN

IND

ERITREA

DEM. REP.
OF THE CONGO
(ZAIRE)

RWANDA

BURUNDI

UGANDA

KENYA

ETHIOPIA

DJIBOUTI

SOMALIA

Gulf of Aden

Rub Al-Khali

YEMEN

Socotra
(Yem.)

Mumbai
(Bombay)

Godavari

Deccan
Plate
Easter

Western Ghats

Arabian Sea

N

TANZANIA

ZAMBIA

MALAWI

MOZAMBIQUE

Lakshadweep
(India)

MALDIVES

INDIAN OCEAN

0   200   400   600   800 Miles

0   200 400 600 800 1000 Kilometers

Copyright by Rand McNally & Co.
Lambert Azimuthal Equal Area Projection

A14

Land Elevation

Meters		Feet
3,000		9,840
2,000		6,560
500		1,640
200		656
0		0

Water Depth

0		0
200		656
2,000		6,560

New Siberian Islands

East Siberian Sea

Arctic Circle

Indigirka

Kolyma

Verkhoyansk Mts.

Lena

I A

e r i a

Stanovoy Range

Lake Baikal

Amur

Greater Khingan Range

Sikhote-Alin Mts.

MONGOLIA

i Desert

Beijing

N A

Qinling Shandi

Chang (Yangtze)

Huang

Xi

Gulf of Tonkin

Red

LAOS

THAILAND

angkok

Mekong

CAMBODIA

VIETNAM

Gulf of Thailand

MALAY PENINSULA

MALAYSIA

Str. of Malacca

Singapore

Sumatra

Jakarta

Java

Bering Sea

Aleutian Islands (U.S.)

Kamchatka Peninsula

Sea of Okhotsk

Sakhalin

Kuril Islands

Tatar Strait

Hokkaido

Honshu

Sea of Japan

Tokyo

Mt. Fuji △ 12,388 ft. 3,776m

JAPAN

NORTH KOREA

SOUTH KOREA

Shikoku

Kyushu

Yellow Sea

Shanghai

East China Sea

TAIWAN

Hainan Island

South China Sea

Luzon Strait

Luzon

Manila

PHILIPPINES

Mindanao

Sulu Sea

BRUNEI

MALAYSIA

Borneo

Celebes Sea

Celebes

Greater Sunda Islands

INDONESIA

Java Sea

EAST TIMOR

Timor

P A C I F I C   O C E A N

Tropic of Cancer

NORTHERN MARIANA ISLANDS (U.S.)

GUAM (U.S.)

Philippine Sea

FEDERATED STATES OF MICRONESIA

PALAU

Equator

Moluccas

Ceram

Banda Sea

New Guinea

PAPUA NEW GUINEA

Arafura Sea

Gulf of Carpentaria

Timor Sea

AUSTRALIA

Coral Sea

30°

170°

180°

20°

10°

0°

10°

20°

150°

140°

130°

120°

116°

100°

A15

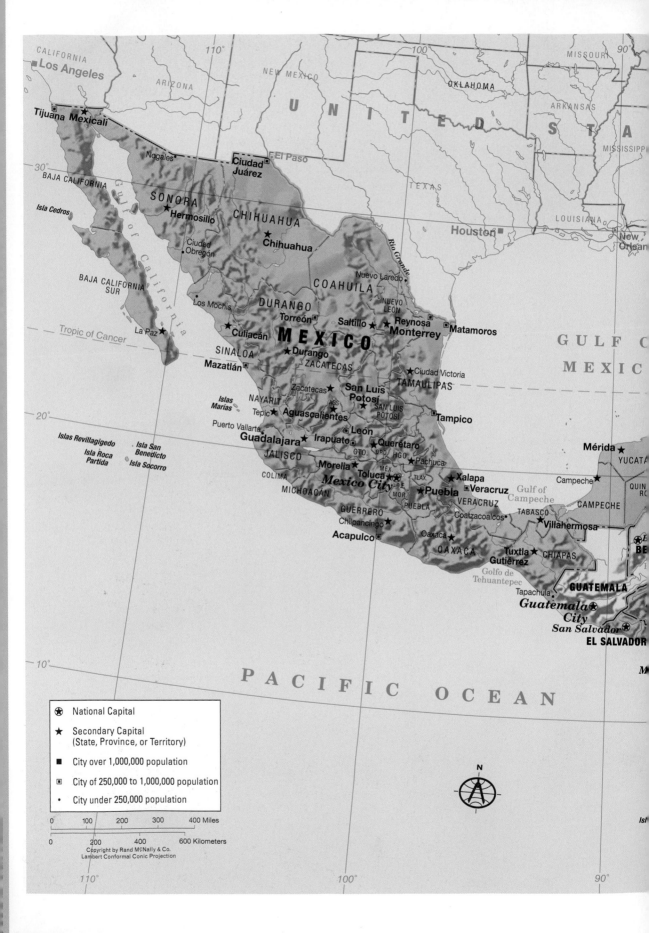

CALIFORNIA
■ Los Angeles

ARIZONA

NEW MEXICO

U N I T E D

OKLAHOMA

ARKANSAS

MISSOURI

MISSISSIPP

Tijuana ★Mexicali

Nogales•

El Paso

Ciudad
Juárez

TEXAS

S T A

30°

BAJA CALIFORNIA

Gulf

of

California

SONORA

CHIHUAHUA

★Hermosillo

Ciudad•
Obregón

★Chihuahua

Houston
□

LOUISIANA

New.
Orlean

Isla Cedros•

BAJA CALIFORNIA
SUR

Río Grande

Nuevo Laredo•

COAHUILA

NUEVO
LEÓN

GULF O

MEXIC

Los Mochis•

DURANGO
Torreón□

Saltillo ★ ★Reynosa
★Monterrey

□Matamoros

Tropic of Cancer

La Paz ★

Culiacán★

MEXICO

SINALOA
Mazatlán□

★Durango
ZACATECAS

Ciudad Victoria•

TAMAULIPAS

20°

Islas Revillagigedo

Isla Roca
Partida

Isla San
Benedicto

Isla Socorro•

Islas
Marías

NAYARIT
Tepic•

Puerto Vallarta•

Zacatecas★

Aguascalientes★

AGS•

★San Luis
Potosí

SAN LUIS
POTOSÍ

□Tampico

Guadalajara★

Irapuato•

León■

GTO.

★Querétaro
QRO.

•Pachuca

Mérida ★

YUCATA

JALISCO

COLIMA

Morelia★

MICHOACÁN

Toluca★
•Mexico City

HGO.

MÉX.

D.F.
★

TLAX.

MOR.

★Xalapa
■Veracruz

Campeche•

Gulf of
Campeche

CAMPECHE

QUIN.
RO

GUERRERO

Chilpancingo•

★Puebla

PUEBLA

VERACRUZ

Coatzacoalcos•

TABASCO

□Villahermosa

Acapulco□

Oaxaca•

OAXACA

Golfo de
Tehuantepec

Tuxtla ★
Gutiérrez CHIAPAS

E

BE

Tapachula•

GUATEMALA

10°

P A C I F I C   O C E A N

Guatemala✪
City

San Salvador✪
EL SALVADOR

M

Isl

✪ National Capital

★ Secondary Capital
    (State, Province, or Territory)

■ City over 1,000,000 population

▣ City of 250,000 to 1,000,000 population

• City under 250,000 population

N

0   100   200   300   400 Miles

0   200   400   600 Kilometers
Copyright by Rand McNally & Co.
Lambert Conformal Conic Projection

110°

100°

90°

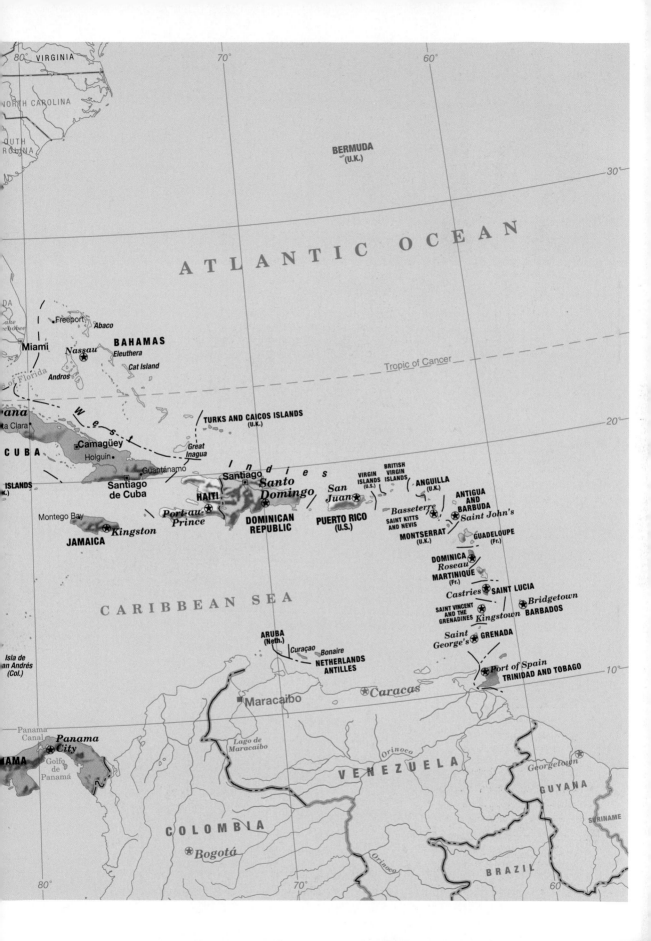

VIRGINIA

80°

NORTH CAROLINA

SOUTH CAROLINA

70°

60°

BERMUDA
(U.K.)

30°

ATLANTIC OCEAN

DA

Lake
Okeechobee

Freeport • Abaco

BAHAMAS

Miami

Nassau

Eleuthera

Cat Island

Tropic of Cancer

Andros

Straits of Florida

20°

ana

anta Clara

West

TURKS AND CAICOS ISLANDS
(U.K.)

CUBA

Camagüey

Holguín •

Guantánamo

Great
Inagua

Indies

VIRGIN
ISLANDS
(U.S.)

BRITISH
VIRGIN
ISLANDS

ANGUILLA
(U.K.)

ANTIGUA
AND
BARBUDA

ISLANDS

K.)

Santiago
de Cuba

Santiago

Santo
Domingo

San
Juan

Saint John's

HAITI

Basseterre
SAINT KITTS
AND NEVIS

GUADELOUPE
(Fr.)

Montego Bay

Port-au-
Prince

DOMINICAN
REPUBLIC

PUERTO RICO
(U.S.)

MONTSERRAT
(U.K.)

JAMAICA

Kingston

DOMINICA
Roseau

MARTINIQUE
(Fr.)

Castries

SAINT LUCIA

CARIBBEAN SEA

SAINT VINCENT
AND THE
GRENADINES

Bridgetown

BARBADOS

Kingstown

Isla de
an Andrés
(Col.)

ARUBA
(Neth.)

Curaçao

Bonaire

NETHERLANDS
ANTILLES

Saint
George's

GRENADA

Port of Spain

TRINIDAD AND TOBAGO

10°

Caracas

Panama
Canal

AMA

Panama
City

Golfo
de
Panamá

Maracaibo

Lago de
Maracaibo

Orinoco

VENEZUELA

Georgetown

GUYANA

COLOMBIA

Bogotá

Orinoco

SURINAME

BRAZIL

80°

70°

60°

A17

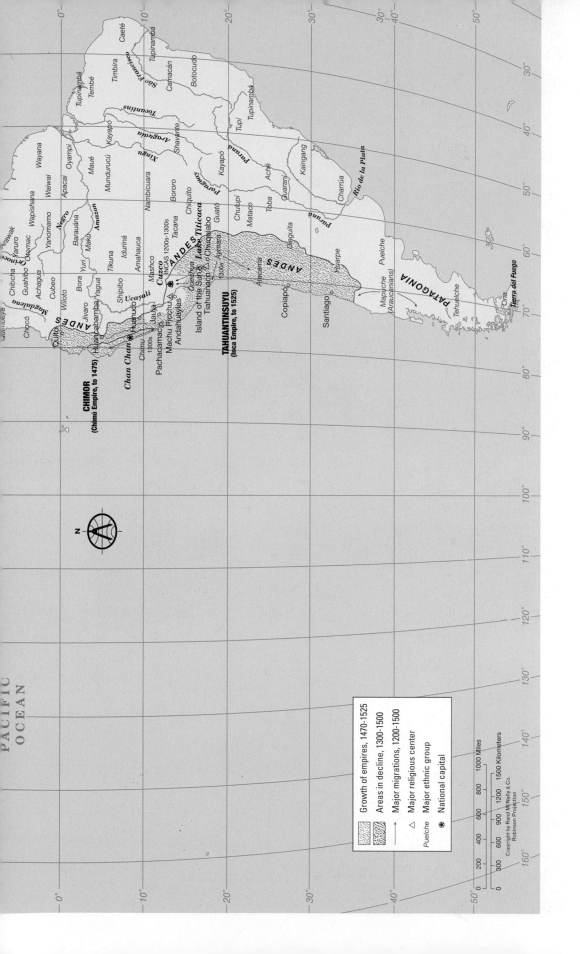

PACIFIC
OCEAN

CHIMOR
(Chimú Empire, to 1475)

TAHUANTINSUYU
(Inca Empire, to 1525)

ANDES

ANDES

PATAGONIA

Lake Titicaca

Chan Chan
Chimú
1300s

Pachacamac
Machu Picchu
Andahuaylas

Cuzco
INCAS 1200s–1300s

Quechua
Island of the Sun
Tiahuanaco
1300s

Aymara

Chucuito

Apatama

Copiapó

Santiago

Mapuche
(Araucanians)

Puelche

Tehuelche

Ona
Tierra del Fuego

Quito
Huancabamba
Huánuco

Jauja
Jivaro

Ucayali
Shipibo
Bora
Yuri
Yagua

Mashco
Tacana
Guató
Chulupí
Matacó
Toba
Guaraní

Huarpe

Chiquito

Amahuaca
Idurina
Tikuna
Makú

Wiloto
Achagua
Cubeo
Yanomamo
Baruáana

Chocó
Cuaiquer
Magdalena
Chibcha
Guahibo
Orinoco
Otomac
Yaruro
Wawak

Wapishana
Waiwai
Apacaí
Maué
Mundurucú
Kayapó
Nambicuara

Negro
Amazon

Wayana
Oyampi
Xingu
Bororo
Shavante
Kayapó

Timbira
Tembé
Tupinambá
Caeté
São Francisco
Tocantins
Araguaia
Camacán
Botocudo

Tupinambá
Tupinambá
Tupi
Aché
Kaingang
Charrúa

Caingang

Paraguay
Pilcomayo
Paraná
Río de la Plata
Paraná

N

	Growth of empires, 1470–1525			
	Areas in decline, 1300–1500			
→	Major migrations, 1200–1500			
△	Major religious center			
Puelche	Major ethnic group			
✵	National capital			

0   200   400   600   800   1000 Miles
0 300 600 900 1200 1500 Kilometers

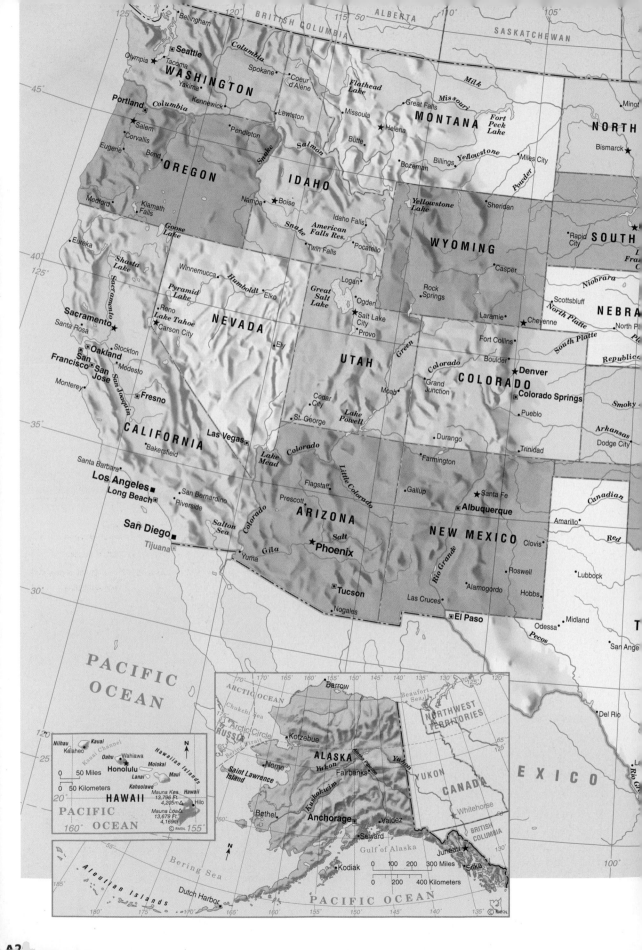

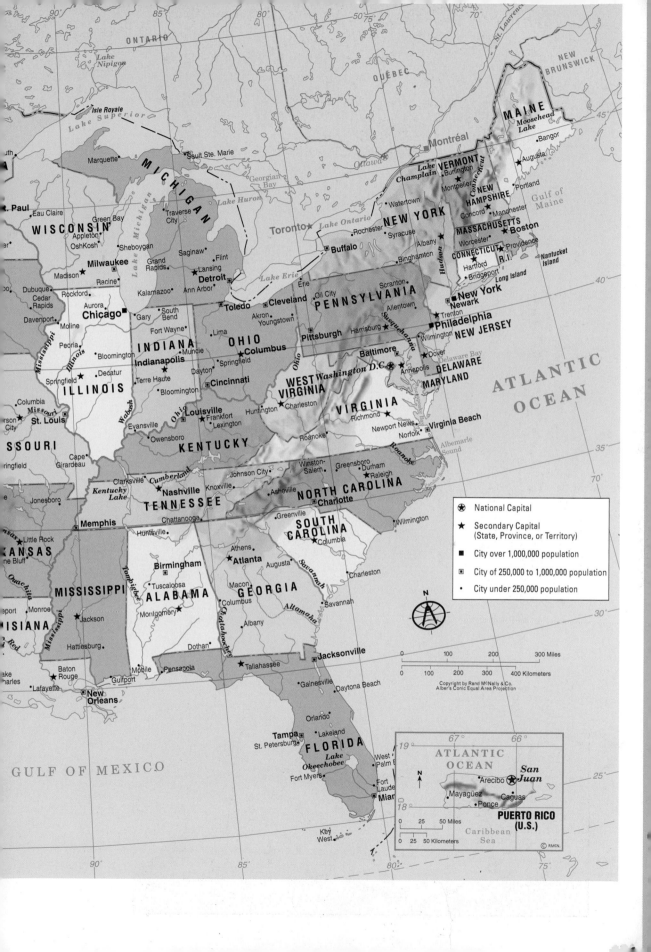

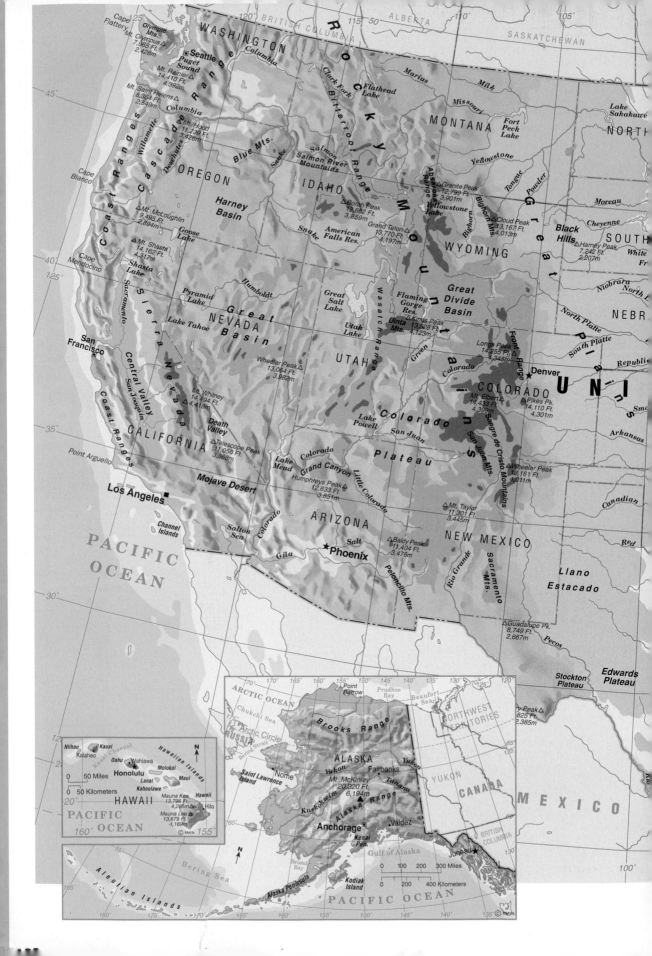

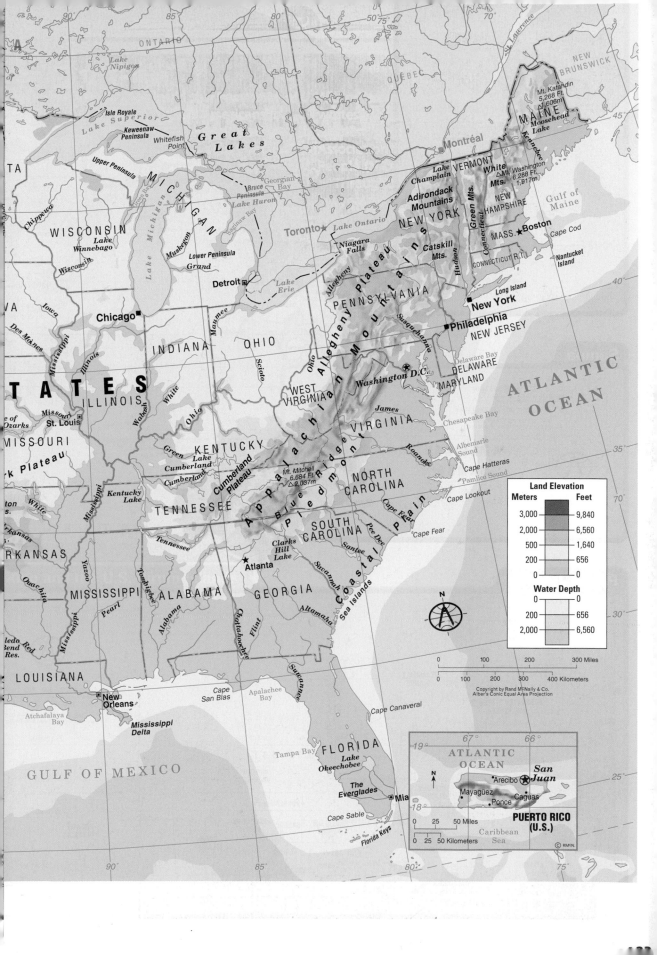

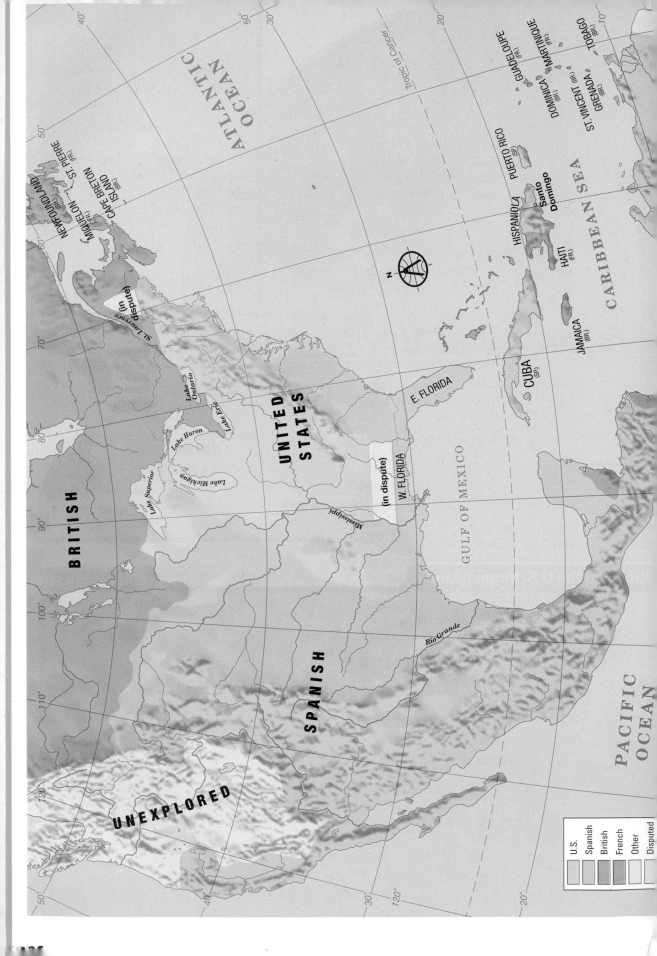

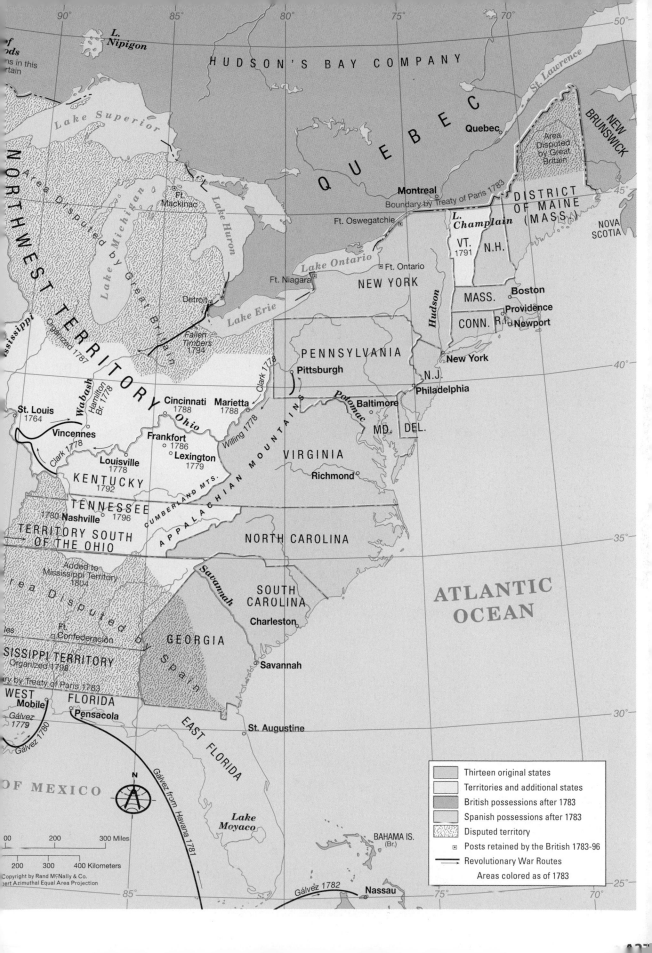

HUDSON'S BAY COMPANY

L. Nipigon

Lake Superior

QUEBEC

Quebec

Montreal

NEW BRUNSWICK

Area Disputed by Great Britain

Boundary by Treaty of Paris 1783

DISTRICT OF MAINE (MASS.)

NOVA SCOTIA

Ft. Oswegatchie

L. Champlain

VT. 1791

N.H.

NORTHWEST TERRITORY

Area Disputed by Great Britain

Lake Michigan

Ft. Mackinac

Lake Huron

Ft. Ontario

Lake Ontario

Ft. Niagara

NEW YORK

MASS.

Boston

Providence

Newport

Detroit

Lake Erie

CONN.

R.I.

Organized 1787

Hudson

Mississippi

Fallen Timbers 1794

New York

Clark 1778

PENNSYLVANIA

N.J.

Philadelphia

Pittsburgh

Wabash

Hamilton Br. 1778

Cincinnati 1788

Marietta 1788

Willing 1778

Potomac

Baltimore

St. Louis 1764

Ohio

MD.

DEL.

Vincennes 1778

Frankfort 1786

Lexington 1779

VIRGINIA

Clark 1778

Louisville 1778

Richmond

KENTUCKY 1792

APPALACHIAN MOUNTAINS

CUMBERLAND MTS.

TENNESSEE 1796

Nashville

1780

NORTH CAROLINA

TERRITORY SOUTH OF THE OHIO

Added to Mississippi Territory 1804

Area Disputed

SOUTH CAROLINA

Savannah

Charleston

Ft. Confederación

MISSISSIPPI TERRITORY Organized 1798

GEORGIA

Spain

Savannah

ATLANTIC OCEAN

Boundary by Treaty of Paris 1783

WEST FLORIDA

Mobile

Pensacola

Gálvez 1779

Gálvez 1780

EAST FLORIDA

St. Augustine

OF MEXICO

N

Gálvez from Havana 1781

Lake Moyaco

BAHAMA IS. (Br.)

100

200

300 Miles

200

300

400 Kilometers

Copyright by Rand McNally & Co.
bert Azimuthal Equal Area Projection

Gálvez 1782

Nassau

	Thirteen original states
	Territories and additional states
	British possessions after 1783
	Spanish possessions after 1783
	Disputed territory
□	Posts retained by the British 1783-96
→	Revolutionary War Routes
	Areas colored as of 1783

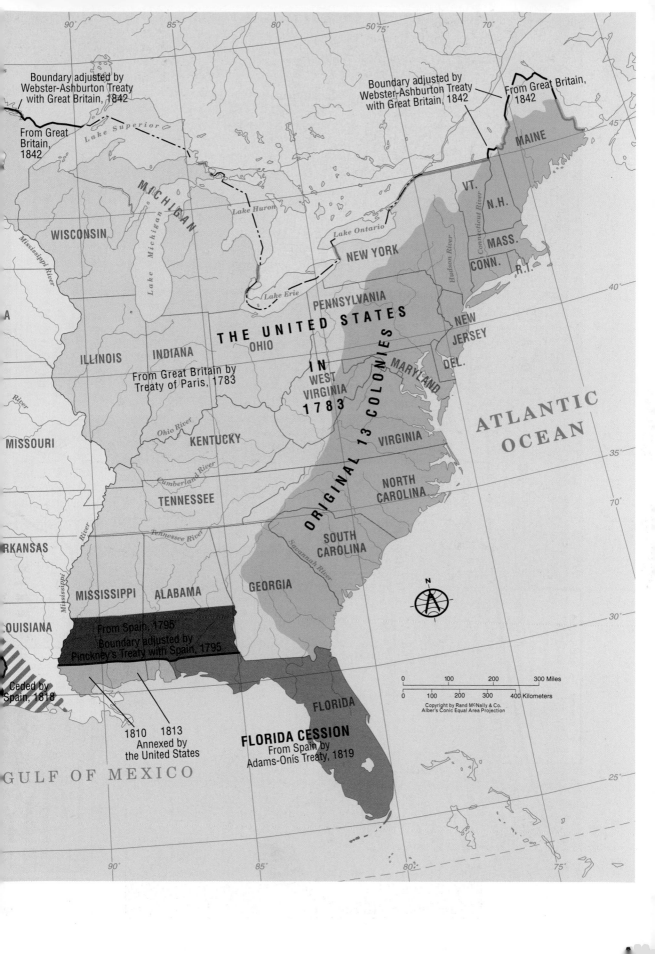

Boundary adjusted by
Webster-Ashburton Treaty
with Great Britain, 1842

From Great
Britain,
1842

Boundary adjusted by
Webster-Ashburton Treaty
with Great Britain, 1842

From Great Britain,
1842

Lake Superior

MICHIGAN

WISCONSIN

Lake Huron

Mississippi River

Lake Michigan

Lake Ontario

NEW YORK

MAINE

VT.

N.H.

MASS.

CONN.

R.I.

Lake Erie

PENNSYLVANIA

THE UNITED STATES

ILLINOIS

INDIANA

OHIO

NEW
JERSEY

DEL.

A

River

From Great Britain by
Treaty of Paris, 1783

IN

WEST
VIRGINIA

1783

MARYLAND

ORIGINAL 13 COLONIES

ATLANTIC
OCEAN

MISSOURI

Ohio River

KENTUCKY

VIRGINIA

35°

Cumberland River

TENNESSEE

NORTH
CAROLINA

70°

RKANSAS

River

Tennessee River

SOUTH
CAROLINA

Savannah River

MISSISSIPPI

ALABAMA

GEORGIA

N

30°

OUISIANA

Mississippi River

From Spain, 1795

Boundary adjusted by
Pinckney's Treaty with Spain, 1795

Ceded by
Spain, 1818

1810   1813
Annexed by
the United States

FLORIDA CESSION
From Spain by
Adams-Onís Treaty, 1819

FLORIDA

0   100   200   300 Miles

0   100   200   300   400 Kilometers

Copyright by Rand McNally & Co.
Alber's Conic Equal Area Projection

GULF OF MEXICO

25°

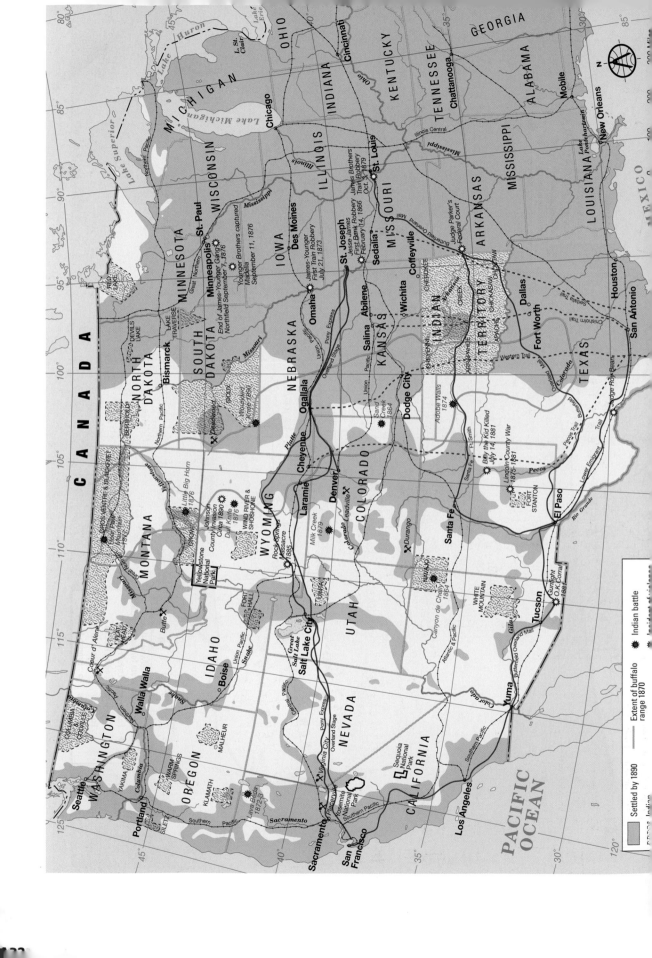

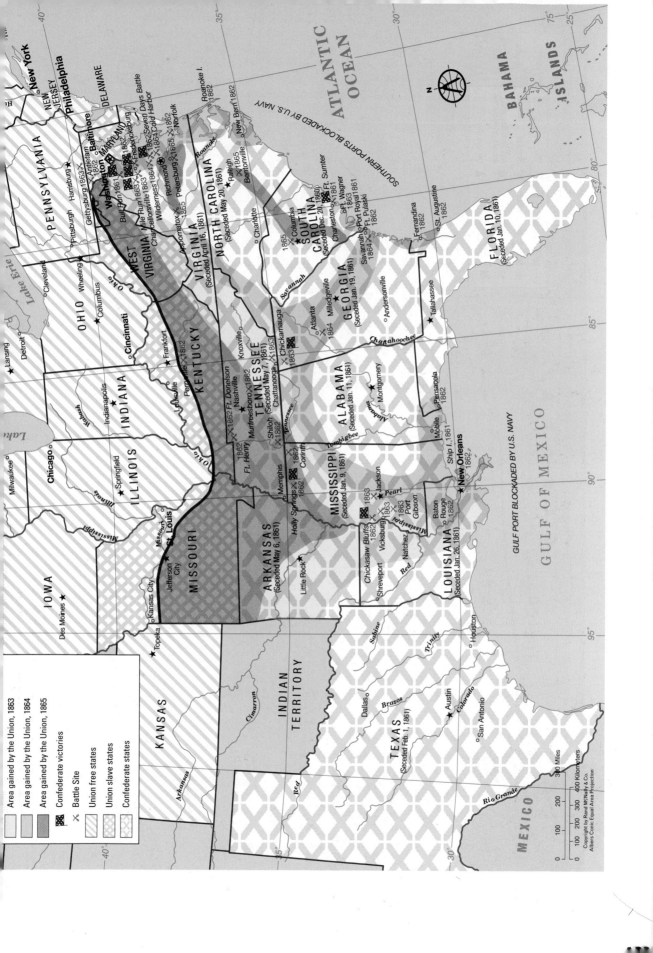

Legend

- Area gained by the Union, 1863
- Area gained by the Union, 1864
- Area gained by the Union, 1865
- Confederate victories
- × Battle Site
- Union free states
- Union slave states
- Confederate states

Copyright by Rand McNally & Co.
Albers Conic Equal Area Projection

0 100 200 300 400 Miles
0 100 200 300 400 Kilometers

ATLANTIC OCEAN

GULF OF MEXICO

BAHAMA ISLANDS

MEXICO

SOUTHERN PORTS BLOCKADED BY U.S. NAVY

GULF PORT BLOCKADED BY U.S. NAVY

New York
NEW JERSEY
Philadelphia
DELAWARE
Baltimore
MARYLAND
Washington 1861
Antietam 1862
Fredericksburg
Bull Run 1861 × 1862 Seven Days Battle
Mile Run 1863 × 1862 × 1864 Cold Harbor
Richmond × 1865 1862
Petersburg × 1865 1864
Chancellorsville 1863 Norfolk
Wilderness 1864 ×
Appomattox × 1865
Roanoke I. 1862
New Bern 1862

PENNSYLVANIA
Gettysburg 1863 ×
Harrisburg
Pittsburgh

Cleveland
Wheeling
Columbus
OHIO
Cincinnati
Frankfort
Louisville
KENTUCKY

Lake Erie

Detroit
Lansing

Milwaukee
Chicago
ILLINOIS
Springfield
Indianapolis
INDIANA

IOWA
Des Moines

St. Louis
Jefferson City
Kansas City
MISSOURI
Topeka
KANSAS

WEST VIRGINIA
(Seceded 1861)

VIRGINIA
(Seceded April 16, 1861)

NORTH CAROLINA
(Seceded May 20, 1861)
Raleigh
Bentonville × 1865

SOUTH CAROLINA
(Seceded Dec. 20, 1860)
Columbia 1865
Charlotte
Charleston × 1861
Ft. Sumter
Ft. Wagner 1863
Ft. Pulaski 1862
Port Royal 1861

GEORGIA
(Seceded Jan. 19, 1861)
Atlanta 1864
Milledgeville
Savannah 1864
Andersonville
Chickamauga × 1863

TENNESSEE
(Seceded May 7, 1861)
Knoxville
Nashville
Murfreesboro × 1862
Chattanooga × 1863
Shiloh × 1862
Ft. Donelson × 1862
Ft. Henry × 1862
Memphis 1862
Corinth
Perryville × 1862

ALABAMA
(Seceded Jan. 11, 1861)
Montgomery
Mobile 1862
Pensacola 1862

FLORIDA
(Seceded Jan. 10, 1861)
Tallahassee
Fernandina 1862
St. Augustine 1862

MISSISSIPPI
(Seceded Jan. 9, 1861)
Jackson 1863
Holly Springs × 1862
Chickasaw Bluffs 1862
Vicksburg 1863
Natchez

ARKANSAS
(Seceded May 6, 1861)
Little Rock

LOUISIANA
(Seceded Jan. 26, 1861)
Baton Rouge 1862
Port Gibson 1863
New Orleans 1862
Ship I. 1861

TEXAS
(Seceded Feb. 1, 1861)
Dallas
Austin
San Antonio
Houston

INDIAN TERRITORY

Rivers labeled: Ohio, Mississippi, Missouri, Wabash, Roanoke, Savannah, Chattahoochee, Tennessee, Tombigbee, Alabama, Pearl, Red, Trinity, Brazos, Colorado, Sabine, Rio Grande, Cimarron, Arkansas

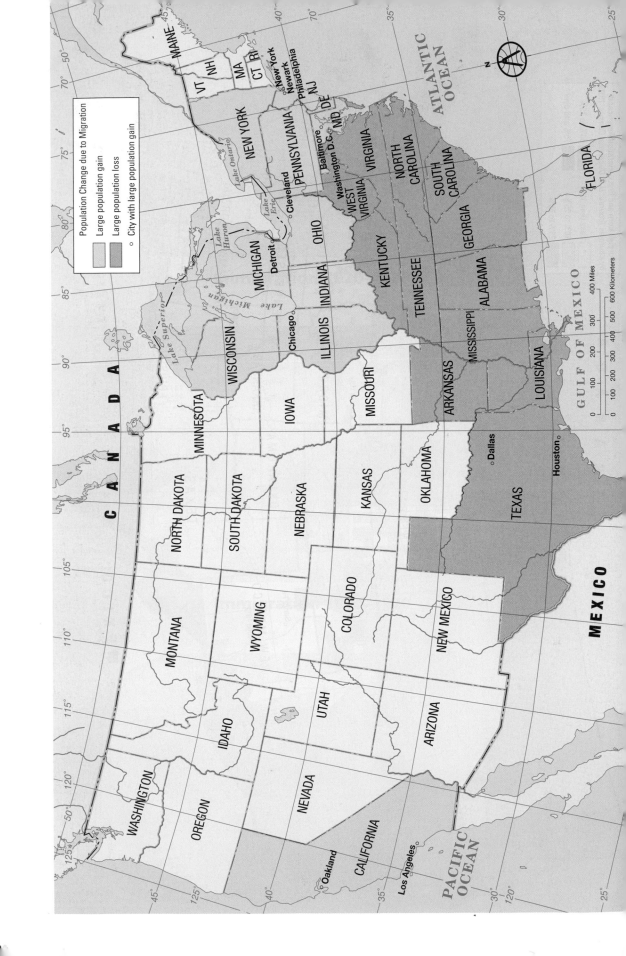

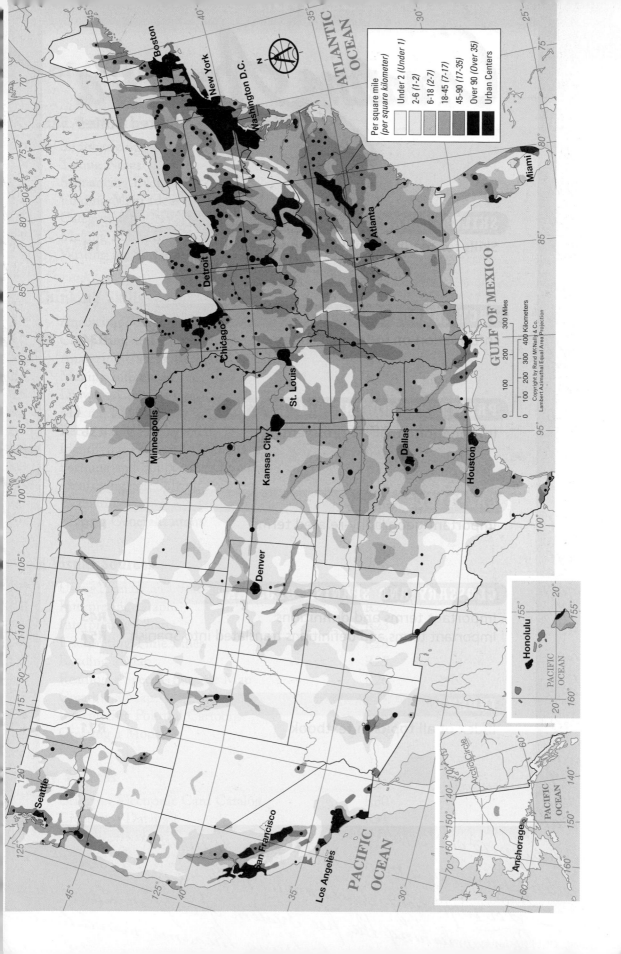

1.1 Summarizing

Defining the Skill

When you **summarize,** you restate a paragraph, passage, or chapter in fewer words. You include only the main ideas and most important details. It is important to use your own words when summarizing.

Applying the Skill

The passage below tells about Harriet Tubman, a prominent member of the Underground Railroad. She helped runaway slaves to freedom. Use the strategies listed below to help you summarize the passage.

How to Summarize

Strategy ❶ Look for topic sentences stating the main idea. These are often at the beginning of a section or paragraph. Briefly restate each main idea—in your own words.

Strategy ❷ Include key facts and any numbers, dates, amounts, or percentages from the text.

Strategy ❸ After writing your summary, review it to see that you have included only the most important details.

HARRIET TUBMAN

❶ One of the most famous conductors on the Underground Railroad was Harriet Tubman. ❷ Born into slavery in Maryland, the 13-year-old Tubman once tried to save another slave from punishment. The angry overseer fractured Tubman's skull with a two-pound weight. She suffered fainting spells for the rest of her life but did not let that stop her from working for freedom. When she was 25, Tubman learned that her owner was about to sell her. Instead, ❷ she escaped.

After her escape, ❷ Harriet Tubman made 19 dangerous journeys to free enslaved persons. The tiny woman carried a pistol to frighten off slave hunters and medicine to quiet crying babies. Her enemies offered $40,000 for her capture, but ❷ no one caught her. "I never run my train off the track and I never lost a passenger," she proudly declared. Among the people she saved were her parents.

Write a Summary

You can write your summary in a paragraph. The paragraph at right summarizes the passage you just read.

Practicing the Skill

Turn to Chapter 6, Section 2, "Colonial Resistance Grows." Read "The Boston Tea Party" and write a paragraph summarizing the passage.

❸ Harriet Tubman was one of the most famous conductors on the Underground Railroad. She had been a slave, but she escaped. She later made 19 dangerous journeys to free other slaves. She was never captured.

2 Taking Notes

Defining the Skill

When you **take notes,** you write down the important ideas and details of a paragraph, page, or chapter. A chart or an outline can help you organize your notes to use in the future.

Applying the Skill

The following passage describes President Washington's cabinet. Use the strategies listed below to help you take notes on the passage.

How to Take and Organize Notes

Strategy ❶ Look at the title to find the main topic of the passage.

Strategy ❷ Identify the main idea and details of the passage. Briefly summarize the main idea and details in your notes.

Strategy ❸ Identify key terms and define them. The term *cabinet* is shown in boldface type and underlined. Both techniques signal that it is a key term.

Strategy ❹ In your notes, use abbreviations to save time and space. You can abbreviate words such as *department (dept.), secretary (sec.), United States (U.S.),* and *president (pres.)* to save time and space.

---

❶ WASHINGTON'S CABINET

❷ The Constitution gave Congress the task of creating departments to help the president lead the nation. The ❷ president had the power to appoint the heads of these departments, which became his ❸ **cabinet**.

Congress created three departments. Washington chose talented people to run them. ❷ For secretary of war, he picked Henry Knox, a trusted general during the Revolution. ❷ For secretary of state, Washington chose Thomas Jefferson. He had been serving as ambassador to France. The State Department oversaw U.S. foreign relations. For secretary of the treasury, Washington turned to the brilliant ❷ Alexander Hamilton.

Make a Chart

Making a chart can help you take notes on a passage. The chart below contains notes on the passage you just read.

Item	Notes
❸ cabinet	heads of ❹ depts; ❹ pres. appoints heads
a. War Dept.	Henry Knox; ❹ sec. of war; former Revolutionary War general
b. State Dept.	Thomas Jefferson; sec. of state; oversees relations between ❹ U.S. and other countries
c. Treasury Dept.	Alexander Hamilton; sec. of the treasury

Practicing the Skill

Turn to Chapter 3, Section 3, "Founding the Middle and Southern Colonies." Read "Maryland and the Carolinas" and use a chart to take notes on the passage.

1.3 Sequencing Events

Defining the Skill

Sequence is the order in which events follow one another. By being able to follow the sequence of events through history, you can get an accurate sense of the relationship among events.

Applying the Skill

The following passage describes the sequence of events involved in Britain's plan to capture the Hudson River Valley during the American Revolution. Use the strategies listed below to help you follow the sequence of events.

How to Find the Sequence of Events

Strategy ① Look for specific dates provided in the text. If several months within a year are included, the year is usually not repeated.

Strategy ② Look for clues about time that allow you to order events according to sequence. Words such as *day, week, month,* or *year* may help to sequence the events.

> ### BRITAIN'S STRATEGY
>
> Burgoyne captured Fort Ticonderoga in ① July 1777. From the[ ]it was 25 miles to the Hudson River, which ran to Alba[ ]② Burgoyne took three weeks to reach the Hudson. On ① Aug[ ]3, Burgoyne received a message from Howe. He would not[ ]coming north, Howe wrote, because he had decided to inva[ ]Pennsylvania to try to capture Philadelphia and Gene[ ]Washington. "Success be ever with you," Howe's message sa[ ]But General Burgoyne needed Howe's soldiers, not his good wish[ ]Howe did invade Pennsylvania. In ① September 1777, he defea[ ]—but did not capture—Washington at the Battle of Brandywine[ ]

Make a Time Line

Making a time line can help you sequence events. The time line below shows the sequence of events in the passage you just read.

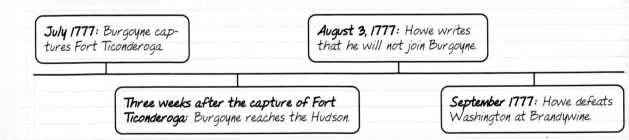

July 1777: Burgoyne captures Fort Ticonderoga.

August 3, 1777: Howe writes that he will *not* join Burgoyne.

Three weeks after the capture of Fort Ticonderoga: Burgoyne reaches the Hudson.

September 1777: Howe defeats Washington at Brandywine.

Practicing the Skill

Turn to Chapter 2, Section 1, "Spain Claims an Empire." Read "Europeans Explore Foreign Lands" and make a time line showing the sequence of events in that passage.

4 Finding Main Ideas

ining the Skill

main idea is a statement that summarizes the main point of a speech, an article, a
n of a book, or a paragraph. Main ideas can be stated or unstated. The main idea
paragraph is often stated in the first or last sentence. If it is the first sentence, it is
ved by sentences that support that main idea. If it is the last sentence, the details
up to the main idea. To find an unstated idea, you must use the details of the para-
as clues.

olying the Skill

ollowing paragraph describes the role of women in the American Revolution. Use
rategies listed below to help you identify the main idea.

to Find the Main Idea

ategy 1 Identify what you
may be the stated main idea.
k the first and last sentences
e paragraph to see if either
d be the stated main idea.

ategy 2 Identify details that
ort that idea. Some details
ain the main idea. Others give
mples of what is stated in the
idea.

> ### WOMEN IN THE REVOLUTION
>
> **1** Many women tried to help the army. Martha Washington and
> other wives followed their husbands to army camps. **2** The wives
> cooked, did laundry, and nursed sick or wounded soldiers.
> **2** A few women even helped to fight. **2** Mary Hays earned the
> nickname "Molly Pitcher" by carrying water to tired soldiers dur-
> ing a battle. **2** Deborah Sampson dressed as a man, enlisted, and
> fought in several engagements.

e a Chart

g a chart can help you identify the main idea and details in a passage or paragraph.
hart below identifies the main idea and details in the paragraph you just read.

ain Idea: Women helped the army during the Revolution.

tail: They cooked and did laundry.
tail: They nursed the wounded and sick soldiers.
tail: They helped to fight.
tail: One woman, Molly Pitcher, carried water to soldiers during battles.

cticing the Skill

o Chapter 5, Section 1, "Early American Culture." Read "Women and the Economy"
reate a chart that identifies the main idea and the supporting details.

1.5 Categorizing

Defining the Skill

To **categorize** is to sort people, objects, ideas, or other information into groups, called categories. Historians categorize information to help them identify and understand patterns in historical events.

Applying the Skill

The following passage contains information about the reasons people went west during the mid-1800s. Use the strategies listed below to help you categorize information.

How to Categorize

Strategy ❶ First, decide what kind of information needs to be categorized. Decide what the passage is about and how that information can be sorted into categories.

For example, find the different motives people had for moving west.

Strategy ❷ Then find out what the categories will be. To find why many different groups of people moved west, look for clue words such as *some, other,* and *another.*

Strategy ❸ Once you have chosen the categories, sort information into them. Of the people who went west, which ones had which motives?

THE LURE OF THE WEST

❶ People had many different motives for going west. ❷ One moti was to make money. ❷ *Some* people called speculators bought hu areas of land and made great profits by selling it to thousands of se tlers. ❷ *Other* settlers included farmers who dreamed of owning the own farms in the West because land was difficult to acquire in t East. ❷ *Another* group to move west was merchants. They hoped earn money by selling items that farmers needed. Finally, ❷ *so* people went west for religious reasons. These people includ ❷ missionaries, who wanted to convert the Native Americans Christianity, and Mormons, who wanted a place where they cou practice their faith without interference.

Make a Chart

Making a chart can help you categorize information. You should have as many columns as you have categories. The chart below shows how the information from the passage you just read can be categorized.

Motives	Money	Land	Religion
❸ Groups	• speculators • merchants	• farmers	• missionaries • Mormons

Practicing the Skill

Turn to Chapter 14, Section 3, "Reforming American Society." Read "Improving Education" and make a chart in which you categorize the changes happening in elementary, high school, and college education.

6 Making Public Speeches

...ining the Skill

...ech is a talk given in public to an audience. Some speeches are given to persuade ...udience to think or act in a certain way, or to support a cause. You can learn how to **public speeches** effectively by analyzing great speeches in history.

...plying the Skill

...ollowing is an excerpt from the "I Have a Dream" speech delivered by Martin Luther ...Jr., in 1963 in Washington, D.C. Use the strategies listed below to help you analyze ...speech and prepare a speech of your own.

...to Analyze and Prepare a Speech

...tegy ❶ Choose one central ...or theme and organize your ...ch to support it. King orga-...l his speech around his dream ...uality.

...tegy ❷ Use words or ...es that will win over your ...nce. King referred to the ...ration of Independence when ...ed the words "all men are ...ed equal."

...tegy ❸ Repeat words or ...es to drive home your main ...—as if it is the "hook" of a ...ong. King repeats the phrase ...ve a dream."

I HAVE A DREAM

❶ I have a dream that one day this nation will rise up and live out the true meaning of its creed—we hold these truths to be ❷ self-evident that all men are created equal.

❸ I have a dream that one day on the red hills of Georgia the sons of former slaves and the sons of former slave owners will be able to sit down together at the table of brotherhood.

❸ I have a dream that my four little children will one day live in a nation where they will not be judged by the color of their skin but by the content of their character.

❸ I have a dream today!

...e an Outline

...g an outline like the one to ...ght will help you make an ...ive public speech.

...cticing the Skill

...o Chapter 12, Section 2, ...son's Policy Toward Native ...cans." Read the section and ...e a topic for a speech. First, ...an outline like the one to ...ght to organize your ideas. ...write your speech. Next, ...ce giving your speech. Make ...ree-minute speech.

Title: I Have a Dream

I. **Introduce Theme:** I have a dream
   A. This nation will live up to its creed
   B. Quote from the Declaration of Independence:
      that all men are created equal

II. **Repeat theme:** I have a dream
   A. Sons of former slaves and slave owners will sit
      together in brotherhood
   B. My four children will be judged by their character,
      not by their skin color

III. **Conclude:** I have a dream

1.7 Writing for Social Studies

Defining the Skill

Writing for social studies requires you to describe an idea, situation, or event. Often, social studies writing takes a stand on a particular issue or tries to make a specific point. To successfully describe an event or make a point, your writing needs to be clear, concise, and factually accurate.

Applying the Skill

The following passage describes Stephen A. Douglas. Notice how the strategies below helped the writer explain Douglas's historical importance.

How to Write for Social Studies

Strategy ❶ Focus on your topic. Be sure that you clearly state the main idea of your piece so that your readers know what you intend to say.

Strategy ❷ Collect and organize your facts. Collect accurate information about your topic to support the main idea you are trying to make. Use your information to build a logical case to prove your point.

Strategy ❸ To express your ideas clearly, use standard grammar, spelling, sentence structure, and punctuation when writing for social studies. Proofread your work to make sure it is well organized and grammatically correct.

STEPHEN A. DOUGLAS, 1813–1861

❶ Stephen A. Douglas was one of the most powerful membe of Congress in the 1850s. In fact, ❷ he was called the "Lit Giant" because he commanded great respect even though he w only five feet four inches tall. The most important issue th Douglas faced in his career was slavery in the territories. ❷ I played a key role in the passage of the Compromise of 1850 well as the Kansas–Nebraska Act, which addressed this issue. 1858, his famous debates with Abraham Lincoln also focused slavery in the territories. ❷ When Douglas ran for president 1860, his position on slavery was critical to his defeat.

Practicing the Skill

Turn to Chapter 15, Section 1, "Growing Tensions Between North and South." Read the section and use the strategies above to write your answer to Question 4 on page 461.

1 Analyzing Points of View

Defining the Skill

Analyzing points of view means looking closely at a person's arguments to understand the reasons behind that person's beliefs. The goal of analyzing a point of view is to understand a historical figure's thoughts, opinions, and biases about a topic.

Applying the Skill

The following passage describes the Panic of 1837 and two politicians' points of view about it. Use the strategies listed below to help you analyze their points of view.

How to Analyze Points of View

Strategy ① Look for statements that show you a person's view on an issue. For example, Van Buren said he believed the economy would improve if he took no action. Clay thought the government should do something to help the people.

Strategy ② Use information about people to validate them as sources and understand why they might disagree. What do you know about Clay and Van Buren that might explain their own biases and disagreements with each other?

Strategy ③ Write a summary that explains why different people take different positions on the issue.

THE PANIC OF 1837

The Panic of 1837 caused severe hardship. People had little money, so manufacturers had few customers for their goods. Almost 90 percent of factories in the East closed. Jobless workers could not afford food or rent. Many people went hungry.

① Whig senator Henry Clay wanted the government to do something to help the people. ① President Van Buren, a Democrat, disagreed. He believed that the economy would improve if left alone. He argued that "the less government interferes with private pursuits the better for the general prosperity." Many Americans blamed Van Buren for the Panic, though he had taken office only weeks before it started. The continuing depression made it difficult for him to win reelection in 1840.

Make a Diagram

Making a diagram can help you analyze points of view. The diagram below analyzes the views of Clay and Van Buren in the passage you just read.

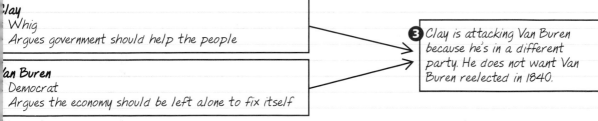

Clay
Whig
Argues government should help the people

Van Buren
Democrat
Argues the economy should be left alone to fix itself

③ Clay is attacking Van Buren because he's in a different party. He does not want Van Buren reelected in 1840.

Practicing the Skill

Turn to the Interactive Primary Sources on pages 238 and 239. Read the selections by James Madison and George Mason. Use their language, information from other sources, and information about each man to validate them as sources. Then make a chart to analyze their different points of view on the Constitution.

3.2 Interpreting Graphs

Defining the Skill

Graphs use pictures and symbols, instead of words, to show information. Graphs are created by taking information and presenting it visually. The graph on this page takes numerical information on immigration and presents it as a bar graph. There are many different kinds of graphs. Bar graphs, line graphs, and pie graphs are the most common. Bar graphs compare numbers or sets of numbers. The length of each bar shows a quantity. It is easy to see how different categories compare on a bar graph.

Applying the Skill

The bar graph below shows numbers of immigrants coming to the United States between 1821 and 1860. Use the strategies listed below to help you interpret the graph.

How to Interpret a Graph

Strategy ❶ Read the title to identify the main idea of the graph. Ask yourself what kinds of information the graph shows. For example, does it show chronological information, geographic patterns and distributions, or something else?

Strategy ❷ Read the vertical axis (the one that goes up and down) on the left side of the graph. This one shows the number of immigrants in thousands. Each bar represents the number of immigrants during a particular decade.

Strategy ❸ Read the horizontal axis (the one that runs across the bottom of the graph). This one shows the four decades from 1821 to 1860.

Strategy ❹ Summarize the information shown in each part of the graph. Use the title to help you focus on what information the graph is presenting.

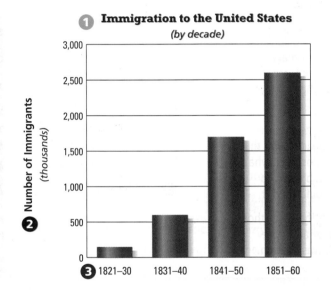

❶ **Immigration to the United States**
(by decade)

❷ Number of Immigrants *(thousands)*

❸ 1821–30   1831–40   1841–50   1851–60

Write a Summary

Writing a summary will help you understand the information in the graph. The paragraph to the right summarizes the information from the bar graph.

Practicing the Skill

Turn to Chapter 2, Section 4, "Beginnings of Slavery in the Americas." Look at the graph entitled "Slaves Imported to the Americas, 1493–1810" and write a paragraph in which you summarize what you learned from it.

❹ Immigration to the United States increased between and 1860. Between 1821 and 1830, fewer than 200,00 immigrants arrived. In the next decade, more than 500,000 immigrants came. During the 1840s, more th 1.5 million immigrants arrived, and that number incre to more than 2.5 million in the 1850s.

3 Interpreting Charts

fining the Skill

ts, like graphs, present information in a visual form. Charts are created by organiz-
summarizing, and simplifying information and presenting it in a format that makes
sy to understand. Tables and diagrams are examples of commonly used charts.

plying the Skill

chart below shows the number of slaves who were imported to the Americas
ween 1601 and 1810. Use the strategies listed below to help you interpret the infor-
on in the chart.

w to Interpret a Chart

ategy ① Read the title. It will
you what the chart is about. Ask
rself what kinds of information
chart shows. For example, does
now chronological information,
graphic patterns and distribu-
s, or something else?

ategy ② Read the labels
ee how the information in the
rt is organized. In this chart, it
rganized by region and years.

ategy ③ Study the data in
chart to understand the facts
the chart intends to show.

ategy ④ Summarize the
rmation shown in each part of
chart. Use the title to help you
s on what information the
rt is presenting.

1601–1810

① **Slaves Imported to the Americas** (in thousands)		
② **REGION/COUNTRY**	**1601–1700**	**1701–1810**
③ British N. America	*	348
British Caribbean	263.7	1,401.3
French Caribbean	155.8	1,348.4
Spanish America	292.5	578.6
Dutch Caribbean	40	460
Danish Caribbean	4	24
Brazil (Portugal)	560	1,891.4

*= less than 1,000

Source: Philip D. Curtin, *The Atlantic Slave Trade*

te a Summary

ing a summary can help you understand the infor-
on given in a chart. The paragraph to the right
marizes the information in the chart "Slaves
orted to the Americas, 1601–1810."

acticing the Skill

to Chapter 17, Section 4, and look at the chart
led "Costs of the Civil War." Study the chart and
yourself what geographic patterns and distribu-
are shown in it. Then write a paragraph in which
summarize what you learned from the chart.

④ *The chart shows how many slaves were imported to
the Americas between 1601 and 1810. It divides the
Americas into seven regions. It also divides the time
period into two parts: 1601–1700 and 1701–1810. The
number of slaves imported increased greatly from the
1600s to the 1700s. More slaves were imported to
Brazil than to any other region.*

3.4 Interpreting Time Lines

Defining the Skill

A **time line** is a visual list of events and dates shown in the order in which they occurred. Time lines can be horizontal or vertical. On horizontal time lines, the earliest date is on the left. On vertical time lines, the earliest date is often at the top.

Applying the Skill

The time line below lists dates and events during the presidencies of John Adams, Andrew Jackson, and Martin Van Buren. Use the strategies listed below to help you interpret the information.

How to Read a Time Line

Strategy ❶ Read the dates at the beginning and end of the time line. These will show the period of history that is covered. The time line below is a dual time line. It includes items related to two topics. The labels show that the information covers U.S. events and world events.

Strategy ❷ Read the dates and events in sequential order, beginning with the earliest one. Pay particular attention to how the entries relate to each other. Think about which events caused later events.

Strategy ❸ Summarize the or main idea, of the time line. T to write a main idea sentence t describes the time line.

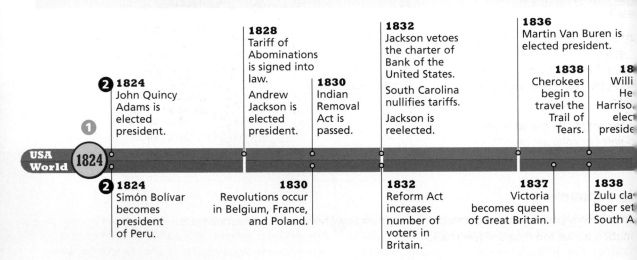

1828
Tariff of Abominations is signed into law.

1830
Indian Removal Act is passed.

1832
Jackson vetoes the charter of Bank of the United States.

South Carolina nullifies tariffs.

Jackson is reelected.

1836
Martin Van Buren is elected president.

1838
Cherokees begin to travel the Trail of Tears.

18
Willi
He
Harriso
elec
preside

❷ 1824
John Quincy Adams is elected president.

❶

Andrew Jackson is elected president.

USA / World 1824

❷ 1824
Simón Bolívar becomes president of Peru.

1830
Revolutions occur in Belgium, France, and Poland.

1832
Reform Act increases number of voters in Britain.

1837
Victoria becomes queen of Great Britain.

1838
Zulu cla
Boer set
South A

Write a Summary

Writing a summary can help you understand information shown on a time line. The summary to the right states the main idea of the time line and tells how the events are related.

Practicing the Skill

Turn to Chapter 15, page 455, and write a summary of the information shown on the time line.

❸ The time line covers the period between 1824, whe Quincy Adams was elected president, and 1840, wh William Henry Harrison was elected president. Du that period of time, Andrew Jackson and Martin Buren also served as president. The time line show the important issues in the United States were ta banking, and relations with Native Americans.

5 Reading a Map

fining the Skill

s are representations of features on the earth's surface. Some maps show political
ures, such as national borders. Other maps show physical features, such as mountains
bodies of water. By learning to use map elements and math skills, you can better
erstand how to read maps.

plying the Skill

following map shows the Battle of Yorktown during the Revolution. Use the strate-
listed below to help you identify the elements common to most maps.

to Read a Map

ategy ❶ Read the title. This
itifies the main idea of the map.

ategy ❷ Look for the grid of
s that form a pattern of squares
r the map. These numbered lines
the lines of latitude (horizontal)
longitude (vertical). They indi-
the location of the area on
earth.

ategy ❸ Read the map key.
usually in a box. This will give
the information you need to
rpret the symbols or colors on
map.

ategy ❹ Use the scale and
pointer, or compass rose, to
rmine distance and direction.

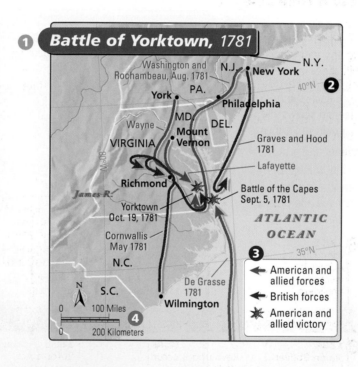

❶ **Battle of Yorktown,** *1781*

e a Chart

art can help you organize information given on maps. The chart below summarizes
mation about the map you just studied.

Title	Battle of Yorktown, 1781
Location	between latitude 40° N and 35° N, just east of longitude 80° W
Map Key Information	blue = American and allied forces, red = British forces
Scale	7/16 in. = 100 miles, 9/16 in. = 200 km
Summary	British commanders Graves and Hood sailed south from New York. They were defeated by De Grasse at the Battle of the Capes. British commander Cornwallis marched north from Wilmington, North Carolina, to Virginia, where he was defeated by American forces.

cticing the Skill

to Chapter 1, Section 5, "Early European Explorers." Read the map entitled "Explor-
Leads to New Sea Routes" and make a chart to identify information on the map.

3.6 Reading a Special-Purpose Map

Defining the Skill

Special-purpose maps help people focus on a particular aspect of a region, such as economic development in the South. These kinds of maps often use symbols to indicate information.

Applying the Skill

The following special-purpose map indicates the products of the Southern colonies. Use the strategies listed below to help you identify the information shown on the map.

How to Read a Special-Purpose Map

Strategy ❶ Read the title. It tells you what the map is intended to show.

Strategy ❷ Read the legend. This tells you what each symbol stands for. This legend shows the crops that were grown in various Southern colonies.

Strategy ❸ Look for the places on the map where the symbol appears. These tell you the places where each crop was grown.

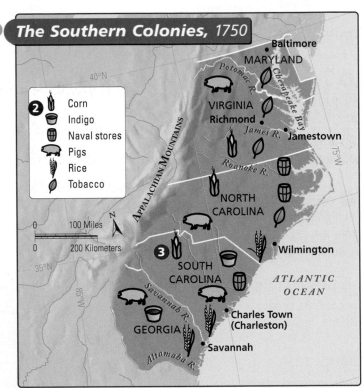

❶ The Southern Colonies, 1750

Legend ❷:
- Corn
- Indigo
- Naval stores
- Pigs
- Rice
- Tobacco

Make a Chart

A chart can help you understand special-purpose maps. The chart below shows information about the special-purpose map you just studied.

	Corn	Indigo	Naval stores	Pigs	Rice	Tobacco
Maryland						x
Virginia	x			x		x
North Carolina	x		x	x	x	x
South Carolina	x	x	x	x	x	
Georgia		x		x	x	

Practicing the Skill

Turn to Chapter 4, Section 1, "New England: Commerce and Religion." Look at the special-purpose map entitled "The New England Colonies" and make a chart that shows information about products from New England.

7 Creating a Map

Defining the Skill

Creating a **map** involves representing geographical information. When you draw a map, it is easiest to use an existing map as a guide. On the map you draw, you can show geographical information. You can also show other kinds of information, such as data on climates, population trends, resources, or routes. Often, this data comes from a graph or a chart.

Applying the Skill

Below is a map that a student created to show information about the number of slaves in 1750. Read the strategies listed below to see how the map was created.

How to Create a Map

Strategy ① Select a title that identifies the geographical area and the map's purpose. Include a date in your title.

Strategy ② Draw the lines of latitude and longitude using short dashes.

Strategy ③ Create a key that shows the colors.

Strategy ④ Draw the colors on the map to show information.

Strategy ⑤ Draw a compass rose and scale.

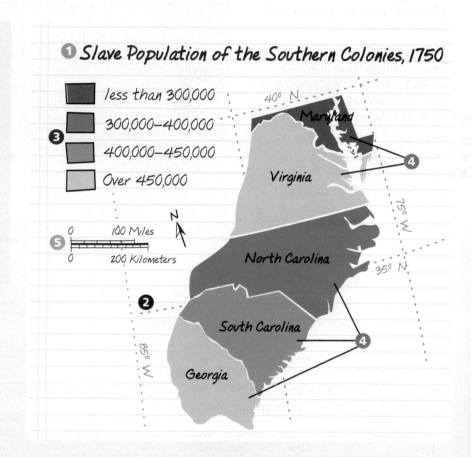

① Slave Population of the Southern Colonies, 1750

less than 300,000
300,000–400,000
400,000–450,000
Over 450,000

0   100 Miles
0   200 Kilometers

40° N
Maryland
75° W
Virginia
North Carolina
35° N
South Carolina
85° W
Georgia

Practicing the Skill

Make your own map. Turn to page 104 in Chapter 3 and study the graph entitled "The 13 Colonies." Use the strategies described above to create a map that shows the colonies and the dates that they were founded. You can use the map on page 102 of the chapter as a guide.

3.8 Interpreting Political Cartoons

Defining the Skill

Political cartoons are cartoons that use humor to make a serious point. Political cartoons often express a point of view on an issue better than words do. Understanding signs and symbols will help you to interpret political cartoons.

Applying the Skill

The cartoon below shows Abraham Lincoln and the other candidates running for the presidency in 1860. Use the strategies listed below to help you understand the cartoon.

How to Interpret a Political Cartoon

Strategy ❶ Identify the subject by reading the title of the cartoon and looking at the cartoon as a whole.

Strategy ❷ Identify important symbols and details. The cartoonist uses the image of a running race to discuss a political campaign. The White House is the finish line.

Strategy ❸ Interpret the message. Why is Lincoln drawn so much taller than the other candidates? How does that make him the fittest candidate?

Make a Chart

Making a chart will help you summarize information from a political cartoon. The chart below summarizes the information from the cartoon above.

Subject	"A Political Race" (The Election of 1860)
Symbols and Details	Running is a symbol for a political campaign. Lincoln is the tallest and fastest candidate.
Message	❸ Lincoln is pulling ahead of the other candidates in the campaign for the presidency.

Practicing the Skill

Turn to Chapter 18, Section 3, "End of Reconstruction." Look at the political cartoon on page 547. It shows a cartoonist's view of corruption in President Grant's administration. Use a chart like the one above and the strategies outlined to interpret the cartoon.

9 Creating a Model

Defining the Skill

When you **create a model,** you use information and ideas to show an event or a situation in a visual way. A model might be a poster or a diagram that explains how something happened. Or, it might be a three-dimensional model, such as a diorama, that depicts an important scene or situation.

Applying the Skill

The following sketch shows the early stages of a model of three ways that people could have traveled from the eastern United States to California during the gold rush. Use the strategies listed below to help you create your own model.

How to Create a Model

Strategy ❶ Gather the information you need to understand the situation or event. In this case, you need to be able to show the three routes and their dangers.

Strategy ❷ Visualize and sketch an idea for your model. Once you have created a picture in your mind, make an actual sketch of an how it might look.

Strategy ❸ Think of symbols you may want to use. Since the model should give information in a visual way, think about ways you can use color, pictures, or other symbols to tell the story.

Strategy ❹ Gather the supplies you will need and create the model. For example, you will need a globe and art supplies, such as yarn, for your model.

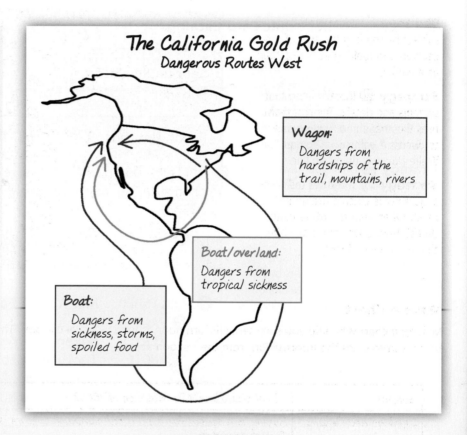

The California Gold Rush
Dangerous Routes West

Wagon: Dangers from hardships of the trail, mountains, rivers

Boat/overland: Dangers from tropical sickness

Boat: Dangers from sickness, storms, spoiled food

Practicing the Skill

Read the History Workshop called "Pack Your Trunk" on pages 450–451. Follow the step-by-step directions to create a model of a trunk that shows what immigrants might have needed to bring with them when they came to America.

4.1 Using an Electronic Card Catalog

Defining the Skill

An **electronic card catalog** is a library's computerized search program that will help you find information about the books and other materials in the library. You can search the catalog by entering a book title, an author's name, or a subject of interest to you. The electronic card catalog will give you information about the materials in the library. This information is called bibliographic information. You can use an electronic card catalog to create a bibliography (a list of books) on any topic you are interested in.

Applying the Skill

The screen shown below is from an electronic search for information about Thomas Jefferson. Use the strategies listed below to help you use the information on the screen.

How to Use an Electronic Card Catalog

Strategy ❶ Begin searching by choosing either subject, title, or author, depending on the topic of your search. For this search, the user chose "Subject" and typed in the words "Jefferson, Thomas."

Strategy ❷ Once you have selected a book from the results of your search, identify the author, title, city, publisher, and date of publication.

Strategy ❸ Look for any special features in the book. This book is illustrated, and it includes bibliographical references and an index.

Strategy ❹ Locate the call number for the book. The call number indicates the section in the library where you will find the book. You can also find out if the book is available in the library you are using. If not, it may be in another library in the network.

```
Search Request:
❶ Subject          Title          Author
─────────────────────────────────────────────
Find  Options  Locations  Backup  Startover  Help

❷ Miller, Douglas T. Thomas Jefferson and the
  creation of America. New York: Facts on File,
  1997.
        ❷ AUTHOR:  Miller, Douglas T.
          TITLE:  Thomas Jefferson and the
                  creation of America/Douglas T.
                  Miller.
  ❷ PUBLISHED:  New York: Facts on File, ©1997.
      ❸ PAGING:  vi, 122p. : ill ; 24 cm.
         SERIES:  Makers of America.
       ❸ NOTES:  Includes bibliographical
                  references (p. 117-118) and index
  ❹ CALL NUMBER:  1. 973.46 N61T 1997-Book Available
```

Practicing the Skill

Turn to Chapter 10, "The Jefferson Era," and find a topic that interests you, such as the Federalists, the Louisiana Purchase, the Lewis and Clark expedition, or the War of 1812. Use the SUBJECT search on an electronic card catalog to find information about your topic. Make a bibliography of books about the subject. Be sure to include the author, title, city, publisher, and date of publication for all the books included.

2 Creating a Database

Defining the Skill

A database is a collection of data, or information, that is organized so that you can find and retrieve information on a specific topic quickly and easily. Once a computerized database is set up, you can search it to find specific information without going through the entire database. The database will provide a list of all information in the database related to your topic. Learning how to use a database will help you learn how to create one.

Applying the Skill

The chart below is a database for the significant battles of the Civil War. Use the strategies listed below to help you understand and use the database.

How to Create a Database

Strategy 1 Identify the topic of the database. The keywords, or most important words, in this title are Civil War and Battles. These words were used to begin the search for this database.

Strategy 2 Ask yourself what kind of data you need to include. For example, what geographic patterns and distributions will be shown? Your choice of data will provide the column headings for the database. The key words Battle, Date, Location, and Significance were chosen to focus the research.

Strategy 3 Identify the entries needed under each heading.

Strategy 4 Use the database to help you find information quickly. For example, in this database you could search for "Union victories" to find a list of significant battles won by the North.

① LOCATION OF SIGNIFICANT CIVIL WAR BATTLES			
② BATTLE	DATE	② LOCATION	SIGNIFICANCE
③ Fort Sumter	April 12, 1861	Charleston, SC	Beginning of the Civil War
First Battle of Bull Run (Manassas)	July 21, 1861	Virginia	Confederate victory
Shiloh	April 6–7, 1862	Tennessee (near Shiloh Church)	④ Union victory
Antietam	September 17, 1862	Sharpsburg, MD	No clear victory; considered bloodiest battle of war
Gettysburg	July 1–3, 1863	Gettysburg, PA	Retreat of Confederacy
Vicksburg	Three-month siege ending July 3, 1863	Vicksburg, MS	Union gained control of Mississippi River
Chattanooga	November 23–25, 1863	Chattanooga, TN	④ Union victory
Atlanta	September 2, 1864	Atlanta, GA	④ Union victory; helped convince Confederacy of defeat

Practicing the Skill

Create a database for U.S. presidents through the Civil War that shows each president's home state, political party, and years served as president. Use the information in "Presidents of the United States" on pages R36–R38 to provide the data. Use a format like the one above for your database.

4.3 Using the Internet

Defining the Skill

The Internet is a computer network that connects to universities, libraries, news organizations, government agencies, businesses, and private individuals throughout the world. Each location on the Internet has a home page with its own address, or URL (universal resource locator). With a computer connected to the Internet, you can reach the home pages of many organizations and services. The international collection of home pages, known as the World Wide Web, is a good source of up-to-date information about current events as well as research on subjects in history.

Applying the Skill

The Web page below shows the links for Chapter 6 of *Creating America.* Use the strategies listed below to help you understand how to use the Web page.

How to Use the Internet

Strategy ❶ Go directly to a Web page. For example, type http://www.mcdougallittell.com in the box at the top of the screen and press ENTER (or RETURN). The Web page will appear on your screen. Then click on ClassZone and find the link to *Creating America.*

Strategy ❷ Explore the *Creating America* links. Click on any one of the links to find out more about a specific subject. These links take you to other pages at this Web site. Some pages include links to related information that can be found at other places on the Internet.

Strategy ❸ When using the Internet for research, you should confirm the information you find. Web sites set up by universities, government agencies, and reputable news sources are more reliable than other sources. You can often find information about the creator of a site by looking for copyright information.

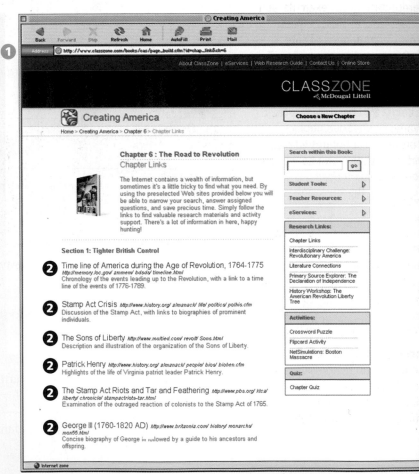

Practicing the Skill

Turn to Chapter 14, Section 2, "American Literature and Art." Read the section and make a list of topics you would like to research. If you have Internet access, go to the McDougal Littell home page at http://www.mcdougallittell.com and click on ClassZone. There you will find links that provide more information about the topics in the section.

4 Creating a Multimedia Presentation

Defining the Skill

Slides, CD-ROMs, television, and computer software are different kinds of media. To create a **multimedia presentation,** you need to collect information in different media and organize them into one presentation.

Applying the Skill

The scene below shows students using computers to create a multimedia presentation. Use the strategies listed below to help you create your own multimedia presentation.

How to Create a Multimedia Presentation

Strategy 1 Identify the topic of your presentation and decide which media are best for an effective presentation. For example, you may want to use slides or posters to show visual images of your topic. Or, you may want to use CDs or audiotapes to provide music or spoken words.

Strategy 2 Research the topic in a variety of sources. Images, maps, props, and background music should reflect the historical period or the event you choose.

Strategy 3 Write the script for the oral portion of the presentation. You could use a narrator and characters' voices to tell the story. Primary sources are an excellent source for script material. Make sure the recording is clear so that the audience will be able to understand the oral part of the presentation.

Strategy 4 Videotape the presentation. Videotaping the presentation will preserve it for future viewing and allow you to show it to different groups of people.

Practicing the Skill

Turn to Chapter 24, "World War I." Choose a topic from the chapter and use the strategies listed above to create a multimedia presentation about it.

Alabama
4,486,508 people
52,218 sq. mi.
Rank in area: 30
Entered Union in 1819

Florida
16,713,149 people
59,909 sq. mi.
Rank in area: 23
Entered Union in 1845

Louisiana
4,482,646 people
49,650 sq. mi.
Rank in area: 31
Entered Union in

Alaska
643,786 people
616,240 sq. mi.
Rank in area: 1
Entered Union in 1959

Georgia
8,560,310 people
58,970 sq. mi.
Rank in area: 24
Entered Union in 1788

Maine
1,294,464 people
33,738 sq. mi.
Rank in area: 39
Entered Union in

Arizona
5,456,453 people
113,998 sq. mi.
Rank in area: 6
Entered Union in 1912

Hawaii
1,244,898 people
6,641 sq. mi.
Rank in area: 47
Entered Union in 1959

Maryland
5,458,137 people
12,297 sq. mi.
Rank in area: 42
Entered Union in

Arkansas
2,710,079 people
53,178 sq. mi.
Rank in area: 28
Entered Union in 1836

Idaho
1,341,131 people
83,570 sq. mi.
Rank in area: 14
Entered Union in 1890

Massachusetts
6,427,801 people
9,240 sq. mi.
Rank in area: 45
Entered Union in

California
35,116,033 people
158,854 sq. mi.
Rank in area: 3
Entered Union in 1850

Illinois
12,600,620 people
57,914 sq. mi.
Rank in area: 25
Entered Union in 1818

Michigan
10,050,446 peopl
96,716 sq. mi.
Rank in area: 11
Entered Union in

Colorado
4,506,542 people
104,093 sq. mi.
Rank in area: 8
Entered Union in 1876

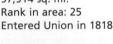
Indiana
6,159,068 people
36,418 sq. mi.
Rank in area: 38
Entered Union in 1816

Minnesota
5,019,720 people
86,938 sq. mi.
Rank in area: 12
Entered Union in

Connecticut
3,460,503 people
5,543 sq. mi.
Rank in area: 48
Entered Union in 1788

Iowa
2,936,760 people
56,271 sq. mi.
Rank in area: 26
Entered Union in 1846

Mississippi
2,871,782 people
48,282 sq. mi.
Rank in area: 32
Entered Union in

Delaware
807,385 people
2,396 sq. mi.
Rank in area: 49
Entered Union in 1787

Kansas
2,715,884 people
82,276 sq. mi.
Rank in area: 15
Entered Union in 1861

Missouri
5,672,579 people
69,704 sq. mi.
Rank in area: 21
Entered Union in

District of Columbia
570,898 people
68 sq. mi.

Kentucky
4,092,891 people
40,409 sq. mi.
Rank in area: 37
Entered Union in 1792

Montana
909,453 people
147,042 sq. mi.
Rank in area: 4
Entered Union in

Sources: U.S. Bureau of the Census, July 1 2002 population estimates.
World Almanac and Book of Facts, 2003
Statistical Abstract of the United States, 2002

Nebraska
1,729,180 people
77,353 sq. mi.
Rank in area: 16
Entered Union in 1867

Ohio
11,421,267 people
44,825 sq. mi.
Rank in area: 34
Entered Union in 1803

Columbus

Texas
21,779,893 people
267,256 sq. mi.
Rank in area: 2
Entered Union in 1845

Austin

Nevada
2,173,491 people
110,560 sq. mi.
Rank in area: 7
Entered Union in 1864

Oklahoma City

Oklahoma
3,493,714 people
69,898 sq. mi.
Rank in area: 20
Entered Union in 1907

Utah
2,316,256 people
84,898 sq. mi.
Rank in area: 13
Entered Union in 1896

Salt Lake City

New Hampshire
1,275,056 people
9,282 sq. mi.
Rank in area: 44
Entered Union in 1788

Salem

Oregon
3,521,515 people
97,126 sq. mi.
Rank in area: 10
Entered Union in 1859

Vermont
616,592 people
9,614 sq. mi.
Rank in area: 43
Entered Union in 1791

Montpelier

New Jersey
8,590,300 people
8,214 sq. mi.
Rank in area: 46
Entered Union in 1787

Harrisburg

Pennsylvania
12,335,091 people
46,055 sq. mi.
Rank in area: 33
Entered Union in 1787

Virginia
7,293,542 people
42,328 sq. mi.
Rank in area: 35
Entered Union in 1788

Richmond

New Mexico
1,855,059 people
121,589 sq. mi.
Rank in area: 5
Entered Union in 1912

Providence

Rhode Island
1,069,725 people
1,231 sq. mi.
Rank in area: 50
Entered Union in 1790

Washington
6,068,996 people
70,634 sq. mi.
Rank in area: 19
Entered Union in 1889

Olympia

New York
19,157,532 people
54,077 sq. mi.
Rank in area: 27
Entered Union in 1788

Columbia

South Carolina
4,107,183 people
31,190 sq. mi.
Rank in area: 40
Entered Union in 1788

West Virginia
1,801,873 people
24,230 sq. mi.
Rank in area: 41
Entered Union in 1863

Charleston

North Carolina
8,320,146 people
52,670 sq. mi.
Rank in area: 29
Entered Union in 1789

Pierre

South Dakota
761,063 people
77,116 sq. mi.
Rank in area: 17
Entered Union in 1889

Wisconsin
5,441,196 people
65,498 sq. mi.
Rank in area: 22
Entered Union in 1848

Madison

North Dakota
634,110 people
70,699 sq. mi.
Rank in area: 18
Entered Union in 1889

Nashville

Tennessee
5,797,289 people
42,143 sq. mi.
Rank in area: 36
Entered Union in 1796

Wyoming
498,703 people
97,813 sq. mi.
Rank in area: 9
Entered Union in 1890

Cheyenne

nited States: Major Dependencies

herican Samoa—68,688 people; 90 sq. mi.
am—160,796 people; 217 sq. mi.
mmonwealth of Puerto Rico—3,957,988 people; 5,324 sq. mi.

- Virgin Islands of the United States—123,498 people; 171 sq. mi.
- Midway Atoll—no indigenous inhabitants; 2 sq. mi.
- Wake Atoll—no indigenous inhabitants; 3 sq. mi.

Here are some little-known facts about the presidents of the United States:

- Only former president to serve in Congress: John Quincy Adams
- First president born in the new United States: Martin Van Buren (eighth president)
- Only president who was a bachelor: James Buchanan
- First left-handed president: James A. Garfield
- Largest president: William H. Taft (6 feet 2 inches, 326 pounds)
- Youngest president: Theodore Roosevelt (42 years old)
- Oldest president: Ronald Reagan (77 years old when he left office in 1989)
- First president born west of the Mississippi River: Herbert Hoover (born in West Branch, Iowa)
- First president born in the 20th century: John F. Kennedy (born May 29, 1917)

1 George Washington
1789–1797
No Political Party
Birthplace: Virginia
Born: February 22, 1732
Died: December 14, 1799

2 John Adams
1797–1801
Federalist
Birthplace: Massachusetts
Born: October 30, 1735
Died: July 4, 1826

3 Thomas Jefferson
1801–1809
Democratic-Republican
Birthplace: Virginia
Born: April 13, 1743
Died: July 4, 1826

4 James Madis
1809–1817
Democratic-Repu
Birthplace: Virgin
Born: March 16,
Died: June 28, 18

5 James Monroe
1817–1825
Democratic-Republican
Birthplace: Virginia
Born: April 28, 1758
Died: July 4, 1831

6 John Quincy Adams
1825–1829
Democratic-Republican
Birthplace: Massachusetts
Born: July 11, 1767
Died: February 23, 1848

7 Andrew Jackson
1829–1837
Democrat
Birthplace: South Carolina
Born: March 15, 1767
Died: June 8, 1845

8 Martin Van B
1837–1841
Democrat
Birthplace: New
Born: December
Died: July 24, 18

9 William H. Harrison
1841
Whig
Birthplace: Virginia
Born: February 9, 1773
Died: April 4, 1841

10 John Tyler
1841–1845
Whig
Birthplace: Virginia
Born: March 29, 1790
Died: January 18, 1862

11 James K. Polk
1845–1849
Democrat
Birthplace: North Carolina
Born: November 2, 1795
Died: June 15, 1849

12 Zachary Taylo
1849–1850
Whig
Birthplace: Virgin
Born: November
Died: July 9, 1850

illard Fillmore
50–1853
hig
irthplace: New York
rn: January 7, 1800
ed: March 8, 1874

14 **Franklin Pierce**
1853–1857
Democrat
Birthplace: New Hampshire
Born: November 23, 1804
Died: October 8, 1869

15 **James Buchanan**
1857–1861
Democrat
Birthplace: Pennsylvania
Born: April 23, 1791
Died: June 1, 1868

16 **Abraham Lincoln**
1861–1865
Republican
Birthplace: Kentucky
Born: February 12, 1809
Died: April 15, 1865

ndrew Johnson
65–1869
tional Union
irthplace: North Carolina
rn: December 29, 1808
ed: July 31, 1875

18 **Ulysses S. Grant**
1869–1877
Republican
Birthplace: Ohio
Born: April 27, 1822
Died: July 23, 1885

19 **Rutherford B. Hayes**
1877–1881
Republican
Birthplace: Ohio
Born: October 4, 1822
Died: January 17, 1893

20 **James A. Garfield**
1881
Republican
Birthplace: Ohio
Born: November 19, 1831
Died: September 19, 1881

hester A. Arthur
81–1885
publican
irthplace: Vermont
rn: October 5, 1829
ed: November 18, 1886

22 **24** **Grover Cleveland**
1885–1889, 1893–1897
Democrat
Birthplace: New Jersey
Born: March 18, 1837
Died: June 24, 1908

23 **Benjamin Harrison**
1889–1893
Republican
Birthplace: Ohio
Born: August 20, 1833
Died: March 13, 1901

25 **William McKinley**
1897–1901
Republican
Birthplace: Ohio
Born: January 29, 1843
Died: September 14, 1901

heodore Roosevelt
01–1909
publican
irthplace: New York
rn: October 27, 1858
ed: January 6, 1919

27 **William H. Taft**
1909–1913
Republican
Birthplace: Ohio
Born: September 15, 1857
Died: March 8, 1930

28 **Woodrow Wilson**
1913–1921
Democrat
Birthplace: Virginia
Born: December 28, 1856
Died: February 3, 1924

29 **Warren G. Harding**
1921–1923
Republican
Birthplace: Ohio
Born: November 2, 1865
Died: August 2, 1923

30 **Calvin Coolidge**
1923–1929
Republican
Birthplace: Vermont
Born: July 4, 1872
Died: January 5, 1933

31 **Herbert C. Hoover**
1929–1933
Republican
Birthplace: Iowa
Born: August 10, 1874
Died: October 20, 1964

32 **Franklin D. Roosevelt**
1933–1945
Democrat
Birthplace: New York
Born: January 30, 1882
Died: April 12, 1945

33 **Harry S. Trun**
1945–1953
Democrat
Birthplace: Misso
Born: May 8, 188
Died: December

34 **Dwight D. Eisenhower**
1953–1961
Republican
Birthplace: Texas
Born: October 14, 1890
Died: March 28, 1969

35 **John F. Kennedy**
1961–1963
Democrat
Birthplace: Massachusetts
Born: May 29, 1917
Died: November 22, 1963

36 **Lyndon B. Johnson**
1963–1969
Democrat
Birthplace: Texas
Born: August 27, 1908
Died: January 22, 1973

37 **Richard M. N**
1969–1974
Republican
Birthplace: Califo
Born: January 9,
Died: April 22, 19

38 **Gerald R. Ford**
1974–1977
Republican
Birthplace: Nebraska
Born: July 14, 1913

39 **James E. Carter, Jr.**
1977–1981
Democrat
Birthplace: Georgia
Born: October 1, 1924

40 **Ronald W. Reagan**
1981–1989
Republican
Birthplace: Illinois
Born: February 6, 1911

41 **George H. W.**
1989–1993
Republican
Birthplace: Mass
Born: June 12, 19

42 **William J. Clinton**
1993–2001
Democrat
Birthplace: Arkansas
Born: August 19, 1946

43 **George W. Bush**
2001–
Republican
Birthplace: Connecticut
Born: July 6, 1946

Gazetteer identifies important places and geographical features
…is book. Entries include a short description, often followed by
…page numbers. The first number refers to a text page on which
…ntry is discussed, and the second, in italics, refers to a map
…e the place appears. (The reference *Atlas* is to the section of
…and world maps on pages R32–R37.) In addition, some entries
…de rounded-off geographical coordinates. There are entries for
…S. states (with capital cities).

…a world's second largest continent. *Atlas*

…ama 22nd state. Capital: Montgomery. *Atlas*

…o Texas mission in San Antonio captured by
…o in 1836. (29°N 98°W), 402, *m405*

…ka 49th state. Capital: Juneau. *Atlas*

…rctica continent at the South Pole. *Atlas*

…tam Maryland creek; site of bloodiest day's
…ng in the Civil War. (39°N 77°W), 497, *m495*

…lachian Mountains mountain range running
…Alabama into Canada. 126, *m127*

…omattox Court House town near Appomattox,
…ia, where Lee surrendered to Grant on April 9,
…(37°N 79°W), 519, *m517*

…na 48th state. Capital: Phoenix. *Atlas*

…nsas 25th state. Capital: Little Rock. *Atlas*

… world's largest continent. *Atlas*

…tic Ocean ocean forming east boundary of the
…d States. *Atlas*

…ralia island country between Indian and Pacific
…s; also the world's smallest continent. *Atlas*

…ria-Hungary one of the Central Powers in
…d War I; after the war, divided into smaller
…ries. 680, *m680*

…c Empire former region of Mexico once under
… control. 63, *m63*

…country identification for former undeveloped
…n beginning in the Appalachian Mountains and
…ding west. 126, *m127*

…more Maryland city on Chesapeake Bay.
…77°W), 332, *m331*

…gia former land bridge connecting Asia with
…America and now under waters of Bering Strait.
…169°W), 27, *m28*

…on capital of Massachusetts; site of early colonial
…t and conflict. (42°N 71°W), 165, *m172*

…Run stream 30 miles southwest of Washington,

D.C.; site of first land battle of Civil War. (39°N 78°W),
485, *m495*

Bunker Hill hill now part of Boston; its name
misidentifies Revolutionary War battle fought at
nearby Breed's Hill. (42°N 71°W), 177

Cahokia Illinois Mound Builders site; village taken
from British by Clark in 1778. (39°N 90°W), 31, *m203*

California 31st state. Capital: Sacramento. *Atlas*

Canada nation sharing northern U.S. border. *Atlas*

Caribbean Sea expanse of the Atlantic Ocean
between the Gulf of Mexico and South America. *Atlas*

Central America area of North America between
Mexico and South America. *m72, Atlas*

Charleston as Charles Town, largest Southern
colonial city; South Carolina site of first Civil War shots,
at offshore Fort Sumter. (33°N 80°W), 481, *m483*

Charlestown former town, now part of Boston;
site of both Bunker and Breed's hills. (42°N 71°W),
177, *m172*

Chicago large Illinois city on Lake Michigan.
(42°N 88°W), 602, *Atlas*

China large nation in Asia. *Atlas*

Colorado 38th state. Capital: Denver. *Atlas*

Concord Massachusetts city and site of second battle
of the Revolutionary War. (42°N 71°W), 172, *m172*

Confederate States of America nation formed
by 11 Southern states during the Civil War. Capital:
Richmond, Virginia. 473 and 482, *m483*

Connecticut 5th state. Capital: Hartford. *Atlas*

Cuba Caribbean island south of Florida. 662, *m665*

Delaware 1st state. Capital: Dover. *Atlas*

District of Columbia (D.C.) self-governing federal
district between Virginia and Maryland, made up
entirely of the city of Washington, the U.S. capital.
(39°N 77°W), 305, *Atlas*

Dominican Republic nation sharing the island of
Hispaniola with Haiti. 673, *m672*

England southern part of Great Britain. *Atlas*

English Channel narrow waterway separating Great Britain from France. 69

Erie Canal all-water channel dug out to connect the Hudson River with Lake Erie. 355, *m355*

Europe second smallest continent, actually a peninsula of the Eurasian landmass. *Atlas*

Florida 27th state. Capital: Tallahassee. *Atlas*

Fort McHenry fort in Baltimore harbor where 1814 British attack inspired U.S. national anthem. (39°N 77°N), 332, *m331*

Fort Sumter fort in Charleston, South Carolina, harbor where 1861 attack by Confederates began the Civil War. (33°N 80°W), 481, *m483*

France nation in western Europe; it aided America in the Revolutionary War. *Atlas*

Gadsden Purchase last territory (from Mexico, 1853) added to continental United States. 411, *m410*

Georgia 4th state. Capital: Atlanta. *Atlas*

Germany nation in central Europe; once divided into West and East Germany, 1949–1990. *Atlas*

Gettysburg Pennsylvania town and site of 1863 Civil War victory for the North that is considered war's turning point. (40°N 77°W), 513, *m514*

Ghana first powerful West African trading empire. 40, *m40*

Great Britain European island nation across from France; it consists of England, Scotland, and Wales. *Atlas*

Great Lakes five connected lakes—Ontario, Erie, Huron, Michigan, and Superior—on the U.S. border with Canada. 355, *m355*

Great Plains vast grassland region in the central United States. 393, *m395*

Gulf of Mexico body of water forming southern U.S. boundary from east Texas to west Florida. *Atlas*

Haiti nation sharing the island of Hispaniola with Dominican Republic. *Atlas*

Harpers Ferry village today in extreme eastern West Virginia where John Brown raided stored U.S. weapons in 1859. (39°N 78°W), 469, *m495*

Hawaii 50th state. Capital: Honolulu. *Atlas*

Hispaniola West Indies island (shared today by Dominican Republic and Haiti) that Columbus mistook for Asia. 52, *m51*

Hudson River large river in eastern New York. 100, *m95*

Idaho 43rd state. Capital: Boise. *Atlas*

Illinois 21st state. Capital: Springfield. *Atlas*

Indiana 19th state. Capital: Indianapolis. *Atlas*

Indian Territory area, mainly of present-day Oklahoma, that in the 1800s became land for relo Native Americans. 376, *m376*

Iowa 29th state. Capital: Des Moines. *Atlas*

Ireland island country west of England whose m 1800s famine caused more than one million peopl emigrate to America. 426, *Atlas*

Israel Jewish nation in the Middle East. 864, *Atla*

Italy nation in southern Europe. *Atlas*

Jamestown community in Virginia that was the permanent English settlement in North America. 87, *m87*

Japan island nation in east Asia. *Atlas*

Kansas 34th state. Capital: Topeka. *Atlas*

Kentucky 15th state. Capital: Frankfort. *Atlas*

Latin America region made up of Mexico, Carib Islands, and Central and South America, where La based languages of Spanish, French, or Portugues spoken. 359, *m672*

Lexington Massachusetts city and site of first Revolutionary War battle in 1775. (42°N 71°W), 173, *m172*

Little Bighorn River Montana site of Sioux and Cheyenne victory over Custer. (46°N 108°W), 565, *m*

Louisiana 18th state. Capital: Baton Rouge. *Atla*

Louisiana Purchase land west of the Mississipp River purchased from France in 1803. 319, *m320*

Lowell Massachusetts city built in early 1800s as planned factory town. (43°N 71°W), 342

Maine 23rd state. Capital: Augusta. *Atlas*

Mali early West African trading empire succeedir Ghana empire. 41, *m40*

Maryland 7th state. Capital: Annapolis. *Atlas*

Massachusetts 6th state. Capital: Boston. *Atlas*

Mexico nation sharing U.S. southern border. *Atla*

Michigan 26th state. Capital: Lansing. *Atlas*

Minnesota 32nd state. Capital: St. Paul. *Atlas*

Mississippi 20th state. Capital: Jackson. *Atlas*

Mississippi River second longest U.S. river, sout from Minnesota to the Gulf of Mexico. 146, *m153*

Missouri 24th state. Capital: Jefferson City. *Atlas*

...ouri River longest U.S. river, east from the Rockies ... Mississippi River. 321, *m320*

...tana 41st state. Capital: Helena. *Atlas*

...aska 37th state. Capital: Lincoln. *Atlas*

...da 36th state. Capital: Carson City. *Atlas*

...England northeast U.S. region made up of Maine, ...Hampshire, Vermont, Massachusetts, Rhode Island, ...onnecticut. 109, *m110*

...France first permanent French colony in North ...ica. 70, *m148*

...Hampshire 9th state. Capital: Concord. *Atlas*

...Jersey 3rd state. Capital: Trenton. *Atlas*

...Mexico 47th state. Capital: Santa Fe. *Atlas*

...Netherland early Dutch colony that became ...York in 1664. 70

...Orleans Louisiana port city at mouth of the ...sippi River. *Atlas*

...Spain former North American province of the ...sh Empire, made up mostly of present-day Mexico ...he southwest United States. 71, *m72*

...York 11th state. Capital: Albany. *Atlas*

...York City largest U.S. city, at the mouth of the ...on River; temporary U.S. capital, 1785–1790. *Atlas*

...h America continent of Western Hemisphere ... of Panama-Colombia border. *Atlas*

...h Carolina 12th state. Capital: Raleigh. *Atlas*

...h Dakota 39th state. Capital: Bismarck. *Atlas*

...hwest Territory U.S. land north of the Ohio River ...e Great Lakes and west to the Mississippi River; ...red in 1783. 223, *m226*

... 17th state. Capital: Columbus. *Atlas*

... River river that flows from western Pennsylvania ...e Mississippi River. *Atlas*

...homa 46th state. Capital: Oklahoma City. *Atlas*

...on 33rd state. Capital: Salem. *Atlas*

...on Country former region of northwest North ...ica claimed jointly by Britain and the United States ...1846. 318, *m320*

...on Trail pioneer wagon route from Missouri to ...Oregon Territory in the 1840s and 1850s. *m395*, 396

...fic Ocean world's largest ocean, on the west coast ...e United States. *Atlas*

...ma Canal ship passageway cut through Panama ...ntral America, linking Atlantic and Pacific oceans. ...80°W), 670, *m670*

Pearl Harbor naval base in Hawaii; site of surprise Japanese aerial attack in 1941. (21°N 158°W), 661 *m660*

Pennsylvania 2nd state. Capital: Harrisburg. *Atlas*

Philadelphia large port city in Pennsylvania; U.S. capital, 1790–1800. (40°N 76°W), 229, *Atlas*

Philippine Islands Pacific island country off the southeast coast of China. 662, *m665*

Plymouth town on Massachusetts coast and site of Pilgrim landing and colony. (42°N 71°W), 93, *m95*

Portugal nation in southwestern Europe; leader in early oceanic explorations. 49, *m51*

Potomac River historic river separating Virginia from Maryland and Washington, D.C. 496, *m495*

Puerto Rico Caribbean island that has been U.S. territory since 1898. 667, *m665*

Quebec major early Canadian city; also a province of eastern Canada. 146, *m148*

Rhode Island 13th state. Capital: Providence. *Atlas*

Richmond Virginia capital that was also the capital of the Confederacy. (38°N 77°W), 482, *m483*

Rio Grande river that forms part of the border between the United States and Mexico. *Atlas*

Roanoke Island island off the coast of North Carolina; 1585 site of the first English colony in the Americas. (36°N 76°W), 85, *m87*

Rocky Mountains mountain range in the western United States and Canada. *Atlas*

Russia large Eurasian country, the major republic of the former Soviet Union (1922–1991). 680, *m680*

St. Augustine oldest permanent European settlement (1565) in the United States, on Florida's northeast coast. (30°N 81°W), 68, *m63*

St. Lawrence River Atlantic-to-Great Lakes waterway used by early explorers of mid-North America. 146, *m148*

St. Louis Missouri city at the junction of the Missouri and Mississippi rivers. (39°N 90°W), 320, *Atlas*

San Antonio Texas city and site of the Alamo. (29°N 99°W), 402, *m405*

San Francisco major port city in northern California. (38°N 123°W), 416, *m592*

San Salvador West Indies island near the Bahamas where Columbus first landed in the Americas. (24°N 74°W), 52, *m51*

Santa Fe Trail old wagon route from Missouri to Santa Fe in Mexican province of New Mexico. 395, *m395*

Songhai early West African trading empire succeeding Mali empire. 42, *m40*

South America continent of Western Hemisphere south of Panama-Colombia border. *Atlas*

South Carolina 8th state. Capital: Columbia. *Atlas*

South Dakota 40th state. Capital: Pierre. *Atlas*

Spain nation in southwestern Europe; early empire builder in the Americas. 50, *m51*

Tennessee 16th state. Capital: Nashville. *Atlas*

Tenochtitlán Aztec Empire capital; now site of Mexico City. 64, *m63*

Texas 28th state. Capital: Austin. *Atlas*

Utah 45th state. Capital: Salt Lake City. *Atlas*

Valley Forge village in southeast Pennsylvania and site of Washington's army camp during winter of 1777–1778. (40°N 75°W), 202, *m209*

Vermont 14th state. Capital: Montpelier. *Atlas*

Vicksburg Mississippi River site of major Union victory (1863) in Civil War. (32°N 91°W), 516, *m517*

Virginia 10th state. Capital: Richmond. *Atlas*

Washington 42nd state. Capital: Olympia. *Atlas*

Washington, D.C. capital of the United States s 1800; makes up whole of District of Columbia (D.C (39°N 77°W), 305, *Atlas*

West Africa region from which most Africans w brought to the Americas. 39, *m40*

Western Hemisphere the half of the world tha includes the Americas. 75, *m74*

West Indies numerous islands in the Caribbean between Florida and South America. 111, *m111*

West Virginia 35th state. Capital: Charleston. *Ai*

Wisconsin 30th state. Capital: Madison. *Atlas*

Wounded Knee South Dakota site that was scer 1890 massacre of Sioux. (43°N 102°W), 566, *m563*

Wyoming 44th state. Capital: Cheyenne. *Atlas*

Yorktown Virginia village and site of American victory that sealed British defeat in Revolutionary (37°N 77°W), 209, *m209*

...tion (AB uh LIHSH uhn) *n.* the movement to end ...very. (p. 440)

...dge (uh BRIHJ) *v.* to reduce. (p. 266)

n. the American Expeditionary Force, U.S. forces during World War I. (p. 686)

...mation (AF uhr MAY shuhn) *n.* a statement declaring that something is true. (p. 257)

...an Diaspora (AF rih kuhn dy AS puhr uh) *n.* the ...ced removal of Africans from their homelands to ...ve as slave labor in the Americas. (p. 78)

...ny Plan of Union *n.* the first formal proposal to ...ite the American colonies, put forth by Benjamin ...anklin. (p. 149)

...n and Sedition (si DISH uhn) **Acts** *n.* a series of ...ur laws enacted in 1798 to reduce the political power ...recent immigrants to the United States. (p. 306)

...s (AL yz) *n.* an alliance of Serbia, Russia, France, ...eat Britain, Italy, and seven other countries during ...orld War I. (p. 680)

... (AL eye) *n.* a country that agrees to help another ...untry achieve a common goal. (p. 200)

...rican Federation of Labor (AFL) *n.* a national ...ganization of labor unions founded in 1886. (p. 603)

...rican System *n.* a plan introduced in 1815 to make ...e United States economically self-sufficient. (p. 354)

...conda (AN uh KAHN duh) **Plan** *n.* a strategy by ...nich the Union proposed to defeat the Confederacy ...the Civil War. (p. 484)

...el Island *n.* the first stop in the United States for ...ost immigrants coming from Asia. (p. 615)

...federalist (AN tee FED uhr uh list) *n.* a person who ...pposed the ratification of the U.S. Constitution. (p. 234)

...-Imperialist (AN tee im PEER y uh LIZT) **League** *n.* ...group of well-known Americans that believed the ...nited States should not deny other people the right ...govern themselves. (p. 667)

...alachian (AP uh LAY chee uhn) **Mountains** *n.* a ...ountain range that stretches from eastern Canada ...uth to Alabama. (p. 126)

...ellate (uh PEL it) *adj.* having power to review court ...ecisions. (p. 260)

Appomattox (AP uh MAT uhks) **Court House** *n.* the Virginia town where Robert E. Lee surrendered to Ulysses S. Grant in 1865, ending the Civil War. (p. 519)

apprentice (uh PREN tis) *n.* a beginner who learns a trade or a craft from an experienced master. (p. 137)

appropriation (uh PROH pree AY shuhn) *n.* public funds set aside for a specific purpose. (p. 253)

archaeologist (AHR kee AHL uh jist) *n.* a scientist who studies the human past by examining the things people left behind. (p. 27)

armistice (AHR mi stis) *n.* an end to fighting. (p. 690)

Articles of Confederation *n.* a document, adopted by the Continental Congress in 1777 and finally approved by the states in 1781, that outlined the form of government of the new United States. (p. 222)

artifact (AHR tuh FAKT) *n.* a tool or other object made by humans. (p. 27)

artillery (ahr TIL uhr ee) *n.* a cannon or large gun. (p. 177)

artisan (AHR ti zuhn) *n.* a skilled worker, such as a weaver or a potter, who makes goods by hand; a craftsperson. (p. 117)

assimilation (uh SIM uh LAY shuhn) *n.* the process of blending into society. (p. 616)

B

baby boom *n.* the term for the generation born between 1946 and 1961, when the U.S. birthrate sharply increased following World War II. (p. 722)

Backcountry *n.* a colonial region that ran along the Appalachian Mountains through the far western part of the New England, Middle, and Southern colonies. (p. 109)

Bacon's Rebellion *n.* a revolt against powerful colonial authority in Jamestown by Nathaniel Bacon and a group of landless frontier settlers that resulted in the burning of Jamestown in 1676. (p. 89)

bail (bayl) *n.* money paid as security by arrested persons to guarantee they will return for trial. (p. 268)

Battle of Antietam (an TEE tuhm) *n.* a Civil War battle in 1862 in which 25,000 men were killed or wounded. (p. 497)

Battle of Fallen Timbers *n.* in 1794, an American army defeated 2,000 Native Americans in a clash over control of the Northwest Territory. (p. 299)

Battle of Gettysburg (GET eez BURG) *n.* an 1863 battle in the Civil War in which the Union defeated the Confederacy, ending hopes for a Confederate victory in the North. (p. 513)

Battle of Quebec (kwi BEK) *n.* a battle won by the British over the French, and the turning point in the French and Indian War. (p. 150)

Battle of Shiloh (SHY loh) *n.* an 1862 battle in which the Union forced the Confederacy to retreat in some of the fiercest fighting in the Civil War. (p. 494)

Battle of Yorktown *n.* the last major battle of the Revolutionary War, which resulted in the surrender of British forces in 1781. (p. 210)

Battle of the Alamo (AL uh MOH) *n.* in 1836, Texans defended a church called the Alamo against the Mexican army; all but five Texans were killed. (p. 403)

Battle of the Little Bighorn *n.* an 1876 battle in which the Sioux and the Cheyenne wiped out an entire force of U.S. troops. (p. 565)

Battle of the Thames (temz) *n.* an American victory over the British in the War of 1812, which ended the British threat to the Northwest Territory. (p. 332)

Battles of Saratoga (SAR uh TOH guh) *n.* a series of conflicts between British soldiers and the Continental Army in 1777 that proved to be a turning point in the Revolutionary War. (p. 199)

bayonet (BAY uh net) *n.* a long steel knife attached to the end of a gun. (p. 202)

Bear Flag Revolt *n.* the 1846 rebellion by Americans against Mexican rule in California. (p. 409)

Benin (buh NIN) *n.* a West African kingdom that arose near the Niger River delta in the 1300s. (p. 43)

Bessemer (BES uh muhr) **steel process** *n.* a new way of making steel that was developed in the 1850s and caused steel production to soar. (p. 587)

bill of attainder (uh TAYN duhr) *n.* a law that condemns a person without a trial in court. (p. 255)

Bill of Rights *n.* the first ten amendments to the U.S. Constitution, added in 1791, and consisting of a formal list of citizens' rights and freedoms. (p. 237)

black code *n.* a law passed by Southern states that limited the freedom of former slaves. (p. 534)

blockade *n.* when armed forces prevent the transportation of goods or people into or out of an area. (p. 484)

boomtown *n.* a town that has a sudden burst of e nomic or population growth. (p. 558)

border state *n.* a slave state that bordered states i which slavery was illegal. (p. 482)

Boston Massacre (MAS uh kuhr) *n.* a clash betweer British soldiers and Boston colonists in 1770, in whi five of the colonists, including Crispus Attucks, wer killed. (p. 165)

Boston Tea Party *n.* the dumping of 342 chests of into Boston Harbor by colonists in 1773 to protes Tea Act. (p. 167)

bounty (BOWN tee) *n.* a reward or cash payment g by a government. (pp. 271, 508)

Boxer Rebellion *n.* in 1900, Chinese resentment toward foreigners' attitude of cultural superiority resulted in this violent uprising. (p. 669)

boycott (BOI KOT) *n.* a refusal to buy certain goods. (p.

buck *n.* a buckskin from an adult male deer was a u of money for settlers. (p. 127)

buffalo soldier *n.* a name given by Native America to African Americans serving in the U.S. army in t West. (p. 571)

business cycle *n.* the pattern of good times and b times in the economy. (p. 586)

C

cabinet *n.* a group of department heads who serve the president's chief advisers. (p. 294)

California gold rush *n.* in 1849, large numbers of ple moved to California because gold had been d ered there. (p. 413)

caravel (KAR uh VEL) *n.* a ship with triangular sails that allowed it to sail into the wind and with square sails carried it forward when the wind was at its back. (p.

cash crop *n.* a crop grown by a farmer to be sold fc money rather than for personal use. (p. 115)

cavalry *n.* soldiers on horseback. (p. 496)

Centennial (sen TEN ee uhl) **Exhibition** *n.* an exhi tion in Philadelphia in 1876 that celebrated Ameri 100th birthday. (p. 588)

Central Powers *n.* an alliance of Austria-Hungary, Germany, the Ottoman Empire, and Bulgaria durir World War I. (p. 680)

rter *n.* a written contract issued by a government iving the holder the right to establish a colony. (p. 87)

cks and balances *n.* the ability of each branch of overnment to exercise checks, or controls, over the ther branches. (p. 246)

nese Exclusion Act *n.* enacted in 1882, this law anned Chinese immigration for ten years. (p. 617)

l disobedience (DIS uh BEE dee uhns) *n.* peacefully efusing to obey laws one considers unjust. (p. 431)

lization (SIV uh li ZAY shuhn) *n.* a form of culture haracterized by city trade centers, specialized work-rs, organized forms of government and religion, sys-ems of record keeping, and advanced tools. (p. 29)

l rights *n.* rights granted to all citizens. (p. 535)

a *n.* a large group of families that claim a common ncestor. (p. 127)

yton Antitrust Act *n.* a law passed in 1914 that aid down rules forbidding business practices that less-ned competition; it gave the government more ower to regulate trusts. (p. 648)

d War *n.* the state of hostility, without direct military onflict, that developed between the United States nd the Soviet Union after World War II. (p. 717)

umbian (kuh LUM bee uhn) **Exchange** *n.* the trans-er of plants, animals, and diseases between the Western and the Eastern hemispheres. (p. 74)

mittee of correspondence *n.* a group of people n the colonies who exchanged letters on colonial ffairs. (p. 166)

mon law *n.* a system of law developed in England, ased on customs and previous court decisions. (p. 268)

npromise of 1850 *n.* a series of Congressional laws ntended to settle the major disagreements between ree states and slave states. (p. 461)

npromise of 1877 *n.* the agreement that resolved n 1876 election dispute: Rutherford B. Hayes became resident and then removed the last federal troops rom the South. (p. 548)

pulsory process *n.* a required procedure. (p. 267)

estoga (KON i STOW guh) **wagon** *n.* a vehicle with vide wheels, a curved bed, and a canvas cover used by American pioneers traveling west. (p. 117)

federate States of America *n.* the confederation ormed in 1861 by the Southern states after their ecession from the Union. (p. 473)

conquistador (kon KWIS tuh DAWR) *n.* a Spaniard who traveled to the Americas as an explorer and a con-queror in the 16th century. (p. 63)

conscription (kuhn SKRIP shuhn) *n.* a law that required men to serve in the military or be drafted. (p. 508)

Constitutional Convention *n.* a meeting held in 1787 to consider changes to the Articles of Confederation; resulted in the drafting of the Constitution. (p. 229)

containment (kuhn TAYN muhnt) *n.* the blocking by one nation of another nation's attempts to spread influence—especially the efforts of the United States to block the spread of Soviet Communism during the late 1940s and early 1950s. (p. 718)

Continental Army *n.* a colonial force authorized by the Second Continental Congress in 1775, with George Washington as its commanding general. (p. 177)

convene (kuhn VEEN) *v.* to call together. (p. 259)

convoy system *n.* a heavy guard of destroyers that escorts merchant ships during wartime. (p. 687)

cooperative (koh OP uhr uh tiv) *n.* an organization owned and run by its members. (p. 577)

Copperheads *n.* Abraham Lincoln's main political oppo-nents; they favored peace with the South. (p. 508)

corporation *n.* a business owned by investors who buy part of the company through shares of stock. (p. 594)

cotton gin *n.* a machine invented in 1793 that cleaned cotton much faster and far more efficiently than human workers. (p. 348)

counterculture (KOWN tuhr KUL chuhr) *n.* a group of young people with values and lifestyles in opposition to those of the established culture. (p. 725)

Crittenden (KRIT uhn duhn) **Plan** *n.* a compromise introduced in 1861 that might have prevented secession. (p. 475)

Crusades (kroo SAYDZ) *n.* a series of wars to capture the Holy Land, launched in 1096 by European Christians. (p. 45)

culture (KUL chuhr) *n.* a way of life shared by people with similar arts, beliefs, and customs. (p. 28)

Dawes (dawz) **Act** *n.* a law, enacted in 1887, that distributed reservation land to individual owners. (p. 567)

Declaration of Independence n. the document, written in 1776, in which the colonies declared independence from Britain. (p. 180)

department store n. a store that sells everything from clothing to furniture to hardware. (p. 627)

depression n. a severe economic slump. (p. 386)

desert (di ZURT) v. to leave military duty without intending to return. (p. 203)

direct primary n. voters, rather than party conventions, choose candidates to run for public office. (p. 640)

diversity (di VUR si tee) n. a variety of people. (p. 117)

doctrine of nullification (NUL uh fi KAY shuhn) n. a right of a state to reject a federal law that it considers unconstitutional. (p. 381)

domestication (doh MES ti KAY shuhn) n. the practice of breeding plants or taming animals to meet human needs. (p. 28)

Dred Scott* v. *Sandford n. an 1856 Supreme Court case in which a slave, Dred Scott, sued for his freedom because he had been taken to live in territories where slavery was illegal; the Court ruled against Scott. (p. 467)

due process of law n. fair treatment under the law. (p. 267)

elector n. a voter. (p. 249)

Ellis Island n. the first stop in the United States for most immigrants coming from Europe. (p. 614)

Emancipation (i MAN suh PAY shuhn) **Proclamation** n. an executive order issued by Abraham Lincoln on January 1, 1863, freeing the slaves in all regions in rebellion against the Union. (p. 504)

Embargo (em BAHR goh) **Act of 1807** n. an act that stated that American ships were no longer allowed to sail to foreign ports, and it also closed American ports to British ships. (p. 328)

emigrant (EM i gruhnt) n. a person who leaves a country. (p. 423)

encomienda (en koh mee YEN duh) n. a grant of Native American labor. (p. 72)

English Bill of Rights n. an agreement signed by William and Mary to respect the rights of English citizens and of Parliament, including the right to free elections. (p. 144)

enlightenment (en LYT n muhnt) n. an 18th-century movement that emphasized the use of reason and the scientific method to obtain knowledge. (p. 140)

enumeration (i NOO muh RAY shuhn) n. an official count, such as a census. (p. 249)

equity (EK wi tee) n. a system of justice not covered under common law. (p. 269)

Erie (EER ee) **Canal** n. completed in 1825, this waterway connected New York City and Buffalo, New York. (p.)

Espionage (ES pee uh NAHZH) **Act** n. passed in 1917, law set heavy fines and long prison terms for antiwar activities and for encouraging draft resisters. (p. 69)

European Middle Ages n. a period from the late 4 to about the 1300s, during which Europeans turned feudalism and the manor system. (p. 44)

exoduster (EKS suh duhs tuhr) n. an African America who left the South for the West and compared him self or herself to Biblical Hebrews who left slavery Egypt. (p. 575)

ex post facto (EKS pohst FAK toh) **law** n. a law that would make an act a criminal offense after it was committed. (p. 255)

factory system n. a method of production that brought many workers and machines together into one building. (p. 341)

fall line n. the point at which a waterfall prevents la boats from moving farther upriver. (p. 126)

famine (FAM in) n. a severe food shortage. (p. 426)

fascism (FASH iz uhm) n. a political philosophy that advocates a strong, centralized, nationalistic government headed by a powerful dictator. (p. 712)

federalism n. a system of government where power shared among the central (or federal) government and the states. (pp. 234, 245)

Federalists n. supporters of the Constitution. (p. 234)

Federalist Papers n. a series of essays defending an explaining the Constitution. (p. 235)

eral Judiciary (joo DISH ee ER ee) **Act** *n.* it helped create a court system and gave the Supreme Court six members. (p. 294)

eral Reserve Act *n.* a law passed in 1913 that "created" the nation's banking system and instituted a flexible currency system. (p. 648)

ny (FEL uh nee) *n.* a serious crime. (p. 253)

dalism (FYOOD l IZ uhm) *n.* a political system in which the king allows nobles the use of his land in xchange for their military service and their protection f people living on the land. (p. 44)

eenth Amendment *n.* passed in 1870, this amendment to the U.S. Constitution stated that citizens could ot be stopped from voting "on account of race, color, r previous condition of servitude." (p. 546)

a Massachusetts Regiment *n.* one of the first frican-American regiments organized to fight for the nion in the Civil War. (p. 506)

t Battle of Bull Run *n.* an 1861 battle of the Civil War in which the South shocked the North with a ictory. (p. 485)

eign (FAWR in) **policy** *n.* relations with the governments of other countries. (p. 304)

Sumter *n.* a federal fort located in the harbor of harleston, South Carolina; the Southern attack on Fort umter marked the beginning of the Civil War. (p. 481)

y-niner *n.* a person who went to California to find old, starting in 1849. (p. 412)

rteen Points *n.* President Woodrow Wilson's goals or peace after World War I. (p. 695)

rteenth Amendment *n.* an amendment to the .S. Constitution, passed in 1868, that made all persons born or naturalized in the United States—including former slaves—citizens of the country. (p. 535)

t Continental Congress *n.* a meeting of delegates n 1774 from all the colonies except Georgia to uphold olonial rights. (p. 171)

edmen's Bureau *n.* a federal agency set up to help ormer slaves after the Civil War. (p. 533)

edmen's school *n.* a school set up to educate newly eed African Americans. (p. 541)

e Soil Party *n.* a political party dedicated to stoping the expansion of slavery. (p. 459)

French and Indian War *n.* a conflict in North America from 1754 to 1763 that was part of a worldwide struggle between France and Britain; Britain defeated France and gained French Canada. (p. 147)

frontier (frun TEER) *n.* unsettled or sparsely settled area occupied largely by Native Americans. (p. 557)

Fugitive Slave Act *n.* an 1850 law to help slaveholders recapture runaway slaves. (p. 462)

French Revolution *n.* in 1789, the French launched a movement for liberty and equality. (p. 301)

Fundamental Orders of Connecticut *n.* a set of laws that were established in 1639 by a Puritan congregation who had settled in the Connecticut Valley and that expanded the idea of representative government. (p. 95)

G

generator *n.* a machine that produces electric current. (p. 587)

Ghana (GAH nuh) *n.* a West African empire in the 8th–11th centuries A.D. (p. 39)

Gilded (gil did) **Age** *n.* an era during the late 1800s of fabulous wealth. (p. 596)

"Glorious Revolution" *n.* the overthrow of English King James II in 1688 and his replacement by William and Mary. (p. 144)

gold standard *n.* a policy under which the government backs every dollar with a certain amount of gold. (p. 577)

Grange (graynj) *n.* formed in 1867, the Patrons of Husbandry tried to meet the social needs of farm families. (p. 577)

Great Awakening *n.* a revival of religious feeling in the American colonies during the 1730s and 1740s. (p. 139)

Great Compromise *n.* the Constitutional Convention's agreement to establish a two-house national legislature, with all states having equal representation in one house and each state having representation based on its population in the other house. (p. 232)

Great Depression *n.* a period, lasting from 1929 to 1941, in which the U.S. economy was in severe decline and millions of Americans were unemployed. (p. 709)

Great Migration *n.* the movement of Puritans from England to establish settlements around the world, including 20,000 who sailed for America (p. 94); the movement of African Americans between 1910 and 1920 to northern cities from the South. (p. 693)

Great Plains *n.* the area from the Missouri River to the Rocky Mountains. (p. 557)

Great Society *n.* a program started by President Lyndon Johnson that provided help to the poor, the elderly, and women, and also promoted education and outlawed discrimination. (p. 724)

greenback *n.* paper currency issued by the federal government during the Civil War. (p. 509)

gristmill (GRIST MIL) *n.* a mill in which grain is ground to produce flour or meal. (p. 115)

guerrilla (guh RIL uh) *n.* a soldier who weakens the enemy with surprise raids and hit-and-run attacks. (p. 207)

H

hacienda (HAH see EN duh) *n.* a large farm or estate. (p. 72)

Harlem Renaissance *n.* a flowering of African-American artistic creativity during the 1920s, centered in the Harlem community of New York City. (p. 709)

Harpers Ferry *n.* a federal arsenal in Virginia that was captured in 1859 during a slave revolt. (p. 469)

Hausa (HOW suh) *n.* a West African people who lived in what is now northern Nigeria after A.D. 1000. (p. 42)

Haymarket affair *n.* in 1886, a union protest resulted in about 100 dead after an unknown person threw a bomb, and police opened fire on the crowd. (p. 602)

Holocaust (HOL uh KAWST) *n.* the systematic killing by Germany during World War II of about six million Jews as well as millions from other ethnic groups. (p. 716)

homestead *n.* land to settle on and farm. (p. 568)

Homestead Act *n.* passed in 1862, this law offered 160 acres of land free to anyone who agreed to live on and improve the land for five years. (p. 574)

House of Burgesses *n.* created in 1619, the first representative assembly in the American colonies. (p. 88)

Hudson River school *n.* a group of artists living in the Hudson River Valley in New York. (p. 430)

Hull House *n.* founded in 1889, a model for other settlement houses of the time. (p. 613)

hygiene (HY JEEN) *n.* conditions and practices that promote health. (p. 490)

I

immigrant *n.* a person who settles in a new country (p. 423)

immunity *n.* legal protection. (p. 262)

impeachment *n.* the process of accusing a public official of wrongdoing. (p. 249)

imperialism *n.* the policy by which stronger nations extend their economic, political, or military control over weaker nations or territories. (p. 659)

impressment *n.* the act of seizing by force. (p. 327)

inaugurate (in AW gyuh RAYT) *v.* to swear in or induct into office in a formal ceremony. (p. 293)

income tax *n.* a tax on earnings. (p. 509)

indentured servant *n.* a person who sold his or her labor in exchange for passage to America. (p. 88)

Indian Removal Act *n.* this 1830 act called for the government to negotiate treaties that would require Native Americans to relocate west. (p. 376)

Indian Territory *n.* present-day Oklahoma and parts Kansas and Nebraska to which Native Americans w moved under the Indian Removal Act of 1830. (p.

indictment (in DYT muhnt) *n.* a written statement iss by a grand jury charging a person with a crime. (p. 2

indigo *n.* a plant grown in the Southern colonies tha yields a deep blue dye. (p. 121)

individual right *n.* a personal liberty and privilege g anteed to U.S. citizens by the Bill of Rights. (p. 247)

Industrial Revolution *n.* in late 18th-century Britai factory machines began replacing hand tools and manufacturing replaced farming as the main form work. (p. 341)

inferior court *n.* a court with less authority than the Supreme Court. (p. 260)

inflation *n.* an increase in the price of goods and ser ices and a decrease in the value of money. (p. 386)

initiative (i NISH uh tiv) *n.* the procedure that allows voters to propose a law directly. (p. 640)

inoperative *adj.* no longer in force. (p. 274)

insurrection (IN suh REK shuhn) *n.* open revolt again government. (p. 271)

erchangeable part *n.* a part that is exactly like another part. (p. 343)

olerable Acts *n.* a series of laws enacted by Parliament in 1774 to punish Massachusetts colonists for the Boston Tea Party. (p. 170)

nclad *n.* a warship covered with iron. (p. 491)

quois (IR uh KWOH) **League** *n.* a 16th-century alliance of the Cayuga, Mohawk, Oneida, Onondaga, and Seneca Native American groups living in the eastern Great Lakes region. (p. 37)

gation *n.* the practice of bringing water to crops. (p. 29)

am (is LAHM) *n.* a religion founded by the prophet Muhammad in the 600s, which teaches that there is one God, named Allah. (p. 41)

ksonian democracy *n.* the idea of spreading political power to all the people, thereby ensuring majority rule. (p. 370)

nestown *n.* the first permanent English settlement in North America. (p. 87)

's Treaty *n.* the agreement that ended dispute over American shipping during the French Revolution. (p. 302)

z *n.* a new kind of music in the 1920s that captured the carefree spirit of the times. (p. 708)

Crow *n.* laws meant to enforce separation of white and black people in public places in the South. (p. 621)

nt-stock company *n.* a business in which investors pool their wealth in order to turn a profit. (p. 86)

icial (joo DISH uhl) **review** *n.* the principle that the Supreme Court has the final say in interpreting the Constitution. (p. 317)

iciary (joo DISH ee ER ee) **Act of 1801** *n.* a law that increased the number of federal judges, allowing President John Adams to fill most of the new spots with Federalists. (p. 316)

isas-Nebraska Act *n.* an 1854 law that established the territories of Kansas and Nebraska and gave their residents the right to decide whether to allow slavery. (p. 464)

ak (KY AK) *n.* a small boat made of animal skins. (p. 33)

King Cotton *n.* cotton was called king because cotton was important to the world market, and the South grew most of the cotton for Europe's mills. (p. 484)

King Philip's War *n.* a war between the Puritan colonies and Native Americans in 1675–1676. (p. 96)

Knights of Labor *n.* an organization of workers from all different trades formed after the Civil War. (p. 601)

Ku Klux Klan *n.* a group formed in 1866 that wanted to restore Democratic control of the South and to keep former slaves powerless. (p. 544)

L

labor union *n.* a group of workers who band together to seek better working conditions. (p. 434)

Land Ordinance of 1785 *n.* a law that established a plan for surveying and selling the federally owned lands west of the Appalachian Mountains. (p. 223)

land speculator *n.* a person who buys huge areas of land for a low price and then sells off small sections of it at high prices. (p. 394)

League of Nations *n.* an organization set up after World War I to settle international conflicts. (p. 695)

leisure (LEE zhuhr) *n.* free time. (p. 627)

Lewis and Clark expedition *n.* a group led by Meriwether Lewis and William Clark who explored the lands of the Louisiana Purchase beginning in 1803. (p. 320)

Lexington and Concord *n.* sites in Massachusetts of the first battles of the American Revolution. (p. 173)

limited government *n.* the principle that requires all U.S. citizens, including government leaders, to obey the law. (p. 247)

lode *n.* a deposit of mineral buried in rock. (p. 558)

Lone Star Republic *n.* the nickname of the republic of Texas, given in 1836. (p. 405)

long drive *n.* taking cattle by foot to a railway. (p. 560)

Louisiana (loo EE zee AN uh) **Purchase** *n.* the 1803 purchase of the Louisiana Territory from France. (p. 319)

Lowell mills *n.* textile mills located in the factory town of Lowell, Massachusetts, founded in 1826. (p. 342)

Loyalist *n.* an American colonist who supported the British in the American Revolution. (p. 173)

M

mail-order catalog *n.* a publication that contains pictures and descriptions of items so that people can order by mail. (p. 627)

Magna Carta *n.* "Great Charter;" a document guaranteeing basic political rights in England, approved by King John in 1215. (p. 141)

Mali (MAH lee) *n.* a West African empire from the 13th–15th centuries that grew rich from trade. (p. 41)

manifest destiny *n.* the belief that the United States was destined to stretch across the continent from the Atlantic Ocean to the Pacific Ocean. (p. 407)

manor system *n.* a system in which lords divided their lands into estates, which were farmed mostly by serfs who received protection from the lord in return. (p. 45)

Marbury v. Madison *n.* an 1803 case in which the Supreme Court ruled that it had the power to abolish laws by declaring them unconstitutional. (p. 317)

mass culture *n.* a common culture experienced by large numbers of people. (p. 626)

matrilineal (MAT ruh LIN ee uhl) *adj.* a society in which ancestry is traced through the mother. (p. 36)

Mayflower Compact *n.* an agreement established by the men who sailed to America on the *Mayflower*, which called for laws for the good of the colony and set forth the idea of self-government. (p. 93)

melting pot *n.* a place where cultures blend. (p. 616)

mercantilism (MUHR kuhn tee LIZ uhm) *n.* an economic system in which nations increase their wealth and power by obtaining gold and silver and by establishing a favorable balance of trade. (p. 61)

mercenary (MUR suh NER ee) *n.* a professional soldier hired to fight for a foreign country. (p. 195)

Mexican Cession (sesh uhn) *n.* a vast region given up by Mexico after the War with Mexico; it included the present-day states of California, Nevada, Utah, most of Arizona, and parts of New Mexico, Colorado, and Wyoming. (p. 411)

Mexicano (may hi KAH noh) *n.* a person of Spanish descent whose ancestors had come from Mexico and settled in the Southwest. (p. 570)

Middle Passage *n.* the middle leg of the triangular trade route—the voyage from Africa to the Americas—that brought captured Africans into slavery. (p. 78)

migrate *v.* to move from one location to another. (p. 27)

militarism *n.* the belief that a nation needs a large military force. (p. 679)

militia (muh LISH uh) *n.* a force of armed civilians pledged to defend their community during the American Revolution. (p. 170); an emergency military force that is not part of the regular army. (p. 254)

minié (MIN ee) **ball** *n.* a bullet with a hollow base. (p. 4

Minuteman *n.* a member of the colonial militia who w trained to respond "at a minute's warning." (p. 170)

misdemeanor (mis di MEE nuhr) *n.* a violation of the law. (p. 259)

mission *n.* a settlement created by the Church in ord to convert Native Americans to Christianity. (p. 72)

missionary *n.* a person sent by the Church to preach, teach, and convert native peoples to Christianity. (p.

Missouri Compromise *n.* a series of laws enacted in 1820 to maintain the balance of power between sla states and free states. (p. 358)

monopoly *n.* a company that eliminates its competit and controls an industry. (p. 595)

Monroe Doctrine *n.* a policy of U.S. opposition to a European interference in the Western Hemisphere, announced by President Monroe in 1823. (p. 359)

Mormon *n.* a member of a church founded by Josep Smith in 1830. (p. 397)

Mound Builder *n.* an early Native American who bu large earthen structures. (p. 31)

mountain man *n.* a fur trapper or explorer who opened up the West by finding the best trails throu the Rocky Mountains. (p. 393)

muckraker *n.* around 1900, the term for a journalist who exposed corruption in American society. (p. 64

Muslim (MUZ luhm) *n.* a follower of Islam. (p. 41)

N

nationalism *n.* a feeling of pride, loyalty, and protec tiveness toward one's country. (p. 354)

nativist *n.* a native-born American who wanted to el inate foreign influence. (p. 428)

natural-born citizen *n.* a citizen born in the United States or a commonwealth of the United States or parents who are U.S. citizens living outside the cou try. (p. 257)

turalization *n.* a way to give full citizenship to a person born in another country. (pp. 253, 270)

vigation Acts *n.* a series of laws passed by Parliament, beginning in 1651, to ensure that England made money from its colonies' trade. (p. 112)

vigator *n.* a person who plans the course of a ship while at sea. (p. 49)

zi (NAHT see) **Party** *n.* the National Socialist German Workers' Party; came to power under Adolf Hitler in the 1930s. (p. 712)

utral (NOO truhl) *adj.* not siding with one country or the other. (p. 302)

utrality (noo TRAL i tee) *n.* refusing to take sides in a war. (p. 682)

w Deal *n.* President Franklin Roosevelt's programs to fight the Great Depression. (p. 710)

w France *n.* a fur-trading post established in 1608 that became the first permanent French settlement in North America. (p. 70)

w immigrant *n.* a person from southern or eastern Europe who entered the United States after 1900. (p. 614)

w Jersey Plan *n.* a plan of government proposed at the Constitutional Convention in 1787 that called for a one-house legislature in which each state would have one vote. (p. 231)

eteenth Amendment *n.* an amendment to the U.S. Constitution, ratified in 1920, which gave women full voting rights. (p. 653)

rthwest Ordinance *n.* it described how the Northwest Territory was to be governed and set conditions for settlement and settlers' rights. (p. 223)

rthwest Territory *n.* territory covered by the Land Ordinance of 1785, which included land that formed the states of Ohio, Indiana, Michigan, Illinois, Wisconsin, and part of Minnesota. (p. 223)

en Door Policy *n.* in 1899, the United States asked nations involved in Asia to follow a policy in which no one country controlled trade with China. (p. 669)

gon Trail *n.* a trail that ran westward from Independence, Missouri, to the Oregon Territory. (p. 396)

rseer *n.* a worker hired by a planter to watch over and direct the work of slaves. (p. 122)

P

pacifist (PAS uh fist) *n.* a person morally opposed to war. (p. 209)

Palmer raids *n.* in 1920, federal agents and police raided the homes of suspected radicals. (p. 697)

Panama (PAN uh MAH) **Canal** *n.* a shortcut through Panama that connects the Atlantic and the Pacific oceans. (p. 670)

Panic of 1837 *n.* a financial crisis in which banks closed and the credit system collapsed. (p. 386)

Panic of 1873 *n.* a financial crisis in which banks closed and the stock market collapsed. (p. 547)

Parliament (PAHR luh muhnt) *n.* England's chief lawmaking body. (p. 142)

patent *n.* a government document giving an inventor the exclusive right to make or sell his or her invention for a specific number of years. (p. 586)

Patriot *n.* an American colonist who sided with the rebels in the American Revolution. (p. 173)

patroon (puh TROON) *n.* a person who brought 50 settlers to New Netherland and in return received a large land grant and other special privileges. (p. 101)

petroleum *n.* an oily, flammable liquid. (p. 585)

philanthropist (fil LAN thruh pist) *n.* a person who gives large sums of money to charities. (p. 596)

Pickett's Charge *n.* General George Pickett led a direct attack on Union troops during the 1863 Civil War battle at Gettysburg; the attack failed. (p. 513)

piedmont *n.* a broad plateau that leads to the foot of a mountain range. (p. 126)

Pilgrim *n.* a member of the group that rejected the Church of England, sailed to America, and founded the Plymouth Colony in 1620. (p. 92)

Pinckney's (PINGK neez) **Treaty** *n.* a 1795 treaty with Spain that allowed Americans to use the Mississippi River and to store goods in New Orleans; made the 31st parallel the southern U.S. border. (p. 302)

plantation *n.* a large farm that raises cash crops. (p. 73)

platform *n.* a statement of beliefs. (p. 471)

Platt Amendment *n.* a result of the Spanish-American War, which gave the United States the right to intervene in Cuban affairs when there was a threat to "life, property, and individual liberty." (p. 666)

Plessy v. Ferguson *n.* an 1896 case in which the Supreme Court ruled that separation of the races in public accommodations was legal. (p. 621)

political machine *n.* an organization that influences enough votes to control a local government. (p. 613)

political party *n.* a group of people that tries to promote its ideas and influence government, and also backs candidates for office. (p. 304)

Pontiac's (PON tee AKS) **Rebellion** *n.* a revolt against British forts and American settlers in 1763, led in part by Ottawa war leader Pontiac, in response to settlers' claims of Native American lands and to harsh treatment by British soldiers. (p. 151)

popular sovereignty (SOV uhr in tee) *n.* a government in which the people rule (p. 244); a system in which the residents vote to decide an issue. (p. 463)

Populist Party *n.* also known as the People's Party and formed in the 1890s, this group wanted a policy that would raise crop prices. (p. 577)

prejudice (PREJ uh dis) *n.* a negative opinion that is not based on facts. (p. 427)

printing press *n.* a machine invented about 1455 by Johannes Gutenberg. (p. 47)

privateer (PRY vuh TEER) *n.* a privately owned ship that has government permission during wartime to attack an enemy's merchant ships. (p. 204)

Proclamation (PRAHK luh MAY shuhn) **of 1763** *n.* an order in which Britain prohibited its American colonists from settling west of the Appalachian Mountains. (p. 151)

profit *n.* money a business makes, after subtracting the costs of doing business from the income. (p. 48)

progressivism (pruh GREHS ih VIHZ uhm) *n.* an early 20th-century reform movement seeking to return control of the government to the people, to restore economic opportunities, and to correct injustices in American life. (p. 639)

propaganda (PRAHP uh GAN duh) *n.* an opinion expressed for the purpose of influencing the actions of others. (p. 692)

proprietary (pruh PRY ih TEHR ee) **colony** *n.* a colony with a single owner. (p. 101)

pro tempore (proh TEHM puh ree) *adv.* Latin phrase meaning "for the time being." (p. 250)

Pullman Strike *n.* a nationwide railway strike that spread throughout the rail industry in 1894. (p. 603)

Puritan *n.* a member of a group from England that se[t]tled the Massachusetts Bay Colony in 1630 and soug[ht] to reform the practices of the Church of England. (p. 94)

push-pull factor *n.* a factor that pushes people out [of] their native lands and pulls them toward a new pla[ce] (p. 424)

Quaker (KWAY kuhr) *n.* a person who believed all pe[o]ple should live in peace and harmony; accepted diff[er]ent religions and ethnic groups. (p. 101)

quarter *v.* to give a place to stay. (p. 267)

Quartering Act *n.* a law passed by Parliament in 176[5] that required the colonies to house and supply Brit[ish] soldiers. (p. 160)

quorum (KWAWR uhm) *n.* the minimum number of members that must be present for official business [to] take place. (p. 251)

racial (RAY shuhl) **discrimination** (dih SKRIHM uh NA[Y] shuhn) *n.* different treatment based on a person's race. (p. 620)

racism (RAY SIHZ uhm) *n.* the belief that some people [are] inferior because of their race. (p. 79)

radical (RAD ih kuhl) *n.* a person who takes extreme political positions. (p. 313)

Radical Republican (rih PUHB lih kuhn) *n.* a congre[ss]man who, after the Civil War, favored using the go[v]ernment to create a new order in the South and to give African Americans full citizenship and the righ[t] [to] vote. (p. 533)

ragtime *n.* a blend of African-American songs and European musical forms. (p. 629)

ratification (RAT uh fih KAY shuhn) *n.* official approv[al] (p. 264)

recall *v.* to vote an official out of office. (p. 640)

Reconstruction *n.* the process the U.S. government used to readmit the Confederate states to the Unio[n] after the Civil War. (p. 533)

Red Scare *n.* in 1919–1920, a wave of panic from fea[r of] a Communist revolution. (p. 697)

referendum (REHF uh REHN duhm) *n.* when a propos[ed] law is submitted to a vote of the people. (p. 640)

rmation *n.* a 16th-century religious movement to rrect problems in the Roman Catholic Church. (p. 47)

issance (REHN ih SAHNS) *n.* a period of European tory, lasting from the 1300s to 1600, that brought creased interest in art and learning. (p. 46)

ezvous (RAHN day VOO) *n.* a meeting. (p. 197)

ieve (rih PREEV) *n.* a delay or cancellation of nishment. (p. 259)

blic (rih PUHB lihk) *n.* a government in which peo- elect representatives to govern for them. (p. 222)

blicanism (rih PUHB lih keh NIHZ uhm) *n.* the belief at government should be based on the consent of e people; people exercise their power by voting for litical representatives. (pp. 214, 245)

blican Party *n.* the political party formed in 1854 opponents of slavery in the territories. (p. 466)

rvation *n.* land set aside by the U.S. government r Native American tribes. (p. 562)

nue (REHV uh noo) *n.* income a government collects cover expenses. (pp. 160, 252)

al (rih VY vuhl) *n.* a meeting designed to reawaken igious faith. (p. 433)

n. a gun with a grooved barrel that causes a bullet spin through the air. (p. 491)

er baron *n.* a business leader who became wealthy rough dishonest methods. (p. 594)

anticism (roh MAN tih SIHZ uhm) *n.* a European tistic movement that stressed the individual, imagi- tion, creativity, and emotion. (p. 429)

sevelt Corollary (KAWR uh lehr ee) *n.* a 1904 addi- on to the Monroe Doctrine allowing the United ates to be the "policeman" in Latin America. (p. 672)

gh Rider *n.* a member of the First United States olunteer Cavalry, organized by Theodore Roosevelt uring the Spanish-American War. (p. 665)

l colony *n.* a colony ruled by governors appointed a king. (p. 103)

tary (SAL yuh TEHR ee) **neglect** *n.* a hands-off policy England toward its American colonies during the st half of the 1700s. (p. 144)

Sand Creek Massacre (MAS uh kuhr) *n.* an 1864 attack in which more than 150 Cheyenne men, women, and children were killed by the Colorado militia. (p. 564)

Santa Fe (SAN tuh FAY) **Trail** *n.* a trail that began in Missouri and ended in Santa Fe, New Mexico. (p. 395)

secede (sih SEED) *v.* to withdraw. (p. 473)

secession (sih SEHSH uhn) *n.* withdrawal. (p. 383)

Second Battle of the Marne (mahrn) *n.* a 1918 battle during World War I that marked the turning point in the war; allied troops along with Americans halted the German advance into France. (p. 689)

Second Continental Congress *n.* a governing body whose delegates agreed, in May 1775, to form the Continental Army and to approve the Declaration of Independence. (p. 177)

Second Great Awakening *n.* the renewal of religious faith in the 1790s and early 1800s. (p. 433)

sectionalism (SEHK shuh nuh LIHZ uhm) *n.* the placing of the interests of one's own region ahead of the interests of the nation as a whole. (p. 357)

Sedition (sih DIHSH uhn) **Act** *n.* a 1918 law that made it illegal to criticize the war; it set heavy fines and long prison terms for those who engaged in antiwar activities. (p. 692)

segregation (SEHG rih GAY shuhn) *n.* separation, espe- cially of races. (p. 621)

Seneca (SEHN ih kuh) **Falls Convention** *n.* a women's rights convention held in Seneca Falls, New York, in 1848. (p. 444)

separation of powers *n.* the division of basic govern- ment roles into branches. (p. 246)

servitude (SUR vih TOOD) *n.* a state of belonging to an owner or master. (p. 270)

Seven Days' Battles *n.* an 1862 Civil War battle in which the Confederacy forced the Union to retreat before it could capture the Southern capital of Richmond. (p. 496)

Seventeenth Amendment *n.* an amendment to the U.S. Constitution, ratified in 1913, that provided for the direct election of U.S. senators. (p. 648)

sharecropping *n.* a system in which landowners gave farm workers land, seed, and tools in return for a part of the crops they raised. (p. 543)

Shays's (SHAY zuhz) **Rebellion** *n.* an uprising of debt- ridden Massachusetts farmers in 1787. (p. 225)

Sherman Antitrust Act *n.* a law passed in 1890 that made it illegal for corporations to gain control of industries by forming trusts. (p. 641)

Siege (seej) **of Vicksburg** *n.* an 1863 Union victory in the Civil War that enabled the Union to control the entire Mississippi River. (p. 516)

Sixteenth Amendment *n.* an amendment to the U.S. Constitution, ratified in 1913, that gave Congress the power to create income taxes. (p. 647)

slash-and-burn agriculture (ag rih kuhl chuhr) *n.* a farming method in which people clear fields by cutting and burning trees and grasses, the ashes of which fertilize the soil. (p. 37)

slave code *n.* a law passed to regulate the treatment of slaves. (p. 79)

slavery *n.* the practice of holding a person in bondage for labor. (p. 76)

slum *n.* a neighborhood with overcrowded and dangerous housing. (p. 612)

smuggle *v.* to illegally import or export goods. (p. 112)

social gospel (GAHS puhl) *n.* a movement aimed at improving the lives of the poor. (p. 612)

socialism *n.* an economic system in which all members of a society are equal owners of all businesses; members share the work and the profits. (p. 602)

sodbuster *n.* a farmer on the frontier. (p. 575)

Songhai (SAWNG HY) *n.* a West African empire that succeeded Mali and controlled trade from the 1400s to 1591. (p. 42)

Sons of Liberty *n.* a group of colonists who formed a secret society to oppose British policies at the time of the American Revolution. (p. 161)

Spanish-American War *n.* a war in 1898 that began when the United States demanded Cuba's independence from Spain. (p. 664)

Spanish Armada (ahr MAH duh) *n.* a fleet of ships sent in 1588 by Philip II, the Spanish king, to invade England and restore Roman Catholicism. (p. 69)

sphere of influence *n.* an area where foreign nations claim special rights and economic privileges. (p. 669)

spiritual *n.* a religious folk song. (p. 351)

spoils system *n.* the practice of winning candidates giving government jobs to political backers or supporters. (p. 373)

Stamp Act *n.* a 1765 law passed by Parliament th required all legal and commercial documents to carry an official stamp showing a tax had been (p. 160)

standard time *n.* a system adopted in 1918 that div the United States into four time zones. (p. 592)

states' rights *n.* theory that said that states had th right to judge when the federal government had passed an unconstitutional law. (p. 307)

steerage *n.* the cheapest deck or place on a ship. (p

Stono (STOH noh) **Rebellion** *n.* a 1739 uprising of slaves in South Carolina, leading to the tightening already harsh slave laws. (p. 123)

strategy *n.* an overall plan of action. (p. 196)

strike *v.* to stop work to demand better working conditions. (p. 434)

subsistence farm *n.* a farm that produces enough food for the family with a small additional amour for trade. (p. 110)

suffrage *n.* the right to vote. (pp. 262, 444)

Sugar Act *n.* a law passed by Parliament in 1764 th placed a tax on sugar, molasses, and other produc shipped to the colonies; also called for harsh puni ment of smugglers. (p. 160)

sweatshop *n.* a place where workers labored long hours under poor conditions for low wages. (p. 6(

Tammany (TAM uh nee) **Hall** *n.* a famous political machine, located in New York City in the late 19th century. (p. 613)

tariff *n.* a tax on imported goods. (p. 296)

Tariff of Abominations *n.* an 1828 law that raised tariffs on raw materials and manufactured goods; upset Southerners who felt that economic interes the Northeast were determining national econom policy. (p. 381)

technology *n.* the use of tools and knowledge to n human needs. (p. 32)

Tejano (tuh HAH noh) *n.* a person of Spanish heritag who considered Texas his or her home. (p. 400)

temperance movement *n.* a campaign to stop th drinking of alcohol. (p. 434)

tender *n.* money. (p. 255)

ment *n.* an apartment building that is usually run-own and overcrowded. (p. 611)

eenth Amendment *n.* an amendment to the U.S. nstitution, adopted in 1865, banning slavery and voluntary servitude in the United States. (p. 521)

e-Fifths Compromise *n.* the Constitutional nvention's agreement to count three-fifths of a ate's slaves as population for purposes of representa-on and taxation. (p. 232)

nshend (TOWN zuhnd) **Acts** *n.* a series of laws ssed by Parliament in 1767 that suspended New rk's assembly and established taxes on goods ought into the British colonies. (p. 163)

of Tears *n.* the tragic journey of the Cherokee ople from their homeland to Indian Territory tween 1838 and 1839; thousands of Cherokee ed. (p. 377)

scendentalism (TRAN sen DEN tl IZ uhm) *n.* a 19th-ntury philosophy that taught the spiritual world is ore important than the physical world and that peo-e can find truth within themselves through feeling d intuition. (p. 431)

scontinental (TRANS kon tuh NEN tl) **railroad** *n.* a ilroad that spanned the entire continent. (p. 590)

ty of Ghent (gent) *n.* treaty, signed in 1814, which ded the War of 1812; no territory exchanged hands d trade disputes were not resolved. (p. 333)

ty of Greenville *n.* a 1795 agreement in which 12 ative American tribes surrendered much of present-y Ohio and Indiana to the U.S. government. (p. 300)

ty of Guadalupe Hidalgo (GWAHD loop hi DAH oh) *n.* the 1848 treaty ending the U.S. war with exico; Mexico ceded nearly one-half of its land to e United States. (p. 410)

ty of Paris *n.* the 1763 treaty that ended the ench and Indian War; Britain gained all of North merica east of the Mississippi River. (p. 150)

ty of Paris of 1783 *n.* the treaty that ended the evolutionary War, confirming the independence of e United States and setting the boundaries of the ew nation. (p. 212)

ty of Tordesillas (TAWR duh SEE uhs) *n.* the 1494 eaty in which Spain and Portugal agreed to divide e lands of the Western Hemisphere between them d moved the Line of Demarcation further west. . 61)

ty of Versailles (vuhr SY) *n.* the 1919 treaty that ded World War I. (p. 696)

trench warfare *n.* a kind of warfare during World War I in which troops huddled at the bottom of trenches and fired artillery and machine guns at each other. (p. 680)

triangular trade *n.* the transatlantic system of trade in which goods, including slaves, were exchanged between Africa, England, Europe, the West Indies, and the colonies in North America. (p. 111)

tribunal (try BYOO nuhl) *n.* a court. (p. 253)

trust *n.* a legal body created to hold stock in many com-panies, often in the same industry. (p. 595)

tundra (TUN druh) *n.* a treeless plain that remains frozen under its top layer of soil. (p. 33)

U

unanimous (yoo NAN uh muhs) **consent** *n.* complete agreement. (p. 264)

Uncle Tom's Cabin *n.* a novel published by Harriet Beecher Stowe in 1852, which portrayed slavery as brutal and immoral. (p. 462)

unconstitutional *n.* something that contradicts the law of the Constitution. (p. 317)

Underground Railroad *n.* a series of escape routes used by slaves escaping the South. (p. 442)

urbanization *n.* growth of cities resulting from industrialization. (p. 609)

U.S.S. *Maine* *n.* a U.S. warship that mysteriously exploded and sank in the harbor of Havana, Cuba, on February 15, 1898. (p. 663)

V

vaquero (vah KAIR oh) *n.* a cowhand that came from Mexico with the Spaniards in the 1500s. (p. 560)

vaudeville (VAWD vil) *n.* a form of live stage entertain-ment with a mixture of songs, dance, and comedy. (p. 629)

viceroyalty (VYS ROI uhl tee) *n.* a province ruled by a viceroy, who ruled in the king's name. (p. 71)

Vietnam War (vee ET NAHM) *n.* a military conflict from 1957 to 1975 between the North Vietnam Communists and the non-Communist forces of South Vietnam sup-ported by the United States. (p. 719)

vigilante (vij uh LAN tee) *n.* a person willing to take the law into his or her own hands. (p. 561)

Virginia Plan *n.* a plan proposed by Edmund Randolph, a delegate to the Constitutional Convention in 1787, that proposed a government with three branches and a two-house legislature in which representation would be based on a state's population or wealth. (p. 231)

W

war bond *n.* a low-interest loan by civilians to the government, meant to be repaid in a number of years. (p. 691)

War Hawk *n.* a westerner who supported the War of 1812. (p. 329)

Watergate scandal *n.* a scandal resulting from the Nixon administration's attempt to cover up its involvement in the 1972 break-in at the Democratic National Committee headquarters in the Watergate apartment complex in Washington, D.C. (p. 720)

Webster-Hayne debate *n.* an 1830 debate between Daniel Webster and Robert Hayne over the doctrine of nullification. (p. 382)

Whig (hwig) **Party** *n.* a political party organized in 1834 to oppose the policies of Andrew Jackson. (p. 387)

Whiskey Rebellion *n.* a 1794 protest against the government's tax on whiskey, which was valuable to the livelihood of backcountry farmers. (p. 301)

Wilderness Road *n.* the trail into Kentucky that woodsman Daniel Boone helped to build. (p. 221)

Wilmot (WIL muht) **Proviso** (pruh VY zoh) *n.* an 1846 proposal that outlawed slavery in any territory gained from the War with Mexico. (p. 459)

World War II *n.* a war fought from 1939 to 1945, in which Great Britain, France, the Soviet Union, the United States, and other allies defeated Germany, Italy, and Japan. (p. 713)

Wounded Knee Massacre *n.* the massacre by U.S. soldiers of 300 unarmed Native Americans at Wounded Knee Creek, South Dakota, in 1890. (p. 566)

writ (rit) **of assistance** *n.* a search warrant that allowed British officers to enter colonial homes or businesses to search for smuggled goods. (p. 164)

X

XYZ Affair *n.* a 1797 incident in which French officials demanded a bribe from U.S. diplomats. (p. 306)

Y

yellow journalism *n.* a style of journalism that exaggerates and sensationalizes the news. (p. 663)

Yoruba (YOH roo bah) *n.* a West African people who formed several states southwest of the Niger River. (p.)

Z

Zimmermann telegram *n.* a message sent in 1917 the German foreign minister to the German ambassador in Mexico, proposing a German-Mexican alliance and promising to help Mexico regain Texas, New Mexico, and Arizona if the United States entered World War I. (p. 682)

abolition [abolición] s. movimiento para eliminar la esclavitud. (p. 440)

abridge [abreviar] v. reducir. (p. 266)

AEF s. Fuerza Expedicionaria Estadounidense, fuerzas de EE. UU. durante la primera guerra mundial. (p. 686)

affirmation [afirmación] s. declaración de que algo es cierto. (p. 257)

African Diaspora [diáspora africana] s. traslado forzado de los africanos, desde su patria a las Américas para trabajar allí como esclavos. (p. 78)

Albany Plan of Union [Plan de la Unión de Albany] s. primera propuesta formal para unir las colonias norteamericanas, presentado por Benjamín Franklin. (p. 149)

Alien and Sedition Acts [leyes de Extranjeros y Sedición] s. serie de cuatro leyes promulgadas en 1798 para reducir el poder político de inmigrantes recién llegados a Estados Unidos. (p. 306)

Allies [aliados] s. alianza de Serbia, Rusia, Francia, Gran Bretaña, Italia y otros siete países durante la primera guerra mundial. (p. 680)

ally [aliado] s. país que acuerda ayudar a otro país a alcanzar un objetivo común. (p. 200)

American Federation of Labor (AFL) [Federación Norteamericana del Trabajo] s. organización nacional de sindicatos obreros fundada en 1886. (p. 603)

American System [Sistema Americano] s. plan presentado en 1815 para hacer autosuficiente a Estados Unidos. (p. 354)

Anaconda Plan [Plan Anaconda] s. estrategia de tres pasos mediante la cual la Unión se proponía derrotar a la Confederación durante la guerra civil estadounidense. (p. 484)

Angel Island [isla del Ángel] s. primera parada en Estados Unidos para la mayoría de los inmigrantes que venían de Asia. (p. 615)

Antifederalist [antifederalista] s. persona que se oponía a la ratificación de la Constitución de los Estados Unidos. (p. 234)

Anti-Imperialist League [Liga Antiimperialista] s. grupo de estadounidenses importantes que creían que Estados Unidos no debía negarle a otras personas el derecho de gobernarse a sí mismas. (p. 667)

Appalachian Mountains [montes Apalaches] s. cadena de montañas que se extiende desde el este de Canadá hacia el sur, hasta Alabama. (p. 126)

appellate [de apelación] adj. que tiene el poder de reexaminar decisiones de las cortes. (p. 260)

Appomattox Court House [Appomattox] s. pueblo de Virginia donde Robert E. Lee se rindió a Ulysses s. Grant en 1865, finalizando así la guerra civil. (p. 519)

apprentice [aprendiz] s. joven que aprende un oficio o una artesanía de un maestro experto. (p. 137)

appropiation [apropiación] s. fondos públicos que se reservan para un propósito específico. (p. 253)

archaeologist [arqueólogo] s. científico que estudia el pasado humano examinando artículos que dejó la gente. (p. 27)

armistice [armisticio] s. suspensión de la lucha en una guerra. (p. 690)

Articles of Confederation [Artículos de Confederación] s. documento, adoptado por el Congreso Continental en 1777 y finalmente aprobado por los estados en 1781, que delineaba la forma de gobierno de los nuevos Estados Unidos. (p. 222)

artifact [artefacto] s. herramienta u otro artículo hecho por seres humanos. (p. 27)

artillery [artillería] s. cañón o arma grande. (p. 177)

artisan [artesano] s. obrero especializado, como un tejedor a telar o un alfarero, que hace artículos a mano; artífice. (p. 117)

assimilation [asimilación] s. proceso de integrarse a una sociedad. (p. 616)

B

baby boom s. término para la generación que nació en Estados Unidos entre 1946 y 1961, cuando el índice de natalidad aumentó marcadamente después de la segunda guerra mundial. (p. 722)

Backcountry [tierras fronterizas] s. región colonial que se extendía a lo largo de los montes Apalaches a través de la sección oeste de Nueva Inglaterra y las colonias del centro y del sur. (p. 109)

Bacon's Rebellion [Rebelión de Bacon] s. levantamiento contra la poderosa autoridad colonial de Jamestown por Nathaniel Bacon y un grupo de habitantes de la frontera que resultó en la quema de Jamestown en 1676. (p. 89)

bail [fianza] s. dinero que pagan como fianza las personas arrestadas para garantizar que van a regresar para el juicio. (p. 268)

Battle of Antietam [batalla de Antietam] s. batalla de la guerra civil, en 1862, en que murieron o resultaron heridos 25,000 hombres. (p. 497)

Battle of Fallen Timbers s. en 1794 el ejército estadounidense derrotó a 2,000 amerindios en un enfrentamiento por el control del territorio del Noroeste. (p. 299)

R

racial quota, 750–751

racism, 79, 620–623, 698

Radical Republicans, 534–536, i535, 542

radicals, 313

radio, 708

ragtime, i629

railroads, 356, 590–593
antitrust suit against, 642
after Civil War, 523
cattle industry and, 559–561
government promotion of, 575
growth of, c584, 587
immigrants and, 426, 571
organized labor and, 602
Panic of 1837 and, 547
settling of Great Plains and, 558
shipment of crops and, 577
transcontinental, m592
westward expansion and, 569, i574

Railroad Strike of 1877, 601

Rainey, Joseph, 546

Raleigh, Walter, 86

ranching, 560–561

Randolph, Edmund, i228, 231, i291, 295

Raza Unida, La, 724

Reagan, Ronald, i258, 720, i721, i725, i726, R38

reapers, 576

recall, 640

recession, 725

Reconstruction, 532–539
aftermath of, 545–550
civil rights amendments and laws in, c271, c549
daily life in, 540–544
Ku Klux Klan and, 544
problems of, c532

Reconstruction Acts of 1867, 535–536, 542

redcoats, 165

Red River, 322

Red Scare, 697–698

referendum, 640

Reformation, 47

reform movements, 433–439, 440–445
in Progressive Era, 638, 639–642
women and, 650–652

Reform Party, 467

Regents of the University of

California v. *Bakke,* 750–751

regimental flag, i514

region, 4, 13

relative location, 4

religion
education and, 138
freedom of, 215, 237, 266
Great Awakening and, 140
immigration and, 424
in Middle Colonies, 102, 116
Pilgrims and, 92
Puritans and, 94
slaves and, 351–352
utopian communities and, 437

Renaissance, 46–48

rendezvous system, 394

reparations, 696

representative government, 95, 134, 141–144, 168, 245

reprieves, 259

republic, 222

republicanism, 214–215

Republican Party
development of, i386, 466–467
in election of 1860, m473
Grant's presidency and, 545–547
Ku Klux Klan and, 544
Reagan and, i258
in Reconstruction, 534

reservation, 564, 566

reserved powers, 245

Revels, Hiram, 536, i546

revenue, 252

revenue tariffs, i380

Revere, Paul, i165, m172

revival, 139, i433

Revolutionary War. *See* American Revolution.

Reynolds v. *Sims,* 748–749

Rhode Island
facts about, R35, R41
founding of, m95
mills in, 342
ratification of U.S. Constitution by, 237

rice, 121

Richmond, Va., 518
in Confederacy, 482, m483, 484, 496, 507
in Reconstruction, i537
transportation system in, 611

Richthofen, Manfred von, 681

Rickenbacker, Eddie, 686, 689

Ridge, Tom, 733

rifle, 491

rights of accused persons, 2[?]

rights of people, 268
to bear arms, 267
to privacy, 267
to a speedy, public trial, 2[?]
to vote, i243, 271, 546

Rio Grande, 322–323, 407

riots, 509

"Rip Van Winkle," 429

river mouth, i14

roads, 355

Roanoke Island, 85, 86, m87

Roaring Twenties, 707–708

robber baron, 594

Robinson projection, i9

Rochambeau, Jean, 210

Rockefeller, John D., i584, 595–596, i595, 640

Rockefeller University, 596

Rock Springs, Wyo., 623

Rocky Mountains, i11, 393, 558–559

Rocky Mountains, The, i310

Rolfe, John, 88

Roman Catholic Church, 45, 50–51, 72

Roman Catholics, 426, 428

romanticism, 429

Roosevelt, Franklin Delano, 710–711, i711, 713, 714, R38

Roosevelt, Theodore, i643, R[?]
and conservation moveme[?]
643–645, i644
and Latin America, 672
and Progressive Era, i637, [?]
in Spanish-American War, 664–666, i666
square deal policy of, 641

Roosevelt Corollary, 672

Ross, Betsy, i199

rotary printing press, i339

Rothschild, Alexander, 426

Rough Riders, 665, i666

roundup, i560

Rowlandson, Mary, 138

royal colony, 103

royal governor, 143, c144

Royall, Anne Newport, 432

rule of law, i247

Rush-Bagot Agreement, 356–[?]

Russell, Charles M., i554

Russia, 318, 359

Russian Revolution, 683

vurm, John, 435
, Babe, i708

gawea, 321–322, i324
o and Vanzetti, 697–698
amento, Cal., 416
dahoc, 86, m87
r family, 396
ugustine, Fla., i68
awrence River, 70
eger, Barry, 196–197
ouis, Mo., 320
orld's fair in, i632, 633
m, Mass., 96
tax, 647
ary neglect, 144
oset, 93
pson, Deborah, 195
Antonio, Tex., 402
d Creek Massacre, m563, 564
doz, Mari, 568
Francisco, Cal.
inatown in, 416
rthquake of 1906 in, 611
migrants in, 615
d westward expansion,
c569, i569
Jacinto, Battle of, 404
Juan Hill, 665
Salvador, 52
ta Anna, Antonio López de,
402–404, 408, 409, 410
ta Fe, N.M., 395
ta Fe Trail, 395–396, m395
ta Maria, 51
ah, Plain and Tall, i571
atoga, Battle of, 198–199
annah, Ga.
American Revolution,
206–207, m209
Civil War, 517
awags, 536
e, 7
ndinavians, 424–425, m425
begoats, 97
rlet Letter, The, 432
enck, Charles, 744
enck v. United States,
692–693, 744–745
ool of Athens, i47
ool of Manners, The, i138

schools. See education.
Scots-Irish, 127
Scott, Abigail, i568
Scott, Dred, 467, i468, 740, i741
Scott, Winfield, 377, 410, 484
Scotts Bluff, i364
sea dogs, 68
sea level, i14
search and seizure, 267
search warrants, 159
secession, 473–474, m477, 482,
m483
South Carolinan threat of, 383
Second Amendment, 267
secondary sources, using, R21
Second Bank of the United
States, i384, i385
Second Continental Congress, 177
adoption of Declaration of
Independence, 179–180,
i180
Articles of Confederation and,
222
war actions of, 194, 203, 213
Second Great Awakening, 433
Second Seminole War, 378
secretary of state, 294
secretary of treasury, 294, 295
secretary of war, 294
sectionalism
in pre-Civil War America,
357–358
slavery debate and, 457–461,
462–465
Southern secession and,
473–475
tariffs and, 379–381
Sedition Act, 692
segregation, i506, 620–623, 742
in schools, 746–747
Seguín, Juan, 403, i404
Selective Service Act, 686
self-government, 238
Seminole people, 357, 374–375,
i376, 378
Senate
constitutional provisions for,
249, 250
direct election of, 272
Great Compromise and, 232
role in legislation, c252
terms in, c250
Seneca Falls Convention, 444
separate ballots, 314

separate but equal, 621,
742–743, 746–747
separation of powers, 246
September 11 terrorist attack,
721, i721, 732, i733, 734
effect on air travel of, 733
impact of, 721, 732–737
New York City and, 732, 733
sequencing, c84, c158, c192, R4
Sequoia National Park, 12, i644
Sequoya, i374
Serapis, 205
settlement houses, 612, 650–651
Seven Days' Battle, 496
Seventeenth Amendment, 272,
c653
Seventh Amendment, 142, 261,
268
Seven Years' War, 148
Seward, William, 522, 660
sewing machine, 589
Shakers, 437
sharecropping, 543–544, c543,
597
Shays's Rebellion, 224–225, i225,
229
sheriff, 561
Sherman, Roger
Great Compromise and, 232
Sherman, William Tecumseh,
494–495, i501, 516–519
Sherman Antitrust Act, 641, 642
Shiloh, Battle of, 494–495
shipping, 116
Sholes, Christopher Latham, 588
Shoshone people, 322, i324
Shreve, Henry Miller, 344–345
sick pay, 603
Sierra Nevada, 413
silver, 558–559
Sinclair, Upton, 642
Singer, Isaac, 589
Singleton, Benjamin "Pap," 575
Sioux people, 564, 565
Sitting Bull, i565
Sixteenth Amendment, 272,
647–648, c647, c653
Sixth Amendment, 267
skills for studying history
categorizing, c26, c392, c608,
c706, R6
causes and effects, analyzing, c48,
c96, c108, c323, c329, c333,
c340, c416, c456, c523, c584,
604, c678, c697, c720, R11

488 Bureau of Archives and History, New Jersey State Library; 489 Corbis-Bettmann; 490 Culver Pictures; 491 The Granger Collection, New York; 492 Illustration by Alexander Verbitsky; 493 Library of Congress; 496 U.S. Signal Corps photo no. 111-B-4146 (Brady Collection) in the National Archives; 497 Chicago Historical Society; 498 *left, center* Photos by Larry Sherer. Copyright © Time-Life Books Inc.; *bottom right* Fort Sumter National Park.

Chapter 17, 500–501 Detail of *Cavalry Charge at Yellow Tavern, VA, May 11, 1864* (1871), H.W. Chaloner. West Point Museum Art Collection, United States Military Academy; 500 *left* The Granger Collection, New York; *right* © Paul Almasy/Corbis; 501 *left* The Granger Collection, New York; *right* Library of Congress; 502 *top left, top right, bottom left* Library of Congress; *bottom right* The Granger Collection, New York; 503 Corbis; 504 The Granger Collection, New York; 505 *top* Copyright © Archive Photos; *bottom* Library of Congress; 506 Defense Visual Information Center, Linda Delatorre, Researcher; 507 Culver Pictures; 508 The Granger Collection, New York; 510 American Red Cross; 511 *background* Corbis; *foreground* Massachusetts Commandery Military Order of the Loyal Legion and the U.S. Army Military History Institute; 512 The Pejepscot Historical Society; 513 Copyright © 1994 Kunio Owaki/The Stock Market; 514–515 *background* Illustration by Ken Goldammer; 514 *center* Library of Congress; *bottom left* From *Echoes of Glory: Arms & Equipment of The Union.* Photo by Larry Sherer. Copyright © 1991 Time-Life Books Inc.; *bottom right* The Museum of the Confederacy, Richmond, Virginia. Photo by Katherine Wetzel; 515 *bottom* From *Echoes of Glory: Arms & Equipment of The Union.* Photo by Larry Sherer. Copyright © 1991 Time-Life Books Inc.; 516 Library of Congress; 518 *top left* Courtesy of Stamatelos Brothers Collection. Photo by Larry Sherer. Copyright © 1991 Time-Life Books Inc.; *bottom* Courtesy Reserve-Kunhardt Collection, Mount Kisco, New York; 520 Copyright © Robert M. Anderson/Uniphoto, Inc.; 522 National Archives; 526 *top right* Manassas National Battlefield Park, National Park Service. Photo by Larry Sherer; *bottom right* Collection of Old Capitol Museum of Mississippi History; 528 *center left, center* High Impact Photography/Copyright © Time-Life Books Inc.; *center right* Courtesy of Stamatelos Brothers Collection. Photo by Larry Sherer. Copyright © 1991 Time-Life Books Inc.; 529 Photos by Sharon Hoogstraten.

Chapter 18, 530–531 National Archives; 530 © Bettmann/Corbis; 531 *top left* © Bettmann/Corbis; *bottom left* © Corbis; *right* Library of Congress; 533, 534 The Granger Collection, New York; 535 Corbis; 536 *His First Vote* (1868), Thomas Waterman Wood. Cheekwood Museum of Art, Nashville, Tennessee; 537, 538–539 *background* The Granger Collection, New York; 538 *top right,* 540, 541 Corbis; 542 Library of Congress; 544 The Granger Collection, New York; 545 Library of Congress; 546, 547 The Granger Collection, New York; 548 Library of Congress; 551 *bottom* The Granger Collection, New York.

Unit 6

552–553 The Granger Collection, New York.

Chapter 19, 554–555 © Corbis; 554 *left* The Granger Collection, New York; *right* © Corbis; 555 *left* © Bettmann/Corbis; *right* © Bettmann/Corbis; 557 Denver Public Library; 559 *top* The Granger Collection, New York; *bottom* Copyright © Dan Guravich/Photo Researchers, Inc.; 560 *California Vaqueros* (1875),

James Walker. Oil on canvas, 31" x 46". Courtesy of The Anschutz Collection. Photo by William J. O'Connor; 561 Culver Pictures; 562 *background* The Granger Collection, New York; *foreground* State Historical Society of North Dakota; 564 *Custer's Last Stand* (1899), Edgar S. Paxson. Oil on canvas, 7 1/2" x 106". Buffalo Bill Historical Center, Cody, Wyoming; 565 *top* The Granger Collection, New York; *center* Culver Pictures; *bottom* Library of Congress; 566 Western History Collection, University of Oklahoma Libraries; 567 Library of Congress; 568 The Kansas State Historical Society, Topeka, Kansas; 569 *top View of San Francisco [Formerly Yerba Buena]* (1847), attributed to Victor Prevost. Oil on canvas, 25" x 30". California Historical Society, gift of the Ohio Historical Society; *bottom* The Bancroft Library, University of California, Berkeley; 570 *top* The Granger Collection, New York; *center* Courtesy of the Arizona Historical Society/Tucson; *bottom* The Granger Collection, New York; 571 Photofest; 572–573 Wyoming Division of Cultural Resources; *top* Library of Congress; 574 *foreground, Northern Pacific Railroad. The Pioneer Route to Fargo Moorhead Town Bismarck Dakota and Montana and the Famous Valley of the Yellowstone* (about 1885), Creator–Poole Brothers, Printers. Broadside. Chicago Historical Society; 575 Solomon D. Butcher Collection, Nebraska State Historical Society; 577 The Granger Collection, New York; 578 Culver Pictures; 579 *Rush for the Oklahoma Land* (1894), John Steuart Curry. Department of the Interior.

Chapter 20, 582–583 The Granger Collection, New York; 582 National Museum of American History/Smithsonian Institution; *bottom* © Hulton-Deutsch Collection/Corbis; 583 *left* © Michael Maslan Historic Photographs/Corbis; *right* © Bettmann/Corbis; 584 The Newberry Library, Chicago; 585 Corbis-Bettmann; 587 Library of Congress; 588 *background* U.S. Dept. of Commerce–Patent & Trademark Office, Washington, D.C.; *left foreground* The Granger Collection, New York; *right foreground* Courtesy AT&T; 589 *left background* U.S. Dept. of Commerce—Patent & Trademark Office, Washington, D.C.; *left foreground* First Church of Christ, Lynn, Massachusetts; 590 Special Collections Division, University of Washington Libraries. Negative no. 2315; 591 *top* Courtesy Colorado Historical Society; *bottom, The Last Spike* (1869). William T. Garrett Foundry, San Francisco. 17 6/10 carat gold, alloyed with copper. 5 9/16" x 7/16" x 1/2" (shaft including head), 1/2" x 1 3/8" x 1 1/4". Iris & B. Gerald Cantor Center for Visual Arts at Stanford University. Gift of David Hewes, 1998.11; 593 Copyright © United States Postal Service; 594 Corbis-Bettmann; 595 *left, John Davison Rockefeller* (1967), Adrian Lamb, after the 1917 oil by John Singer Sargent. Oil on canvas, 58 3/4" x 45 3/4". National Portrait Gallery, Smithsonian Institution/Art Resource, New York; *right* National Portrait Gallery, Smithsonian Institution/Art Resource, New York; 596 *left The Hatch Family* (1871), Eastman Johnson. Oil on canvas, 48 x 73 3/8". The Metropolitan Museum of Art, Gift of Frederic H. Hatch, 1926 (26.97). Photograph copyright © 1999 The Metropolitan Museum of Art. *right, Room in a Tenement Flat* (about 1910), photo by Jessie Tarbox Beals. The Jacob A. Riis Collection, Museum of the City of New York; 598 *top right* Library of Congress; *center left* Chicago Historical Society; *bottom right* Library of Congress; 598 *bottom left,* 599 *center left* Corbis-Bettmann; 599 *bottom* Chicago Historical Society; 600, 601 Corbis-Bettmann; 602 Brown Brothers.

Chapter 21, 606–607 The Granger Collection, New York; 606 *left* The Granger Collection, New York; *right* © Corbis; 607 *top* © Corbis; *bottom* The Granger Collection, New York; 609

stration by Patrick Ghan; 611 The Granger Collection, New k; 613 Corbis-Bettmann; 614 The Granger Collection, New k; 616 Brown Brothers; 617 Michael S. Yamashita/Corbis; 618 stration by Ronald Himler. Copyright © 1995 HarperCollins blishers. Bottom background copyright © Bill Pogue; 619 bis; 620 Copyright © Jacques Chenet/Liaison Agency; 621 top eph Schwartz Collection/Corbis; bottom Corbis; 622 Library of ngress; 623 The Granger Collection, New York; 626, 627 rbis-Bettmann; 628 top Lake County Museum/Corbis; center, ttom The Granger Collection, New York; 629 Corbis-ttmann; 631, 632 top right The Granger Collection, New York; 2 bottom left Culver Pictures; 633 Photos by Sharon ogstraten.

nit 7

4–635 Brown Brothers.

hapter 22, 636 top Family Making Artificial Flowers (about 10), photo by Jessie Tarbox Beals. The Jacob A. Riis Collection, useum of the City of New York; center © Bettmann/Corbis; bttom © Bettmann/Corbis; 637 top Library of Congress; center Corbis; bottom © Bettmann/Corbis; 638 Brown Brothers; 639, 0, 641 Library of Congress; 642 bottom Brown Brothers; left set Doubleday, Page and Company, New York, 1906, second sue; 643 Theodore Roosevelt (date unknown), John Singer argent. White House Collection. Copyright © 1992 White House istorical Association; 644 center Culver Pictures; bottom left opyright © F. Sieb/H. Armstrong Roberts; bottom right Copyright W. Bertsch/H. Armstrong Roberts; 645 bottom Copyright © J. lank/H. Armstrong Roberts; 646 Eugene V. Debs ollection/Tamiment Institute Library, New York University; 648, 49 Culver Pictures; 650 top, Lillian Wald 1867-1940, public health urse, social worker. William Valentine Schevill, 1864-1951. Oil on ardboard, 71.7 x 71.7 cm (28 1/4 : 28 1/4 in.) feigned circle, 1919. NPG. 76.37 National Portrait Gallery, Smithsonian Institution. Gift of the Visiting Nurse Service of New York/Art Resource, NY; bottom, A Short Cut over the Roofs of the Tenements; A Henry Street Visiting Nurse (1908), photo by Jessie Tarbox Beals. Museum of the City of New York. Lent by the Visting Nurse Service of New York; 651 The Granger Collection, New York; 652 left Copyright © 1994 FPG International.

Chapter 23, 656–657 Great White Fleet, Harry Reuterdahl. Courtesy of the U.S. Naval Academy Museum; 656 left The Granger Collection, New York; right © Bettmann/Corbis; 657 left © Charles & Josette Lenars/Corbis; right, © Lake County Museum/Corbis; 658 The Granger Collection, New York; 659 Corbis; 661 Portrait of Queen Lliuokalani, date and artist unknown. Bishop Museum; 662 The Granger Collection, New York; 663 Chicago Historical Society; 664, 666 The Granger Collection, New York; 667 From Puerto Rico: A Political and Cultural History, Arturo Morals Carrion; 668 U.S. Naval Academy Museum; 671 Illustration by Nick Rotondo; center left Corbis-Bettmann; 673 Copyright © Caren Firouz/Black Star/PNI; 674, 675 bottom The Granger Collection, New York.

Chapter 24

Chapter 24, 676–677 The Granger Collection, New York; 676 top © Bettmann/Corbis; bottom © Swim Ink/Corbis; 677 left Library of Congress; right © Bettmann/Corbis; 678 The Granger Collection, New York; 679 The Granger Collection, New York; 681 top center Copyright © Mike Fizer/Check Six; top right Copyright © Hulton Getty/Tony Stone Images; bottom left Hulton-Deutsch Collection/Corbis; bottom right Copyright © Hulton Getty/Tony Stone Images; 682 The

Enormous Room by E. E. Cummings, Penguin Twentieth Century Classics Edition. Cover painting Prisoner's Round (1890), Vincent Van Gogh, after Dore. Pushkin Museum of Fine Arts, Moscow. Photo courtesy Scala/Art Resource, New York; right Book cover from A Farewell to Arms by Ernest Hemingway. Cover illustration by Cathie Bleck. Reprinted by permission of Scribner, a Division of Simon & Schuster (New York: Scribner/Simon & Schuster, 1995); 691 Wyoming Division of Cultural Resources; 692 Culver Pictures; 693 Panel no. 1: "During the World War There Was a Great Migration North by Southern Negroes" from The Migration of the Negro mural series (1940–41), Jacob Lawrence. Tempera on masonite, 12″ × 18″. Acquired through Downtown Gallery, 1942. The Phillips Collection, Washington, D.C.; 695 Corbis; 696 The Granger Collection, New York; 697 right, 701 bottom The Granger Collection, New York; 702 Culver Pictures; 703 Photos by Sharon Hoogstraten.

Epilogue

704–705 top, left to right LIFE cover (July 1, 1926) Fred Coope The Granger Collection, New York; National Archives; U.S. A Force; bottom, left to right Used by permission, Elvis Presley Enterprises, Inc.; James P. Blair/National Geographic Image Collection; Larry Burrows/TimePix; © R. Ian Lloyd/Masterfile; 704 left © Getty Images; 705 left Courtesy Ronald Reagan Library; right © Owen Franken/Corbis. 706 Copyright © The Washington Post. Reprinted with permission; 707 Brown Brothers; 708 top Culver Pictures; center Copyright © Blank Archives/Archive Photos; bottom Movie Still Archives; 710 National Museum of American Art, Smithsonian Institution/Art Resource, New York; 711 Photo by Margaret Suckley/Franklin D. Roosevelt Library; 712 Photo courtesy o Margaret Bourke-White Estate/Life Magazine, copyright © Time Inc.; 713 Copyright © Hulton Getty/Liaison Agency; 71 top Copyright © 1999 Owen H. K./Black Star; bottom The Granger Collection, New York; 716 UPI/Corbis-Bettmann; 71 AP/Wide World Photos; 718 U.S. Air Force Photo; 719 top NASA; bottom UPI/Corbis-Bettmann; 721 Copyright © Dirck Halstead/Liaison Agency; 722 top Copyright © 1970 Elliott Erwitt/Magnum Photos, Inc.; bottom AP/Wide World Photo 723 Copyright © 1963 Bob Adelman/Magnum Photos, Inc.; 724 Copyright © 1978 George Ballis/Take Stock; 725 top W McNamee/Corbis; bottom From the Collection of David J. a Janice L. Frent; 726 AP/Wide World Photos; 727 Copyright Robert Brenner/PhotoEdit/PNI; 728–729 background NASA; 728 top right Copyright © 1996 Tom Stewart/The Stock Market; bottom left Copyright © Scott McKlernan/Zuna Images/The Stock Market; 729 center Copyright © The New Yorker Collection 1999 Mick Stevens from cartoonbank.cor All rights reserved.

Special Report

733 top, bottom AP/Wide World Photos; 735 top, bottom AP/Wide World Photos; 736 AP/Wide World Photos; 737 le Mario Tama/Getty Images; right © Reuters NewMedia Inc./Corbis.

Historic Decisions of the Supreme Court

738 top left Corbis; bottom left Copyright © 1994 North Wi Pictures; bottom center The Granger Collection, New York; b tom right Copyright © 1999 North Wind Pictures; 739 top Corbis; bottom left Corbis-Bettmann; bottom right AP/Wide

ctures; **742** Corbis; **743** *left* Culver Pictures; *right* The Granger
ollection, New York; **744** Corbis; *bottom right* The Granger
ollection, New York; **745** Copyright © 1999 North Wind
ctures; **746** Corbis; **747** *left* The Granger Collection, New York;
ght Lincoln University Archives, Langston Hughes Memorial
brary, Lincoln University, Penn.; **748** *top left* Corbis; *bottom
ght* The Granger Collection, New York; **749** AP/Wide World
otos; **750** *top left* Corbis; **751** Wally Mcnamee/Corbis; **752** *top
ft* Corbis; *bottom right* AP/Wide World Photos; **753** Corbis; **754**
p left* Corbis; *bottom right* Corbis-Bettmann; **756** *top left*
ven Franken/Corbis; *bottom right,* **757** AP/Wide World Photos.

R15 Library of Congress; **R28** Courtesy of the Lloyd Ostendor
Collection.

Presidents of the United States

R36-R38 The Oval Office Collection™ *except Clinton and
George W. Bush;* **R38** *Clinton* AP/Wide World Photos; *Georg
W. Bush* Bush-Cheney 2000, Inc.

Maps created by Mapping Specialists

McDougal Littell has made every effort to locate the copyright holders of all copyrighted material in this book and to
make full acknowledgment for its use.